Janson's
History of Art

THE RENAISSANCE THROUGH ROCOCO

Janson's History of Art

THE RENAISSANCE THROUGH ROCOCO

Eighth Edition

Portable Edition | Book 3

PENELOPE J. E. DAVIES

WALTER B. DENNY

FRIMA FOX HOFRICHTER

JOSEPH JACOBS

ANN M. ROBERTS

DAVID L. SIMON

Prentice Hall
Upper Saddle River   London   Singapore
Toronto   Tokyo   Sydney   Hong Kong   Mexico City

Editorial Director: Leah Jewell
Editor in Chief: Sarah Touborg
Senior Sponsoring Editor: Helen Ronan
Editorial Project Manager: David Nitti
Editorial Assistant: Carla Worner
Media Director: Brian Hyland
Media Editor: Alison Lorber
Director of Marketing: Brandy Dawson
Senior Marketing Manager: Laura Lee Manley
Marketing Assistant: Ashley Fallon
Senior Managing Editor: Ann Marie McCarthy
Assistant Managing Editor: Melissa Feimer
Senior Operations Specialist: Brian Mackey
Production Liaisons: Barbara Cappuccio and Marlene Gassler
AV Project Manager: Gail Cocker
Cartography: Peter Bull Art Studio
Senior Art Director: Pat Smythe
Site Supervisor, Pearson Imaging Center: Joe Conti
Pearson Imaging Center: Corin Skidds, Robert Uibelhoer, and Ron Walko
Cover Printer: Lehigh-Phoenix Color
Printer/Binder: Courier/Kendallville

This book was produced by
Laurence King Publishing Ltd, London.
www.laurenceking.com

Senior Editor: Susie May
Copy Editor: Robert Shore
Proofreader: Lisa Cutmore
Picture Researcher: Amanda Russell
Page and Cover Designers: Nick Newton and Randell Harris
Production Controller: Simon Walsh

Cover image: View of Florence, Italy, with dome of the Florence Cathedral by Filippo
Brunelleschi, 1420–1436; lantern completed 1471. © Ocean/Corbis

Library of Congress Cataloging-in-Publication Data
Janson, H. W. (Horst Woldemar)
Janson's history of art : the western tradition / Penelope J.E. Davies ... [et. al]. -- 8th ed.
p. cm.
Includes bibliographical references and index.
ISBN 978-0-205-68517-2 (hardback)
1. Art--History. I. Davies, Penelope J. E., II. Janson, H. W. (Horst Woldemar), History of art.
III. Title. IV. Title: History of art.
N5300.J29 2009b
709--dc22
2009022617

10 9 8 7 6 5 4 3 2 1

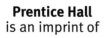

Prentice Hall
is an imprint of

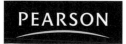

www.pearsonhighered.com

ISBN 10: 0-205-16114-6
ISBN 13: 978-0-205-16114-0
Exam Copy ISBN 10: 0-205-16755-1
ISBN 13: 978-0-205-16755-5

Contents

PART THREE
THE RENAISSANCE THROUGH ROCOCO

Preface

WELCOME TO THE EIGHTH EDITION OF JANSON'S CLASSIC TEXTBOOK, officially renamed *Janson's History of Art* in its seventh edition to reflect its relationship to the book that introduced generations of students to art history. For many of us who teach introductory courses in the history of art, the name Janson is synonymous with the subject matter we present.

When Pearson/Prentice Hall first published the *History of Art* in 1962, John F. Kennedy occupied the White House, and Andy Warhol was an emerging artist. Janson offered his readers a strong focus on Western art, an important consideration of technique and style, and a clear point of view. The *History of Art*, said Janson, was not just a stringing together of historically significant objects, but the writing of a story about their interconnections—a history of styles and of stylistic change. Janson's text focused on the visual and technical characteristics of the objects he discussed, often in extraordinarily eloquent language. Janson's *History of Art* helped to establish the canon of art history for many generations of scholars.

Although revised to remain current with new discoveries and scholarship, this new edition continues to follow Janson's lead in important ways: It is limited to the Western tradition, with a chapter on Islamic art and its relationship to Western art. It keeps the focus of the discussion on the object, its manufacture, and its visual character. It considers the contribution of the artist as an important part of the analysis. This edition maintains an organization along the lines established by Janson, with separate chapters on the Northern European Renaissance, the Italian Renaissance, the High Renaissance, and Baroque art, with stylistic divisions for key periods of the modern era. Also embedded in this edition is the narrative of how art has changed over time in the cultures that Europe has claimed as its patrimony.

WHAT'S NEW IN *JANSON'S HISTORY OF ART*?

"The history of art is too vast a field for anyone to encompass all of it with equal competence."

H. W. JANSON, from the Preface to the first edition of *History of Art*

Janson's History of Art in its eighth edition is once again the product of careful revision by a team of scholars with different specialties, bringing a readily recognized knowledge and depth to the discussions of works of art. We incorporate new interpretations such as the reidentification of the "Porticus Aemilia" as Rome's Navalia, or ship-shed (p. 186); new documentary evidence, such as that pertaining to Uccello's *Battle of San Romano* (p. 538); and new interpretive approaches, such as the importance of nationalism in the development of Romanticism (Chapter 24).

Organization and Contextual Emphasis

Most chapters integrate the media into chronological discussions instead of discussing them in isolation from one another, which reflected the more formalistic approach used in earlier editions. Even though we draw connections among works of art, as Janson did, we emphasize the patronage and function of works of art and the historical circumstances in which they were created. We explore how works of art have been used to shore up political or social power.

Interpreting Cultures

Western art history encompasses a great many distinct chronological and cultural periods, which we wish to treat as distinct entities. So we present Etruscan art as evidence for Etruscan culture, not as a precursor of Roman or a follower of Greek art. Recognizing the limits of our knowledge about certain periods of history, we examine how art historians draw conclusions from works of art. The boxes called *The Art Historian's Lens* allow students to see how the discipline works. They give students a better understanding of the methods art historians use to develop art-historical arguments. *Primary Sources*, a distinguishing feature of Janson for many editions, have been incorporated throughout the chapters to support the analysis provided and to further inform students about the cultures discussed, and additional documents can be found in the online resource, MyArtsLab. (See p. xv for more detail.)

Women in the History of Art

Women continue to be given greater visibility as artists, as patrons, and as an audience for works of art. Inspired by contemporary approaches to art history, we also address the representation of women as expressions of specific cultural notions of femininity or as symbols.

Objects, Media, and Techniques

Many new objects have been incorporated into this edition to reflect the continuous changes in the discipline. The mediums we discuss are broad in scope and include not only modern art forms such as installations and earth art, but also the so-called minor arts of earlier periods—such as tapestries, metalwork, and porcelain. Discussions in the *Materials and Techniques* boxes illuminate this dimension of art history.

The Images

Along with the new objects that have been introduced, every reproduction in the book has been reexamined for excellence in quality, and when not meeting our standards has been replaced. Whenever possible we obtain our photography directly from the holding institutions to ensure that we have the most accurate and authoritative illustrations. Every image that could be obtained in color has been acquired. To further assist both students and teachers, we have sought permission for electronic educational use so that instructors who adopt *Janson's History of Art* will have access to an extraordinary archive of high quality (over 300 dpi) digital images for classroom use. (See p. xv for more detail on the Prentice Hall Digital Art Library.)

New Maps and Timelines

A new map program has been created to both orient students to the locations mentioned in each chapter and to better tell the story of the chapter narrative. Readers now can see the extent of the Eastern and Western Roman Empires, as well as the range of the Justinian's rule (p. 236). They can trace the migration routes of tribes during early medieval times (p. 314) and the Dutch trade routes of the seventeenth century (p. 702). This enriching new feature provides an avenue for greater understanding of the impact of politics, society, and geography on the art of each period. End of chapter timelines recap in summary fashion the art and events of the chapter, as well as showing key contemporaneous works from previous chapters (for example, pp. 345 and 759).

Chapter by Chapter Revisions

The following list includes the major highlights of this new edition:

CHAPTER 1: PREHISTORIC ART

Expands upon the methods scholars (both art historians and anthropologists) use to understand artwork, including, for instance, feminist interpretations. Includes new monuments such as Skara Brae and Mezhirich. A new box explains dating techniques.

CHAPTER 2: ANCIENT NEAR EASTERN ART

This chapter is expanded to include a discussion of Jerusalem.

CHAPTER 3: EGYPTIAN ART

Now includes a tomb painting from the pre-Dynastic age, and a discussion of jewelry. A new box names the major Egyptian gods.

CHAPTER 4: AEGEAN ART

Improved images and a reconstruction of Mycenae enhance the discussion of Aegean art.

CHAPTER 5: GREEK ART

This chapter is tightened to allow space for longer discussion of Greek sanctuaries, and the inclusion of Hellenistic works outside of the Greek mainland, such as the Pharos at Alexandria. The issue of homosexuality in fifth-century Athens is addressed, as well as women's roles in life and art. A new box deals with the issue of repatriation of works of art such as the Elgin marbles.

CHAPTER 6: ETRUSCAN ART

The range of artworks is increased to include, for instance, terra-cotta revetments and terra-cotta portraits.

CHAPTER 7: ROMAN ART

This chapter includes new interpretations such as the reidentification of the "Porticus Aemilia" as Rome's Navalia or ship-shed. It also has been tightened to allow space for more Republican works (such as the terracotta pediment from Via di San Gregorio and the Praeneste mosaic) and a wider discussion of life in Pompeii. There is some rearrangement of art works to improve the chronological flow.

CHAPTER 8: EARLY CHRISTIAN AND BYZANTINE ART

A new section on early Jewish art is added, including three images of early synagogue wall paintings and mosaics (Dura Europos and Hammath Tiberias). Coverage of Late Byzantine art is increased, as is discussion of liturgical and social history.

CHAPTER 9: ISLAMIC ART

The relationship of Islamic art to early Jewish and Christian medieval art is accentuated.

CHAPTER 10: EARLY MEDIEVAL ART

Includes an expanded discussion and reorganization of Viking art, which is now placed later in the chapter.

CHAPTER 11: ROMANESQUE ART

Coverage of secular architecture is broadened to include the bridge at Puente la Reina on the pilgrimage route to Santiago de Compostela and a new section on the crusades and castle architecture.

CHAPTER 12: GOTHIC ART

This chapter is tightened to allow space for added focus on secular objects and buildings with the inclusion of a Guillaume de Machaut manuscript illumination and Westminster Hall from the royal palace in London. There is also expanded discussion of courtly art and royal iconography in later Gothic monuments.

CHAPTER 13: ART IN THIRTEENTH- AND FOURTEENTH-CENTURY ITALY

Organization now places less emphasis on religious architecture. Siena's Palazzo Pubblico is added. There is a more focused discussion of Tuscany, and a briefer treatment of Northern Italy and Venice. Images of key works of art, including Nicola and Giovanni Pisano and the Arena chapel are improved. Two maps in the chapter outline Italian trade routes and the spread of the plague in the 1340s.

CHAPTER 14: ARTISTIC INNOVATIONS IN FIFTEENTH-CENTURY NORTHERN EUROPE

Discussion of the *Tres Riches Heures* is enlarged, and reproductions contrasting aristocratic "labors" and the images of peasants are added. Treatment of works by Van Eyck, Van der Weyden and Bosch is revised and sharpened. A new map of centers of production and trade routes in Northern Europe illustrates the variety of media produced in the region.

CHAPTER 15: THE EARLY RENAISSANCE IN FIFTEENTH-CENTURY ITALY

Reorganized for better flow and student comprehension, chapter now begins with the Baptistery competition illustrating reliefs by both Ghiberti and Brunelleschi. It then looks at architectural projects by Brunelleschi and Alberti in Florence as a group, considering their patronage and function as well as their form. New art illustrates Brunelleschi's innovations at the Duomo, while his work at San Lorenzo is expanded to include the Old Sacristy.

Section on domestic life has been revised, but it still offers a contextualized discussion of works such as Donatello's *David*, Uccello's *Rout of San Romano* and Botticelli's *Birth of Venus*. This section now includes the Strozzi cassone at the Metropolitan Museum in New York and Verrocchio's *Lady with Flowers*. The discussion of Renaissance style throughout Italy is revised for greater clarity.

CHAPTER 16: THE HIGH RENAISSANCE IN ITALY, 1495–1520

A discussion of the portrait of Ginevra de' Benci is now included, permitting a revised discussion of the *Mona Lisa*. The section on the Stanza della Segnatura is revamped to focus on the *School of Athens*. Treatment of Giorgione and Titian is reorganized and revised to reflect current discussions of attribution and collaboration. A new Titian portrait, *The Man with a Blue Sleeve*, is included.

CHAPTER 17: THE LATE RENAISSANCE AND MANNERISM IN SIXTEENTH-CENTURY ITALY

Florence in the sixteenth century is reorganized and refreshed with new images, including a view of the architectural context for Pontormo's *Entombment*. Michelangelo's New Sacristy is treated in terms of architecture as well as sculpture. Ducal Palaces of the Uffizi and the Pitti and of the Boboli Gardens receives a new focus. Cellini's *Saltceller* is discussed in its Florentine context. Treatment of Il Gesu is revamped. New images enliven the Northern Italian art section and Sophonisba Anguissola's *Self Portrait* is compared to Parmagianino's. There is a revised consideration of Palladio, and a new Titian, *The Rape of Europa*, exemplifies the artist's work for elite patrons.

CHAPTER 18: RENAISSANCE AND REFORMATION IN SIXTEENTH-CENTURY NORTHERN EUROPE

Discussion of France, as well as Spain, is revised and images are improved. Includes new images and discussions of Cranach and Baldung: Cranach's *Judgment of Paris* in New York replaces another version of this theme, while Baldung is represented by his woodcut of the *Bewitched Groom* of 1544. The discussion of Holbein is enlivened by consideration of his *Jean de Dinteville and Georges de Selve* ('The Ambassadors'), allowing examination of him as an allegorist as well as a portraitist. Gossaert is now represented by the *Neptune and Amphitrite* of 1516, while a new Patinir, the *Triptych of Saint Jerome in the Wilderness*, represents the landscape specialty of that region.

CHAPTER 19: THE BAROQUE IN ITALY AND SPAIN

Chapter content benefits from insights gained through recent exhibitions and from the inclusion of new architectural image components. New illustrations better expand understanding of the Roman Baroque and the role of the Virgin in Spanish art, including a view of the Piazza Navonna that shows Bernini's *Four Rivers Fountain* and as well as Borromini's church of *S. Agnese*, a cut-away of Borromini's complex star-hexagon shaped church, S. Ivo, and one of Murillo's many depictions of the *Immaculate Conception* (St. Petersberg).

CHAPTER 20: THE BAROQUE IN THE NETHERLANDS

The importance of trade, trade routes and interest in the exotic is explored in this chapter. Gender issues—and the relationship between men and women—and local, folk traditions (religious and secular) play a role here in the exploration of the visual culture and social history. New images include: Peter Paul Rubens, *The Raising of the Cross*—the entire open altarpiece; Peter Paul Rubens, *Four Studies of the Head of a Negro*; Jacob Jordaens, *The King Drinks*; Judith Leyster, *The Proposition*; Rembrandt van Rijn, *Bathsheba with King David's Letter* and Vermeer, *Officer and Laughing Girl*.

CHAPTER 21: THE BAROQUE IN FRANCE AND ENGLAND

New scholarship from the *Poussin and Nature: Arcadian Visions* exhibition in 2008 informs a more developed discussion of this artist's work. A fuller discussion of the role of the 1668 Fire of London and the re-building of St. Paul's Cathedral, in addition to a 3-D reconstruction of St. Paul's and a modern reconstruction of Sir Christopher Wren's plan of the city of London drawn just days after the fire, expands the coverage of this architect.

CHAPTER 22: THE ROCOCO

Expresses in greater depth the concept of the Rococo, the role of Madame da Pompadour and the expansion of the Rococo style in Germany. New images include Francois Boucher, *Portrait of Madame de Pompadour* (Munich); Jean-Simeon Chardin, *The Brioche (the Dessert)* and Egid Quirin Asam, interior and altar of the Benedictine Church at Rohr. Sections of this chapter are reorganized to accommodate the removal of Élisabeth-Louise Vigée-le Brun, Sir Thomas Gainsborough and Sir Joshua Reynolds to Chapter 23.

CHAPTER 23: ART IN THE AGE OF THE ENLIGHTENMENT, 1750-1789

Slightly restructured, the chapter keeps Neoclassicism and early Romanticism separated, thus making them more clearly defined. Joshua Reynolds, Thomas Gainsborough, and Elizabeth Vigée-Lebrun are placed here and into the context of Neoclassicism and Romanticism. Antonio Canova also is moved to this chapter to emphasize his importance in the development of Neoclassicism. Image changes include Joseph Wright's more clearly Romantic *Old Man and Death*; Ledoux's Custom House with the entrance to Salt Works at Arc-et-Senans; as well as the addition of Canova's tomb of Archduchess Maria Christina.

CHAPTER 24: ART IN THE AGE OF ROMANTICISM, 1789-1848

This chapter is tightened and has several new images. William Blake is now represented by *Elohim Creating Adam* and Corot by *Souvenir Montrefontaine (Oise)*. Frederick Church's *Twilight in the Wilderness* is added. The discussion of architecture is changed by placing the Empire style at the very end, thus keeping the Neoclassical revival together.

CHAPTER 25: THE AGE OF POSITIVISM: REALISM, IMPRESSIONISM, AND THE PRE-RAPHAELITES, 1848-1885

Includes a number of image changes to better focus discussions. These include: Monet, *Gare St. Lazare*; Rossetti, *Proserpine*; Nadar, *Portrait of Manet*; and Gustav, *Brig on the Water*.

CHAPTER 26: PROGRESS AND ITS DISCONTENTS: POST-IMPRESSIONISM, SYMBOLISM, AND ART NOUVEAU, 1880-1905

Now incorporates discussions of vernacular, or snapshot, photography, represented by Henri Lartigue's *Woman in Furs on the Avenue in the Bois de Bologne*, and the advent of film, represented by Thomas Edison's *Train Crossing the Brooklyn Bridge*.

CHAPTER 27: TOWARD ABSTRACTION: THE MODERNIST REVOLUTION, 1904-1914

Discussion of the formal and stylistic developments between 1904 and 1914 that culminated in abstractionism is tightened and the number of images reduced.

CHAPTER 28: ART BETWEEN THE WARS

More compact discussion structured around the impact of World War I and the need to create utopias and uncover higher realities, especially as seen in Surrealism.

CHAPTER 29: POSTWAR TO POSTMODERN, 1945-1980

Polke is placed here from Chapter 30, thus putting him within the context of an artist influenced by Pop Art. David Hammons is moved to Chapter 30. Betye Saar's *Shield of Quality* adds a woman to the discussion of African-American artists.

CHAPTER 30: THE POSTMODERN ERA: ART SINCE 1980

Architecture is reduced, and fine art is expanded. Neo-Expressionism benefits from the addition of Julian Schnabel's *Exile*. The multi-culturalism of the period receives greater emphasis, especially feminism. Barbara Kruger is placed in a more feminist context with inclusion of a new image, *We Won't Play Nature to Your Culture*. The discussion of African-American identity is broadened by the placement of David Hammons here, and by the addition of Kara Walker's *Insurrection*. Fred Wilson's *Mining the Museum* is also included. The discussion of Gonzalez-Torres now stresses his involvement with the AIDS crisis. The importance of large-scale photography for the period is reinforced by the addition of Andreas Gursky's *Shanghai*. The truly global nature of contemporary art is strengthened by the addition of El Antsui's *Dzeii II*.

Acknowledgments

We are grateful to the following academic reviewers for their numerous insights and suggestions on improving Janson:

Amy Adams, College of Staten Island
Susan Benforado Baker, University of Texas Arlington
Jennifer Ball, Brooklyn College
Dixon Bennett, San Jacinto College – South
Diane Boze, Northeastern State University
Betty Ann Brown, California State University – Northridge
Barbara Bushey, Hillsdale College
Mary Hogan Camp, Whatcom Community College
Susan P. Casteras, University of Washington
Cat Crotchett, Western Michigan University
Tim Cruise, Central Texas College
Julia K. Dabbs, University of Minnesota - Morris
Adrienne DeAngelis, University of Miami
Sarah Diebel, University of Wisconsin-Stout
Douglas N. Dow, Kansas State University
Kim Dramer, Fordham University
Brian Fencl, West Liberty State College
Monica Fullerton, Kenyon College
Laura D. Gelfand, The University of Akron
Alyson A. Gill, Arkansas State University
Maria de Jesus Gonzalez, University of Central Florida

Bobette Guillory, Carl Albert State College
Bertha Steinhardt Gutman, Delaware County Community College
Marianne Hogue, University of North Carolina - Wilmington
Stephanie Jacobson, St. John's University
Ruth Keitz, University of Texas - Brownsville
Joanne Kuebler, Manhattan College
Adele H. Lewis, Arizona State University
Lisa Livingston, Modesto Junior College
Diane Chin Lui, American River College
B. Susan Maxwell, University of Wisconsin-Oshkosh
Paul Miklowski, Cuyahoga Community College
Charles R. Morscheck Jr., Drexel University
Elaine O'Brien, California State University - Sacramento
Matthew Palczynski, Temple University
Jason Rosenfeld, Marymount Manhattan College
Phyllis Saretta, The Metropolitan Museum of Art
Onoyom Ukpong, Southern University and A & M College
Kristen Van Ausdall, Kenyon College
Marjorie S. Venit, University of Maryland
Linda Woodward, Montgomery College
Ted M. Wygant, Dayton Beach Community College

The contributors would like to thank John Beldon Scott, Whitney Lynn, and Nicole Veilleux for their advice and assistance in developing this edition. We also would like to thank the editors and staff at Pearson Education including Sarah Touborg, Helen Ronan, Barbara Cappuccio, Marlene Gassler, Cory Skidds, Brian Mackey, David Nitti, and Carla Worner who supported us in our work. At Laurence King Publishing, Susie May, Kara Hattersley-Smith, Julia Ruxton, Amanda Russell, and Simon Walsh oversaw the production of this new edition.

Faculty and Student Resources for Teaching and Learning with *Janson's History of Art*

PEARSON/PRENTICE HALL is pleased to present an outstanding array of high quality resources for teaching and learning with *Janson's History of Art*. Please contact your local Prentice Hall representative (use our rep locator at www.pearsonhighered.com) for more details on how to obtain these items, or send us an email at art.service@pearson.com.

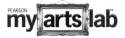 www.myartslab.com Save time, improve results. MyArtsLab is a robust online learning environment providing you and your students with the following resources:

Complete and dynamic e-book
Illustrated and printable flashcards
Unique "Closer Look" tours of over 125 key works of art
Pre-and post-tests for every chapter of the book
Customized study plan that helps students focus in on key areas
Primary Sources with critical thinking questions
Writing Tutorials for the most common writing assignments

Available at no additional charge when packaged with the text. Learn more about the power of MyArtsLab and register today at www.myartslab.com

 THE PRENTICE HALL DIGITAL ART LIBRARY. Instructors who adopt *Janson's History of Art* are eligible to receive this unparalleled resource containing every image in *Janson's History of Art* in the highest resolution (over 300 dpi) and pixilation possible for optimal projection and easy download. Developed and endorsed by a panel of visual curators and instructors across the country, this resource features images in jpeg and in PowerPoint, an instant download function for easy import into any presentation software, along with a zoom and a save-detail feature.

COURSESMART eTEXTBOOKS ONLINE is an exciting new choice for students looking to save money. As an alternative to purchasing the print textbook, students can subscribe to the same content online and save up to 50% off the suggested list price of the print text. With a CourseSmart eTextbook, students can search the text, make notes online, print out reading assignments that incorporate lecture notes, and bookmark important passages for later review. For more information, or to subscribe to the CourseSmart eTextbook, visit www.coursesmart.com.

CLASSROOM RESPONSE SYSTEM (CRS) IN CLASS QUESTIONS. (ISBN: 0-205-76375-8) Get instant, classwide responses to beautifully illustrated chapter-specific questions during a lecture to gauge students' comprehension—and keep them engaged. Contact your local Pearson representative for details.

MYTEST (ISBN: 0-205-76391-X) is a commercial-quality computerized test management program available for both Microsoft Windows and Macintosh environments.

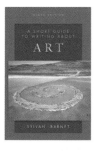 **A SHORT GUIDE TO WRITING ABOUT ART, 10/e** (ISBN: 0-205-70825-0) by Sylvan Barnet. This best-selling text has guided tens of thousands of art students through the writing process. Students are shown how to analyze pictures (drawings, paintings, photographs), sculptures and architecture, and are prepared with the tools they need to present their ideas through effective writing. Available at a discount when purchased with the text.

INSTRUCTOR'S RESOURCE MANUAL WITH TEST BANK (ISBN: 0-205-76374-X, download only) is an invaluable professional resource and reference for new and experienced faculty, containing sample syllabi, hundreds of sample test questions, and guidance on incorporating media technology into your course.

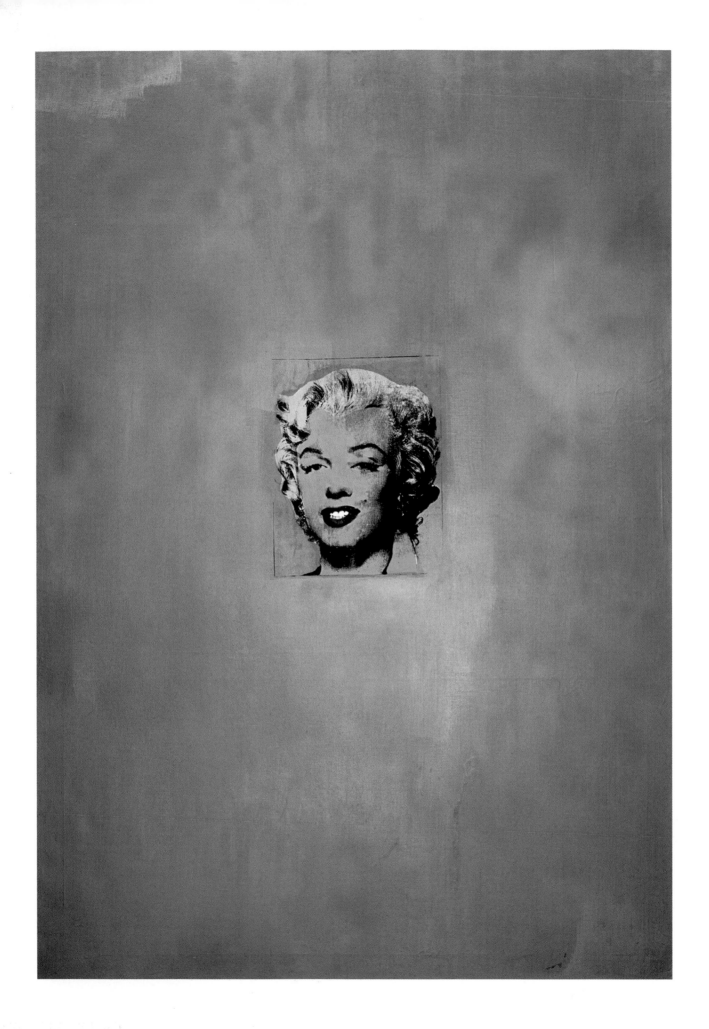

Introduction

WHY IN 1962 DID ANDY WARHOL MAKE A PAINTING ENTITLED *Gold Marilyn Monroe* (fig. **I.1**)? This almost 7-foot-high canvas was produced shortly after the death of the Hollywood screen star and sex symbol. It was not commissioned and obviously Monroe never "sat" for it, an activity that we generally associate with portraiture. Instead, Warhol

worked from a press photograph, a still from the 1953 movie *Niagara*, which he cropped to his liking and then transferred onto canvas using **silkscreen**. This process involves mechanically transferring the photograph onto a mesh screen, or in this case several screens, one for each color, and pressing printing ink through them onto canvas. Warhol then surrounded Marilyn's head with a field of broadly brushed gold paint.

Warhol's painting is not a conventional portrait of Monroe but rather a pastiche of the public image of the film star as propagated by the mass media. Warhol imitates the sloppy, gritty look and feel of color newspaper reproductions of the period, when the colors were often misregistered, aligning imperfectly with the image, and the colors themselves were "off," meaning not quite right. The Marilyn we are looking at is the impersonal celebrity of the media, the commodity being pushed by the film industry. She is supposedly glamorous, with her lush red lipstick and bright blond hair, but instead she appears pathetically tacky because of the grimy black ink and the garish color of her blond hair as it becomes bright yellow and her flesh tone turns pink. Her personality is impenetrable, reduced to a sad, lifeless public smile. Prompted by Monroe's suicide, *Gold Marilyn Monroe* presents the real Marilyn—a depressed, often miserable person, who, in

this textureless, detailless, unnaturalistic image, is becoming a blur fading into memory. Warhol has brilliantly expressed the indifference of the mass media, whose objective is to promote celebrities by saturating a thirsty public with their likenesses but which tells us nothing meaningful about them and shows no concern for them. Monroe's image is used simply to sell a product, much as the alluring and often jazzy packaging of Brillo soap pads or Campbell's soup cans is designed to make a product alluring without telling us anything about the product itself. The packaging is just camouflage. As a sentimental touch, Warhol floats Marilyn's head in a sea of gold paint, embedding her in an eternal realm previously reserved for use in icons of Christ and the Virgin Mary, which immerse these religious figures in a spiritual aura of golden, heavenly light (see fig. 13.22). But Warhol's revered Marilyn is sadly dwarfed by her celestial gold surrounding, adding to the tragic sense of this powerful portrait, which trenchantly comments on the enormous gulf existing between public image and private reality.

If we turn the clock back some 200 years and look at a portrait by the Boston painter John Singleton Copley, we again see an image of a woman (fig. **I.2**). But, made as it was in a different time and context, the story surrounding the painting is entirely different. The sitter is Freelove Olney Scott, and she is presented as a refined-looking woman, born, we would guess, into an aristocratic family, used to servants and power. As a matter of fact, we have come to accept Copley's portraits of colonial Bostonians, such as Mrs. Joseph Scott, as accurate depictions of their subjects

I.1 Andy Warhol, *Gold Marilyn Monroe*. 1962. Synthetic polymer paint, silk-screened, and oil on canvas, 6'11¼" × 4'9" (2.11 × 1.44 m). Museum of Modern Art, New York. Gift of Philip Johnson 316.1963

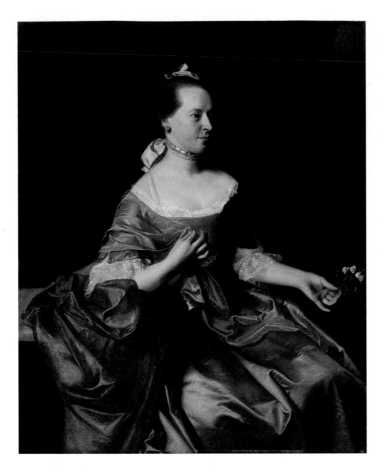

1.2 John Singleton Copley, *Mrs. Joseph Scott*.
Oil on canvas, 69½ × 39½" (176.5 × 100 cm).
The Newark Museum, Newark, New Jersey. 48.508

and lifestyles. But many, like Mrs. Scott, were not what they appear to be. So, who was Mrs. Scott? Let's take a closer look at the context in which the painting was made.

Copley is recognized as the first great American painter. Working in Boston from about 1754 to 1774, he became the most sought-after portraitist of the period. Copley easily outstripped the meager competition, most of whom actually earned their living painting signs and coaches. After all, no successful British artist had any reason to come to America. The economically struggling colonies were not a strong market for art. Only occasionally was a portrait commissioned, and typically, artists were treated like craftsmen rather than intellectuals. Like most colonial portraitists, Copley was largely self-taught, learning his trade by looking at black-and-white prints of paintings by the European masters.

As we can see in *Mrs. Joseph Scott*, Copley was a master of painting textures, which is all the more astonishing when we remember that he had no one to teach him the tricks of the painter's trade. His pictorial illusions are so convincing, we think we are looking at real silk, ribbons, lace, pearls, skin, hair, and marble, quite the opposite of Warhol's artificial Marilyn. Copley's contemporaries also marveled at his sleight of hand. No other colonial painter attained such a level of realism.

But is Copley just a "face painter," as portraitists were derogatorily called at the time, offering mere resemblances of his sitters and their expensive accoutrements? Is this painting just a means to replicate the likeness of an individual in an era before the advent of photography? The answer to both questions is a resounding "no." Copley's job was not just to make a faithful image of Mrs. Scott, but to portray her as a woman of impeccable character, limitless wealth, and aristocratic status. The flowers she holds are a symbol of fertility, faithfulness, and feminine grace, indicating that she is a good mother and wife, and a charming woman. Her expensive dress was imported from London, as was her necklace. Copley undoubtedly copied her pose from one of the prints he had of portraits of British or French royalty.

Not only is Mrs. Scott's pose borrowed, but most likely her clothing is as well, for her necklace appears on three other women in Copley portraits. In other words, it was a studio prop, as the dress may have been too. In fact, except for Mrs. Scott's face, the entire painting is a fiction designed to aggrandize the wife of a newly wealthy Boston merchant who had made his fortune selling provisions to the occupying British army. The Scotts were *nouveau-riche* commoners, not titled aristocrats. By the middle of the eighteenth century, rich Bostonians wanted to distinguish themselves from the multitude, and so, after a century of trying to escape their British roots, from which many had fled to secure religious freedom, they now sought to imitate the British aristocracy, even to the point of taking tea in the afternoon and owning English Spaniels, a breed that in England only aristocrats were permitted to own.

Joseph Scott commissioned this painting of his wife, as well as a portrait of himself, not just to record their features, but to show off the family's wealth. The pictures were extremely expensive and therefore status symbols, much as a Rolls-Royce or a Tiffany diamond ring are today. The portraits were displayed in the public spaces of their house so that they could be readily seen by visitors. Most likely they hung on either side of the mantel in the living room, or in the entrance hall. They were not intended as intimate affectionate resemblances destined for the bedroom. If patrons wanted cherished images of their loved ones, they would commission miniature portraits, which captured the likeness of the sitter in amazing detail and were often so small they could be encased in a locket that a woman would wear on a chain around her neck, or a gentleman would place in the inner breastpocket of his coat, close to the heart.

Warhol and Copley worked in very different times, a fact that has tremendous effect on the look and meaning of their portraits. Their paintings were made to serve very different purposes, and consequently they tell very different stories. And because art always serves a purpose, it is impossible for an artist to make a work that does not represent a point of view and tell a story, sometimes many stories. As we will see, great artists tell great and powerful stories. We shall find that an important key to unraveling these stories is understanding the context in which the work was made.

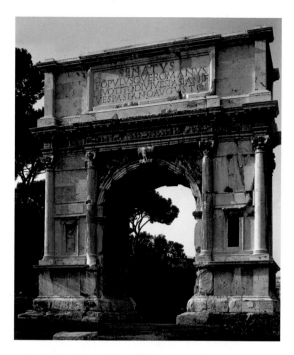

I.4   Arch of Titus, Forum Romanum, Rome. ca. 81 CE (restored)

THE POWER OF ART AND THE IMPACT OF CONTEXT

In a sense, art is a form of propaganda, for it represents an individual's or group's point of view, and this view is often presented as truth or fact. For centuries, art was used by church and state to propagate their importance, superiority, and greatness. *The Alba Madonna* (fig. **I.3**), for example, was designed to proclaim the idealized, perfect state of existence attainable through Catholicism in sixteenth-century Italy, while the Arch of Titus (fig. **I.4**) was erected to reinforce in the public's mind the military prowess of the first-century Roman emperor. Even landscape

paintings and still lifes of fruit, dead game, and flowers made in the seventeenth century are loaded with moral messages, and are far from simple attempts to capture the splendor and many moods of nature or show off the painter's finesse at creating a convincing illusionistic image.

Epitomizing the power of art is its ability to evoke entire historical periods. The words "ancient Egypt" will conjure up in most people's minds images of the pyramids, the Sphinx, and flat stiff figures lined up sideways across the face of stone (fig. **I.5**). Or look at the power of Grant Wood's famous 1930 painting

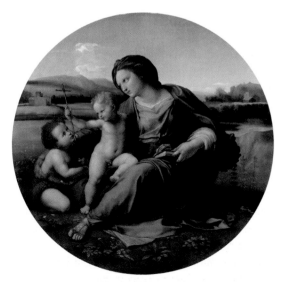

I.3   Raphael, *The Alba Madonna*. ca. 1510. Oil on panel transferred to canvas, diameter 37¼" (94 cm). Image courtesy of the Board of Trustees, National Gallery of Art, Washington, D.C., Andrew W. Mellon Collection, 1937.1.24. (24)

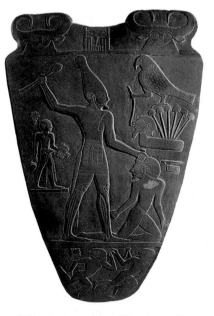

I.5   Palette of King Narmer, from Hierakonpolis. ca. 3150–3125 BCE. Slate, height 25" (63.5 cm). Egyptian Museum, Cairo

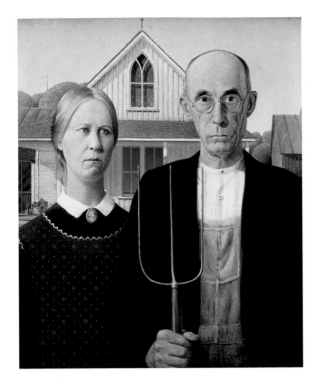

I.6 Grant Wood, *American Gothic*. 1930. Oil on beaverboard, 30¹¹/₁₆″ × 25¹¹/₁₆″ (78 × 65.3 cm). Unframed. Friends of American Art Collection. 1930.934. The Art Institute of Chicago

Many art historians, critics, and other viewers found the picture remarkably beautiful—glittering and shimmering with a delicate, ephemeral otherworldy aura. Many, especially Catholics, however, were repulsed by Ofili's homage to the Virgin and were infuriated. Instead of viewing the work through Ofili's eyes, they placed the painting within the context of their own experience and beliefs. Consequently, they interpreted the dung and graphic imagery—and perhaps even the black Virgin, although this was never mentioned—as sacrilegious. Within days of the opening of the exhibition, the painting had to be placed behind a large Plexiglas barrier. One artist hurled horse manure at the façade of the Brooklyn Museum, claiming, "I was expressing myself creatively," a defense often offered for Ofili. Another museum visitor sneaked behind the Plexiglas barrier and smeared the Virgin with white paint in order to cover her up. The biggest attack came from New York's mayor, Rudolph Giuliani, a Catholic, who was so outraged that he tried, unsuccessfully, to stop city funding for the museum. The public outrage at Ofili's work is just part of a long tradition that probably goes back to the beginning of image making. Art has consistently provoked anger, just as it has inspired pride, admiration, love, and respect, and the reason is simple: Art is never an empty container but rather a vessel loaded with meaning, subject to multiple interpretations, and always representing someone's point of view.

American Gothic (fig. **I.6**), which has led us to believe that humorless, austere, hardworking farmers dominated the American hinterlands at the time. The painting has virtually become an emblem of rural America for the period.

American Gothic has also become a source of much sarcastic humor for later generations, which have adapted the famous pitchfork-bearing farmer and his sour-faced daughter for all kinds of agendas unrelated to the artist's original message. Works of art are often later appropriated to serve purposes quite different from those initially intended, with context heavily influencing the meaning of a work. The reaction of some New Yorkers to *The Holy Virgin Mary* (fig. **I.7**) by Chris Ofili reflects the power of art to provoke and spark debate, even outrage. The work appeared in an exhibition titled *Sensation: Young British Artists from the Saatchi Collection*, presented at the Brooklyn Museum in late 1999. Ofili, who is a Briton of African descent, made an enormous picture of a black Virgin Mary using tiny dots of paint, glitter, map pins, and collaged images of genitalia from popular magazines. Instead of hanging on the wall, this enormous painting rested on two large wads of elephant dung, which had been a signature feature of the artist's large canvases since 1991. Elephant dung is held sacred in some African cultures, and for Ofili, a devout Catholic who periodically attends Mass, the picture was a modernization of the traditional presentation of the elemental sacredness of the Virgin, with the so-called pornographic images intended to suggest both procreation and hovering naked angels. While intentionally provocative, the picture was not conceived as an attack on the Catholic religion.

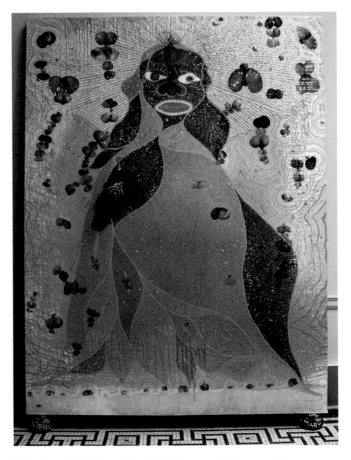

I.7 Chris Ofili, *The Holy Virgin Mary*. 1996. Paper, collage, oil paint, glitter, polyester resin, map pins, and elephant dung on linen, 7′11″ × 5′11⅝″ (2.44 × 1.83 m). Victoria Miro Gallery, London

Because the context for looking at art constantly changes, our interpretations and insights into art and entire periods evolve as well. For example, when the first edition of this book was published in 1962, women artists were not included, which was typical for textbooks at the time. America, like most of the world, was male-dominated and history was male-centric. Historically, women were expected to be wives and mothers, and to stay in the home and not have careers. They were not supposed to become artists, and the few known exceptions were not taken seriously by historians, who were mostly male. The feminist movement, beginning in the mid-1960s, overturned this restrictive perception of women. As a result, in the last 40 years, art historians—many of them female—have "rediscovered" countless women artists who had attained a degree of success in their day. Many of them were outstanding artists, held in high esteem during their lifetimes, despite the enormous struggle to overcome powerful social and even family resistance against women becoming professional artists.

One of these "lost" women artists is the seventeenth-century Dutch painter Judith Leyster, a follower, if not a student, of the famed Frans Hals. Over the subsequent centuries, Leyster's paintings were either attributed to other artists, including Hals and Gerrit van Honthorst, or they were labeled "artist unknown." At the end of the nineteenth century, however, Leyster was rediscovered in her own right through an analysis of her signature, documents, and style, and her paintings were gradually restored to her name. It was only with the feminist movement that she was elevated from a minor figure to one of the more accomplished painters of her generation, one important enough to be included in basic histories of art. The feminist movement provided a new context for evaluating art, one that had an interest in rather than a denial of women's achievements and a study of issues relating to gender and how they appear in the arts.

A work like Leyster's *Self-Portrait* (fig. **I.8**) is especially fascinating from this point of view. Its size and date (ca. 1633) suggest that this may have been the painting the artist submitted as her presentation piece for admission into the local painters' guild, the Guild of St. Luke of Haarlem. Women were not generally encouraged to join the guild, which was a male preserve that reinforced the professional status of men. Nor did women artists generally take on students. Leyster bucked both traditions, however, as she carved out a career for herself in a man's world. In her self-portrait, she presents herself as an artist armed with many brushes, suggesting her deft control of the medium—an idea that the presentation picture itself was meant to demonstrate. On the easel is a segment of a genre scene of which several variations are known. We must remember that at this time artists rarely showed themselves working at their easels, toiling with their hands: They wanted to separate themselves from mere artisans and laborers, presenting themselves as intellectuals belonging to a higher class. As a woman defying male expectations, however, Leyster needed to declare clearly that she was indeed an artist. But she cleverly elevates her status by not dressing as an artist would when painting. Instead, she appears as her patrons do in their portraits, well-dressed and well-off. Her mouth is open, in what is called a

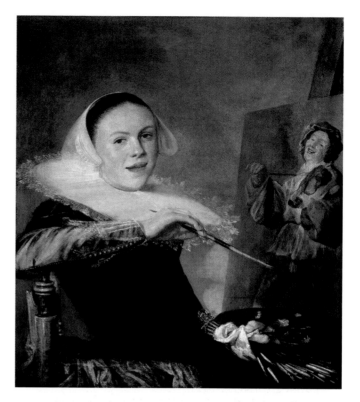

I.8 Judith Leyster, *Self-Portrait*. ca. 1633. Oil on canvas, 29⅜ × 25⅝" (72.3 × 65.3 cm). National Gallery of Art, Washington, D.C. Gift of Mr. and Mrs. Robert Woods Bliss

"speaking likeness" portrait, giving her a casual but self-assured animated quality, as she appears to converse on equal terms with a visitor, or with us. Leyster, along with Artemisia Gentileschi and Marie-Louise-Élisabeth Vigée-Lebrun, who also appear in this book, was included in a major 1976 exhibition titled *Women Artists 1550–1950*, which was shown in Los Angeles and Brooklyn, and played a major role in establishing the importance of women artists.

WHAT IS ART?

Ask most people "What is art?," and they will respond with the words "an oil painting" or "a marble or bronze sculpture." Their principal criterion is that the object be beautiful—whatever that may be—although generally they will probably define this as the degree to which a painting or sculpture is real looking or adheres to their notion of naturalism. Technical finesse or craft is viewed as the highest attribute of art making, capable of inspiring awe and reverence. Epitomizing these values is Greek and Roman sculpture, such as the fourth-century BCE sculpture the *Apoxyomenos (Scraper)* (fig. **I.9**), which for centuries was considered the high point of fine art. To debunk the myth that art is only about technique and begin to get at what it is really about, we return to Warhol's *Gold Marilyn Monroe*. The painting is rich with stories, one of which is how it poses questions about the meaning of art, how it functions, and how it takes on value, both financial and aesthetic. Warhol even begs the question of the significance of technical finesse in art making, an issue raised by the fact that he wants to give us the impression that he may not have even touched this painting himself. We have already seen how he appropriated someone else's photograph of Monroe, not even taking his own. Warhol then instructed his assistants to make the screens for the printing process. They may also have prepared the canvas, screened the image with the colors Warhol selected, and even painted the gold to Warhol's specifications.

By using assistants to make his work, Warhol is telling us that art is not necessarily about the artist's technical finesse, but about communicating an idea using visual language. The measuring stick for quality in art is the quality of the statement being made, or its philosophy, as well as the quality of the technical means for making this statement, even if not executed by the artist. Looking at *Gold Marilyn Monroe* in the flesh at New York's Museum of Modern Art is a powerful, even unforgettable experience. Standing in front of this large canvas, we cannot help but feel the

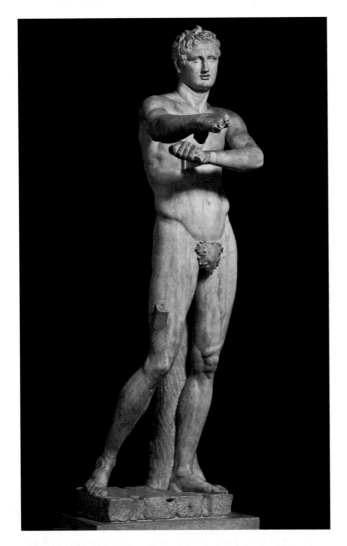

I.9 *Apoxyomenos (Scraper)*. Roman marble copy, probably after a bronze original of ca. 330 BCE by Lysippos. Height 6'9" (2.1 m). Musei Vaticani, Rome

empty glory of America's most famous symbol of female sexuality and stardom. Because the artist's vision, and not his touch, is the relevant issue for the production of this particular work, it is of no consequence that Warhol makes it seem as though he never laid a hand on the canvas except to sign the back. We shall see shortly, however, that the artist's touch is indeed often critical to the success of a work of art, which is especially true for art made before 1900.

Warhol openly declared that his art was not about his technical ability when he named his midtown Manhattan studio "The Factory." By doing so, he told us that art was a commodity, and that he was manufacturing a product, even a mass-produced one. The factory churned out over a thousand paintings and prints of Marilyn based on the same publicity still. All Warhol appeared to do for the most part was sign them, his signature reinforcing the importance people placed on the idea of the artist's signature itself being an essential part of the work. Ironically, most Old Master paintings, dating from the fourteenth through the eighteenth centuries, are not signed; and despite giving the public the impression that he had little involvement in his work, Warhol was a workaholic and very hands-on in the production of his art.

Moreover, artists have been using assistants to help make their pictures for centuries. Peter Paul Rubens, an Antwerp painter working in the first half of the seventeenth century and one of the most famous artists of his day, had an enormous workshop that cranked out many of his paintings, especially the larger works. His assistants often specialized in particular elements such as flowers, animals, or clothing, for example, and many went on to become successful artists in their own right. Rubens would design the painting, and then assistants, trained in his style, would execute individual parts. Rubens would then come in at the end and pull the painting together as needed. The price the client was willing to pay often determined how much Rubens himself participated in the actual painting of the picture: Many of his works were indeed made entirely by him, and therefore commanded the highest prices. Rubens's brilliant flashy brushwork was in many respects critical to the making of the picture. Not only was his handling of paint considered superior to that of his assistants, the very identity of his paintings—their very life, so to speak—was linked to his unique genius in applying paint to canvas, almost as much as it was to the dynamism of his dramatic compositions. His brushwork complemented his subject matter. The two went hand in hand.

Warhol was not the first artist to make art that intentionally raised the issue of what art is and how it functions. This distinction belongs to the humorous and brilliant Parisian Marcel Duchamp, one of the most influential artists of the twentieth century. In 1919, Duchamp took a postcard reproduction of Leonardo da Vinci's *Mona Lisa*, which hangs in the Louvre Museum in Paris, and drew a moustache on the sitter's face (fig. I.10). Below he wrote the letters, "L.H.O.O.Q.," which when pronounced in French is *elle a chaud au cul*, or "She's got the hots." Duchamp was poking fun at the public's fascination with the mysterious smile on the Mona Lisa, which had intrigued

and while intellectually engaging us in a most serious manner, it can also provide us with a smile, if not a good belly laugh. Many historians today consider *Mona Lisa (L.H.O.O.Q)* as important as Leonardo's *Mona Lisa*, and put the two artists on the same plane of importance.

ART AND AESTHETICS: THE ISSUE OF BEAUTY

Mona Lisa (L.H.O.O.Q.) also raised the issue of aesthetics, which is the study of theories surrounding art, including the definition of beauty and the meaning and purpose of art. Duchamp selected the *Mona Lisa* for appropriation for many reasons, one of them no doubt being that many people considered it the greatest and therefore the most beautiful painting ever made. Certainly, it was one of the most famous paintings in the world, if not the most famous. In 1919, most of those who held such a view had probably never seen it and only knew if from reproductions, probably no better than the one Duchamp used in *Mona Lisa (L.H.O.O.Q.)*. And yet, they would describe the original painting as beautiful, but not Duchamp's comical version.

Duchamp called altered found objects such as *Mona Lisa (L.H.O.O.Q.)* "readymades" (for other examples, see *Bicycle Wheel*, fig. 27.29, and *Fountain*, fig. 28.2), and he was adamant that these works had no aesthetic value whatsoever. They were not to be considered beautiful; they were aesthetically neutral. What interested Duchamp were the ideas that these objects embodied once they were declared art.

Despite his claim, Duchamp's readymades can be perceived as beautiful, in ways, of course that are quite different from Leonardo's *Mona Lisa*, but beautiful all the same. *Mona Lisa (L.H.O.O.Q.)* has an aura about it, an aura of wit and ideas that are specific to Duchamp. As a result, this slightly altered cheap color postcard is a compelling work of art. The qualities that attract us to it, which we can describe as its beauty, could not be further from those of Leonardo's *Mona Lisa*, which have more to do with composition, color, and paint handling. Ultimately, beauty, in many respects, can be equated with quality, which to a large degree hinges on the power of the statement, not some pre-conceived notion of visual beauty.

Beauty is not just a pretty colorful picture or a perfectly formed, harmonious nude marble figure such as the *Apoxymenos*. Beauty resides as well in content and how successfully this content is made visual. This book is intended to suggest the many complex ways that quality, and thus beauty, manifests itself in art. Some of the greatest paintings are grotesque, depicting horrific scenes that many people do not find acceptable, but they are nonetheless beautiful—scenes such as beheadings, crucifixions (fig. **I.11**), death and despair, emotional distress, and the brutal massacre of innocent women and children. Like Duchamp's *Mona Lisa (L.H.O.O.Q.)*, these works possess an aura that makes them riveting, despite the repulsiveness of their subject matter. They have quality, and to those who recognize and feel this quality, this

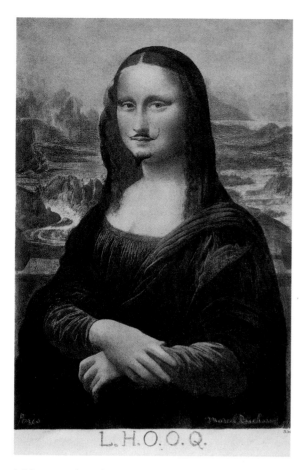

I.10 Marcel Duchamp, *Mona Lisa (L.H.O.O.Q.)*. 1919. Rectified readymade; pencil on a postcard reproduction, 7 × 4⅞" (17.8 × 12 cm). Private collection

viewers for centuries and eluded suitable explanation. Duchamp irreverently provided one: She is sexually aroused. With the childish gesture of affixing a moustache to the image, Duchamp also attacked bourgeois reverence for Old Master painting, as well as the age-old ideal of oil painting representing the pinnacle of art.

Art, Duchamp is saying, can be made by merely drawing on a mass-produced reproduction. Artists can use any imaginable medium in any way in order to express themselves: not just oil on canvas or cast bronze or chiseled marble sculpture He is announcing that art is about ideas that are made visually, and not necessarily about craft. In this deceptively whimsical work, which is actually rich in ideas, Duchamp is telling us that art is anything someone wants to call art—which is not the same as saying it is good art. Furthermore, he is proclaiming that art can be small, since *Mona Lisa (L.H.O.O.Q.)* is a fraction of the size of its source, the *Mona Lisa*. By appropriating Leonardo's famous picture and interpreting it very differently from traditional readings (see pages 564–66), Duchamp suggests that the meaning of art is not fixed forever by the artist, that it can change and be reassigned by viewers, writers, collectors, and museum curators, who may use it for their own purposes. Lastly, and this is certainly one of Duchamp's many wonderful contributions to art, he is telling us that art can be fun, that it can defy conventional notions of beauty,

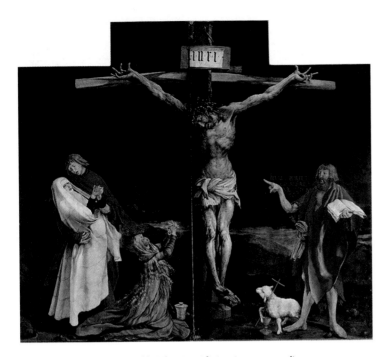

I.11 Matthias Grünewald, *The Crucifixion* (center panel).
ca. 1509/10–15. Oil on panel, 9'9½" × 10'9" (2.97 × 3.28 m).
Musée d'Unterlinden, Colmar, France

makes them beautiful. Others will continue to be repulsed and offended by them, or at best fail to find them interesting.

ILLUSIONISM AND MEANING IN ART

The Roman historian Pliny tells the story about the competition between the Greek painters Zeuxis and Parrhasius to see who could make the most realistic work. Zeuxis painted grapes so real that birds tried to eat them. But it was Parrhasius who won the competition when he made a painting of a curtain covering a painting. So realistic was the work that Zeuxis asked him to pull back the curtain covering his painting only to discover that he was already looking at the painting.

Pliny's story is interesting, because despite a recurring emphasis on illusionism in art, the ability to create illusionistic effects and "fool the eye" is generally not what determines quality in art, and if it were, thousands of relatively unknown artists today would be considered geniuses. As we just discussed, quality in art comes from ideas *and* execution. Just being clever and fooling the eye is not enough.

A look at the sculpture of twentieth-century artist Duane Hanson shows us how illusionism can be put in the service of meaning to create a powerful work of art. Hanson's 1995 sculpture *Man on a Mower* (fig. **I.12**) is a work that is too often appreciated only for its illusionistic qualities, while the real content goes unnoticed. Yet, it is the content, not the illusionism itself, that makes this sculpture so powerful. Hanson began making his sculptures in the late 1960s, casting his figures in polyester resin, and then meticulously painting them. He then dressed them in

real clothing, used real accessories (including wigs and artificial eyeballs), and placed them with real bits of furniture. Most viewers are startled to discover his sculptures are not real people, and many have tried to interact with his characters, which include museum guards, tourists, shoppers, house painters, and sunbathers.

But Hanson's art is about more than just a visual sleight of hand. He is also a realist and a moralist, and his art is filled with tragic social commentary. By "realist," we mean that his sculpture is not limited to attractive, beautiful, and ennobling people, objects, and situations, but instead focuses on the base, crude, and unseemly. In *Man on a Mower*, which, with the exception of the lawnmower and aluminum can, is painted cast bronze, we see an overweight man clutching a diet soda. He dwarfs the riding mower he sits on. His T-shirt, baseball hat, pants, and sneakers are soiled. He is ordinary, and the entire sculpture is remarkably prosaic.

Man on a Mower is a tragic work. We see disillusionment in the man's eyes as he blankly stares off into space. The diet soda he holds suggests that he is trying to lose weight but is losing the battle. Cutting grass is another metaphor for a losing battle, since the grass is going to grow back. This work also represents the banality of human existence. What is life about? The monotony of cutting grass. In this last work, made when he knew he was dying of cancer, Hanson captured what he perceived to be the emptiness of human existence and contemporary life in the modern world. The illusionism of the sculpture makes this aura of alienation and lack of spirituality all the more palpable. This man is us, and this is our life, too. He embodies no poetry, nobility, or heroism. Our twentieth-century *Man on a Mower* has no fine causes or beliefs to run to as he confronts the down-to-earth reality of life and death.

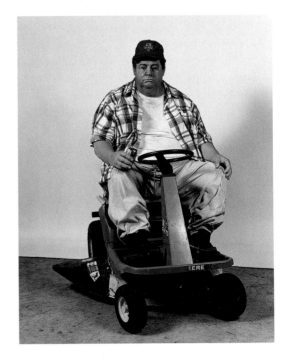

I.12 Duane Hanson, *Man on a Mower*. 1995.
Bronze, polychromed in oil, with mower. Life-size.
Courtesy Van de Weghe Fine Art, New York

CAN A MECHANICAL PROCESS BE ART? PHOTOGRAPHY

The first edition of this book did not include photography, reflecting on attitude dating back to the introduction of photography in 1839 that the medium, because it was largely a mechanical process, was not an art form, or certainly not one that had the same merit as painting and sculpture. Within the last 25 years, however, photography has been vindicated. Along with video and film, it has been elevated to the status of one of the most important artistic mediums, perhaps even outstripping painting. Pictures from the nineteenth and twentieth centuries that had interested only a handful of photography insiders suddenly became intensely sought-after, with many museums rushing to establish photography departments and amass significant collections. In other words, it took well over 125 years for people to understand photography and develop an eye for the special qualities and beauties of the medium, which are so radically different from those of the traditional twin peaks of the visual arts, painting and sculpture.

We need only look at a 1972 photograph titled *Albuquerque* (fig. **I.13**) by Lee Friedlander to see how photography operates as an artistic medium. In his black-and-white print, called a gelatin silver print since the pre-exposed paper surface consists of silver in a gelatin solution, Friedlander portrays a modern America which, he suggests, has been rendered vacuous and lifeless by modernity and twentieth-century technology. How does he make such a statement? The picture obviously has a haunting emptiness, for it contains no people and is instead filled with strange vacant spaces of walkway and street that appear between the numerous objects, such as a fire hydrant, street signs, and traffic light, that pop up everywhere. A hard, eerie geometry prevails, as seen in the strong verticals of poles, buildings, and wall. Cylinders, rectangles, and circles can be found throughout the composition, even in the background apartment building and the brick driveway in the foreground.

Despite the stillness and sense of absence, the picture is busy and restless. The vertical elements create a vibrant staccato rhythm, which is reinforced by the asymmetrical composition lacking a focus or center, and by the powerful intersecting diagonals of the street and foreground wall. Friedlander crafted his composition so carefully he gets the shadow of the hydrant to parallel the street. Disturbing features appear everywhere. There is a lopsided telephone pole, suggesting collapse. And there is the pole for a street sign, the top of which has been cropped, that visually cuts a dog in two while casting a mysterious shadow on a nearby wall. The fire hydrant appears to be mounted incorrectly, sticking too far out of the ground. The car on the right has been brutally cropped and appears to have a light pole sprouting from its hood. The entire picture is dominated by technology and synthetic, industrial, or mass-produced objects. Nature has been cemented over, reduced to a few straggly trees in the middle ground and distance and the thriving weeds surrounding the

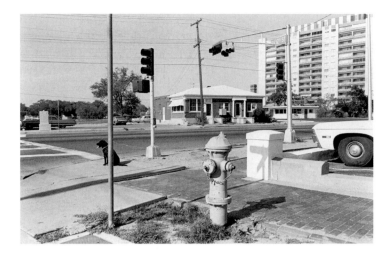

I.13 Lee Friedlander, *Albuquerque*. 1972. Gelatin silver print, 11 × 14" (27.9 × 35.6 cm)

hydrant. In this brilliant print, Friedlander powerfully suggests that technology, mass-produced products, and a fast fragmented lifestyle are spawning alienation and a disconnection with nature. Friedlander also suggests that modernization is also making America homogeneous—if it were not for the title, we would have no idea that this photograph was taken in Albuquerque, New Mexico.

Friedlander did not just find this composition. He very carefully made it. He not only wanted a certainly quality of light for his picture, but probably even waited for the sun to cast shadows that aligned perfectly with the street. When framing the composition, he meticulously incorporated a fragment of the utility cover in the lower left foreground, while axing a portion of the car on the right. Nor did the geometry of the picture just happen. He made it happen. Instead of a soft focus that would create an atmospheric blurry picture, he used a deep focus that produces a sharp crisp image filled with detail, allowing, for example, the individual rectangular bricks in the pavement to be clearly seen. The strong white tones of the vertical rectangles of the apartment building, the foreground wall, and the utility box blocking the car on the left edge of the picture were most likely carefully worked up in the darkroom, as was the rectangular columned doorway on the house. Friedlander has exposed the ugliness of modern America in this hard, cold, dry image, and because of the power of its message has made an extraordinarily beautiful work of art, the kind of image that has elevated photography into the pantheon of art.

HOW ARCHITECTURE TELLS STORIES

An art form that is basically abstract and functional might be seen as a poor candidate for telling stories, conveying messages, and disseminating propaganda. And yet it can. We see Gianlorenzo Bernini doing it in 1657 when he was asked by Pope Alexander XVII to design a large open space, or piazza, in front of St. Peter's

Cathedral in Rome. Bernini's solution was to create a plaza that was defined by a colonnade, or row of columns, resembling arms that appear to embrace visitors maternally, welcoming them into the bosom of the church (fig. **I.14**). He thus anthropomorphized the building by emphasizing the identification of the church with the Virgin Mary. At the same time, the French architect Claude Perrault was commissioned to design the façade of Louis XIV's palace, the Louvre in Paris (fig. **I.15**). To proclaim the king's grandeur, he made the ground floor, where the day-to-day business of the court was carried out, a squat podium. In contrast, the second floor, where the royal quarters were located and Louis would have held court, was much higher and grander and served as the main floor, clearly supported by the worker-bee floor. Perrault articulated this elevated second story with a design that recalled Roman temples, thus associating Louis XIV with imperial Rome and worldly power. The severe geometry and symmetry of the building reflect the regimented order and tight control of Louis XIV's reign.

At first glance, it seems hard to project any story onto Frank Lloyd Wright's Solomon R. Guggenheim Museum (fig. **I.16**), a museum that, when it was built between 1956 and 1959, was largely dedicated to abstract art. Located on upper Fifth Avenue in New York and overlooking Central Park, the building resembled for many a flying saucer; it was certainly radically different from the surrounding residential apartment buildings, and for that matter, almost anything built anywhere up to that time. But if we had to guess, we would probably first divine that the building might be a museum, for the exterior resembles a work of art— a giant nonobjective sculpture. Made of reinforced concrete, the building even seems as though it were made from an enormous mold that formed its continuous upward spiral, which from any one side appears to consist of enormous, weighty, massive horizontal bands. There is no mistaking this structure for an apartment complex or office building.

Wright conceived the Guggenheim in 1945–46, when he received the commission, and his personal goal was to create an organic structure that deviated from the conventional static rectangular box filled with conventional rectangular rooms. The building is designed around a spiral ramp (fig. **I.17**), which is meant to evoke a spiral shell, and this ramp is what defines the design of the exterior. Wright also thought of the interior as a ceramic vase, for it is closed at the bottom, widens as it rises, and is "open" at the top since it is capped by a spectacular light-filled, cone-shaped glass roof. Essentially, the museum is a single ramp-lined space, although there are a handful of galleries off the ramp and separate spaces for offices, auditorium, and bookstore, for example. Wright expected visitors to take an elevator to the top of the ramp, and then slowly amble down its 3 percent gradient, gently pulled along by gravity. Because the ramp was relatively narrow, viewers could not stand too far back from the art, which seemed to float on the curved walls, enhancing the fluid effect of Wright's curved, organic design. As a result, visitors were forced into a more intimate relationship with the art. At the same time, however, they could look back across the open space of the room

to see where they had gone, comparing the work in front of them to a segment of the exhibition presented on a sweeping distant arc, Or they could look ahead as well, to get a preview of where they were going.

Not only do visitors see the art, they also see other visitors, sometimes just as distant specks, winding their way down the ramp. The building has a sense of continuity and mobility that Wright viewed as an organic experience, analogous to traveling along the continuous winding paths of the adjacent Central Park, which was designed in the nineteenth century to capture and preserve nature in the encroaching urban environment. Wright's enormous "room" reflects nature not only in its spiral shell design, but also in the organic concave and convex forms that can be seen from the top of ramp and that reflect the subtle eternal movement of nature. Wright even placed a lozenge-shaped pool on the ground floor, directly opposite the light entering from the skylight above, the two architectural touches reinforcing a sense of nature. Art historians have also likened the sense of constant

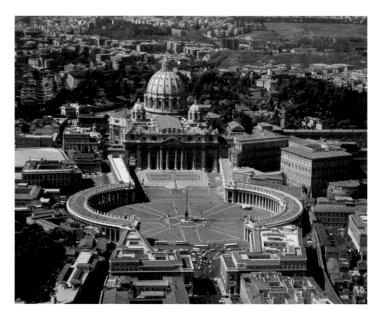

I.14   St. Peter's, Rome. Nave and façade by Carlo Maderno, 1607–15; colonnade by Gianlorenzo Bernini, designed 1657

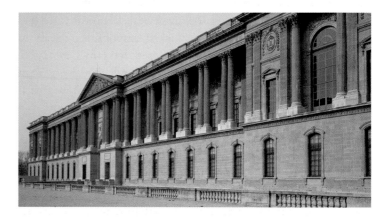

I.15   Claude Perrault. East front of the Louvre, Paris. 1667–70

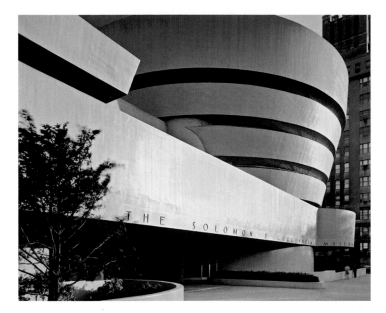

1.16 Frank Lloyd Wright. The Solomon R. Guggenheim Museum, New York. 1956–59

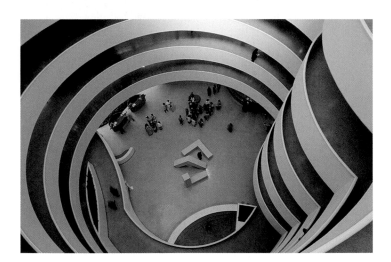

I.17 Frank Lloyd Wright. Interior of the Solomon R. Guggenheim Museum, New York. 1956–59

movement in Wright's seemingly endless ramp—which most people now ascend rather than descend because exhibitions begin at the foot of the ramp—to the American frontier, the ramp embodying "the expansive, directionless response of the frontiersman to limitless space," as expressed by James Fenimore Cooper's Natty Bumppo, Herman Melville's whaling chase, Mark Twain's Mississippi, and Walt Whitman's Open Road. Far-fetched as this may sound, we must remember that Wright was born in the Midwest in the nineteenth century, when it was still rural, and beginning with his earliest mature buildings, his designs, such as the Robie House (see fig. 26.39), were meant to capture the vast spread of the plains and were carefully integrated into the land.

If Wright's austere, abstract sculptural design for both the exterior and interior undermines his attempt to evoke nature, the building still retains a sense of open space and continuous

movement. Unlike any other museum, the Guggenheim has a sense of communal spirit, for here everyone is united in one large room and traveling the same path.

EXPERIENCING ART

You will be astonished when you see first-hand much of the art in this book. No matter how accurate the reproductions here, or in any other text, they are no more than stand-ins for the actual objects. We hope you will visit some of the museums where the originals are displayed. But keep in mind that looking at art, absorbing its full impact, takes time and repeated visits. In many respects, looking at art is no different than reading a book or watching a film—it requires extensive, detailed looking, a careful reading of the image or object, perhaps even a questioning of why every motif, mark, or color is used. Ideally, the museum will help you understand the art. Often, there are introductory text panels that tell you why the art has been presented as it is and what it is about, and ideally there will be labels for individual works that provide further information. Major temporary exhibitions generally have a catalog, which adds further information and sometimes another layer of interpretation. But text panels, labels, and catalogues generally reflect one person's reading of the art: Keep in mind there are usually many other ways to approach or think about it.

Art museums are relatively new. Before the nineteenth century art was not made to be viewed in museums, so when you are looking at work in a museum, you are often viewing it out of the original context in which it was meant to be seen. Much work can still be seen in its original context—churches, cathedrals, chateaux, public piazzas, and archaeological sites. Ultimately, however, art can be found everywhere—in commercial galleries, corporate lobbies and offices, places of worship, and private homes. It is displayed in public spaces, from subway stations and bus stops to public plazas and civic buildings such as libraries, performing arts centers, and city halls. University and college buildings are often filled with art, and the buildings themselves are art. The chair you are sitting in and the house or building you are reading this book in are also works of art—maybe not great art, but art all the same, as Duchamp explained. Even the clothing you are wearing is in a sense art, and for you it is a way to make a personal statement. Everywhere you find art, it is telling you something, and supporting a point of view.

Art is not a luxury, as many people would have us believe, but an integral part of daily life. It has a major impact on us, even when we are not aware of it, for we feel better about ourselves when we are in environments that are visually enriching and exciting. Most important, art stimulates us to think. Even when it provokes and outrages us, it broadens our experience by making us question our values, attitudes, and worldview. This book is an introduction to this fascinating field that is so intertwined with our lives. After reading it, you will find that the world will no longer look the same.

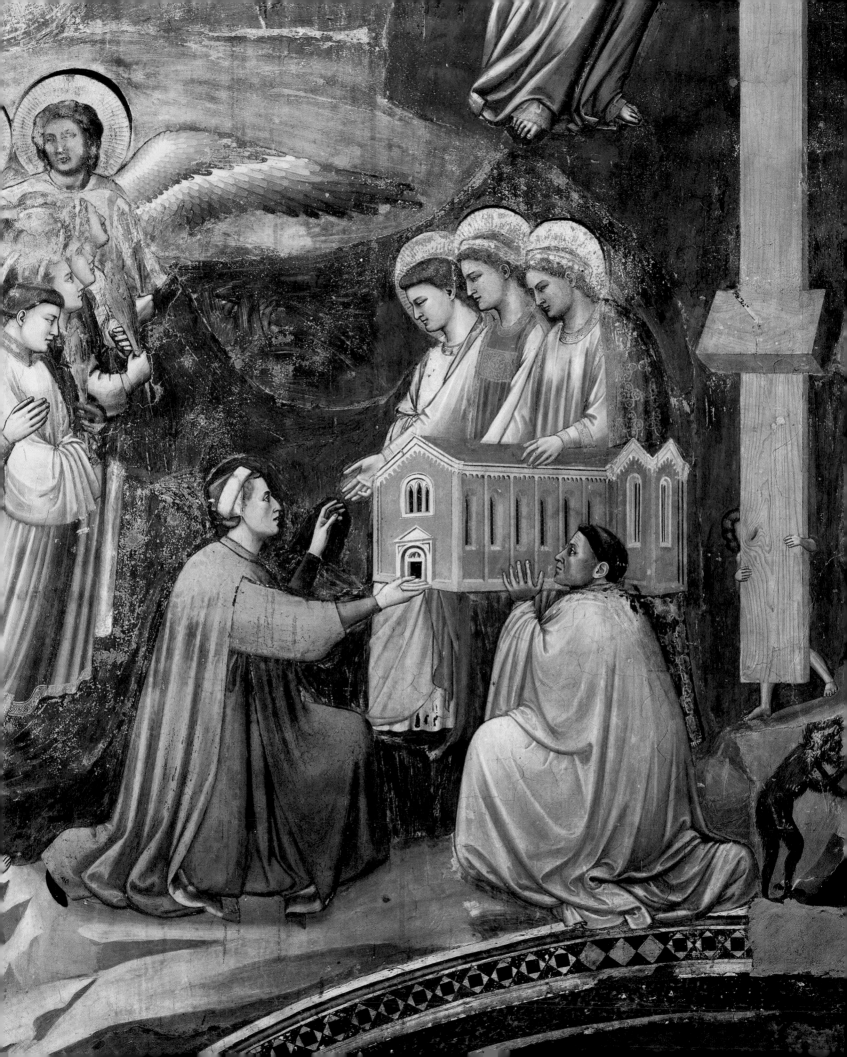

CHAPTER 13

Art in Thirteenth- and Fourteenth-Century Italy

THE MAP OF THE ITALIAN PENINSULA (MAP 13.1) HINTS AT THE forces that shaped life and art there in the thirteenth and fourteenth centuries. Although the Alps separate the peninsula from the rest of Europe, branches of the Mediterranean Sea surround it, providing access by water to the rest of the world. As the heart of the Roman Empire, the

peninsula abounded in the physical remains of Rome. Italy was also the center of the Catholic Church for much of the Middle Ages, bringing church officials and ambassadors from Europe to its cities. The culture formed by this geography was distinctive and cosmopolitan.

The length of the coastline encouraged trade by sea, while Italy's location made it a natural link between Europe and Africa and Asia. Coastal cities, such as Pisa, Genoa and Venice, controlled these important trade routes. Italian vessels carried goods from as far away as Constantinople and the Baltics to its cities. Merchants traveled over land, too, even reaching the court of the Great Khan in China.

This geography had profound effects on Italian society. In the absence of a strong central authority, the cities controlled the regions around them, so that there was no single political unit called Italy. Unlike many other parts of Europe, political power lay not in the hands of the hereditary aristocracy, but in the hands of urban elites. Monarchs controlled only a few regions: Lombardy in the north and Naples in the south. Instead, the wealthiest and most influential cities, including Florence and Siena, were organized as representative republics, with political offices held by mercantile oligarchs. As a check on inherited

Detail of figure 13.18, the Last Judgment, Giotto, showing Enrico Scrovegni Offering the Chapel. Interior of Arena (Scrovegni) Chapel, Padua.

power, some cities even excluded the landed aristocracy from participating in their political processes.

The larger powers of Europe, especially the two international institutions of the Holy Roman Empire and the papacy, often interfered in Italian politics, though sometimes from a distance. The emperors usually remained north of the Alps, though they claimed to control portions of Italy. The papacy left Italy for southern France in the fourteenth century, underscoring the power and influence of the French king. The prestige of the French monarchy enhanced the appeal of the **Gothic** style of building born near Paris and its related pictorial innovations, which artists in Italy adapted to their traditions.

The context in which Italian artists developed their skills differed from the rest of Europe. Throughout the Middle Ages, Roman and Early Christian art served as an inspiration for Italian architects and sculptors, as is visible in such works as the **cathedral** of Pisa (see fig. 11.33). In the mid-thirteenth century, the Holy Roman emperor Frederick II (1194–1250), who lived for a time in southern Italy, deliberately revived imperial Roman style to express his own political ambitions as heir to the Roman Empire. The other empire, Byzantium, kept a presence throughout Italy, too— through mosaics at Ravenna, Sicily, and Venice, and through the circulation of artists and **icons** such as the *Madonna Enthroned* (see fig. 8.49). A further element added to the vocabulary of Italian artists was the French Gothic style, created in the Paris region and introduced through the travels of artists and patrons.

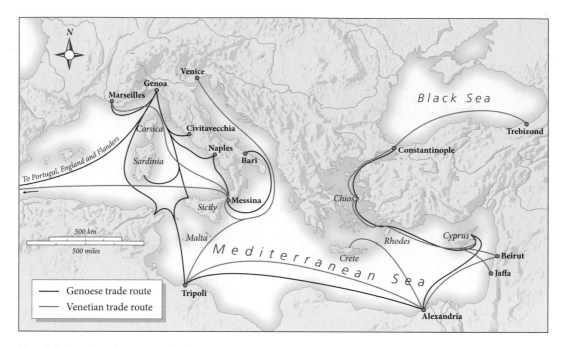

Map 13.1   The Italian Peninsula's key sea trade-routes

One of those travelers, the poet churchman, and scholar Francesco Petrarch, exemplifies another aspect of fourteenth-century Italian culture: a growing interest in the creative works of individuals. Petrarch and his contemporaries Dante Alighieri and Giovanni Boccaccio belong to a generation of thinkers and writers who turned to the study of ancient works of literature, history, and art to seek out beautiful and correct forms. Petrarch also sought to improve the quality of written Latin, and thereby to emulate the works of the Roman authors Vergil and Cicero. This study of ancient thought and art led to a search for moral clarity and models of behavior, a mode of inquiry that came to be known as **humanism**. Humanists valued the works of the ancients, both in the literary and the visual arts, and they looked to the classical past for solutions to modern problems. They particularly admired Roman writers who championed civic and personal virtues, such as service to the state and stoicism in times of trouble. Humanists considered Roman forms the most authoritative and, therefore, the most worthy of imitation, though Greek texts and ideas were also admired.

The study of the art of Rome and Greece would profoundly change the culture and the art of Europe by encouraging artists to look at nature carefully and to consider the human experience as a valid subject for art. These trends found encouragement in the ideals and theology of late medieval groups, such as the Dominicans, who valued classical learning, and the Franciscans, whose founder saw God in the beauty of nature. These bodies, called mendicants because they originally supported themselves from alms, became an important stimulus to thirteenth- and fourteenth-century patronage.

THE GROWTH OF THE MENDICANT ORDERS AND THE VISUAL ARTS IN ITALY

The two major mendicant groups were the Franciscans and the Dominicans. They established international "orders," as many monastic groups had done in the Middle Ages, although their missions differed from those of traditional monks. Both orders were founded to minister to the lay populations in the rapidly expanding cities; they did not retreat from the world, but engaged with it. Each order of friars (brothers) built churches in the cities so that sermons could be preached to crowds of people. The Dominicans, founded by Dominic de Guzmán in 1216, were especially concerned with combating heresy. The Franciscan order, founded by Francis of Assisi in 1209, worked in the cities to bring deeper spirituality and comfort to the poor. Taking vows of poverty, Franciscans were committed to teaching the laity and to encouraging them to pursue spiritual growth. Toward this goal, they told stories and used images to explain and affirm the teachings of the Church. Characteristically, Franciscans urged the faithful to visualize events such as the Nativity in tangible ways, including setting up Nativity scenes (crèches) in churches as an aid to devotion. Both orders played important roles in late medieval religious and artistic life, though the Franciscans held a special place in Italy since their founder was a native son.

The Franciscans at Assisi and Florence

The charismatic Francis died in 1226 and was named a saint two years later. His home town and burial place was the site of a huge

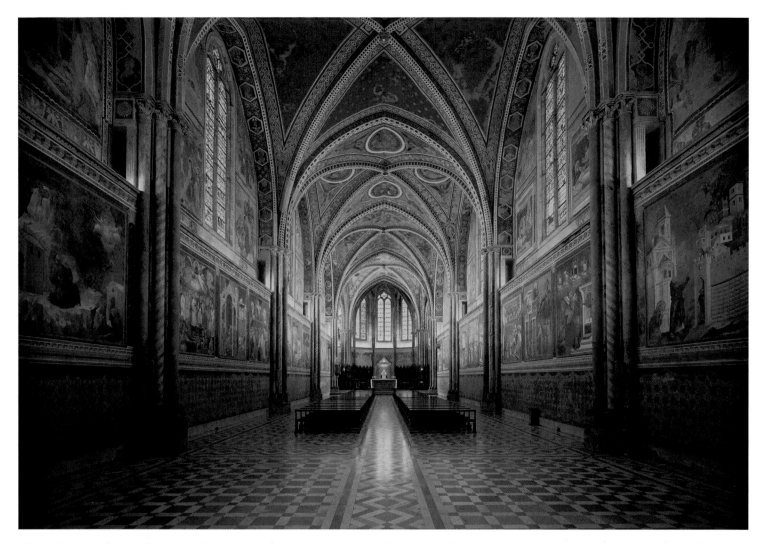

13.1   Interior of Upper Church, Basilica of San Francesco, Assisi. Begun 1228; consecrated 1253

church built in his honor. The pope sponsored its construction, which began shortly after Francis's canonization in 1228; the church was consecrated in 1253. Because it held the body of the popular saint, it was built as a large, multistoried structure in order to accommodate the numerous pilgrims it attracted. Most pilgrims would first encounter the large hall of the Upper Church, before descending to a church below. The Upper Church (fig. **13.1**) consists of a single long **nave,** or central hall, where crowds could gather. Whereas French churches of the same period reduced wall surfaces in their naves in favor of large stained-glass windows and complex vertical supports, as is the case at Chartres (see fig. 12.12), San Francesco at Assisi has relatively small windows and large expanses of wall surface. As in the northern churches, at San Francesco a brick **vault,** supported by Gothic pointed **arches,** covers the nave. Yet San Francesco is neither as high nor as spatially complex as French Gothic churches. The elimination of lower side **aisles** along the length of the nave simplifies the space and makes the walls more prominent. These wall surfaces became a magnet for artists, especially below the windows in the nave of the Upper Church. Their paintings were executed in the fresco technique, which Italian artists had

used throughout the Middle Ages. (See *Materials and Techniques,* page 441.)

The scale of the painting program at Assisi required teams of artists drawn from all over Italy and the work took many years to complete. From the 1270s through the early fourteenth century, papal sponsorship brought together artists from Rome, Siena, Florence, and elsewhere. Assisi became a laboratory for the development and dissemination of fourteenth-century Italian art. The frescoes flanking the nave windows depict biblical scenes from the book of Genesis and the life of Christ. But the most visible frescoes in the nave were painted below the windows; these depict the life and achievements of Francis himself.

The artists responsible for the St. Francis cycle had to devise images that conveyed both the events of Francis's life and their significance to Christian history. The events chosen for depiction came from biographies of Francis's life composed by his followers. One important theme found in these texts is the saint's veneration of nature as a manifestation of divine workmanship. The scene *St. Francis Preaching to the Birds* (fig. **13.2**) expresses this theme and Francis's attitude that all creatures are connected. The fresco depicts Francis in his brown habit standing in a landscape

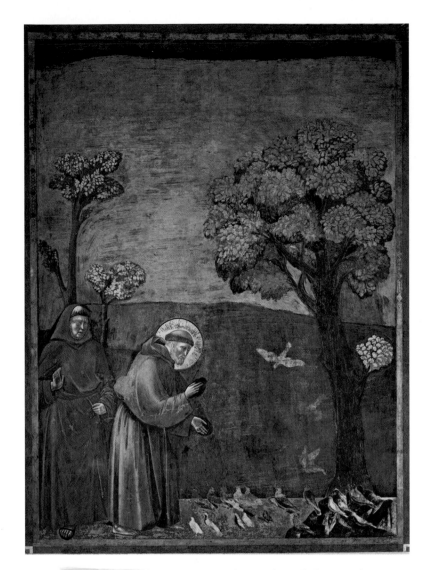

13.2 Anonymous. *St. Francis Preaching to the Birds*, from Basilica of San Francesco, Assisi. Begun 1290 (?). Fresco

and speaking to a flock of birds. To the astonished eyes of his companion, Francis appears to be able to communicate with the birds, who gather at his feet to listen.

The artist sets the scene outdoors by framing the figures with trees and painting the background blue. A narrow shelf of earth creates a platform on which the bulky figures stand. Francis and his companion are rendered naturalistically, as the artist describes light washing over their forms to suggest their mass and weight. Francis's figure becomes the focal point of the image, through his central position, the halo around his head, and his downward glance. His body language—the bent-over stance, the movement of his hands—express his intense engagement with the birds as representatives of nature. The simplicity of the composition makes the fresco easily legible and memorable.

The identities of the artists responsible for the frescoes in the nave of San Francesco are uncertain and controversial. One of the artists mentioned as a primary designer and painter is the Roman Pietro Cavallini; another is the Florentine Giotto di Bondone. But documentary evidence is lacking, and the opinions of connoisseurs vary. Some prefer to assign these frescoes to an anonymous master, or masters, named either after the paintings at Assisi or subgroups among them. Since many painters worked in the same space, they competed with and influenced each other, thus affecting the future direction of Italian art.

Franciscan women served God within the walls of their convents, through their vocations as nuns, and their prayers for their neighbors. Like the friars, these women devoted themselves to poverty and simplicity, and their convents and churches were often less wealthy than many of the masculine institutions. Franciscan nuns belonged to the branch of the order founded by Francis's associate, St. Clare, who was canonized in 1255. The thirteenth-

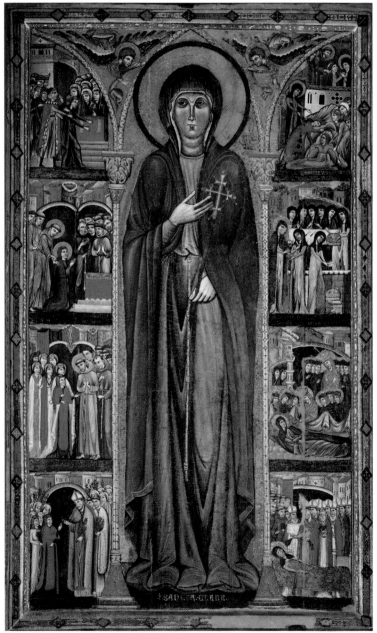

13.3 *Altarpiece of St. Clare*. ca. 1280. Tempera on panel, 9 × 5'6" (2.73 × 1.65 m). Convent of Santa Chiara, Assisi

Fresco Painting and Conservation

Fresco is a technique for applying paint to walls that results in an image that is both durable and brilliant. Frescoed surfaces are built up in layers: Over the rough wall goes a layer of rough lime-based plaster called *arriccio*. The artist then draws preliminary sketches onto this layer of plaster. Because they are done in red, these sketches are called *sinopie* (an Italian word derived from ancient Sinope, in Asia Minor, which was famous as a source of red-colored pigment). Then a finer plaster called *intonaco* is applied in areas just large enough to provide for a day's worth of painting—the *giornata* (from *giorno*, the Italian word for "day"). While the plaster is still wet, the artist applies pigments suspended in lime water. As the plaster dries, the pigments bind to it, creating a *buon fresco*, or "true fresco." Plaster dries in a day, which is why only the amount of wet plaster that can be painted during that time can be applied. The work has to be done on a scaffold, so it is carried out from top to bottom, usually in horizontal strips about 4 to 6 feet long. As each horizontal level is completed, the scaffolding is lowered for the next level. To prevent chemical interactions with the lime of the plaster, some colors have to be applied *a secco* or dry; many details of images are applied this way as well. *Fresco secco* does not bond to the plaster as surely as *buon fresco* does, so it tends to flake off over time. Consequently, some frescoes have subsequently been touched up with tempera paints.

Although durability is the key reason for painting in fresco, over the centuries wars and floods have caused damage. Modern conservators have developed techniques for removing frescoes from walls and installing them elsewhere. After the Arno River flooded in 1966, many Florentine frescoes were rescued in this way, not only preserving the artworks but greatly adding to the knowledge and technology required for this task. When a fresco is removed, series of cuts are made around the image. Then, a supporting canvaslike material is applied to the frescoed surface with a water-soluble glue. The surface to which the canvaslike material has been glued can then be pulled off gently and transferred to a new support to be hung elsewhere, after which the canvas can be removed. Such removals have exposed many *sinopie*, such as the one shown here. The fresco, attributed to Francesco Traini

(see fig. 13.30), was badly damaged by fire in 1944 and had to be detached from the wall in order to save what was left of it. This procedure revealed the plaster underneath, on which the composition had been sketched out. These drawings, of the same size as the fresco itself, are much freer-looking in style than the actual fresco. They often reveal the artist's personal style more directly than the painted version, which was carried out with the aid of assistants.

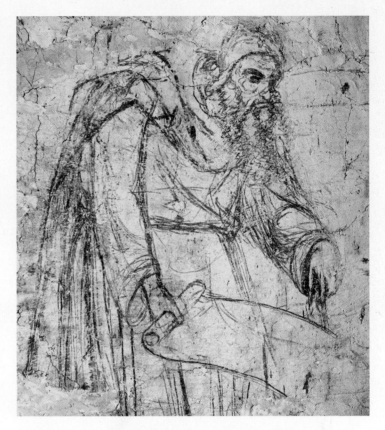

Anonymous (Francesco Traini?). Sinopia drawing for *The Triumph of Death* (detail). Camposanto, Pisa

century convent in Assisi dedicated to St. Clare does not boast a large fresco cycle but preserves a painted panel (fig. **13.3**) intended to sit on an **altar** (an **altarpiece**). A tall rectangle of wood covered with egg-based **tempera** paints, it was executed around 1280. It is dominated by the figure of St. Clare, dressed in the habit of her order, standing frontally and holding the staff of an abbess. The image does not portray her specific features as a portrait would, but represents her as a saintly figure of authority, whose large staring eyes and frontal posture have roots in Byzantine art. Alongside the saint eight tiny narratives convey stories about her life, death, and miracles. These **vignettes** relate her commitment to her vocation, her obedience to Francis and the Church, and her service to her fellow nuns. The narratives make little pretense at three-dimensional form or spatial structure, keeping the focus on the figures and their actions the better to tell the story.

Churches and Their Furnishings in Urban Centers

Franciscan churches began to appear all over Italy as the friars ministered to the spiritual lives of city dwellers. A characteristic example in Florence is the church of Santa Croce (Holy Cross), begun around 1295 (figs. **13.4** and **13.5**). The architect was probably the Tuscan sculptor Arnolfo di Cambio. Like San Francesco in Assisi, Santa Croce shares some features with Gothic churches in northern Europe, but it differs from them too. Its form is a **basilica** (a standard church plan including nave, side aisles, and apse), though the eastern end, where the high altar and many chapels are located, terminates in mostly rectilinear forms. Only the **apse** (or projecting niche), where the altar stands, is polygonal. This simplified design for the most sacred spaces in the

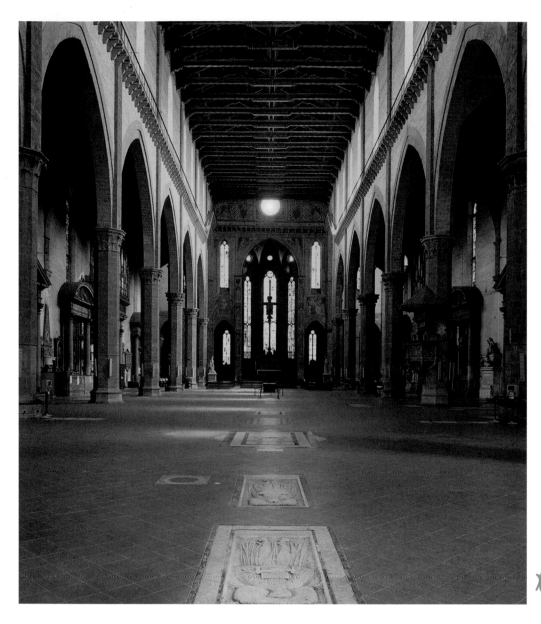

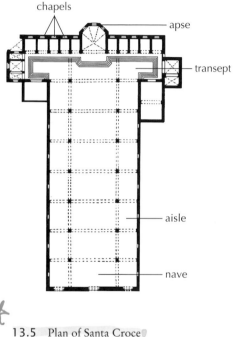

13.4 Arnolfo di Cambio (?). Nave and choir of Santa Croce, Florence. Begun ca. 1295

13.5 Plan of Santa Croce

church probably comes from monastic churches, especially of the reform-minded Cistercian order; for example, the plan of Fontenay Abbey (see fig. 11.21). The nave's proportions are broad and expansive rather than vertical. The nave **arcade** uses a Gothic pointed arch, while vertical moldings pull the eye up to the ceiling. Where in a French Gothic church, however, such moldings would support a vaulted ceiling, at Santa Croce wooden **trusses** (beams or rafters joined together) span the nave. The only vaults are at the apse and several chapels at the ends of the **transept**, the perpendicular space between the nave and the apse.

As the stone vaults of San Francesco in Assisi, the order's mother church, indicate that the friars were not averse to such structures, the choice of a wooden roof at Santa Croce may need explanation. This preference perhaps originates in a Tuscan tradition, as the great **Romanesque** cathedral of nearby Pisa (fig. 11.34) also has a wooden roof. Santa Croce's broad nave with high arches is also reminiscent of Early Christian churches (see fig. 8.9), so the choice may also spring from a desire to evoke the simplicity of Early Christian basilicas and thus link Franciscan poverty with the traditions of the early Church. A vaulted nave would have been much more expensive.

Santa Croce served the growing population of Florence by providing room for elite burials in its aisles and chapels. The church's wide spaces also held large crowds so they could hear the friars' sermons.

Pulpits in Pisan Churches

For reading Scripture at services and for preaching, churchmen often commissioned monumental pulpits with narrative or symbolic images carved onto them. Several monumental pulpits were made by members of a family of sculptors who worked in Pisa, including Nicola Pisano (ca. 1220/25–1284) and his son Giovanni Pisano (1265–1314). Though the two men worked at various sites throughout Italy, they executed important pulpits for the cathedral and baptistery at Pisa.

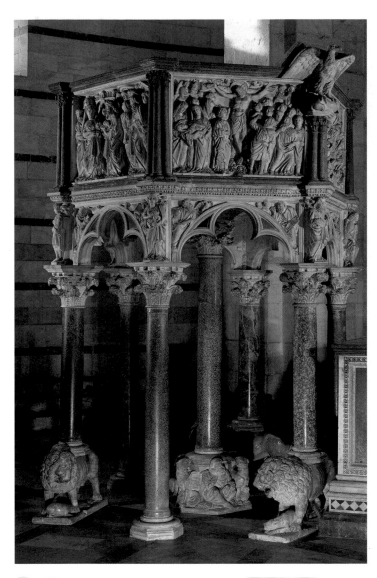

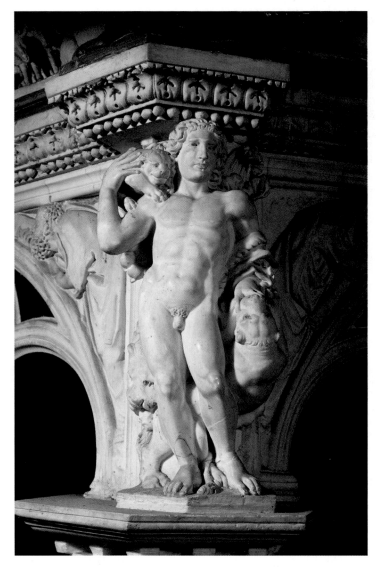

13.6 Nicola Pisano. Pulpit. 1259–60. Marble, height 15' (4.6 m). Baptistery, Pisa

13.7 Nicola Pisano. *Fortitude*, detail of pulpit

For the Pisan baptistery, Nicola Pisano and his workshop carved a hexagonal marble pulpit finished around 1260 (fig. **13.6**). Rising to about 15 feet high, so the assembly could see and hear the speaker, the six sides of the pulpit rest on colored marble columns supporting classically inspired **capitals**. Above the capitals, carved into leaf shapes, small figures symbolizing the virtues stand between cusped arches, while figures of the prophets sit in the **spandrels** (the areas above the curves) of these arches. Surprisingly, one of these figures (fig. **13.7**) is a male nude with a lion cub on his shoulder and a lion skin over his arm. His form and the lion skin should identify him as the Greek hero Herakles (Hercules in Latin). Some scholars, however, have interpreted these same details to identify him as Daniel, the biblical hero whose faith allowed him to survive the lion's den. In either case, in the program of the pulpit, he stands for the Christian virtue of Fortitude. His anatomy, his proportions, and his stance are probably the product of Nicola Pisano's study of Roman and Early Christian sculpture. The figure's heroic nudity and his posture, with the

weight balanced on one leg to suggest movement, seem to be inspired by ancient models. Pisano had worked for Frederick II in southern Italy and at Rome, but his deep knowledge of ancient art may also derive from study of Roman artifacts in Pisa.

Nicola's study of the Roman past informs many other elements in his pulpit, including the narratives he carved for the six rectangular sides of the pulpit itself. These scenes from the life of Christ are carved in **relief**, so they project from the background. The Nativity scene in figure **13.8** is a densely crowded composition that combines the Annunciation with the Birth of Christ. The relief is treated as a shallow box filled with solid convex shapes in the manner of Roman **sarcophagi** (carved stone coffins), which Pisa's monumental cemetery preserved in good numbers. The Virgin has the dignity and bearing of a Roman matron. Pisano also knew Byzantine images of the Nativity, for the recumbent figure of the Virgin reflects that tradition. As the largest and most central figure, the reclining Virgin overpowers all the other elements in the composition. Around her, the details of

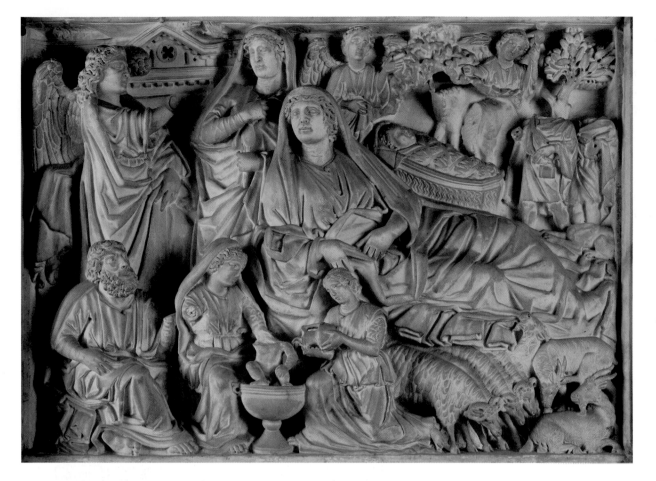

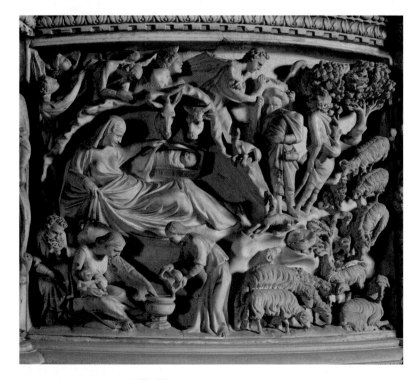

13.9 Giovanni Pisano, *Nativity*, detail of pulpit. 1302–10. Marble. Pisa cathedral

the narrative or setting, such as the midwives washing the child and Joseph's wondering gaze at the events, give the relief a human touch. Using forms inspired by both Byzantine and Roman models, Nicola uses broad figures, wrapped in **classicizing** draperies, to endow the scene with gravity and moral weight.

When his son Giovanni Pisano carved a pulpit about 50 years later for the cathedral of Pisa, he chose a different emphasis. Though executed at the same size and using the same material, his relief of the Nativity from the cathedral pulpit (fig. **13.9**) makes a strong contrast to his father's earlier work. Depicting the Nativity and the Annunciation to the shepherds, Giovanni dwells on the landscape and animal elements: Sheep and trees fill the right edge of the composition, while the Nativity itself takes place in a shallow cave in the Byzantine tradition. The Virgin still dominates the composition, but she is no longer a dignified matron staring out of the image. Instead, she is a young mother whose gaze and tender attention focus on her newborn child. Her proportions are elongated rather than sturdy. Rather than echoing Roman or Classical models, Giovanni has clearly studied contemporary French works to bring elegance and a detailed observation of nature to the image. Giovanni's swaying figures move more comfortably in the space they occupy. Where Nicola's *Nativity* is dominated by convex, bulging masses, Giovanni's appears to be made up of cavities and shadows. The play of lights and darks in Giovanni's relief exhibits a dynamic quality that contrasts with the serene calm of his father's work.

Expanding Florence Cathedral

The building and adornment of Pisa's cathedral complex were a civic as well as a religious duty for the town's citizens. As Italian cities grew and prospered, their religious centers grew with them. East of Pisa, along the Arno River, the increasing wealth of Florence inspired that town to undertake major projects for its cathedral and baptistery in order to compete with its neighbors. One of Nicola Pisano's students, Arnolfo di Cambio (ca. 1245–1302), was chosen to design a new cathedral for Florence to replace a smaller church that stood on the site. The cathedral was begun in 1296 (figs. **13.10**, **13.11**, and **13.12**). The project took the skills and energy of several generations, and the plan was modified more than once. For example, in 1357 Francesco Talenti (active 1325–1369) took over the project and dramatically extended the building to the east. By 1367, a committee of artists consulted by the overseers of the construction decided to cover the eastern zone with a high **dome**. The west façade and other portals continued to be adorned with sculpture throughout the **Renaissance** period, but the marble cladding on the building was not completed until the nineteenth century. Florence's Duomo (dome) was intended to be a grand structure that would not only serve as the spiritual center of the city, but as a statement of its wealth and importance.

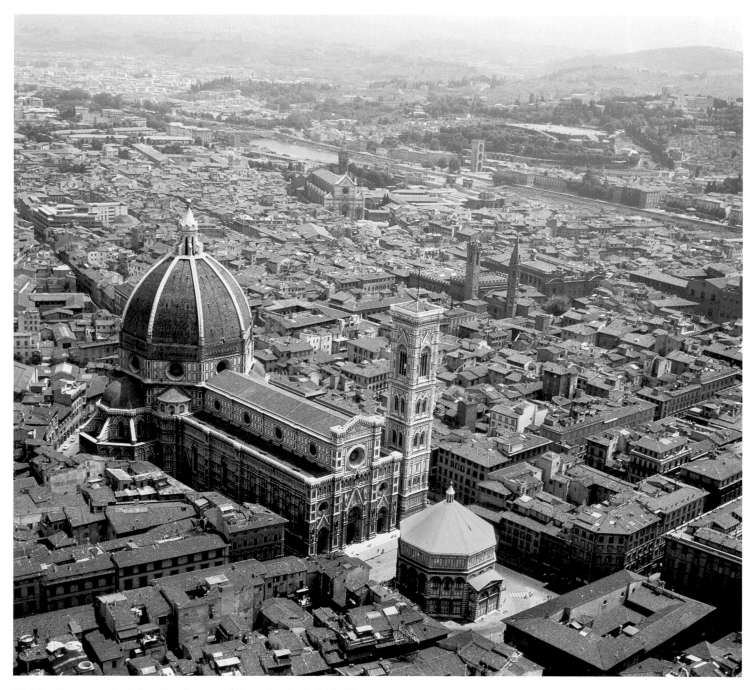

13.10   Florence cathedral and baptistery seen from the air. Cathedral begun 1296

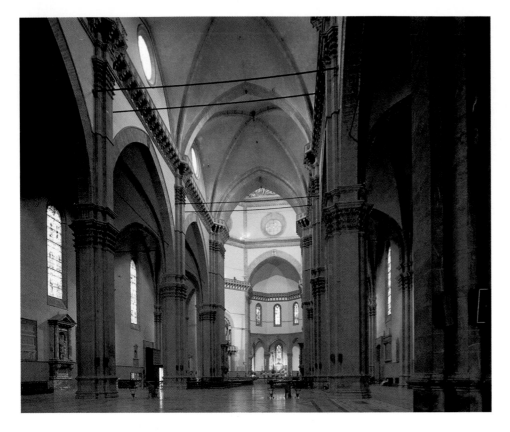

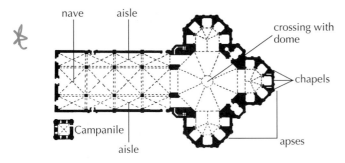

13.12   Plan of Florence cathedral and campanile

Arnolfo's original design provided for a large basilica with a high arcade and broad proportions that differs sharply from contemporary Gothic structures in France, even as it employs some of the technology of French Gothic. High pointed arches in the nave arcade rest on **piers** (vertical supports) articulated with leaf-shaped capitals. Flat moldings rise to the **clerestory** level, above the arcade. Windows in the clerestory and aisles are relatively small, leaving much more wall surface than in French cathedrals. Although the original plan called for a trussed wooden roof like the one at Santa Croce, by the mid-fourteenth century the plan had been altered to include **ribbed groin vaults** (stone vaults comprised of four sections with reinforcing along their edges), a detail closer to the northern Gothic taste. The later plans enlarged the eastern zone to terminate in three faceted arms which meet to form an octagonal space (the **crossing**) that would be covered by a dome. (This design appears in the fresco in fig. 13.31.) While this project included **flying buttresses** like French Gothic churches, these were never built. The scale of the proposed dome presented engineering difficulties that were not solved until the early fifteenth century. Instead of tall western towers incorporated into the façade, which was the norm in Gothic France, the cathedral has a **campanile** (bell tower) as a separate structure in the Italian tradition. The campanile is the work of the Florentine painter Giotto and his successors. If Florence's cathedral has Gothic elements in its vaults and arches, these foreign forms are tempered by local traditions.

Opposite the cathedral's west front stands the venerable baptistery of Florence, built in the eleventh century on much older foundations, which the Florentines believed to be Roman; they saw the glory of their own past in the structure's age. St. John the Baptist is a patron saint of the city of Florence; newborns became citizens of Florence by being baptized in this structure. The baptistery was the site of important artistic projects throughout the Renaissance. In 1330, its overseers commissioned another sculptor from Pisa, Andrea Pisano (ca. 1295–1348; no relation to Nicola or Giovanni) to cast a new pair of bronze doors for the baptistery. These were finished and installed in 1336 (fig. **13.13**). Cast of bronze and gilded, the project required 28 separate panels across the two panels of the door. They mostly represent scenes from the life of John the Baptist. Each vignette is framed by a Gothic **quatrefoil**, such as those found on the exteriors of French cathedrals. Yet within most of the four-lobed frames, Andrea provides a projecting ledge to support the figures and the landscape or architectural backgrounds. The relief showing the Baptism of Christ demonstrates Andrea's clear compositional technique:

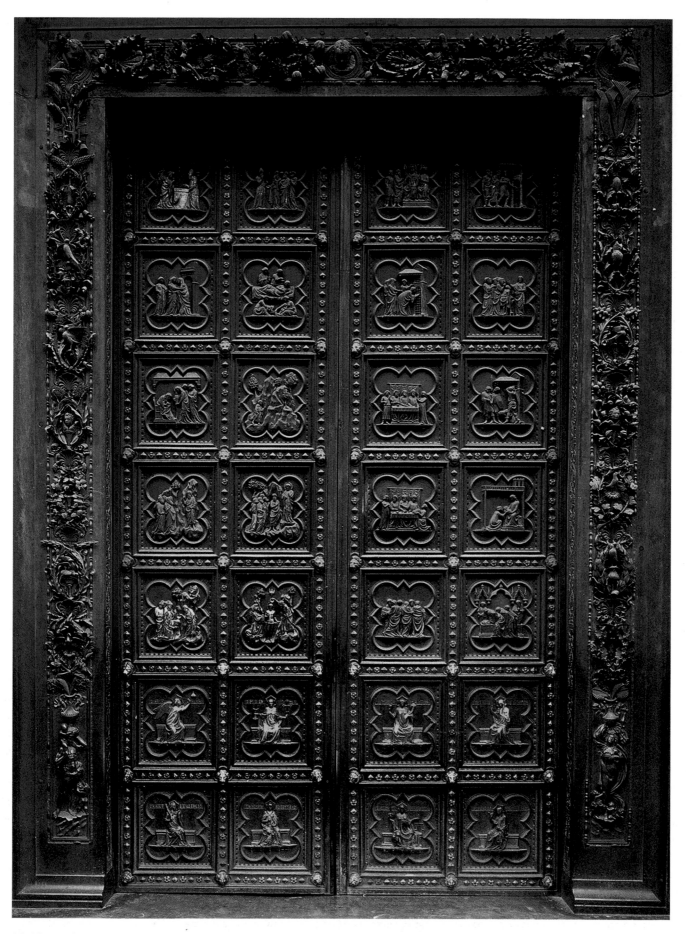

13.13 Andrea Pisano. South doors, baptistery of San Giovanni, Florence. 1330–36. Gilt bronze

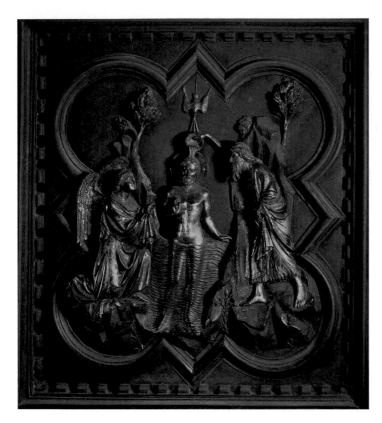

13.14 Andrea Pisano, *The Baptism of Christ*, from the south doors, baptistery of San Giovanni, Florence. 1330–36. Gilt bronze

Christ stands at the center, framed by John on the right in the act of baptism and an angelic witness on the left (fig. **13.14**). The dove symbolizing the Holy Spirit appears above Christ's head. The emphasis is on the key figures, with little detail to distract from the main narrative; only a few small elements suggest the landscape context of the Jordan River. If the beautiful torso of Christ in the river recalls the Fortitude figure from Nicola Pisano's Pisa Baptistery, the simplicity of the landscape and composition recall the frescoes at Assisi.

Building for the City Government: The Palazzo della Signoria

While the citizens of Florence were building the huge cathedral, the political faction that supported the papacy instead of the Holy Roman Empire consolidated its power in the city. The pro-papal party (the Guelphs) was largely composed of wealthier merchants who sought to contain the dynastic ambitions of aristocratic families who supported the emperor (the Ghibellines). The pro-papal group commissioned a large structure to house their governing council and to serve as the symbol of the political independence of the city. They probably chose Arnolfo di Cambio to design the Palazzo della Signoria (fig. **13.15**). It was begun in 1298 and completed in 1310, though it has been subject to later expansion and remodeling. It became known as the Palazzo Vecchio (or old palace) during the sixteenth century, when the ruling Medici family moved to another palace.

Similar to fortified castles in the region, the Palazzo boasts thick stone walls, heavy **battlements** (defensive parapets), and a tall tower. Few windows pierce the walls of the lowest level, whose stones are left rough and uneven (or **rusticated**) to create the appearance of greater strength. The two upper stories display smoother masonry and more elegant pointed windows. The tower serves not only as a symbol of civic pride, but as a defensive structure. It sits slightly off-center for two reasons: This part of the building rests on the foundations of an earlier tower, and its position makes it visible from a main street in the city. Boasting the highest civic tower in the city, the Palazzo della Signoria dominated the skyline of Florence and expressed the power of the communal good over powerful individual families.

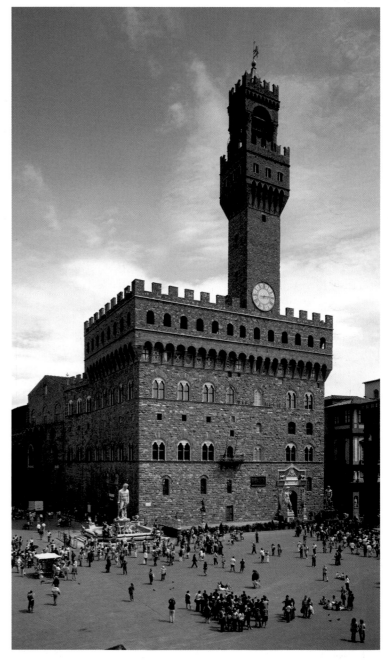

13.15 Palazzo della Signoria (Palazzo Vecchio), Florence. Begun 1298

PAINTING IN TUSCANY

As with other art forms in the thirteenth century, Italian painting's stylistic beginnings are different from those of the rest of Europe, although they shared traits and ideas. Italy's ties to the Roman past and the Byzantine present would inspire Italian painters to render forms in naturalistic and monumental images. Throughout the Middle Ages, Byzantine mosaics and murals were visible to Italian artists. Venice had long-standing trading ties with the Byzantine Empire, while the crusades of the twelfth and thirteenth centuries had brought Italy in even closer contact with Byzantium, including the diversion of the Fourth Crusade in 1204 to Constantinople itself.

One result of the short-lived occupation of Constantinople by western Europeans, from 1204 to 1261, was an infusion of Byzantine art forms and artists into Italy, which had a momentous effect on the development of Italian art in the thirteenth century. Later observers of the rapid changes that occurred in Italian painting from 1200 to 1550 described the starting point of these changes as the "Greek manner," by which they meant Byzantine art. Writing in the sixteenth century, the biographer and artist Giorgio Vasari reported that in the mid-thirteenth century, "Some Greek painters were summoned to Florence by the government of the city for no other purpose than the revival of painting in their midst, since that art was not so much debased as altogether lost." Vasari assumes that medieval Italian painting was all but nonexistent and attributes to Byzantine art great influence over the development of Italian art in the thirteenth century. Italian artists were able to absorb the Byzantine tradition far more thoroughly at this time than ever before. When Gothic style from northern Europe began to influence artists working in this Byzantinizing tradition, a revolutionary synthesis of the two was accomplished by a generation of innovative and productive painters in Tuscan cities.

Cimabue and Giotto

One such artist was Cimabue of Florence (ca. 1250–after 1300), whom Vasari claimed had been apprenticed to a Greek painter. His presence has also been noted in Assisi, Rome, and Pisa. In the 1280s, he painted a large panel depicting the Madonna Enthroned (fig. **13.16**), or Madonna in Majesty (Maestà), to sit on an altar in the church of Santa Trinità in Florence; the large scale of the altarpiece—it is more than 12 feet high—made it the devotional focus of the church. Its composition recalls Byzantine icons, such asthe *Madonna Enthroned* (see fig. 8.49), but its scale and verticality are closer to the *Altarpiece of St. Clare* (fig. 13.3) and similar thirteenth-century altarpieces than to Byzantine prototypes. Mary and her son occupy a heavy golden throne, flanked by rows of angels on either side. Hebrew Bible prophets holding scrolls appear below, as if forming a foundation for Mary's throne; the relationship between the Hebrew Bible and the New Testament is an important theme in Christian art. The Virgin's toweringscale and the brilliant blue of her gown against

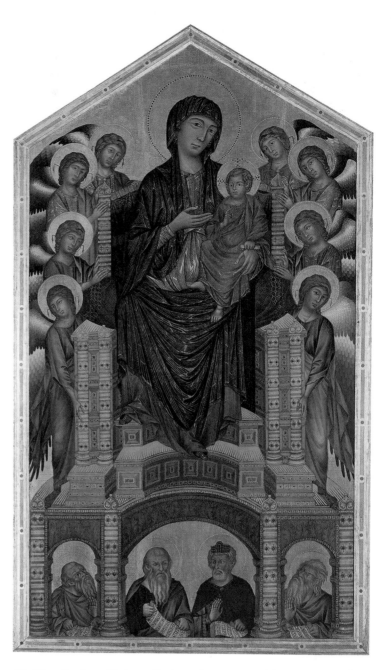

13.16 Cimabue, *Madonna Enthroned.* ca. 1280–90. Tempera on panel, 12'7½" × 7'4" (3.9 × 2.2 m). Galleria degli Uffizi, Florence

the gold-leaf background draw a viewer's eye to her; with her gesture she emphasizes the presence of her son. Like Byzantine painters, Cimabue uses linear gold elements to enhance her dignity, but in his hands the network of gold lines follows the line of her body instead of creating abstract patterns. The severe design and solemn expression are appropriate to the monumental scale of the painting.

Later artists in Renaissance Italy, such as Lorenzo Ghiberti (see Chapter 15) and Giorgio Vasari (see Chapter 16) claimed that Cimabue was the teacher of Giotto di Bondone (ca. 1267–1336/37), one of the key figures in the history of art. If so, Giotto may have learned from him the "Greek Manner" in which Cimabue worked. Some scholars believe that Giotto also worked

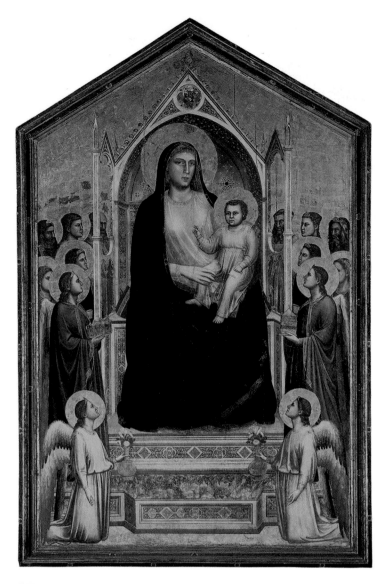

13.17 Giotto, *Madonna Enthroned*. ca. 1310. Tempera on panel, 10'8" × 6'8" (3.3 × 2 m). Galleria degli Uffizi, Florence

at Assisi, while documents tell us that Giotto worked in Rome where examples of both ancient and Early Christian art were available for artists to study. Equally important, however, was the influence of the Pisani—Nicolo and Giovanni—with their blend of **classicism** and Gothic **naturalism** to express strong emotional content. (See figs. 13.8 and 13.9.)

We can see Giotto's relationship to, but difference from, Cimabue in a tall altarpiece showing the Madonna Enthroned, which he painted around 1310 for the church of All Saints (Ognissanti) in Florence (fig. **13.17**). Like Cimabue's Santa Trinità Madonna, Giotto depicts the Queen of Heaven and her son enthroned among holy figures against a gold background. The Virgin's deep blue robe and huge scale bring a viewer's eye directly to her and to the Christ Child in her lap. All the other figures gaze at them, both signaling and heightening their importance. Unlike Cimabue, Giotto models the figures in light, so that they appear to be solid, sculptural forms. Where Cimabue turns light into a network of golden lines, Giotto achieves a gradual

movement from light into dark, so that the figures appear to be three-dimensional forms.

The throne exhibits some features of contemporary Italian architecture, such as the high pointed arches, though Giotto uses them to create a nichelike structure. This encloses the Madonna on three sides, setting her apart from the gold background, and defines the space that she inhabits. Giotto further suggests space by placing angels kneeling before the throne and by the overlapping figures of saints, who seem to stand behind one another on a level surface. The throne's lavish ornamentation includes a feature that is especially interesting: the colored marble surfaces of the base and of the quatrefoil within the **gable**. Such illusionistic stone textures had been highly developed by ancient painters (see fig. 7.56), and their appearance here is evidence that Giotto was familiar with whatever ancient murals could still be seen in medieval Rome.

THE ARENA CHAPEL IN PADUA Giotto's innovative ideas about light and space were accompanied by a gift for storytelling. Although scholars are not certain that he was among the artists who painted the nave frescoes at Assisi, his fresco cycles share formal and narrative characteristics with those images (see fig.

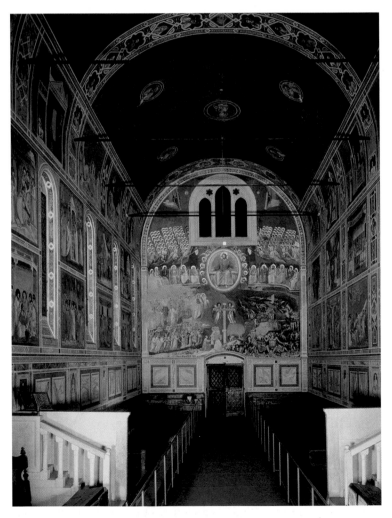

13.18 Interior of Arena (Scrovegni) Chapel, Padua. 1305–06

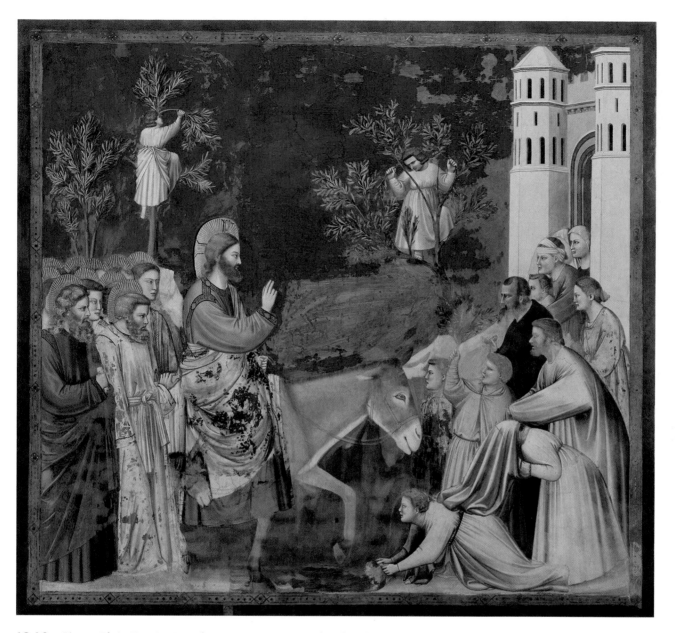

13.19 Giotto, *Christ Entering Jerusalem*, Arena (Scrovegni) Chapel, Padua. 1305–06. Fresco

13.2). Of Giotto's surviving murals, those in the Arena, or Scrovegni, Chapel in Padua, painted in 1305 and 1306, are wonderfully preserved and recently restored. It is known variously as the Arena Chapel because the site once housed a Roman arena, and the Scrovegni Chapel because it was built by Enrico Scrovegni, a Paduan banker, next to his palace, where he intended it to serve as his burial chapel. Dedicated to "Our Lady of Charity", the structure is a one-room hall covered with a **barrel vault** (fig. **13.18**).

Giotto and his assistants painted the whole chapel from floor to ceiling in the fresco technique. A blue field with gold stars symbolic of Heaven dominates the barrel vault, below which the walls are divided into three **registers** or horizontal rows. Each register contains rectangular fields for narrative scenes representing the lives of the Virgin and Christ. The Annunciation appears at the altar end of the room; this represents the archangel Gabriel

announcing to Mary that she has been chosen to bear the son of God. The theme commemorates the Incarnation of Christ and marks the beginning of the plan of Salvation, according to Catholic belief. At the other end of the chapel, Giotto depicted the Last Judgment (the events predicted for the end of time). At the foot of the Last Judgment, Giotto has included the figure of the donor, Enrico Scrovengi, offering his chapel to the Virgin and angels (see page 436). Along the length of the wall, the top register depicts stories of the early life of Mary and her parents; the center register focuses on stories of Christ's life and miracles; and the lowest register depicts his Passion, Death, and Resurrection. Below the narratives, the walls resemble marble panels interspersed with reliefs, but everything is painted.

One scene in the middle register, *Christ Entering Jerusalem*, depicts the event commemorated by Christians on Palm Sunday (fig. **13.19**). The Gospels report that the citizens welcomed

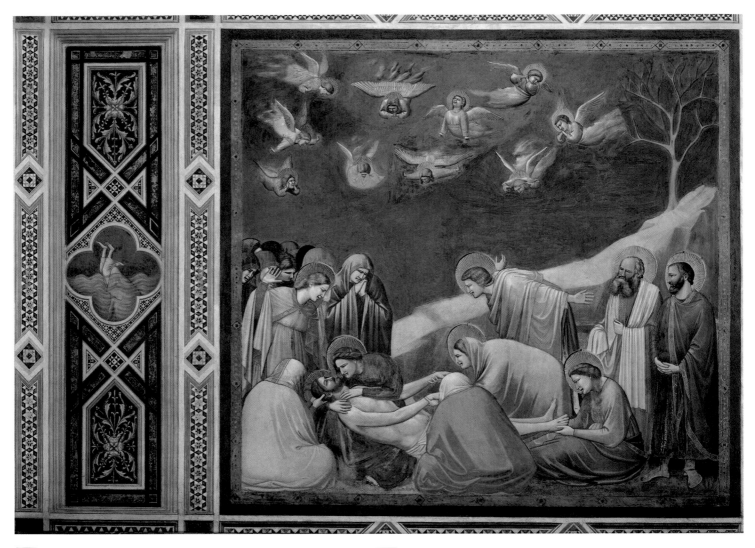

13.20 Giotto, *The Lamentation*, Arena (Scrovegni) Chapel, Padua. 1305–06. Fresco

Jesus with palm fronds and cheers as he entered Jerusalem riding a donkey; Christ's arrival on a humble mount fulfilled a Hebrew Bible prophecy. Giotto places the entire scene in the foreground of his image, which brings the events very close to a viewer. Furthermore, Giotto gives his forms such a strong three-dimensional quality that they almost seem as solid as sculpture. The rounded forms create the illusion of space in which the actors exist.

Giotto deliberately leaves the setting spare for this event, except for the trees in which children climb and the city gate on the right. His large simple forms, strong grouping of figures, and the limited depth of his stage give his scenes a remarkable spatial coherence. The massed verticals of the block of apostles on the left contrast with the upward slope of the crowd welcoming Jesus on the right; but Jesus, alone in the center, bridges the gap between the two groups. His isolation and dignity, even as he rides the donkey toward the city where he will die, give the painting a solemn air.

Giotto's skill at perfectly matching composition and meaning may also be seen in the scenes on the lowest register, which focus on the Passion. A viewer gazing at these frescoes sees them straight on, so the painter organizes the scenes to exploit that relationship. One of the most memorable of these paintings depicts the Lamentation, the moment of last farewell between Jesus and his mother and friends (fig. **13.20**). Although this event does not appear in the Gospels, by the end of the Middle Ages versions of this theme had appeared in both Byzantine and in Western medieval art.

The tragic mood of this Lamentation, found also in religious texts of the era, is created by the formal rhythm of the design as well as by the gestures and expressions of the participants. The low center of gravity and the hunched figures convey the somber quality of the scene, as do the cool colors and bare sky. With extraordinary boldness, Giotto sets off the frozen grief of the human mourners against the frantic movement of the weeping angels among the clouds. It is as if the figures on the ground are restrained by their obligation to maintain the stability of the composition, while the angels, small and weightless as birds, are able to move—and feel—freely.

Once again, the simple setting heightens the impact of the drama. The descending slope of the hill acts as a unifying element that directs attention toward the heads of Christ and the Virgin, which are the focal point of the scene. Even the tree has a twin function. Its barrenness and isolation suggest that all of nature shares in the sorrow over Christ's death. Yet it also carries a more precise symbolic message: It refers to the Tree of Knowledge, which the sin of Adam and Eve had caused to wither and which was to be restored to life through Christ's sacrificial death.

Giotto's frescoes in the Arena Chapel established his fame among his contemporaries. In the *Divine Comedy*, written around 1315, the great Italian poet Dante Alighieri mentions the rising reputation of the young Florentine: "Once Cimabue thought to hold the field as painter, Giotto now is all the rage, dimming the luster of the other's fame." (See www.myartslab.com.) Giotto continued to work in Florence for 30 years after completing the chapel frescoes, in 1334 being named the architect of Florence cathedral, for which he designed the campanile (see figs. 13.10 and 13.12). His influence over the next generation was inescapable and was felt by artists all over Italy.

Siena: Devotion to Mary in Works by Duccio and Simone

Giotto's slightly older contemporary Duccio di Buoninsegna of Siena (ca. 1255–before 1319) directed another busy and influential workshop in the neighboring Tuscan city of Siena. The city of Siena competed with Florence on a number of fronts—military, economic, and cultural—and fostered a distinct identity and visual tradition. Its wealth came from agriculture and trade. After a key military victory against Florence in 1260, Siena took the Virgin Mary as its protector and patron. The Sienese chose a representative form of government—a republic—directed by the *Nove* (the Nine), who were chosen from the elite merchants of the city. By the end of the thirteenth century, this government had taken up the project of building a town hall (fig. **13.21**), the Palazzo Pubblico, as an expression of their city's wealth and status.

Begun by 1298, the Palazzo Pubblico served not only to house the city government, but to frame a public space, the Piazza del

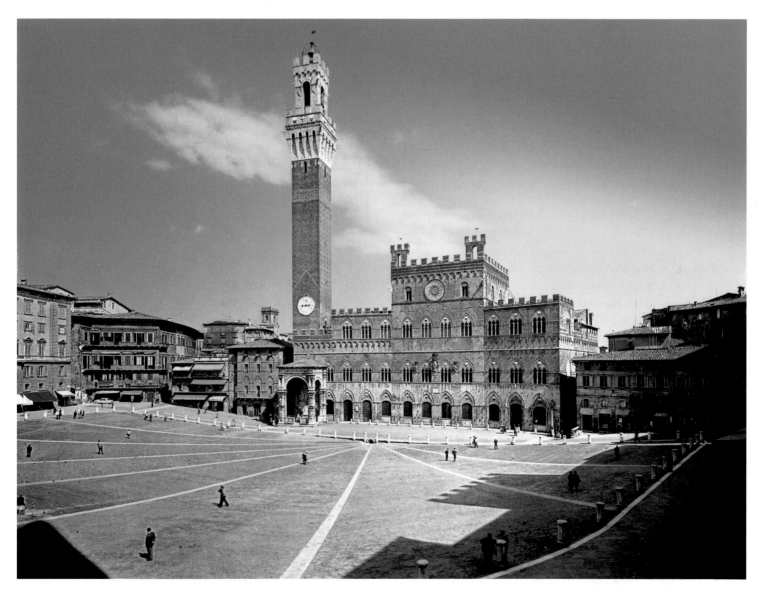

13.21 Palazzo Pubblico, Siena. Begun ca. 1298

PRIMARY SOURCE

Agnolo di Tura del Grasso

From his *Chronicle*

Duccio's Maestà *(see fig. 13.22) stood on the main altar of Siena cathedral until 1506, when it was removed to the transept. It was sawed apart in 1771, and some panels were acquired subsequently by museums in Europe and the United States. This local history of about 1350 describes the civic celebration that accompanied the installation of the altarpiece in 1311.*

These paintings [the *Maestà*] were executed by master Duccio, son of Nicolò, painter of Siena, the finest artist to be found anywhere at his time. He painted the altarpiece in the house of the Muciatti outside the gate toward Stalloreggi in the suburb of Laterino. On the 9th of June [1311], at midday, the Sienese carried the altarpiece in great devotion to the cathedral in a procession, which included Bishop Roger of Casole, the entire clergy of the cathedral, all monks and nuns of the city, and the Nine Gentlemen [Nove] and officials of the city such as the podestà and the captain, and all the people. One by one the worthiest, with lighted candles in their hands, took their places near the altarpiece. Behind them came women and children with great devotion. They accompanied the painting up to the cathedral, walking in procession around the Campo, while all the bells rang joyfully. All the shops were closed out of devotion, all through Siena many alms were given to the poor with many speeches and prayers to God and to his Holy Mother, that she might help to preserve and increase the peace and well being of the city and its jurisdiction, as she was the advocate and protection of said city, and deliver it from all danger and wickedness directed against it. In this way the said altarpiece was taken into the cathedral and placed on the main altar. The altarpiece is painted on the back with scenes from the Old Testament and the Passion of Jesus Christ and in front with the Virgin Mary and her Son in her arms and many saints at the sides, the whole decorated with fine gold. The altarpiece cost 3000 gold florins.

Source: Teresa G. Frisch, *Gothic Art 1140–c 1450* (Englewood Cliffs, NJ: Prentice Hall, 1971)

Campo, where the city's economic, political, religious, and social life was played out. Both the timing and the character of the Palazzo Pubblico point to the city's rivalry with Florence, which was then building the Palazzo della Signoria. Built of brick and stone, Siena's Palazzo Pubblico rises to three stories and supports a tower, as does Florence's Palazzo. It also terminates in castlelike battlements at the roofline. But it has many more windows and other openings, and a more ornamental and elegant façade. The tower, not completed until the 1340s, is intentionally taller than that of the Palazzo della Signoria.

The city also concerned itself with adorning its cathedral, dedicated to the Virgin. For the high altar of the cathedral the directors of the cathedral works hired Duccio to paint a large altarpiece, called the *Maestà* as it depicts the Virgin and Child in Majesty (fig. **13.22**). Commissioned in 1308, the *Maestà* was installed in the cathedral in 1311 amidst processions and celebrations in the city. (See *Primary Source*, above, and *The Art Historian's Lens*, page 455.) Duccio's signature at the base of the throne expresses his pride in the work: "Holy Mother of God, be the cause of peace to Siena, and of life to Duccio because he has painted you thus."

Painted in tempera, Duccio's image measures approximately 7 by 13 feet without its architectural frame and many subsidiary elements. It takes the shape of a **polyptych**, or multipaneled work. The regal figures of the Virgin and Child in the *Maestà* sit on a complex throne draped in golden cloth. The Virgin is by far the largest and most impressive figure in this assembly, swathed in the rich blue reserved for her by contemporary practice. Surrounding her is a carefully balanced arrangement of saints and angels, each bearing a golden halo. In the front row kneel Siena's other patron saints, all gesturing and gazing at her. The Virgin may seem much like Cimabue's (see fig. 13.16) which Duccio probably knew, as both originated in the Greek manner.

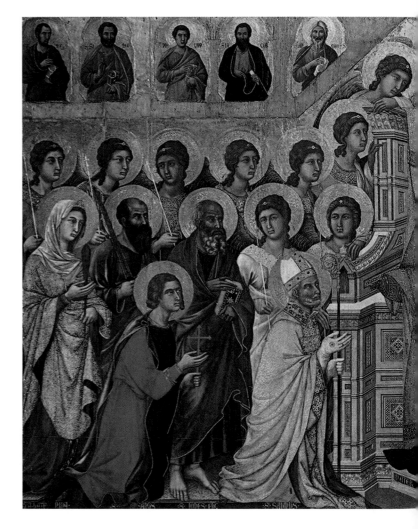

Duccio, however, relaxes the rigid, angular draperies of that tradition so that they give way to an undulating softness. The bodies, faces, and hands of the many figures seem to swell with three-dimensional life as the painter explores the fall of light on their

The Social Work of Images

The report of the celebrations held in Siena when Duccio's *Maestà* was installed in the city's cathedral attests to the importance of this painting for the entire community. It was a source of pride for the citizens of Siena, but also a powerful embodiment of the Virgin's protection of the city. Although modern audiences expect to find and react to works of art hanging in museums, art historians have demonstrated that art served different purposes in late medieval Europe. Few in the West today believe that a work of art can influence events or change lives. But in fourteenth-century Europe, people thought about images in much more active terms. Art could be a path to the sacred or a helper in times of trouble.

During a drought in 1354, for example, the city fathers of Florence paraded a miracle-working image of the Virgin from the village of Impruneta through the city in hopes of improving the weather. People with illness or health problems venerated a fresco of the Annunciation in the church of the Santissima Annunziata in Florence; they gave gifts to the image in hopes of respite from their problems. When the plague came to Florence, artists were commissioned to paint scenes depicting St. Sebastian and other saints who were considered protectors against this deadly disease.

Images were also called upon for help outside the sacred space of the church. Continuing a tradition begun in the fourteenth century, street corners in Italy are often adorned with images of the Virgin, to whom passersby may pray or show respect. Candles may be lit or gifts offered to such images in hopes of the Virgin's assistance. Art historians are also studying how works of art functioned among late medieval populations to forge bonds among social groups and encourage group identity. For example, outside the confines of monasteries, groups of citizens formed social organizations that were dedicated to a patron saint, whose image would be an important element of the group's identity.

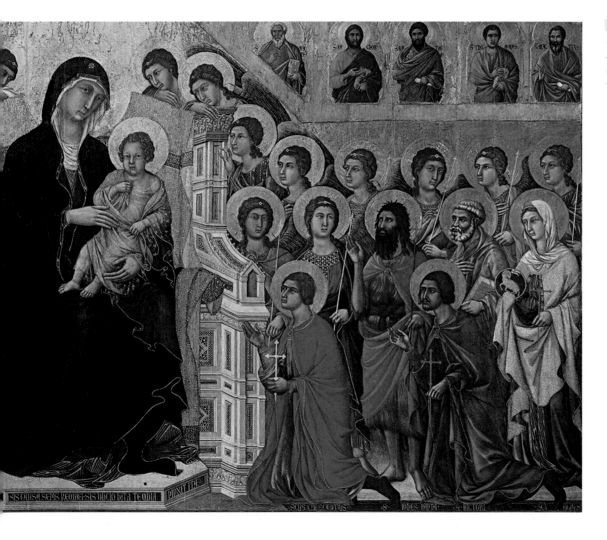

13.22 Duccio, *Madonna Enthroned*, center of the *Maestà Altar*. 1308–11. Tempera on panel, height 6'10½" (2.1 m). Museo dell'Opera del Duomo, Siena

forms. Byzantine painting preserved aspects of ancient illusionism, which inspired Duccio to a profound degree. Nonetheless, Duccio's work also reflects contemporary Gothic sensibilities in the fluidity of the drapery, the appealing naturalness of the figures, and the glances by which the figures communicate with each other. An important source of this Gothic influence was probably Giovanni Pisano, who worked in Siena from 1285 to 1295 as the sculptor-architect in charge of the cathedral façade.

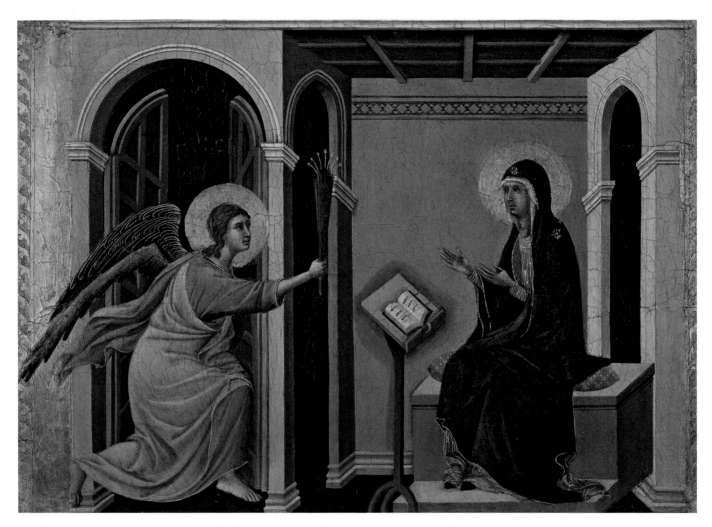

13.23 Duccio, *Annunciation of the Death of the Virgin*, from the *Maestà Altar*. Museo dell'Opera del Duomo, Siena

Some evidence hints that Duccio may have traveled to Paris, where he would have encountered French Gothic style directly.

In addition to the principal scene, the *Maestà* included on its front and back numerous small scenes from the lives of Christ and the Virgin. In these panels, Duccio's synthesis of Gothic and Byzantine elements exploits a new kind of picture space and, with it, a new treatment of narrative. The *Annunciation of the Death of the Virgin* (fig. **13.23**), which originally stood above the main image on the front of the altarpiece, represents two figures enclosed by an architectural interior; Duccio implies space for the figures to inhabit by representing walls and ceiling beams as receding into depth (called **foreshortening**). His architecture integrates the figures within the drama. In a parallel scene to the Annunciation (see fig. 13.25, for comparison), this panel depicts the archangel Gabriel returning to the mature Virgin to warn her of her impending death. The architecture places the two figures in the same uncluttered room, but enframes them separately. Despite sharing the space, each figure is isolated. Duccio's innovative use of architecture to enhance the narrative of his paintings inspired his younger French contemporary, Jean Pucelle, who adapted this composition for the *Annunciation* in the *Hours of Jeanne d'Evreux* (see fig. 12.39).

The architecture keeps its space-creating function even in the outdoor scenes on the back of the *Maestà*, such as in *Christ Entering Jerusalem* (fig. **13.24**), a theme that Giotto had treated only a few years before in Padua. Where Giotto places Christ at the center of two groups of people, Duccio places him closer to the apostles and on one side of the composition. He conveys the diagonal movement into depth not by the figures, who have the same scale throughout, but by the walls on either side of the road leading to the city, by the gate that frames the crowd welcoming Christ, and by the buildings in the background. Where Giotto reduces his treatment of the theme to a few figures and a bare backdrop, Duccio includes not only detailed architectural elements, some of which resemble contemporary Tuscan buildings, but also many figures, including one peering at the crowd in the streets from a first-floor window. Duccio gives a viewer a more complete description of the event than Giotto, whose work stresses the doctrinal and psychological import of the moment. The goals of the two painters differ, and so do the formal means they use to achieve them.

Duccio trained the next generation of painters in Siena. One distinguished disciple was Simone Martini (ca. 1284–1344), who also worked in Assisi but spent the last years of his life in

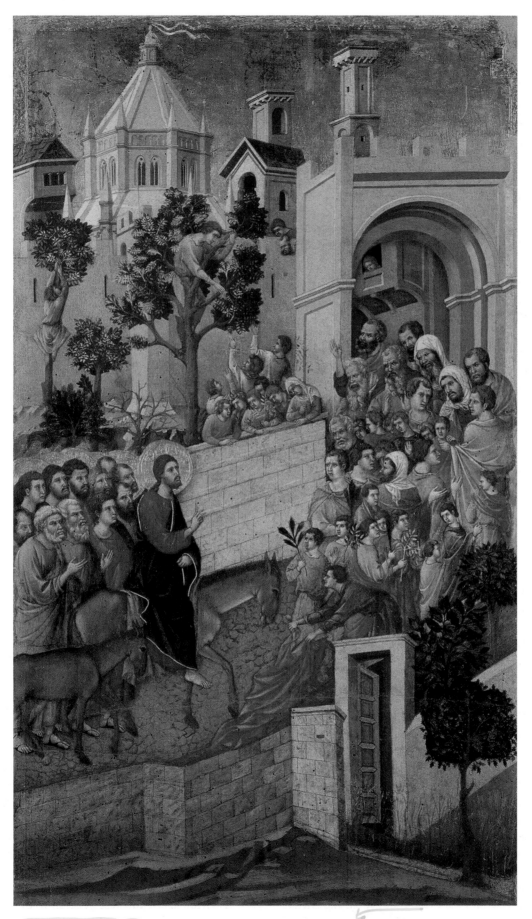

13.24 Duccio, *Christ Entering Jerusalem*, from the back of the *Maestà Altar*. 1308–11.
Tempera on panel, 40½ × 21⅛" (103 × 53.7 cm). Museo dell'Opera del Duomo, Siena

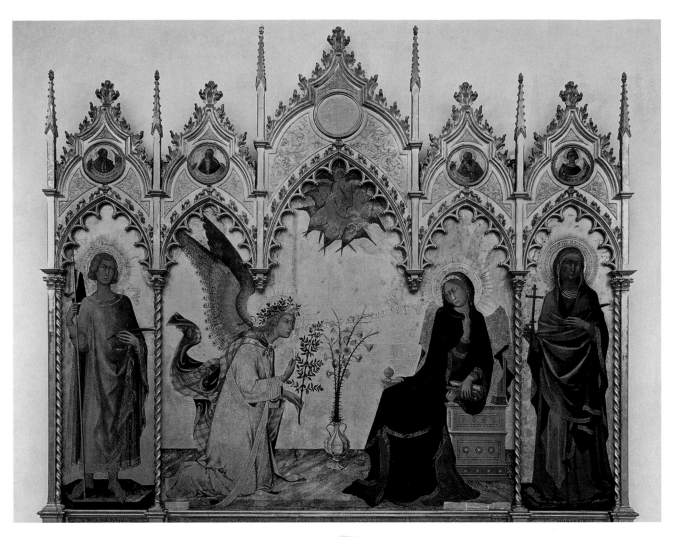

13.25 Simone Martini, *Annunciation*. ca. 1330. Tempera on panel, 10′ × 8′9″ (3 × 2.7 m). Galleria degli Uffizi, Florence

Avignon, the town in southern France that served as the residence of the popes during most of the fourteenth century. In 1333, the directors of Siena cathedral commissioned Simone to make another altarpiece to complement Duccio's *Maestà*. His *Annunciation* (fig. **13.25**) in its restored cusped and gilded frame hints at what has been lost in the dismemberment of Duccio's *Maestà*, which had a complex Gothic frame. Simone's altarpiece, in the form of a **triptych** or three-part structure, depicts the Annunciation flanked by two local saints set against a brilliant gold ground. To connect her visually to the *Maestà*, Simone's Virgin sits in a similar cloth-covered throne and wears similar garments.

In Simone's picture, the angel Gabriel approaches Mary from the left to pronounce the words "*Ave Maria gratia plena Dominus tecum*" ("Hail Mary, full of grace, the Lord is with you"). These words are familiar to believers as a popular prayer. Simone renders the words in relief on the surface of this painting, covering them in the same gold leaf that transforms the scene into a heavenly vision. Details like the marble floor, the lilies symbolic of purity, and the sumptuous garment worn by the angel add to the richness of the image. Simone adds an element of doubt to the narrative, as the Virgin responds to her visitor with surprise and

pulls away from him. The dove of the Holy Spirit flies toward her in anticipation of her momentous acceptance of her role as the mother of Jesus, thereby beginning the process of Salvation. Like Giotto, Simone has reduced the narrative to its simplest terms, but like Duccio, his figures have a lyrical elegance that lifts them out of the ordinary and into the realm of the spiritual.

Pietro and Ambrogio Lorenzetti

Another altarpiece commissioned for the cathedral at Siena takes a more down-to-earth approach to representing the life of the Virgin. This is the *Birth of the Virgin* (fig. **13.26**) painted in 1342 by Pietro Lorenzetti (active ca. 1306–1348). Pietro and his brother Ambrogio (active ca. 1317–1348), learned their craft in Siena in Duccio's workshop, though their work also shows the influence of Giotto. Pietro has been linked to work at Assisi, and Ambrogio enrolled in the painters' **guild** of Florence in the 1330s. Like Simone's, Pietro's altarpiece is a triptych, though it has lost its original frame. In this triptych, Pietro has related the painted architecture to the real architecture of the frame so closely that the two are seen as a single system. Moreover, the vaulted room

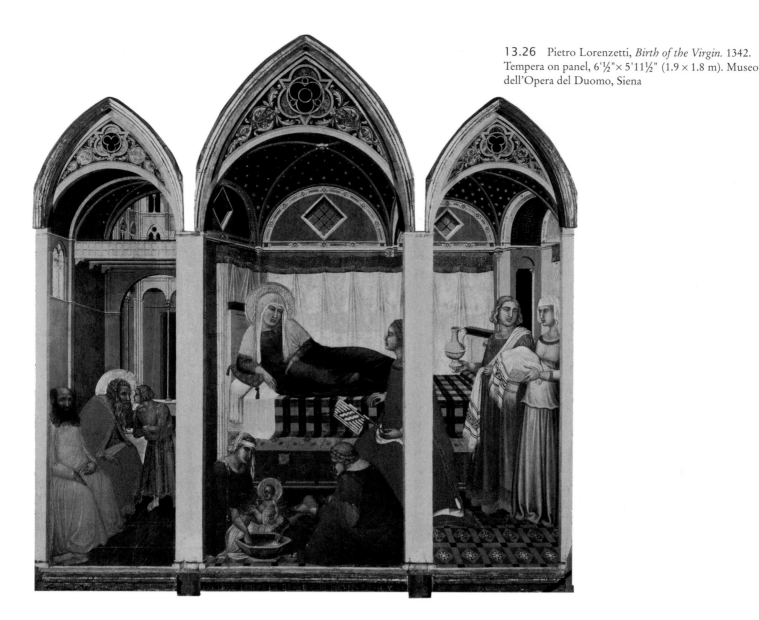

13.26 Pietro Lorenzetti, *Birth of the Virgin.* 1342. Tempera on panel, 6'½"× 5'11½" (1.9 × 1.8 m). Museo dell'Opera del Duomo, Siena

where the birth takes place occupies two panels and continues unbroken behind the column that divides the center from the right wing. The left wing represents a small chamber which opens onto a Gothic façade. Pietro's achievement of spatial illusion here is the outcome of a development that began three decades earlier in the work of Giotto and Duccio. Pietro treats the painting surface like a transparent window *through* which—not *on* which—a viewer experiences a space comparable to the real world. Pietro uses the architecture in his painting to carve out boxes of space that his figures appear to inhabit, but he is also inspired by Giotto's technique of giving his figures such mass and weight that they seem to create their own space. His innovation served the narrative and liturgical needs of Siena cathedral by depicting another key moment in the life of the Virgin, her birth, which was also an important feast day in the Church. St. Anne rests in her childbed, while midwives attend the newborn Virgin and other women tend to the mother. The figure of the midwife pouring water for the baby's bath seems to derive from the figure seen from the back in Giotto's *Lamentation* (see fig. 13.20). The father, Joachim, waits for a report of the birth outside the room.

GOOD AND BAD GOVERNMENT Pietro's brother, Ambrogio Lorenzetti, combined these same influences in a major project for the Palazzo Pubblico, executed between 1338 and 1340. The ruling Council of Nine commissioned several local artists to adorn the building, including Simone Martini. For their council room, they hired Ambrogio to paint an **allegory**, or moralizing narrative, contrasting good and bad government. In the room where the council deliberated, these frescoes aimed to inspire its members to achieve good government. Although the negative example of the effects of Bad Government has been severely damaged, the frescoes that depict the positive example of Good Government are remarkably well preserved (fig. **13.27**). On the short wall of the room, Ambrogio depicted the *Allegory of Good Government* as an assembly of figures personifying virtues who flank the large enthroned figure of the Common Good. To the left, another enthroned figure personifies Justice, who is inspired by Wisdom. Below the virtues stand 24 members of the Sienese judiciary under the guidance of the personification of Concord.

On the long wall, the fresco of *Good Government in the City* (fig. **13.28**) bears an inscription praising Justice and the many

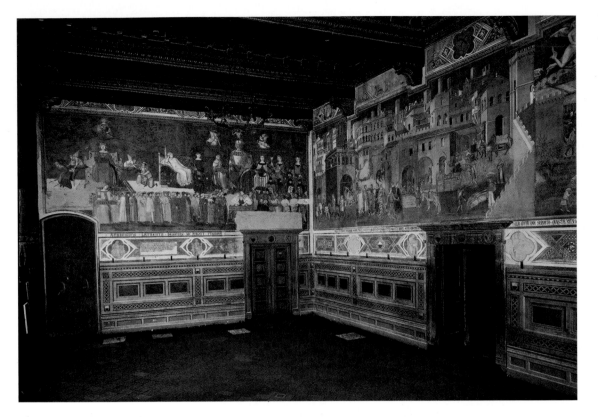

benefits that derive from her. (See *Primary Source*, page 461.) In this fresco, Ambrogio renders an architectural portrait of Siena. To show the life of a well-ordered city-state, the artist fills the streets and houses with activity. Within the city, merchants do business, teachers conduct classes, buildings go up, and the streets teem with people. On the right, outside the city walls, *Good*

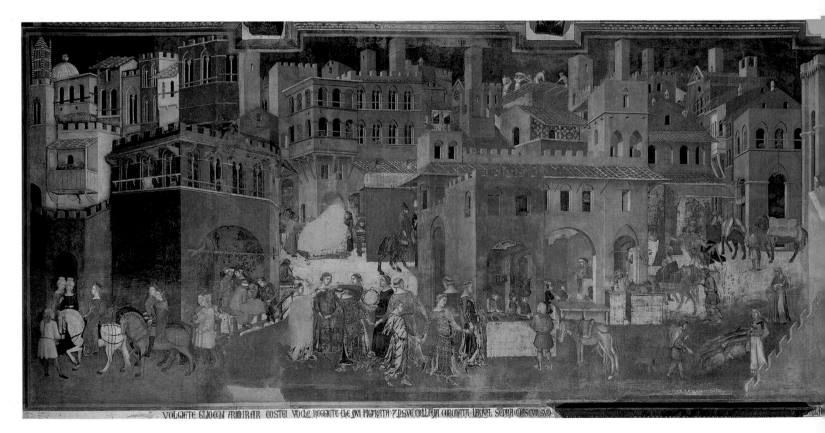

13.28   Ambrogio Lorenzetti, *Good Government in the City*

PRIMARY SOURCE

Inscriptions on the Frescoes in the Palazzo Pubblico, Siena

The first inscription is painted in a strip below the fresco of Good Government *(see figs. 13.27 and 13.28), which is dated between 1338 and 1340. The second is held by the personification of Security, who hovers over the landscape in figure 13.29.*

> Turn your eyes to behold her,
> you who are governing, [Justice] who is portrayed here,
> crowned on account of her excellence,
> who always renders to everyone his due.
> Look how many goods derive from her
> and how sweet and peaceful is that life

of the city where is preserved
this virtue who outshines any other.
She guards and defends
those who honor her, and nourishes and feeds them.
From her light is born
Requiting those who do good
and giving due punishment to the wicked.

Without fear every man may travel freely
and each may till and sow,
so long as this commune
shall maintain this lady [Justice] sovereign,
for she has stripped the wicked of all power.

Source: Randolph Starn and Loren Partridge, *Arts of Power: Three Halls of State in Italy, 1300-1600* (Berkeley: University of California Press, 1992)

Government in the Country provides a view of the Sienese farmland, fringed by distant mountains (fig. **13.29**) and overseen by a personification of Security. It is a true landscape—the first since ancient Roman times (see fig. 7.55). It represents a sweeping view of the orderly hillside: vineyards, farms, and pastures result from a fruitful nature possessed by well-governed humans. Ambrogio observes the peasants at their seasonal labors, which support the life within the city, even as the countryside is safe for travelers, merchants, and pleasure-seekers.

Artists and Patrons in Times of Crisis

Ambrogio's ideal vision of the city and its surroundings reveals how the citizens of Siena imagined their government and their city at a moment of peace and prosperity. The first three decades of the fourteenth century in Siena, as in Florence, were a period of political stability and economic expansion, as well as of great artistic achievement. In the 1340s, however, both cities suffered a series of catastrophes whose effects were to be felt for many years.

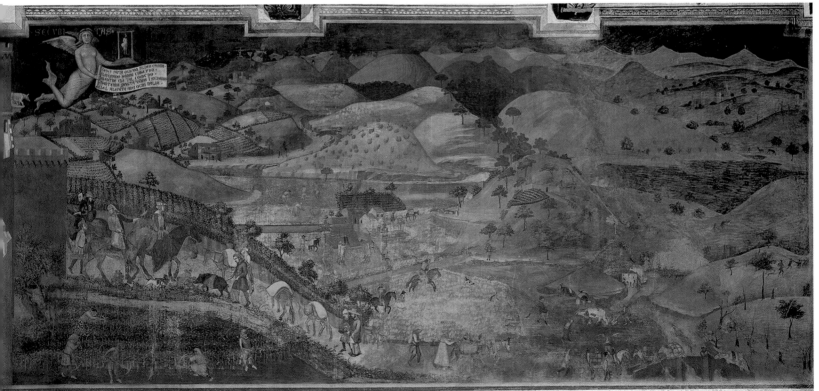

13.29   Ambrogio Lorenzetti, *Good Government in the Country*

"peaceful country"

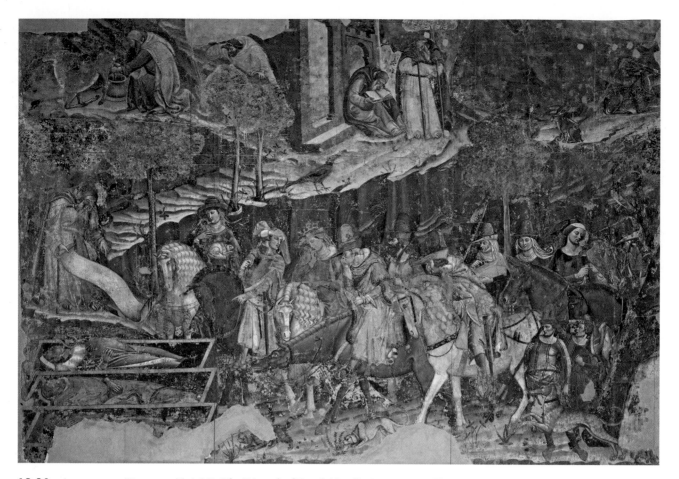

13.30 Anonymous (Francesco Traini ?), *The Triumph of Death* (detail), Camposanto, Pisa. ca. 1325–50. Fresco

Constant warfare pushed scores of banks and merchants into bankruptcy, internal upheavals shook governments, and there were repeated crop failures and famine. Then, in 1348, the pandemic of bubonic plague—the Black Death—that spread throughout Europe wiped out more than half the population of the two cities (see map **13.2**). Flea-infested rats swarmed into cities from the barren countryside in search of food and so spread the disease. Popular reactions to these events were mixed. Many people saw them as signs of divine wrath, warnings to a sinful humanity to forgo the pleasures of this earth. In such people, the Black Death intensified an interest in religion and the promise of heavenly rewards. To others, such as the merry company who entertain each other by telling stories in the Florentine humanist Giovanni Boccaccio's (1313–1375) book the *Decameron*, finished around 1353, the fear of death intensified the desire to enjoy life while there was still time. (See www.myartslab.com.)

Late medieval people were regularly confronted with the inevitability and power of death. A series of frescoes painted on the walls of the Camposanto, the monumental cemetery building next to Pisa cathedral, offers a variety of responses to death. Because of its somber message, these frescoes were once dated after the outbreak of the plague, but recent research has pushed the date closer to the 1330s. The painter is not known, though some scholars attribute the work to a Pisan artist named Francesco Traini (documented ca. 1321–1363). The huge fresco

cycle, which was damaged in 1944 as a result of bombings in World War II, included a powerful *Last Judgment* and an image called *The Triumph of Death*, which asserts that death comes to all, rich or poor, saint or sinner. In a particularly dramatic detail (fig. **13.30**), the elegantly costumed men and women on horseback have suddenly come upon three decaying corpses in open coffins. Even the animals are terrified by the sight and smell of rotting flesh. The hermit St. Macarius, having renounced all earthly pleasures, points out the lesson of the scene. His scroll reads: "If your mind be well aware, keeping here your view attentive, your vainglory will be vanquished and you will see pride eliminated. And, again, you will realize this if you observe that which is written." As the hermits in the hills above make clear, the way to salvation is through renunciation of the world in favor of the spiritual life. The artist's style recalls the realism of Ambrogio Lorenzetti, although the forms are harsher and more expressive.

It is likely that the Lorenzetti brothers perished in the Black Death of 1348–49, along with thousands of other people throughout Tuscany. Scholars have studied the impact of the plague on artists and patrons of works of art in the second half of the fourteenth century to determine its effect on style and subject matter. We can assume that many painters died, so the number of artists probably diminished. Documentary research reveals that the number of endowed chapels, tombs, and funeral masses rose as people worried about their mortality. Many such burials and endowments were made in mendicant churches, such as the Franciscan Santa Croce and the Dominican Santa Maria Novella in Florence.

At Santa Maria Novella, a Florentine merchant named Buonamico Guidalotti, who died in 1355, provided funds in his will for a new chapterhouse for the Dominican community in which he could be buried. The chapel served as a meeting room for the friars and as such was painted with frescoes expressing the role of Dominicans in the struggle for salvation. A fresco on one of the walls of the Guidalotti Chapel, painted by Andrea Bonaiuti (also known as Andrea da Firenze, active 1346–1379) between 1365 and 1367, depicts the actions of Dominicans to assure the access of the faithful to Heaven, hence its title: *The Way of Salvation* (fig. **13.31**). In the lower section of the fresco, spiritual and temporal leaders gather before a representation of the then-unfinished cathedral of Florence. The fresco depicts a model of the church rather than its actual state of construction. Groups of Dominicans preach to the laity and convert heretics amidst black and white dogs (a punning reference to the order—the *Domini canes*, or the dogs of the Lord). On the upper right, some heedless

aristocrats enjoy the pleasures of the senses, while at the center, a Dominican shows the more spiritually minded the path to Heaven, whose gate is guarded by St. Peter. Andrea's fresco reveals the influence both of Ambrogio Lorenzetti's *Allegory of Good Government* (see fig. 13.27) and the fresco on the walls of the cemetery near Pisa cathedral (see fig. 13.30). Nonetheless, the fresco's symmetry and the sense of order reveal a didactic function: It seeks legibility rather than illusion, and serenity rather than emotion.

Florence, however, did not complete its cathedral in the fourteenth century, and it was not to enjoy the calm atmosphere portrayed in Andrea's fresco. The plague returned in 1363, the political elite clashed with the papacy, and an uprising among the working classes created social and economic turmoil. The wealthier classes restored their power in 1381. Florence overcame these disasters to flourish in the fifteenth century as a center of economic energy, political astuteness, and cultural leadership. As the fifteenth century began, a new generation of Florentine artists would look to the art of Giotto and his contemporaries in their search for new forms of visual expression.

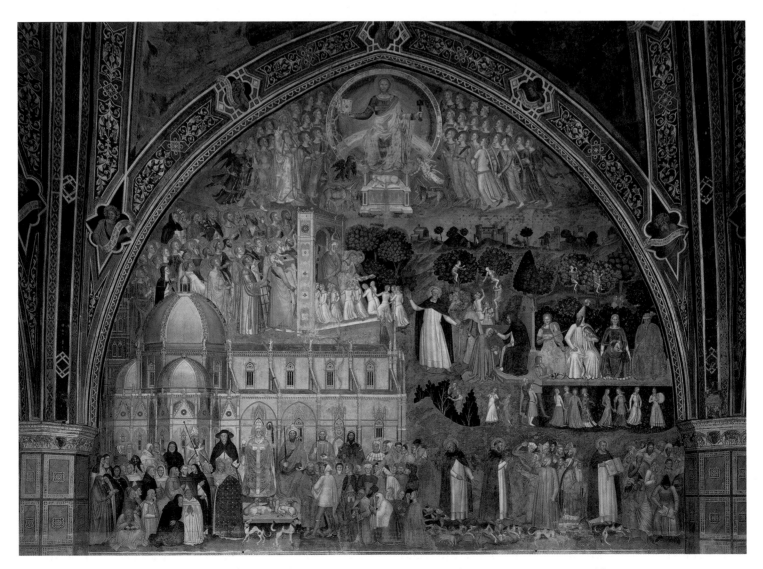

13.31   Andrea da Firenze, *The Way of Salvation*, Guidalotti Chapel, Santa Maria Novella, Florence. 1365–67. Fresco, width 38' (11.6 m)

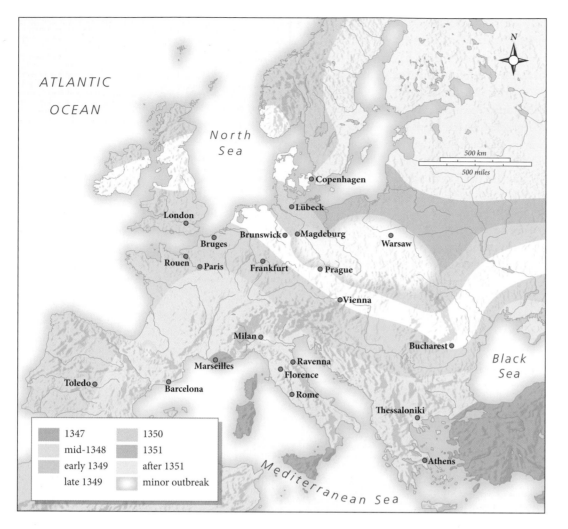

Map 13.2 The Bubonic Plague spreads across Europe, 1347–1351

1347
mid-1348
early 1349
late 1349
1350
1351
after 1351
minor outbreak

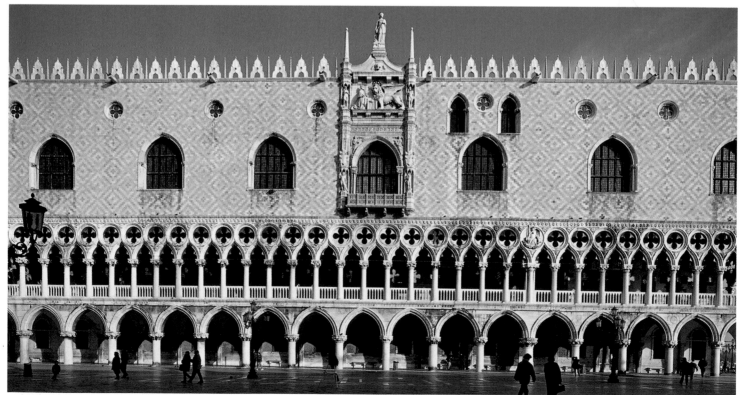

13.32 Doge's Palace, Venice. Begun 1340

NORTHERN ITALY

Political struggles did not disturb Venice in the fourteenth century. Unlike Florence, which was riven by warring factions, the city enjoyed political stability. Since 1297, it had closed off membership in the merchant oligarchy that participated in government, and the city's leader (the Doge) was elected from this group. This created a stable social climate, so neither Venetian palaces nor their communal buildings required the defensive architecture seen in Florentine structures such as the Palazzo della Signoria (see fig. 13.15). A somewhat different atmosphere existed in Milan, west of Venice in Lombardy, where a monarchical government lay in the hands of a single family with great dynastic ambitions. In Lombardy, the main political and cultural connections were with northern Europe, which had important results for the type and the style of art produced there.

Venice: Political Stability and Sumptuous Architecture

The differing political situations in Florence and Venice affected palace design. Whereas the Florentine palace was solid and impenetrable, the Venetian equivalent is airy and open, full of windows and arcades that are anything but defensible. Venetian architects borrowed from Gothic, Byzantine, and Islamic precedents in an elegant display of the city's wealth and security. When a larger meeting space was needed for the Great Council, the city decided to enlarge the Doge's Palace near St. Mark's cathedral in 1340 (fig. 13.32). Work continued here until the mid-fifteenth century. In contrast to the fortresslike Palazzo della Signoria in Florence, the Doge's Palace is open at the base, the weight of its upper stories resting on two stories of pointed arcades. The lower arcade provides a covered passageway around the building, the upper a balcony. The lavish moldings and the quatrefoils of the arcades give the structure an ornamentality accented by the doubling of the rhythm in the upper arcade. The walls of the structure are ornamented with stonework in a diamond pattern, making them both visually lighter and more ornate.

Milan: The Visconti Family and Northern Influences

Lombardy had a different political structure and a closer relationship with Gothic France, which found expression in its visual arts. The Visconti family had acquired great wealth from the products of this richly agricultural region. Besides controlling Lombardy, the Visconti positioned themselves among the great families of Europe through marriage ties to members of the Italian and European nobility. By 1395, Giangaleazzo Visconti had been named duke of Milan, had married the daughter of the king of France, and had wed his daughter to the French king's brother, Louis, duke of Orleans.

The authoritarian nature of Visconti rule in Milan may be seen in the tomb of Giangaleazzo's uncle Bernabò Visconti (fig. 13.33).

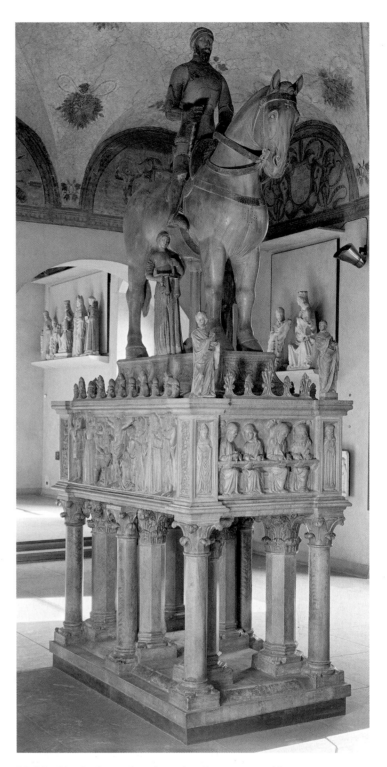

13.33   Tomb of Bernabò Visconti. Before 1363. Marble, 19'8" (6 m). Castello Sforzesco, Milan

Completed around 1363, perhaps by the local sculptor Bonino da Campione (active ca. 1357–1397), the marble structure includes a sarcophagus that supports a sculpted figure of Bernabò on horseback. Though now in a museum, Bernabò's equestrian monument originally stood over the altar of a church in Milan. The figure stands rather than sits on the horse, forcefully commanding the space over the high altar. The idea of the equestrian image of a ruler goes back to antiquity, with the *Equestrian Statue of Marcus Aurelius* (see fig. 7.33) visible in Rome throughout the Middle Ages.

The ruling aristocracy of Europe claimed for themselves the prerogative of equestrian imagery. In this sculpture, Bernabò is rigid and formal in his bearing; originally the figure was covered with silver and gold leaf to further enhance its impressiveness. Yet the treatment of the horse, with its sensitive proportions and realistically observed anatomy, points to a Lombard interest in the natural depiction of form, which may be a result of contact with contemporary French art.

Bernabò's nephew, who deposed him to claim power, used the visual arts as part of his own campaign to be named duke of Milan. Giangaleazzo Visconti encouraged the construction of a new cathedral in Milan in 1386 and commissioned expensive illuminated manuscripts like his French peers. His **Book of Hours** was begun around 1395 by Giovannino dei Grassi (active ca. 1380–1398) and features numerous personal representations and references to the duke. The page in figure **13.34** begins one of the Psalms with an illuminated initial "D" wherein King David appears. David is both the author of the text and a good biblical

exemplar of a ruler. An unfurling ribbon ornamented with the French *fleur-de-lis* forms the "D"; shields at the corners bear the Visconti emblem of the viper. Below the text appears a portrait of Giangaleazzo in the profile arrangement that was familiar from ancient coins. Although the portrait is naturalistic, it is set into an undulating frame that supports the rays of the sun, another Visconti emblem. Around the portrait Giovannino has painted images of stags and a hunting dog, paying great attention to the accurate rendering of these natural forms. Such flashes of realism amidst the splendor of the page reflect both the patrons and the artist's contribution to the developing International Gothic style. Commissioning such lavish books was an expression of the status and power that Giangaleazzo attempted to wield. His ambition to bring most of northern Italy under his control would profoundly affect the arts in Tuscany in the early fifteenth century.

Starting from the local traditions of Italy and the inspiration of Byzantine and French Gothic style, Italian artists of the thirteenth and fourteenth centuries created works of art with pronounced elements of naturalism and featuring increasingly complex imagery. Their accomplishments provided a foundation for the artists of the subsequent century in Italy and the rest of Europe.

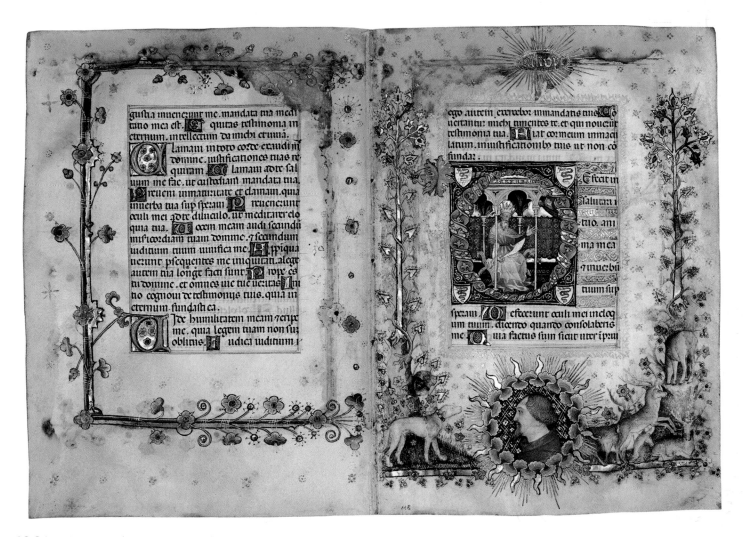

13.34 Giovannino dei Grassi, *Hours of Giangaleazzo Visconti.* ca. 1395. Tempera and gold on parchment, 9¾ × 6⅞" (24.7 × 17.5 cm). Banco Rari, Biblioteca Nazionale, 397 folio 115/H, Florence

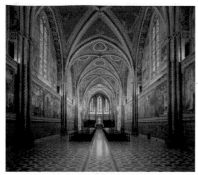

1228 Work begins on San Francesco, Assisi

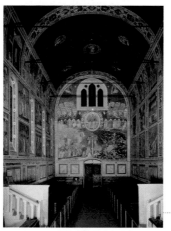

1260 Nicola Pisano's Pisa pulpit

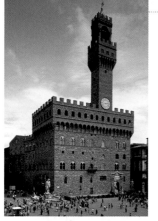

1298 Palazzo della Signoria begun in Florence

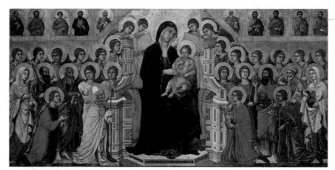

1305 Giotto's Arena Chapel frescoes

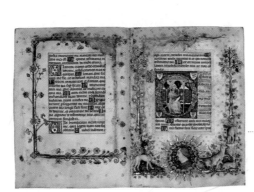

1311 Duccio's *Maestà* completed in Siena

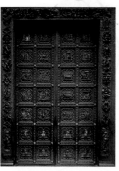

1330 Doors of baptistery of Florence

1395 *Hours of Giangaleazzo Visconti*

Art in Thirteenth- and Fourteenth- Century Italy

1200

◄ *1204 Europeans in Fourth Crusade conquer Constantinople*

1225

◄ *1234 Canonization of Dominic de Guzmán*

1250

◄ *1250 Death of Emperor Frederick II*

1262 Saint-Urbain at Troyes begun

◄ *1271–95 Marco Polo travels to China*

1275

1295 Prayer Book of Philip the Fair

◄ *1297 Venetian oligarchy closes ranks*

1300

◄ 1305–78 Papacy in Avignon, France

1310 Queen Mary Psalter

ca. 1314 Tomb of Oljeytu, Sultaniya, Iran

1325

1339 Virgin of Jeanne d'Évreux

◄ 1347–48 Black Death ravages Europe

1350

1351 Peter Parler adds choir to church of Heiligenkreuz, Schwäbisch-Gmünd, Germany

1375

◄ *1378 Wool workers (Ciompi) revolt in Florence*

1400

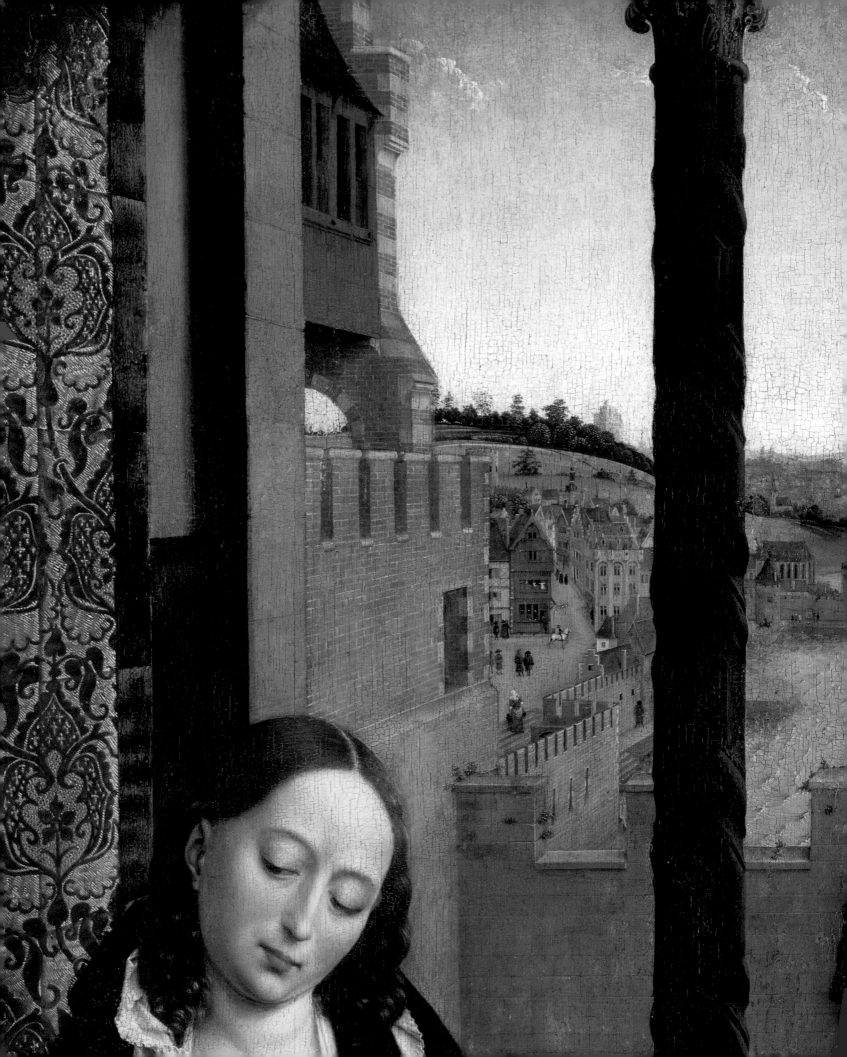

CHAPTER 14

Artistic Innovations in Fifteenth-Century Northern Europe

THE GREAT CATHEDRALS OF EUROPE'S GOTHIC ERA—THE PRODUCTS of collaboration among church officials, rulers, and the laity—were mostly completed by 1400. As monuments of Christian faith, they exemplify the medieval outlook. But cathedrals are also monuments of cities, where major social and economic changes would set the stage for the

modern world. As the fourteenth century came to an end, the medieval agrarian economy was giving way to an economy based on manufacturing and trade, activities that took place in urban centers. A social shift accompanied this economic change. Many city dwellers belonged to the middle classes, whose upper ranks enjoyed literacy, leisure, and disposable income. With these advantages, the middle classes gained greater social and cultural influence than they had wielded in the Middle Ages, when the clergy and aristocracy had dominated. This transformation had a profound effect on European culture, including the development of the visual arts.

Cities such as Paris, London, Prague, Bruges, Barcelona, and Basel were home to artisans, dayworkers, and merchants as well as aristocrats. Urban economies based more on money and wages than landed wealth required bankers, lawyers, and entrepreneurs. Investors seeking new products and markets encouraged techno-logical innovations, such as the printing press, an invention with sweeping consequences. Some cities specialized in manufacturing specific goods, such as tapestries, or working in specific materials, such as metalworking (map **14.1**). The raw materials for such products came from mines or farms from all over Europe, as well as Asia and Africa, following organized trade routes. Trade put more liquid wealth into the hands of merchants and artisans, who

were emboldened to seek more autonomy from the traditional aristocracy, who sought to maintain the feudal status quo.

Two of the most far-reaching changes concerned increased literacy and changes in religious expression. In the fourteenth century, the pope left Rome for Avignon, France, where his successors resided until 1378. On the papacy's return to Rome, however, a faction remained in France and elected their own pope. This created a schism in the Church that only ended in 1417. But the damage to the integrity of the papacy had already been done. Such scandals undermined confidence in the institutional Church, leading many laypeople to turn to religious movements that encouraged them to read sacred texts on their own, to meditate on Scripture, and to seek a personal relationship with God. One such movement was called the Modern Devotion, but mendicant friars and other clerics also encouraged this new lay piety. Although the Church was not wholly comfortable with this phenomenon, the persuasiveness of the preachers supporting it spread the new outlook. These religious impulses and increasing literacy fueled a demand for books in vernacular (local) languages, including translations of Scripture. The printing press made books more available, further stimulating the development and spread of knowledge.

Books and the ideas within them spread easily in an era when political changes brought significant changes to northern Europe whose boundaries now began to resemble those of present-day European nations. The Hundred Years' War between France and

Detail of figure 14.16, Rogier van der Weyden, *St. Luke Drawing the Virgin*

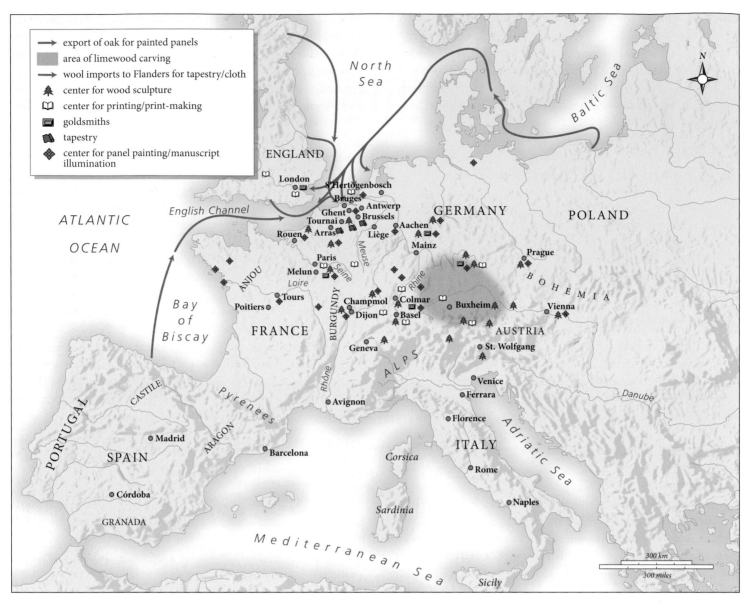

Map 14.1   Craft and manufacturing specialties in Northern Europe in the Early Modern period

England finally ended in 1453. This allowed the French monarchy to recover, but civil war kept England politically unstable until late in the fifteenth century. French kings, however, had to contend with their Burgundian cousins, who controlled the trading hub of northern Europe: the rich lands of Flanders in the southern Netherlands (present-day Belgium) and the northern Netherlands (present-day Holland). Indeed, Duke Philip the Good of Burgundy (r. 1419–1467) was one of the most powerful men of the century.

Duke Philip's son, Charles, wanted to create his own kingdom out of the regions he inherited, a matter on which he unsuccessfully petitioned the Holy Roman emperor. The emperor had nominal control of much of Central Europe, but local rulers within this region often flouted his authority. On the Iberian peninsula, the marriage between Queen Isabella of Castile and King Ferdinand of Aragon created a unified Spanish kingdom that became increasingly powerful. Competition among the

regions of Europe for trade routes led to the voyages of Christopher Columbus, which would enrich the Spanish crown and bring European culture to another hemisphere.

A new style of visual art that stressed naturalism accompanied these political and social changes. As in the medieval era, aristocrats and churchmen continued to commission works, but the new ranks of society—bureaucrats and merchants—also became art patrons. For the merchants and middle-class patrons in urban centers, painters made images in a new medium with a new character. Using oil paints, artists in the Netherlands made paintings that still astonish viewers today by their close approximation to optical reality. By midcentury, this strongly naturalistic style became the dominant visual language of northern Europe, attracting patrons from all classes and many countries.

This transition was gradual and by no means universal. Faced with a growing middle class, the traditional aristocracy attempted to maintain their privileges and status. Among the aristocratic courts of France, the Holy Roman Empire, England, and the Burgundian Netherlands, many of which were linked by treaty or marriage, a preference emerged for a highly refined form of Gothic art, which has been termed International Gothic. Yet within these courtly images were the seeds of the heightened naturalism that would blossom in the fifteenth century.

COURTLY ART: THE INTERNATIONAL GOTHIC

As the fourteenth century came to an end, aristocratic patrons throughout Europe indulged a taste for objects made of sumptuous materials with elegant forms, based on the Gothic style. The latter had been born in France and was linked with the powerful French monarchy, so its latest manifestation owed a great deal to the forms and traditions of France. Cosmopolitan courts such as Avignon and Paris attracted artists from many regions and allowed them to exchange ideas. These circumstances produced the style historians call the International Gothic. The artists of the International Gothic also adapted some elements from fourteenth-century Italy, including devices to imply spatial settings borrowed from Duccio and Pietro Lorenzetti, and certain themes and compositions, such as aristocrats enjoying the countryside (see figs. 13.30 and 13.31). The chronological limits of this style are somewhat fluid, as some objects ascribed to the International Gothic date from the mid-fourteenth century, whereas others may date as late as the mid-fifteenth.

International Gothic artists came from Italy, France, Flanders, Germany, Spain, Bohemia, Austria, England, and elsewhere. They produced works of exquisite craftsmanship, with sometimes very complex iconographies, out of expensive materials for elite patrons. In making these objects, artists followed Gothic principles, which used geometric patterns to impose order on natural forms to idealize them (as we saw for example in fig. 12.19, in the work of Villard de Honnecourt), but they added details directly observed from nature, too. Many scholars see the detailed naturalism that appears in the International Gothic as a key stimulus for the more thoroughgoing naturalism of the early Flemish painters and their followers in the fifteenth century.

Sculpture for the French Royal Family

The French royal family was among the most active patrons of the International Gothic. King Charles V had three brothers, all of whom were active patrons of the arts. The youngest of them, Philip the Bold, became duke of Burgundy in 1363; then he added the title of count of Flanders through his marriage to Margaret of Mâle. Through these territorial acquisitions, the dukes of Burgundy became powerbrokers in the military and economic struggles of the fifteenth century. Works of art helped further Philip's status, providing an important example for his successors.

In his domain of Burgundy, Duke Philip the Bold established a Carthusian monastery, the Chartreuse de Champmol, outside Dijon. Although the monastery was almost completely destroyed in the late eighteenth century during the anti-aristocratic riots of the French Revolution, some parts of the building survive. For the construction of this monastery, which Philip intended to serve as his family mausoleum, he assembled a team of artists, many of them from the Netherlands. Chief among them was the sculptor Claus Sluter (ca. 1360–1406) who came from Brussels. Remnants of Sluter's work at the Chartreuse de Champmol include tombs, portal sculptures and other sculptural projects.

THE WELL OF MOSES AT THE CHARTREUSE DE CHAMPMOL The most emblematic among those of the International Gothic style is *The Well of Moses* (fig. 14.1). At one time, this hexagonal well, surrounded by statues of Hebrew Bible prophets, was topped by a life-size Calvary scene with Christ on the Cross flanked by his mother and saints. This served as a visual expression of the fulfillment by the New Testament of the Hebrew Bible. With the loss of most of the Calvary scene, however, it is the six figures of Hebrew Bible prophets on the base who must represent Sluter's achievement for us. Supported on a narrow console and framed by slim colonnettes. The majestic Moses wears a long flowing beard and drapery that envelops his body like an ample shell. The swelling forms of the prophets seem to reach out

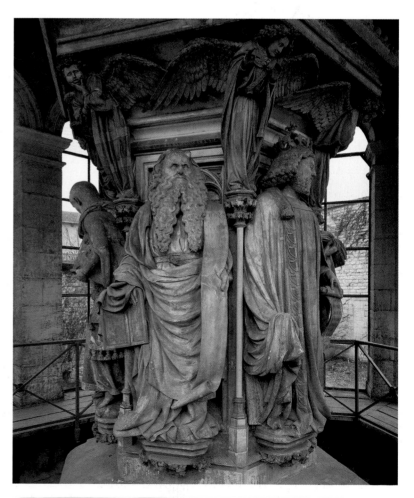

14.1 Claus Sluter, *The Well of Moses*, Chartreuse de Champmol, France. 1395–1406. Stone, height of figures approx. 6' (1.8 m)

into the surrounding space to interact directly with a viewer. Each prophet carries a scroll with texts that predict the death of Christ, and each bears an attribute that identifies him. To Moses' right stands King David, wearing the crown and robe of monarchy. The intense, staring Moses bears a pair of horns to identify him; this detail arose from a mistranslation of the Hebrew word for "ray" during the early Christian period. The horns describe Moses, holding the tablets of the Ten Commandments, after his encounter with God on Sinai. The lifelike feeling created by Moses' size and naturalistic rendering must have been greatly enhanced by the colors added to the stone by the painter Jean Malouel; these have now largely disappeared. Sluter gave one of the prophets a pair of bronze spectacles to further the connection to the real world. This attachment to the specific distinguishes Sluter's naturalistic style from that of the earlier period and is one of the hallmarks of the International Gothic.

THE ALTARPIECE AT THE CHARTREUSE DE CHAMPMOL

In addition to sculptural projects for the Chartreuse de Champmol, Duke Philip commissioned an altarpiece for its church that was executed between 1394 and 1399. The ensemble included an elaborately carved relief for the central section by Jacques de Baerze (showing the Adoration of the Magi, the Crucifixion, and the Entombment) and wings by the Flemish painter Melchior Broederlam (ca. 1355–1410) (fig. **14.2**). (Their complex shape results from the format of the central section.) Each panel of these wings depicts two scenes from the infancy of Christ: The left wing depicts the Annunciation and the Visitation (when the pregnant Virgin visited her cousin Elizabeth, who was herself expecting John the Baptist); the right, the presentation of the infant Christ to the rabbi Simeon in the Temple and the flight of the holy family from Bethlehem into Egypt to escape the persecution of Herod. The painter uses landscape and architectural elements to define the narratives and to fill in available spaces. Broederlam arranges the architecture so a viewer can see inside, as if into a doll's house; the spatial arrangements, however, derive from Duccio and the Lorenzetti (see figs. 13.23 and 13.26). Details of the landscape are out of scale with the figures, yet the panels convey a strong feeling of depth thanks to the subtlety of the modeling. The softly rounded shapes and the dark, velvety

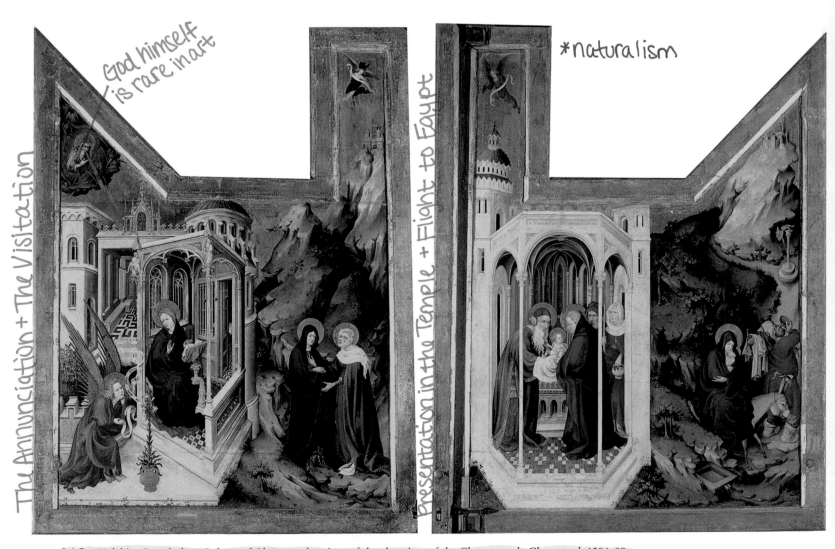

14.2 Melchior Broederlam, *Infancy of Christ* panels, wings of the altarpiece of the Chartreuse de Champmol. 1394–99. Tempera on panel, each 65 × 49¼" (167 × 125 cm). Musée des Beaux-Arts, Dijon, France

shadows create the illusion of weight, as do the ample, loosely draped garments, reminiscent of the sculpture of Sluter.

Broederlam's panels display another feature of the International Gothic style: the realistic depiction of small details. Observing nature in detail was certainly not new; similar realism may be seen in some Gothic sculpture (see fig. 12.28) and among some drôleries (small designs, often of fables or scenes from everyday life) in the margins of manuscripts such as the *Hours of Jeanne d'Évreux* (fig. 12.39). In Broederlam's Annunciation panel, such realism is evident in the carefully rendered foliage and flowers of the enclosed garden behind Gabriel at the left. In the right-hand panel, touches of naturalistic detail include the delightful donkey, the tiny fountain at its feet, and the rustic figure of St. Joseph, who looks like a simple peasant in contrast with the delicate, aristocratic beauty of the Virgin. These painstaking touches give Broederlam's work the flavor of an enlarged miniature rather than of a large-scale painting, even though the panels are more than 5 feet tall. But they do more than merely endow the image with small flashes of realism: They contribute to its meaning. In the left-hand panel, for example, the lily signifies Mary's virginity, as does the enclosed garden next to her, which is inspired by a metaphor from the biblical Song of Songs: "A garden enclosed is my sister, my spouse; a spring shut up, a fountain sealed." Even the architecture contributes to the meaning. The contrasting Romanesque and Gothic buildings stand for the Hebrew Bible and New Testament respectively. Broederlam both enchants and instructs in this painting.

Illuminated Manuscripts: Books of Hours

Broederlam's work in these painted altarpiece wings reflects the influence of manuscript illuminations, which had been an important medium in northern Europe throughout the Middle Ages. The French court prized these expensive, custom-made objects. Philip the Bold's older brother, Jean, duke of Berry in central France, commissioned many of these sumptuous books, amassing a huge collection in his lifetime.

The luxurious book of hours known as *Les Très Riches Heures du Duc de Berry* (*The Very Rich Hours of the Duke of Berry*), is one of the most famous of the duke's books and a prime example of the International Gothic style. The artists responsible for it were Pol de Limbourg and his two brothers, Herman and Jean. They were introduced to the court by their uncle, Jean Malouel, the painter who had applied the colors to Sluter's *The Well of Moses*, and came to share an appointment as court painters to the duke, reflecting the high regard they enjoyed. One or more of the brothers must have visited Italy, for their work includes numerous motifs and whole compositions borrowed from the artists of Tuscany and Lombardy.

The Limbourg Brothers began the *Très Riches Heures* about 1413 and left it unfinished when they died in 1416, probably of the plague. As a result, some pages were completed long after their deaths. The most famous pages in the book are devoted to the calendar and depict human activities and the cycle of nature.

Such image cycles, originally consisting of 12 single figures each performing an appropriate seasonal activity, were an established tradition in medieval art. In this manuscript, the calendar pages depict aristocrats and peasants in detailed and elegant images in activities appropriate to the month represented.

The page for January, for example (fig. **14.3**), shows a scene of feasting, a traditional choice for the cold winter months. But the Limbourgs flatter their patron by depicting the duke himself at the table, seated before a large fireplace, whose wicker screen serves to frame him. Wearing a fur cap and embroidered blue garment, Duke Jean sits beneath a wall hanging adorned with his coat of arms and swans, his personal emblem. Before him, a feast is laid out on golden plates and sumptuous vessels. He discourses with a clergyman seated near him, while expensively dressed courtiers

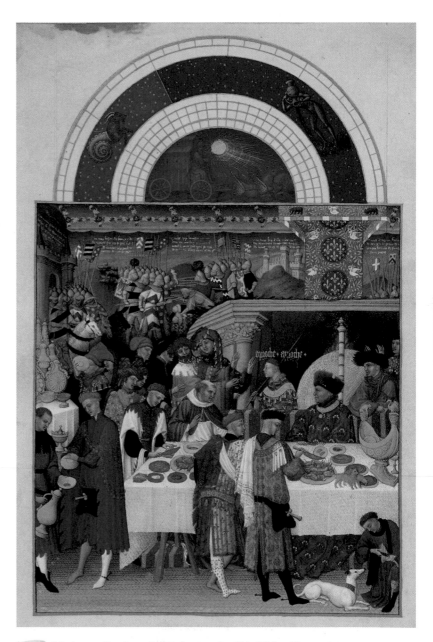

14.3 Limbourg Brothers. January page, *Les Très Riches Heures du Duc de Berry*. 1413–16. 8⅞ × 5⅜" (22.5 × 13.7 cm). Musée Condé, Chantilly, France

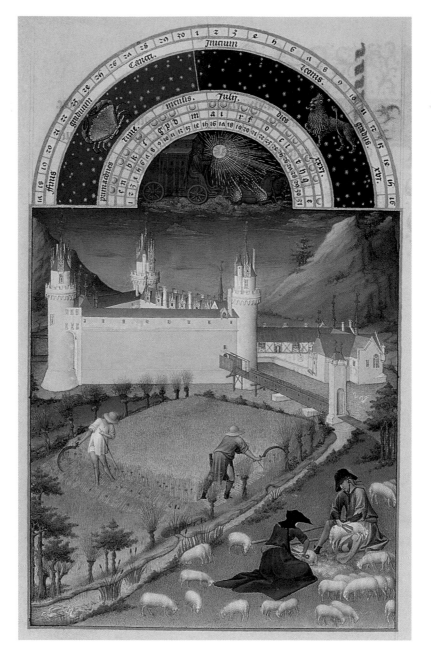

14.4 Limbourg Brothers. July page, *Les Très Riches Heures du Duc de Berry.* 1413–16. 8⅞ × 5⅜" (22.5 × 13.7 cm). Musée Condé, Chantilly, France

wait on the duke or warm themselves at the fire. Painted tapestries hang on the wall next to and above the mantel. Using brilliant colors, the artists reproduce the table setting, the items on the menu, the patterns in the draperies, even the texture of the floor covering. Such detailed observation records the pleasures of the winter season for the duke, who could literally see himself in the page.

The chronological elements above the interior scene on this page are unfinished, but they are complete in another page of the book for the summer season. The calendar page for July (fig. **14.4**) notes the passage of time in several ways: A semicircular section at the top marks the days numerically and includes the astrological signs for the month. Below this, the labor of the month is performed, as peasants harvest wheat and shear sheep in the fields, beneath a precisely rendered castle, Jean de Berry's Chateau du Clain (Poitiers), now destroyed but well documented. The page depicts the orderly harvesting of a fruitful earth by the peaceful peasantry for the eyes of the man who owns the castle. This idealized view of the social order of feudalism is achieved by combining the portrait of the castle and naturalistic details of the sheep or the scythes with an artificial space that rises up the picture plane rather than receding into depth. The carefully crafted composition links the three major zones into triangular elements that fit together like a jigsaw puzzle. The jewel-like color and splashes of gold leaf in the calendar zone contribute to the sumptuous effect of the page. The prestige of the patron and the sheer innovation of the images, especially on the calendar pages, in the *Très Riches Heures* inspired many later copies.

Bohemia and England

Other courts and regions in Europe shared the French taste for the International Gothic. In Central Europe, the city of Prague, the capital of Bohemia, became a major cosmopolitan center thanks to Emperor Charles IV (1316–1378). Charles was educated in Paris at the court of the French king Charles IV, whose daughter he married and in whose honor he changed his name from Wenceslaus. After returning to Prague and succeeding his father as king of Bohemia, Charles was named Holy Roman emperor by the German Electors at Aachen in 1349 and crowned as such in Rome in 1355.

Charles wanted to make Prague a center of learning, and in 1348 he established a university modeled on the one in Paris. It soon attracted many of the best minds in Europe. He also became a patron of the arts and founded a guild for artists. In addition to encouraging local talent, Charles brought artists from all over Europe to his city. In his castle of Karlstein, just outside of Prague, he built a chapel dedicated to the Holy Cross that imitated Louis IX's Sainte Chapelle (fig. 12.32). Instead of stained glass, however, the walls of this chapel were covered in paintings done by Master Theodoric, the first head of the painters' guild of Prague. The paintings were executed between 1357 and 1367.

St. Matthew and the Angel (fig. **14.5**) comes from this project. As one of the authors of the Gospels, Matthew holds a book while an angel whispers in his ear. A long-standing medieval tradition assigned symbols to each of the four Evangelists, in Matthew's case an angel. Master Theodoric makes the angel an active participant in the work of the saint. Matthew himself is rendered as a three-dimensional figure, whose blue garment falls across his body in softly modeled folds of drapery. This style probably derives from Theodoric's study of Italian artists, either in his native Austria or Prague.

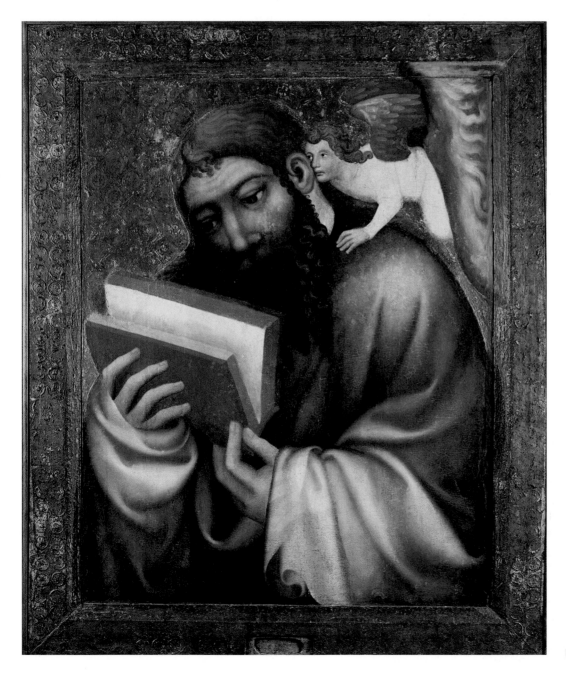

14.5 Master Theodoric, *St. Matthew and the Angel*. ca. 1360–65. Panel, 45¼ × 37" (1.15 × 0.93 m). National Gallery, Prague

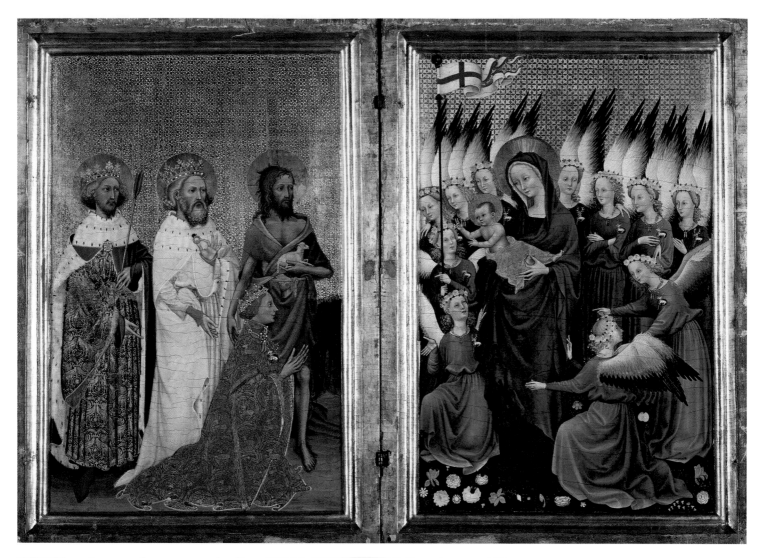

14.6 *The Wilton Diptych.* ca. 1400. Panel, 20⅞ × 14⅝" (53 × 37 cm). National Gallery of Art, London

In a pattern typical among late medieval dynasties, the emperor Charles IV's daughter, Anne of Bohemia, married the English king Richard II in 1382. Richard, who ruled from 1377 to 1399, is the figure depicted in a painting called (for the collector who once owned it) *The Wilton Diptych* (fig. **14.6**). A **diptych** is a double panel that opens on a hinge at the center like a book. This diptych represents King Richard II kneeling before his patron saints to venerate the Virgin Mary and her Child. The gazes of the figures connect across the panels as they stare at the Virgin and Child, who playfully reaches out toward the king. Angels accompany the elegant figure of the Virgin, who appears like a queen surrounded by her palace guard, yet because the angels wear badges with emblems of Richard himself, it is his guard that surrounds her. The sumptuous colors and tall weightless figures stand in an eternal setting defined by a beautifully tooled gold background. Yet the drapery worn by the angels is modeled in the same natural light as Master Theodoric's *St. Matthew.* Scholars are still debating whether the unidentified artist who achieved this combination of Gothic otherworldliness and natural observation came from France, England, Bohemia, or somewhere else.

URBAN CENTERS AND THE NEW ART

Many of the artists whom the patrons in the courts preferred for their projects came from the cities of the southern Netherlands: Bruges, Brussels, Ghent, and Tournai. These were centers of international commerce in whose streets many languages could be heard as merchants from all over Europe gathered to do business. They were very jealous of their status as independent entities with special privileges to govern themselves, set trade tariffs, and establish militias. Their claims for independence often clashed with the desires of aristocratic overlords to tax and control their inhabitants. Buildings like the Town Hall of Bruges (fig. **14.7**), built between 1376 and 1402, were designed to provide a setting for town councils and to serve as symbols of the independence and privileges the cities claimed. The Town Hall is one of the earliest such structures in northern Europe. Set on a major town square, it looks like an ecclesiastical structure, with its high gabled roof, traceried windows, and vaulted interior. The façade emu-lates Gothic churches, too, with its many sculpted figures depicting not saints, but the local rulers, the counts of Flanders.

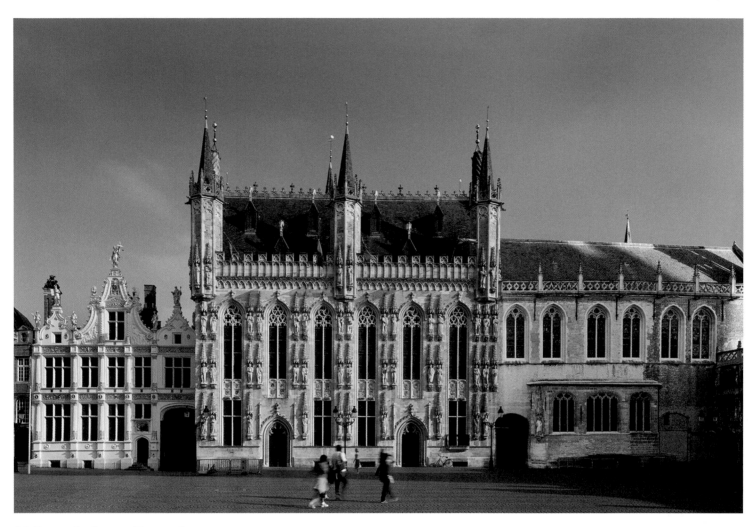

14.7 Façade of Bruges Town Hall. Begun 1376

(The building was damaged during the French Revolution, and the statues on the façade today are modern.) While the interior of the structure functioned as a council hall for self-rule and issuing judgments, the exterior sculpture expressed the nominal rule of the counts of Flanders.

It is in the cities of Flanders that the beginnings of an artistic revolution may be seen. Working either for courts or for citizens, artists began to make images in oil paint that represent sacred figures as if they existed in the natural world, giving tangible form to spiritual concepts.

Robert Campin in Tournai

An early pioneer of this naturalistic revolution is Robert Campin (1378–1444), the foremost painter in Tournai, an important trade center in southwestern Belgium. Campin ran a busy workshop, from which several other successful painters emerged, including Rogier van der Weyden.

THE MÉRODE TRIPTYCH The most famous work attributed to Campin is the *Mérode Triptych* (fig. **14.8**), dated on the basis of style to around 1425. The name derives from an early owner of

the painting, but the subject of the central panel is the Annunciation, frequently depicted in earlier Christian art. Typically, those earlier representations of the Annunciation set the event in an ecclesiastical building (see fig. 14.2) or other sacred space (see fig. 13.25), but Campin places the Virgin and the angel Gabriel in what appears to be the main room of a bourgeois house, complete with open shutters, well-used fireplace, and cushioned bench. Despite the supernatural events, a viewer has the sense of actually looking through the surface of the panel into a world that mimics reality. Campin uses several devices to create this effect. He fits the objects and figures into boxes of space aligned with the parts of the triptych. Sometimes the fit isn't comfortable, but he renders details in such a way as to make every object as concrete as possible in its shape, size, color, and texture. He also paints two kinds of light. One is of a diffused kind that creates soft shadows and delicate gradations of brightness; the other is more direct and enters through the two round windows, casting shadows on the wall. Campin's color scheme, with its muted tonality, unifies all three panels; his bright colors have richness and depth, and he achieves smooth transitions from lights into darks. These effects were made possible by the use of oil. (See *Materials and Techniques*, page 479.) Although medieval artists

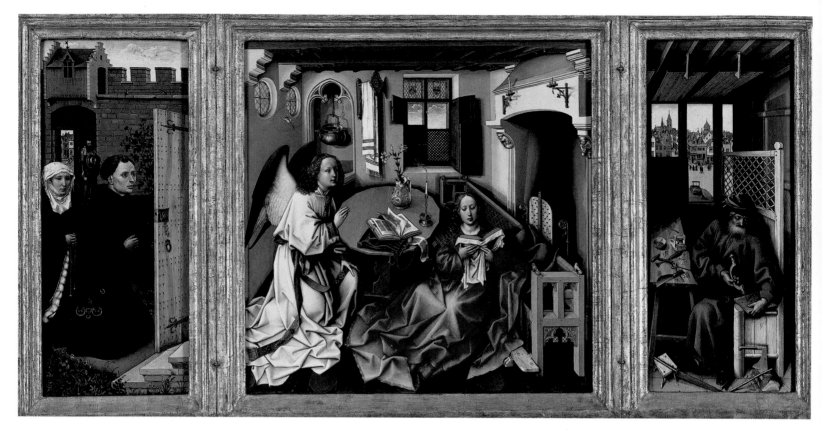

14.8 Robert Campin and workshop. *Mérode Triptych.* ca. 1425–30. Oil on oak, center panel 25¼ × 24⅞" (64.1 × 63.2 cm), each wing approx. 25⅜ × 10⅞" (64.5 × 27.4 cm). Metropolitan Museum of Art, New York, The Cloisters Collection, 1956. 56.70a-c

had knowledge of oil paint, Campin and his contemporaries expanded its possibilities for painting on panels. Its use allowed him to create a much more thorough illusion of reality than the flashes of natural detail seen in the work of court artists.

Campin was no court painter but a townsman who catered to the tastes of fellow citizens, such as the two donors shown here piously kneeling outside the Virgin's chamber. A coat of arms painted in the window of the central panel points to a family of merchants who had settled in Tournai by 1427. Obviously they were wealthy enough to commission this triptych, probably for their own dwelling, as it is too small for installation in a public church. Perhaps it was this function that inspired the artist to break with tradition in the picture. This Annunciation takes place in a fully equipped domestic interior with figures that are rendered as real people, with mass and weight. The drapery of their garments falls in deep folds, anchoring the figures to the floor, as in the sculpture of Claus Sluter (see fig. 14.1). Gabriel adopts a not-quite-kneeling, not-quite-standing position as he raises his right hand to speak. Mary's red dress draws attention to her as she sits on the floor, book in hand. Between them, a table supports another book, a vase of lilies, and a candle. Above and behind Gabriel, the tiny figure of a baby holding a cross, who must be Christ, floats downward toward Mary. In the left wing panel, the donors kneel in a garden, as though looking through the open door to witness this event. The whole effect is of time frozen: Something important is about to happen. Where Simone Martini

had rendered Gabriel and the Virgin as slim, weightless figures set against an eternal gold ground (see fig. 13.25), Campin depicts their substantial bodies in a recognizably earthly setting for the eyes of the donor couple. They see the event taking place in their world, not in Heaven.

The right wing panel depicts Joseph, the carpenter, at work, though just what he is making is debatable. Scholars have identified the mysterious boxlike object on the window ledge as a mousetrap, an object that the Christian theologian St. Augustine used metaphorically to explain God's plan for salvation when he said, "The Cross of the Lord was the devil's mousetrap." The mousetrap could be a visual cue to the reason for Christ's incarnation, which is about to occur in the central panel. Equally puzzling is the object in Joseph's hand, identified by some as a fire screen (like the one in the central panel) and by others as part of a press through which grapes are forced to make wine (which would refer to the wine used in the sacrament of the Eucharist).

Such carefully chosen details have persuaded many scholars that Campin used these forms as symbols to convey spiritual messages. We have seen some of these symbols before: The flowers, for example, are associated with the Virgin as emblems of her purity and other virtues; they appeared in Simone Martini's Annunciation (see fig. 13.25). Interpreting other details, such as the smoking candle next to the vase of lilies, has been more difficult. Its glowing wick and the curl of smoke indicate that it has just been extinguished. To explain why a candle had been lit

Panel Painting in Tempera and Oil

In the fourteenth and fifteenth centuries, painters worked with liquid pigments on wooden panels. The type of wood used varied from region to region, though oak panels were preferred in northern Europe because they could be sawn into thin planks to serve as supports for the paint. Pine, fruitwoods, and poplar were also used. Once the panels had been formed, and often inserted into a frame by a carpenter, the flat surface would be covered with a film of gesso (a type of fine plaster) to create a smooth surface for the image. Often an underdrawing would be laid onto the gesso as a guide for the painter or his assistants.

For pigments, artists used oxides, plants, minerals, or semiprecious stones. They ground these materials into powders that had to be mixed with some sort of liquid medium to bind them to the panel. The basic medium of medieval panel painting had been tempera, in which the finely ground pigments were mixed ("tempered") with diluted egg yolk. This produced a thin, tough, quick-drying coat that was well suited to the medieval taste for high-keyed flat color surfaces. However, in tempera the different tones on the panel could not be blended smoothly, and the progression of values necessary for three-dimensional effects was difficult to achieve.

While medieval artists had used oil-based paints for special purposes, such as coating stone surfaces or painting on metal, artists like Jan van Eyck and Robert Campin in Flanders exploited it for panel paintings. Oil, a viscous, slow-drying medium, can produce a variety of effects, from thin, translucent films (called **glazes**) to a thick layer of creamy, heavy-bodied paint (called **impasto**). The tones can also yield a continuous scale of hues, including rich, velvety dark shades. Oil painting offers another advantage over egg tempera, **encaustic**, and fresco: It allows artists to change their minds and rework their paintings. As the use of oil paints spread across Europe, some artists adopted a mixed technique, using tempera for the base layers and covering these with oil glazes. Although pigments continued to be mixed with tempera for some time, oil has been the painter's basic medium until very recently.

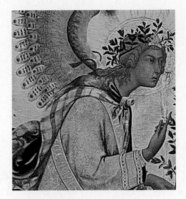 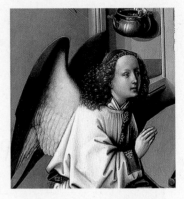

Simone Martini's image of the angel Gabriel is painted in tempera, which dries quickly; consequently, the layers of paint do not blend, and individual strokes of the brush are visible on the surface.

Campin's Gabriel is painted with oil, which dries slowly and is translucent. Each layer of color merges with the one below it to create a mirrorlike finish.

---

on a sunny day, and what had snuffed out its flame, scholars have pointed to the arrival of Christ on a beam of light coming through the round window: In theological terms, the arrival of the true light (Christ) extinguishes the mundane one.

The appearance in Campin's picture of so many carefully delineated objects suggests that these details constitute a symbolic program, which either the artist or the patron conceived. Theologians or scholars may have provided Campin with the more learned aspects of the symbolism, but it was the artist who found the means to express these complex ideas in symbolic terms using forms observed in the visible world. Modern scholars also debate the reasons why Campin and his contemporaries wanted to record the world with such fidelity. Some have argued that philosophies about nature and the natural world had changed, along with religious practices. Others have suggested that pragmatic merchants demanded directly observed renderings of things they could see.

The Annunciation certainly has liturgical and theological import, but it is also a story about the conception of a child. The couple on the left kneel devoutly before the image of these events. From their perspective, the triptych may be an expression of their own desire for children or their reverence for the Holy Family as a model for their own. Such personalized approaches to holy figures and sacred dramas enlivened religious life at the end of the Middle Ages. Believers were encouraged in sermons, Passion plays, and written texts to visualize the sacred in terms they could understand and to meditate on events from Christ's life in order to increase their empathy and devotion. Although monks and nuns had long practiced such contemplation, the religious movement called the Modern Devotion helped to spread these ideas among the laity. New texts, such as the *Imitation of Christ* by Thomas à Kempis, provided guidance for laypeople wishing to emulate Christ. Artists like Campin may have been responding to the call to see the physical world as a mirror of divine truths and to create moving and pious images of sacred events occurring in everyday environments.

Jan van Eyck in Bruges

The visual revolution achieved in paintings such as the *Mérode Triptych* was recognized and admired not only by patrons in Flanders but also by patrons in Italy. Italian observers provide the earliest external assessments of the Flemish innovators. They recognized that the technical achievement of oil painting contributed to the striking naturalism and evocation of religious feeling in Flemish painting, and they credited the "invention" of oil painting to Jan van Eyck (1390–1441). (See www.myartslab.com.) As a result, his is one of the more famous names of fifteenth-century art, and he is a figure about whom we know a good deal.

Jan worked first for the count of Holland and then for the reigning duke of Burgundy, Philip the Good, from 1425 until his death in Bruges in 1441. Both a townsman and a court painter, Jan was highly esteemed by Philip the Good, who occasionally sent him on diplomatic errands. Unusual for his time, he signed and dated several surviving pictures, which has allowed historians to identify his artistic output and to assign unsigned works to him based on the signed ones.

THE *GHENT ALTARPIECE* The *Ghent Altarpiece* is one of the most famous of early Flemish paintings. From the moment it was installed in a chapel of the cathedral of St. John in Ghent (see fig. 14.12), it began to draw a crowd. Albrecht Dürer visited it in 1520, and much later artists like the nineteenth-century French painter Ingres drew inspiration from it. An inscription on the now-lost frame identified Jan van Eyck as the artist who finished this multipaneled altarpiece in May 1432 and alluded to the collaboration of his older brother, Hubert, who died in 1426. The basic form of this complex altarpiece is a triptych (consisting of three hinged panels), but here each of the three units consists of four panels. Since the wings are also painted on both sides, the altarpiece contains a total of 20 images of various shapes and sizes. Discontinuities among the many panels suggest alterations took place as the work progressed. It appears that Jan took over a number of panels left unfinished by Hubert, completed them, added some of his own, and assembled the whole at the request of the wealthy donor, Jodicus Vijd. Vijd's portrait with that of his wife, Elizabeth Borluut, appears on the outer panels of the altar when the triptych is closed (fig. **14.9**).

Their portraits appear on the lower tier with two other figures, each in a separate niche framed by painted Gothic tracery. Next to

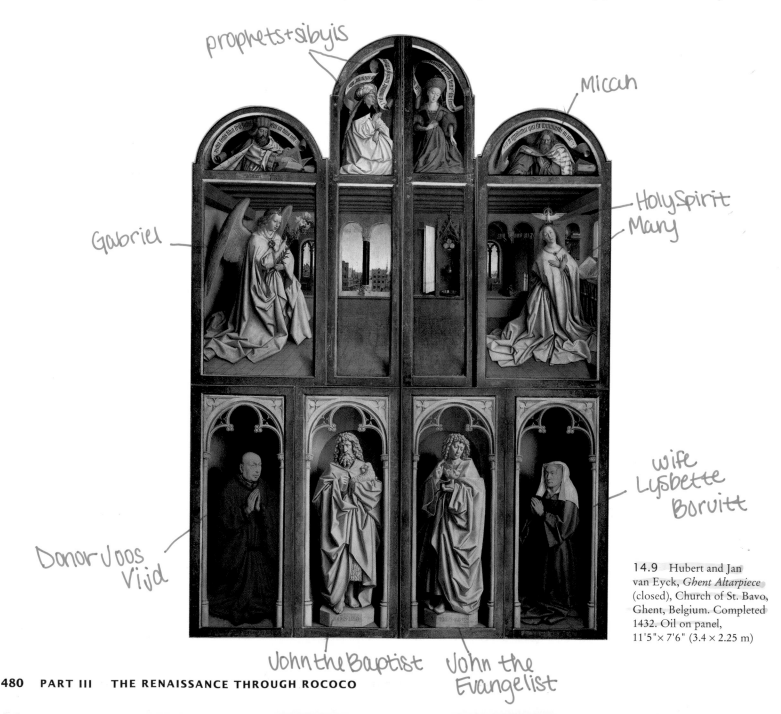

14.9 Hubert and Jan van Eyck, *Ghent Altarpiece* (closed), Church of St. Bavo, Ghent, Belgium. Completed 1432. Oil on panel, 11'5" × 7'6" (3.4 × 2.25 m)

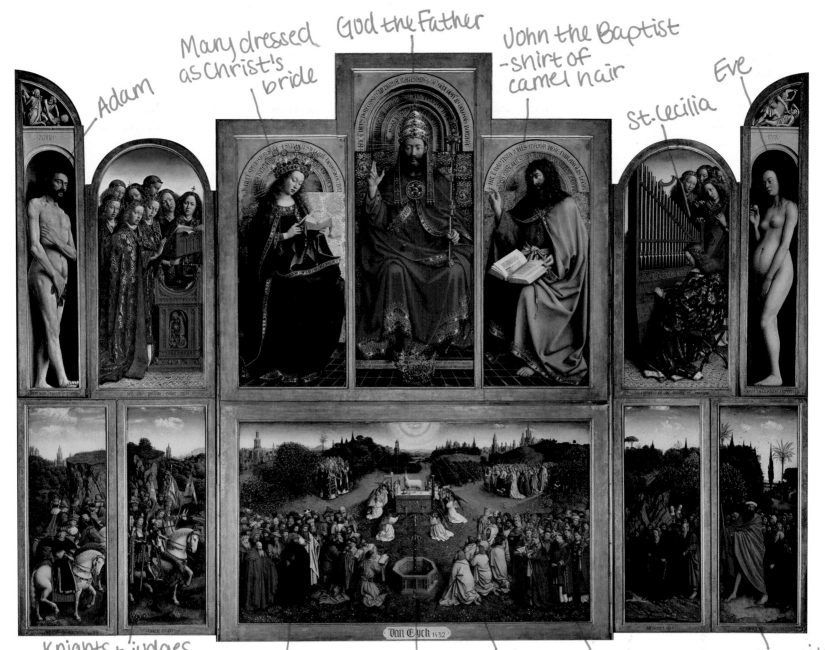

Handwritten annotations on image:
- Adam
- Mary dressed as Christ's bride
- God the Father
- John the Baptist - shirt of camel hair
- St. Cecilia
- Eve
- knights + judges
- saints prophets
- fountain
- Lamb of God
- apostles in white + saints in red
- hermits + pilgrims

14.10 Hubert and Jan van Eyck, *Ghent Altarpiece* (open). 11'5" × 15'1" (3.4 × 4.5 m)

the donors are John the Baptist and John the Evangelist, the patrons of the cathedral, painted in **grisaille** (a monochrome; in this case to imitate the grayish color of statues). The upper tier has two pairs of panels of different width. The artist has made a virtue of this awkward necessity by combining all four into one interior, whose foreshortened timber ceiling crosses all four panels. In addition to the continuous space, Jan heightens the illusion by painting shadows on the floor of the Virgin's chamber as if they were cast by the frames of the panels. Prophets and sibyls occupy an upper story, their prophecies written in Gothic script in scrolls above their heads. In such altarpieces, the wings stayed closed except on Sundays, specific feast days, and when other liturgically important moments required them to be opened.

When the wings are opened (fig. **14.10**) the viewer sees a detailed rendering of a celestial assembly: Across the bottom tier, groups of figures converge on a central image of an altar, upon which stands a haloed Lamb. This assembly includes angels, apostles, popes, theologians, virgin martyrs, hermits, pilgrims, knights, and judges (including, possibly, a reference to Jan's employer, Duke Philip the Good). A verdant landscape provides the setting for this mystic Mass, with towers of numerous churches in the skyline. Above this earthly paradise reigns an imposing Court of Heaven, with the Lord in a bright red robe at the center. Flanking him are Mary and John the Baptist. To the left and right, choirs of angels sing and play musical instruments. At the outer edges of this upper tier stand Adam and Eve, rendered as nudes in shallow niches, below grisaille images of Abel and Cain. The almost life-size nudes are portrayed with careful attention to their anatomy and caressed by a delicate play of light and shade (fig. **14.11**).

The figures' poses are comparable to those in Gothic manuscripts, but here the artist breathes life into the forms by rendering

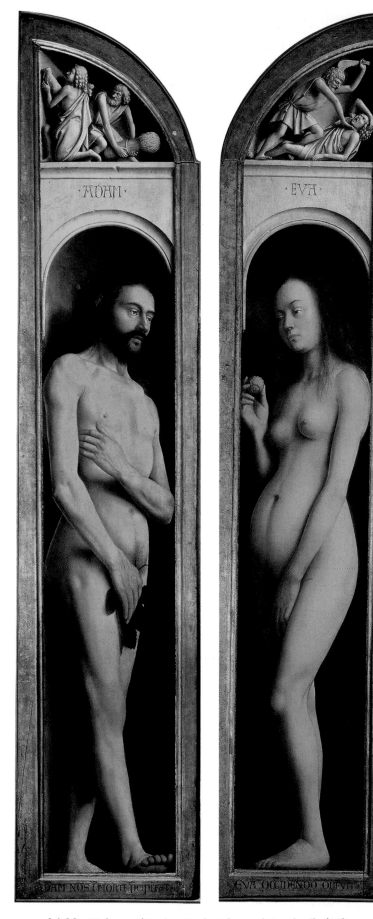

14.11 Hubert and Jan van Eyck, *Adam and Eve*, detail of *Ghent Altarpiece*. Left and right wings

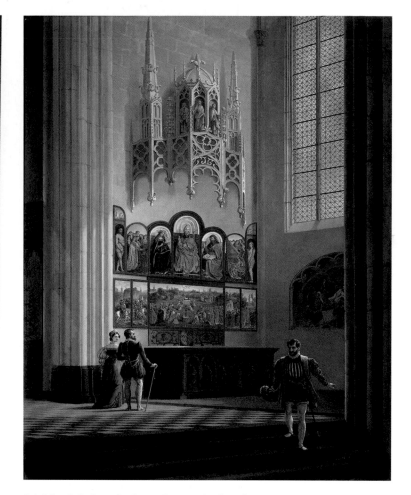

14.12 Painting of *Ghent Altarpiece* in chapel. Rijksmuseum, Amsterdam

the textures and colors of the bodies with great accuracy. Seeing this work on the altar of the Vijd Chapel in Ghent cathedral (fig. **14.12**), a viewer could not fail to be impressed by the scale and setting of the painting. The tone and majesty of this ensemble are very different from the domestic intimacy of the *Mérode Triptych*. The function of the altarpiece is to elucidate the **liturgy** performed in front of it. When open, its subject is the Mass itself, here shown in a paradisiacal setting. The number of books represented and the many erudite inscriptions celebrating Christian learning suggest that a cleric or theologian may have advised Jan in developing the program. But Jan accomplished the difficult task of bringing the disparate panels together and welding them into an imposing and memorable experience.

Jan's work is large in scale but full of naturally observed details and glowing color. His technique of building up color in layers of glazes results in highly saturated hues, while the slow, methodical application of paint blends brushstrokes to a mirrorlike finish. Jan offers a glimpse into Heaven to stimulate devotion. If, as some scholars believe, the whole altarpiece was set into a Gothic architectural frame, one meaning of the image becomes the importance of the Church itself as an institution and as a pathway to salvation.

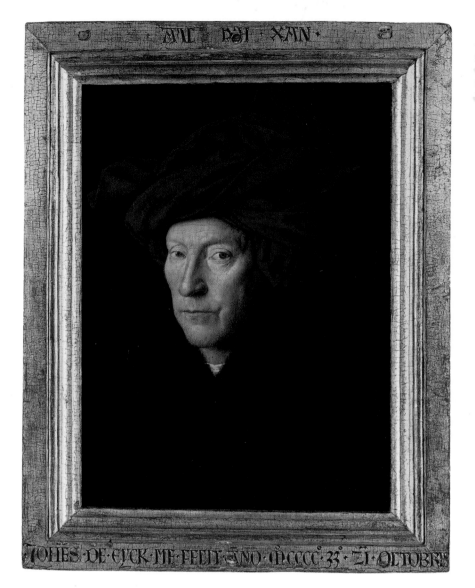

14.13 Jan van Eyck, *Man in a Red Turban (Self-Portrait?)*. 1433. Oil on panel, 13⅛ × 10¼" (33 × 25.8 cm). The National Gallery, London

SECULAR IMAGES Jan van Eyck also made purely secular paintings, fulfilling the commissions of the court and of the middle-class citizens of Flemish towns. One example is Jan's *Man in a Red Turban* (fig. **14.13**), signed and dated 1433, which represents a middle-aged man in a three-quarters pose whose face is framed by his dramatic headgear. Warm light bathes the distinctive face emerging from the dark background of this painting and reveals every detail of shape and texture with almost microscopic precision. The artist does not explore the sitter's personality, yet the man gazes out of the picture to make eye contact with the viewer. This innovation, and the slight strain about the eyes which may come from gazing into a mirror, suggests that the painting may be a self-portrait. The self-consciousness that such a project demands may relate to the text painted on the frame: An inscription reads "*ALS ICH KAN*" ("As I can" or "As best I can"). This motto appears on other works by Jan, too, perhaps challenging other artists to do better, for he has done all he can. Though transposed into Greek letters, the phrase is Flemish; this implies that Jan saw himself in competition with the ancients as well as with his contemporaries. Whatever his reason may have been, we can read the motto as another sign of Jan's self-consciousness about his work as an artist and his place in history.

The next example demonstrates that Jan van Eyck's signatures complicate the task of interpreting his work. One of the most studied and yet still mysterious of his surviving images represents a man and a woman standing in a richly furnished room, equipped with a brass chandelier, a mirror, and a canopied bed (fig. **14.14**). Jan signed the painting, not on the frame, as he did in many of his other paintings, but within the panel itself. Above the painted mirror in a formal script, the translated signature reads, "Jan van Eyck was here, 1434." The features of the man, if not the lady, are specific enough to be a portrait, and the image is unusual enough that scholars have been able to use later documents to identify the subject as Giovanni Arnolfini, an Italian merchant living in Bruges. For many years, scholars believed that his companion should be identified as Giovanna Cenami, Arnolfini's wife; recent research, however, makes this doubtful, as that marriage took place much later than 1434.

Whatever their names, the painted couple appear in the main room of a fifteenth-century house that is somewhat more

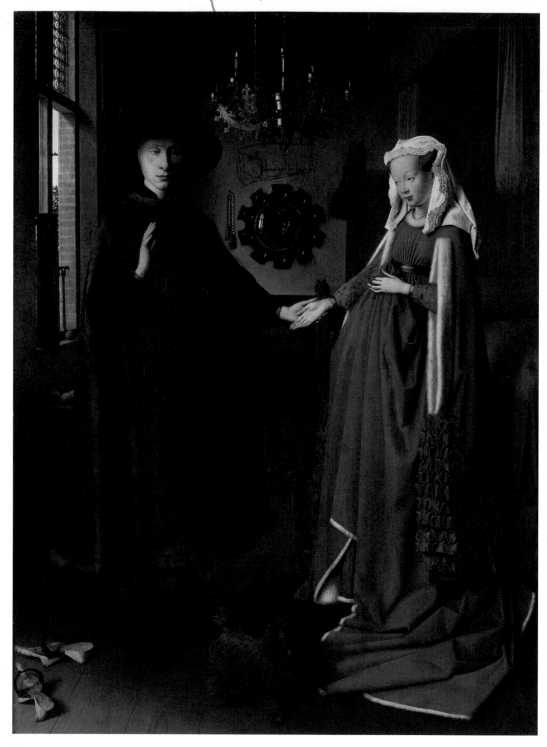

artist's signature

14.14 Jan van Eyck, *The "Arnolfini Portrait."* 1434. Oil on panel, 33 × 22½" (83.7 × 57 cm). The National Gallery, London

expensively furnished than the room in the *Mérode Triptych*. The two join hands, with the man raising his right hand as if in a solemn oath, seemingly quite alone in the room. In the mirror behind them, however, is the reflection of two men. Because the signature appears right above the mirror, many scholars believe that one of these men must be Jan van Eyck himself, perhaps the figure wearing the red headdress. The combination of the signature, with its flourishes and phrasing, and the image of the men in

the mirror suggests to some that Jan is acting as a witness to whatever is occurring in the room.

Traditionally, scholars have argued that this panel represents either the wedding or the engagement of the couple shown, either of which would have required a legal and financial contract between their two families. By this reading, the painting commemorates the union of the couple. If so, the second man in the mirror may be the bride's father, who would have made the

Cyriacus of Ancona (1449)

Rogier van der Weyden probably visited Italy, and sources reveal that he made several paintings for prominent Italian patrons, including the Este family of Ferrara. One of Rogier's most discussed images in Italy drew the praise of Cyriacus of Ancona, a humanist and diplomat who had traveled widely in the service of Italian princes.

After that famous man from Bruges, Johannes the glory of paint-ing [i.e., Jan van Eyck], Roger in Brussels is considered the outstanding painter of our time. By the hand of this most excellent painter is a magnificently wrought picture which the illustrious prince Lionello of Este showed me in Ferrara on July 8, 1449. In it one sees our first progenitors, and in a most pious image the ordeal of the Deposition of the God-Incarnate, with a large crowd of men and women standing about in deep mourning. All this is admirably depicted with what I would call divine rather than human art. There you could see those faces come alive and breathe which he wanted to show as living, and likewise the deceased as dead, and in particular, many garments, multicolored soldiers' cloaks, clothes prodigiously enhanced by purple and gold, pearls, precious stones, and everything else you would think to have been produced not by the artifice of human hands but by all-bearing nature itself.

Source: *Northern Renaissance Art 1400–1600: Sources and Documents*, ed. Wolfgang Stechow (Evanston, IL: Northwestern University Press, 1989).

contract for the marriage of his daughter. The woman's gesture to lift her heavy gown may suggest her wish for children, and the bed behind her may suggest the consummation of the marriage. Another recent interpretation sees the image as a commemoration of a wife who died giving birth, which might explain her general-ized features and the carved figure of St. Margaret, to whom preg-nant women prayed for safe delivery.

Given the scene's secular nature, scholars have debated whether the realistic touches serve simply as an accurate record of an event and its domestic setting, or whether those details carry more symbolic weight. The couple may have taken off their shoes as a matter of custom, or the artist may want to imply that they are standing on "holy ground." (This symbol has its origins in stories of Moses removing his sandals at the burning bush on Mount Sinai; that is, in the presence of God.) The little dog may be a beloved pet, like those in the January page of the *Très Riches Heures* (see fig. 14.3), or it could be an emblem of fidelity. (*Fides* is Latin for faithfulness, the origin of the traditional dog name, Fido.) The other furnishings of the room suggest other questions. Here is yet another candle (in the chandelier) burning in broad daylight, but no holy figure is present as in the *Mérode Triptych*. Pieces of fruit on the window sill may be expressions of the cou-ple's wealth, or refer to the temptation of Adam and Eve. Tiny images of Christ's Passion and Resurrection in the small medal-lions that surround the mirror sound the only unambiguously religious note in the picture. Scholars are still investigating the function and patronage of this image as they are now much less certain about the meaning of the image than they used to be. Jan van Eyck's carefully crafted image incites much scholarly fascina-tion, just as his work garnered much praise from his employer, the duke of Burgundy.

Rogier van der Weyden in Brussels

His status as a court painter exempted Jan van Eyck from the restrictions that governed other artists in Flemish towns. Regulations for the training of artists and the market for works of art came from the guilds, professional organizations of artists established to protect the interests of their members. Aspiring artists learned their trade as apprentices in the workshop of a certified master. After a fixed period, an apprentice became a jour-neyman (or dayworker) who could then hire out his services to others but not open his own shop. Journeymen often traveled to learn from artists other than their master. Becoming a master required completing a "masterpiece" that was evaluated by the leaders of the guild. Guilds not only controlled training but limited competition from artists outside their towns, investigated disputes among members, and saw to the social and economic needs of members, such as providing for burials, pensions, and the care of widows. Guilds were both economic and social institu-tions, assuring the quality of their products and seeing to the well-being of their members.

One illustrious graduate of the guild system was Rogier van der Weyden (1399/1400–1464), a painter who trained with Robert Campin in Tournai, and who certainly knew the work of Jan van Eyck. By 1435, Rogier had established a flourishing workshop in Brussels which took commissions from as far away as Italy and Spain. Perhaps his most influential work is the *Descent from the Cross* (fig. **14.15**), which dates from about 1435. The crossbow-men's guild of Louvain (near Brussels) commissioned it as the center of an altarpiece for a church there. In this work, Rogier depicted the moment when Christ's followers lower his body from the Cross; the mourners crowd into a shallow box of space. Rogier modeled the forms carefully to suggest sculptural pres-ence, and included enough detail to show every nuance of texture.

Rogier's goal is to increase the expressive content of his pictures. He emphasizes the emotional impact of the scene on its participants. Their faces and postures express the grief of the fig-ures. John the Evangelist on the left and Mary Magdalen on the right are bowed in pain. The Virgin's swoon echoes the pose and expression of her son. Rogier depicts her intense pain and grief in order to inspire the same compassion in a viewer. He has staged his scene in a shallow niche or shrine, not against a landscape. This bold device focuses a viewer's attention on the foreground and allows the artist to mold the figures into a coherent group. Furthermore, the emphasis on the body of Christ at the center of the composition refers to the celebration of the Eucharist, which takes place before the altarpiece during the Mass. Rogier could

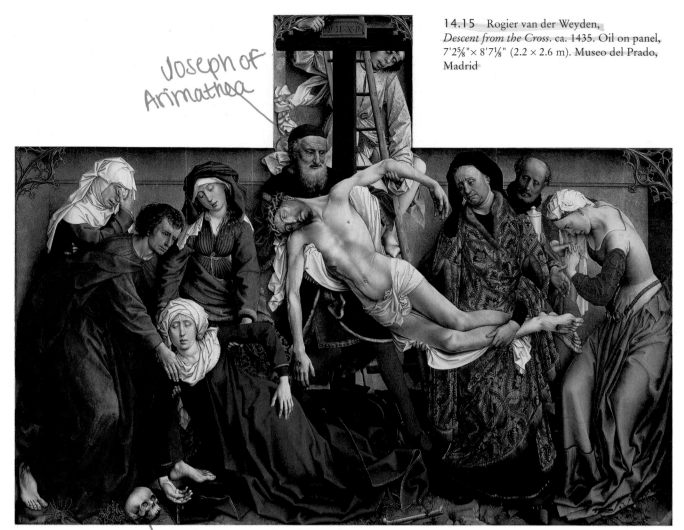

Joseph of Arimathea [handwritten annotation]

Skull of Adam = Golgatha [handwritten annotation]

14.15 Rogier van der Weyden, *Descent from the Cross.* ca. 1435. Oil on panel, 7'2⅝"× 8'7⅛" (2.2 × 2.6 m). Museo del Prado, Madrid

find precedents for these grief-stricken gestures and faces in earlier sculpture; these figures share the strong emotion of the mourners on the Naumburg choir screen (see fig. 12.57) or the Virgin in the *Roettgen Pietà* (see fig. 12.60). Rogier's memorable painting inspired many copies, in both painting and sculpture.

The heightened emotion with which Rogier imbues his works was noted and admired by the Italian diplomat Cyriacus of Ancona, who saw another painting by Rogier on this theme in 1449. (See *Primary Source*, page 485.) This commentator singled out the naturalism in Rogier's work, as he admired the figures who seemed to come alive in Rogier's painting. Other Italian scholars remarked on Flemish painting's naturalism and piety as well. Viewers in Flanders would have brought their own interest in meditating on the sacrifice of Christ to their experience of Rogier's painting.

Rogier's depiction of *St. Luke Drawing the Virgin*, dated between 1435 and 1440 (fig. **14.16**), reveals his debt to earlier Flemish artists. The figure of Mary nursing her son in this image shows the continuing influence of Campin, while the composition is based on a work by Jan van Eyck. In contrast to the *Descent from the Cross*, here Rogier creates a deep landscape that moves into the distance. The figures inhabit a room that opens onto a

garden protected by fortifications. A man and a woman peer over these battlements toward a busy Flemish city in the distance, where shopkeepers open for the day and citizens walk the street.

The painting represents St. Luke the Evangelist in a different role, as the portrayer of the Virgin and Christ Child. A Byzantine tradition explained that the Madonna appeared miraculously to Luke, so that he could take her portrait. This legend helped to account for numerous miraculous images of the Madonna in the later Middle Ages. Rogier depicts Luke drawing the features of the Virgin in **silverpoint** (a drawing technique using a stylus of silver scraped across prepared paper) as she appears before him. (Such drawings were the starting point for most paintings of the period.) Because of this story, St. Luke became the patron of painters' guilds throughout Europe. Later documents describe a painting like this one in the chapel of the Brussels Guild of St. Luke. Since this image depicts the making of an image, Rogier's painting may be a self-conscious statement about the dignity of painting and painters. It was copied numerous times in the fifteenth century, even by Rogier's own workshop. In recent years, scholars have been studying such paintings with new scientific tools that examine the techniques used by the artists. (See *The Art Historian's Lens*, page 488.)

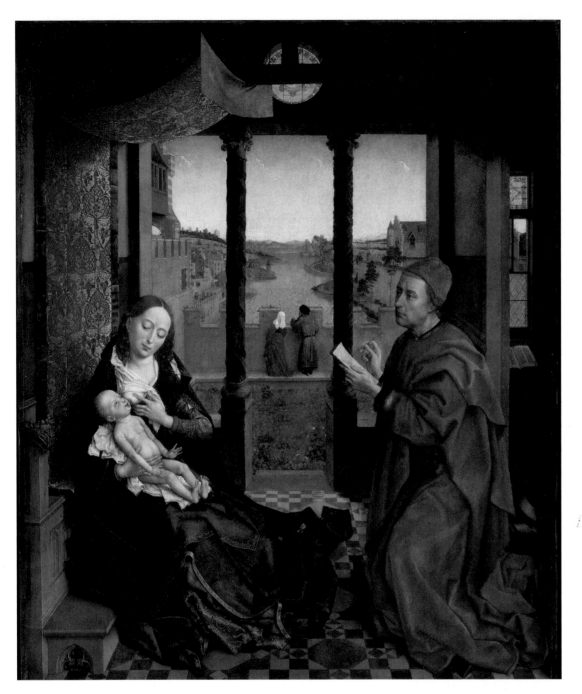

14.16 Rogier van der Weyden, *St. Luke Drawing the Virgin*. ca. 1435–40. Oil and tempera on panel, 54⅛ × 43⅝" (1.38 × 1.11 m). Museum of Fine Arts, Boston. Gift of Mr. and Mrs. Henry Lee Higginson, 1893. Photograph © 2006, Museum of Fine Arts, Boston. 93.153

LATE FIFTEENTH-CENTURY ART IN THE NETHERLANDS

The paintings of Robert Campin, Jan van Eyck, and Rogier van der Weyden offered powerful examples for other artists to follow, in the Netherlands and beyond. In the later fifteenth century, court patrons continued to prefer objects made of expensive materials, particularly gold. They also commissioned illuminated manuscripts and tapestries. At the same time, patronage by the merchant class continued to grow, and painters found work in commissions from the middle classes. Nonetheless, the medium of painting gained in prestige as the century wore on, attracting interest and patronage in aristocratic circles. Despite the increasing market for paintings, large-scale sculpture continued to find a market in the fifteenth-century Netherlands, though little has survived the ravages of war, social and religious upheavals, and changes of taste. Even rarer are survivals of objects made in precious metals, as the very valuable raw material was easily recycled when money was scarce.

Aristocratic Tastes for Precious Objects, Personal Books, and Tapestries

Aristocratic patrons commissioned small-scale precious objects throughout the fifteenth century. One, whose brilliance makes us mourn the loss of others, is the *Statuette of Charles the Bold*, preserved in the treasury of the cathedral of Liège in eastern Belgium

Investigative tools used in the contemporary scientific study of materials are providing new information about the practices of artists in the past. The very materiality of works of art makes them appropriate for the same sort of study as archaeological discoveries. Chemical analysis of paints and pigments is providing information on the recipes for making paints that artists used. This information can be used to examine workshop practices, to establish authenticity of given objects, and to suggest methods of conservation.

Modern scholars use a variety of techniques to investigate paintings. **X-radiographic** imaging penetrates painted surfaces and produces a photographic analysis of the use of lead in the painting process. Because lead white was used to lighten pigments, x-radiographs allow an investigator to examine how an artist modeled forms with lighter colors. X-radiographs also reveal details about an artist's brushwork or changes made as the painting progressed. Another technique uses **infrared light**, which can see through painted surfaces to distinguish dark marks on the white ground of a panel. Aided by special infrared cameras (a technique called **infrared reflectography**), analysts can photograph the underdrawings and initial paint layers below painted surfaces; computers match these photos to produce images of the preparatory layers of the painting. This information is invaluable for studying the creative process. It has also aided in determining which of the many versions of Rogier's *St. Luke Drawing the Virgin* (see fig. 14.16) was executed first.

Because many Renaissance panels are painted on wood, scholars have been able to determine the age of a particular panel from the number of tree rings in it, using a technique known as *dendrochronology*. The number of tree rings in a panel is then compared to a database of tree rings that have been dated to define the time when the tree was probably cut down. This can then provide additional evidence for dating the painting. Such evidence has caused some scholars to date Bosch's *The Garden of Earthly Delights* (see fig. 14.22) to around 1480. Similar techniques have revealed the composition of the limestone used in Gothic sculpture and the chemical makeup of ancient bronzes.

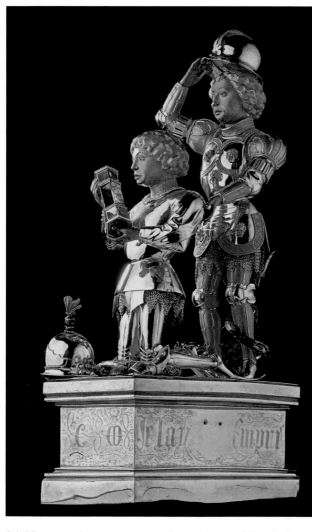

14.17 Gerard Loyet, *Statuette of Charles the Bold.* ca. 1471. 21 × 12½ × 7" (53 × 32 × 17.5 cm). Cathedral treasury, Liège

(fig. **14.17**). Duke Charles the Bold of Burgundy commissioned the goldsmith Gerard Loyet (before 1442–1500) to make this figure; he then gave it to the cathedral in Liège in 1471, perhaps to assert his control over that rebellious city. Made of gold and silver gilt with enamel details, the 21-inch-high statuette represents Duke Charles holding a reliquary; behind him stands St. George, Charles's favorite patron saint, who lifts his helmet in greeting. The duke is dressed in armor, kneeling on a pillow to make his offering. The object demonstrates Loyet's skill and the prestige of such objects in the Burgundian court. The composition derives from a painting by Jan van Eyck, and so reflects the rising status of panel painters as creative innovators.

The taste of the court also ran to expensive books. Despite the introduction of the printing press (see pages 499–502), among the traditional elites, the manuscript book—custom-made to celebrate the purchaser's status and interests—retained its appeal. Books of hours, in which prayers were organized into cycles according to the hours of the day, appealed especially to women. A striking example of a complex and lavish illuminated book is the *Hours of Mary of Burgundy*, which includes the coat of arms of Mary, daughter of Charles the Bold and last duchess of Burgundy, evidence that she owned the book before her death in 1482.

Mary herself may be the woman depicted in figure **14.18**. In this full-page miniature, the anonymous artist (named after this book of hours) depicts an elegantly dressed young woman reading from a book of hours similar to the *Hours of Mary of Burgundy*. Her costume and surroundings indicate her status: Golden brocades, transparent veils, jewelry, and flowers surround her, and a little dog rests on her lap. She sits in a private chapel, whose windows open onto a view of a light-filled Gothic church. Through the window the viewer sees the Virgin Mary with her child seated in the sanctuary, surrounded by angels. To the right

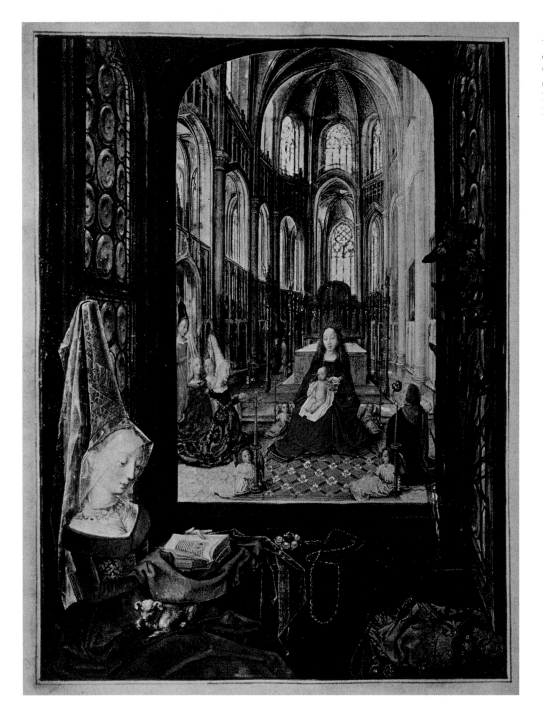

14.18 Mary of Burgundy Painter, page
with *Mary at Her Devotions*, from the *Hours
of Mary of Burgundy*. ca. 1480 (before 1482).
Colors and ink on parchment, 7½ × 5¼"
(19.1 × 13.3 cm). Österreichisches
Nationalbibliothek, Vienna.
E 28.560-C, Cod. 1857. fol. 14v

of these sacred figures kneels a group of noble women, whose access to the child and his mother may be what the woman in the foreground prays for.

The artist creates a picture within a picture here, as the glimpse into the church is completely framed by the architecture of the lady's chapel. Earlier manuscript artists (like the Limbourg Brothers) usually put floral or other decorative motifs in the border and created a spatial context only for the main image. This artist, however, treats the border as a spatial entity in its own right that links the border and the main image. The artist takes care to record the tactile and sensuous quality of the dog's fur, the transparency of the glass vase, and the reflective qualities of the pearls on the ledge. The manuscript page has the impact of a painted panel.

The court was also the key market for the flourishing industry in tapestries. Major workshops practiced in Brussels, Tournai, and Arras; the latter city's name became synonymous with the art form. Woven with colored threads of wool or silk, tapestries were popular with the courtly class or their peers in the Church. The tapestry fragment of *Penelope Weaving* (fig. **14.19**), for example, was part of a series of "Famous Women" commissioned by the bishop of Tournai around 1480. The image depicts the wife of Odysseus (or Ulysses) working at a loom. According to Homer's *Odyssey*, Penelope fended off her numerous suitors with her weaving; she insisted she would not marry again until she had completed her work, which she unwove every evening. Although a figure from the classical past, Penelope is dressed in the costume

Penelope Weaving (Penelope at Her Loom), a fragment from *The Story of Penelope and the Story of the Cimbri Women.* ca. 1480. Tapestry, 39⅜ × 59¹⁄₁₆" (100 × 150 cm). Museum of Fine Arts, Boston. Maria Antoinette Evans Fund. 26.54

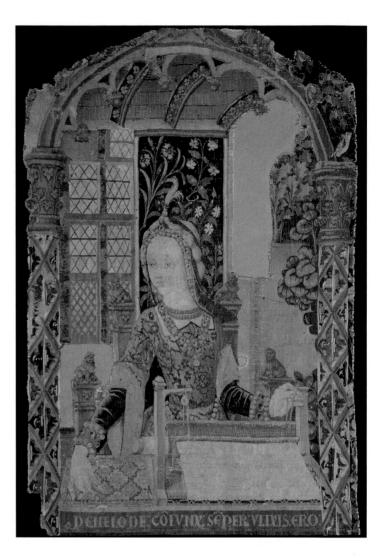

of a fifteenth-century lady. The influence of paintings is apparent in the suggestion of space, the detailed treatment of her gems and garment, and in the figure. On the wall behind Penelope hangs a tapestry within the tapestry, in a two-dimensional pattern of repeated floral forms called *millefleurs*, one of the best-selling designs for tapestry in the fifteenth century. The court of Burgundy shared their Italian contemporaries' interest in stories of the ancients as exemplars for the present, but they envisioned them in familiar, not historic terms. The naturalism of the Flemish painters provided a language for the tapestry weavers to satisfy courtly taste.

Panel Paintings in the Southern Netherlands

While the court collected precious objects, illuminated manuscripts, and tapestries, the middle-class demand for panel paintings continued to grow. International businessmen invested their money and their reputations in commissioning paintings from Flemish artists like Hugo van der Goes (ca. 1440–1482). Having served as dean of the painters' guild of Ghent, Hugo entered a monastery near Brussels as a lay brother in 1475. He continued to paint there until his death in 1482. His best-known work is the huge altarpiece commissioned around 1474 by an agent of the

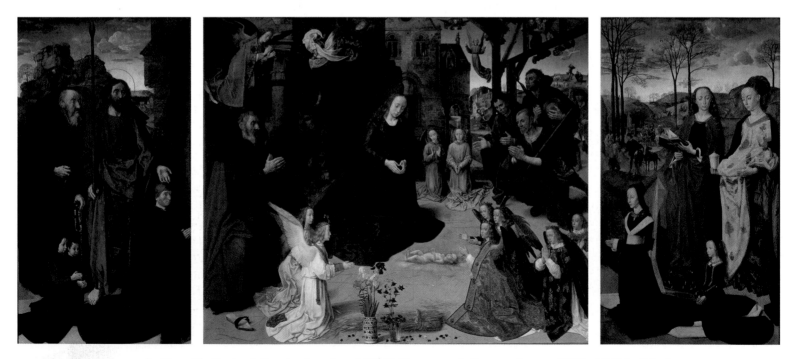

14.20 Hugo van der Goes, *The Portinari Altarpiece* (open). ca. 1474–76. Tempera and oil on panel, center 8'3½"× 10' (2.5 × 3.1 m), wings each 8'3½"× 4'7½" (2.5 × 1.4 m). Galleria degli Uffizi, Florence

Medici bank in Bruges, who shipped it to Florence (fig. **14.20**). The 10-foot-wide central panel represents the Virgin, St. Joseph, and shepherds adoring the newborn Christ Child in Bethlehem. In the wings, members of the donor family, including Tommaso Portinari, his wife, Maria Maddelena Baroncelli, and their children, kneel to face the central image. A spacious landscape unites all three wings as a continuous space, with the bare trees and December sky suggesting not the Holy Land but Flanders itself. Objects in the distance have turned the blue of the atmosphere; this use of **atmospheric perspective** (a technique that recognizes the loss of color in distant objects) infuses the panel with a cool tonality. Hugo filled this setting with figures and objects rendered with precise detail in deeply saturated colors.

Despite Hugo's realistic renderings of both landscape and figures, the image contains numerous contradictions for expressive effect. Figures vary greatly in scale: The angels and kneeling members of the Portinari family are dwarfed by the other figures; the patron saints in the wings are the same size as Joseph, the Virgin Mary, and the shepherds of the Nativity in the center panel. These shifts of scale undermine the pictorial space that the artist has provided for his figures. Another contrast occurs between the raucous intrusion of the shepherds and the ritual solemnity of all the other figures. These fieldhands gaze in breathless wonder at the newborn Christ Child, who is the focus of all the figures ranged around him. Mary, however, sits at the physical center of the

composition. Such deliberate contrasts between the pictorial and psychological focal points, between the scale of the historical and the contemporary figures, and between the static and kinetic postures of the figures contribute to the unsettling effect of the work.

The background is populated with narratives that support the main theme. Behind the figures in the left-hand panel, Mary and Joseph travel toward Bethlehem. Behind the saints on the right, the Magi progress toward the center. And in the center, angels flicker across the surface, lit by both natural and supernatural light. Strategically placed at the front of the picture is a beautiful **still life** of flowers and a sheaf of wheat. As with so many other realistic details in Flemish paintings, these have been interpreted symbolically. The wheat refers to the bread of the Eucharist and the flowers to the Virgin. Portinari brought the triptych to Florence in 1483 and installed it in the family chapel attached to the hospital of Sant' Egidio. There it proclaimed the taste, wealth, and piety of the donor. Judging from their imitation of it, Italian painters who saw the work there especially admired its naturalism and its unidealized representation of the shepherds.

Triptychs were often intended for liturgical spaces. For more domestic spaces, patrons wanted smaller objects. For example, the young up-and-coming citizen of Bruges Martin van Nieuwenhove commissioned a diptych from Hans Memling in 1487 (fig. **14.21**). Born in Germany (ca. 1435–1494), Memling worked in Bruges, where his refined style, based on Rogier and

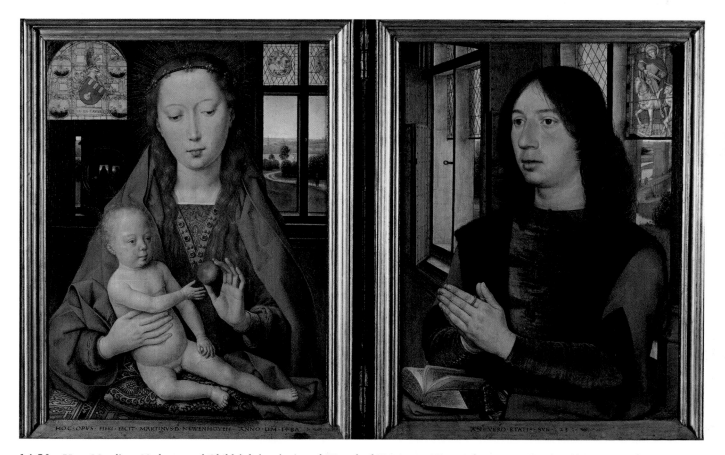

14.21 Hans Memling, *Madonna and Child*, left-hand wing of *Diptych of Martin van Nieuwenhove*. 1487. Panel, 17⅜ × 13" (44 × 33 cm). Hans Memling Museum, Musea Brugge, Sint-Jans Hospital, Bruges

Jan van Eyck, brought him commissions from patrons from all over Europe. Italians in Bruges especially preferred his workshop, as did local patricians like Van Nieuwenhove. An inscription on the frame of his diptych identifies the patron and gives his age, while his stylish garment and gilt-edged prayer book express his social status. Behind him a piece of stained glass represents his patron saint, Martin. The young man focuses his gaze on the left-hand panel, where an image of the Virgin and Child appears. Martin's family coat of arms in the window behind them implies that the Virgin and Child are visiting him in his own home. The reflection in the mirror further expresses this conceit: the artist has included the reflections of both the Virgin and young man appearing in the same space. Memling has borrowed the concave mirror Jan van Eyck used in *The "Arnolfini Portrait"* (see fig. 14.14) to unite the two halves of the diptych.

Memling's image demonstrates a new trend in portraiture: In addition to rendering the features, he creates a believable setting for the figure. This contrasts to the inky blackness behind the figure in Jan van Eyck's *Man in a Red Turban* (see fig. 14.13). Access to the divine remains a preoccupation for otherwise worldly men; in this light-filled room, Martin kneels in permanent prayer, so that the image becomes an expression of his devotion. But this object also served as a piece of self-promotion, as the many personal references to the patron display his self-assurance and social status.

The Northern Netherlands

The innovations of the early fifteenth-century painters quickly spread to the northern Netherlands (present-day Holland), the origin of one of the most famous paintings from the era, Hieronymus Bosch's *The Garden of Earthly Delights* (fig. **14.22**). Bosch (ca. 1450–1516) came from a family of painters. He spent his life in the town of 's Hertogenbosch, the seat of a ducal residence, from which his name derives. His patrons included the duke of Burgundy, whose grandson, King Philip II of Spain, owned numerous Bosch paintings in the sixteenth century; it was in Philip's collection that Fray José de Sigüenza encountered Bosch's painting. (See *Primary Source*, page 494.) Sigüenza's account has been an important document for interpreting this complex and surprising painting, whose subject and meaning have been vigorously debated.

Divided into three panels, *The Garden of Earthly Delights* represents humans in the natural world. A continuous landscape unites the three sections; the high horizon and atmospheric perspective imply a deep vista of the earth from an omniscient vantage point. Shades of green create an undulating topography marked by thickets of trees and bodies of water. Throughout, small creatures both human and nonhuman swarm, while strange rock formations and other objects appear at intervals. As Sigüenza says, the left-hand wing appears to represent the Garden of Eden,

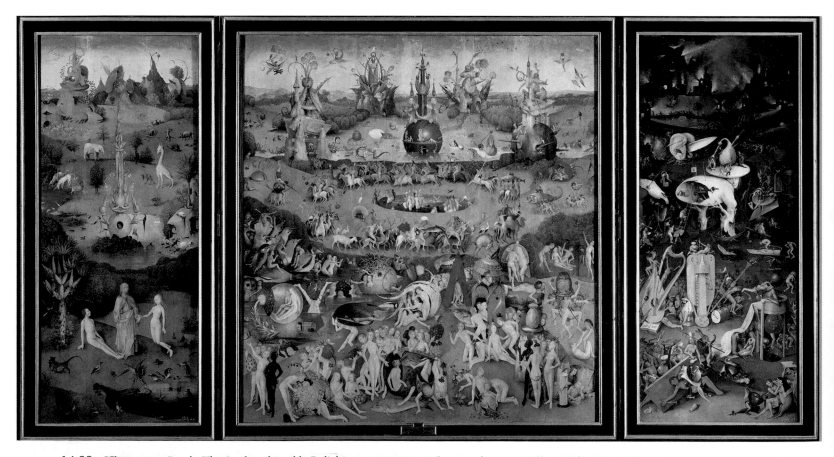

14.22   Hieronymus Bosch, *The Garden of Earthly Delights*. ca. 1480–1515. Oil on panel, center 7'2½"× 6'4½" (2.19 × 1.95 m), each wing 7'2½"× 3'2" (2.19 × 0.96 m). Museo del Prado, Madrid

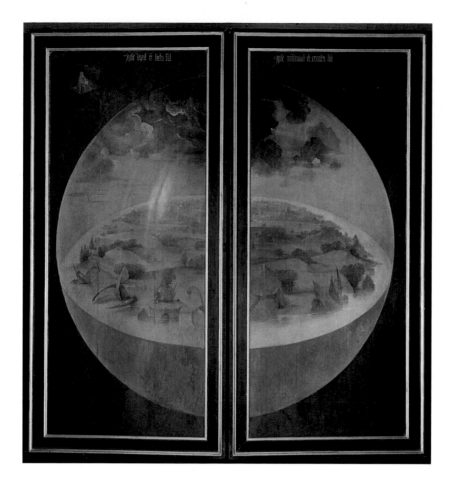

14.23 Hieronymus Bosch, *The Garden of Earthly Delights* (outer wings closed). ca. 1480–1515. Oil on panel, each wing 7'2½"× 3'2" (2.19 × 0.96 m). Museo del Prado, Madrid

where the Lord introduces Adam to the newly created Eve. This airy landscape is filled with animals, including such exotic creatures as an elephant and a giraffe; it also includes strange hybrid monsters. The central panel reveals a world inhabited by tiny humans who frolic among giant fruits, birds, and other creatures. In the middle ground, men parade around a circular basin on the backs of all sorts of beasts. Many of the humans interact with huge birds, fruits, flowers, or marine animals. The right-hand wing depicts an infernal zone, which may be Hell, where strange hybrid creatures torment the tiny humans with punishments appropriate to their sins. When the triptych is closed (fig. **14.23**), its outer wings depict a crystal globe with an image of the earth emerging from the waters, with God watching over the events from above. An inscription from Psalm 33 says: "For he spoke and it came to pass; he commanded it and it stood forth." Some see this image as the third day of creation, others identify it as the flood of Noah.

Despite its triptych format, this is not a traditional altarpiece but a secular work. It belonged to Count Henry III of Nassau, in whose palace in Brussels it was reported to be in 1517, though recent research suggests Bosch could have painted it as early as 1480. Many scholars place it ca. 1500–1505 and assume that Henry of Nassau commissioned it. Scholars have studied many different aspects of Bosch's painting in an effort to find the key to its meaning. Some have looked at the numerous visual references to verbal puns and proverbs. One theory holds that it represents the time of Noah, as shown by the image of a flood on the exterior; another that the many swarming nudes express the views of a heretical group that promoted free love; yet another that the infernal landscape in the right-hand wing demonstrates a moralizing condemnation of carnal sin.

These interpretations suggest that Bosch was a pessimist sermonizing about the depravity of humankind. This is certainly the way that José de Sigüenza described it, although his text also suggests several "allegories or metaphors" embedded in the painting. Yet the image itself is beautifully painted and as seductive as the sirens in the pool in the middle of the central panel. There is an innocence, even a poetic beauty, in this panorama of human activity that suggests something other than outright condemnation of the acts so carefully depicted. This ambivalence has fueled numerous interpretations, including a recent proposal that the image depicts an alternative view of history in which the Original Sin of Adam and Eve does not happen, and therefore humans continue to live in a state of innocence.

Another interpretation of this painting links it to the practice of alchemy as an allegory of redemption. The many strangely shaped rocks and fountains refer to the tools and vessels used in this medieval science. Bosch married an apothecary's daughter, so his use of the visual symbols of that science has a strong historical basis. If we consider its secular function and the interests of his educated patron, however, Bosch's painting seems to warn its audience against too much concern for sensual pleasures in the world.

Fray José de Sigüenza (1544?–1606)

From *The History of the Order of St. Jerome*

The works of Hieronymus Bosch were collected by the Spanish king Philip II (r. 1556–1598) and were displayed in his Escorial Palace near Madrid, where Sigüenza was the librarian. The interpretation of Bosch's work was as difficult then as it is today and caused just as much disagreement. This passage is Sigüenza's attempt to interpret the painting that we call The Garden of Earthly Delights *(see fig. 14.22).*

Among these German and Flemish pictures...there are distributed throughout the house many by a certain Geronimo Bosch. Of him I want to speak at somewhat greater length for various reasons: first, because his great inventiveness merits it; second, because they are commonly called the absurdities of Geronimo Bosque by people who observe little in what they look at; and third, because I think that these people consider them without reason as being tainted by heresy....

The difference that, to my mind, exists between the pictures of this man and those of all others is that the others try to paint man as he appears on the outside, while he alone had the audacity to paint him as he is on the inside....

The...painting has as its basic theme and subject a flower and the fruit of [a] type that we call strawberries.... In order for one to understand his idea, I will expound upon it in the same order in which he has organized it. Between two pictures is one large painting, with two doors that close over it. In the first of the panels he painted the Creation of Man, showing how God put him in paradise, a delightful place...and how He commands him as a test of his obedience and faith not to eat from the tree, and how later the devil deceived him in the form of a serpent. He eats and, trespassing God's rule, is exiled from that wondrous place and deprived of the high dignity for which he was created.... This is [shown] with a thousand fantasies and observations that serve as warnings....

In the large painting that follows he painted the pursuits of man after he was exiled from paradise and placed in this world, and he shows him searching after the glory that is like hay or straw, like a plant without fruit, which one knows will be cast into the oven the next day...and thus uncovers the life, the activities, and the thoughts of these sons of sin and wrath, who, having forgotten the commands of God...strive for and undertake the glory of the flesh....

In this painting we find, as if alive and vivid, an infinite number of passages from the scriptures that touch upon the evil ways of man...many allegories or metaphors that present them in the guise of tame, wild, fierce, lazy, sagacious, cruel, and bloodthirsty beasts of burden and riding animals.... Here is also demonstrated the transmigration of souls that Pythagoras, Plato, and other poets...displayed in the attempt to show us the bad customs, habits, dress, disposition, or sinister shades with which the souls of miserable men clothe themselves—that through pride they are transformed into lions; by vengefulness into tigers; through lust into mules, horses, and pigs; by tyranny into fish; by vanity into peacocks; by slyness and craft into foxes; by gluttony into apes and wolves; by callousness and evil into asses; by stupidity into sheep; because of rashness into goats....

One can reap great profit by observing himself thus portrayed true to life from the inside....And he would also see in the last panel the miserable end and goal of his pains, efforts, and preoccupations, and how...the brief joys are transformed into eternal wrath, with no hope or grace.

REGIONAL RESPONSES TO THE EARLY NETHERLANDISH STYLE

Artists in many regions of Europe responded to the formal and technical achievements of the generation of Robert Campin and Jan van Eyck. Local traditions and tastes influenced these regional responses, but patrons found the naturalism of the new style useful for their religious and social purposes. Many regions of Europe, among them France, Spain, and Central Europe, therefore produced their own variations on this style.

France

The geographic proximity, trade routes, linguistic links, and political relationships between the Burgundian Netherlands and France helped to spread the innovations in technique and style throughout France. Artists either traveled to Flemish cities or developed their own brand of naturalism in imitation of the effects that Rogier van der Weyden or Hugo van der Goes had achieved (see figs. 14.15 and 14.20). Still, French art has its own distinctive characteristics. In the first half of the fifteenth century, the troubles of the Hundred Years' War limited expenditure on art. Citizens of the war-torn cities commissioned very little, but members of the Church and court continued earlier forms of patronage.

After establishing his rule at the close of the Hundred Years' War, King Charles VII of France appointed Jean Fouquet (ca. 1420–1481) of Tours as his court painter. Both a book illuminator and a panel painter, Fouquet traveled to Italy around 1445, where he learned some of the innovations of contemporary Italian art (see Chapter 15). His work, however, owes much to the Netherlandish style in technique, color, and approach. Charles VII's treasurer, Étienne Chevalier, commissioned Fouquet around 1450 to paint a diptych representing himself and his patron saint, Stephen, in proximity to the Virgin and Child, the so-called *Melun Diptych* (figs. **14.24** and **14.25**). Like his Flemish contemporaries, Fouquet records the specific physiognomy of the patron in his fur-lined garment. The head of the saint, who carries a book and a stone (which refers to his martyrdom), seems as individual as that of the donor.

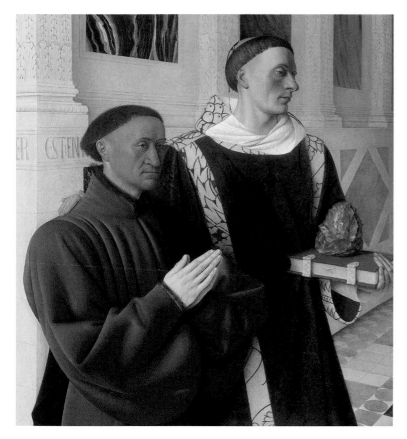

14.24 Jean Fouquet, *Étienne Chevalier and St. Stephen*, left wing of the *Melun Diptych*. ca. 1450. Oil on panel, 36½ × 33½" (92.7 × 85 cm). Staatliche Museen zu Berlin, Gemäldegalerie

The Melun Diptych

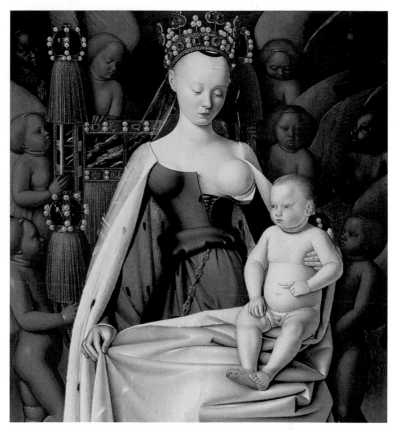

14.25 Jean Fouquet, *Madonna and Child*, right wing of the *Melun Diptych*. ca. 1450. Oil on panel, 36⅝ × 33½" (94.5 × 85.5 cm). Koninklijk Museum Voor Schone Kunsten, Antwerpen Belgie (Musée Royal des Beaux-Arts, Antwerp, Belgium)

They stand in a room with marbled floors and marble panels on the walls, framed by antique-inspired pilasters that recede to suggest space. The two men gaze across the frame toward an image of the enthroned Virgin and Child. According to an old tradition, the Madonna is also a portrait: of Agnès Sorel, Charles VII's mistress. If so, the panel presents an image of courtly beauty, as befits the Queen of Heaven, seen wearing a crown amid a choir of angels. Fouquet deliberately contrasts the earthly and divine realms. The deep space in the left panel differs strikingly from that on the right, organized as a rising triangle, with the cool colors of the Virgin and Child set against the vivid reds and blues of the angels. In contrast to his Flemish counterparts, Fouquet is not interested in suggesting specific textures, and he subordinates details to the overall design. He does not appeal to the emotions. His images are geometrically ordered and rational rather than expressive.

Spain

Netherlandish naturalism reverberated strongly on the Iberian peninsula in the fifteenth century. Artists traveled between Flanders and Spain, and trade, diplomacy, and a dynastic marriage brought the united kingdoms of Castile and Aragon into increasingly close contact with Flanders. These contacts were echoed in the works of art imported into Spain from Flanders and in works of art produced in Spain by local artists.

A powerful example of the Spanish interpretation of Flemish naturalism is the *Pietà* painted in 1490 by Bartolomé Bermejo (ca. 1440–1500) for a deacon of the cathedral of Barcelona (fig. **14.26**). Bermejo was born in Córdoba, but he worked in many regions of Spain, and may have been trained in Bruges. His *Pietà* sets the image of the Virgin grieving for her dead son in a dark and atmospheric landscape dominated by an empty cross. Instead of the historical mourners called for by the narrative, and included by Giotto in his fresco in Padua (see fig. 13.20), Mary and Christ are flanked by St. Jerome to a viewer's left (the lion is his attribute) and a portrait of the deacon to the right. This removes the theme from a strict narrative context and makes the painting function as an image of devotion similar to the *Roettgen Pietà* (see fig. 12.60), though the precise detail of the figures and the landscape derive from Flemish models. In contrast to the cool rationality of Fouquet, Bermejo's work is highly emotional and expressive.

Central Europe

Linked by trade and political ties to the Netherlands, artists and patrons in Central Europe were also receptive to the new style, especially in cities along the Rhine (see map 14.1). One such artist,

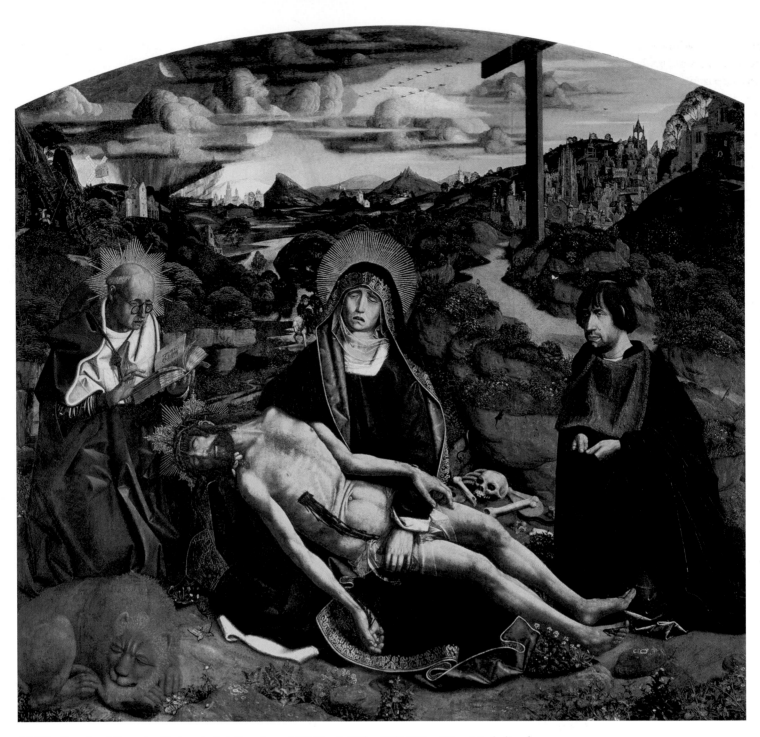

14.26   Bartolomé Bermejo, *Pietà*, cathedral, Barcelona. 1490. Panel, 74⅜ × 68⅞" (189 × 175 cm) including frame

Conrad Witz (1400/10–1445/46) became a citizen of Basel, Switzerland, and a master in the city's guild of painters at just the moment that the Church's Council of Basel concluded. This council, or synod, had met from 1431 to 1434 to debate whether the pope alone or councils of bishops had the right to determine doctrine. These controversial issues inform the paintings Witz made in 1444 for the bishop of Geneva, which were destined for the cathedral of St. Peter.

The panels represent scenes from the life of St. Peter, *The Miraculous Draught of Fishes* (fig. **14.27**) depicts Christ calling St. Peter to walk across the Sea of Galilee to join him. The solidly

modeled figure of Christ dominates the right-hand side of the composition, in part because his red garment contrasts vividly with the green tones of the painting. St. Peter appears twice, once in the boat among other apostles, who are called to be "fishers of men," and again sinking into the waters upon which Christ seems to float. The technique and style owe much to the Flemings, but Witz devotes his attention to the landscape. In place of the Sea of Galilee, Witz substitutes Lake Geneva, emphasizing local topography, such as the distinctive mountain above Christ's head. He accurately depicts every reflection on the water, so that we can see the bottom of the lake in the foreground and a variety of textures

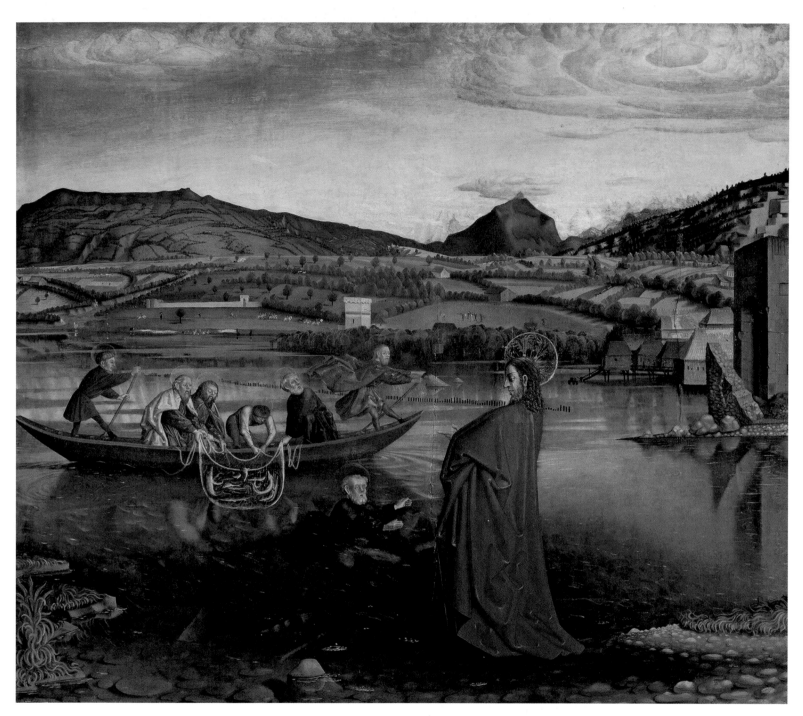

14.27 Conrad Witz, *The Miraculous Draught of Fishes*. 1444. Oil on wood of fir tree, 51 × 61" (132 × 154 cm). Musée d'Art et d'Histoire, Geneva, Switzerland. 1843.11

on the water's surface in the background. Witz places the events of the historical past in the setting of the present. Peter's sinking into the water, suggesting his need for assistance, may be evidence of the bishop's support for the council's role in advising the pope.

AN ALTARPIECE IN ITS ORIGINAL SETTING Witz's panels were originally the wings of an altarpiece, many of which had sculptures as their central element, or **corpus**. In German-speaking regions, altarpieces were usually made of wood, often large and intricately carved. Protestant reformers in the sixteenth century destroyed many sculpted religious images, so surviving

examples are relatively rare. The *St. Wolfgang Altarpiece* (fig. **14.28**) by the Tyrolean sculptor and painter Michael Pacher (ca. 1435–1498) is impressive both because of its scale and because it remains in its original setting.

The surviving contract between the abbot who commissioned it and the painter specifies both the subject matter and the quality of the materials and workmanship. (See *Primary Source*, page 499.) This was the normal pattern for contracts given to artists for expensive projects in the period.

Much as Jan van Eyck did in the *Ghent Altarpiece*, Pacher creates a vision of Heaven: The corpus depicts the coronation of the

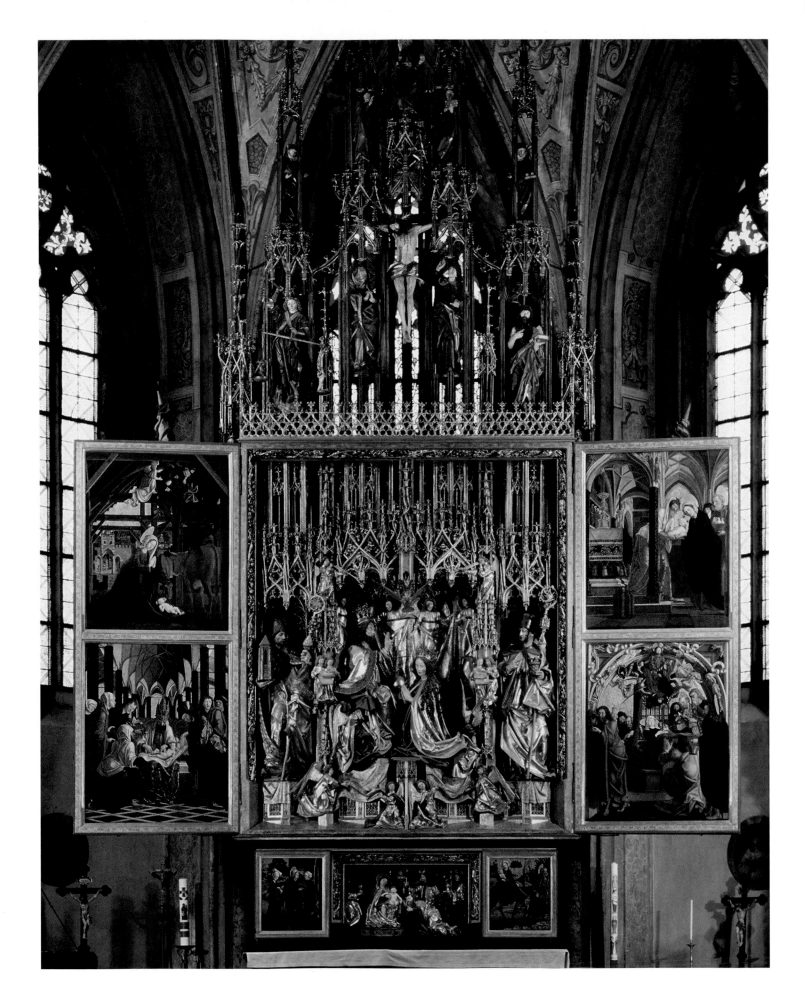

From the Contract for the St. Wolfgang Altarpiece

It took Michael Pacher 11 years (1471–81) to complete this elaborate altarpiece for the pilgrimage church of St. Wolfgang. The altarpiece is still in its original location.

Here is recorded the pact and contract concerning the altar at St. Wolfgang, concluded between the very Reverend, Reverend Benedict, Abbot of Mondsee and of his monastery there, and Master Michael, painter of Bruneck, on St. Lucy's day of the year 1471.

ITEM, it is first to be recorded that the altar shall be made conforming to the elevation and design which the painter has brought to us at Mondsee, and to its exact measurements.

ITEM, the predella shrine shall be guilded on the inside and it shall show Mary seated with the Christ Child, Joseph, and the Three Kings with their gifts; and if these should not completely fill the predella shrine he shall make more figures or armored men, all gilt.

ITEM, the main shrine shall show the Coronation of Mary with angels and gilt drapery—the most precious and the best he can make.

ITEM, on one side St. Wolfgang with mitre, crozier, church, and hatchet; on the other St. Benedict with cap, crozier, and a tumbler, entirely gilded and silvered where needed.

ITEM, to the sides of the altar shall stand St. Florian and St. George, fine armored men, silvered and gilded where needed.

ITEM, the inner wings of the altar shall be provided with good paintings, the panels gilded and equipped with gables and pinnacles, representing four subjects, one each....

ITEM, the outer wings—when the altar is closed—shall be done with good pigments and with gold added to the colors; the subject from the life of St. Wolfgang....

ITEM, at St. Wolfgang, while he completes and sets up the altar, we shall provide his meals and drink, and also the iron work necessary for setting up the altar, as well as help with loading wherever necessary.

ITEM, the contract is made for the sum of one thousand two hundred Hungarian guilders or ducats....

ITEM, if the altar is either not worth this sum or of higher value, and there should be some difference of opinion between us, both parties shall appoint equal numbers of experts to decide the matter.

Source: *Northern Renaissance Art 1400-1600: Sources and Documents*, ed. Wolfgang Stechow (Evanston, IL: Northwestern University Press, 1989)

Virgin as Queen of Heaven flanked by the patron saints of the monastery. Carved of soft wood that permits the sculptor to create deep folds and sharp edges, the lavishly gilt and colored forms make a dazzling spectacle as they emerge from the shadows under Flamboyant Gothic canopies. The figures and setting in the central panel seem to melt into a pattern of twisting lines that permits only the heads to stand out as separate elements.

The complexity and surface ornamentation that dominate the corpus contrast with the paintings of scenes from the life of the Virgin on the interior of the wings. Here, the artist represents large figures, strongly modeled by clear light, and he suggests a deep space for them. He takes a viewer's vantage point into account, so that the upper panels are represented as if seen from below. This kind of **perspective** must have been inspired by developments in contemporary Italian painting. Pacher almost certainly crossed the Alps and visited northern Italy, where some of his works were commissioned and where he had learned to use the Italians' new technique for projecting space. (Compare his perspective to Mantegna's in fig. 15.49.) This type of perspective appears only in the wings, however, where scenes from the historical past are set into spaces that look like the Austrian present. The interior of the temple where the circumcision takes place, for example, has a vault much like ones in Late Gothic churches. Pacher makes the historical scenes in the wings much more down to earth than the spectacle of Heaven in the center.

14.28 Michael Pacher, *St. Wolfgang Altarpiece*, church of St. Wolfgang, Austria. 1471–81. Carved wood, figures about life-size; wings, oil on panel

PRINTING AND THE GRAPHIC ARTS

Along with the new techniques of painting, fifteenth-century Europe saw the development of a new medium: printmaking. The invention of movable type and the printed page would have enormous consequences for Western civilization. Tradition has credited Johann Gutenberg (ca. 1397–1468) with inventing movable type, but the roots of printing actually lie in the ancient Near East 5,000 years ago. The Sumerians were the earliest "printers," for their relief impressions on clay, from stone seals, were carved with both pictures and inscriptions (fig. 2.10). From Mesopotamia the use of seals spread to India and eventually to China. The Chinese applied ink to their seals in order to impress them on wood or silk, and in the second century CE they invented paper. By the ninth century they were printing pictures and books from wooden blocks carved in relief, and 200 years later, they developed movable type. Some of the products of Chinese printing may have reached the medieval West—perhaps through Islamic intermediaries.

The technique for manufacturing paper came to Europe from contact with Islamic regions, though it gained ground as a cheap alternative to parchment only very slowly. While printing on wood blocks was known in the late Middle Ages, it was used solely for ornamental patterns on cloth. All the more astonishing, then, is the sudden development, over the course of a mere century, of a printing technology capable of producing editions of several hundred copies of relatively inexpensive books. The new technology spread quickly across Europe, spawning the new industry of bookmaking. Printed books were far less expensive than handmade volumes, but they were useless to those who

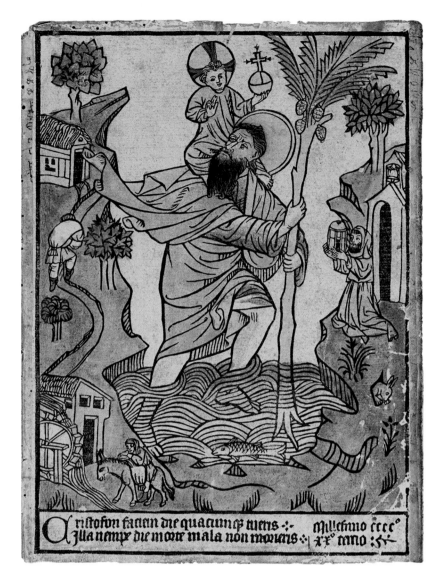

14.29 *Buxheim St. Christopher.* 1423. Handcolored woodcut, 11⅜ × 8⅛" (28.8 × 20.6 cm). John Rylands University Library. The John Rylands University Library of Manchester

could not read. Literacy began to rise among the lower classes, a consequence that would have a profound effect on Western civilization. To compete with illuminated manuscripts, printed books included printed images, which were often handcolored to imitate the more expensive manuscripts. Ultimately, the printed book almost completely replaced the illuminated manuscript.

The pictorial and literary aspects of printing were closely linked from the start. The practice of inking pictorial designs carved on wooden blocks and then printing those designs on paper began in Europe late in the fourteenth century. Early surviving examples of such prints, called **woodcuts**, come from France, the Netherlands, and Germany. Painters or sculptors probably furnished the designs, but specialists did the actual carving of the wood blocks. (For the various techniques of printing, for pictures as well as books, see *Materials and Techniques,* page 501.)

An early dated example of a woodcut is the *Buxheim St. Christopher* (fig. **14.29**), so called because it came from a monastery in that south German town. This single sheet, handcolored woodcut bears the date 1423 and a prayer to the saint;

woodcuts combining image and text like this on a single block were sometimes assembled into popular picture books called **block books**. Simple, heavy lines define the forms in the print, including the fall of the garment around the figures and the contours of objects. Thinner lines in parallel rows—called **hatching**—denote shadows or textures of objects, but the composition is strictly two-dimensional, as the landscape forms rise along the picture plane to surround the figures. According to legend, Christopher, patron saint of travelers, was a giant who ferried people across a river; he was surprised one day by the weight of a child, who turned out to be Christ.

The forms in the *Buxheim St. Christopher* owe a great deal to Late Gothic style, but the audience for prints were not the aristocrats of the Middle Ages. Fifteenth-century woodcuts were popular art. A single wood block yielded thousands of copies, to be sold for pennies apiece, so that for the first time in history almost anyone could own pictures. A detail from a Flemish Annunciation panel of about 1435 in figure **14.30** reveals one use to which people put such prints: A print much like the *Buxheim St. Christopher* is pinned on a wall in a middle-class household.

Printmaking

Printmaking is a technique for making multiple copies of the same image. In the fifteenth century, most prints used dark black ink on paper (though some are printed on parchment). Printmakers used one of several techniques to make these images; the two broad categories are **relief** prints (in which the lines to be printed are raised from the block) and **intaglio** (in which the lines to be printed are cut into a plate). Designs (and text) will print as reversed images as they are transferred to the paper by the force of a press. By 1500, printing technology allowed for the reproduction of pictures by several methods, all developed at the same time as the printing of type.

Woodcut

• lithography
• screenprinting

In a woodcut, the design is cut into a wood block so that raised ridges will print. The thinner the ridges are, the more difficult they are to carve, so specialists took over this phase of the work. Early woodcuts often include inscriptions, but to carve lines of text backward in relief on a wooden block must have been risky—a single slip could ruin an entire page. It is little wonder, then, that printers soon had the idea of putting each letter on its own small block. Wooden movable type carved by hand worked well for large letters but not for small ones, and the technique proved cumbersome for printing long texts such as the Bible. By 1450, this problem had been solved through the introduction of metal type cast from molds, and the stage was set for book production as it was practiced until the late twentieth century. Because the text was carved in relief, it became apparent that accompanying pictures should be carved in relief as well, so that an entire page could be printed with one run of the press over the **matrix**—or form—which held all the information to be printed.

Engraving

The technique of engraving—embellishing metal surfaces with incised pictures—had developed in classical antiquity (see fig. 6.20) and continued to be practiced throughout the Middle Ages (see fig. 11.7). Goldsmiths and designers of armor, in particular, were experts in incising designs on metal surfaces. These skills allowed goldsmiths to engrave a plate that could serve as the matrix for a paper print. Because the lines themselves were incised into the plate, more linear information could be included in the design. In an engraving, lines are V-shaped grooves cut with a special tool, called a **burin**, into a metal plate—usually copper, which is relatively soft and easy to work with. Ink is forced into the grooves made by the burin, the plate is wiped clean of excess ink, and a damp sheet of paper is placed on top of the inked plate; the force of a press transfers the ink—and the design—to the paper.

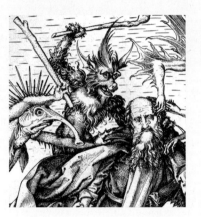

Detail of Schongauer's *The Temptation of St. Anthony.* See fig. 14.31

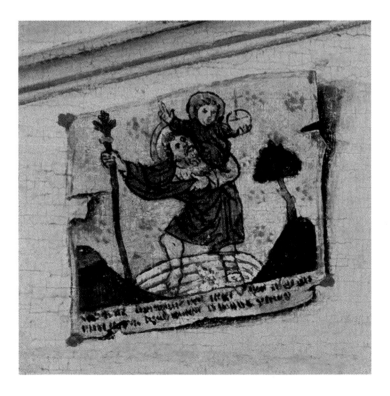

From the start, **engravings** (images taken from incised plates) appealed to a smaller and more sophisticated public. The oldest surviving examples, from about 1430, already show the influence of Flemish painters. Early engravers were usually trained as goldsmiths, but their prints reflect local painting styles. Their forms are systematically modeled with fine hatched lines and are often convincingly foreshortened. Distinctive styles appear even in the earliest engravings, and engravers often included initials and dates in their prints. Consequently, many engravers of the late fifteenth century are known to us by name.

Printing Centers in Colmar and Basel

Martin Schongauer of Colmar, then in Germany (ca. 1435/50 –1491) learned the goldsmith's craft from his father, but he became a printmaker and a painter. He studied the paintings of Rogier van der Weyden, which probably influenced the style of

14.30 Jacques Daret, woodcut of St. Christopher, *Annunciation* (detail). ca. 1435. Musée Royaux d'Art et d'Histoire, Brussels, Belgium

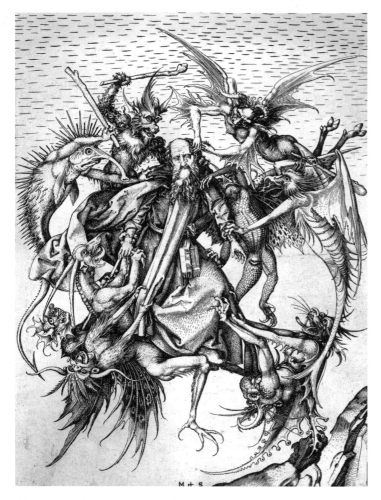

14.31 Martin Schongauer, *The Temptation of St. Anthony*. ca. 1480–90. Engraving, 11½ × 8⅝" (29.2 × 21.8 cm). Metropolitan Museum of Art, New York, Rogers Fund, 1920

· Carrying the cross 1474 - engraving

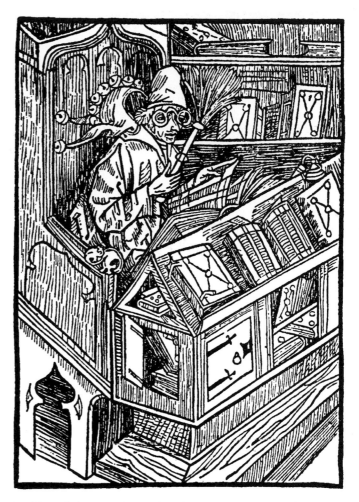

14.32 *Scholar in Study*, woodcut from Sebastian Brant's *Ship of Fools* (Basel, 1494)

his engravings. Their complex designs, spatial depth, and rich textures make them competitors to panel paintings. Some artists found inspiration in them for large-scale pictures. They were also copied by other printmakers. *The Temptation of St. Anthony* (fig. **14.31**) is one of Schongauer's most famous works—known and admired in sixteenth-century Italy. The print represents the climax of St. Anthony's resistance to the Devil. Unable to tempt him to sin, the Devil sent demons to torment him. Varying the type of mark he made on the plate, Schongauer displays a wide range of tonal values and a rhythmic quality of line, and he approximates a wide range of textures—spiky, scaly, leathery, furry—to enhance the expressive impact of the image.

Since the time of Conrad Witz, the Swiss city of Basel had embraced the new technology for printing books to become a major center for publishing. There, a group of reform-minded intellectuals and authors contributed texts for publication, which graphic artists illustrated with woodcuts. One of the best sellers of the period was a satirical text by Sebastian Brant called the *Ship of Fools*, published in Basel in 1494. Brant's text poked fun at many of the ills he perceived in his society, which, as the title implies, he characterized as a boat piloted by Folly. One important theme his

text addresses is contemporary dissatisfaction with the Church. This tide of anticlerical feeling was already rising when Luther's critique of the Church was posted in 1517 in Wittenberg (see page 634). But Brant's satirical eye also fell on his own peers, as the woodcut in figure **14.32** reveals. The image depicts a scholar in his study surrounded by books, but rather than read them, he holds a duster to clean them. The man's costume, including a hood with bells on it, identifies him as a fool. Compared with the *Buxheim St. Christopher*, the unnamed artist who produced this woodcut increases the density of hatching that implies texture and volume and attempts a spatial context for the forms. The practice of coloring prints fell by the wayside as the medium developed its own aesthetic and appeal.

As a period of cultural flowering and great innovation, from the complex naturalistic imagery in the paintings of Campin and Jan van Eyck to the dynamism of the new technology of printing, we could consider the fifteenth century in northern Europe a renaissance. That term is usually linked to this century, but not to this region: Another version of naturalistic representation was developing at the same time in Italy, to which we shall turn in the next chapter.

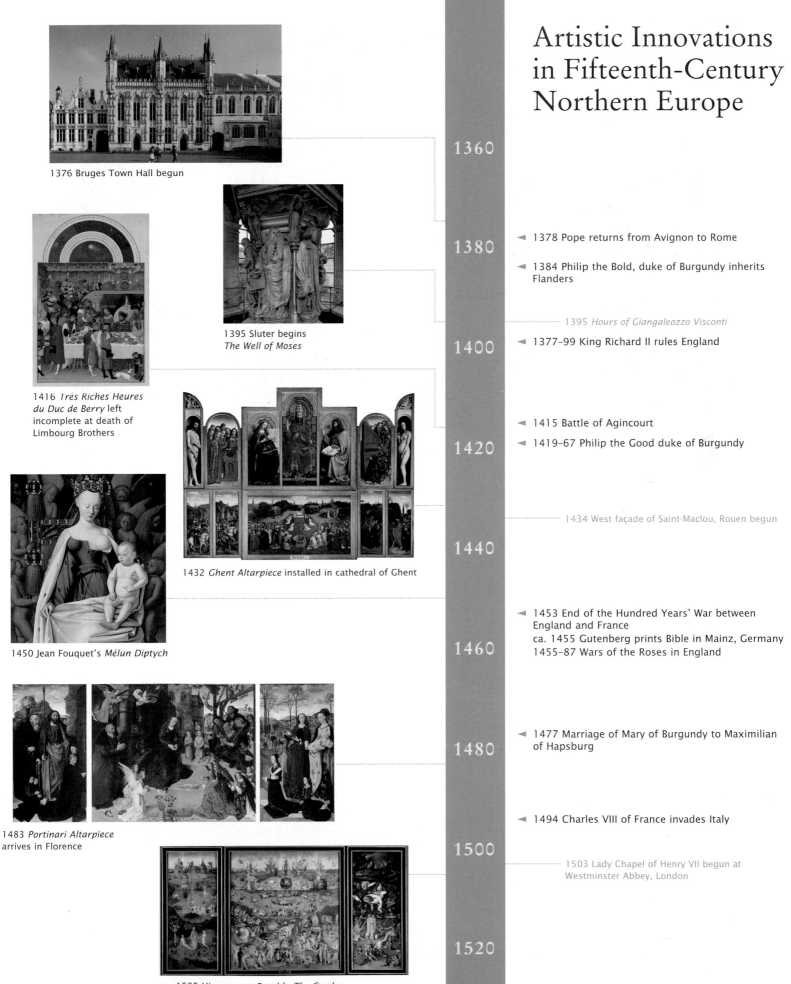

Artistic Innovations in Fifteenth-Century Northern Europe

1376 Bruges Town Hall begun

1395 Sluter begins *The Well of Moses*

1416 *Très Riches Heures du Duc de Berry* left incomplete at death of Limbourg Brothers

1432 *Ghent Altarpiece* installed in cathedral of Ghent

1450 Jean Fouquet's *Mélun Diptych*

1483 *Portinari Altarpiece* arrives in Florence

ca. 1505 Hieronymus Bosch's *The Garden of Earthly Delights*

1360

1380

◄ 1378 Pope returns from Avignon to Rome

◄ 1384 Philip the Bold, duke of Burgundy inherits Flanders

1395 *Hours of Giangaleozzo Visconti*

1400

◄ 1377–99 King Richard II rules England

◄ 1415 Battle of Agincourt

◄ 1419–67 Philip the Good duke of Burgundy

1420

1434 West façade of Saint-Maclou, Rouen begun

1440

◄ 1453 End of the Hundred Years' War between England and France
ca. 1455 Gutenberg prints Bible in Mainz, Germany
1455–87 Wars of the Roses in England

1460

◄ 1477 Marriage of Mary of Burgundy to Maximilian of Hapsburg

1480

◄ 1494 Charles VIII of France invades Italy

1500

1503 Lady Chapel of Henry VII begun at Westminster Abbey, London

1520

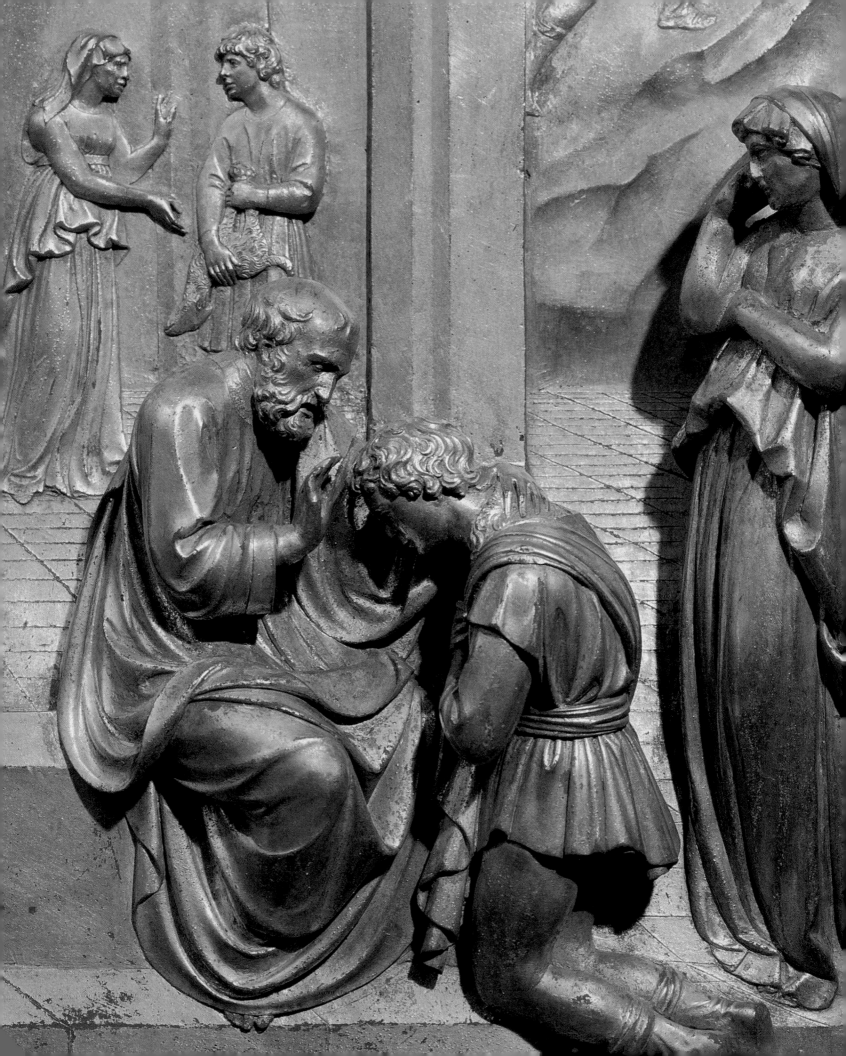

CHAPTER 15

The Early Renaissance in Fifteenth-Century Italy

NEITHER A SCHOLAR WRITING A HISTORY OF FRANCE IN THIRTEENTH-century Paris nor a notary writing a contract in fourteenth-century Bruges could have imagined that hc was living in a "middle" age; he only knew that his age followed the eras of the past. But intellectuals in fifteenth-century Italy thought of themselves as living in a *new* age, one that was

distinct from the immediate past. This consciousness of historical difference separates the thinkers of the fifteenth and sixteenth centuries from their medieval forebears. These thinkers devalued the post-Roman, or medieval world, and believed they could improve their culture by reviving the best features of antiquity, that is, Roman and Greek culture. Their efforts, beginning in the fifteenth century in Italy, sparked a cultural flowering of great significance for the history of Europe.

First called the *rinascimento*, Italian for "rebirth," the period came to be known by its French name, the Renaissance. Its original users defined it as the rebirth of classical learning, literature, and art. Modern historians have divided the Italian Renaissance into stages: an early phase in the fifteenth century, the High Renaissance denoting a period of exceptional achievement, and the Late Renaissance, which is primarily a chronological term. Neither the definition of the Renaissance as the revival of classical forms nor the chronological limits apply easily outside of Italy, but the broader definition of a Renaissance as a cultural or artistic renewal has come to apply elsewhere. In northern Europe, as we have seen in Chapter 14, scholars and artists did not have the same dedication to reviving the ancients, though they did study the past. More significant was an economic and

Detail of figure 15.17, Lorenzo Ghiberti, *The Story of Jacob and Esau*, panel of the *Gates of Paradise*

cultural expansion that resulted in far-reaching technical and cultural achievements.

The causes of the cultural flowering in Italy are complex, as events, people, ideas, and social shifts came together in a revolution that produced many of the characteristics of modern European civilization. For this reason, some scholars refer to this era as the "early modern period." This cultural shift was fundamentally an intellectual one. The followers of the fourteenth-century author Petrarch began to study texts from Greece and Rome both for their moral content and their style. They committed themselves to the *studia humanitatis*—the study of human works, emphasizing rhetoric, literature, history, and moral philosophy. The roots of humanist education lay in the medieval university, which prized theology, but in the Renaissance humanism aimed to create knowledge for practical use in the world—for lawyers, bureaucrats, politicians, diplomats, and merchants.

Humanist scrutiny of ancient texts not only deepened knowledge of Latin authors, but also stimulated the study of the great Greek thinkers such as Aristotle, Plato, Euclid, and Ptolemy. Humanists' analytical approach and empirical observations inspired new thinking in many fields, including mathematics and natural science. Studying history taught the importance of individuals acting in the world to assure their personal fame, yet also encouraged educated people to serve the common good by participating in civic life. Humanist educational ideas spread quickly throughout Italy, aided by the introduction into Italy of

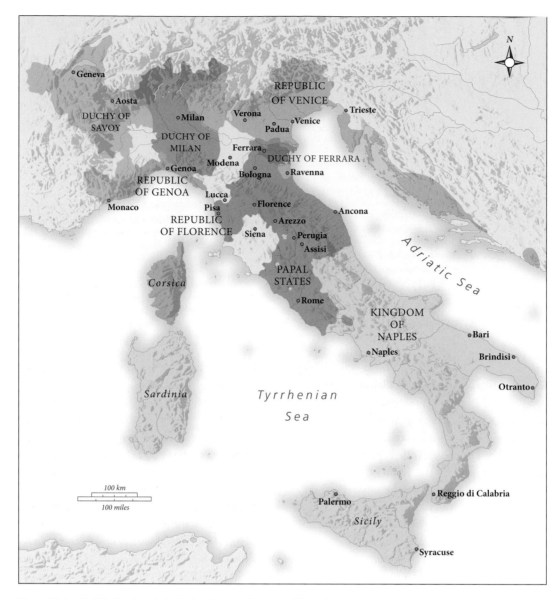

Map 15.1   Political units of the Italian Peninsula in the fifteenth century

the printing press in 1464, which made books more widely available. Governing parties throughout Italy, whether princes, popes, or elected councils, used humanists in their bureaucracies and courts to conduct their business.

Humanist ideas affected artists as well as the patrons who hired them. As humanists studied ancient texts, artists studied ancient artworks, not just to imitate details or motifs, but to understand the principles by which ancient buildings were designed and ancient sculptures achieved their naturalism. Renaissance artists took up the ancient ideal of rivaling nature in their art and brought their practical skills to this intellectual aim. They devised techniques such as perspective and mastered new technologies like oil painting and printmaking to further their goal of reproducing the natural world and to spread their ideas.

Artists employed these ideas and techniques to make art that served spiritual and dynastic functions for their patrons. Medieval

institutions—religious orders, guilds, and the Church—commissioned church buildings, architectural sculpture, wall paintings, altar furnishings, and other objects as they had in earlier centuries, though secular patronage increased. The artists earned personal glory along the way, so that by the end of the century the status of the artist had changed. Through much of the Middle Ages, the social and economic position of artists in society was comparable to that of any other artisan. They were respected for the skill of their hands, but not considered intellectuals. Many artists in fifteenth-century Italy behaved like intellectuals, investigating the past and solving problems scientifically, so the status of the artist rose as a result.

During this period, there was still no single political entity called Italy. Regions of different size and political organization competed with each other economically and often on the battlefield (map 15.1). The Kingdom of Naples in the south was a

In Praise of the City of Florence (ca. 1403–4) by Leonardo Bruni

Though born in Arezzo, Leonardo Bruni (1370–1444) moved to Florence to take up law and humanistic studies. His mentor, Coluccio Salutati, was the chancellor of Florence, to which post Bruni succeeded in 1406. An ardent student of classical literature, he modeled his own writings on those of Greek and Roman authors. He wrote this panegyric to Florence after the death of Giangaleazzo Visconti, which ended the threat to the city from Milan.

Therefore, what ornament does this city lack? What category of endeavor is not fully worthy of praises and grandeur? What about the quality of the forebears? Why are they not the descendants of the Roman people? What about glory? Florence has done and daily continues to do great deeds of honor and virtue both at home and abroad. What about the splendor of the architecture, the buildings, the cleanliness, the wealth, the great population, the healthfulness and pleasantness of the site? What more can a city desire? Nothing at all. What, therefore, should we say now? What remains to be done? Nothing other than to venerate God on account of His great beneficence and to offer our prayers to God. Therefore, our Almighty and Everlasting God, in whose churches and at whose altars your Florentines worship most devoutly; and you, Most Holy Mother, to whom this city has erected a great temple of fine and glimmering marble, where you are at once mother and purest virgin tending your most sweet son; and you, John the Baptist, whom this city has adopted as its patron saint—all of you, defend this most beautiful and distinguished city from every adversity and from every evil.

Source: "Panegyric to the City of Florence," tr. Benjamin G. Kohl in *The Earthly Republic: Italian Humanists on Government and Society* (Philadelphia: University of Pennsylvania Press, 1978)

---

monarchy. Dukes, princes, and despots carved up northern Italy into city-states, including Milan, Mantua, and Urbino. The pope returned to Rome from Avignon to reclaim control of the Papal States which had been lost when the papacy moved to France in 1305. And the major trading cities of Venice and Florence formed republics, where mercantile elites controlled political power. Though the cultural flowering we call the Renaissance occurred throughout Italy, for many modern scholars the city of Florence was its birthplace.

FLORENCE IN THE FIFTEENTH CENTURY

One reason for the prominence of Florence in histories of the Renaissance is that many early humanists were Florentines who patriotically praised their hometown. Florence was an important manufacturing center, a key center for trade, and a major center for international banking, whose wealth and social dynamism attracted talented individuals. Instead of hereditary aristocrats, bankers and merchants controlled the government. Groups of merchants and artisans banded together in guilds (economic and social organizations) to strengthen their positions. The governing council, called the Signoria, consisted of officials elected from members of the guilds and prominent mercantile families. The government was a republic, a word that for Florentines signaled their identity as the heirs of the ancient Roman Republic.

Florentine politicians, such as Coluccio Salutati and Leonardo Bruni, successive chancellors to the Signoria, gave eloquent voice to Florentine aspirations. Urging the city to defy the duke of Milan as he threatened to invade in 1401–02, Salutati called on the city's Roman history as a model to follow. After this threat had passed, Leonardo Bruni declared that Florence had been able to defy Milan because of her republican institutions, her cultural achievements, and the origins of her people. In his *In Praise of the City of Florence* (1403–04), he compared Florence's virtues to those of fifth-century BCE Athens, which had defied the invading Persians. Yet he also praised Florentine piety and devotion, expressed in the building of churches. (See *Primary Source*, above.) Renaissance humanists wished to reconcile the lessons of antiquity with their Christian faith.

Bruni's words may explain why practical Florentines invested so much of their wealth in cultural activity. The Signoria and subsidiary groups commissioned numerous public projects to beautify and improve their city (map 15.2, page 517). It was not only individuals and families who sponsored public projects, so too did merchant guilds, which held competitions among artists for their commissions. The successful accomplishment of projects of great visibility enhanced the prestige of sponsoring individuals and groups and drew artists to the city. Many native sons (daughters were forbidden entry to most guilds, so few women became artists) became sculptors, painters, and goldsmiths. In this climate of humanism, innovation, and display, the Renaissance in Florence opens with a competition.

The Baptistery Competition

Andrea Pisano's bronze doors for the baptistery (see fig. 13.13), completed in 1360, were an impressive example of Florentine taste and piety. Their success inspired the overseers of the works at the baptistery, the Guild of Wool Merchants, to open another competition for a second set of bronze doors. They asked each entrant to make a design on the theme of the Sacrifice of Isaac, while retaining the Gothic quatrefoil shape from Andrea Pisano's first doors for the baptistery (see fig. 13.14). Competing artistsall had to include the same figures and were given the same materials. Seven artists made trial reliefs for this competition,

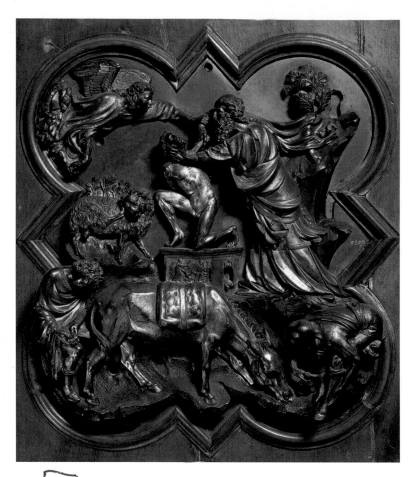

15.1 Filippo Brunelleschi, *The Sacrifice of Isaac.* 1401–03.
Panel, gilt bronze relief, 21 × 17" (53.3 × 43.2 cm).
Museo Nazionale del Bargello, Florence

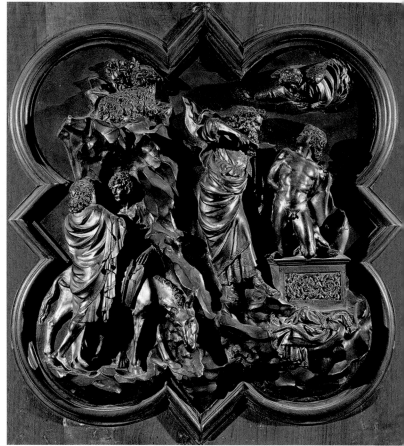

15.2 Lorenzo Ghiberti, *The Sacrifice of Isaac.* 1401–03.
Panel, gilt bronze relief, 21 × 17" (53.3 × 43.2 cm).
Museo Nazionale del Bargello, Florence

though only two of them survive. One is by Filippo Brunelleschi (1377–1446) (fig. **15.1**); the other is by Lorenzo Ghiberti (1381–1455), whom the guild ultimately chose to execute the second doors of the baptistery (fig. **15.2**). Ghiberti left a description of the competition and his acclaim as the victor in his *Commentaries*, written late in his life. (See *Primary Source*, page 509.)

The subject the artists were assigned, from the book of Genesis, recounts how God ordered Abraham to sacrifice his only son; obediently, Abraham led Isaac to an altar on a mountain and lifted his knife to slaughter him when an angel halted the sacrifice. Although Isaac is a figure for Christ in Christian theology, this is also the story of a chosen people avoiding doom through divine intervention, an issue about which Florentines felt strongly in 1402. For the artists, the challenge was to fill the four lobes of the quatrefoil, yet at the same time to convey the narrative succinctly and naturalistically. In his trial relief, Brunelleschi organized the forms to focus on the dynamic figure of Abraham whose arm, lifted to strike Isaac, is grasped by the angel rushing in from the left. Isaac struggles as his father grabs his neck, contorting his posture and increasing the drama. The ram who replaces him as the sacrifice stands next to the altar. Subsidiary figures of shepherds and a donkey fill the lower portions of the quatrefoil;

though their postures are complex (one of them based on an ancient work of art), they do not contribute much to the main theme. Brunelleschi gives his figures great naturalism, and the composition great drama.

Ghiberti's relief reveals the strength of his composition, his skill at rendering the human form, and his observation of natural details. Ghiberti solved the problem of the quatrefoil field by placing narrative details in the margins and the focal point at the center. Thus, the ram on the mountain appears in the upper left and the foreshortened angel on the right. At the center, Abraham gestures dramatically as he moves to sacrifice his son, bound and naked on an altar. Isaac twists to face the spectator, his beautifully formed torso contrasting with the drapery worn by his father. He does not struggle, but seems heroically to accept his fate. A wedge of mountain keeps other figures away from the main scene. Ghiberti's design successfully combines movement, focus, and narrative. At the same time, his interest in the lyrical patterning of the International Gothic tempers the brutality of the scene. Abraham's drapery falls in cascades similar to those of the figure of Moses in Sluter's *The Well of Moses* (see fig. 14.1). In addition to the design, Ghiberti's entry demonstrated a technical finesse that may have persuaded the judges to select him: Unlike Brunelleschi, he cast his entry in one piece.

Lorenzo Ghiberti (ca. 1381–1455)

The Commentaries, from Book 2

Ghiberti's incomplete Commentaries *is an important early document of art history. The first book consists largely of extracts from Pliny and Vitruvius; the second is about art in Italy in the thirteenth and four-teenth centuries and ends with an account of Ghiberti's own work (see fig. 15.2).*

Whereas all gifts of fortune are given and as easily taken back, but disciplines attached to the mind never fail, but remain fixed to the very end ... I give greatest and infinite thanks to my parents, who ... were careful to teach me the art, and the one that cannot be tried without the discipline of letters. ... Whereas therefore through parents' care and the learning of rules I have gone far in the subject of letters or learning in philology, and love the writing of commentaries. I have furnished my mind with these possessions, of which the final fruit is this, not to need any property or riches, and most of all to desire nothing. ... I have tried to inquire how nature proceeds ... and how I can get near her, how things seen reach the eye and how the power of vision works, and how visual ... works, and how visual things move, and how the theory of sculpture and paint-ing ought to be pursued.

In my youth, in the year of Our Lord 1400, I left Florence because of both the bad air and the bad state of the country. ... My mind was largely directed to painting. ... Nevertheless ... I was written to by my friends how the board of the temple of St. John the Baptist was sending for well-versed masters, of whom they wanted to see a test piece. A great many very well qualified masters came through all the lands of Italy to put themselves to this test. ... Each one was given four bronze plates. As the demonstration, the board of the temple wanted each one to make a scene ... [of] the sacrifice of Isaac. ... These tests were to be carried out in a year. ... The competitors were ...: Filippo di ser Brunellesco, Simone da Colle, Niccolo D'Arezzo, Jacopo della Quercia from Siena, Francesco da Valdambrino, Nicolo Lamberti. ... The palm of victory was conceded to me by all the expects and by all those who took the test with me. The glory was conceded to me universally, without exception. Everyone felt I had gone beyond the others in that time, without a single exception, with a great consultation and examination by learned men.

... The judges were thirty-four, counting those of the city and the surrounding areas: the endorsement in my favor of the victory was given by all, and the by the consuls and board and the whole body of the merchants guild, which has the temple of St. John the Baptist in its charge. It was ... determined that I should do this bronze door for this temple, and I executed it with great diligence. And this is the first work; with the frame around it, it added up to about twenty-two thousand florins.

Source: Creighton Gilbert, ed., *Italian Art 1400-1500: Sources and Documents* (Evanston, IL: Northwestern University Press, 1992)

The casting of the doors kept Ghiberti's workshop busy for 20 years. Many of the most sought-after artists of the next generation spent time there, as he completed the doors. The competition between these two artists sets the stage for developments in both architecture and sculpture in Florence during the first half of the fifteenth century.

Architecture and Antiquity in Florence

Although he may have lost the competition for the baptistery doors, Filippo Brunelleschi is a crucial figure for Renaissance art, especially in architecture. While he continued to work in sculp-ture, his study of ancient buildings drew him to solving architec-tural problems. After losing the competition for the doors, Brunelleschi went to Rome with his friend the sculptor Donatello. There he studied ancient structures and reportedly took exact measurements of them. His discovery of linear per-spective (discussed later in this chapter) may well have grown out of his search for an accurate way of recording the appearance of those ancient buildings. He brought his study of ancient buildings to the service of design problems at the Florentine Duomo, at other churches and chapels in Florence, and other structures. Other architects working in Florence took inspiration from his example, among them Leon Battista Alberti. His treatises on both painting and architecture helped to spread Brunelleschi's innovations.

BRUNELLESCHI AND THE DOME OF FLORENCE CATHEDRAL Between 1417 and 1419, Brunelleschi again com-peted with Ghiberti, this time for the job of building the dome for Florence cathedral (fig. **15.3**). The dome had been planned half a century earlier, so at this stage only details could be changed, and its vast size posed a problem of construction. Brunelleschi's pro-posals were the fruit of his study of Gothic, Roman, Byzantine, and maybe even Persian buildings, but the building of the dome was as much a feat of engineering as of style. (See *Materials and Techniques*, page 512.) The project occupied him for most of the rest of his life, and it would come to symbolize Florentine inventiveness, piety, ambition, and skill.

Soaring hundreds of feet above street level, the dome dwarfs all other structures in Florence. Resting visually on the smaller semidomes that surround the cathedral's eastern end, the ribs of the dome rise upward dramatically, terminating in a marble cupola or lantern. Brunelleschi designed this lantern to tie the eight exterior ribs together, but it also marks the crescendo of that upward movement. When the cathedral was dedicated on March 25, 1436, the city rejoiced. Florence had demonstrated its devotion to the Virgin Mary, as well as its ambition to overawe

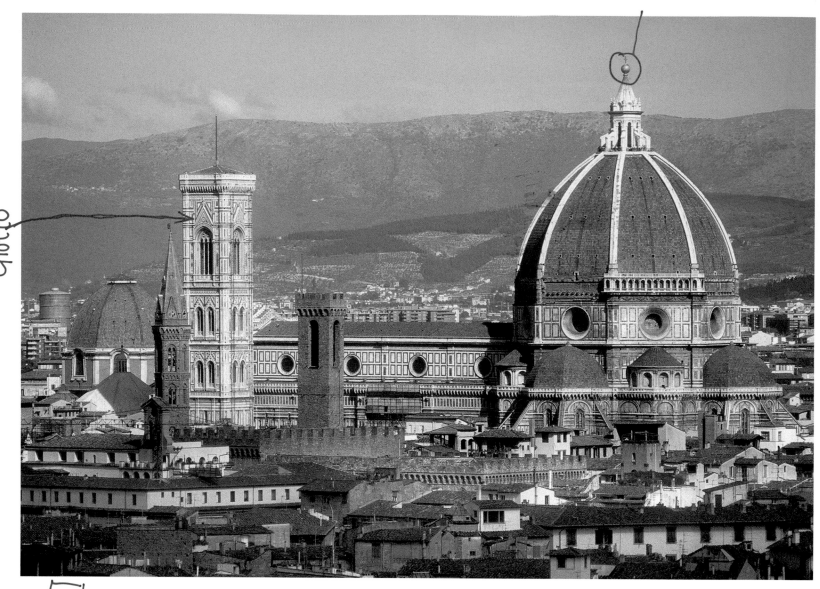

Andrea del Verrocchio (handwritten annotation)

Giotto (handwritten annotation)

15.3 Filippo Brunelleschi. Dome of Florence cathedral (Santa Maria del Fiore). 1420–36. Height 100' (35.5 m), diameter 459' (140 m)

its neighbors culturally. Florentines were justifiably proud that a native son had so cleverly accomplished what previous generations had failed to do. Brunelleschi's forms would influence architecture far beyond Tuscany.

BRUNELLESCHI'S *OSPEDALE DEGLI INNOCENTI* The work at the Duomo came under the purview of the wool merchants' guild, but another guild in Florence sponsored a different sort of public project for the city, intended to address a social problem. The Guild of Silk Manufacturers and Goldsmiths hired Brunelleschi to design a hospital for abandoned children near the church of the Santissima Annunziata. In 1421, construction began on the Ospedale degli Innocenti (Hospital of the Innocents), although building continued long after Brunelleschi's death. The façade of the hospital (fig. **15.4**) consists of a covered walkway, or **loggia**, defined by an arcade raised slightly above ground level. A strong horizontal molding sits above the arcade, and above that is a simple arrangement of **pedimented** windows.

In designing this hospital, Brunelleschi revived the architectural forms of the ancients, as seen in the columns, their capitals, the arches, and the entablatures. Doing so demanded that he work within rigid rules. Unlike a medieval column (see, for example, the colonnettes in the nave of San Francesco in Assisi, fig. 13.1), a Classical column is strictly defined; its details and proportions can vary only within narrow limits. Unlike any other arch (horseshoe, pointed, and so forth), the Classical round arch has only one possible shape: a semicircle. The Classical **architrave**, profiles, and ornaments must all follow similarly strict rules. This is not to say that Classical forms are completely inflexible. But the discipline of the Greek orders, which can be felt even in the most original Roman buildings, demands regularity and discourages arbitrary departures from the norm. Using such "standardized" forms, Brunelleschi designed the façade of this hospital as a series of blocks of space of the same size, defined by the **bays** of the arcade. Each bay establishes a square of space that is covered by a dome resting on **pendentives** (fig. **15.5**). Transverse arches divide the

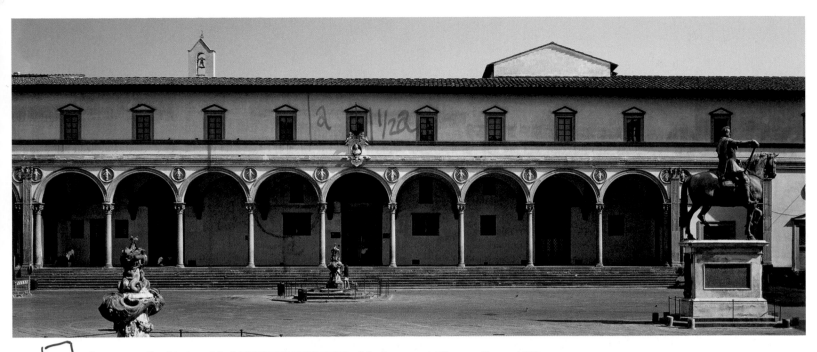

15.4　Filippo Brunelleschi. Ospedale degli Innocenti (Hospital of the Innocents), Florence. Begun 1421

domes inside the arcade. Using contrasting colors of stone, Brunelleschi emphasizes the edges of these units of space without disrupting their rhythmic sequence.

One other principle accounts for the balanced nature of the design. For Brunelleschi, the secret of good architecture lay in choosing the "right" proportions—that is, proportional ratios

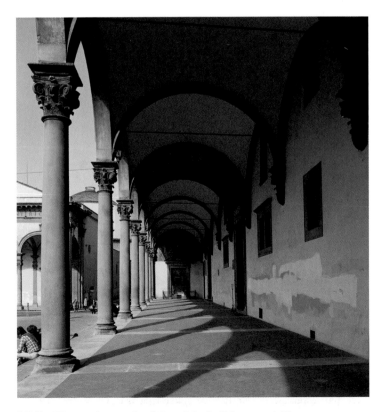

15.5　View under arcade of Ospedale degli Innocenti, Florence

expressed in simple whole numbers—for all the major measurements of a building. For example, the entablature over the columns sits at twice the height of a column for a ratio of 2:1. The ancients had possessed this secret, he believed, and he tried to discover it when he measured their monuments. What he found, and exactly how he applied it, is uncertain, but his knowledge may have been passed to Leon Battista Alberti. In his *Treatise on Architecture*, Alberti argues that the mathematical ratios that determine musical harmony must also govern architecture, for they recur throughout the universe and thus are divine in origin. (See *Primary Source*, page 514.) Similar ideas, derived from the theories of the Greek philosopher Pythagoras, had been current during the Middle Ages, but they had never before been expressed so directly and simply. At the Innocenti, Brunelleschi used ratios to dictate relationships: The windows are centered between the columns, the intervals between columns equal the height of the columns, the span between the columns is the distance from the column to the wall. Proportion locks the composition into a balanced whole. The arcade, with its beautifully proportioned columns supporting arches, made of a dark local sandstone called *pietra serena* (literally, "peaceful stone"), gives the façade a graceful rhythm.

Above the spandrels of the arches, terra-cotta reliefs in later roundels from the della Robbia workshop depict babies, the "innocents" for whom the structure was named. Brunelleschi's Innocenti not only served Florence's poor, it defined a public square. This loggia establishes one side of a piazza perpendicular to the church of the Santissima Annunziata; later, the façades of other buildings formed the remaining limits of the square. Such public spaces were used for social, religious, and political functions, and by echoing the design of the Roman Forum, they expressed the Florentine sense of themselves as the heirs to Rome.

Brunelleschi's Dome

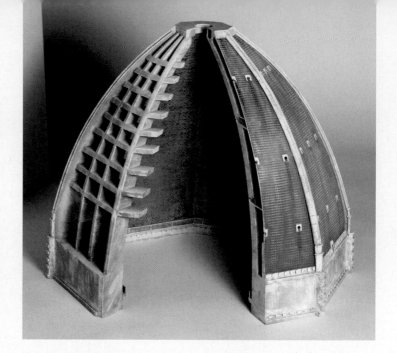

As the basic dimensions and plans for the cathedral of Florence had been established in the fourteenth century, Brunelleschi first determined to lift the dome on a drum above the level of the nave. He proposed to build the dome in two separate shells, which was a method more common in Islamic than Italian architecture, especially in Persia. Compare the fourteenth-century tomb of the Il-Khan Oljeytu in Sultaniya (see fig. 9.20). These two shells were supported by a series of ribs, eight of them visible on the exterior but others hidden; the vertical ribs were themselves linked by rows of horizontal ribs, a system which may have been inspired by the coffered dome of the Pantheon (see fig. 7.25). Both the use of ribs and the pointed profile reflect Gothic practice. The dual shells of the dome lighten the whole mass since their walls are thin relative to their size. Brunelleschi's herringbone-pattern brickwork serves both to resist cracks caused by settling and to lessen the weight as the courses of brick get thinner as they rise.

Along with these design features, Brunelleschi proposed innovations in the construction process. The traditional practice had been to construct a wooden centering across the span of the dome to support it during construction, but this required huge pieces of timber. To avoid this, Brunelleschi designed a new system by which temporary scaffolding was cantilevered out from the walls of the drum, thereby reducing the size and amount of timber needed during building. And

Model of some of the structural features of Brunelleschi's dome

instead of having building materials carried up on ramps to the required level, he designed new hoisting machines. Brunelleschi's entire scheme reflects a bold, analytical mind that was willing to discard conventional solutions if better ones could be devised.

In the revival of classical forms, Renaissance architecture found a standard vocabulary. The theory of harmonious proportions gave it a syntax that had been mostly absent from medieval architecture. Similarly, the revival of classical forms and proportions enabled Brunelleschi to transform the architectural "vernacular" of his region into a stable, precise, and coherent system. Brunelleschi's achievement placed architecture on a firm footing and applied the lessons of classical antiquity for modern Christian ends. Furthermore, his study of the ancients and his practical application of classical geometric proportions probably stimulated his discovery of a system for rendering forms in three dimensions. This technique became known as linear or **scientific perspective**. (See *Materials and Techniques*, page 516.)

BRUNELLESCHI AT SAN LORENZO Brunelleschi's skills also brought him to the notice of private patrons. Early in the fifteenth century, the up-and-coming Medici family began a project to rebuild their parish church. In 1419, Giovanni di Bicci de' Medici commissioned Brunelleschi to add a sacristy to the Romanesque church of San Lorenzo. The sacristy serves two purposes; it provides a liturgical space in which the priest prepares himself for the ritual of the Mass, but Giovanni also intended it as a funerary chapel. Because a later generation of Medici commissioned a sacristy on the opposite side of the church, Brunelleschi's chapel, completed by 1429, became known as the Old Sacristy.

The chapel (fig. **15.6**) consists of a square room oriented toward a niche with an altar. Brunelleschi covered this rectilinear

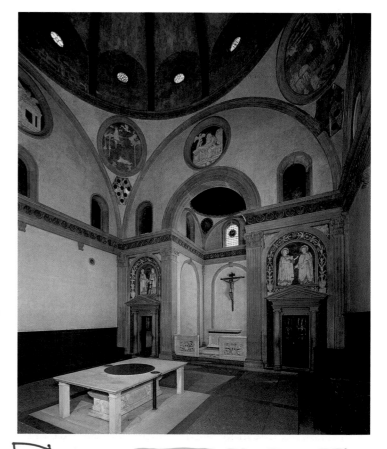

15.6 Filippo Brunelleschi, Old Sacristy, church of San Lorenzo, Florence. 1421–28

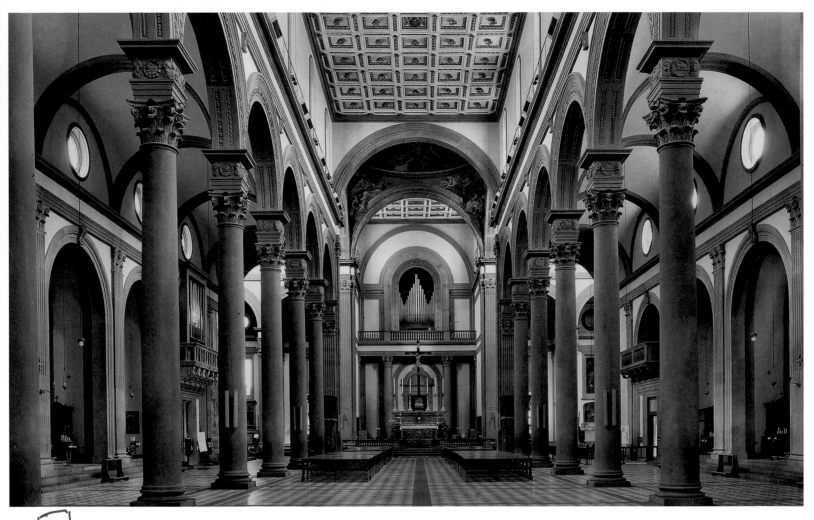

Filippo Brunelleschi. Nave of church of San Lorenzo, Florence. ca. 1421–69

space with a dome resting on triangular pendentives, uniting the circular form of a dome with a square. In plan, the square inscribes the circle. These two forms were thought ideal by ancient architects like Vitruvius, and thus by Brunelleschi and contemporary humanists. Proportion is also important here; Brunelleschi uses a 2:1 measure to determine the height of the architrave as well as further subdivisions of wall and space (such as the height of the doors that flank the altar). He marked these divisions, and in fact all the points where walls and other structural elements meet, with stone moldings that contrast with the wall. The result is a room that seems at once light and stable, spacious and harmonious, and that melds Christian function with forms inspired by antiquity.

The family was so pleased with his plans for this sacristy that they asked Brunelleschi to develop a new design for the entire church. Brunelleschi's work began in the 1420s, but construction proceeded in fits and starts; the nave was not completed until 1469, more than 20 years after the architect's death. (The exterior remains unfinished to this day.) Nevertheless, the building in its present form is essentially what Brunelleschi had envisioned about 1420, and it represents the first full statement of his architectural aims (figs. 15.7 and 15.8).

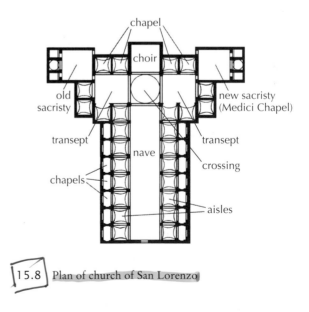

15.8 Plan of church of San Lorenzo

If the sacristy offered a new and exciting solution to issues of space and structure, the plan of the church itself seems at first glance to be more conventional. The plan shows it to be a basilica form, with nave and aisles; it terminates in a square east end and

Leon Battista Alberti on what makes a building beautiful

From the *Ten Books on Architecture* (1452)

Alberti composed his treatise on architecture after studying the treatise by the Roman architect Vitruvius. Originally written in Latin, his treatise prescribes the best way to design and build buildings and was intended for both practicing architects and for their patrons. This passage argues that the key to good building is something Alberti called concinnitus, which means something like consonance or harmony.

When you make judgments on beauty, you do not follow mere fancy, but the workings of a reasoning faculty that is inborn in the mind…Within the form and figure of a building there resides some natural excellence and perfection that excites the mind and is immediately recognized by it. I myself believe that form, dignity, grace and other such qualities depend on it, and as soon as anything is removed or altered these qualities are themselves weakened and perish …

From this we may conclude … that the three principal components of that whole theory into which we inquire are number, what we might call outline, and position. But arising from the composition and connection of these three is a further quality in which beauty shines full face: our term for this is *concinnitas*, which we say is nourished with every grace and splendor. It is the task and aim of *concinnitas* to compose parts that are quite separate from each other by their nature, according to some precise rule, so that they correspond to one another in appearance. That is why when the mind is reached by way of sight or sound, or any other means, *concinnitas* is instantly recognized …

Let us conclude as follows. Beauty is a form of sympathy and consonance of the parts within a body, according to definite number, outline and position, as dictated by *concinnitas*, the absolute and fundamental rule in nature. This is the main object of the art of building, and the source of her dignity, charm, authority and worth.

Source: Leon Battista Alberti, *On the Art of Building in Ten Books*, tr. Joseph Rykwert, Neil Leach and Robert Tavernor (Cambridge, MA: The MIT Press, 1988)

---

limits ornament as in some Cistercian churches (see fig. 11.21). San Lorenzo's unvaulted nave and transept recall Franciscan churches like Santa Croce (see fig. 13.4). Brunelleschi was constrained by the just completed sacristy and the preexisting church. But a new emphasis on symmetry and regularity distinguishes his design for San Lorenzo, accompanied by architectural elements inspired by the past and organized by attention to proportion. The ground plan demonstrates Brunelleschi's technique of composing with units of space in regular square blocks, so that each bay of the nave is twice as wide as its side aisles, and the crossing and choir are each four times the size of each bay of the aisle.

Inside, static order has replaced the flowing spatial movement of Gothic church interiors, such as Chartres (see fig. 12.12). From the portal, a viewer can clearly see the entire structure, almost as if looking at a demonstration of scientific perspective. The effect recalls the "old-fashioned" Tuscan Romanesque, as seen at Pisa cathedral (see fig. 11.34), as well as Early Christian basilicas like Santa Maria Maggiore in Rome (see fig. 8.16). To Brunelleschi, these monuments exemplified the church architecture of antiquity. They inspired his use of round arches and columns, rather than piers, in the nave arcade. Yet these earlier buildings lack the lightness and clarity of San Lorenzo; their columns are larger and more closely spaced, so that they tend to screen off the aisles from the nave. Only the **blind arcade** on the exterior of the Florentine baptistery is as graceful in its proportions as San Lorenzo's, but it has no supporting function (see fig. 11.35). Since the Baptistery was thought to have once been a classical temple, it was an appropriate source of inspiration for Brunelleschi and for the new generation of Medici patrons.

Brunelleschi's innovations in construction techniques, in designing spaces, and in using the architectural vocabulary of antiquity made his work very influential. Some of the next generation of architects, such as Michelozzo (see page 533) trained with him. He was also a friend and correspondent of Leon Battista Alberti (1404–1472), a Florentine humanist, scholar and author; his treatise *On Painting* (which is dedicated to Brunelleschi, refers to "our dear friend" Donatello, and praises Masaccio), completed ca. 1435, helped to spread Brunelleschi's formula for perspective and the author's own ideas about what good painting required. During a stay at the court of Ferrara in 1438, Alberti was asked to restore Vitruvius' treatise on architecture, then known in various manuscripts. Upon his return to Rome five years later, he began a systematic study of the monuments of ancient Rome that led to the *Ten Books on Architecture* (finished 1452 and published 1485)—the first book of its kind since Vitruvius' treatise, on which it is modeled. (See *Primary Source*, above.) Alberti's ideas about architecture had roots in his study of the past, but his emphasis and prescriptions for proportion owe something to Brunelleschi, too. Alberti's writings helped to spread Florentine innovations through Italy and increased the prestige of Florentine artists as well. It brought him important commissions as an architect.

ALBERTI AT SANTA MARIA NOVELLA Few of Brunelleschi's buildings were completed in his lifetime, so we do not know what he would have done with their façades. In fact, few of the major churches of Florence had their façades completed in the Renaissance. (Neither Santa Croce nor the Duomo had complete façades until the nineteenth century; San Lorenzo still has no façade.) One important church in Florence that did have its façade completed, however, is Santa Maria Novella. The exterior of this Dominican church, built largely between 1278 and 1350, had been left unfinished above the row of polychromed Gothic niches with their Gothic portals.

Repairing and improving a church was an act of piety—motivation enough for a neighbor of Santa Maria Novella, the

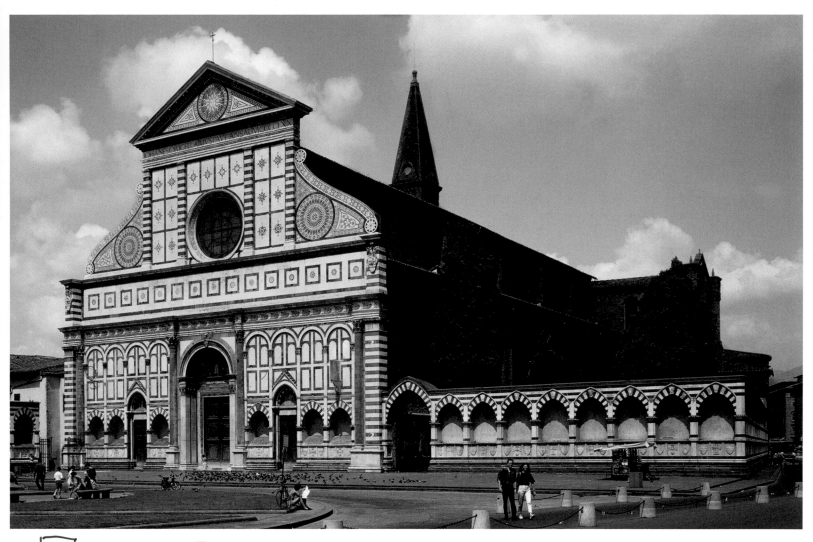

15.9 Leon Battista Alberti. Façade of Santa Maria Novella, Florence. 1458–70

wealthy Giovanni Rucellai, to have this façade completed around 1458 (fig. **15.9**). Rucellai paid Leon Battista Alberti to design and install a marble façade. Multicolored marble façades were traditional in Tuscany. Alberti's models for this project included the cathedral (see fig. 15.3) and other churches in Florence, including the baptistery (see fig. 11.35) and San Miniato al Monte (see fig. 11.36), from which the emphatic arcades may derive.

Other than the doorways and giant round oculus, which were fixed, Alberti's façade masks its relationship to the rest of the church. As he chose not to let the internal structure of the church (with its nave higher than the side aisles) limit him, the architect could use a system of squares to design the façade. Three main squares divide the façade. Two on the lower story flank the extraordinarily classicizing main portal; likewise, the "temple" atop the frieze fits within a square. Mathematical ratios lock these squares into relationships with the whole façade and with the other elements of the composition. Alberti's use of graceful scrolls to bridge the gap between the temple and the frieze was truly innovative and was to prove extremely influential (see fig. 17.23). It also helps to disguise the loose fit of the façade with the

main body of the church by hiding the clerestory. Just below the pediment on the frieze level of the "temple," Alberti includes an inscription that credits Giovanni Rucellai for bringing the work to completion. It is the patron, not the artist, who gains the glory for the work.

Alberti built other influential buildings outside Florence (see page 546). He and Brunelleschi laid the foundations for later architects to design buildings based on their principles of emulating antiquity and designing with an eye to harmonious proportions.

Ancient Inspirations in Florentine Sculpture

While work continued on the baptistery doors and the dome of Florence cathedral, another competition played out nearby at Or San Michele. Begun in 1337, this structure served both as a granary and a shrine holding a locally venerated image of the Virgin and Child. The guilds of Florence oversaw the building, with each one taking responsibility for filling a niche on the exterior with sculpture. In 1406, the city set a deadline to complete the work

Perspective

One of the genuinely transformative inventions of the Renaissance was linear, or scientific, perspective, sometimes called one-point or center-point perspective. The system is a geometric procedure for projecting the illusion of space onto a two-dimensional surface. Its central feature is the **vanishing point**, a single point toward which any set of parallel lines will seem to converge. If these lines are perpendicular to the picture plane, their vanishing point will be on the horizon. (Such lines are called **orthogonals**.) To further clarify the space, lines parallel to the picture plane, called **transversals** (not shown), are laid in at regular intervals, derived geometrically.

Brunelleschi is said to have developed this tool, but artists had been experimenting since antiquity with techniques to create the illusion of depth on a flat surface. At Pompeii, wall painters sometimes used color to suggest deep space (see fig. 7.55), a technique known as atmospheric or aerial perspective. This method recognizes the eye's inability to perceive color at great distances, and that specific colors become light blue or gray at the horizon line. In addition, the forms themselves often become less clear. (See the lower section of fig. 14.10.) Artists also adjusted spatial elements according to how the forms looked to them, sometimes with excellent results, as in Van Eyck's *The "Arnolfini Portrait"* (see fig. 14.14).

In Early Renaissance Italy, scientific perspective systemized the projection of space using mathematics and geometry, overturning the intuitive perspective practices of the past. This "scientific" approach to making images (whether paintings, prints, drawings, or reliefs) became an argument for upgrading the fine arts to become one of the liberal arts. In 1435, Brunelleschi's discovery was described in *On Painting* by Leon Battista Alberti, the first Renaissance treatise on painting. It remains a standard element of drawing instruction to this day.

One advantage of this technique is that the artist can adjust the perspectival system to take account of the presence of a spectator. The method presupposes that a beholder's eye occupies a fixed point in space, so that a perspective picture dictates where the viewer must stand to see it properly. Thus the artist who knows in advance that the image will be seen from above or below, rather than at ordinary eye level, can make the perspective construction correspond to these conditions. (See, for example, fig. 15.55.) Sometimes, however, these vantage points are so abnormal (as when a viewer is looking up at an image on the ceiling) that the design must be foreshortened to an extreme degree. In such cases, the artist may create an "ideal beholder" for the image, regardless of a spectator's actual viewpoint.

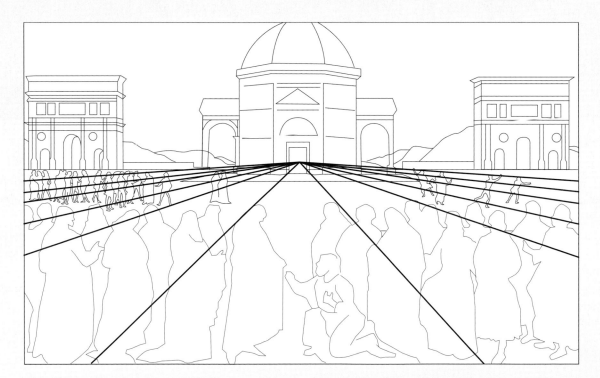

Perspective image with *Delivery of the Keys* (see fig. 15.55)

within ten years. In the decades that followed, the guilds and the sculptors they commissioned competed intensely to create impressive statues of their patron saints. The major guilds commissioned Lorenzo Ghiberti to execute several statues for Or San Michele, while some younger sculptors won commissions from less powerful guilds.

NANNI DI BANCO The Guild of Wood and Stone Carvers hired one of its members, Nanni di Banco (ca. 1380–1421), to fill its niche at Or San Michele with an image of the Four Crowned Saints, called the *Quattro Coronati* (fig. **15.10**). Carved between 1409 and 1416/17, these figures represent four Christian sculptors who were executed for refusing to carve a pagan statue ordered by

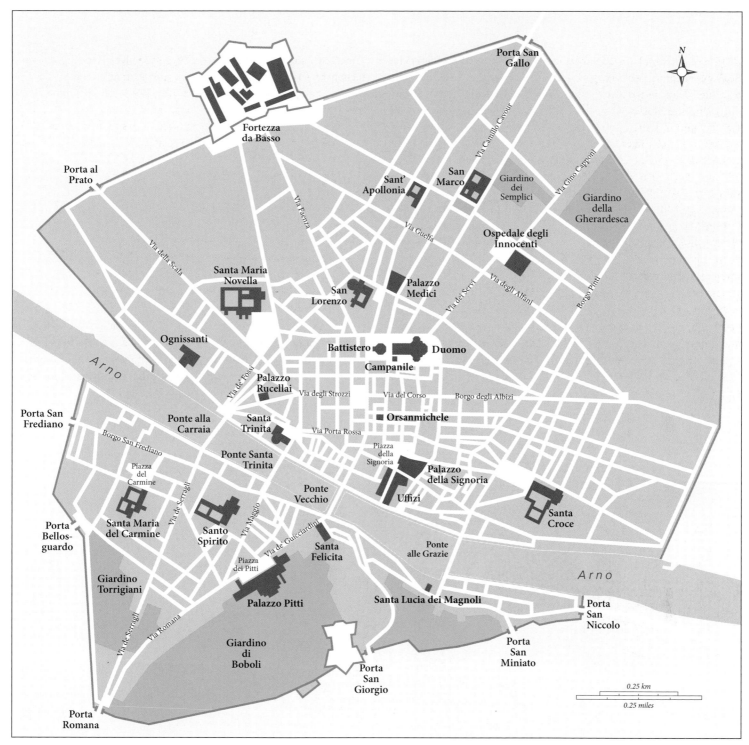

Map 15.2 Key monuments in Renaissance Florence

the Roman emperor Diocletian. The life-size saints stand in a Gothic niche as if discussing their impending fate. Their bodies seem to spill out of the confines of the niche, draped as they are in the heavy folds of their togas. These garments and the heads of the second and third of the *Coronati* directly recall Roman portrait sculpture of the first century CE (see fig. 7.35). It is as if Nanni were situating the martyrs in their historical moment. His

figures emulate Roman verism and monumentality. The relief below the saints represents a sculptor, stonecutters, and a mason at work, both explaining the story of the martyrs and advertising the skills of the patrons who commissioned the work. This double function occurs often in the statues designed for the niches on Or San Michele, reflecting the building's double origin in commerce and piety.

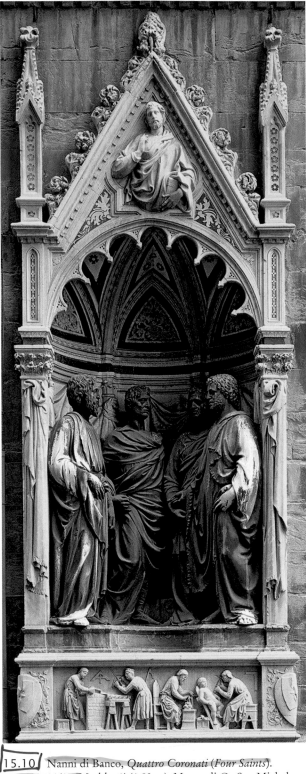

15.10 Nanni di Banco, *Quattro Coronati* (*Four Saints*). ca. 1409–16/17. Marble, 6' (1.83 m). Museo di Or San Michele, Florence

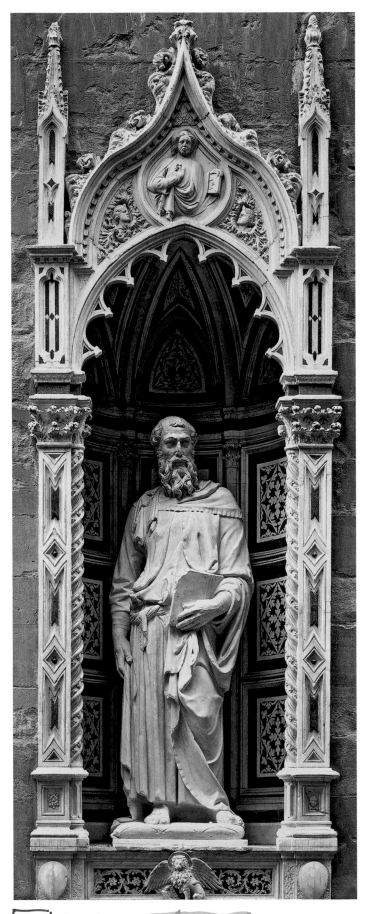

15.11 Donatello, *St. Mark*. ca. 1411–13. Marble, 7'9" (2.4 m). Museo di Or San Michele, Florence

DONATELLO AT OR SAN MICHELE One of Ghiberti's former assistants, the young Donatello (1389–1466) executed several statues for Or San Michele. The linen weavers' guild turned to him to fill its niche with a figure probably completed in 1413 (fig. **15.11**). Their patron, St. Mark, stands almost 8 feet high, but that is only one of the features that makes him so imposing. His large,

verism

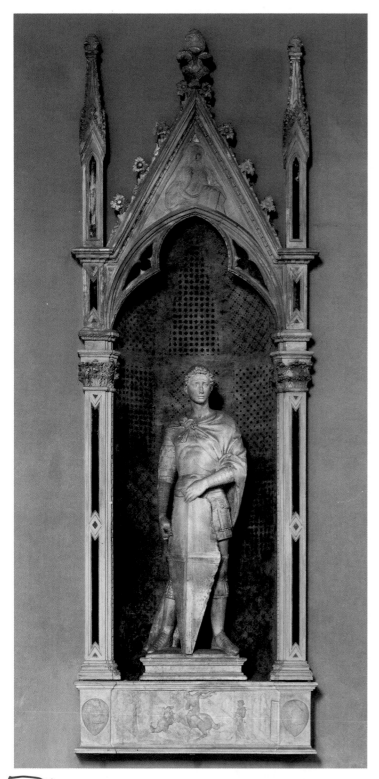

15.12 Donatello, *St. George*, from Or San Michele, Florence. ca. 1410–20. Marble, height of statue 6'10" (2.1 m). Relief 15¼ × 47¼" (39 × 120 cm). Museo Nazionale del Bargello, Florence

powerful hands grip a book (his Gospel). His body stands in a pose Donatello learned from studying the art of the ancients: One leg is flexed while the other holds the body's weight in a **contrapposto** stance (see fig. 5.33). St. Mark's drapery falls in deep folds to reveal and emphasize his posture.

Donatello treats the human body as an articulated structure, capable of movement, and its drapery as a separate element that is based on the shapes underneath rather than on patterns and shapes imposed from outside. Following classical precedents such as the *Doryphoros*, Donatello carefully balances the composition, so the elements on the left (as a viewer sees it) stress the vertical and the static, while those on the right emphasize the diagonal and kinetic. St. Mark's deeply carved eyes and undulating beard give him a powerful personality, while the mass of drapery reminds the viewer of the linen weavers' products. This work reflects Donatello's deep understanding of the principles that guided the artists of antiquity and his commitment to them. *St. Mark* reveals what Donatello learned from studying ancient works of sculpture: an emphasis on naturalistic form, the independence of body and drapery, a balanced but contrasting composition, the potential for movement, and psychological presence.

Donatello finished his *St. George* (fig. **15.12**) for the Guild of Armorers around 1417. The niche is so shallow that the figure seems poised to step out of it. Although dressed in armor, he appears able to move his limbs easily. His stance, with the weight placed on the forward leg, suggests he is ready for combat. Originally, he held a real sword or lance in his right hand, and he wore a real helmet, effectively showcasing the guild's wares. The controlled energy of his body is reflected in his eyes, which seem to scan the horizon for the enemy. St. George is portrayed as a Christian soldier, spiritually akin to the *St. Theodore* at Chartres (see fig. 12.22) and to other figures of chivalry.

Below the niche a relief panel shows the hero's best-known exploit, the slaying of a dragon. The woman on the right is the princess whom he had come to free. Here, Donatello devised a new kind of shallow relief (called **schiacciato**, meaning "flattened-out"), yet he created an illusion of almost infinite depth. In this relief, the landscape behind the figures consists of delicate surface modulations that catch light from varying angles. Every tiny ripple has a descriptive power that is greater than its real depth. The sculptor's chisel, like a painter's brush, becomes a tool for creating shades of light and dark. The energetic figure of the saint on horseback, battling the dragon in the foreground, protrudes from this atmospheric background, while the princess watches. The whole work becomes an image of watchfulness and preparedness for danger.

DONATELLO AT WORK IN SIENA, PADUA, AND FLORENCE Donatello's innovations in Florence soon became known elsewhere in Italy, leading to commissions in other cities, such as Siena and Padua. His career was long and productive making him the most influential sculptor of fifteenth-century Italy. It is worth pausing here to consider the range of his activities from the 1420s until the 1460s, as there is such variety, invention and power in his art.

Donatello's early career may have begun in Ghiberti's workshop, but he ultimately competed with his mentor both at Or San Michele and in Siena. In 1416, Lorenzo Ghiberti was one of a group of artists hired to execute a new baptismal font for that

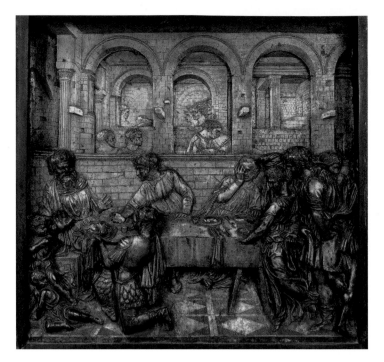

15.13 Donatello, *The Feast of Herod*, Siena cathedral. ca. 1425. Gilt bronze, 23½" (59.7 cm) square

city's baptistery, San Giovanni. Donatello took over one of the relief panels for the sides of the hexagonal basin in 1423. He finished *The Feast of Herod* (fig. **15.13**) by 1427. The relief represents the story of John the Baptist's martyrdom; Salome, the stepdaughter of King Herod, requested the head of the saint as a reward for performing a dance. Donatello combines many stages in the narrative into one space. The focus of the drama—the executioner presenting the head of St. John the Baptist to Herod—is far to the left, while the dancing Salome and most of the spectators are massed on the right. Yet the center is empty. Donatello created this gaping hole to add to the impact of the shocking sight, bolstered by the witnesses' gestures and expressions. Moreover, the centrifugal movement of the figures suggests that the picture space does not end within the panel but continues in every direction. The frame thus becomes a window through which is seen a segment of deepening space. The arched openings within the panel frame additional segments of the same reality, luring the viewer farther into the space.

This architecture, with its round arches and fluted columns and pilasters, reflects the designs of Donatello's friend and colleague Filippo Brunelleschi. More importantly, *The Feast of Herod* is an example of a picture space using Brunelleschi's linear

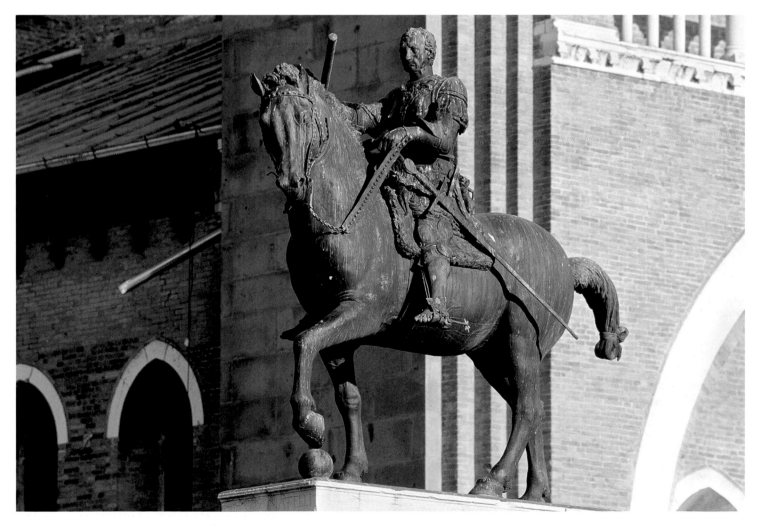

15.14 Donatello, *Equestrian Monument of Gattamelata*. 1445–50. Bronze, approx. 11 × 13' (3.35 × 3.96 m). Piazza del Santo, Padua

perspective. A series of arches set at different depths provides the setting for different figures and moments in the biblical story: In the background, we see the servant carrying the head of the Baptist, which he then presents to Herod in the foreground. Donatello used perspective to organize the action as a continuous narrative, unfolding through space as well as time.

Donatello's successes in Tuscany led to a commission from the Republic of Venice in 1443. The commander of the Venetian armies, Erasmo da Narni (nicknamed "Gattamelata"), had recently died, and Venice sought to honor him with a statue. To this end, Donatello produced his largest free-standing work in bronze: the *Equestrian Monument of Gattamelata* (fig. **15.14**), which still stands in its original position on a tall pedestal near the church of St. Anthony in Padua. Having visited Rome, Donatello certainly knew the tradition of equestrian statues exemplified by that of Marcus Aurelius (see fig. 7.33). The work also reflects the medieval tradition seen in the monument to Bernabò Visconti in Milan (fig. 13.33). Like the *Equestrian Statue of Marcus Aurelius*, the *Gattamelata* is impressive in scale and creates a sense of balance and dignity. The horse, a heavy-set animal fit to carry a man in full armor, is so large that the rider must dominate it by force of personality rather than by size. Like the Visconti work, it belongs to a tradition of representations of military leaders on horseback as funerary monuments. In his vivid portrait of a general, Donatello reenergizes this tradition by the carefully realistic depiction of the armor and fittings, and his powerful characterization of Gattamelata's features.

Despite these "foreign" commissions, Donatello spent most of his career in Florence, where he produced works for the Duomo, the Palazzo della Signoria and for important families like the Medici. For the latter's palace, he apparently executed a bronze *David* (see fig. 15.33), which will be discussed below. In addition to projects in bronze, Donatello worked in less expensive mediums. Although the circumstances of its commission are unclear, Donatello carved a powerful *Mary Magdalen* sometime in mid-century. Rather than marble or bronze, this life-size figure (fig. **15.15**) was carved in poplar wood, then painted and gilded. Our earliest reference to this object dates from around 1500 and describes it as being displayed in the baptistery, although there has been much speculation about its origins and date. Late medieval enhancements of Mary of Magdala's biography reported that she spent the last years of her life in the desert as a hermit in penitence. In his image of her, Donatello carves the soft wood into complex textures to render her rough garment and her hair, and to give her figure a gaunt, emaciated look. Her limbs and face are painted the ruddy color of someone who lives in the desert, while her hair was originally gilded. The artist is less interested in ancient forms here than he is in expressive naturalism.

Even though the date for this figure is uncertain, many scholars see the *Magdalen* as a work of Donatello's old age, and thus in its spiritual intensity they see a change of mood for the artist. In any case, the *Magdalen* demonstrates Donatello's range as a sculptor, as he explores the expressive possibilities of another sculpted medium. He worked in wood, marble, bronze, and terra

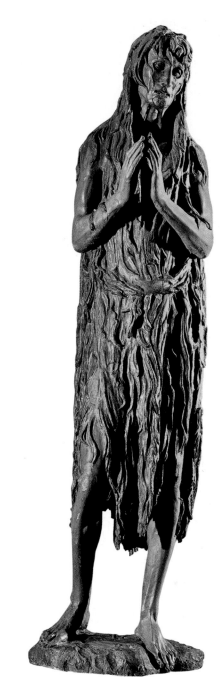

15.15 Donatello, *Mary Magdalen*. ca. 1430–50. Polychrome and gold on wood, height 6'1" (1.85 m). Museo dell'Opera del Duomo, Florence

cotta, leaving a prodigious amount of sculpture behind when he died in 1466.

GHIBERTI AND LATER FLORENTINE SCULPTURE

Donatello's contemporary Lorenzo Ghiberti's work on the bronze doors for the baptistery continued, with the assistance of numerous other artists, until their completion in 1424. This set of doors so impressed the Guild of Wool Merchants, which oversaw the building, that it commissioned him to execute a second pair. These doors, begun in 1425 but not completed until 1452, were ultimately installed in the east entry of the baptistery, facing the

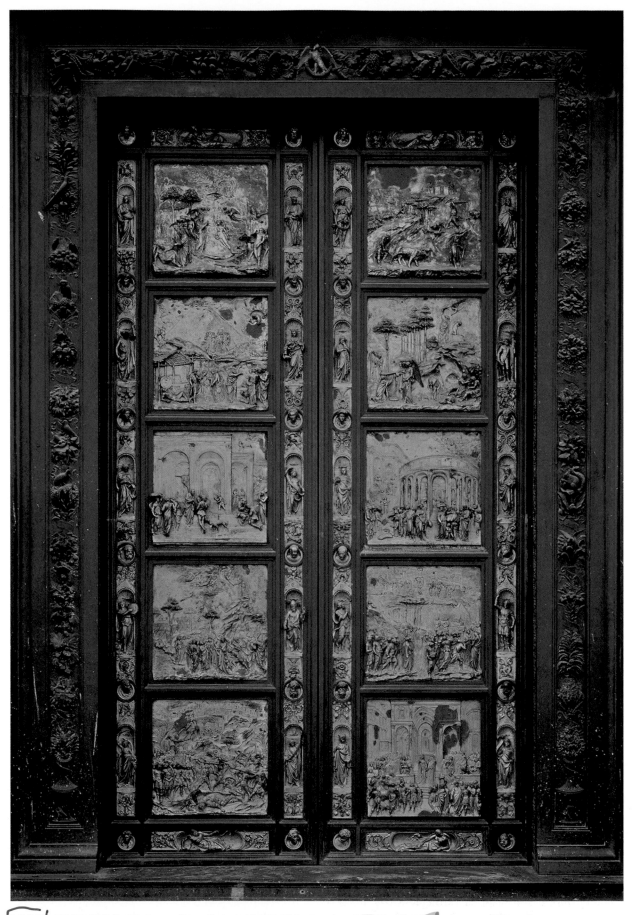

15.16 Lorenzo Ghiberti, *Gates of Paradise*, east doors of the Baptistery of San Giovanni, Florence. 1425–52. Gilt bronze, height 15' (4.57 m)

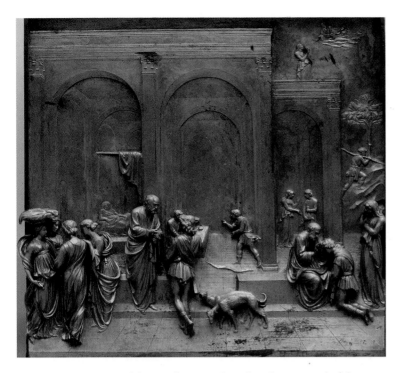

15.17 Lorenzo Ghiberti, *The Story of Jacob and Esau*, panel of the *Gates of Paradise*, Baptistery of San Giovanni, Florence. ca. 1435. Gilt bronze, 31¼" (79.5 cm) square

cathedral; this area is called the Paradise, so the doors were termed the *Gates of Paradise* (fig. **15.16**), a witticism that reportedly originated with Michelangelo. Where the earlier doors by Andrea Pisano and Ghiberti each bore 28 small panels in quatrefoils, these two doors each contain five large panels in simple square frames, creating a larger field for each image. These panels depict scenes from the Hebrew Bible, completing the program of all three doors: One door is devoted to the life of John the Baptist, one to the life of Christ, and one to the Hebrew Bible. Two humanists may have planned the program for the later doors: Ambrogio Traversari (1386–1439) and the chancellor, Leonardo Bruni. The latter prescribed that the doors should be both significant and splendid. To achieve splendor, Ghiberti completely gilded the masterfully crafted bronze reliefs and framed the panels with figures of prophets in niches, portrait heads in roundels, and foliate decorations. Significance was achieved through the selection of themes and the legibility of the narratives.

In designing these reliefs, Ghiberti drew on the new devices for pictorial imagery he and his rivals had pioneered, including the *schiacciato* relief devised by Donatello for the *St. George* at Or San Michele and the linear perspective developed by Brunelleschi. The graceful proportions, elegant stances, and fluid drapery of the figures bespeak Ghiberti's allegiance to the International Gothic style. The hint of depth seen in *The Sacrifice of Isaac* (see fig. 15.2) has grown in *The Story of Jacob and Esau* (fig. **15.17**) into a deeper space defined by the arches of a building planned to accommodate the figures as they appear and reappear throughout the structure in a continuous narrative. The relief tells the story of Isaac mistakenly blessing his younger son, Jacob, instead of the elder, Esau.

The blind Isaac sends Esau off to hunt on the left, but confers his blessing on the disguised Jacob on the right. Isaac's effective preference to the younger Jacob over the older Esau foreshadowed Christianity replacing Judaism for medieval theologians. Ghiberti's spacious hall is a fine example of Early Renaissance architectural design.

A HUMANIST'S TOMB Tomb sculpture was another important form in fifteenth-century Florence. On the death of its illustrious chancellor Leonardo Bruni, the city of Florence honored him with a monument installed in Santa Croce (fig. **15.18**). This humanist and statesman had played a vital part in the city's affairs since the

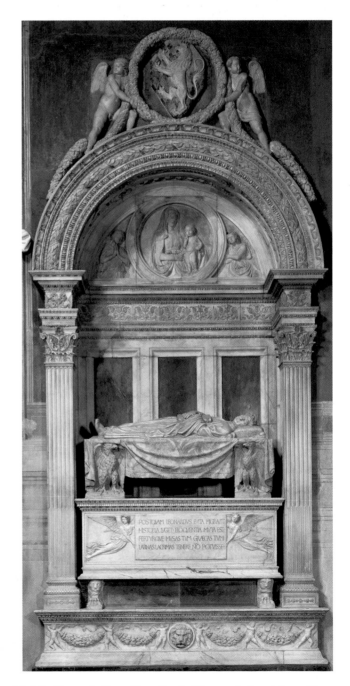

15.18 Bernardo Rossellino, *Tomb of Leonardo Bruni*, Santa Croce, Florence. ca. 1445–50. Marble, height to top of arch 20' (6.1 m)

beginning of the century; when he died in 1444, he received a grand funeral "in the manner of the ancients." Bernardo Rossellino (1409–1464), a sculptor from the countryside around Florence, executed the tomb. Since Bruni had been born in Arezzo, his native town probably contributed to the project and perhaps favored Rossellino, another former resident, for the commission.

Bruni's contributions to the city as politician, historian, and literary figure forged Florentines' notion of themselves as the heirs to Roman culture, so Rossellino's design paid homage to this theme. His effigy lies on a bier supported by Roman eagles, his head wreathed in laurel and his right hand resting on a book (perhaps his own *History of Florence*). On the sarcophagus, two figures with wings hold an eloquent inscription. The only religious element appears in the **lunette**, where the Madonna and Child look down at the effigy from a roundel. Above the arch, a heraldic lion appears in a wreath supported by angels. This symbol of Florence associates Bruni with the city he served and links Florence to his goal of reviving Roman virtues.

LATER SCULPTURE AT OR SAN MICHELE Although many of the guilds had filled their niches by 1430, more sculptural commissions were given at Or San Michele in the second half of the century. Not all groups active in commissioning works of art could afford the expense of bronze or marble; some guilds installed terra-cotta roundels in the façade above the niches. The leading sculptor in this medium was Luca della Robbia (1400–1482), a student of Nanni di Banco, who executed a medallion of the Virgin and Child for the Guild of Doctors and Apothecaries around 1465 (fig. **15.19**). Luca covered the earth-colored clay with enamel-like glazes to mask the surface and

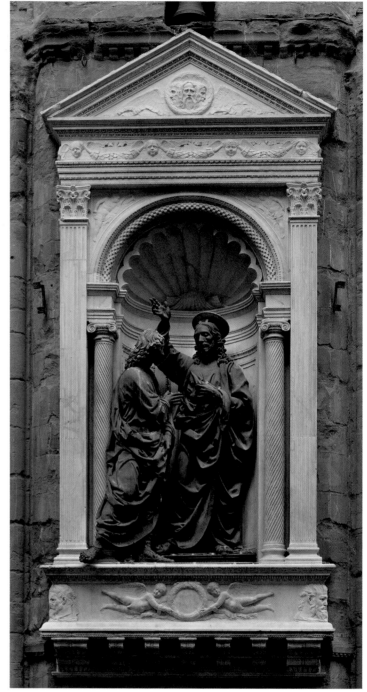

15.20   Andrea del Verrocchio, *The Incredulity of Thomas*. 1467–83. Bronze, height of Christ 7'6½" (2.28 m), Thomas 6'6¾" (2 m). Or San Michele, Florence (copy in niche)

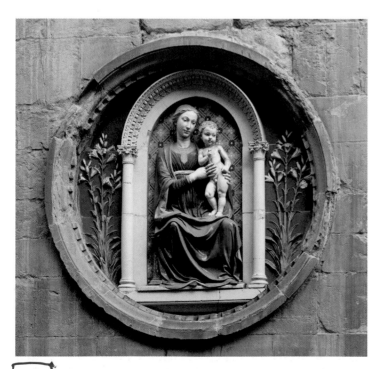

15.19   Luca della Robbia, *Madonna and Child*. ca. 1465. Glazed terra cotta. Or San Michele, Florence

protect it from the weather. This relief depicts the Virgin and Child beneath a Brunelleschian arch, flanked by lilies. The blue background highlights the flowers and the architectural forms. Mother and child form a compact group, their heads echoing each other, as they look downward to make eye contact with a viewer passing by. Such inexpensive substitutes for marble and bronze carvings attracted many customers and the della Robbia workshop became a factory, turning out scores of small Madonna reliefs still visible throughout Florence.

Patronage Studies

Seeing a work of art in a museum, a modern viewer may not be aware of its original function or context, nor of the circumstances that brought it into creation. Many art historians find that an important way to investigate these circumstances is to focus on the patronage of art. Such studies may include finding evidence in documents indicating who paid the artist for the work; considering what role the patron may have had in determining style or subject matter; evaluating the relationship between the artist and the patron; and drawing conclusions about what the patron wanted the work of art to do.

Relationships between patron and artist in the Renaissance varied greatly. In princely courts, an artist could be considered a member of the household staff, with many rather mundane tasks to do, or an esteemed member of the prince's circle, with special status and prestige. In urban centers, artists may have interacted with patrons on a more socially equal level, but the person buying the work of art still had a great deal to say about the finished product. In gifts made to churches, patrons might want their portraits painted into the work of art or their coat of arms prominently displayed to remind a viewer of the identity of the donor, a practice that was widespread by the end of the Middle Ages. The system of patronage in Italy was part of a larger social network. In Florence, the great families of a neighborhood were often the major patrons of large projects for the entire neighborhood (for example, the Medici at San Lorenzo and the Rucellai at Santa Maria Novella). Other families or groups often allied themselves with the great families for political, social, or commercial reasons. In some cases, this resulted in works of art that represented or made reference to the great families. Artists favored by the major patrons could gain other clients among the followers of those patrons. The investigation of these issues has enhanced our understanding of the way works of art functioned in their time.

Later interventions at Or San Michele brought other changes. Sometime after 1462, a sculpture by Donatello was removed and its niche reassigned to the judges of the merchants' guild. This group, responsible for adjudicating commercial cases, hired Andrea del Verrocchio (1435–1488) to fill the niche with an image reflecting their activities, using a theme traditionally associated with justice. The architecture of the niche remained as Donatello had designed it, so Verrocchio executed the figures of *The Incredulity of Thomas* (fig. **15.20**) without backs to squeeze them into the shallow space. The bronze figures stand close together, as the apostle Thomas seeks proof of the miracle of the Resurrection by probing the wound in Christ's side. Verrocchio was a painter as well as a sculptor, and this sculpture shares with contemporary paintings an interest in textures, the play of light and dark in massive drapery folds, and illusionism. The niche can barely contain the oversized figures, so Thomas's foot projects beyond the limits of the frame, linking passersby to the scene. His body twists into the composition, leading a viewer to the gentle features of Christ. The eloquent poses and bold exchange of gestures between Christ and Thomas convey the drama of the scene. Verrocchio lets the active drapery, with its deep folds, suggest the calm of Christ and the disturbance in Thomas's mind. Michelangelo admired the *The Incredulity of Thomas* for the beauty of the figures; and Leonardo da Vinci learned directly from Verrocchio, as his teacher, to create figures whose actions express the passions of the mind.

Sculpture in Florence took many forms, though it was often commissioned in association with buildings. Doors, niches, baptismal fonts, and altars were all adorned with sculpture in relief or with figural works of a scale and impressiveness that almost brings them to life. Materials ranged from less expensive terra cotta to gilded bronze. Renaissance sculptors' study of the ancients and interest in naturalism inspired their increasingly realistic and psychologically charged imagery.

Painting in Florentine Churches and Chapels

Well-funded guilds oversaw the sculptural adornment of public buildings like the baptistery and Or San Michele, and great families often sponsored building programs in churches. Many of the elite families of Florence, having patronage rights in chapels, commissioned paintings rather than sculpture. (See *The Art Historian's Lens*, above.) The stimulus of such fresco and panel commissions led to many innovations in the art of painting. The achievements of the sculptors in realizing vivid sacred characters on the niches of Or San Michele and the tools for projecting space provided by Brunelleschi inspired new directions in Renaissance painting.

GENTILE DA FABRIANO Patrons commissioned chapels in mendicant and parish churches, such as the Gothic church of Santa Trinità. Here the sacristy was endowed by the Strozzi, one of the wealthiest families in Florence. To complete the program, Palla Strozzi hired Gentile da Fabriano to paint the altarpiece, *The Adoration of the Magi*, which Gentile signed and dated in 1423 (fig. **15.21**). Gentile (ca. 1385–1427) worked throughout northern Italy in a style informed by the International Gothic. The lavish, triple-arched gilt frame of the altarpiece, with a **predella** (the base of the altarpiece) and gable figures, encloses a single scene in the central panel: the visit of the Magi to Bethlehem to acknowledge the newborn Jesus as king. A cavalcade of richly dressed courtiers, as well as horses, dogs, and exotic animals (monkeys, leopards, and camels), fills the front plane of the picture as the three kings advance to venerate the child, who sits in his mother's lap to the left. Behind the stable and rock formations that define the frontal plane, the landscape winds upward into the arches of the frame. In those distant vistas appear the Magi wending their way to Bethlehem; towns and castles mark their route. So despite the

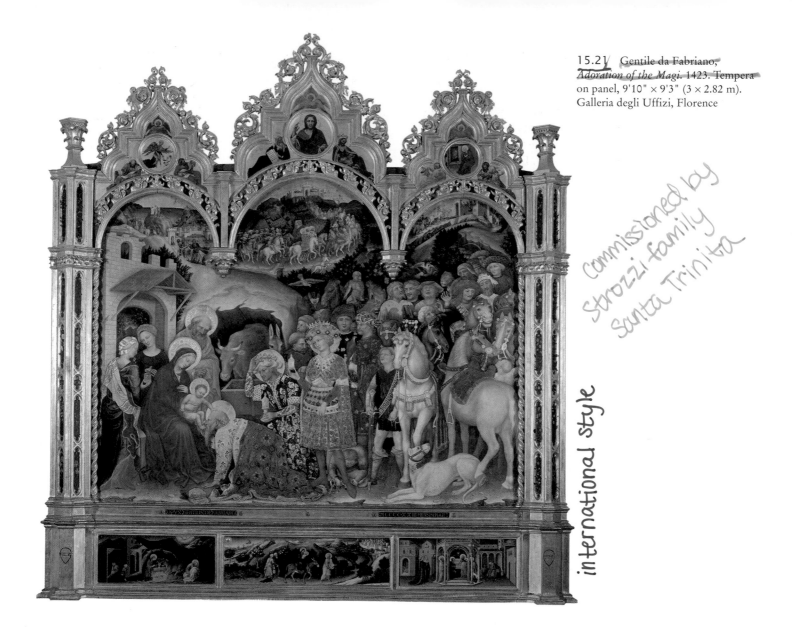

15.21 Gentile da Fabriano, *Adoration of the Magi*. 1423. Tempera on panel, 9'10" × 9'3" (3 × 2.82 m). Galleria degli Uffizi, Florence

Commissioned by Strozzi family Santa Trinita

international style

apparently unified landscape, several episodes of the narrative appear in the center panel. Other moments in the story—the Nativity, the Flight into Egypt, the Presentation in the Temple—appear in the predella. Small images in the gable above the center panel preface the story with images of the Annunciation.

Gentile's altarpiece imagines the events of the Magi's visit in courtly and sumptuous terms. Not only is the image full of elegant figures, garbed in brilliant brocades and surrounded by colorful retainers, but the panel also shines with gold leaf and tooled surfaces. (The haloes of the Virgin and St. Joseph bear pseudo-kufic

15.22 Gentile da Fabriano, *The Nativity*, detail of *Adoration of the Magi* predella. 1423. Tempera on panel, 12¼ × 29½" (31 × 75 cm)

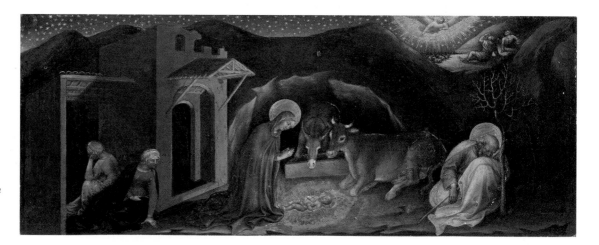

inscriptions, attesting to Gentile's contact with Islamic works, probably in Venice.) The kings, also given halos, stand not only for the international acknowledgement of Christ's divinity, but for the three ages of man: youth, middle age, and old age. The artist crowds the space, and the festive pageant almost overwhelms the Holy Family with its profusion of men and beasts, including some marvelously rendered horses. Despite this crowding, a golden light unites the whole image, illuminating the bodies of the animals, the faces of the humans, and parts of the landscape. These forms are softly modeled to suggest volume for the figures and to counteract the strong flattening effect of the gold. The predella scene of the Nativity (fig. **15.22**) demonstrates this aspect of Gentile's art further, as it stresses the function of light over line to delineate the forms. What is more, the source for the light that models the figures and the shed in the predella is the mystical light emanating from the Christ Child himself. Gentile's picture reveals his awareness of light as a carrier of meaning.

MASACCIO AT SANTA MARIA NOVELLA Gentile's refined style made him very popular among aristocratic patrons throughout Italy, but it was his approach to light that would strongly influence younger painters. One such was Masaccio (Tommaso di Ser Giovanni di Mone Cassai, 1401–1428). Leon Battista Alberti, a contemporary of Massaccio, celebrated the young painter's work in his treatise "On Painting," finished around 1435. Vasari noted that many sixteenth-century artists admired Masaccio, but nonetheless, in the 1560s, he covered up one of Masaccio's most famous works in Santa Maria Novella (fig. **15.23**) when he remodeled the church. Ultimately, this action probably saved Masaccio's work, but much about its commissioning and meaning remains obscure.

Because the fresco originally stood above a tomb slab for the Lenzi family, many scholars have concluded that they commissioned Masaccio to paint the fresco depicting the Holy Trinity in the company of the Virgin, St. John the Evangelist, and the two donors. The lowest section depicts a skeleton lying on a sarcophagus. An inscription (in Italian) reads, "What I once was, you are; what I am, you will become." The large scale, balanced composition, and sculptural volume of the figures in this painting have their origins in the art of Giotto (see figs. 13.17–13.20). But although Giotto was a starting point for Masaccio, in Giotto's work, body and drapery form a single unit, whereas Masaccio's figures, like Donatello's, are "clothed nudes," whose drapery falls in response to the body underneath.

The setting reveals the artist's awareness of Brunelleschi's new architecture and of his system of perspective. (See *Materials and Techniques*, page 516.) The tall pilasters next to the painted columns recall the pilasters Brunelleschi designed for the Old Sacristy, as do the simple moldings that define the arch and the entablature of this fictive chapel. Masaccio's use of perspective gives the spectator all the data needed to measure the depth of this painted interior, to draw its plan, and to envision the structure in three dimensions. This barrel-vaulted chamber is not a shallow niche, but a deep space in which the figures can move freely. The

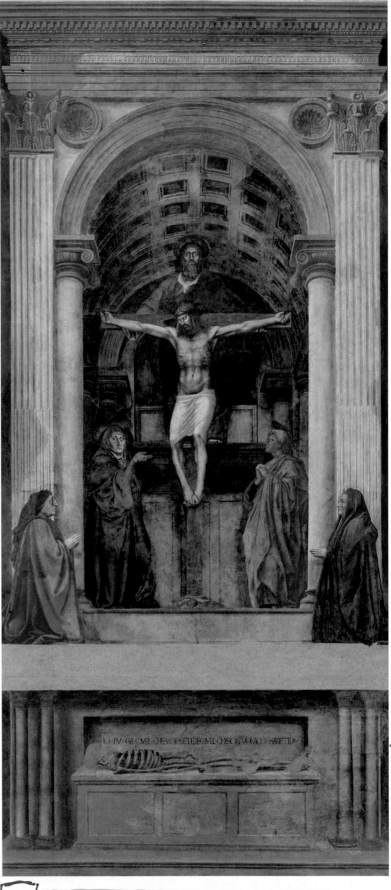

First fully-developed + accurate use of perspective

15.23 Masaccio, *The Holy Trinity with the Virgin, St. John, and Two Donors.* ca. 1425. Fresco, detached from wall, 21'10⅝ × 10'4¾" (6.67 × 3.17 m). Santa Maria Novella, Florence

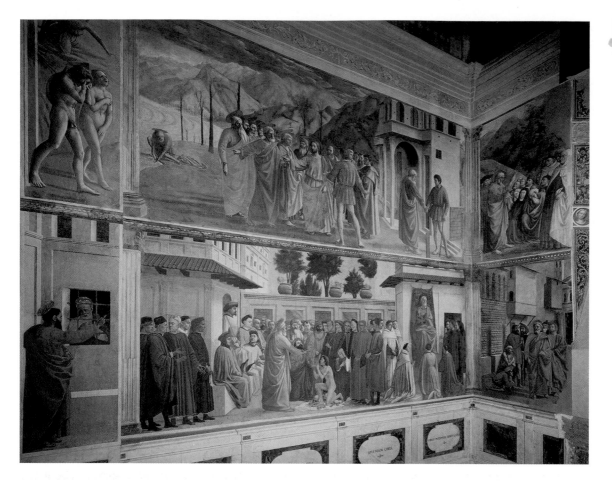

15.24 Left wall of Brancacci Chapel, Florence, with frescoes by Masaccio and others, Santa Maria del Carmine, Florence

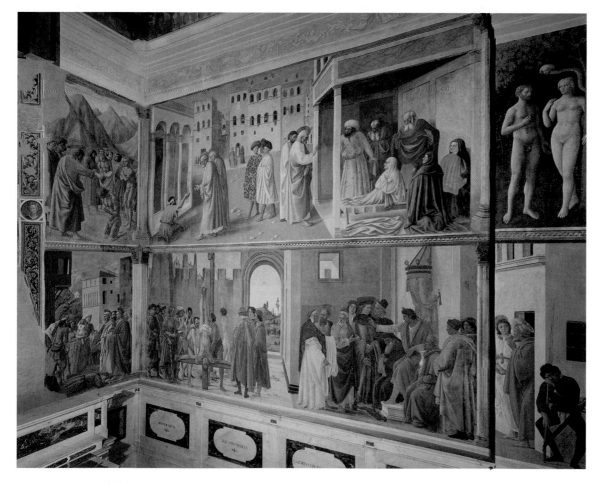

15.25 Right wall of Brancacci Chapel, Florence, with frescoes by Masaccio, Masolino, and Filippino Lippi, Santa Maria del Carmine, Florence

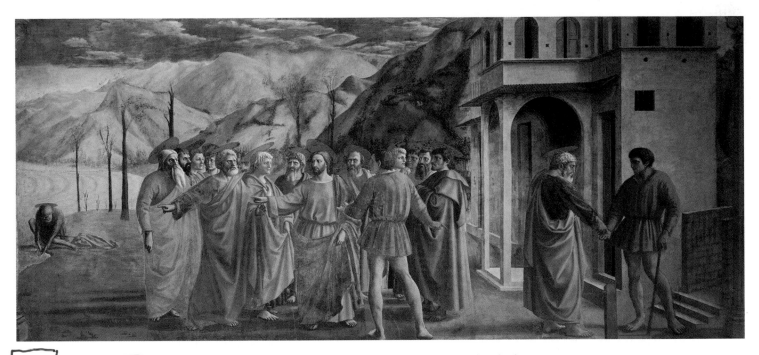

15.26 Masaccio, *The Tribute Money*. ca. 1425. Fresco, 8'1" × 19'7" (1.87 × 1.57 m). Brancacci Chapel, Florence

picture space is independent of the figures; they inhabit the space, but they do not create it. Masaccio used Brunelleschi's invention to create an illusion of space where none exists.

All the lines perpendicular to the picture plane converge toward a point below the foot of the Cross, on the platform that supports the kneeling donors. To see the fresco correctly, we must face this point, which is at an eye level somewhat more than 5 feet above the floor of the church. The figures within the chamber are 5 feet tall, slightly less than life-size, while the donors, who are closer to the viewer, are fully life-size. The framework therefore is "life-size," too, since it is directly behind the donors. The chapel that opens out behind them seems to belong to the same scale: It moves backward into space, covered by a barrel vault. That vault is subdivided by square **coffers**, an echo of the dome of the Pantheon (see fig. 7.25). The space seems measurable, palpable. However, the position of God the Father is puzzling. His arms support the Cross, close to the front plane, while his feet rest on a ledge attached to a wall. It is difficult to measure the distance to the ledge; if it is against the back wall, then the figure of God destroys the spatial effect. But why should the laws of perspective constrain God? Another possibility is that Masaccio intended to locate the ledge directly behind the Cross, as we can tell by the strong shadow that St. John casts on the wall below.

God the Father holds his son while the dove of the Holy Spirit is a further link between them. Masaccio further expresses the theme of the Trinity by the triangular composition that begins with the donors and rises to the halo of God. Color balances the composition, too, as opposing reds and blues unite in the garment worn by God. The whole scene has a tragic air, made more solemn by the calm gesture of the Virgin, as she points to the Crucifixion, and by the understated grief of St. John the Evangelist. The reality

of death but promise of resurrection is an appropriate theme for a funerary commemoration.

THE BRANCACCI CHAPEL If we are uncertain about the identity of the donors for the *Trinity* fresco, we do know who paid for the largest group of Masaccio's surviving works. To fulfill a bequest from his uncle Pietro, Felice Brancacci, a wealthy silk merchant and sometime ambassador, underwrote the frescoes in the Brancacci Chapel in Santa Maria del Carmine (figs. **15.24** and **15.25**). The frescoes depict the life of St. Peter. Work began in the chapel around 1425, when Masaccio collaborated with a slightly older painter named Masolino (1383–ca. 1440). The project was left incomplete when both artists were called away to work on other commissions. Masaccio went to Rome, where he died in 1428. The chapel remained unfinished until the Florentine painter Filippino Lippi (1457/58–1504) finally completed the lower tier on either side in the 1480s. These frescoes transform the space of the chapel into a display of narratives from Scripture.

The most famous of the frescoes is *The Tribute Money* by Masaccio, located in the upper tier (fig. **15.26**). It depicts the story told in the Gospel of Matthew (17:24–27) as a continuous narrative. In the center, Christ instructs Peter to catch a fish, whose mouth will contain money for the tax collector. On the far left, in the distance, Peter takes the coin from the fish's mouth, and on the right he gives it to the tax collector. Masaccio uses perspective to create a deep space for the narrative and to link the painting's space to the space of a viewer, Masaccio models the forms in the picture with light that seems to have its source in the real window of the chapel. He also uses atmospheric perspective in the subtle tones of the landscape to make the forms somewhat hazy, seen as well in the *Ghent Altarpiece* by Hubert and Jan van Eyck (see fig.

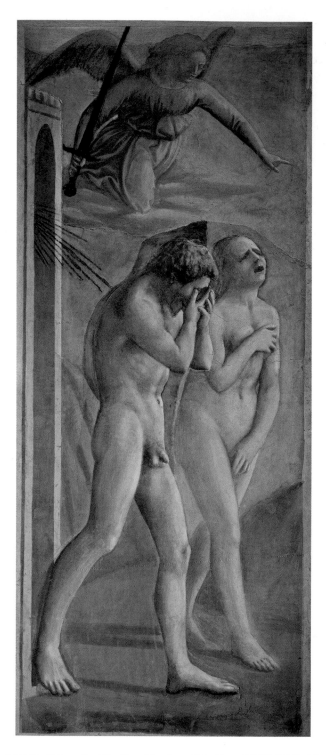

15.27 Masaccio, *The Expulsion from Paradise*. ca. 1425. Fresco, 7'1¼" × 10'35½" (214 × 90 cm). Brancacci Chapel, Florence.

14.10). The effect also recalls the setting used a decade earlier in Donatello's small relief of St. George (see fig. 15.12).

The figures in *The Tribute Money*, even more than those in the *Trinity* fresco, show Masaccio's ability to merge the weight and volume of Giotto's figures with the new functional view of body and drapery. The organization of the central group surrounding Christ seems to draw from Nanni di Banco's *Quattro Coronati* (see fig. 15.10), yet their balanced contrapposto poses may be

inspired by Donatello. Fine vertical lines scratched in the plaster establish the axis of each figure from the head to the heel of the engaged leg. In accord with this dignified approach, the figures seem rather static. Instead of employing violent physical movement, Masaccio's figures here convey the narrative by their intense glances and a few strong gestures.

In *The Expulsion from Paradise* just to the left (fig. **15.27**), however, Masaccio shows the human body in motion. The tall, narrow format of this fresco leaves little room for a spatial setting. The gate of Paradise is barely indicated, and in the background are a few shadowy, barren slopes. Yet the soft, atmospheric modeling, and especially the boldly foreshortened angel, convey a sense of unlimited space. Masaccio's grief-stricken Adam and Eve are striking representations of the beauty and power of the nude human form.

In contrast to the fluid grace of Gentile da Fabriano's painting (see figs. 15.21 and 15.22), Masaccio's paintings represent a less beautiful reality. However, at the Brancacci Chapel and elsewhere, Masaccio worked alongside Masolino, who had been strongly influenced by Gentile. The two painters worked well together and even collaborated on some of the frescoes. (The head of Christ in *The Tribute Money* may be by Masolino.) Nowhere is the contrast between the two artists' styles more striking than in *The Temptation* by Masolino (visible in the upper right of fig. 15.25). Where Masolino's figures of Adam and Eve are serenely beautiful nudes bathed in a diffuse natural light, Masaccio's express powerful emotion through their sheer physicality. Before he could finish the Brancacci Chapel, Masaccio left for Rome to work on another commission; he died there at a very young age, but his work stimulated other painters to experiment with perspectival space.

Florentine Painters in the Age of the Medici

Florentine politics played a role in delaying the completion of the Brancacci Chapel. The patron, Felice Brancacci, was the son-in-law of Palla Strozzi and part of a political faction that drove Cosimo de' Medici into exile in 1433. When Cosimo returned to Florence in 1434, he expelled both the Strozzi and the Brancacci from the city. The Medici family consolidated their power to become the most powerful family in Florence, a position they maintained until 1494.

Across four generations, Medici men were active in government and in business, while Medici women contributed to the social and religious life of the city. The family's wealth came from their mercantile and banking interests and the wise political alliances they struck both within Florence and in other Italian centers. As bankers to the pope, the Medici became leaders in the Florentine pro-papal party, and ultimately became the *de facto* rulers of the city.

Their fortunes had been made at the end of the fourteenth century by the shrewd investments of Giovanni di Bicci de' Medici (1360–1429). His son Cosimo (1389–1464) was involved in the factional disputes of the 1430s, resulting in his exile from the city in 1433. But in 1434 his party triumphed, and Cosimo returned as the leader of the Florentine government. Cosimo's sons Piero (1416–1469) and Giovanni (1421–1463) followed their father's example; and Piero's son, Lorenzo, called "The Magnificent" (1449–1492), became one of the most celebrated and well-connected men of the century. In addition to creating links to other prominent families in Florence and beyond, the Medici family promoted the literary and educational innovations of Florentine humanists, and actively used works of art to express their political and social status. This period of Medici domination saw the continued development of the stylistic innovations of the early fifteenth century along with new themes in art. Painters working in Florence from the 1430s to the 1460s were profoundly affected by the achievements of Masaccio and Donatello, Brunelleschi's antiquity-inspired architecture, and the drive toward greater naturalism. In addition, this generation of painters became very proficient at the technique of linear perspective. Their works executed for religious settings throughout the city treat sacred figures with a new reality.

FRA ANGELICO AT SAN MARCO With the support of Cosimo de' Medici, the Dominicans built a second convent for their friars in Florence in 1436. Among the members of this community was a talented painter from the Florentine countryside, Fra (Brother) Giovanni da Fiesole, called Fra Angelico (ca. 1400–1455). For this new community, Angelico painted altarpieces, books, and many frescoes in the friars' living quarters. His *Annunciation* fresco, executed between 1440 and 1445, is placed prominently at the entry to the dormitory (fig. **15.28**). Angelico sets the angel and Mary into a vaulted space very similar to the real architecture of the convent, itself inspired by Brunelleschi. A perspectival scheme defines the space, although the figures are too large to stand comfortably in it. The Virgin and the angel Gabriel glance at each other across the space; they humbly fold their hands, expressing their submission to divine will. The forms are graceful, and the overall scene is spare, rather than extravagant. The colors are pale, the composition has been pared to the minimum, and the light bathes all the forms in a soft glow. Angelico's composition has the simplicity and spatial sophistication of Masaccio (see fig. 15.26), with figures that are as graceful as Gentile da Fabriano's (see fig. 15.21). An inscription at the base of the fresco calls on the friars who pass by to say an Ave Maria. The fresco enhanced their life of prayer and contemplation, as was the goal of such imagery in religious communities.

CASTAGNO AT SANT'APOLLONIA Florence was home to many convents of women whose residents also wished to adorn their establishments. Unlike Fra Angelico, however, few nuns had the opportunity to train as painters to do the work themselves. Thus, professional painters like Andrea del Castagno (ca. 1423–1457) were hired to provide convent spaces with appropriate imagery. For the Benedictine convent of Sant'Apollonia,

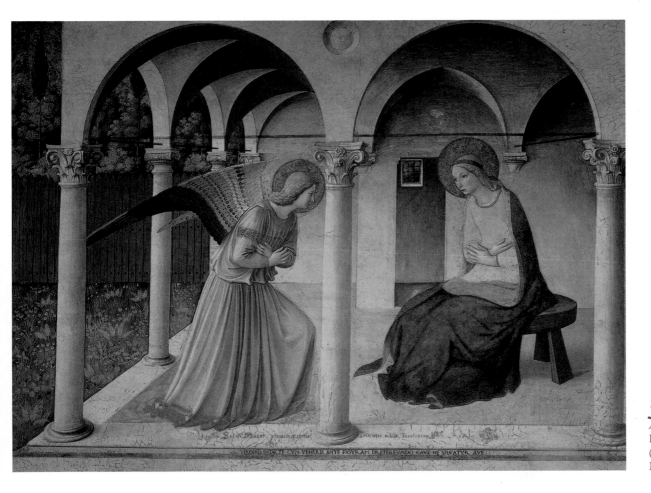

15.28 Fra Angelico, *Annunciation*. ca. 1440–45. Fresco, 7'1" × 10'6" (2.1 × 3.2 m). Museo di San Marco, Florence

Castagno painted his most famous fresco, *The Last Supper* (fig. **15.29**) around 1447. This fresco is the best preserved of a series he painted in the refectory (dining hall) of the convent. The image depicts the events of Holy Thursday, when Jesus and his apostles gather to dine, and Jesus reveals that he will be betrayed. Castagno sets the event in a richly paneled alcove framed by classicizing pilasters and other antique decorative elements. By skillfully using perspective, Castagno creates a stagelike space for the event. Strong contrasts of light and dark define sculpturally imagined figures seated around the table. As in medieval representations of the subject, Judas sits alone on the near side of the table. The symmetry of the architecture, emphasized by the colorful inlays, imposes a similar order among the figures and threatens to imprison them. There is little communication among the apostles—only a glance here, a gesture there—so that a brooding silence hovers over the scene. Breaking with the demands of tradition and perspective, Castagno used a daring device to disrupt the symmetry and focus on the drama of the scene. Five of the six marble panels on the wall behind the table are filled with subdued colored marble, but above the heads of St. Peter, Judas, and Jesus, the marble's veining is so garish and explosive that a bolt of lightning seems to descend on Judas' head to focus attention on these key figures. This theme often adorned Florentine refectories as the monks or nuns imitated Christ and the apostles as they dined. The sisters who dined in front of this fresco could see in it examples to follow and to avoid.

DOMENICO VENEZIANO AT SANTA LUCIA DEI MAGNOLI

Religious imagery adorned the altars of parish churches to instruct the laity. An important shift occurred in the design of altar panels in the 1440s, perhaps at the hands of Fra Angelico, that was soon adopted by many painters. Earlier altarpieces, like Gentile's *Adoration of the Magi* (see fig. 15.21), were complex ensembles with elaborately carved frames, but the newer altarpieces emphasized gilded carpentry less and geometric clarity more. For the main altar of the church of Santa Lucia dei Magnoli in Florence, Domenico Veneziano (ca. 1410–1461) executed the *Madonna and Child with Saints* around 1445 (fig. **15.30**). As his name suggests, Domenico was from Venice; he came to Florence in search of work in 1439. A letter he addressed to the son of Cosimo de' Medici in 1438 reveals that he knew about the commissions being awarded there (see *Primary Source*, page 534), while his work shows that he had studied Florentine artists. The altarpiece he painted for Santa Lucia depicts an enthroned Madonna and Child framed by architecture and surrounded by saints, including Zenobius, a patron saint of Florence, and Lucy, an early Christian martyr, who holds a dish containing her eyes.

The theme of the central Madonna surrounded by saints and sometimes angels is often termed a *sacra conversazione* (sacred conversation), which suggests that the image is not a narrative, but a glimpse of a heavenly court peopled by dignified and decorous courtiers. Domenico imagines this gathering in a light-filled loggia articulated with pink and green marble. The architecture is clear and convincing, yet the space it defines is an ideal one elevated above the everyday world. Domenico may have modeled this space on Masaccio's *Holy Trinity* fresco (see fig. 15.23), for his St. John (second from left) looks at us while pointing toward the Madonna, repeating the glance and gesture of Masaccio's Virgin. Domenico's perspective setting is worthy of Masaccio's, although his architectural forms have Gothic proportions and arches. The slim, sinewy bodies of the male saints, with their highly individualized, expressive faces, show Donatello's influence (see fig. 15.12).

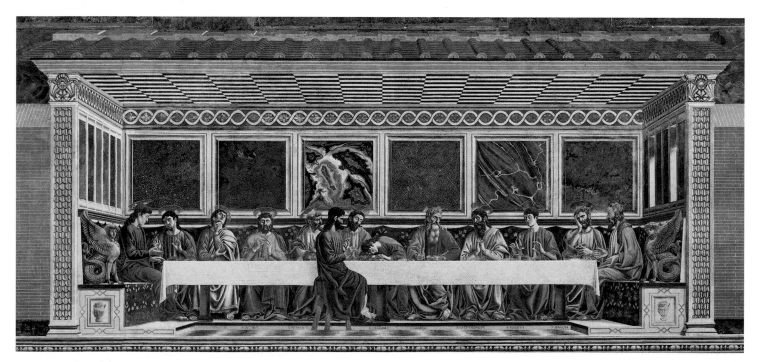

15.29   Andrea del Castagno, *The Last Supper*. ca. 1445–50. Fresco. Sant'Apollonia, Florence

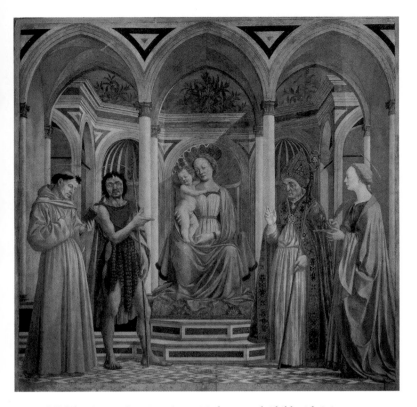

15.30 Domenico Veneziano, *Madonna and Child with Saints*. ca. 1445. Tempera on panel, 6'10" × 7' (2.08 × 2.13 m). Galleria degli Uffizi, Florence

Domenico treats color as an integral part of his work. This *sacra conversazione* is as noteworthy for its **palette** as for its composition. The blond tonality—its harmony of pink, light green, and white set off by spots of red, blue, and yellow—reconciles the brightness of Gothic panel painting with natural light and perspectival space. The sunlight streams in from the right, as revealed by the cast shadow behind the Madonna. The surfaces reflect the light so strongly that even the shadowed areas glow with color. Color, light, and space come together in this painting to make a heavenly vision in which the faithful may take comfort.

DOMESTIC LIFE: PALACES, FURNISHINGS, AND PAINTINGS IN MEDICEAN FLORENCE

Patrons like Giovanni Rucellai or Cosimo de' Medici asked artists to create works of art for their homes as well as for their churches. As family fortunes rose, palaces needed building or remodeling to provide an appropriate setting for family life and civic display. Furnishings within the home had to express the status of the family. Sculptures and paintings of new sorts, such as **cassone** paintings (see page 537), proclaimed the alliances between families. Works of art depicted new subjects, many of them inspired by antique art, which reflected the humanist educations of both artists and patrons. In sculpture, the long-lived Donatello was an

inspiration for younger sculptors like Pollaiuolo. Painters tacked between the grave simplicity of Masaccio and the idealized elegance of Gentile da Fabriano to find the right language to depict imagery drawn from the ancient world. Architects such as Michelozzo built family homes endowed with great dignity by their use of classical forms.

Palace Architecture

As their status rose in Florence, the Medici required a more lavish palace to house them and accommodate political and diplomatic functions. Nevertheless, Cosimo de' Medici turned down a design by Brunelleschi for this project, perhaps because he found it ostentatious. The commission went instead to a younger architect, Michelozzo di Bartolomeo (1396–1472), who had worked as a sculptor with both Ghiberti and Donatello. His design (fig. **15.31**) recalls the fortresslike Florentine palaces of old; it may have been this conservatism that appealed to Cosimo. (The windows on the ground floor were added by Michelangelo in 1516–17, and the whole was extended by the Riccardi family in the seventeenth century.)

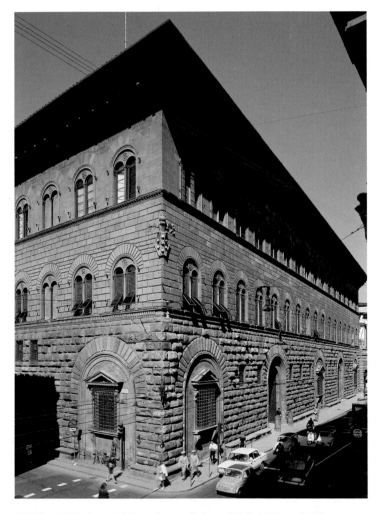

15.31 Michelozzo di Bartolomeo. Palazzo Medici-Riccardi, Florence. Begun 1444

Domenico Veneziano Solicits Work

The Venetian painter wrote to Piero de' Medici in 1438 requesting that he be considered for a commission that the family was about to award. The letter reveals Domenico's knowledge of the work to be done, and his arguments for why he should do it.

To the honorable and generous man Piero di Cosimo de' Medici of Florence. ...

Honorable and generous sir. After the due salutations. I inform you that by God's grace I am well. And I wish to see you well and happy. Many, many times I have asked about you. ... [A]nd having first learned where you were, I would have written to you for my comfort and duty. Considering that my low condition does not deserve to write to your nobility, only the perfect and good love I have for you and all your people gives me the daring to write, considering how duty-bound I am to do so.

Just now I have heard that Cosimo [Piero's father] has decided to have an altarpiece made, in other words painted, and wants a magnificent work, which pleases me very much. And it would please me more if through your generosity I could paint it. And if that happens, I am in hopes with God's help to do marvelous things, although there are good masters like Fra Filippo [Lippi] and Fra Giovanni [Angelico] who have much work to do. Fra Filippo in particular has a panel going to Santo Spirito which he won't finish in five years working day and night, it's so big. But however that may be, my great good will to serve you makes me presume to offer myself. And in case I should do less well than anyone at all, I wish to be obligated to any merited punishment, and to provide any test sample needed, doing honor to everyone. And if the work were so large that Cosimo decided to give it to several masters, or else more to one than to another, I beg you as far as a servant may beg a master that you may be pleased to enlist your strength favorably and helpfully to me in arranging that I may have some little part of it ... and I promise you my work will bring you honor. ...

By your most faithful servant Domenico da Veneziano painter, commending himself to you, in Perugia, 1438, first of April.

Source: Creighton Gilbert, ed., *Italian Art 1400–1500: Sources and Documents* (Evanston, IL: Northwestern University Press, 1992)

Michelozzo borrowed the rustication from the Palazzo della Signoria (see fig. 13.15), but he lightened the forms significantly. The three stories form a graded sequence: The lowest features

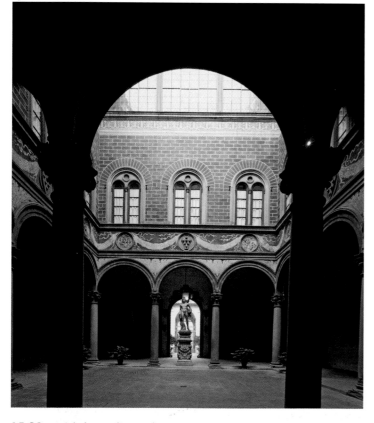

15.32 Michelozzo di Bartolomeo. Courtyard of Palazzo Medici-Riccardi

rough-hewn, "rusticated" masonry; the second has smooth-surfaced blocks; and the third has an unbroken surface. The building seems heavier on the bottom and lighter above. On top of the structure rests, like a lid, a strongly projecting cornice of the sort found on Roman temples. Inside, the spaces of the palace open to a central courtyard defined by an arcade resting on Brunelleschian classicizing columns (fig. **15.32**). The arcade supports a frieze with carved medallions featuring symbols favored by the Medici (the seven balls are on the Medici coat of arms) and **sgraffito ornament** (incised decorative designs). The double-lancet windows of the façade reappear here. The effect of the whole is to provide a splendid setting for Medici affairs: familial, social, commercial, and governmental. Thus, the large courtyard that dominates the interior is ceremonial as well as practical.

DONATELLO'S *DAVID* One of the most debated works of the Renaissance, Donatello's bronze *David* (fig. **15.33**), once stood on a high pedestal in the courtyard of the Medici palace. The *David* may be the first free-standing, life-size nude statue made since antiquity. The sheer expense of casting a whole figure of this sort in bronze, and with gilt parts, required a patron with the wealth of the Medici to pay for it. Using the lost-wax method of casting (see *Materials and Techniques*, page 128), Donatello composed the figure to be seen from every side, as the contrapposto stance and high finish of the work demand that a viewer walk around it.

Both the date of the *David* and its interpretation have sparked controversy. The evidence for its date is unclear; the only firm documentation places it in the Medici palace by 1469; scholars have proposed dates from the 1420s to 1460s. Much in the figure is difficult to square with the biblical story. The young David stands with his left foot atop the severed head of the giant

accentuate his nudity. David wields Goliath's sword, which is too large for him, and his gaze seems impassive when we consider the terror he has just confronted.

One key to the meaning of the *David* may be an inscription once written on its base that identified David as the defender of the fatherland: Since David had been venerated as a patron of the city, the Medici chose to appropriate this symbol of Florentine civic virtue and install it in their residence. (Donatello had earlier sculpted a marble image of David that stood in the Palazzo della Signoria, so even the choice of sculptor may be significant.) But scholars have debated the specific associations of the statue: one proposal is that the *David* celebrates a particular Florentine military victory, or perhaps a Medici political victory; another proposal is that it represents Florentine vigilance, or is a symbol of republican victory over tyranny. At the same time, its presence in the Medici palace may turn it into a symbol of dynastic power. All of this is made more complicated by the figure's youth and nudity. Our understanding of how fifteenth-century Florentines viewed the sculpture is still developing.

HERCULEAN IMAGES The Medici family appear to have made a habit of borrowing Florentine civic imagery for their palace. Sometime around 1475, Antonio del Pollaiuolo (1431–1498) executed the *Hercules and Antaeus* (fig. 15.34) for the family. Unlike

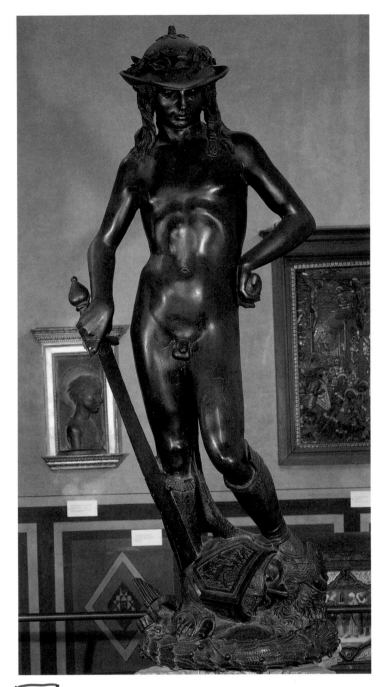

15.33 Donatello, *David*. ca. 1420s–60s. Bronze, height 5'2¼" (1.58 m). Museo Nazionale del Bargello, Florence

Goliath, whom he has miraculously defeated. Nonetheless, Donatello depicts the already victorious David still holding the stone that bought Goliath down. Most untraditionally, he also depicts David nude, which may be intended to suggest his status as a hero in the ancient mode. But instead of depicting him as a full-grown youth like the athletes of Greece, Donatello chose to model an adolescent boy with a softly sensuous torso, like Isaac in Ghiberti's competition panel (see fig. 15.2). The *David*'s contrapposto alludes to ancient sources, but it also gives the nude youth a languid pose, which some critics have seen as sexually suggestive. The broad-brimmed hat and knee-high boots seem to

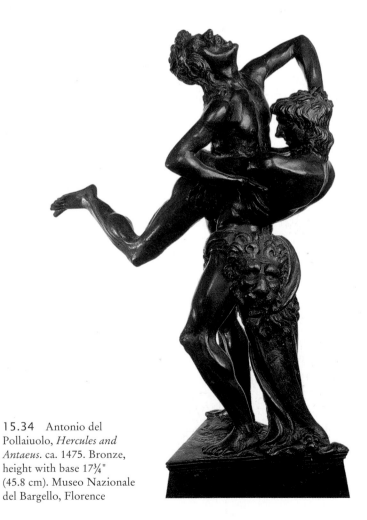

15.34 Antonio del Pollaiuolo, *Hercules and Antaeus*. ca. 1475. Bronze, height with base 17¾" (45.8 cm). Museo Nazionale del Bargello, Florence

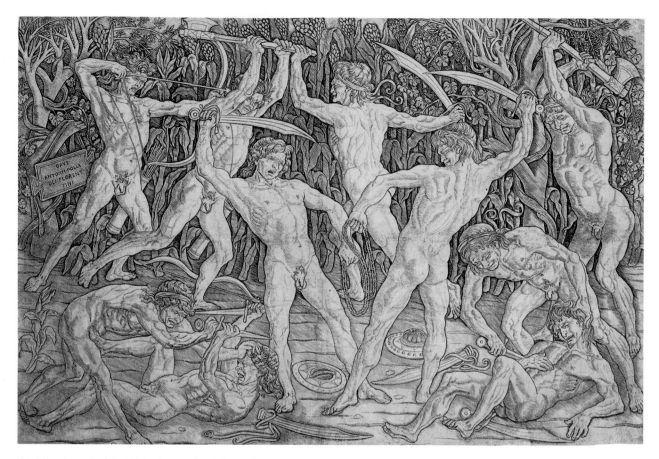

15.35 Antonio del Pollaiuolo, *Battle of the Nudes*. ca. 1465–70. Engraving, 15⅛" × 23¼" (38.3 × 59 cm). Cincinnati Art Museum, Ohio. Bequest of Herbert Greer French. 1943.118

the *David*, this is a table statue, only about 18 inches high, but it has the visual impact of a much larger object. It represents Hercules—another patron of Florence—battling Antaeus, the son of an earth goddess. Antaeus gains strength from contact with the earth, so Hercules must lift him off the ground to defeat him. Pollaiuolo had been trained as a goldsmith and metalworker, probably in the Ghiberti workshop, but was deeply impressed by the work of Donatello and Andrea del Castagno, as well as by ancient art. All these sources influence the distinctive style of the statuette.

To create a free-standing group of two struggling figures, even on a small scale, was a daring idea. There is no precedent for this design among earlier statuary groups, whether from antiquity or the Renaissance. Even bolder is the centrifugal force of the composition. Limbs seem to move outward in every direction, so the viewer must examine the statuette from all sides. Despite its violent action, the group is in perfect balance. To stress the central axis, Pollaiuolo in effect grafted the upper part of Antaeus onto the lower part of Hercules as he lifts him in a stranglehold. Pollaiuolo was a painter and engraver as well as a bronze sculptor, and we know that about 1465 he did a closely related painting of Hercules and Antaeus for the Medici.

Few of Pollaiuolo's paintings have survived, and only one engraving, the *Battle of the Nudes* (fig. **15.35**). The latter is one of Pollaiuolo's most elaborate designs. Its subject is not known, though it may derive from an ancient text. One purpose the engraving serves is to display the artist's mastery of the nude body in action and thus to advertise his skill. This may account for the prominent signature in the print; he signs it *"Opus Antonii Pollaioli Florentini"* ("The work of Antonio Pollaiuolo of Florence"). In 1465–70, when the print must have been produced, depicting the nude in action was still a novel problem, which Pollaiuolo explored in his paintings, sculptures, and prints. He realized that a full understanding of movement demanded a detailed knowledge of anatomy, down to the last muscle and sinew. These naked men look almost as if their skin has been stripped off to reveal the play of muscles underneath. So, to a lesser extent, do the two figures of Pollaiuolo's statuette *Hercules and Antaeus*.

Paintings for Palaces

The interiors of patrician palaces served not only as private quarters and settings for family life, but as public spaces where family members performed civic roles. A visitor would find paintings and perhaps sculptures, many on religious subjects, in these buildings. Indeed, early in the fifteenth century, one of the leading clerics of Tuscany urged that religious images be displayed in private homes. In a treatise written in 1403, Cardinal Giovanni Dominici counseled that images of Christ, Mary, and saints in the home would encourage children to emulate those holy figures. (See *Primary Source*, page 539.)

Patrician homes also showcased **cassoni** (sing. cassone), carved or painted chests for storing valuables. The product of collaboration between skilled carpenters, woodworkers, and painters, such chests were usually decorated, sometimes with military imagery, like the one in figure **15.36**, which bears the arms of the Strozzi family. This chest probably came from the busy workshop of Apollonio di Giovanni (1414–1465) and Marco del Buono Giamberti (1402–1489). Its front panel depicts the conquest of Trebizond (a town on the Black Sea) by Turkish forces in 1461; as a result, Venetian traders were expelled and Florence increased its influence in the Mediterranean. The busy composition features small figures battling in front of a city wall; their armor is gilded to create a sumptuous surface. Antique-inspired scrolls flank the narrative, while the heavy lid and base shine with gold.

Cassoni were also adorned with scenes from mythology, history, and romance. Pairs of cassoni were usually given to a bride on her wedding; they mark the union of two families, and thus reflect family status as much as nuptial concerns. Edifying or learned stories on cassoni often derived from studies of ancient authors such as Plutarch, Ovid, or Vergil. Thus, cassone panels displayed a family's wealth, their learning and interest in humanism, sometimes their patriotism, and very often lessons for a bride to take with her to her new home.

Another type of domestic decoration was the circular painting, or **tondo**, which was something of a Florentine specialty. Many of the leading painters of the middle and later decades of the fifteenth century produced tondi, including Fra Filippo Lippi

(ca. 1406–1469), to whom has been attributed the *Madonna and Child with the Birth of the Virgin* (fig. **15.37**). The Florentine banker Lionardo Bartolini Salimbeni may have commissioned this panel to commemorate a birth in his family. Lippi presents the Madonna and infant Jesus as an exemplary mother and child. Fra Filippo's youthful Mary has a slender elegance and gentle sweetness that may derive from Fra Angelico's work (see fig. 15.28), although his figures and setting are more complicated and ornate. The curly edge of the Virgin's headdress and the curved folds of her mantle streaming to the left, which accentuate her turn to the right, add a lyrical quality to her figure. The child Jesus picks seeds out of a pomegranate, an emblem of eternal life. At the same time, the seeds may also symbolize fertility, since the secondary theme here is St. Anne giving birth to the Virgin.

Behind the Virgin is a stagelike scene that is surprisingly cluttered, created by a perspective scheme with several vanishing points. In the background to the left is a domestic interior showing the Virgin's birth, with St. Anne in childbed. To the right is the meeting of St. Anne and her husband, St. Joachim at the Golden Gate of Jerusalem, after an angel had appeared to them separately and promised them a child. In contrast to all other depictions of this legend, the event in this painting is presented as if it were taking place before the entrance to a private house.

Lippi could have learned to use this kind of continuous narrative from reliefs by Donatello and Ghiberti: Compare *The Feast of Herod* (see fig. 15.13) and *The Story of Jacob and Esau* (see fig. 15.17), which incorporate similarly complex spaces to tell their stories. Lippi quotes from Ghiberti's relief in this tondo in the figure of the maidservant to the right of the Virgin. After Masaccio's

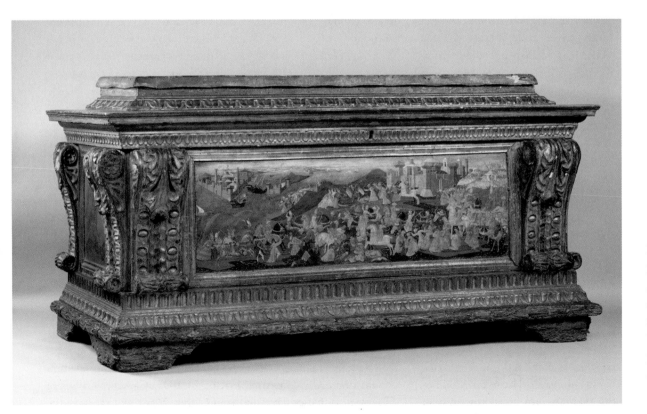

15.36 Marco del Buono Giamberti and Apollonio di Giovanni di Tomaso. Cassone with the Conquest of Trebizond. ca. 1461–65. Tempera, gold, and silver on wood, 39½ × 77 × 32⅞" (100.3 × 195.6 × 83.5 cm). Metropolitan Museum of Art, New York. John Stewart Kennedy Fund, 1914 (14.39)

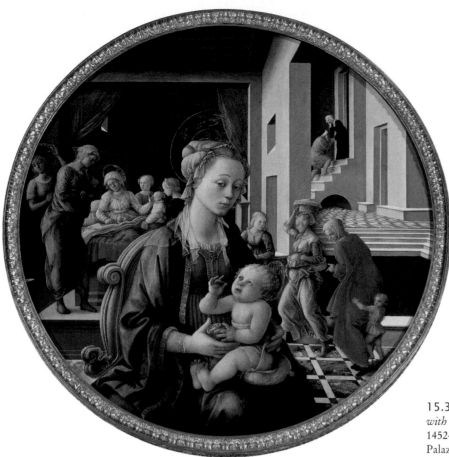

15.37 Fra Filippo Lippi, *Madonna and Child with the Birth of the Virgin* (*The Bartolini Tondo*). 1452–53. Tempera on panel, diameter 53" (134.6 cm). Palazzo Pitti, Florence

death, the age, experience, and prestige of Donatello and Ghiberti gave them an authority unmatched by any other painter active at the time. Their influence, and that of the Flemish masters, on Fra Filippo's outlook was of great importance, since he played a vital role in setting the course of Florentine painting during the second half of the century.

UCCELLO'S *BATTLE OF SAN ROMANO* The same family linked to Lippi's tondo commissioned a set of wall paintings with a fascinating history. The Florentine artist Paolo Uccello (1397–1475) painted the *Battle of San Romano* (fig. **15.38**) as one of three panels depicting a battle between Florence and Lucca in 1432. Florence's victory in this battle was one of the factors that led to Cosimo de' Medici's consolidation of power. Uccello depicts the charge of the Florentine forces led by Cosimo's ally, Niccolò da Tolentino, the man on the white horse wielding a general's baton at the center of the painting. Because of the importance of this subject to the Medici, scholars long believed that they commissioned this painting. The series was identified as one described as hanging in Lorenzo de' Medici's bedroom in a document of 1492. Recent research, however, shows that it was Lionardo Bartolini Salimbeni, who was a member of the governing council of Florence during the battle, who commissioned Uccello to paint these panels for his town house in Florence around 1438. After his death, Lorenzo de' Medici sought to

obtain them, first by purchase and, when that failed, by force. The sons of the original owner filed a lawsuit for their return. These circumstances suggest the importance of the paintings for both families.

Uccello's painting seems to record a ceremony rather than a war, as the plastic shapes of the figures and horses march across a grid consisting of discarded weapons and pieces of armor. These objects form the orthogonals of a perspective scheme that is neatly arranged to include a fallen soldier. A thick hedge of bushes defines this foreground plane, beyond which appears a landscape that rises up the picture plane rather than receding deeply into space. Spots of brilliant color and a lavish use of gold reinforce the surface pattern, which would have been more brilliant originally, as some of the armor is covered in silver foil that has now tarnished. Such splendid surfaces remind us of the paintings of Gentile da Fabriano (see fig. 15.21). Uccello's work owes much to International Gothic displays of lavish materials and flashes of natural observation, with the added element of perspectival renderings of forms and space.

MYTHOLOGIES FOR MEDICI PALACES In addition to acquiring paintings in Florence through commission, purchase, or force, the Medici had numerous contacts with northern Europe, not only through diplomatic exchanges, but through their banking business. Medici agents in Bruges sent many works of art to Florence, as inventories confirm. In this, the Medici behaved as

Giovanni Dominici Urges Parents to Put Religious Images in Their Homes

Florentine by birth, Dominici entered the Dominican order, where he became involved with reform. Among his writings was the Regola del governo di cura familiare *(Rule for the Management of Family Care) of 1403, from which this excerpt is taken.*

Part IV [on the management of children]. In the first consideration, which is to bring them up for God … you should observe five little rules. … The first is to have paintings in the house, of holy little boys or young virgins, in which your child when still in swaddling clothes may delight, as being like himself, and may be seized upon by the like thing, with actions and signs attractive to infancy. And as I say for painting, so I say of sculptures. The Virgin Mary is good to have, with the child on her arm, and the little bird or the pomegranate in his fist. A good figure would be Jesus suckling, Jesus sleeping on his mother's lap, Jesus standing politely before her, Jesus making a hem and the mother sewing that hem. In the same way he may mirror himself in the holy Baptist, dressed in camel skin, a small boy entering the desert, playing with birds, sucking on the sweet leaves, sleeping on the ground. It would do no harm if he saw Jesus and the Baptist, the little Jesus and the Evangelist grouped together, and the murdered innocents, so that fear of arms and armed men would come over him. And so too little girls should be brought up in the sight of the eleven thousand virgins, discussing, fighting and praying. I would like them to see Agnes with the fat lamb, Cecilia crowned with roses, Elizabeth with many roses, Catherine on the wheel, with other figures that would give them love of virginity with their mothers' milk, desire for Christ, hatred of sins, disgust at vanity, shrinking from bad companions, and a beginning, through considering the saints, of contemplating the supreme saint of saints. … I warn you if you have paintings in your house for this purpose, avoid frames of gold and silver, lest they become more idolatrous than faithful, since, if they see more candles lit and more hats removed and more kneeling to figures that are gilded and adorned with precious stones than to the old smoky ones, they will only learn to revere gold and jewels, and not the figures, or rather, the truths represented by those figures.

Source: Creighton Gilbert, ed., *Italian Art 1400–1500: Sources and Documents* (Evanston, IL: Northwestern University Press, 1992)

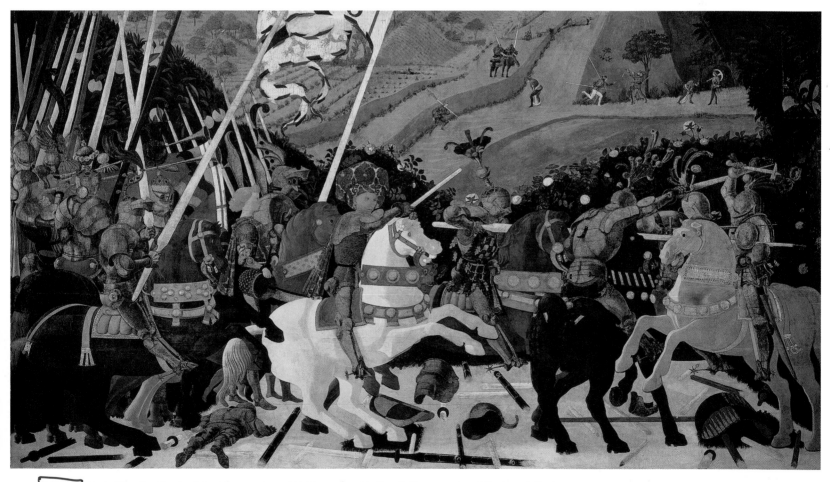

15.38 Paolo Uccello, *Battle of San Romano*. ca. 1438. Tempera and silver foil on wood panel, 6' × 10'5¾" (1.8 × 3.2 m). The National Gallery, London.

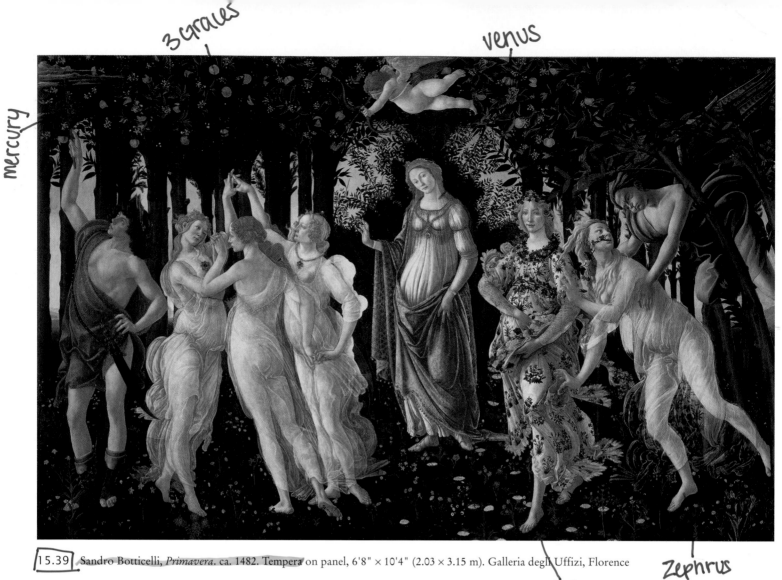

15.39 Sandro Botticelli, *Primavera*. ca. 1482. Tempera on panel, 6'8" × 10'4" (2.03 × 3.15 m). Galleria degli Uffizi, Florence

did many of the ruling families of Italy, for Flemish art was widely admired in places as disparate as Naples, Venice, Ferrara, Urbino, and Milan. Through such acquisitions, the Medici palace was filled with panel paintings and tapestries from the North. These objects made a profound impression on Florentine artists like Paolo Uccello, Filippo Lippi, Domenico Ghirlandaio, and the young Sandro Botticelli.

Botticelli (1445–1510), who had trained with Fra Filippo Lippi, became one of the favorite painters of the Medici circle—the group of nobles, scholars, and poets surrounding Lorenzo the Magnificent, the head of the Medici family and, for all practical purposes, the real ruler of the city from 1469 until 1492. The *Primavera* (*Spring*) (fig. **15.39**) was probably painted for a cousin who grew up in the household of Lorenzo the Magnificent. This work, and two others on the theme of love, may have been commissioned for the young man's wedding, which took place in 1482, the date often proposed for the painting.

Scholars have proposed numerous interpretations of this image. The painting depicts Venus in her sacred grove, with Eros flying overhead. Her companions, the Three Graces and Hermes (the Roman god Mercury), stand on the left; to the right, the wind-god Zephyr reaches for the nymph Chloris, whom he

then transforms into Flora, the goddess of flowers. One interpretation links the *Primavera* to the writings of the Neo-Platonist philosopher Marsilio Ficino (1433–1499), who was widely read and admired at the Medici court. Ficino assigned to Venus the virtues (or graces) desirable in women. With her modest garment and gentle gestures, Venus is the reigning divinity in this fertile garden. At left, Mercury keeps clouds away, while Flora embodies fertility. Other readings of the *Primavera* see it as an allegory about the immortality of the soul (drawing a parallel between the story of Chloris and the Rape of Persephone). Since the painting was made in connection with a wedding, it may be a celebration of marriage and fertility, as the dense thicket of orange trees and carpet of flowers seem to suggest.

Often paired with the *Primavera* in the public imagination is Botticelli's most famous image, *The Birth of Venus* (fig. **15.40**), which also once hung in a Medici villa. It may have been painted several years later, however. In this painting, too, the central figure in the composition is Venus, though here she floats slowly toward the shore, where a flower-clad woman waits to enfold her in a flowered robe. Her movement is aided by Zephyr accompanied by Chloris (Flora). Unlike the *Primavera*, here the space behind the figures seems to open out into the distance, with the

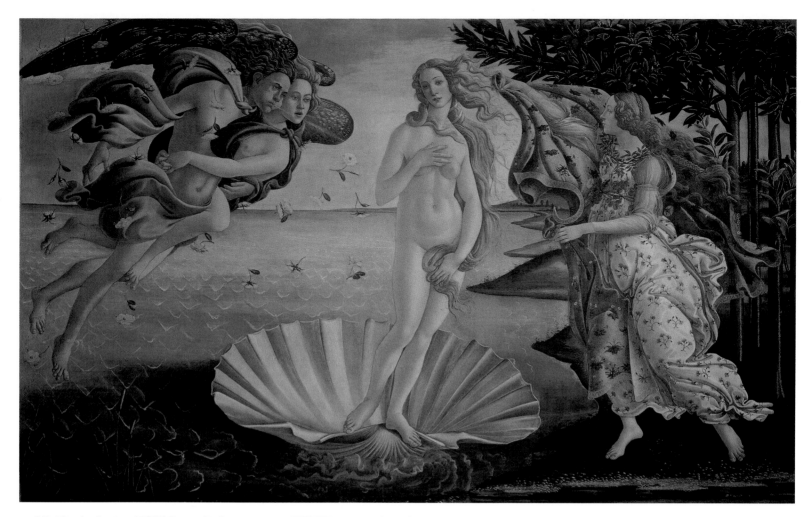

15.40   Sandro Botticelli, *The Birth of Venus*. ca. 1485. Tempera on panel, 5'8⅞" × 9'1⅞" (1.8 × 2.8 m). Galleria degli Uffizi, Florence

sky and water creating a light, cool tonality for the painting. In the figures, though, the shallow modeling and emphasis on outline produce an effect of low relief rather than of solid, three-dimensional shapes. The bodies seem to be drained of all weight, so that they float even when they touch the ground.

These ethereal figures re-create ancient forms. Botticelli's figure of *Venus* depends on a variant of the *Aphrodite of Knidas* by Praxiteles (see fig. 5.56). The subject itself seems related to the Homeric *Hymn to Aphrodite*, which begins: "I shall sing of beautiful Aphrodite…who is obeyed by the flowery sea-girt land of Cyprus, whither soft Zephyr and the breeze wafted her in soft foam over the waves. Gently the golden-filleted Horae received her, and clad her in divine garments." Still, no single literary source accounts for the pictorial conception. It may owe something to Ovid and the poet Poliziano, who was, like Botticelli, a member of the Medici circle. But again, the thinking of Marsilio Ficino may play a role here. Among the Neo-Platonists, Venus appears in two guises, a celestial Venus and a mundane Venus; the former was a source of divine love, the latter of physical love. *The Birth of Venus* may be an allegory of the origin of the celestial Venus for an audience attuned to the nuances of Neo-Platonic philosophy. The elegant forms and high finish of the painting,

combined with the erudite subject matter based on ancient thought, exemplify the taste of the Medici court.

Portraiture

Images of history, of contemporary events, or of ancient myths demonstrate the increasing interest in secular themes in the art of the Renaissance. Another genre of image in great demand was the portrait. In addition to dynastic images for kings, or monuments to war heroes, the second half of the fifteenth century saw the spread of portraits of merchants, brides, and artists.

The idea of recording specific likenesses was inspired by the fifteenth century's increasing awareness of the individual, but also by the study of Roman art, where portraits abound. Artists were already making donor portraits like Masaccio's *Trinity* fresco (see fig. 15.23), funerary monuments like Bruni's tomb (fig. 15.18), and commemorations of public figures like Donatello's *Gattamelata* (fig. 15.14), but new forms of portraiture developed in the fifteenth century.

The Florentine painter Domenico Ghirlandaio (1449–1494) inserted portraits of his patrons and their families into the many fresco cycles he painted, but he also made portraits as stand-alone

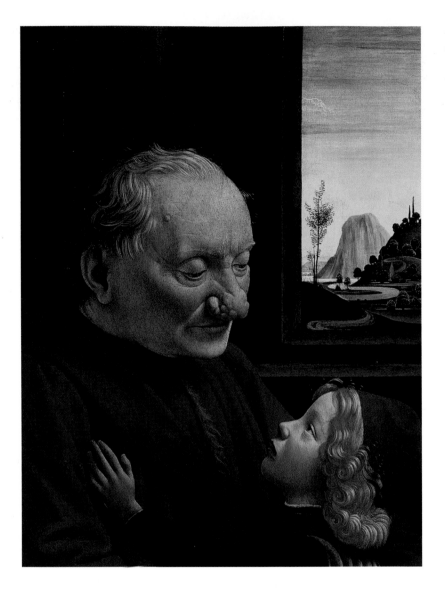

15.41 Domenico Ghirlandaio, *An Old Man and a Young Boy*. ca. 1480. Tempera and oil on wood panel, 24⅛ × 18" (61.2 × 45.4 cm). Musée du Louvre, Paris

paintings. Florentine artists before Ghirlandaio, as he himself did too, produced profile portraits in emulation of Roman coins. But around 1480, both Ghirlandaio and his younger colleague Botticelli began to adopt the three-quarter view (the sitter half turned toward the viewer, between profile and frontal gaze) in their portraits, and the practice soon became widespread. Both profile and three-quarter views appear in Ghirlandaio's most touching individual portrait, *An Old Man and a Young Boy* (fig. 15.41), usually dated to around 1480. Despite the very specific physiognomy of the old man, whose nose has been disfigured by rosacea (a skin disorder), the sitters and their relationship to each other are unknown. Their intimate gestures suggest that they represent two generations of one family; if so, the painting depicts the continuity of the family line. Leon Battista Alberti defined the function of portraits as being "to make the absent present," which may be the case with this image; it appears to be based on a drawing taken at the time of the old man's death. The connection between generations depicted in this family group may be more symbolic than real. Even though the textures are somewhat generalized and the composition geometrically ordered, Ghirlandaio's attention to detail may reflect his acquaintance with

Netherlandish art. The landscape view through the window that breaks up the picture plane was also a northern European idea (see fig. 14.21). But the most important contribution was the three-quarter view of the human face, which had been used in Flanders since the 1420s.

Portraits in three dimensions enjoyed a certain vogue in the fifteenth century, too, especially among the wealthiest families. The Medici commissioned numerous family likenesses for their palaces and for their friends, but they preferred the **portrait bust**, a shoulder-length sculptural likeness. This form was most likely to draw parallels between themselves and Roman families who owned numerous busts of their ancestors (see fig. 7.12). The Florentine busts celebrated the living, however, not the dead, and were made of marble, bronze, or terra cotta by some of the leading sculptors of the century. Piero de' Medici and his wife, Lucrezia Tornabuoni, were recorded in such busts, as were their sons, Giuliano and Lorenzo de' Medici. The format was used for portraits of both men and women, including that shown in figure 15.42. Dated to around 1475–80, this marble bust by Verrocchio depicts a young woman holding a bouquet. It is unusual in showing the sitter in half-length, which gives the artist room to render her

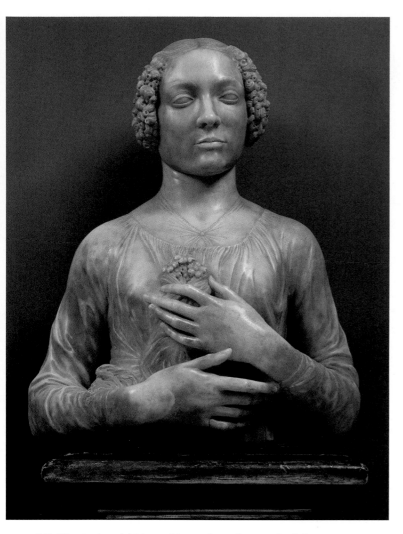

15.42 Andrea del Verrocchio, *Lady with a Bunch of Flowers*. ca. 1475. Marble, height 23²/₃" (60 cm). Museo Nazionale del Bargello, Florence

Savonarola, who attacked the "cult of paganism" and the materialism he saw in Florentine culture. Savonarola's exhortations to repentance and his strong criticism of corruption, not only in Florence but in the church hierarchy, made him many enemies, and he was executed in 1498. As the fifteenth century came to an end, Florence was battling for its life against the stronger powers of the papacy, Spain, and France.

RENAISSANCE ART THROUGHOUT ITALY, 1450–1500

Artists from all over Italy and well beyond found in the innovations being explored in Florence a stimulus for their own work, though they responded to the new styles in individual ways. Additionally, patrons throughout Italy saw the advantages of expressing their authority through visual and textual references to antiquity. By midcentury, linear perspective was in widespread use, and Florentine techniques for rendering form through light were being practiced by many artists. Piero della Francesca blended his own fascination with mathematics, the ancient world, and Flemish painting to create a personal style that found favor in several Italian courts. The Florentine humanist and architect Leon Battista Alberti designed influential buildings in northern Italy, including one for the marquis of Mantua, who had also attracted the services of the painter-archaeologist Andrea Mantegna. The city of Venice commissioned Florentine artists, such as Andrea del Verrocchio, for major projects, but local traditions in architecture and painting remained strong. Venetian painters like Giovanni Bellini developed an influential school that rivaled the Florentine style. As the papacy regained its control in Rome, Perugino and Luca Signorelli created projects designed to celebrate papal power.

Piero della Francesca in Central Italy

One of the most distinctive and original artists of the second half of the fifteenth century was Piero della Francesca (ca. 1420–1492), who visited Florence while training with Domenico Veneziano (see fig. 15.30). Piero came from Borgo San Sepolcro in southeastern Tuscany, where he completed some of his earliest commissions. He worked for patrons in Tuscany, Rimini, and Ferrara, and executed several important works for Federico da Montefeltro, a *condottiere* (mercenary general) turned ruler of Urbino (southeast of Tuscany) around 1470. Piero's early training with Domenico Veneziano may be seen in his use of color, while his experience of Masaccio is apparent in the solidity and simplicity of his forms and the solemn character of his compositions. The early fifteenth-century systemization of perspective was critical for Piero, who became such an expert at mathematically determining perspective and at rendering figures in space that he wrote a treatise about it. It is likely that Piero made contact with Leon Battista Alberti, with whom he shared patrons, as well as an interest in art theory.

expressive hands. Her hair is arranged fashionably, though her garment is simple. Verrocchio manipulates the marble to distinguish textural effects of hair, eyebrows, flowers, and the transparent undergarment buttoned at her neck. The slight tilt of her head and the placement of her hands give the figure movement and grace. Although speculation about her identity has suggested a connection to Lorenzo de' Medici, the identity of the lady in this lyrical portrait remains unknown.

The court around Lorenzo the Magnificent was learned, ambitious, and very cultivated. Lorenzo was the patron of numerous humanists, philosophers, poets, and artists, including the young Michelangelo. Yet this brilliant court did not outlast Lorenzo's death in 1492. His heir, Piero de' Medici, did not share his father's diplomatic gifts. What is more, he faced an increasingly unstable economy (the bank failed in 1494) and invading armies from France and Spain. Piero's inept handling of these crises encouraged an uprising in Florence in 1494, which expelled the Medici faction and sought to restore republican government. The power vacuum was filled for a time by the Dominican friar Girolamo

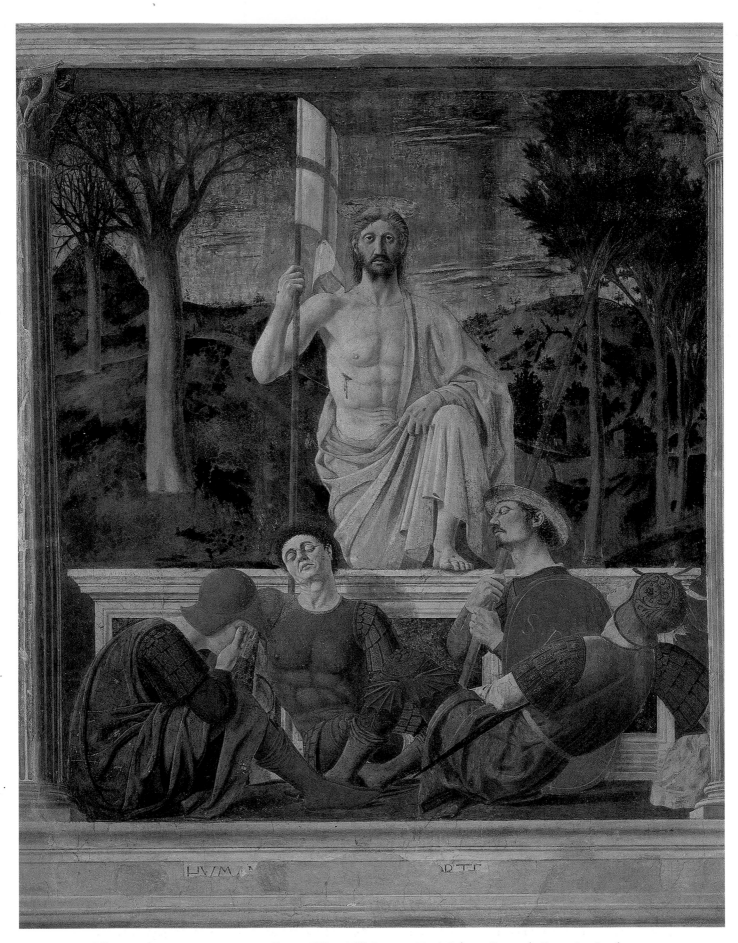

15.43   Piero della Francesca, *Resurrection*. ca. 1463. Fresco, 7'5" × 6'6½" (2.25 × 1.99 m). Palazzo Comunale, Borgo San Sepolcro

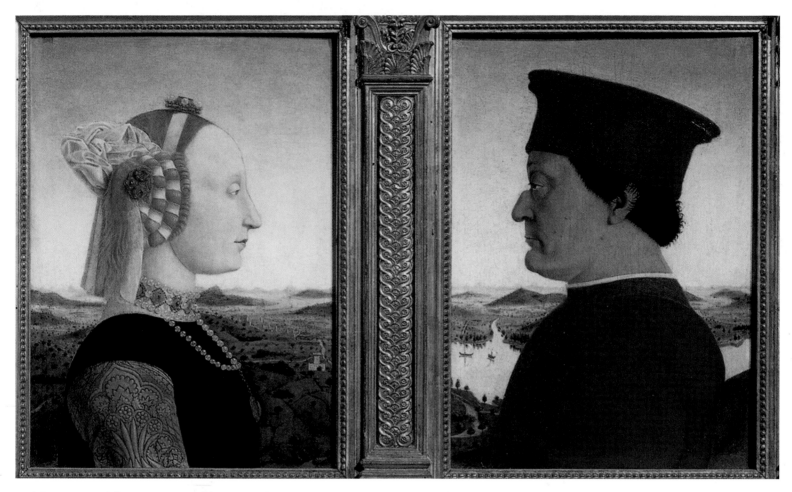

15.44 Piero della Francesca, *Double Portrait of Battista Sforza and Federico da Montefeltro*. ca. 1474. Oil and tempera on panel, each panel 18½ × 13" (47 × 33 cm). Galleria degli Uffizi, Florence

A work that Piero made for his hometown reflects this combination of influences on his art. The city of Borgo San Sepolcro commissioned him to paint a fresco for its Palazzo Comunale, probably around 1460. Befitting the name of the town, which means the "Holy Sepulcher," Piero's theme is Christ Resurrected stepping out of his tomb (fig. **15.43**). The figure of Christ dominates the composition: His frontality and the triangular composition may derive from works like the *Trinity* fresco by Masaccio (see fig. 15.23), but the light of sunrise and the pale colors reflect the art of Domenico Veneziano. The contrast offered by the dead trees on the left and the living ones on the right adds to the theme of resurrection. Piero pays special attention to the arrangement of the Roman soldiers asleep in front of the sepulcher; they are variations on a theme of bodies in space. The spectator must look up to see the glorified body of Christ, so perfect in his anatomy and so serene in his aspect as he triumphs over death. Columns, soldiers, and tomb are all rendered as if seen from below, displaying Piero's mastery of perspective.

Piero's art brought him to the attention of the cultivated Duke Federico da Montefeltro, who attracted artists from all over Europe to his court at Urbino. There, Piero came into contact, and perhaps competition, with artists not only from Italy but also from Spain and Flanders. From them, Piero learned the new technique of painting with oil glazes and became an early practitioner of this technique in central Italy. Piero's quiet, spatially complex paintings were thus enriched with more brilliant colors and surface textures in the style of Flemish art. Piero painted a double portrait of the duke and duchess (fig. **15.44**) about 1474. This painting demonstrates Piero's mastery of spatial representation and clarity of form by using the rich hues and varied textures made possible by oil painting. The diptych portrays both the duke and his wife in profile facing each other in front of a deep, continuous landscape. Presented in a complex gilded frame, the diptych appears much larger and monumental than it really is. Federico, whose face had been disfigured in a tournament, shows his good side. He is depicted on the reverse of his portrait in ducal garb, suggesting a date for the painting after 1474. His wife, Battista, had been dead for two years by then, six months after providing him with a son and heir. Piero gives her the place of honor to the viewer's left. Her pale features are framed by her complicated hairstyle and her gems and brocades. A shadow falls over the landscape behind her, while the landscape behind her husband is lighter and busier. The rigid profiles placed against the low horizon and deep landscape give the figures an unapproachable and monumental appearance. Piero's balanced and spacious composition results in an image of calm authority and triumph.

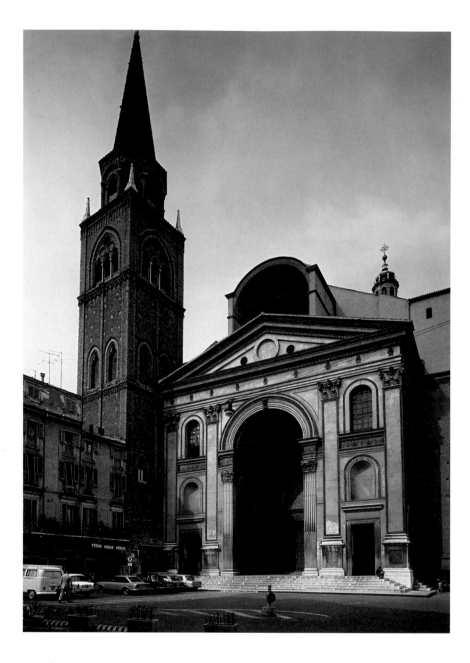

15.45 Leon Battista Alberti. Church of Sant'Andrea, Mantua. Designed 1470

Alberti and Mantegna in Mantua

Duke Federigo was a relative newcomer to power in Urbino, but Mantua, in the northern Po Valley, had been dominated for more than a century by the Gonzaga family. They created a brilliant court, peopled with humanists, educators, and artists. Marquis Ludovico Gonzaga had married a German princess, Barbara of Brandenburg, and the court was very cosmopolitan. Works such as the *Ten Books on Architecture* (ca. 1452) brought Leon Battista Alberti great prominence and the Gonzaga lured him to their service.

In 1470, Alberti had designed the church of Sant'Andrea in Mantua, his last work (fig. **15.45**). The majestic façade expresses Alberti's ultimate goal of merging classical temple forms with the traditional basilican church. Here, he interweaves a triumphal arch motif, now with a huge recessed center niche to serve as the portal, with a classical temple front. To keep the two competing forms in equilibrium, he uses flat pilasters that stress the primacy of the wall surface. Two sizes of pilaster achieve this balance: The smaller pilasters support the arch over the huge central niche, and the larger ones support the unbroken architrave and the strongly outlined pediment. The larger pilasters form what is known as a **colossal order**, meaning that it is more than one story high. These tall pilasters balance the horizontal and vertical elements of the design.

To further unify the façade, Alberti inscribed the entire design within a square, even though it made the façade much lower than the height of the nave. (The effect of the west wall protruding above the pediment appears more disturbing in photographs than from street level, where it can hardly be seen.) While the façade is distinct from the main body of the structure, it offers a "preview" of the interior, where the same colossal order, the same proportions, and the same triumphal-arch motif reappear on the walls of the nave (fig. **15.46**). Unlike the façade of Santa Maria Novella (see fig. 15.9), Alberti announced the interior elevation on the exterior.

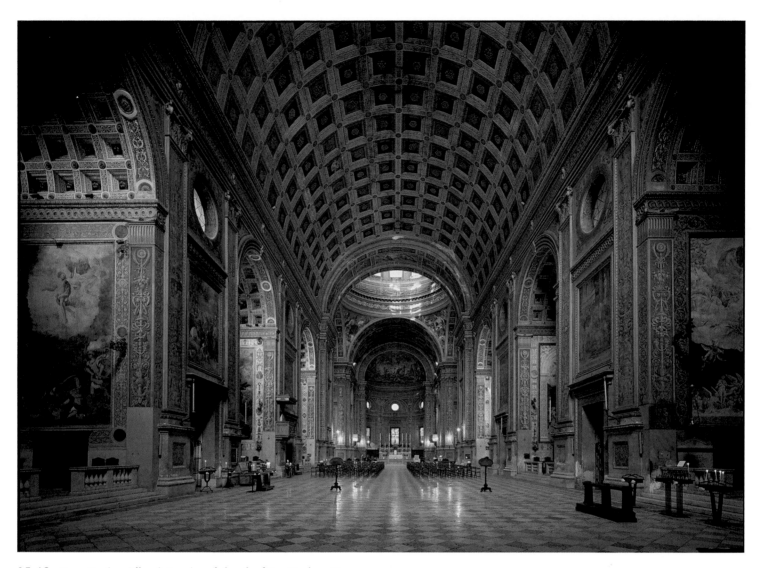

15.46   Leon Battista Alberti. Interior of church of Sant'Andrea, Mantua

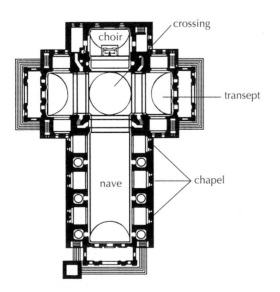

15.47   Plan of Sant'Andrea (transept, dome, and choir are later additions)

Compared with Brunelleschi's San Lorenzo (see fig. 15.8), the plan (fig. **15.47**) is extraordinarily compact. Had the church been completed as planned, the difference would be even more marked. Alberti's design had no transept, dome, or choir—all of these were added in the mid-eighteenth century; he planned only a nave ending in an apse. Following the example of the Basilica of Constantine (see figs. 7.60 and 7.61), Alberti replaced the aisles with alternating large and small vaulted chapels and eliminated the clerestory. The colossal pilasters and the arches of the large chapels support a coffered barrel vault of impressive size. (The nave is as wide as the façade.) Here, Alberti has drawn upon his study of the massive vaulted halls in ancient Roman baths and basilicas, but he interprets these models freely to create a structure that can truly be called a "Christian temple." Such a synthesis of ancient forms and Christian functions was a primary goal of fifteenth-century humanists and their patrician sponsors. Alberti's accomplishment of this goal at Sant'Andrea would inspire many other architects to do the same.

The humanist court at Mantua played host for many years to one of the most intellectually inclined artists of the century,

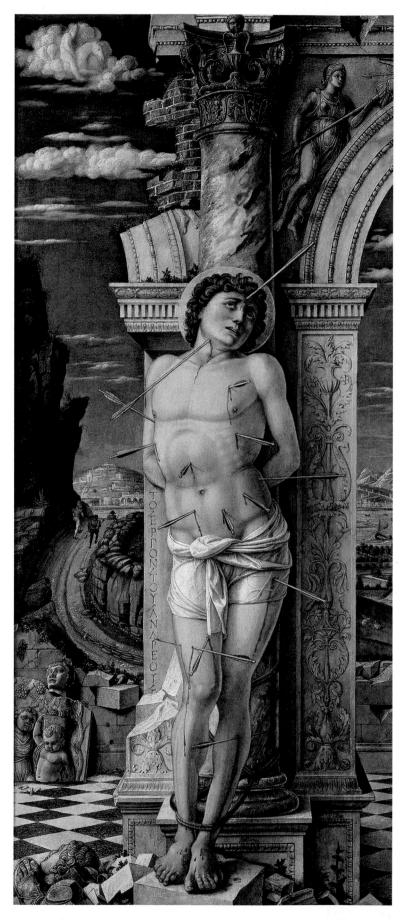

15.48 Andrea Mantegna, *St. Sebastian*. ca. 1450s. Tempera on panel, 26¾ × 11⅞" (68 × 30.6 cm). Kunsthistorisches Museum, Vienna

Andrea del Mantegna (1431–1506). Trained in Padua, but aware of artistic currents in Venice, Florence, and Rome and brother-in-law to Giovanni Bellini, Mantegna became court painter to the Gonzaga in 1460, a position he held until his death at age 75. His interests as a painter, humanist, and archaeologist can be seen in the panel depicting *St. Sebastian* (fig. **15.48**), probably painted in the 1450s. Sebastian was an early Christian martyr who was condemned to be executed by archers. (He recovered from these wounds, which may explain why he was invoked so often against the plague.) Mantegna depicts the anatomically precise and carefully proportioned body of the saint tied to a classical column. These forms are crisply drawn and modeled to resemble sculpture. Architectural and sculptural classical ruins lie at his feet and behind him, and next to him, on the left, is the artist's signature in Greek. A road leads into the distance, traversed by the archers who have just shot the saint; through this device, Mantegna lets the perspectively constructed space denote the passage of time. Beyond these men appears an atmospheric landscape and a deep-blue sky dotted with soft white clouds. The scene is bathed in warm late-afternoon sunlight, which creates a melancholy mood. The light-filled landscape in the background indicates Mantegna's awareness of Flemish paintings, which had reached Florence as well as Venice by 1450, where Mantegna would have encountered them.

Mantegna's patron for the *St. Sebastian* is unknown, but as a court painter, he served the marquis of Mantua. For the marquis' palace in Mantua, he painted a room that has come to be called the *Camera Picta*, or painted room (fig. **15.49**). This was a multipurpose vaulted room—sometimes bedroom, sometimes reception hall—which Mantegna finished in 1474. On the walls he painted portraits of the Gonzaga family, their retainers, their children, and their possessions. The room celebrates the marquis's brilliant court, his dynastic accomplishments, and his wealth, in a witty display that became an attraction for visiting humanists, politicians, artists, and princes. In such ways, princes used art to improve their social and political positions. The *Camera Picta* also celebrates Mantegna's skill and brought him fame among his contemporaries.

Mantegna used the actual architecture of the room—the **corbels** supporting the vaults, the mantel over the fireplace—to create an illusionistic glimpse of the Gonzaga family at home. Trompe-l'oeil pilasters serve as window frames through which a viewer sees members of the family out-of-doors; the figures of Ludovico and his son Francesco, recently made a cardinal, are observed by servants with a horse and dogs on the other side of the main door. In addition to the specific features of the people and the naturalism of the details, Mantegna's mastery of perspective allows him to connect the painted world to the real world of the spectator. The centerpiece of this illusion occurs at the crown of the vault (fig. **15.50**), where Mantegna paints a fictive oculus through which a spectator sees the sky. Framing this window is a foreshortened balustrade on which little *putti* (small boys) climb and over which court ladies peer. Mantegna uses many devices to create illusions in this room, including drapery that appears to be

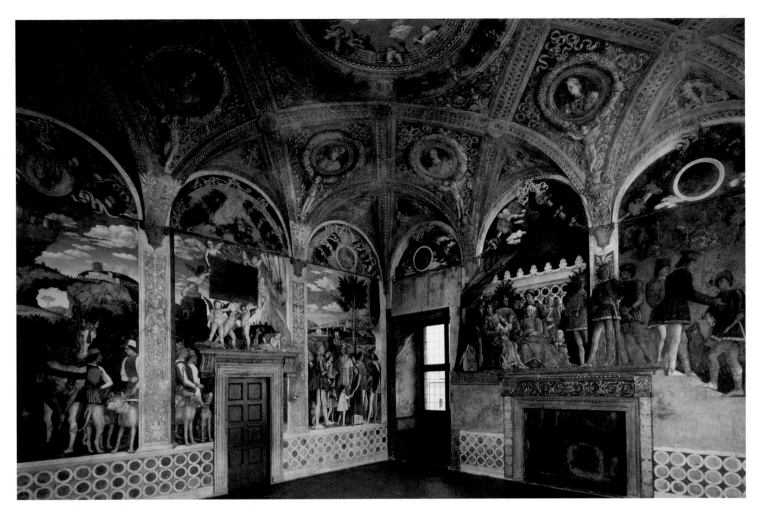

15.49 Andrea Mantegna, *Camera Picta*. 1465–74. Fresco. Ducal Palace, Mantua

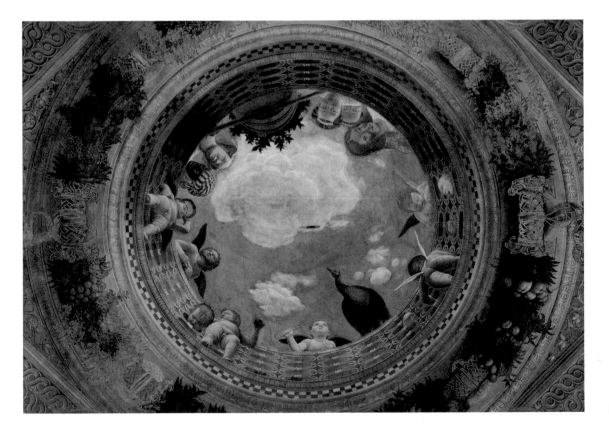

15.50 Andrea Mantegna, *Camera Picta*, detail of ceiling

fluttering in the outside breeze and trompe l'oeil reliefs of Roman emperors on the vaults. Above the mantel, Ludovico appears again, this time in a more formal setting, surrounded by family and courtiers. The brilliance of the court is wonderfully captured by Mantegna's splendid paintings.

Venice

While it extended control over its neighbors, Venice maintained a stable republican government throughout the fifteenth century. Protected from outsiders by its lagoon, it was ruled by a merchant aristocracy so firmly established that there was little internal conflict and the Doge's Palace (see fig. 13.32) could forgo any fortifications. Similarly, the houses of Venetian patricians were not required to serve as fortresses, with the result that they developed into graceful, ornate structures. The Ca' d'Oro (fig. **15.51**) was built beginning in 1421 for Marino Contarini, whose family had long prospered from trade. To assert his status, Contarini spared no expense on his dwelling on the Grand Canal. It received its name ("house of gold") from the lavish gold leaf that once adorned the façade.

The design in part reflects the different functions of the building. The ground floor was used as a shipping center and warehouse, while the second story is devoted mainly to a large reception hall, with several smaller rooms to the right. Private quarters are found mainly on the upper floor. The intersecting ribs of arches form a delicate latticework on the façade, which combine with the brilliant colors and the use of gold to express the family's wealth, position, and ambition.

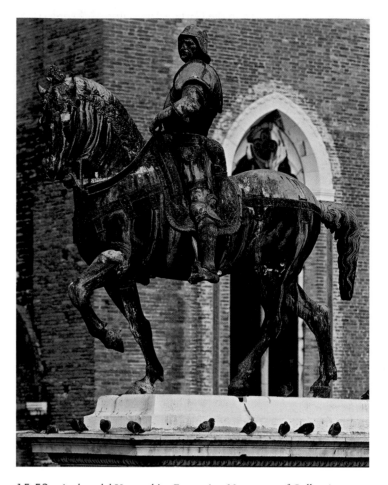

15.52 Andrea del Verrocchio, *Equestrian Monument of Colleoni*. ca. 1483–88. Bronze, height 13' (3.9 m). Campo Santissimi Giovanni e Paolo, Venice

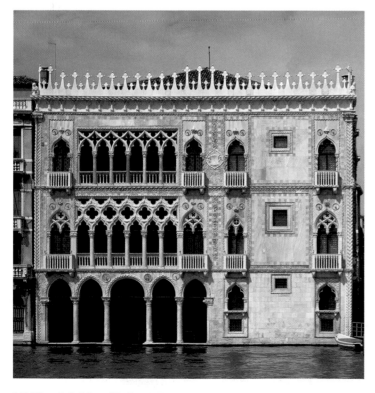

15.51 Ca' d'Oro, Venice. 1421–40

ECHOES OF DONATELLO'S *GATTAMELATA* Local Venetian traditions gave way slowly to the revival of interest in ancient art coming from Florence. Several Florentine artists, including Donatello and Andrea del Castagno, were called to Venice to execute important commissions. Flemish painting was admired and collected in Venice, which as a center for international trade housed colonies of merchants from northern Europe. By the end of the century, Venice had also adopted the new techniques and references to ancient art as useful tools for expressing itself. A good example of this is the commission given by the republic to Verrocchio to execute a large bronze equestrian statue commemorating a Venetian army commander, the *condottiere* Bartolommeo Colleoni (fig. **15.52**). Colleoni had requested such a statue in his will, in which he also left a large fortune to the city-state. Colleoni obviously knew the Gattamelata statue (see fig. 15.14) by Donatello, and wanted the same honor for himself. Verrocchio likely viewed Donatello's work as the model for his statue, yet he did more than simply imitate it, bringing his painter's skills to the rendering of the textures and details of the monument.

Colleoni's horse is graceful and spirited; its thin hide reveals veins, muscles, and sinews, in contrast to the rigid surfaces of the armored figure bestriding it. Since the horse is also smaller in relation to its rider than in the Gattamelata statue, Colleoni looms in the saddle as the very image of forceful dominance. Legs straight, one shoulder thrust forward, he surveys the scene before him with the same concentration we saw in Donatello's *St. George* (see fig. 15.12). Like Donatello's work, the Colleoni statue reminds a viewer of the contributions its subject made to his city.

BELLINI AND OIL PAINTING In addition to the revival of Roman forms, the traditions of Venice were further enhanced late in the fifteenth century by an exploration of the new medium of oil painting. A crucial intermediary in introducing this technique to Venice was probably Antonello da Messina, a painter from southern Italy who may have traveled to Flanders to learn it; he is documented in Venice in the 1470s. In the work of Giovanni Bellini (ca. 1430–1507), Mantegna's brother-in-law and a member of a family of painters, the technique of painting in oil pioneered

by the Flemish is combined with Florentine spatial systems and Venetian light and color.

Bellini's *St. Francis in the Desert* (fig. **15.53**), dating from about 1480, displays the artist's synthesis of these elements to create a wholly original image. In this painting, St. Francis has just stepped out of his hermit's cell, fitted out with a desk under an arbor. He has left his wooden sandals behind and looks up ecstatically to the sky. Some scholars believe the painting shows Francis receiving the stigmata (the wounds of Christ) on the Feast of the Holy Cross in 1224, when a crucified seraph reportedly appeared to him on Mount La Verna, in Tuscany. Others have argued that the scene "illustrates" the *Hymn of the Sun*, which Francis composed the next year, after his annual fast at a hermitage near his hometown of Assisi. Whichever narrative moment is depicted, the painting expresses Franciscan ideals. For St. Francis, "Brother Sun, who gives the day…and…is beautiful and radiant with great

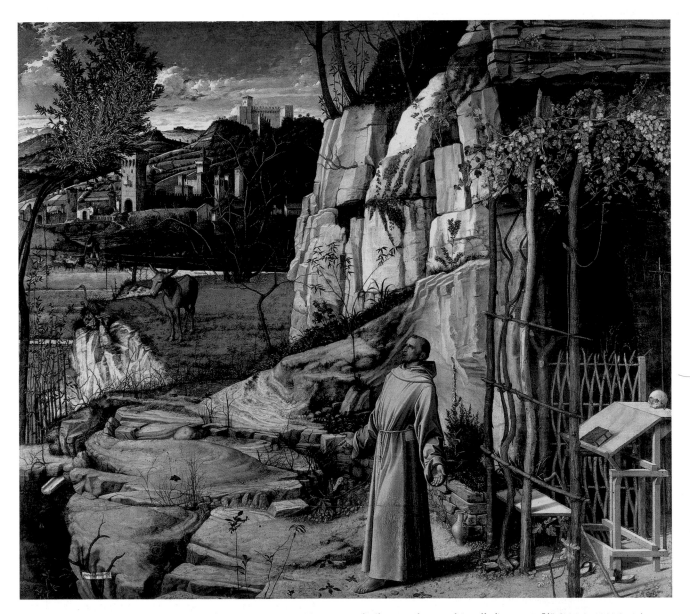

15.53   Giovanni Bellini, *St. Francis in the Desert*. ca. 1480. Tempera and oil on poplar panel (cradled), 49 × 57⅞" (124.4 × 141.9 cm). The Frick Collection, New York

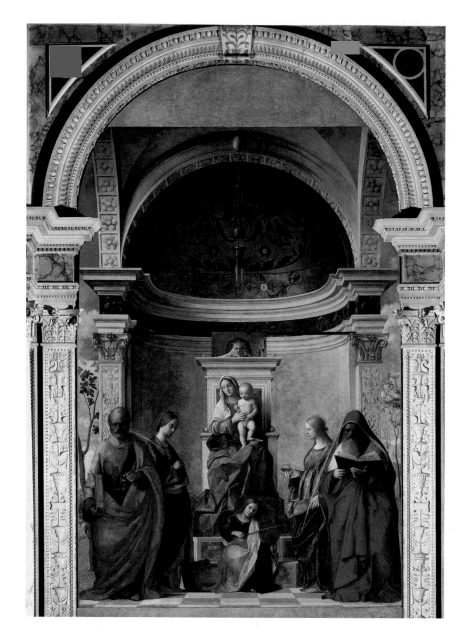

15.54 Giovanni Bellini, *Madonna and Saints*. 1505. Oil on panel, 16'5⅛" × 7'9" (5 × 2.4 m). San Zaccaria, Venice

splendor," was a symbol of the Lord. What he sees in the painting is not the sun itself, which is obscured by a cloud, but God revealed as the light divine. This miraculous light is so intense that it illuminates the entire scene.

In the background is a magnificent expanse of Italian countryside. St. Francis is so small compared to the landscape setting that he seems almost incidental. Yet his mystic rapture before the beauty of the visible world guides a viewer's response to the vista, which is ample and intimate at the same time. St. Francis believed that God created nature for the benefit of humanity. Bellini uses the tools of the Renaissance artist to re-create a vision of natural beauty. In this deep space, derived using the rules of perspective, he depicts detailed textures and forms to populate the landscape. Some of these forms may express Franciscan values. For Francis, the road to salvation lay in the ascetic life of the hermit, symbolized by the cave. The donkey may stand for St. Francis himself, who referred to his body as Brother Ass, which must be disciplined. The other animals—heron, bittern, and rabbit—are,

like monks, solitary creatures in Christian lore. Yet Bellini's soft colors and glowing light infuse the painting with a warmth that makes such a solitary life not only bearable, but enviable.

As the foremost artist of Venice, Bellini produced a number of altarpieces of the *sacra conversazione* type. The last known and most monumental is the *Madonna and Saints* (fig. **15.54**), done in 1505 for the Benedictine convent of San Zaccaria. Here, the Queen of Heaven is raised up on a throne with her Child, while SS. Peter, Catherine, Lucy, and Jerome stand before her. The placement of the female saints may reflect the interests of the nuns for whom the altarpiece was made. (When the painting was fitted with its present frame a decade later, it was cut at the sides, and a piece, since removed, was added at the top.) Compared with Domenico Veneziano's *sacra conversazione* of 60 years earlier (see fig. 15.30), the setting is simpler but even more impressive. Instead of a Gothic canopy, the saints are gathered below a semidome covered with mosaic in the Venetian medieval tradition (see fig. 8.47). It is as if the celestial assembly is taking place in Venice itself. Bellini's figures are comfortably inserted into the apse in a stable pyramid composition. The structure is obviously not a real church, for its sides are open and the scene is flooded with sunlight.

What distinguishes this altar from earlier Florentine examples is not only the spaciousness of the design but its calm, meditative mood. Here, the figures seem isolated and deep in thought. The silence is enhanced by the way the artist has bathed the scene in a delicate haze. There are no harsh contrasts. Light and shadow blend in almost imperceptible gradations, and colors glow with a new richness. Bellini creates a glimpse of a heavenly court peopled by ideal figures in an ideal space.

Rome and the Papal States

Long neglected during the papal exile in Avignon (see page 469), Rome once more became a major artistic center in the late fifteenth century. As the papacy regained power on Italian soil, the popes began to beautify both the Vatican and the surrounding city. They also reasserted their power as temporal lords over Rome and the Papal States. These popes believed that the monuments of Christian Rome should outshine those of the pagan past. To achieve this goal, they called many artists from Florence and the surrounding areas to Rome in the fifteenth century, including Leon Battista Alberti, Gentile da Fabriano, Masaccio, Fra Angelico, Piero della Francesca, and Sandro Botticelli. Like the other courts of Italy, the papacy saw the value of spending money on adorning both ecclesiastical and domestic structures.

THE SISTINE CHAPEL Pope Sixtus IV della Rovere (r. 1471–1484) sponsored several important projects in the last quarter of the century. One of these was the building at the Vatican of a new chapel for the pope, called the Sistine Chapel after Sixtus IV. Around 1481–82, Sixtus commissioned a cycle of frescoes for the walls of the chapel depicting events from the life of Moses (on the left wall) and Christ (on the right wall), representing the Hebrew Bible and New Testament. To execute them, he hired most of the key painters from central Italy, among them Botticelli, Ghirlandaio, and Pietro Vanucci, called Perugino (ca. 1450–1523). Born near Perugia in Umbria (the region southeast of Tuscany), Perugino maintained close ties with Florence. He completed the Sistine Chapel fresco *The Delivery of the Keys* (fig. **15.55**) in 1482.

The gravely symmetrical design conveys the special importance of the subject in this particular setting: The authority of St. Peter as the first pope, as well as of all those who followed him, rests on his having received the keys to the Kingdom of Heaven from Christ himself. The figures have the crackling drapery and idealized features of Verrocchio (see fig. 15.20) in whose workshop Perugino spent some time. Along with the other apostles, a number of bystanders with highly individualized features witness the solemn event.

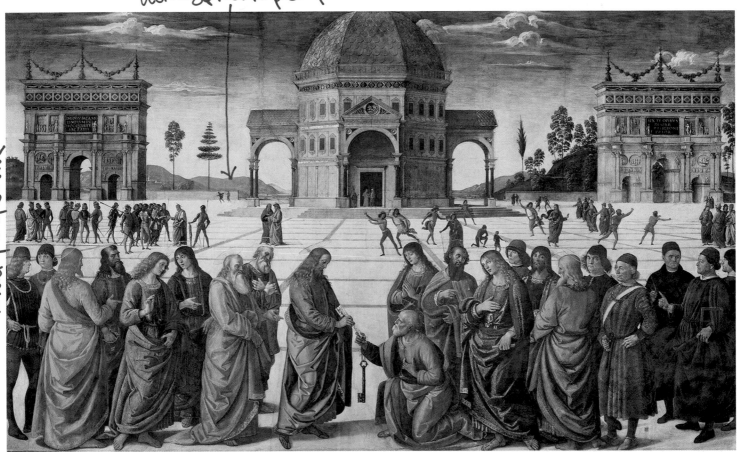

15.55 Pietro Perugino, *The Delivery of the Keys*. 1482. Fresco, 11'5½" × 18'8½" (3.5 × 5.7 m). Sistine Chapel, Vatican Palace, Rome

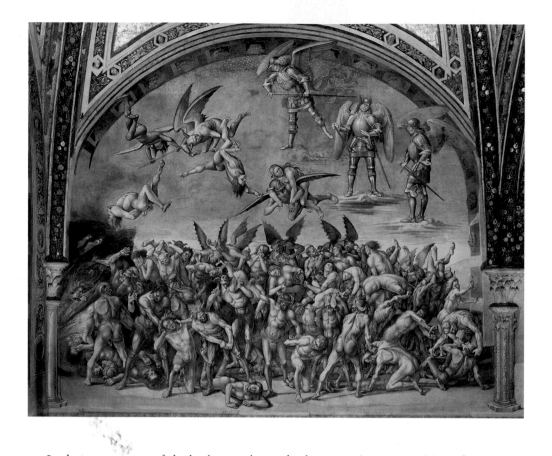

15.56 Luca Signorelli, *The Damned Cast into Hell*. 1499–1500. Fresco, width approx. 23' (7 m). San Brizio Chapel, Orvieto

In the vast expanse of the background, two further narratives appear: To the left, in the middle distance, is the story of the tribute money; to the right, the attempted stoning of Christ. The inscriptions on the two Roman triumphal arches (modeled on the Arch of Constantine; see fig. 7.70) favorably compare Sixtus IV to Solomon, who built the Temple of Jerusalem. These arches flank a domed structure seemingly inspired by the ideal church of Alberti's *Treatise on Architecture*. Also Albertian is the mathematically exact perspective, which lends the view its spatial clarity. The symmetry and clear space of the image express the character of the rule of Sixtus IV, not only in spiritual but also in temporal terms.

SIGNORELLI AND THE CHAPEL OF SAN BRIZIO Sixtus's claims over the Papal States were taken up by his successor, Alexander VI, who pursued temporal power with armies as well as spiritual weapons. Such activities drew the censure of other Christians, both in Italy and elsewhere, fueling the anticlerical feelings of the next century. The city of Orvieto in Umbria had shown great allegiance to the papacy, and in return, the pope adorned the chapel of San Brizio in the city's cathedral with a series of frescoes beginning in 1499. The commission for the project went to Luca Signorelli (1445/50–1523), a Tuscan painter who had studied with Piero della Francesca. The theme chosen for the frescoes is the end of the world, as predicted in the book of Revelation, and further elaborated by St. Augustine, Thomas Aquinas, and Dante, as well as the fifteenth-century Dominican preacher Vincent Ferrer. One of the most memorable of these frescoes is *The Damned Cast into Hell* (fig. **15.56**). Signorelli

envisions the scene as a mass of bodies pressed forcefully downward to be tormented by devils and licked by the flames of Hell, while the archangel Michael oversees the punishment. Inspired by the muscular forms of Pollaiuolo, Signorelli uses the nude body as an expressive instrument: The damned twist and turn, their bodies expressing the torments they face. The chaotic composition and compressed space contrasts strikingly with the rational calm of Perugino's *The Delivery of the Keys* (see fig. 15.55). Signorelli's frightening image of the end of time was painted as the year 1500 approached, a date which many believed would signal the end of days.

The late 1490s were a time of great uncertainty in Italy. The Medici were expelled from Florence; the French invaded in 1494; the plague returned to ravage cities; and the Turks continued their incursions into Europe. (The Turks had crushed the Christian forces at Lepanto, Greece, in 1499, a defeat that would be avenged in a second, more famous battle at the same site in 1571.) Fears that the "end of days" were coming were fanned by the sermons of Savonarola and other preachers.

By this time, however, the artists and patrons of Italy lived in a much different world. Despite Savonarola's charges of "paganism" in late fifteenth-century Italy, the revival of ancient thought and art was there to stay. Under the influence of the ancients and their humanist contemporaries, the artists of Renaissance Italy had transformed the look and design of buildings, the scale and significance of sculpture, and the forms and techniques of painting. They developed new means to render the world in their images, using perspective and naturalism, and created works of art that united ancient forms with contemporary content.

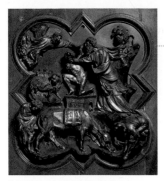

1401 Brunelleschi's and Ghiberti's competition panels for northern doors of the Baptistery of Florence

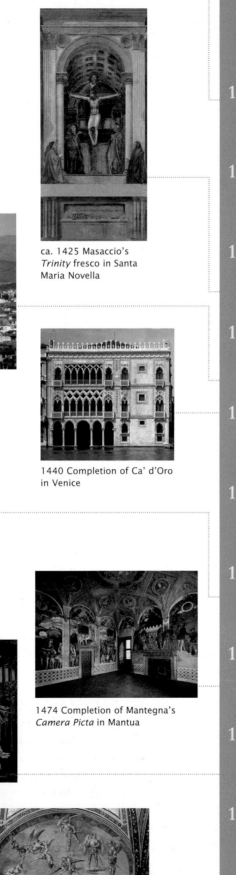

ca. 1425 Masaccio's *Trinity* fresco in Santa Maria Novella

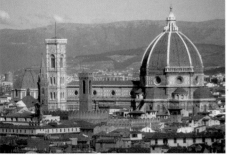

1436 Dedication of the Florentine cathedral with Brunelleschi's dome

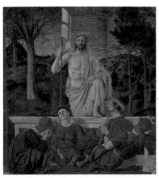

ca. 1463 Piero della Francesca *Resurrection*

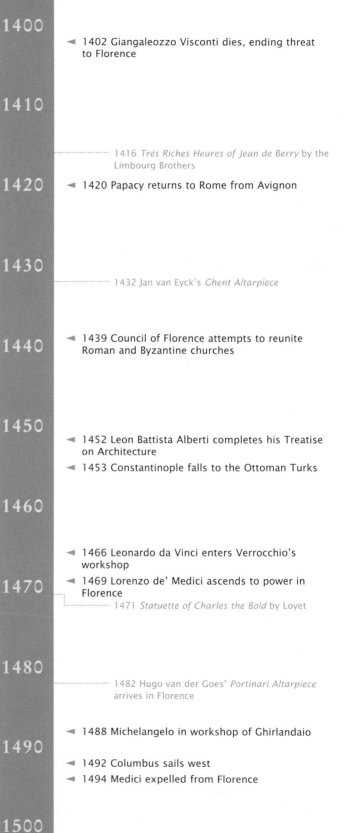

1440 Completion of Ca' d'Oro in Venice

1474 Completion of Mantegna's *Camera Picta* in Mantua

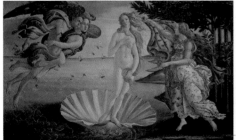

ca. 1485 Botticelli's *Birth of Venus*

1499 Signorelli's *Damned Cast into Hell*

The Early Renaissance in Fifteenth-Century Italy

1400

◄ 1402 Giangaleozzo Visconti dies, ending threat to Florence

1410

1416 *Très Riches Heures of Jean de Berry* by the Limbourg Brothers

1420 ◄ 1420 Papacy returns to Rome from Avignon

1430

1432 Jan van Eyck's *Ghent Altarpiece*

1440 ◄ 1439 Council of Florence attempts to reunite Roman and Byzantine churches

1450 ◄ 1452 Leon Battista Alberti completes his Treatise on Architecture
◄ 1453 Constantinople falls to the Ottoman Turks

1460

◄ 1466 Leonardo da Vinci enters Verrocchio's workshop
1470 ◄ 1469 Lorenzo de' Medici ascends to power in Florence
1471 *Statuette of Charles the Bold* by Loyet

1480

1482 Hugo van der Goes' *Portinari Altarpiece* arrives in Florence

◄ 1488 Michelangelo in workshop of Ghirlandaio

1490 ◄ 1492 Columbus sails west
◄ 1494 Medici expelled from Florence

1500

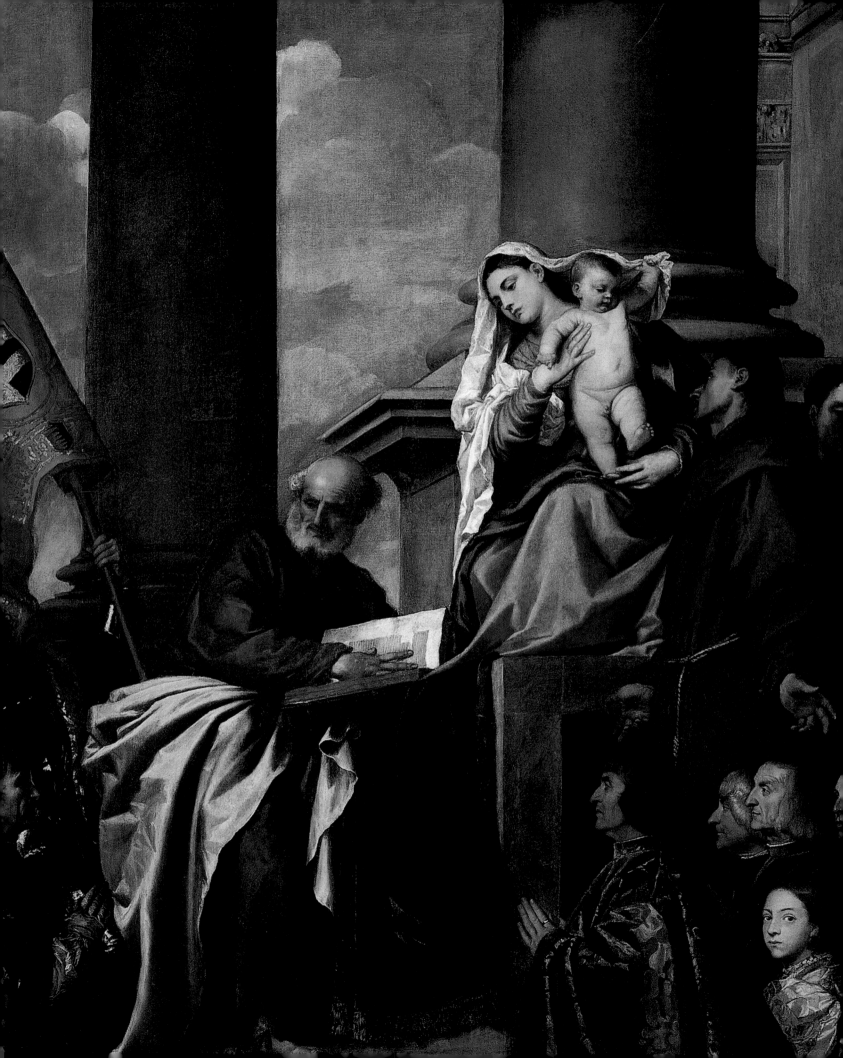

CHAPTER 16

The High Renaissance in Italy, 1495–1520

L OOKING BACK AT THE ARTISTS OF THE FIFTEENTH CENTURY, THE artist and art historian Giorgio Vasari wrote in 1550, "Truly great was the advancement conferred on the arts of architecture, painting, and sculpture by those excellent masters." From Vasari's perspective, the earlier generation had provided the groundwork that enabled sixteenth-century artists to

"surpass the age of the ancients." Later artists and critics agreed with Vasari's judgment that the artists who worked in the decades just before and after 1500 attained a perfection in their art worthy of admiration and emulation.

For Vasari, the artists of this generation were paragons of their profession. Following Vasari, artists and art teachers of subsequent centuries have used the works of this 25-year period between 1495 and 1520, known as the High Renaissance, as a benchmark against which to measure their own. Yet the idea of a "High" Renaissance presupposes that it follows something "lower," which seems an odd way to characterize the Italian art of the inventive and dynamic fifteenth century. For this and other reasons, this terminology has been reconsidered in the past few decades. Nonetheless, however we label it, this brief period saw the creation of what are still some of the most revered works of European art. These were created by the most celebrated names in the history of art, as chronicled in Vasari's *The Lives of the Most Eminent Painters, Sculptors and Architects of Italy*. Vasari's book placed the biography of the artist at the center of the study of art, and his *Lives* became a model for art-historical writing. Indeed, the celebrity of artists is a distinctive characteristic of the early sixteenth century.

Leonardo, Bramante, Michelangelo, Raphael, Giorgione, and Titian were all sought after in early sixteenth-century Italy, and the two who lived beyond 1520, Michelangelo and Titian, were internationally celebrated during their lifetimes. This fame was part of a wholesale change in the status of artists that had been occurring gradually during the course of the fifteenth century and which gained strength with these artists. Despite the qualities of their births, or the differences in their styles and personalities, these artists were given the respect due to intellectuals and humanists. Their social status was on a par with members of the great royal courts. In some cases, they were called "genius" or "divine." Some among them were raised to the nobility.

Part of this cult of fame was owed to the patrons who commissioned this small number of gifted and ambitious men to make works of art for them. This period saw the coming together of demanding patrons—rulers, popes, princes—and innovative artists. Patrons competed for works by these artists and in so doing set the artists into competition with each other; this pattern had already begun in early fifteenth-century Florence. The artists tested their skills against each other to inspire them to produce innovations in technique and in expression. The prestige of their patrons contributed to the mystique that developed around the artists, even as the reputations of the artists enriched the prestige of the patrons.

What is truly remarkable about this group of artists is their mastery of technique in their chosen mediums and in their styles of expression. Each of these artists developed a distinctive visual

Detail of figure 16.32, Titian, *Madonna with Members of the Pesaro Family*

style that grew out of the ideas of the fifteenth century, but which, through their personal vision, their awareness of intellectual trends, and their hard work, gave rise to works of art that their contemporaries claimed surpassed both nature and the ancients. Their pictorial works share certain features: an approach to the imitation of nature that idealizes forms even as they are rendered to replicate nature; understanding of and reliance on the forms of antiquity; balance and clarity in their compositions; and emotional power.

Also remarkable is that works of such authority and harmony were produced during a quarter-century of crisis and instability. During this period, Italy was threatened by the Turkish expansion from Istanbul, invaded by the French, and torn apart by internal wars. Florence saw the exile of the Medici, the rise of Girolamo Savonarola, the establishment of a republic, and the return of the Medici. Venice saw its territories stripped away by its rivals. Milan was ruled by a despot, then conquered by the French. The papacy began a program of territorial reclamation and expansion that brought it into conflict with its neighbors; the Roman Church also had to contend with the shock of a theological challenge offered by Martin Luther's critique of Catholic dogma and practice. All of Europe was astonished by reports of new lands and new peoples across the ocean, which challenged their notion of the world itself.

THE HIGH RENAISSANCE IN FLORENCE AND MILAN

Florence's reputation as a center for the arts made it a magnet for artists and patrons as the fifteenth century came to a close. The brilliance of the court around Lorenzo de' Medici came to an end with his death in 1492 and the subsequent failure of his son as the leader of the city. Many Florentines heeded the warnings of the preacher Girolamo Savonarola, who encouraged them to reform their faith and their lives; in response, they rejected the worldly culture of the Medici court. Under his influence, "pagan" texts and works of art were burned in bonfires in the Piazza della Signoria; the painter Sandro Botticelli destroyed several of his paintings at these bonfires. Yet the penitential furor that Savonarola urged did not outlive the preacher's execution in 1498. Florence restored its republican form of government, which lasted only until the next generation of Medici politicians took

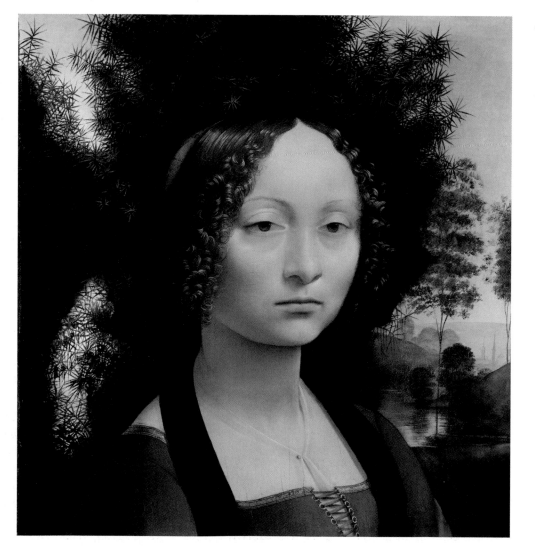

<u>16.1</u> Leonardo da Vinci, *Portrait of Ginevra de' Benci*, ca. 1474–78 Oil on panel, 16¹³⁄₁₆ × 14⁹⁄₁₆" (42.7 × 37 cm). National Gallery of Art, Washington, D.C. Ailsa Mellon Bruce Fund.1967.6.1.a

back the reins of government in 1512. The political ferment seems to have inspired tremendous artistic innovation, as witnessed in the works of Leonardo da Vinci and Michelangelo Buonarotti.

Leonardo da Vinci in Florence

Leonardo da Vinci was at once a scientist, painter, sculptor, musician, architect, and engineer. Born the son of a notary in the little Tuscan town of Vinci in 1452, Leonardo trained as a painter in Florence in Verrocchio's busy workshop. He left Florence around 1482 to work for Ludovico Sforza, the duke of Milan, primarily as a military engineer and only secondarily as an artist. On Sforza's removal by the French in 1499, Leonardo made his way to Venice, Rome, and Florence, where he executed several commissions between 1503 and 1505. From 1506 through 1516 he worked in Rome and Florence and again in Milan, whose French overlord, Francis I, invited him to retire to a chateau in the Loire Valley. Leonardo died there in 1519.

During his twenties, as a student and then assistant in the workshop, Leonardo collaborated with his teacher Verrocchio before taking commissions on his own. Several works from this period remained unfinished, but one that he completed is the *Portrait of Ginevra de' Benci*, usually dated between 1474 and 1478 (fig. **16.1**). Vasari described this painting in his Life of Leonardo, and most authorities recognize it as an early work by his hand.

The sitter's identity is known, both from what Vasari says and elements of the painting itself. The young woman stands before a thick hedge of juniper, which is a pun on her name (juniper is *ginepro* in Italian); it is also a symbol of chastity. The reverse of this panel depicts another sprig of juniper and a painted scroll that says, "She adorns her beauty with virtue." The portrait was cut down in size at some point in its history, and it likely originally included the sitter's hands, in an arrangement much like that of the marble *Lady with Flowers* by Verrocchio (see fig. 15.42). Among the Florentine elite, Ginevra de' Benci was a celebrated beauty and a poet, though little of her poetry survives. She was married in 1474, and this may be the reason for the commission of the portrait.

Marriage or betrothal occasioned the painting of portraits of women, usually setting them in interiors, wearing expensive jewelry and garments, and often in profile arrangements. Leonardo breaks this mold, by setting the young woman (she was 16 when she married) out of doors in an atmospheric landscape and in a three-quarter view. Flemish portraits (see fig. 14.21) that had made their way to Florence probably inspired these choices. Flemish works definitely informed Leonardo's use of oil as the medium for his paintings. Other artists in late fifteenth-century Florence adopted these same elements, including Domenico Ghirlandaio (see fig. 15.41). What is extraordinary here is what these tools achieve in Leonardo's hands. As in Ghirlandaio's lovely portrait of an old man, we see the three-quarter pose, brilliant color, and a view of a landscape. Both artists use atmospheric perspective to suggest the lack of local color in the distant

landscape, but Leonardo's landscape is much more believable and humid-looking. He exploits the oil technique here to blend his brushstrokes very subtly so as to diminish the appearance of contour lines. His figures seem to exist only as the result of light falling on three-dimensional objects. This method of modeling is called **chiaroscuro**, the Italian word for "light and dark." Starting from a middle tone laid all over the panel, Leonardo renders deep shadows and bright highlights for his forms. Instead of standing side by side in a vacuum, forms share in a new pictorial unity created by the softening of contours in an envelope of atmosphere. These early experiments in the oil medium and the intelligence he gives to his sitter point to directions his art would take in the future.

Leonardo in Milan

Leaving behind several incomplete commissions, Leonardo left Florence for Milan in 1481, where he entered the employ of Ludovico Sforza, duke of Milan. He stayed there until 1499, working as an engineer, court artist, and military designer. As had Brunelleschi before him, Leonardo turned to analysis and research to solve a variety of problems, both artistic and scientific. He believed the world to be intelligible through mathematics, which formed the basis for his investigations. Thus, the artist must know not only the rules of perspective, but all the laws of nature. To him, the eye was the perfect means of gaining such knowledge. The extraordinary range of his inquiries can be seen in the hundreds of drawings and notes that he made and hoped one day to turn into an encyclopedic set of treatises. He was fascinated by all elements of nature: animals, water, anatomy, and the workings of the mind. How original he was as a scientist is still a matter of debate, but he pioneered modern scientific illustration, an essential tool for anatomists and biologists. His drawings, such as the *Embryo in the Womb* (fig. **16.2**), combine his own vivid observations with the analytic clarity of diagrams—or, to paraphrase Leonardo himself, sight and insight. The sheet of studies shown here is a product of his skill at rendering what he saw, and of his dispassionate recording of details both in visual terms and in his notes, written backward in mirror-writing.

Like other fifteenth-century scholars, he read ancient authorities to assist his inquiries. To prepare himself for human dissections, Leonardo read the works of the Greek physician Galen. His interest in architecture and engineering led him to the works of the Roman architect Vitruvius, whose treatise had inspired Alberti earlier in the century. A drawing from the late 1480s (fig. **16.3**) visualizes Vitruvius' notion that the human body may be used to derive the perfect geometrical forms of the circle and the square. This is a powerful image of the value that humanists and architects placed on these geometric elements, as carriers of profound meaning as well as visual forms. Like other humanists, Leonardo was interested in the place of man in the world.

His patrons consulted with Leonardo on several sorts of building and engineering projects. He seems, however, to have been less concerned with actual building than with tackling

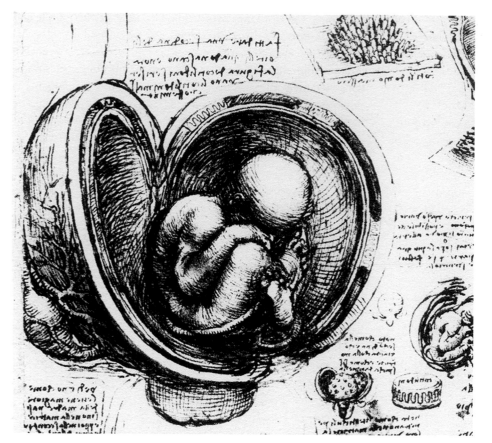

16.2 Leonardo da Vinci, *Embryo in the Womb*. ca. 1510. Pen drawing, 11⅞ × 8⅜" (30.4 × 21.5 cm). Windsor Castle, Royal Library

16.3 (BELOW LEFT) Leonardo da Vinci, *Vitruvian Man*. ca. 1487. Pen and ink, 13½ × 9½" (34.3 × 24.5 cm). Gallerie dell'Accademia, Venice

16.4 (BELOW) Leonardo da Vinci, *Project for a Church* (Ms. B). ca. 1490. Pen drawing, 9⅛ × 6¾" (23 × 17 cm). Bibliothèque de l'Arsenal, Paris

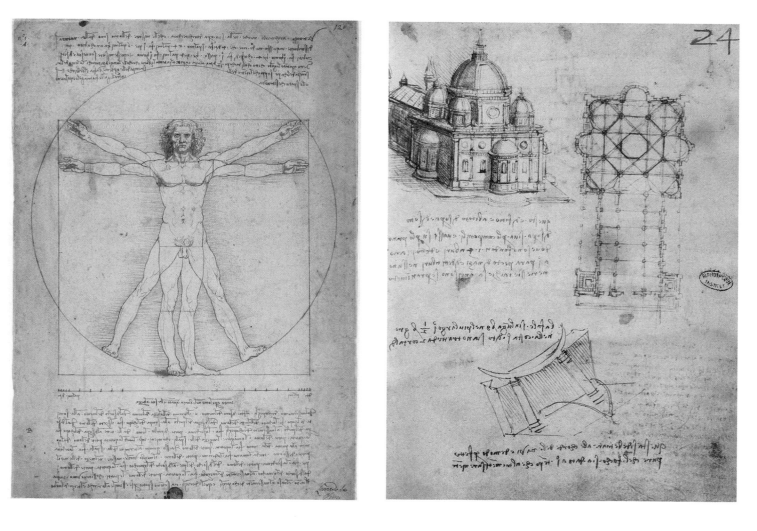

theoretical problems of structure and design. The many architectural projects still to be seen in his notebooks were intended to remain on paper. Yet these sketches, especially those of his Milanese period, reveal Leonardo's probing of the design problems faced by his forebears Brunelleschi and Alberti, as well as by his contemporaries. The domed central-plan churches of the type shown in figure **16.4** hold particular interest to architectural history. In this drawing, Leonardo imagines a union of circle and square, controlled by proportion, and articulated by classical orders. In conception, this design stands halfway between the dome of Florence cathedral and the most ambitious structure of the sixteenth century, the new basilica of St. Peter's in Rome.

Soon after arriving in Milan, Leonardo began painting *The Virgin of the Rocks* (fig. **16.5**) for a confraternity (lay brotherhood)

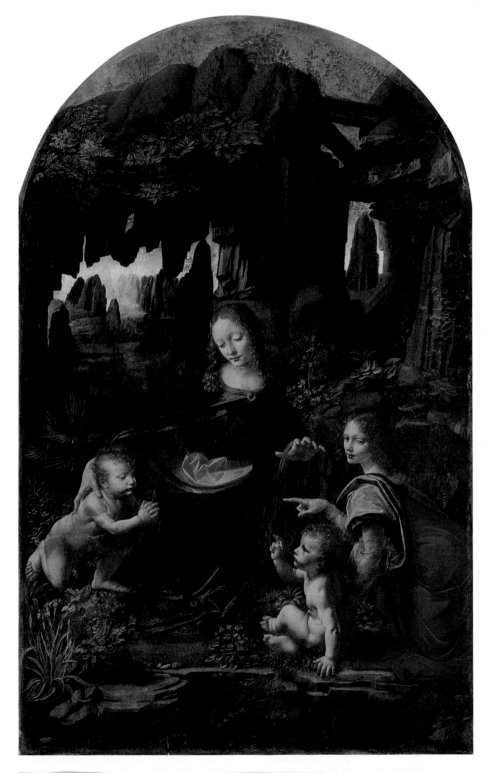

16.5   Leonardo da Vinci, *The Virgin of the Rocks*. ca. 1485. Oil on panel transferred to canvas, 6'6" × 4' (1.9 × 1.2 m). Musée du Louvre, Paris

Leonardo Da Vinci (1452–1519)

From his undated manuscripts

Leonardo, the consummate High Renaissance man, wrote on a variety of topics. The comparison of the arts, or paragone, *was a common subject in High Renaissance scholarship.*

He Who Depreciates Painting Loves Neither Philosophy nor Nature

If you despise painting, which is the sole imitator of all visible works of nature, you certainly will be despising a subtle invention which brings philosophy and subtle speculation to bear on the nature of all forms—sea and land, plants and animals, grasses and flowers—which are enveloped in shade and light. Truly painting is a science, the true-born child of nature. For painting is born of nature; to be more correct we should call it the grandchild of nature, since all visible things were brought forth by nature and these, her children, have given birth to painting. Therefore we may justly speak of it as the grandchild of nature and as related to God.

A Comparison Between Poetry and Painting

The imagination cannot visualize such beauty as is seen by the eye, because the eye receives the actual semblances or images of objects and transmits them through the sense organ to the understanding where they are judged. But the imagination never gets outside the understanding;...it reaches the memory and stops and dies there if the imagined object is not of great beauty; thus poetry is born in the mind or rather in the imagination of the poet who, because he describes the same things as the painter, claims to be the painter's

equal! ... The object of the imagination does not come from without but is born in the darkness of the mind's eye. What a difference between forming a mental image of such light in the darkness of the mind's eye and actually perceiving it outside the darkness!

If you, poet, had to represent a murderous battle you would have to describe the air obscured and darkened by fumes from frightful and deadly engines mixed with thick clouds of dust polluting the atmosphere, and the panicky flight of wretches fearful of horrible death. In that case the painter will be your superior, because your pen will be worn out before you can fully describe what the painter can demonstrate forthwith by the aid of his science, and your tongue will be parched with thirst and your body overcome by sleep and hunger before you can describe with words what a painter is able to show you in an instant.

Of the Sculptor and Painter

The sculptor's art requires more physical exertion than the painter's, that is to say, his work is mechanical and entails less mental effort. Compared with painting, there is little scientific research; for the sculptor's work consists in only taking off and the painter's in always putting on. The sculptor is always taking off from the same material, while the painter is always putting on a variety of materials. The sculptor gives all his attention to the lines that circumscribe the material which he is carving, and the painter studies these same lines, but he has besides to study the shade and light, the color and the foreshortening. With respect to these the sculptor is helped throughout by nature, which supplies the shade and light and the perspective. While the painter has to acquire these by dint of his ingenuity and has himself to play the part of nature, the sculptor always finds them ready made.

Source: *The Literary Works of Leonardo da Vinci*, ed. Jean Paul Richter (London: Phaidon Press, 1975)

dedicated to the Immaculate Conception, which maintained a chapel in San Francesco Grande in Milan. (Completion of the project was delayed because it became the subject of a dispute with the patrons.) The subject—the infant St. John adoring Jesus in the presence of the Virgin—enjoyed a certain popularity in Florence in the late fifteenth century. Speculation on the early life of Jesus and his cousin, the Baptist, led to stories about their meeting as children. Franciscan preachers encouraged believers to meditate on the "human" side of Jesus' life and stories like this were the result. Such tales report the young Baptist spending his life as a hermit; because of this, artists represented him wearing a hair shirt. Leonardo imagines this meeting almost as a vision of Christ appearing to the infant Baptist in the wilderness. The young Baptist kneels on the left and looks toward Jesus, who blesses him. The Virgin Mary is the link between the two boys, as she protectively reaches for the Baptist with one hand and holds the other open-palmed over her son. An angel with a billowing red cloak steadies Jesus and points toward the Baptist, while looking out at the viewer.

The scene is mysterious in many ways. The secluded rocky setting, the pool in the foreground, and the carefully rendered plant life suggest symbolic meanings, but scholars are still debating the details. The figures emerge from the semidarkness of the grotto, enveloped in a moist atmosphere that delicately veils their forms. This fine haze, called **sfumato** (smokiness), lends an unusual warmth and intimacy to the scene. The light draws attention to the finely realized bodies of the children and the beautiful heads of the Virgin and the angel. Leonardo arranges the figures into a pyramid of form, with the figures establishing a solid geometric shape in space which has the Virgin's head at the apex. As a result, the composition is stable and balanced, but the gestures lead the eye back and forth to suggest the relationships among the figures. The selective light, quiet mood, and tender gestures create a remote, dreamlike quality, and make the picture seem a poetic vision rather than an image of reality.

Leonardo had much to say about the relationship between poetry and painting. He thought sight was the superior sense and that painters were better equipped to represent what the eye could

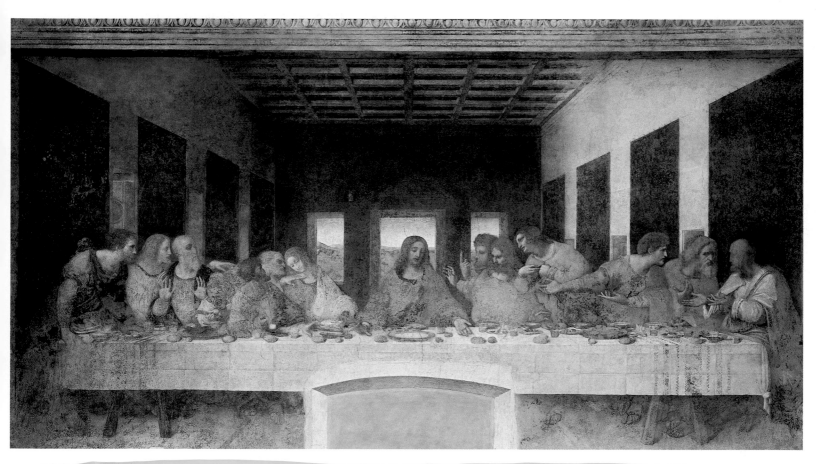

16.6 Leonardo da Vinci, *The Last Supper*. ca. 1495–98. Tempera wall mural, 15'2" × 28'10" (4.6 × 8.8 m). Santa Maria delle Grazie, Milan

see or imagine. His notebooks include many comments on the *paragone*, or comparison, between painting and poetry. This competition between art forms was rooted in the Roman poet Horace's statement that poetry is like painting ("*ut pictura poesis*"), which artists of the High Renaissance reinterpreted to mean that painting and poetry seek similar effects. (See *Primary Source*, page 562.) Leonardo's musings on the rivalry between poetry and painting extended to that between painting and sculpture. He argued that painting was superior to sculpture primarily because it provided the possibility for creating the sort of illusionary spaces and textures seen in *The Virgin of the Rocks*. Additionally, the painter could dress elegantly for his work, and not subject himself to the clouds of dust or the brute force needed to make sculpture. Not all of his contemporaries agreed. Michelangelo, for one, defended the art of sculpture as superior to painting, precisely because it created fully three-dimensional forms while painting merely created illusions.

Leonardo's skill at creating such illusions and his experimental approach to achieving them is apparent in *The Last Supper* (fig. **16.6**), executed between 1495 and 1498. Leonardo's patron, Duke Ludovico, commissioned him to decorate the refectory (dining hall) of the Dominican monastery of Santa Maria delle Grazie, which housed the duke's family chapel. The resulting painting became instantly famous and was copied numerous times by other artists, but a modern viewer can only imagine its original splendor, despite the painting's recent restoration. Dissatisfied with the limitations of the traditional fresco technique, Leonardo experimented with an oil-tempera medium on dry plaster that did not adhere well to the wall in the humidity of Milan. What is more, the quality of the painting has been diminished by renovations and damage done to the wall. Yet what remains is more than adequate to account for its tremendous impact.

The theme of the Last Supper was conventional for monastic refectories, as a comparison with Castagno's *The Last Supper* (see fig. 15.29), painted half a century before, reveals. Monks or nuns dined in silence before images of the apostles and Christ at table. Like Castagno, Leonardo creates a spatial setting that seems like an annex to the real interior of the room, though deeper and more atmospheric than the earlier fresco. The central vanishing point of the perspective system is located behind the head of Jesus in the exact middle of the fresco; it thus becomes charged with symbolic significance. Equally symbolic is the opening in the wall behind Jesus: It acts as the architectural equivalent of a halo. Rather than Castagno's explosion of marble veining or an artificial disk of gold, Leonardo lets natural light enframe Jesus. All elements of the picture—light, composition, colors, setting—focus the attention on Jesus.

He has presumably just spoken the fateful words, "One of you shall betray me." The disciples ask, "Lord, is it I?" The apostles who flank Jesus do not merely react to these words. Rather,

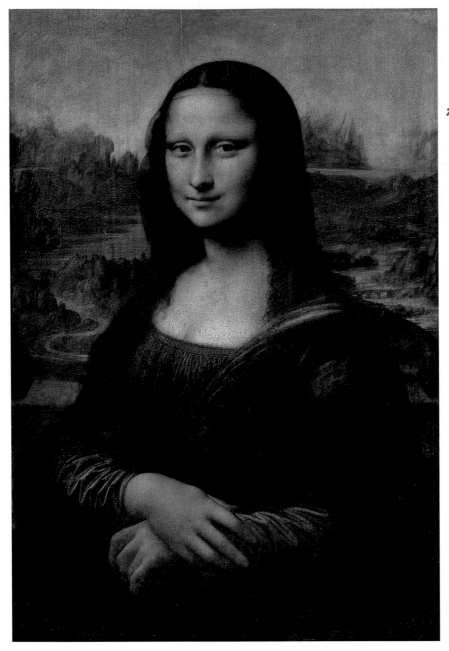

16.7 Leonardo da Vinci, *Mona Lisa*. ca. 1503–05. Oil on panel, 30¼ × 21" (77 × 53.5 cm). Musée du Louvre, Paris

sfumato= smoky technique

each reveals his own personality, his own relationship to Jesus. In the group to his right, Peter impulsively grabs a knife; next to him John seems lost in thought; and Judas (the figure leaning on the table in the group to Jesus' right) recoils from Jesus into shadow. Leonardo has carefully calculated each pose and expression so that the drama unfolds across the picture plane. The figures exemplify what the artist wrote in one of his notebooks—that the highest and most difficult aim of painting is to depict "the intention of man's soul" through gestures and movements of the limbs.

But to view this scene as just one moment in a psychological drama does not do justice to Leonardo's aims, which went well beyond a literal rendering of the biblical narrative. He clearly wanted to condense his subject, both physically (by the compact, monumental grouping of the figures) and spiritually (by presenting many levels of meaning at one time). Thus, Jesus' gesture is one both of submission to the divine will and of offering. His calm presence at the center of the table suggests that, in addition to the drama of the announcement, Jesus also institutes the Eucharist, in which bread and wine become his body and blood. Such multiple meanings would serve as spiritual food for the Dominican friars who lived in the presence of this image.

Leonardo Back in Florence and Elsewhere

In 1499, the duchy of Milan fell to the French, so Leonardo returned to Florence after brief trips to Mantua and Venice. He must have found the political climate very different from what he remembered. Florentines had become unhappy with the rule of Lorenzo de' Medici's son, Piero, and had expelled the Medici;

until their return in 1512, the city was a republic again. For a while, Leonardo seems to have been active mainly as an engineer and surveyor. Then, in 1503, the city commissioned him to do a mural for the council chamber of the Palazzo della Signoria, which he abandoned in 1506 and returned to Milan.

THE *MONA LISA* =mylady While working on the mural, Leonardo also painted the portrait of a woman, whom Vasari identified as Lisa Gherardini, wife of Francesco del Giocondo, the so-called *Mona Lisa* (fig. **16.7**). (Because of her husband's name, the French call her "La Giocanda,") Much recent research has tended to confirm this identity. If it is indeed the Lady Lisa (Mona is a contraction of Madonna), who married in 1495 at age 16, she was about 25 when the portrait was made. For reasons that are now unclear, Leonardo kept this painting, possibly continuing to work on it. After his death in France, the portrait entered the collection of King Francis I. From the royal collection, it became a key possession of the Musée du Louvre. To some extent its fame is a product of its ownership.

But the *Mona Lisa* is also famous for its formal qualities. We may be able to see them more clearly in comparison to his earlier portrait of Ginevra de' Benci (see fig. 16.1). Both paintings break with the fifteenth-century tradition of depicting young women in profile. Leonardo depicts both of these young women in three-quarter poses against landscape backgrounds. He also depicts the women in simple garments, without the jewels and brocades that adorned most brides, to concentrate on their features. As he had originally done with Ginevra, Leonardo represents Mona Lisa at half-length, so that her hands are included in the image. The whole composition thus forms a stable pyramid. Compared to Ginevra, however, Mona Lisa seems a creature of a different order. Leonardo renders the subtle movement of light washing over her figure to draw attention to her features. Having mastered the oil technique, he builds the forms from layers of glazes so thin that the panel appears to glow with a gentle light from within, despite the dirty varnish that now obscures the painting. Mona Lisa sits before an evocative landscape, whose mountainous elements emerge from a cool sfumato backdrop, while the rivers and bridges winding through it echo the highlights on her drapery; the landscape envelops her, where for Ginevra it seems a mere backdrop. The beautifully observed details of Mona Lisa's high brow and crossed hands give her as much character as her famous smile. Vasari helped to spread the fame of the painting, for he claimed the portrait exemplified "how faithfully art can imitate nature." (See www.myartslab.com.) This skill, for Vasari, was the root of Leonardo's genius. For later generations, the *Mona Lisa* has served as the consummate example of his art.

ROME RESURGENT

By the end of the fifteenth century, the papacy had firmly reestablished itself in Rome. Along with their spiritual control of the Church, the popes reasserted political and military control over the Papal States in the area around Rome. Rebuilding the city was an expression of the papal intentions to rule there, as Sixtus IV had demonstrated with his building of the Sistine Chapel, among other projects. Alexander VI, who became pope in 1492, used his papacy to enlarge papal domains through the marriages of his daughter, Lucrezia Borgia, and through the military exploits undertaken by his son Cesare Borgia. He also made the papal court the peer of any princely court in Italy. On Alexander's death, the new pope Julius II (r. 1503–1513) made his aim the physical renewal of Rome, hoping that it would rival the glory of the ancient city. He invested vast sums in large-scale projects involving architecture, sculpture, and painting, and he called on numerous artists to work for him. The ancient city's Roman and medieval monuments inspired a variety of projects in the Renaissance city (map **16.1**). Under Julius, Rome became the crucible of the High Renaissance.

Bramante in Rome

The most important architect in Julius's Rome was Donato Bramante (1444–1514). A native of Urbino, he began his career as a fresco painter. Influenced by Piero della Francesca and Andrea Mantegna, Bramante became skilled at rendering architectural settings in correct perspective. Leonardo may also have had some influence on Bramante, as the two were colleagues at the court of Milan. Bramante's architectural works take Brunelleschi and Alberti as their main points of departure.

After Milan fell to the French in 1499, Bramante went to Rome, where he experienced Roman buildings first hand. There, the Spanish-born pope Alexander VI had begun the process of enlarging and enhancing papal holdings, in which endeavor he had the support of the powerful Spanish monarchs, Ferdinand and Isabella. The Spanish rulers commissioned Bramante around 1500 to build a structure to mark the supposed site of St. Peter's crucifixion, attached to the church of San Pietro in Montorio (fig. **16.8**). Because of its powerful evocation of Roman circular temples, it was called the Tempietto, or "little temple." This structure serves as a **martyrium**, a special chapel associated with a martyr.

In early Christian Rome, such structures were often centralized in plan. Bramante, however, seems as much inspired by the precepts of Alberti and the experiments of Leonardo as he is by the experience of Rome itself. A contemporary, Sebastiano Serlio, recorded Bramante's design in an architectural treatise that was published in the 1540s. According to this plan, Bramante intended to surround the Tempietto by a circular, colonnaded courtyard that would entirely respond to the structure. This conception was as bold and novel as the design of the chapel itself (fig. **16.9**), for not only does the chapel's colonnade dictate the courtyard's colonnade, the walls of the courtyard open into concave niches that echo the façade of the chapel.

This façade, with its three-step platform and use of the plain Tuscan Doric order, recalls Roman temple architecture more directly than does any fifteenth-century building (see fig. 7.23). Moreover, the entire design is based on the **module** of the

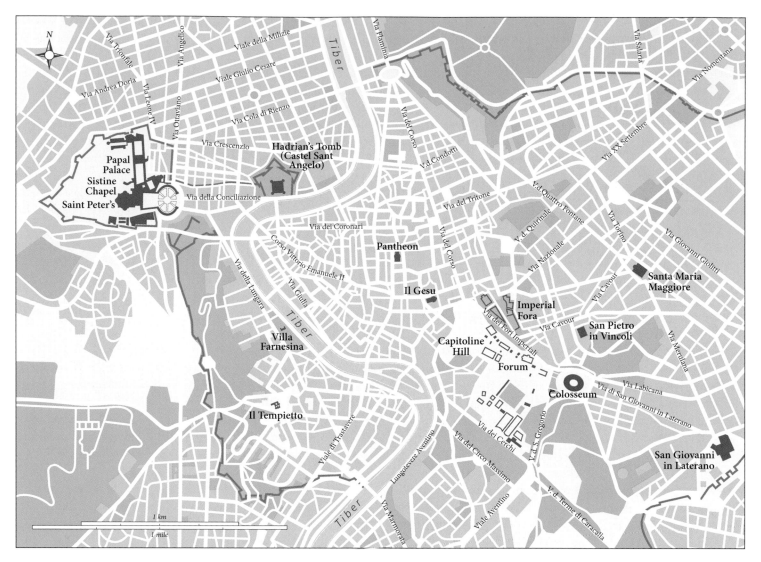

Map 16.1 Renaissance and earlier monuments in Rome

columns: For example, the distance between the columns is four times their diameter, and they are placed two diameters from the wall. This insistent logic follows the rules of temple design established by Vitruvius. Equally striking is Bramante's use of the "sculptured wall" in the Tempietto itself and the courtyard, as shown in the plan. Deeply recessed niches in the upper story are counterbalanced by the convex shape of the dome and by strongly projecting moldings and **cornices**. As a result, the Tempietto has a monumentality that belies its modest size. The building, including the sculptural decoration in the metopes and frieze around the base, is a brilliant example of papal propaganda. The Tempietto proclaims Christ and the popes (considered the successors of St. Peter) as the direct heirs of Rome. Bramante used the language of ancient Rome to express the claims of the modern pope. The publication of the design by Serlio helped spread the specific elements

16.8 Donato Bramante. Tempietto, San Pietro in Montorio, Rome. 1502–11

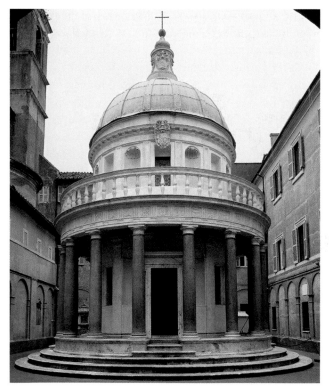

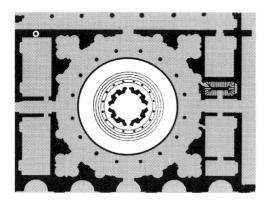

16.9   Plan of Bramante's Tempietto (after
Serlio, in *Regole generali di architettura*)

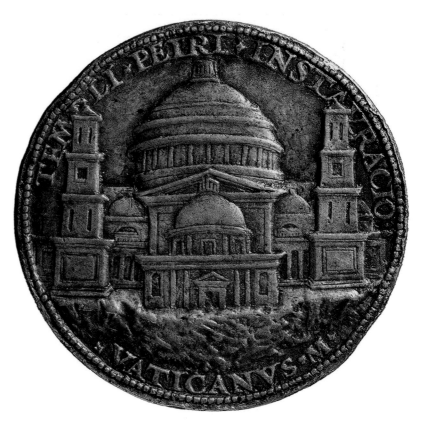

16.11   Cristoforo Foppa Caradosso. Bronze medal showing
Bramante's design for St. Peter's. 1506. The British Museum, London

and the underlying design concepts of this building, and it became
a very influential structure.

Such work brought Bramante to the notice of Alexander VI's
successor, Julius II. The nephew of Sixtus IV, Giuliano delle
Rovere, as Pope Julius II, had great ambitions for the Church and
for Rome. He used art and artists as tools in his goal of restoring
papal authority over Christendom. This is nowhere more evident
than in Julius's decision to replace the Constantinian basilica of St.
Peter's (see fig. 8.8), which was in poor condition, with a church
so magnificent that it would overshadow all the monuments of
imperial Rome. He gave the commission to Bramante and laid the
cornerstone for the project in 1506. Because of later changes, we
know Bramante's original design mostly from a plan (fig. **16.10**)
and from the medal commemorating the start of the building
campaign (fig. **16.11**), which shows the exterior in general terms.
These reveal the innovative approach that Bramante took in this
project, which was grand both in scale and in conception.

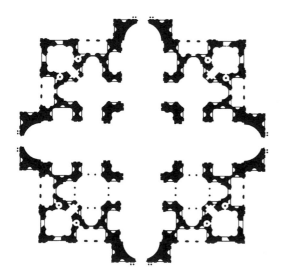

16.10   Donato Bramante. Original plan for St. Peter's,
Rome. 1506 (after Geymuller)

The plan and commemorative medal indicate that Bramante
envisioned a huge round dome, similar to the Pantheon's, to
crown the crossing of the barrel-vaulted arms of a Greek cross,
that is, a cross with four arms the same length. Four lesser domes,
each surmounting a chapel that echoes the main space, and tall
corner towers were planned around the central dome. As Alberti
prescribed and Leonardo proposed, Bramante's plan is based
on the circle and the square. Not only had the ancients revered
these perfect forms, Bramante's contemporaries saw them as
appropriate symbols for the Christian empire that Julius planned.
Bramante envisioned four identical façades dominated by classical
forms: domes, half-domes, colonnades, and pediments. The
principal dome would have been encircled by a colonnade as
well. The whole façade would have been a unified, symmetrical
sculptural form, united by proportion and the interplay of
geometric elements.

But this logical interlocking of forms would have been accompanied by the structure's huge scale, for Julius's church was
intended to be more than 500 feet long. Such a monumental
undertaking required vast sums of money, and the construction of
St. Peter's progressed so slowly that in 1514, when Bramante died,
only the four crossing piers had been built. For the next three
decades the project was carried on by other architects, who
altered his design in a number of ways. A new and decisive phase
in the history of St. Peter's began in 1546, when Michelangelo

Michelangelo Interprets the Vatican Pietà

The Pietà for Cardinal Jean de Villiers de la Groslaye, now in St. Peter's, helped to establish Michelangelo's reputation as a sculptor. In his Life of Michelangelo Buonarotti, *first published in 1553, Michelangelo's friend and biographer, Ascanio Condivi, quotes the sculptor explaining features of the work.*

A little later on, the Cardinal of Saint-Denis ... commissioned him to make from one piece of marble that marvelous statue of Our Lady ... [she] is positioned seated on the rock, in which the cross was sunk, with her dead Son on her lap, and of such and so rare a beauty, that no one sees her without being inwardly moved to pity. An image truly worthy of the humanity which belongs properly to the Son of God and to such a mother; although there are some who make the reproach that the mother is shown as too young, in relation to her Son. But when I was discussing this with Michelangelo one day, he replied to me: "Don't you know that chaste women remain far fresher than those who are not chaste? So much more the Virgin, in whom never has the least lascivious desire ever arisen that might alter her body. Moreover, let me add this, that besides such freshness and flower of youth being maintained in her in this natural way it may be believed to have been assisted by divine power to prove to the world the virginity and perpetual purity of the mother. This was not necessary in the Son; rather completely the opposite; because to show that, as He did, the Son of God took a truly human body, and was subjected to all that an ordinary man endures, except sin, there was no need for the divine to hold back the human, but to leave it to its order and course, so that the time of life He showed was exactly what it was. Consequently you are not to wonder if for these reasons I have made the most Holy Virgin, mother of God, far younger in comparison with her Son than her age would ordinarily require, and that I left the Son at his own age."

This reflection would be worthy of any theologian. ... When he made this work, Michelangelo would have been 24 or 25 years old. He acquired great fame and reputation from this effort, and indeed it was already everyone's opinion that he had not only surpassed all his contemporaries, and those who came before him, but that he also contended with the ancients.

Source: *Michelangelo, Life, Letters and Poetry*, ed. and tr. George Bull (Oxford: Oxford University Press, 1987)

took charge. It was then altered again in the seventeenth century. Nevertheless, Bramante's original plan for St. Peter's was to put Roman imperial and Early Christian forms at the service of a Renaissance pope's spiritual and temporal ambitions.

Michelangelo in Rome and Florence

Julius's ambitions were also the spur for one of the crucial figures in the history of art, Michelangelo di Lodovico Buonarroti Simoni (1475–1564). Acclaimed by his contemporaries, admired by his successors, and hailed as "divine" by Vasari, Michelangelo is one of the most influential and imitated artists in history. Gifted, driven, he has become the archetype of the genius, whose intellect and talents enabled him to work in many mediums; he was a sculptor, architect, painter, and poet. Pope Julius encouraged him in his ambition to outdo the artists of antiquity, by giving him opportunities to produce some of his most inspired and famous works.

Unlike Leonardo, for whom painting was the noblest of the arts because it embraced every visible aspect of the world, Michelangelo was a sculptor to the core. More specifically, he was a carver of marble statues. The limitations of sculpture, which Leonardo condemned as mechanical, unimaginative, and dirty, were virtues in Michelangelo's eyes. Only the "liberation" of real, three-dimensional bodies from recalcitrant matter could satisfy Michelangelo. Painting, for him, should imitate the roundness of sculptured forms. Architecture, too, ought to share the organic qualities of the human figure.

Michelangelo's belief in the human image as the supreme vehicle of artistic expression gave him a sense of kinship with ancient sculptors, more so than with other Renaissance practitioners. Among Italian masters, he nonetheless admired Giotto, Masaccio, and Donatello more than his contemporaries. Although his family came from the nobility, and therefore initially opposed his desire to become an artist, Michelangelo was apprenticed to Ghirlandaio, from whom he learned painting techniques. He came to the attention of Lorenzo de' Medici, who invited him to study the antique statues in the garden of one of the Medici houses. The overseer of this collection, Bertoldo di Giovanni (ca. 1420–1491), a pupil of Donatello, may have taught Michelangelo the rudiments of sculpture. From the beginning, however, Michelangelo was a carver rather than a modeler. He rarely worked in clay, except for sketches; he preferred harder materials, especially marble, which he shaped with his chisel.

The young artist's mind was decisively shaped by the cultural climate of Florence during the 1480s and 1490s, even though the troubled times led him to flee the city for Rome in 1496. Lorenzo de' Medici's death in 1492 put an end to the intellectual atmosphere that he had fostered. The subsequent expulsion of the Medici, and the rise to power of the fiery preacher Girolamo Savonarola, brought calls for a spiritual awakening and a rejection of "paganism" and materialism. Both the Neo-Platonism of Marsilio Ficino and the religious reforms of Savonarola affected Michelangelo profoundly. Just as he conceived his statues as human bodies released from their marble prisons, so he saw the body as the earthly prison of the soul—noble perhaps, but a prison nonetheless. This dualism of body and spirit endows his figures with extraordinary pathos. Although outwardly calm, they seem stirred by an overwhelming psychic energy that finds no release in physical action.

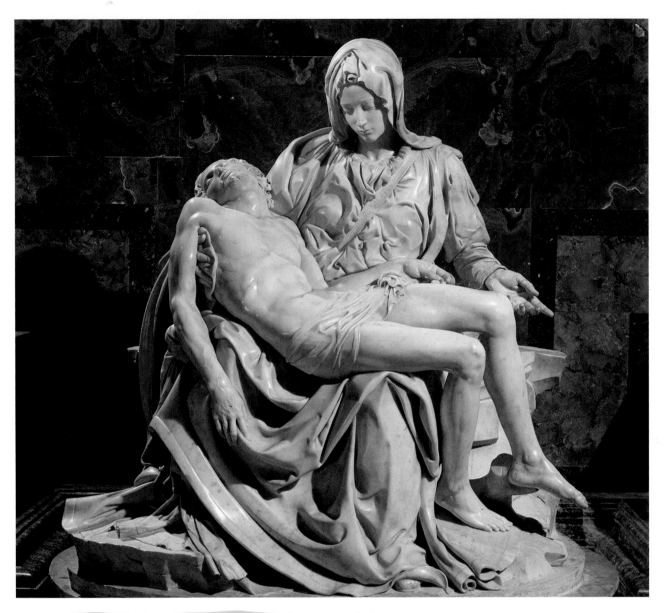

16.12 Michelangelo, *Pietà*. ca. 1498. Marble, height 68½" (173.9 cm). St. Peter's, Rome

PIETÀ Having left Florence after the exile of the Medici, Michelangelo worked in Bologna and then Rome, where a French cardinal commissioned him in 1498 to carve a Pietà for his tomb chapel close to St. Peter's (fig. **16.12**). In the contract, Michelangelo promised to carve "the most beautiful work of marble in Rome." The subject of the Pietà was more familiar in northern Europe than in Italy, appearing in such works as the *Roettgen Pietà* (see fig. 12.60), although the theme of the Virgin's lamentation for her dead son had appeared in works such as Giotto's Arena Chapel frescoes (see fig. 13.20). Michelangelo, however, imagines the farewell between mother and son as a calm and transcendent moment rather than a tortured or hopeless one. The composition is stable; the over-large figure of the Virgin with her deeply carved robe easily supports the weight of her dead son.

The Virgin seems far too young to be holding her grown son, so in addition to the Pietà, the image echoes the theme of the Madonna and Child. Michelangelo himself intended her youth to express her perpetual virginity, according to his friend and biographer, Ascanio Condivi. (See *Primary Source*, page 568.) Michelangelo doesn't merely tell a story, he offers viewers the opportunity to contemplate the central mystery of Christian faith—Christ as God in human form who sacrificed himself to redeem Original Sin—with the same serenity as Mary herself. When the *Pietà* was first displayed in 1499, some controversy surrounded its authorship; Michelangelo put it to rest by carving his name on the Virgin's sash. The inscription proudly asserts his authorship and his origin in Florence. At 24, his fame was assured.

DAVID When this project was completed, Michelangelo returned to Florence, which had reestablished a republican form of government. There, in 1501, directors of the works for Florence cathedral commissioned him to execute a figure to be

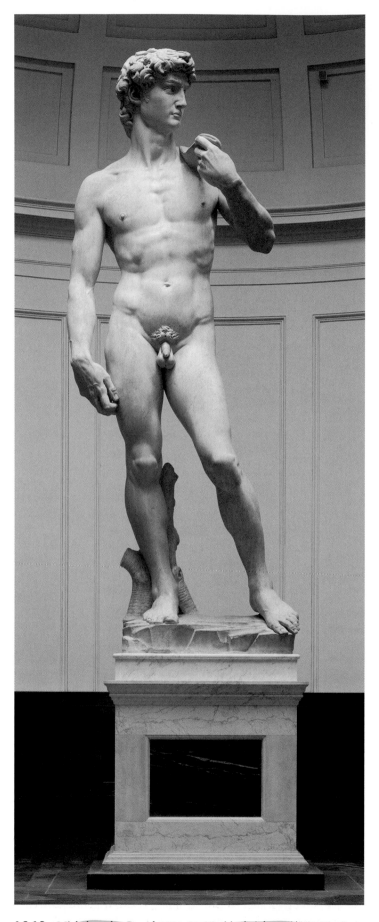

installed on one of the buttresses of the façade. The 18-foot-high block of marble for this project had been partly carved by an earlier sculptor, but Michelangelo accepted the challenge to create something memorable from it. The result was the gigantic figure of the *David* (fig. **16.13**). When it was completed in 1504, a committee of civic leaders and artists decided instead to put it in front of the Palazzo della Signoria, the seat of the Florentine government. They placed a circlet of gilt bronze leaves around the statue's hips and put a gilt bronze wreath on David's head. The city of Florence claimed the figure as an emblem of its own republican virtues.

Michelangelo treated the biblical figure not as a victorious hero, but as the ever-vigilant guardian of the city. Unlike Donatello in his bronze *David* for the Medici (see fig. 15.33), Michelangelo omits the head of Goliath; instead David nervously fingers a slingshot, as his eyes focus on an opponent in the distance. Although both Donatello and Michelangelo rendered David as a nude, the style of the later sculpture proclaims an ideal very different from the wiry slenderness of Donatello's youth. Michelangelo had just spent several years in Rome, where he had been deeply impressed with the emotion-charged, muscular bodies of Hellenistic sculpture, which were being avidly collected there. (See *The Art Historian's Lens*, page 157.) Their heroic scale, their superhuman beauty and power, and the swelling volume of

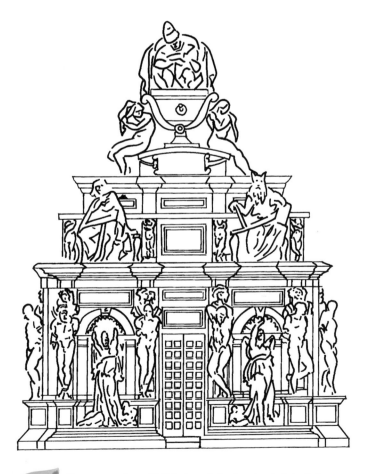

16.13 Michelangelo, *David*. 1501–04. Marble, height 17'⅛" (5.22 m). Galleria dell'Accademia, Florence

16.14 Reconstruction of Michelangelo's plan (ca. 1505) of the Tomb of Pope Julius II (after Tolnay)

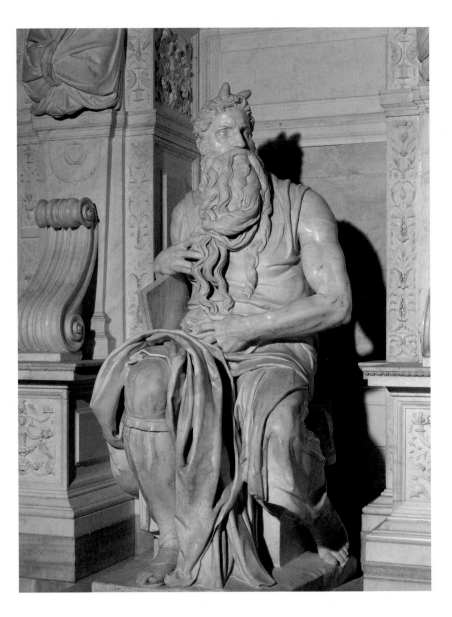

16.15 Michelangelo, *Moses*.
ca. 1513–15. Marble, height 7'8½" (2.35 m).
San Pietro in Vincoli, Rome

their forms became part of Michelangelo's own style and, through him, of Renaissance art in general. In the *David*, Michelangelo competes with antiquity on equal terms and replaces its authority with his own. But instead of the emotionally wrought figures he saw in Hellenistic works, Michelangelo crafted the *David* to be at once calm and tense, active yet static, full of the potential for movement rather than its actual expression.

Michelangelo in the Service of Pope Julius II

The ambition to create powerful works of art is a hallmark of Michelangelo's career. It is seen again in the project he undertook for the Tomb of Julius II, planned for the new St. Peter's. The commission was given in 1505, but Julius interrupted it, then died in 1513, leaving the project incomplete. His heirs negotiated with Michelangelo over the next 30 years to produce a reduced version of the original plan. The initial plan, reconstructed in figure **16.14**, combined sculpture and architecture into a grand statement of the glory of the pope. Julius's sarcophagus was to sit at the apex of

this architectural mass, intended in the first plan to enclose a burial chamber.

On lower levels of the structure Michelangelo planned a figure of St. Paul and one of the Hebrew Bible hero, Moses (fig. **16.15**). This figure was completed about ten years later. The *Moses*, meant to be seen from below, has the awesome force Vasari called *terribilità*—a concept similar to the "sublime" (see page 790). It strikes fear in a viewer from its sheer force. His pose, both watchful and meditative, suggests a man capable of wise leadership as well as towering wrath. Moses has just received the Ten Commandments, which he holds close to his massive torso. The horns, a traditional attribute based on a mistranslation of the Hebrew word for "ray" in the Vulgate (Latin Bible), which is also seen in Sluter's *The Well of Moses* (see fig. 14.1), signify the divine favor bestowed on Moses, whose face shone after he came down from Mount Sinai (Exodus 34). Michelangelo planned other figures for the project, including bound men, whose meaning is still obscure, as well as personifications of the active and contemplative life. Some of these, including the *Moses*, were assembled into the monument

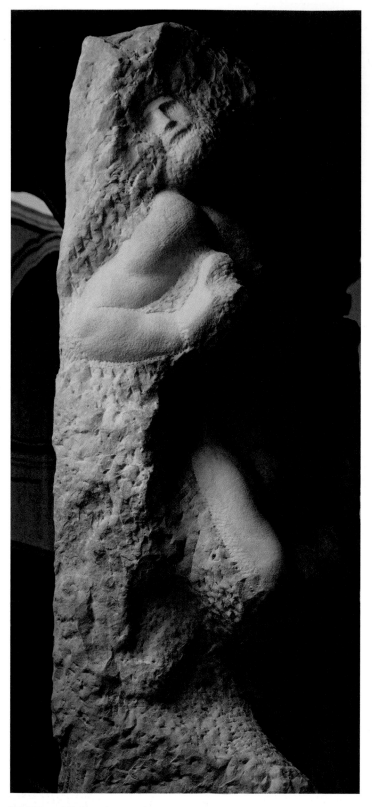

16.16 Michelangelo, *Awakening Prisoner*. ca. 1525. Marble, height 8'11" (2.7 m). Galleria dell'Accademia, Florence

for Julius installed in the church of San Pietro in Vincoli in Rome, on a scale much reduced from the initial plan.

One later figure for the tomb, the unfinished *Awakening Prisoner* (fig. **16.16**), provides invaluable insights into Michelangelo's artistic personality and working methods. For

him, the making of a work of art was both joyous and painful, full of surprises, and not mechanical in any way. It appears that he started the process of carving a statue by trying to perceive a figure in the block as it came to him from the quarry. (At times he may even have visualized figures while picking out his material on the spot.) He may have believed that he could see "signs of life" within the marble—a knee or an elbow pressing against the surface. This attitude is expressed in one of his most famous sonnets, written around 1540:

> Not even the best of artists has any conception
> That a single marble block does not contain
> within its excess, and *that* is only attained
> by the hand that obeys the intellect.

Source: James Saslow's translation, from *The Poetry of Michelangelo* (New Haven, CT: Yale University Press, 1991), page 302

To get a firmer grip on the dimly felt image that he believed was inside the stone, Michelangelo made numerous drawings, and sometimes small models in wax or clay, before daring to assault the marble itself. His practice was to draw the main view on the front of the block. Once he started carving, every stroke of the chisel would commit him more and more to a specific conception of the figure hidden in the block. The marble would permit him to free the figure only if his guess about its shape was correct. Sometimes the stone refused to give up some essential part of the figure within it, and he left the work unfinished. Michelangelo himself may have appreciated the expressive qualities of incomplete works. Although he abandoned *Awakening Prisoner* for other reasons, every gesture seems to record the struggle for liberation of the figure.

Pope Julius interrupted Michelangelo's work on the tomb at an early stage. The pope's decision to enlarge St. Peter's, a commission he gave to Bramante in 1506, altered his patronage priorities, and this so angered Michelangelo that he left Rome. Two years later, the pope half-forced, half-coaxed him to return to paint frescoes on the ceiling of the Sistine Chapel in the Vatican.

FRESCOES FOR THE SISTINE CHAPEL CEILING The Sistine Chapel takes its name from Pope Sixtus IV, Julius's uncle, who had it built and adorned between 1477 and 1482. Driven by his desire to resume work on the tomb, Michelangelo finished the ceiling in only four years, between May 1508 and November 1512 (fig. **16.17**). In this brief period of intense creation in a medium that he never felt was his own, Michelangelo produced a work of truly epochal importance.

The ceiling is a shallow barrel vault interrupted over the windows by the triangular spandrels that support it. Michelangelo treated this surface as a single entity, with hundreds of figures distributed rhythmically within a painted architectural framework. Several different themes intersect throughout this complex structure (fig. **16.18**). In the center, subdivided by ten illusionistic

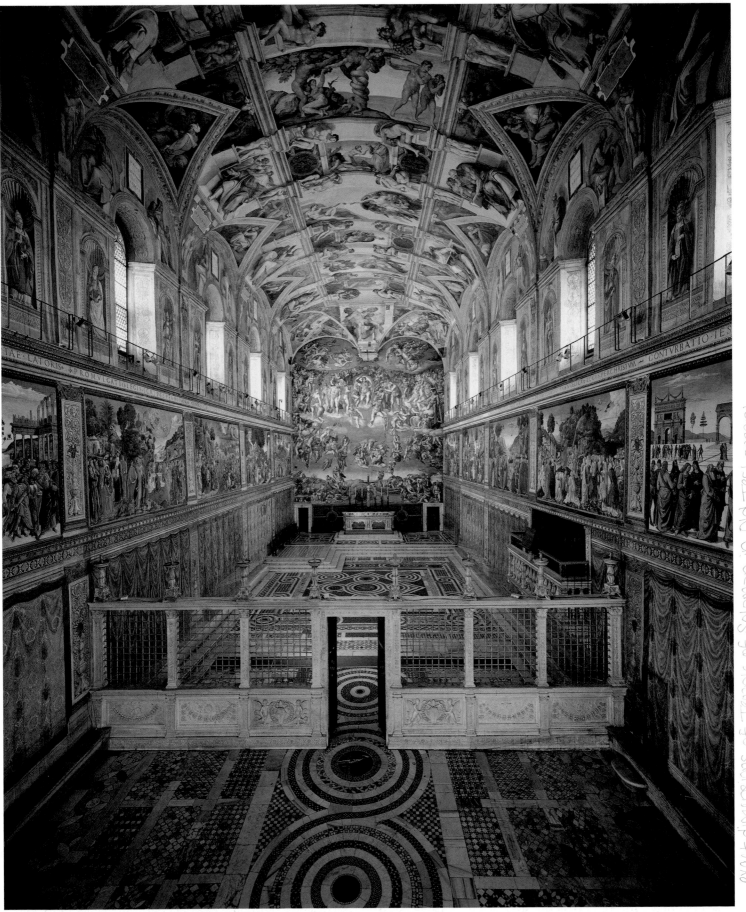

handwritten: exact dimensions of Temple of Solomon in Old Testament

16.17 Interior of the Sistine Chapel showing Michelangelo's ceiling fresco, Vatican, Rome

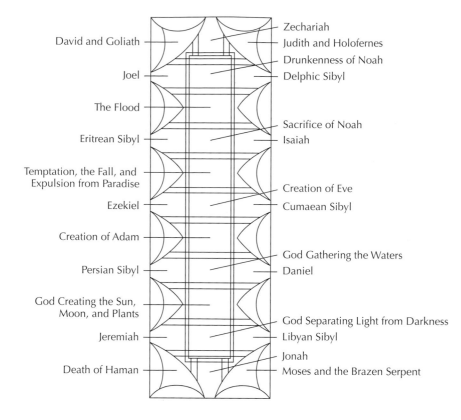

16.18 Diagram of subjects in Sistine Chapel, Vatican, Rome

David and Goliath

Joel

The Flood

Eritrean Sibyl

Temptation, the Fall, and Expulsion from Paradise

Ezekiel

Creation of Adam

Persian Sibyl

God Creating the Sun, Moon, and Plants

Jeremiah

Death of Haman

Zechariah

Judith and Holofernes

Drunkenness of Noah

Delphic Sibyl

Sacrifice of Noah

Isaiah

Creation of Eve

Cumaean Sibyl

God Gathering the Waters

Daniel

God Separating Light from Darkness

Libyan Sibyl

Jonah

Moses and the Brazen Serpent

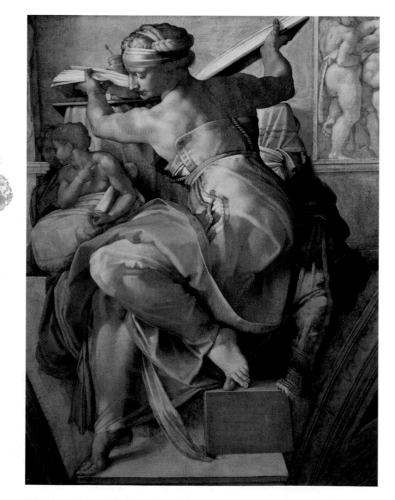

16.19 Libyan Sibyl portion of the Sistine Chapel ceiling

transverse arches, are nine scenes from the book of Genesis, from the Creation of the World (at the altar end) to the Drunkenness of Noah (near the entry door); large figures of prophets and sibyls flank these narratives. In the triangular spandrels sit the ancestors of Christ, who also appear in the lunettes flanking the windows. Further narrative scenes occur at the corner pendentives, focusing on the Hebrew Bible heroes and prophets who **prefigured** Christ. Scholars are still debating the theological import of the whole program and whether Michelangelo consulted with advisors in the development of the themes. While the Creation and Fall of Man occur at the center of the ceiling, the prophets and ancestors predict the salvation of humanity in Christ. Except for the architecture, these themes are expressed almost entirely by the human figure.

The Sistine Chapel ceiling swarms with figures, most of them in the sort of restless posture seen in the *Moses*. For example, as seen in figure **16.19**, the Libyan Sibyl (a sibyl was a pagan prophetess, in whose prophecies Christians saw evidence for the coming of Christ) barely sits on her throne, but twists backward to close her book. Her muscular forms derive from Michelangelo's life drawings of young men. (See *Materials and Techniques*, page 575.) These figures also stem from Michelangelo's deep study of ancient sculpture, which he hoped to surpass. Since the cleaning of the frescoes in the 1980s, scholars have come to appreciate the brilliance of Michelangelo's colors, and the pairing of complementary colors he used in the draperies. (See *The Art Historian's Lens*, page 578.)

A similar energy pervades the center narratives. *The Fall of Man* and *The Expulsion from the Garden of Eden* (fig. **16.20**) show

Drawings

Medieval artists had used the technique of drawing to record monuments they had seen or to preserve compositions for future use. These drawings were usually made with pen and ink on parchment. During the Renaissance, the increasing availability of paper expanded the uses of drawings and encouraged artists to use a variety of mediums in making them.

Pen and ink on paper were used most often, as the liquid ink could be transferred to the paper by means of a sharp quill pen or stylus. Sometimes the forms drawn with ink were further elaborated with a wash (usually diluted ink) applied with a brush. Some artists preferred to work with liquid mediums and thin brushes to render all the forms.

Artists also drew on the relatively rough surface of paper using charcoal or chalk. These naturally occurring materials are both dry and crumbly enough to leave traces when the artist applies them to the paper. The lines they leave can be thick or thin, rendered with carefully descriptive marks or with quick evocative strokes. Artists could smudge these soft mediums to soften contours and fill in shadows, or to produce parallel lines called hatching to describe shadows. See, for example, the variety of strokes Michelangelo used to make the red chalk study for the Libyan Sibyl on the Sistine Chapel ceiling.

More difficult to master was the technique of silverpoint. This entailed using a metal stylus to leave marks on a surface. Silver was the most prized metal for this technique, though lead was also used. Mistakes could not be undone, so it took great skill to work in silverpoint. To make silver leave traces on paper, the paper had to be stiffened up by coating it with a mixture of finely ground bone and size (a gluelike substance). Such coatings were sometimes tinted. When the silver stylus is applied, thin delicate lines are left behind that darken with age.

Renaissance artists also expanded the uses of drawings. Apprentices learned how to render forms using drawings; artists worked out solutions to visual problems with drawings. Drawings were also used to enable artists to negotiate contracts and to record finished works as a kind of diary or model book.

Artists also made **cartoons**, or full-scale patterns, for larger works such as frescoes or tapestries (see fig. 16.26). Transferring designs from drawings onto larger surfaces could be achieved in a number of ways. A grid could be placed over the design to serve as a guide for replicating the image on a larger scale. Or cartoons for frescoes could

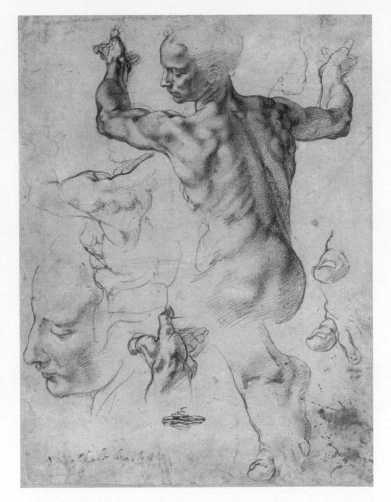

Michelangelo Buonarroti, *Studies for the Libyan Sibyl*. 1508–12. Red chalk, 11⅜ × 8⁷⁄₁₆" (28.9 × 21.4 cm). Metropolitan Museum of Art, New York. Joseph Pulitzer Bequest, 1924 (24.197.2)

be pricked along the main lines of the design; through these tiny holes a powder was forced to reproduce the design on the wall. This is called **pouncing**.

In the sixteenth century, drawings became prized in their own right and were collected by artists, patrons, and connoisseurs. The drawing was thought to reveal something that a finished work could not: the artist's process, the artist's personality, and ultimately, the artist's genius.

the bold, intense hues and expressive body language that characterize the whole ceiling. Michelangelo's figures are full of life, acting out their epic roles in sparse landscape settings. To the left of the Tree of Knowledge, Adam and Eve form a spiral composition as they reach toward the forbidden fruit, while the composition of *The Expulsion from the Garden of Eden* is particularly close to Masaccio's (see fig. 15.27) in its intense drama. The nude youths (*ignudi*) flanking the main sections of the ceiling play an important visual role in Michelangelo's design. They are found at regular intervals, forming a kind of chain linking the narratives. Yet their meaning remains uncertain. Some scholars have proposed

that they represent the world of pagan antiquity. Others have debated whether they are angels or images of human souls. They hold acorns, a reference to the pope's family name, delle Rovere (*rovere* means "oak"). The *ignudi* also support bronze medallions that look like trophies, reminding the viewer of Julius's military campaigns throughout Italy.

The most memorable of the center narratives is *The Creation of Adam* (fig. **16.21**). The fresco depicts not the physical molding of Adam's body, but the passage to him of the divine spark—the soul. The expressive composition conveys a profound conception of the relationship between God and humankind. Michelangelo's

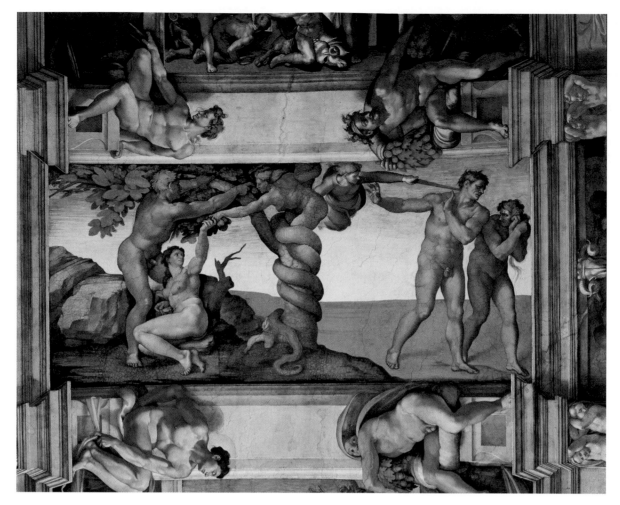

16.20 Michelangelo, *The Fall of Man* and *The Expulsion from the Garden of Eden*. 1508–12.
From the Sistine Chapel ceiling, Vatican, Rome.

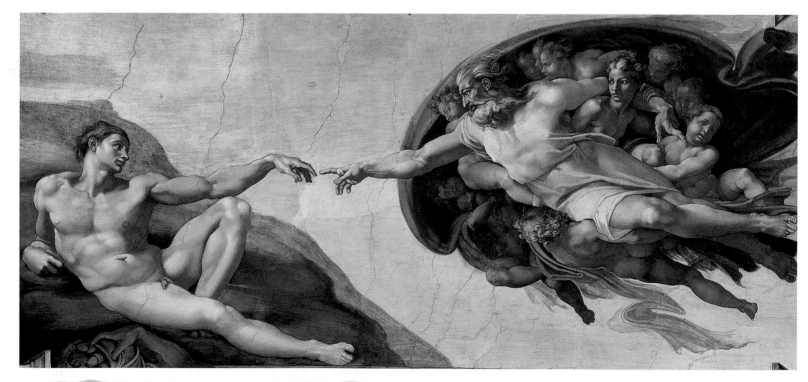

16.21 Michelangelo, *The Creation of Adam*. 1508–12. Portion of the Sistine Chapel ceiling

design contrasts the earthbound Adam, who has been likened to an awakening river-god, with the dynamic figure of God rushing through the sky. Adam gazes not only toward his Creator, he also looks toward the figures in the shelter of God's left arm. The identity of these figures has been vigorously debated: The female may be Eve, awaiting her creation in the next panel; another proposal is that she may be Mary, with Jesus at her knee, foreordained to redeem fallen humanity. The entire image has come to be seen as the perfect expression of Michelangelo's view of his own artistic creativity.

After the death of Julius II in 1513, Michelangelo returned to his work on the pope's tomb. But when Leo X (the son of Lorenzo de' Medici) acceded to the papacy, he sent Michelangelo back to Florence, to work on projects for the Medici family, which had been restored to power. There, his style developed and changed, until his eventual return to Rome in the 1530s.

Raphael in Florence and Rome

If Michelangelo represents the solitary genius, Raphael of Urbino (Raffaello Sanzio, 1483–1520) belongs to the opposite type: the artist as a man of the world. The contrast between them was clear to their contemporaries, and both enjoyed great fame. Vasari's book, with its championing of Michelangelo, helped to inspire later generations' veneration of Michelangelo over Raphael, in part because of the two men's biographies. Where Michelangelo's dramatic conflicts with his art and with his patrons made a good narrative, Raphael's career seems too much a success story, his work too marked by effortless grace, to match the tragic heroism of Michelangelo. Raphael's gifts were in his technical brilliance, his intelligent approach to composing pictures, and his dialogue with the other artists of his time. He is the central painter of the High Renaissance. During his relatively brief career he created the largest body of Renaissance pictorial work outside of Titian's, one that is notable for its variety and power. He also oversaw a lively and large workshop, from which many artists of the next generation emerged, effectively putting his stamp on the whole period.

RAPHAEL'S EARLY MADONNAS Raphael had a genius for synthesis that enabled him to merge the qualities of Leonardo and Michelangelo. His art is lyrical and dramatic, pictorially rich and sculpturally solid. These qualities are already present in the Madonnas he painted in Florence (1504–08) after his apprenticeship with Perugino. The meditative calm of the so-called *La Belle Jardinière* (*Beautiful Gardener*) (fig. **16.22**) still reflects the style of his teacher; the forms are, however, more ample and the chiaroscuro expertly rendered. The young Jesus and John the Baptist have perfect little bodies, posed in graceful postures to interact with each other and the Virgin. For this image, Raphael reworks a composition by Leonardo, but he replaces the enigmatic gestures in *The Virgin of the Rocks* with a gentle, rhythmic interplay. Raphael substitutes for Leonardo's intricate grouping a stable pyramid whose severity is relieved by Mary's billowing cape. Equally striking is the carefully observed landscape, whose

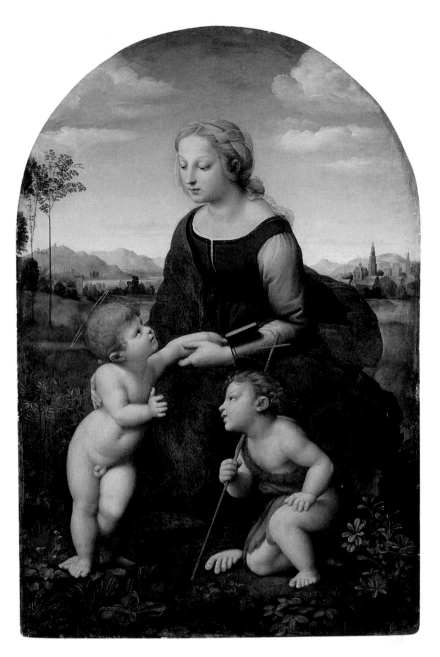

16.22 Raphael, *La Belle Jardinière*. 1507. Oil on panel, 48 × 31½" (122 × 80 cm). Musée du Louvre, Paris

bright light and natural beauty provide an appropriate setting for the figure group.

One of the reasons *La Belle Jardinière* looks different from *The Virgin of the Rocks* (see fig. 16.5), to which it is otherwise so clearly indebted, is Michelangelo's influence, which is seen in the figural composition. The full force of this influence can be felt only in Raphael's Roman works, however. In 1508, at the time Michelangelo began to paint the Sistine Chapel ceiling, Julius II summoned Raphael from Florence at the suggestion of Bramante, who also came from Urbino. At first, Raphael mined ideas he had developed under his teacher Perugino, but Rome utterly transformed him as an artist, just as it had Bramante, and he underwent an astonishing growth.

Cleaning and Restoring Works of Art

One of the most controversial topics in contemporary art history is whether and how to clean venerable but soiled works of art. Heated exchanges, accusations, and lawsuits regularly accompany cleaning and restoration projects. Cleaning means just that—removing soot, grime, pollutants, and sometimes layers of varnish or other protective materials earlier generations of owners put on a work. Restoration may involve replacing missing elements in a work to suggest to a viewer what an object looked like on its completion. Both processes are hotly debated today.

Many of the most famous images from the Renaissance have been at the center of these controversies: Giotto's Arena Chapel, Masaccio's Brancacci Chapel, Leonardo's *Last Supper*, Michelangelo's frescoes at the Sistine Chapel, and Michelangelo's *David*. Questions arise because of the jarring outcomes that can result from cleaning projects. For example, when the Sistine Chapel ceiling was cleaned in the 1980s, critics complained that the process removed the top layer of the paint, leaving only "garish" underpainting. Michelangelo's reputation as a colorist has been permanently changed by the cleaning of the ceiling frescoes.

The techniques of cleaning vary according to the medium and condition of the work, but conservators try to use the least damaging solvents possible, and they document every step they take. Work can be very slow, as in the case of *The Last Supper*. The project took 20 years, as cleaners had to contend with the work of earlier "restorers," who had filled in missing sections of the image with new paint.

Current cleaning removed overpaints, and filled in missing areas with removable water-based pigment. Restorers today are careful to add only materials that can be removed without damaging the original object.

Museums routinely clean objects in their care to conserve them. Major museums keep large conservation laboratories staffed by art historians, chemists, and artists to treat works of art. Often the impetus and funding for such projects comes when an object is requested for an important exhibition. In the case of the Sistine Chapel ceiling, a corporation underwrote the cleaning of the ceiling in exchange for the rights to make a film about the process. Philanthropic and corporate donors have supported many recent cleaning projects.

The *David* offers a good example of why objects need cleaning. The statue stood in the Piazza della Signoria for almost four centuries, subjected to pollutants and humidity, until it was removed to the Galleria dell'Accademia in Florence in 1873. (A copy now stands in the Piazza.) In 2003, a cleaning program was undertaken, again amidst protests: Critics wanted a minimally invasive dry cleaning (like a careful dusting), but the curators used a distilled water, clay, and cellulose paste to draw pollutants out of the marble. Mineral spirits (solvents) were used to remove wax on the marble.

Perhaps the one object from the High Renaissance most in need of cleaning today—but unlikely to receive it—is Leonardo's *Mona Lisa*. The current directors of the Louvre have said that no such cleaning is planned.

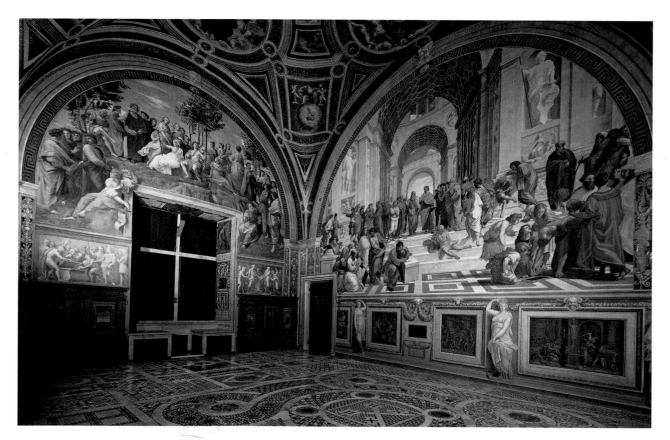

16.23   Raphael. Frescoes of the Stanza della Segnatura, Vatican Palace, Rome. 1508–11

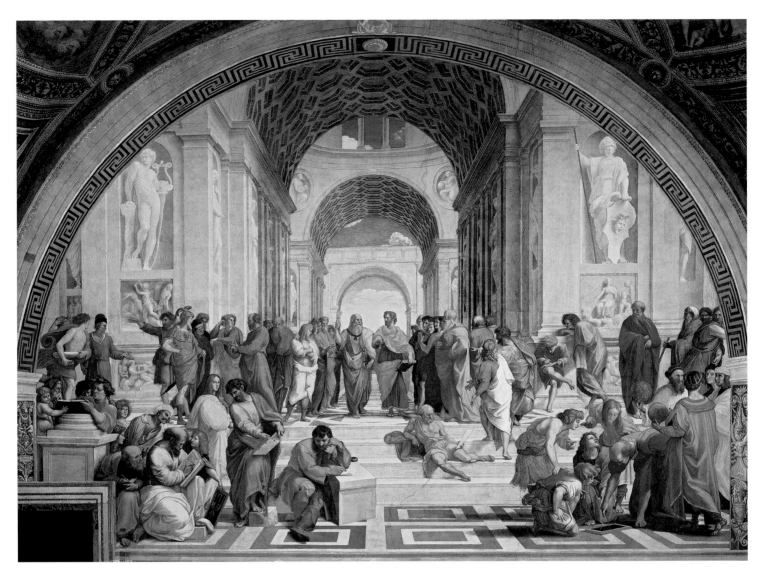

16.24 Raphael, *The School of Athens*, Stanza della Segnatura, Vatican Palace, Rome. 1508–11. Fresco

FRESCOES FOR THE STANZA DELLA SEGNATURA The results can be seen in the Stanza della Segnatura (fig. **16.23**), the first in a series of rooms which Julius commissioned him to decorate at the Vatican Palace. The frescoes painted by Raphael in this room show an almost endless fertility in the creation of daring narrative compositions. The "Room of the Signature," as it is translated, derives its name from its later function as the place where papal bulls (documents) were signed, though originally it housed Julius II's personal library. Beginning in 1508, Raphael painted a cycle of frescoes on its walls and ceiling that refer to the four domains of learning: theology, philosophy, law, and the arts. In general, the Stanza represents a summation of High Renaissance humanism, for it attempts to represent the unity of knowledge in one grand scheme. Raphael probably had a team of scholars and theologians as advisors, yet the design is his alone.

To represent these subjects, Raphael depicted figures from history and mythology in illusionistic spaces. For the arts, for example, the space above and flanking a window depicts Parnassus, the sacred mountain of Apollo. The god appears playing a lyre in a grove of laurel trees surrounded by the Nine Muses and great poets from antiquity down to the artist's own time. Dante stands on the left, near the blind Homer, Petrarch stands to the right, while Sappho appears to lean on the window frame at lower left. Her figure and that of the poet opposite her connect the painted Parnassus with the space of the room. Raphael uses the same illusionistic device that Mantegna exploited in the *Camera Picta* in Mantua (see fig. 15.49). The painting reflects the papal court's dream of a Golden Age under Julius II, in which the Vatican Hill would become the new Parnassus.

Of all the frescoes in the Stanza della Segnatura, *The School of Athens* (fig. **16.24**) has long been acknowledged as Raphael's masterpiece and the embodiment of the classical spirit of the High Renaissance. The title was only assigned later, and the subject of the painting has been much debated. The fresco seems to represent a group of famous Greek philosophers gathered around Plato and Aristotle, each in a characteristic pose or activity. Raphael may have already studied parts of the Sistine Chapel ceiling, then nearing completion: He owes to Michelangelo the expressive energy, the physical power, and dramatic grouping of his figures. Yet he has not simply borrowed Michelangelo's gestures and poses. He has absorbed them into his own style and thus given them a different meaning. Body and spirit, action and emotion are balanced harmoniously, and all members of this great assembly play their roles with magnificent, purposeful clarity.

The conception of *The School of Athens* suggests the spirit of Leonardo's *The Last Supper* (see fig. 16.6), as Raphael organizes his figures into groups like Leonardo's. He further distinguishes the relationships among individuals and groups, and links them in a formal rhythm. (The artist worked out the poses in a series of drawings, many made from life.) Also in the spirit of Leonardo is the symmetrical design, as well as the interdependence of the figures and their architectural setting. Like Leonardo's work, an opening in the building serves as a frame for the key figures. But Raphael's building plays a greater role in the composition than the hall does in *The Last Supper*. With its lofty dome, barrel vault, and colossal statuary, it is classical in spirit, yet Christian in meaning. Inspired by Bramante, who, Vasari informs us, helped Raphael with the architecture, the building seems like an advance view of the new St. Peter's, then being constructed. Capacious, luxurious, overpowering, the building is more inspired by Roman structures, such as the Basilica of Maxentius and Constantine (see fig. 7.60), than by anything Greek. Yet two illusionistically rendered sculptures of Greek divinities preside over this gathering of learned men of the Greek past: Apollo, patron of the arts with his lyre to the left, and Athena, in her guise as Minerva, goddess of wisdom, on the right.

The program of *The School of Athens* reflects the most learned humanism of the day, which commentators are still elucidating. Since Vasari's time, historians have attempted to identify the figures inhabiting this imposing space. At center stage, Plato (whose face resembles Leonardo's) holds his book about cosmology and numerology, *Timaeus*, which provided the basis for much of the Neo-Platonism that came to pervade Christianity. To Plato's left (a viewer's right), his pupil Aristotle grasps a volume of his *Ethics*, which, like his science, is grounded in what is knowable in the material world. The tomes explain why Plato is pointing rhetorically to the heavens, Aristotle to the earth. The figures represent the two most important Greek philosophers, whose approaches, although seemingly opposite, were deemed complementary by many Renaissance humanists. In this composition, the two schools of philosophy come together.

Some believe that Raphael organized his array of philosophers to reflect the two camps: the idealists and the empiricists. To Plato's right is his mentor, Socrates, who addresses a group of disciples by counting out his arguments on his fingers. Standing before the steps are figures representing mathematics and physics (the lower branches of philosophy that are the gateway to higher knowledge). Here appears the bearded Pythagoras, for whom the truth of all things is to be found in numbers. The diagrams and sums on the tablets at his feet symbolize the importance of number in philosophy. On the other side of the same plane, Raphael

borrowed the features of Bramante for the head of Euclid, seen drawing or measuring two overlapping triangles with a pair of compasses in the foreground to the lower right. Behind him, two men holding globes may represent Zoroaster the astronomer and Ptolemy the geographer. Vasari tells us that the man wearing a black hat behind these scientists is a self-portrait of Raphael, who places himself in the Aristotelian camp.

Despite the competition between them, Raphael added Michelangelo at the last minute (as revealed by his insertion of a layer of fresh plaster or *intonaco* on which to paint the new figure), whom he has cast as Heraclitus, a sixth-century BCE philosopher, shown deep in thought sitting on the steps in the Platonic camp. (Heraclitus was often paired with Diogenes the Cynic, shown here lying at the feet of Plato and Aristotle.) Scholars have remarked that this figure is not only a portrait of the sculptor, but is rendered in the style of the figures on the nearby Sistine Chapel ceiling. The inclusion of so many artists among, as well as in the guise of, famous philosophers is testimony to their recently acquired—and hard-won—status as members of the learned community.

PAPAL AND PRIVATE COMMISSIONS After Julius II died in 1513, Raphael was hired by his successor, Leo X, who ordered

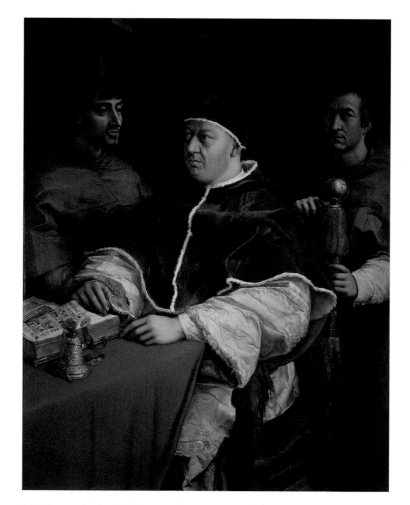

16.25 Raphael, *Portrait of Pope Leo X with Cardinals Giulio de' Medici and Luigi de' Rossi*. ca. 1517. Oil on panel, 60⅝ × 46⅞" (154 × 119 cm). Galleria degli Uffizi, Florence

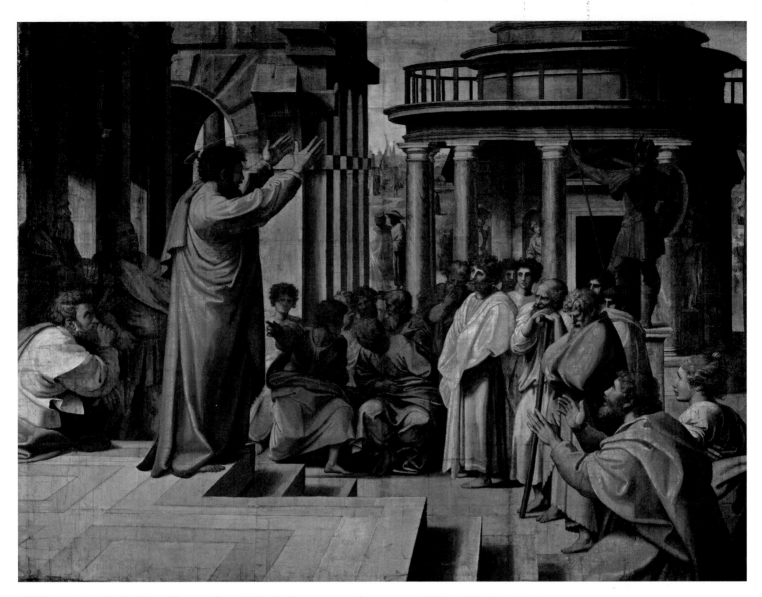

16.26 Raphael, *St. Paul Preaching at Athens*. 1515–16. Cartoon, gouache on paper, 11'3" × 14'6" (3.4 × 4.4 m). Victoria & Albert Museum, London

him to finish painting the papal apartments. The pope also sat for portraits. In the *Portrait of Pope Leo X with Cardinals Giulio de' Medici and Luigi de' Rossi* (fig. **16.25**), painted about 1517, Raphael did little to improve the heavy-jowled features of the pope, or the faces of his associates. (Giulio de' Medici, on the left, became pope himself in 1523, as Clement VII.) The three men are gathered around a table, on which rests a beautifully worked bell and an illuminated manuscript. Rather than a spiritual being or a warrior, the pope is represented as a collector and connoisseur, shown examining a precious object. The textures of the brocades and fur-lined garment only add to the sensual experience. Light enters this space from a window on the right whose shape is reflected in the brass ball of the chair's finial, a reference to the Medici coat of arms. This meditation on the sense of sight owes a debt to Netherlandish art. Leo sent the portrait to Florence to serve as his stand-in during wedding festivities for his Medici cousins there.

Raphael's work clearly pleased the new pope. After Bramante's death in 1514, Raphael was named the architect of St. Peter's and subsequently superintendent of antiquities in Rome. In 1516, Pope Leo X sent Michelangelo to Florence to work at San Lorenzo, leaving Raphael as the leading artist in Rome. He was flooded with commissions, and of necessity depended increasingly on his growing workshop.

In 1515–16, the pope commissioned Raphael to design a set of tapestries on the theme of the Acts of the Apostles for the Sistine Chapel. The commission placed him in direct competition with Michelangelo; consequently, Raphael designed and executed the ten huge cartoons (see *Materials and Techniques*, page 575) for this series with great care and enthusiasm. Because the cartoons were sent to Flanders to be woven, they helped to spread High Renaissance ideas from Italy to northern Europe. One of the most influential of these cartoons is *St. Paul Preaching at Athens* (fig. **16.26**), which demonstrates Raphael's synthesizing genius.

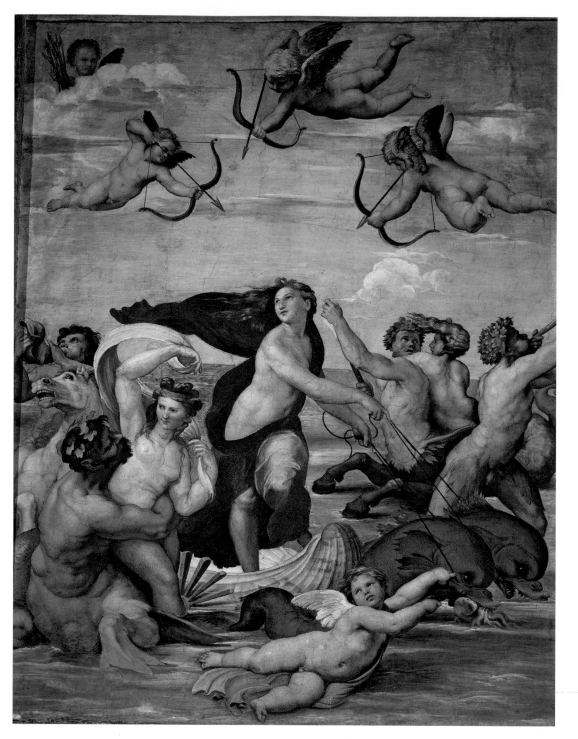

16.27   Raphael, *Galatea*, Villa Farnesina, Rome. ca. 1513. Fresco, 9'8⅛" × 7'4" (3 × 2.2 m)

For the imposing figure of St. Paul, Raphael has adapted the severity and simplicity of Masaccio's Brancacci Chapel frescoes (see figs. 15.24–15.27). The power of the saint's words is expressed not only by his gestures, but by the responses of the voluminously clad audience. Bramante inspires the architecture that defines the space; the plain Tuscan order of the columns in the round temple in the background recalls the Tempietto (see fig. 16.8). Instead of allowing the eye to wander deeply into the distance, Raphael limits the space to a foreground plane, into which a viewer is invited by the steps in the foreground. The simplicity

and grandeur of the conception conveys the narrative in bold, clear terms that are only enhanced by the large scale of the figures.

Other patrons in Rome also engaged Raphael's busy workshop; the powerful Sienese banker Agostino Chigi hired Raphael to adorn his new villa in Rome, now called the Villa Farnesina after a later owner. The building served as the setting for Chigi's interests: in the antique, in conspicuous display, and in love. Throughout the villa he commissioned frescoes on themes from the pagan past. For this setting, Raphael painted the *Galatea* around 1513 (fig. **16.27**). The beautiful nymph Galatea,

On Raphael's Death

Raphael died in Rome in April of 1520. In a letter to Isabella d'Este, the duchess of Mantua, the humanist Pandolfo Pico della Mirandola tells her about the artist's death and the reaction of Rome to his loss.

... now I shall inform you of ... the death of Raphael of Urbino, who died last night, that is, on Good Friday, leaving this court in the greatest and most universal distress because of the loss of hope for the very great things one expected of him that would have given glory to our time. And indeed it is said about this that he gave promise for everything great, through what one could already see of his works and through the grander ones he had begun. ... Here one speaks of nothing else but of the death of this good man, who at thirty-three years of age has finished his first life; his second one, however, that of fame which is not subject to time and death, will be eternal, both through his works and through the men of learning that will write in his praise.

Source: Konrad Oberhuber, *Raphael. The Paintings* (Munich and New York: Prestel, 1999)

vainly pursued by the giant Polyphemus, belongs to Greek mythology, known to the Renaissance through the verses of Ovid. Raphael's *Galatea* celebrates the sensuality of the pagan spirit as if it were a living force. Although the composition of the nude female riding a seashell recalls Botticelli's *The Birth of Venus* (see fig. 15.40), a painting Raphael may have known in Florence, the resemblance only serves to emphasize their profound differences. Raphael's figures are vigorously sculptural and arranged in a dynamic spiral movement around the twisting Galatea. In Botticelli's picture, the movement is not generated by the figures but imposed on them by the decorative, linear design that places all the figures on the same plane. Like Michelangelo, Raphael uses the arrangement of figures, rather than any detailed perspective scheme, to call up an illusion of space and to create a vortex of movement.

Raphael's statuesque, full-bodied figures suggest his careful study of ancient Roman sculpture which, like Michelangelo, he wanted to surpass. An even more direct example of his use of antique sources is his design for the engraving of *The Judgment of Paris* by Marcantonio Raimondi, executed about 1520 (fig. **16.28**). Collectors increasingly desired to own Raphael's drawings, so he used the skills of the engraver to record and to spread his designs. Raphael based this one on a Roman sarcophagus panel, which he has interpreted rather than copied. The engraving depicts the Judgment of Paris witnessed by the Olympian gods in heaven and a group of river-gods on the lower right. The statuesque figures are firmly defined in the engravings through the strong contours and chiaroscuro, and they occupy a frontal plane across the images. In images like this, Raphael translated the art of antiquity for generations of artists to come.

Raphael's life was cut short in 1520, when he died after a brief illness. Roman society mourned him bitterly, according to the reports of witnesses. (See *Primary Source*, above.) Befitting the new status assigned to artists, he was buried in the Pantheon. Significantly, many of the leading artists of the next generation emerged from Raphael's workshop and took his style as their point of departure.

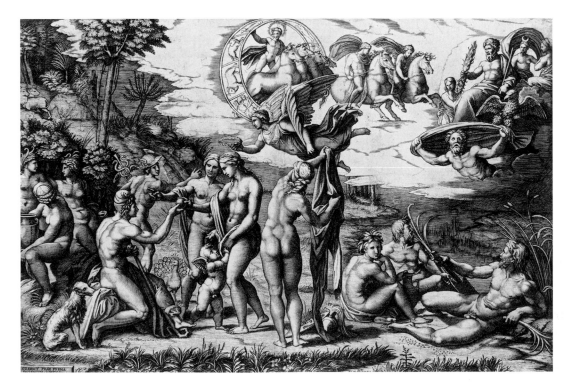

16.28 Marcantonio Raimondi, after Raphael, *The Judgment of Paris*. ca. 1510–20. Engraving, 11⁷/₁₆ × 17³/₁₆" (29.1 × 43.7 cm). Metropolitan Museum of Art, New York. Rogers Fund, 1919. (19.74.1)

VENICE

As Rome became the center of an imperial papal style of art, Venice endured the enmity of its neighbors and the dismantling of its northern Italian empire. Having gradually expanded its influence over northeastern Italy, in 1509 the Republic of Venice faced a threat from the League of Cambrai, an international military alliance aimed against it. Yet, by 1529, Venice had outlasted this menace to its power and reclaimed most of its lost territory. Resisting the invasions of Europe by the Turks, Venice's navy fought determinedly in the eastern Mediterranean to hold off this threat. In the midst of this turmoil, artists in Venice built on the traditions of the fifteenth century and the innovations of Giovanni Bellini to create a distinct visual language. Two artists in particular, Giorgione and Titian, created new subjects, approaches to images, and techniques.

Giorgione

Giorgione da Castelfranco (1478–1510) left the orbit of Giovanni Bellini (see figs. 15.53 and 15.54) to create some of the most mysterious and beguiling paintings of the Renaissance. Although he painted some religious works, he seems to have specialized in smaller-scale paintings on secular themes for the homes of wealthy collectors. His death at a young age, probably from the plague, left the field open for his young colleague, Titian, who worked in his shop for some time. Some of the works traditionally ascribed to Giorgione have, in fact, been argued for Titian in recent years. Many of his works defy attempts to interpret them.

This is the case with Giorgione's *The Tempest* (fig. **16.29**). Documents record the picture in the collection of the patrician Gabriele Vendramin, one of Venice's greatest patrons of the arts. Scholars have offered many possible explanations of this image, which depicts a stormy landscape inhabited by a male figure on the left and a nursing mother on the right. The male has been identified as a shepherd, a warrior, or an angel; the nude woman has been identified as Eve, as Hagar, as Venus, or Nature herself. The figures, and thus any narrative content, remain enigmatic. In fact, Giorgione's landscape seems to provide the key to interpretation. With its verdant setting and humid atmosphere, the scene is like an enchanted idyll, a dream of pastoral beauty soon to be swept away, as the fury of a summer thunderstorm lights the sky. While the painting is very similar in mood to that conjured by the *Arcadia* of Jacopo Sannazaro, a poem about unrequited love that was popular in Giorgione's day, even such parallels do not account for all the details in the image. Scholars have argued that *The Tempest* initiates what was to become an important new tradition in art, the making of pictorial equivalents to poetry or *poesie*, as contemporaries called them: atmospheric images that set a mood rather than convey a story. Nonetheless, what the original audience may have read into the image continues to perplex modern viewers.

A similar problem confronts the viewer of the so-called *Fête Champêtre* or *Pastoral Concert* (fig. **16.30**). The picture has been on display in the Louvre in Paris since the nineteenth century, where it arrived from the French royal collection. It depicts a group of young people gathered in a lush landscape to make music when a shepherd and his flock come upon them. Attempts to find a narrative subject to attach to this image have proven fruitless: No single literary source seems to account for it. Most puzzling are the nude women, one of whom is about to play a recorder, while another takes water from a fountain. One proposal identifies them as the Muses, ancient female divinities who inspire the arts. The forms are rendered in a soft chiaroscuro technique so that they emerge from the atmospheric landscape as soft round shapes. The landscape moves from dark to light to dark passages, receding into the atmospheric distance. There is some evidence that the young Titian may have intervened in this work. Instead of telling a story, the painting seems designed to evoke a mood.

Vasari criticized Giorgione for not making drawings as part of his process of painting. (See www.myartslab.com.) Steeped in the Florentine tradition of Leonardo, Michelangelo, and Raphael, Vasari argued that drawing, or *disegno* was fundamental to good painting. The Venetians, however, valued light and color above all else to create their sensual images. Vasari dismissed this as mere *colore*, which he argued was secondary to the process of drawing. The resulting competition between *disegno* and *colore* provided

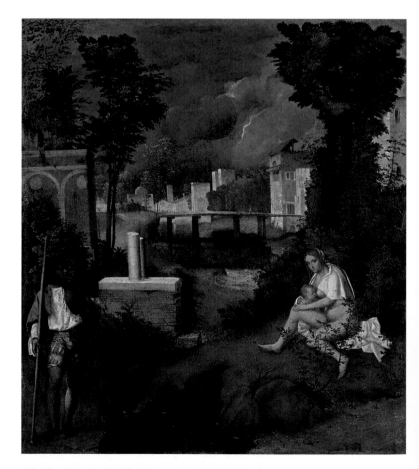

16.29 Giorgione, *The Tempest*. ca. 1505. Oil on canvas, 31¼ × 28¾" (79.5 × 73 cm). Galleria dell'Accademia, Venice

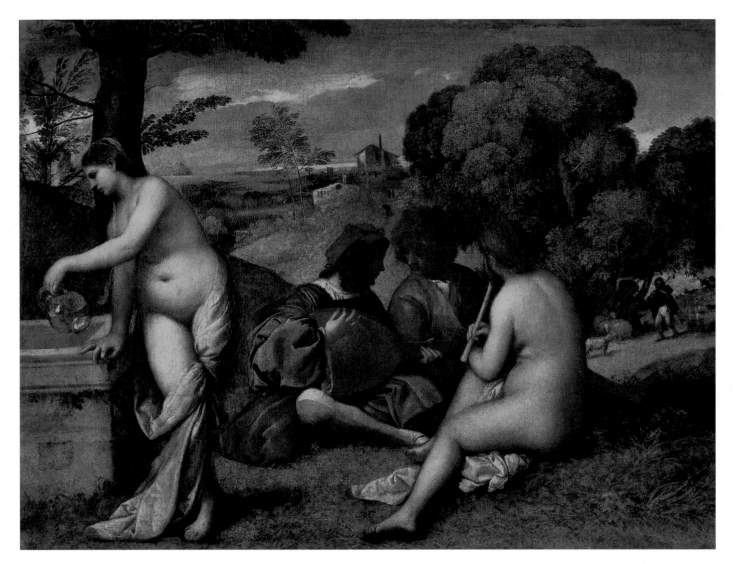

16.30   Giorgione (and Titian?), *Fête Champêtre* (*Pastoral Concert*). ca. 1509–10. Oil on canvas,
43¼ × 54⅜" (105 × 136.5 cm). Musée du Louvre, Paris

the grounds for criticizing or praising paintings well beyond the sixteenth century.

Titian

Giorgione died before he could fully explore the sensuous, lyrical world he had created in the *Fête Champêtre*. This task was taken up by Titian (Tiziano Vecellio, 1488/90–1576), who trained with Bellini and then with Giorgione and even repainted some of their works. Titian would dominate Venetian painting for the next half-century. Throughout his long life, he earned commissions from the most illustrious patrons in Europe; he trained many of the most important Venetian artists of the next century.

Titian's interpretation of the legacy of Giorgione may be seen in the *Bacchanal* (fig. **16.31**), commissioned around 1518 by Alfonso d'Este, the duke of Ferrara, for his Camerino d'Alabastro (Little Room of Alabaster). In this painting Titian attempted to remake a Roman painting known only from descriptions by the Roman author Philostratus. The theme is the effect of a river of

wine on the inhabitants of the island of Andros. Titian depicts a crowd of figures in various stages of undress hoisting jugs of wine and generally misbehaving. The painting thus competes with both antique art and literature. Titian's landscape, rich in contrasts of cool and warm tones, has all the poetry of Giorgione, but the figures are of another breed. Active and muscular, they move with a joyous freedom that recalls Raphael's *Galatea* (see fig. 16.27).

By this time, many of Michelangelo's and Raphael's compositions had been engraved; it was from these reproductions that Titian became familiar with the Roman High Renaissance. At least one figure, the man bending over to fill his jug in the river, may be copied from Michelangelo. A number of the figures in his *Bacchanal* also reflect the influence of classical art. Titian's approach to antiquity, however, is very different from Raphael's. He visualizes the realm of ancient myths as part of the natural world, inhabited not by animated statues but by beings of flesh and blood. The nude young woman who has passed out in the lower right corner is posed in such a way as to show off her beautiful young body for the viewer's pleasure. The figures of the

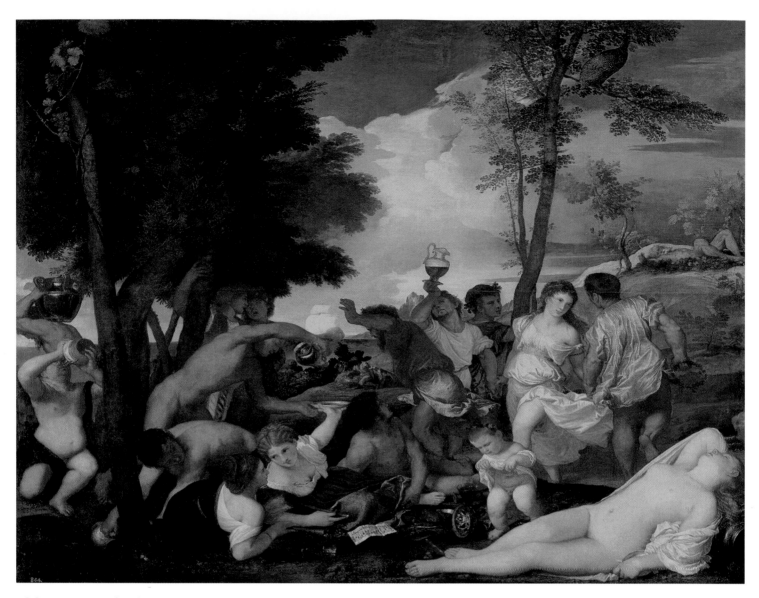

16.31 Titian, *Bacchanal*. ca. 1518. Oil on canvas, 5'8⅝" × 6'4" (1.7 × 1.9 m). Museo del Prado, Madrid

Bacchanal are idealized just enough to persuade us that they belong to a long-lost Golden Age. They invite us to share their blissful state in a way that makes the *Galatea* seem cold and remote by comparison.

Titian's ability to transform older traditions can also be seen in his *Madonna with Members of the Pesaro Family* (fig. **16.32**), commissioned in 1519 and installed in 1526 on the altar of the Immaculate Conception of the Franciscan church of Santa Maria Gloriosa dei Frari. Here, he takes a *sacra conversazione* in the tradition of Domenico Veneziano and Giovanni Bellini (see figs. 15.30 and 15.54) and reimagines both the composition and the figures. He sets the Virgin and Child at the apex of a triangular arrangement of figures, but replaces the familiar frontal view with an oblique one that is far more active. The infant Jesus is as natural as the child in the *Bacchanal*, pudgy and innocently playing with his mother's veil. More solemnly, the Virgin and St. Peter turn to the donor, Jacopo Pesaro, seen kneeling in devotion at the

left. On the other side are the donor's brothers and sons with SS. Francis and Anthony of Padua.

Titian places the Virgin's throne on the steps of a monumental church. The huge columns, which are the key to the setting, represent the gateway to Heaven, traditionally identified with Mary herself; the painting celebrates her as the Immaculate Conception, who was born without Original Sin. Because the view is diagonal, open sky and clouds fill most of the background. Except for the kneeling donors, every figure seems to move. The officer with the flag bearing the coats of arms of Pesaro and of Pope Alexander VI seems ready to lead a charge up the steps. He is probably

16.32 Titian, *Madonna with Members of the Pesaro Family*. 1526. Oil on canvas, 16' × 8'10" (4.9 × 2.7 m). Santa Maria Gloriosa dei Frari, Venice

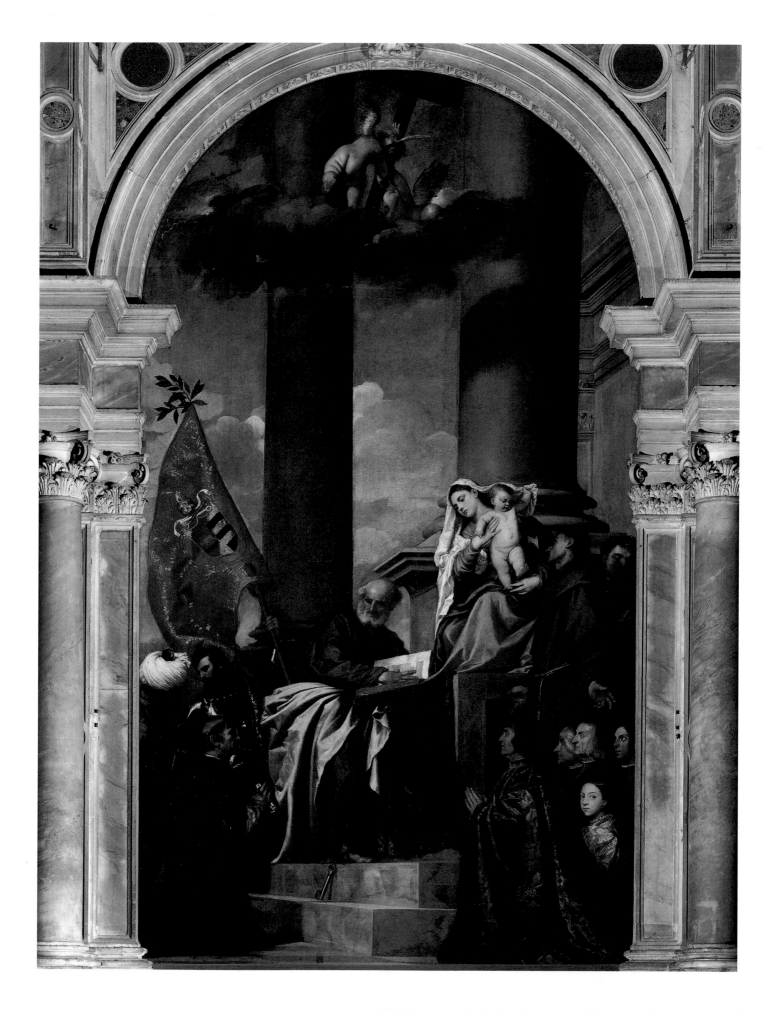

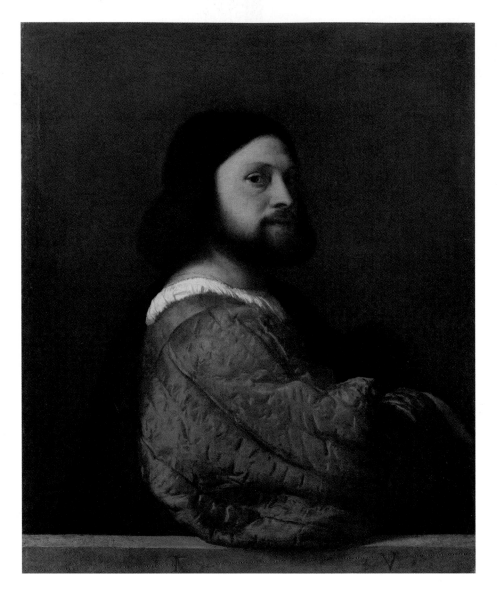

16.33 Titian, *Man with a Blue Sleeve*. ca. 1520. Oil on canvas, 32 x 26" (81.2 × 66.3 cm). The National Gallery, London

St. Maurice, namesake of the battle at Santa Mauro. There, the papal fleet commanded by Pesaro, bishop of Paphos, and the Venetian navy, under his cousin Benedetto Pesaro, defeated the Turks in 1502—note the turbaned figure beside him. St. Peter, identified by the key near his foot, represents the Catholic Church victorious over Islam and, as Pesaro's patron saint, acts as his intercessor with the Madonna. The design remains harmoniously self-contained, despite the strong drama. Brilliant sunlight makes every color and texture sparkle, in keeping with the joyous spirit of the altar. The only hint of tragedy is the cross held by the two little angels. Hidden by clouds from the participants in the *sacra conversazione*, it adds a note of poignancy to the scene.

After Raphael's death, Titian became the most sought-after portraitist of the age. His immense gifts, evident in the donors' portraits in the *Pesaro Madonna*, are equally striking in the *Man with a Blue Sleeve* (fig. 16.33). Titian places his sitter against a nonspecific backdrop behind a stone parapet, on which his initials ("T. V." for Tiziano Vecellio) appear. This is an arrangement pioneered by Flemish painters. The man turns to look at a viewer,

making eye contact. His self-confident air is expressed not only by his cool glance, but also by the commanding presence of the man's projecting arm, which appears to reach out into a viewer's space. The man also wears a fur robe: His garment indicates his elite social status. Titian records the textures of hair, cloth, and stone with great fidelity, all the while wrapping his figure in an atmospheric space through his use of chiaroscuro. The identity of the sitter is not known, but Titian attempts to record his personality as well as his appearance. An early tradition identified the man as the poet Ariosto; another hypothesis identifies him as a Venetian patrician for whose family Titian worked; yet another would claim this as a self-portrait. In any case, Titian's links to Bellini and to Giorgione shine through in this image.

Titian's career was to last long into the sixteenth century. His art is based on nature, whose likeness he records with great skill. He endows his figures with grace and personality, and wraps them in atmospheric light. Titian's gift for compositions using naturalistic forms inspired by the ancient world make him a true representative of the High Renaissance.

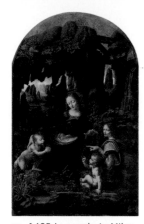

ca. 1485 Leonardo in Milan begins *The Virgin of the Rocks*

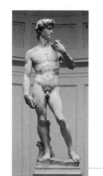

1501 Michelangelo begins work on the *David*

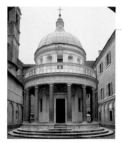

1502–11 Bramante's Tempietto

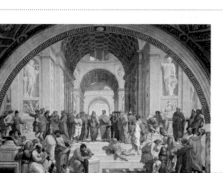

1508–11 Raphael's *The School of Athens*

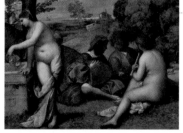

ca. 1509–10 Giorgione's *Fête Champêtre*

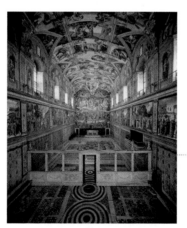

1512 Michelangelo's Sistine Chapel ceiling completed

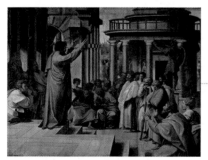

1515 Raphael's cartoon for tapestry of *St. Paul Preaching at Athens*

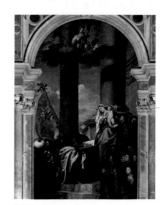

1526 Titian's *Madonna with Members of the Pesaro Family*

The High Renaissance in Italy, 1495–1520

1480

1490

1500

1510

1520

1530

◄ 1492 Death of Lorenzo de' Medici

◄ 1494 *Ship of Fools* published in Basel

◄ 1498 Execution of Savonarola in Florence

◄ 1503 Pope Julius II assumes papal throne

1505 Giovanni Bellini's *Madonna and Saints*

◄ 1509 League of Cambrai formed against Venice

◄ 1512 Florentine Republic dismantled; Medici return
◄ 1513 Leo X pope

◄ 1517 Luther posts his *Ninety-five Theses*, sparking the Reformation

◄ 1519 Leonardo dies in France

◄ 1521 Hernán Cortés conquers Mexico for Spain

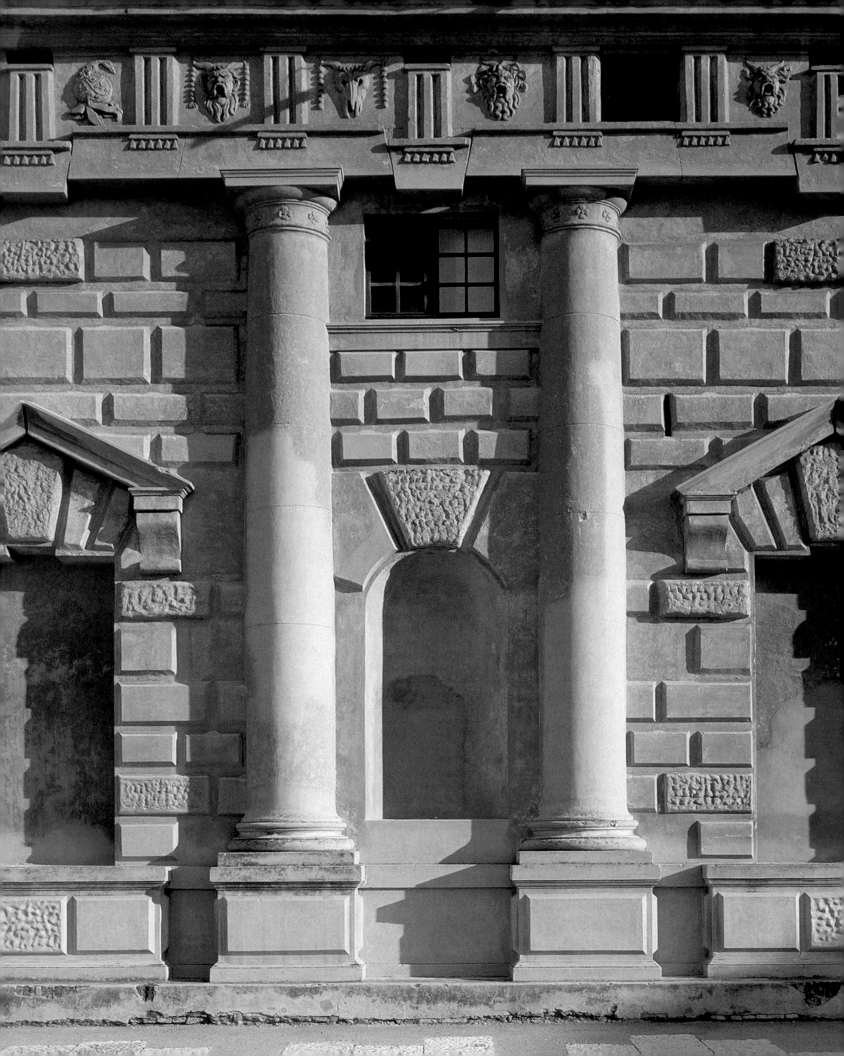

CHAPTER 17

The Late Renaissance and Mannerism in Sixteenth-Century Italy

FROM THE MOMENT THAT MARTIN LUTHER POSTED HIS CHALLENGE to the Roman Catholic Church in Wittenberg in 1517, the political and cultural landscape of Europe began to change. Europe's ostensible religious unity was fractured as entire regions left the Catholic fold. The great powers of France, Spain, and Germany warred with each other on the Italian

peninsula, even as the Turkish expansion into Europe threatened all. The spiritual challenge of the Reformation and the rise of powerful courts affected Italian artists in this period by changing the climate in which they worked and the nature of their patronage. No single style dominated the sixteenth century in Italy, though all the artists working in what is conventionally called the Late Renaissance were profoundly affected by the achievements of the High Renaissance.

The authority of the generation of the High Renaissance would both challenge and nourish later generations of artists. In the works of Leonardo, Raphael, Bramante, and Giorgione, younger artists could observe their elders' skillful rendering of chiaroscuro, perspective, and sfumato, as well as the elder generation's veneration of antiquity. The new generations imitated their technical expertise, their compositions, and their themes. At the same time, the artists of the High Renaissance continued to seek new ways to solve visual problems. Indeed, two of the key figures of the older generation lived to transform their styles: Michelangelo was active until 1564, and Titian until 1576.

The notion of the artist as an especially creative figure was passed on to later generations, yet much had changed. International interventions in Italy came to a head in 1527 when Rome itself was invaded and sacked by imperial troops of the

Habsburgs; three years later, Charles V was crowned Holy Roman emperor in Bologna. His presence in Italy had important repercussions: In 1530, he overthrew the reestablished Republic of Florence and restored the Medici to power. Cosimo I de' Medici became duke of Florence in 1537 and grand duke of Tuscany in 1569. Charles also promoted the rule of the Gonzaga of Mantua and awarded a knighthood to Titian. He and his successors became avid patrons of Titian, spreading the influence and prestige of Italian Renaissance style throughout Europe.

The Protestant movement spread quickly through northern Europe, as Luther, Zwingli, Calvin, and other theologians rejected papal authority and redefined Christian doctrine. Some of the reformers urged their followers to destroy religious images as idolatrous, leading to widespread destruction of images, stained glass, and other religious art. Italy itself, home of the Roman Catholic Church, resisted the new faiths. Nonetheless, through the first half of the sixteenth century, pressures for reform within the Catholic Church grew. The Roman Church had traditionally approved the role of images as tools for teaching and for encouraging piety, and through the efforts of reformers, this was now affirmed as official Church policy. (See www.myartslab.com.) But with its authority threatened by the Protestant Reformation, the Catholic Church asserted even more control over the content and style of images to assure doctrinal correctness. As it sought to define itself against the Protestant Reformation, religious imagery became increasingly standardized.

Detail of figure 17.24, Giulio Romano. *Courtyard of the Palazzo del Te*

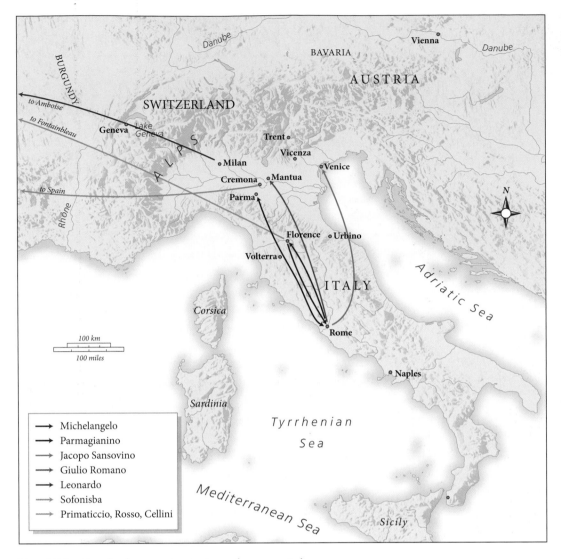

Map 17.1 Travels of some artists in sixteenth-century Italy

Artists responded to all these phenomena. The Sack of Rome in 1527 scattered Roman-based artists throughout Italy and Europe (map **17.1**). Commissions came mostly from the princely courts, so artists' works reflected the taste and concerns of this powerful elite. The connections among the courts helped to spread a new style, usually labeled Mannerist, which lasted through much of the century. The style was typically used for paintings and sculptures, though some works of architecture exhibit Mannerist tendencies.

The term derived from the word *maniera*, meaning manner or style, which was used approvingly by contemporaries. Building on the achievements of Raphael and Michelangelo, above all, artists of the 1520s and later developed a style that emphasized technical virtuosity, erudite subject matter, beautiful figures, and deliberately complex compositions that would appeal to sophisticated tastes. Mannerism became a style of utmost refinement, which emphasized grace, variety, and virtuoso display instead of clarity and unity. Mannerist artists self-consciously explored new definitions of beauty: Rather than repeat ancient forms, they experimented with proportions, ideal figure types, and unusual compositions. Like the artists of the High Renaissance, they aimed for originality and personal expression, which they considered their due as privileged creators.

Just what Mannerism represented continues to spark debate. Some have argued that it signified a decline, because it rejected the standards of the High Renaissance. (These critics, of course, prefer the "classical" works of the High Renaissance.) But the reasons that artists rejected the stability, assurance, and ideal forms of the High Renaissance are not well understood. Perhaps the new generation was attempting to define itself as different from its elders. Or, Mannerism may be seen as an expression of cultural crisis. Some scholars relate it to the spiritual crises brought on by the Reformation and the Catholic Counter-Reformation, while others see Mannerism as the product of an elite class's identity and taste. Even as scholars debate its origins and meanings, it is clear that Mannerism's earliest products appear in Florence in the 1520s, which was very different from the Florence of 1505.

LATE RENAISSANCE FLORENCE: THE CHURCH, THE COURT, AND MANNERISM

Under Medici rule, from 1512 to 1527, Florentine artists absorbed the innovations of the High Renaissance. Pope Leo X sent Michelangelo from Rome to Florence to work on projects for the Medici. The artistic descendants of Raphael came to the city as

well. Having contributed so much to the development of the Early and High Renaissance, Florentine artists now developed a new style that seems to reject the serenity and confidence of High Renaissance art. Using the techniques of naturalism, chiaroscuro, and figural composition learned from Leonardo, Michelangelo, and Raphael, this generation of artists made images that are less balanced and more expressive than those of the earlier generation. In works of the 1520s, a group of Florentine artists created images of deep spiritual power in this new style. This spiritual resurgence may be a reaction to the challenges of the Reformation, or it may be due to the legacy of the fiery preacher Savonarola, who had preached repentance in Florence in the 1490s.

Florentine Religious Painting in the 1520s

An early expression of the new style appears in *The Descent from the Cross* (fig. **17.1**) by Rosso Fiorentino (1495–1540), whose style is very idiosyncratic. A religious society of flagellants, Catholics whose penitential rituals included whipping themselves to express penitence, hired Rosso to paint this altarpiece in 1521. The Company of the Cross of the Day in the Tuscan city of Volterra chose the theme of the lowering of the body of Christ from the Cross, the subject of Rogier van der Weyden's painting of 1438 (see fig. 14.15). To reference the name of the sponsoring group, Rosso has given a great deal of emphasis to the Cross itself. While the composition looks back in part to Early Renaissance art, such as Masaccio's *Trinity* fresco (see fig. 15.23), the composition is much less stable than the triangle used by Masaccio. Instead of moving slowly and carefully back into space, the forms all appear on the same plane. The muscular bodies of the agitated figures recall Michelangelo, but the draperies have brittle, sharp-edged planes. The low horizon line sets the figures against a dark sky, creating a disquieting effect. The colors are not primaries but sharply contrasting, and the brilliant light seems to fall on the bodies irrationally. Unlike the orderly calm and deep space of Leonardo's *The Last Supper* (see fig. 16.6), Rosso creates an unstable composition within a compressed space staffed by figures that move frantically to lower the body of Christ. Only Christ's figure appears serene in the midst of this emotionally charged image. The Mannerist rejection of High Renaissance ideals allows Rosso to create in *The Descent from the Cross* a work that was especially appropriate to the piety of the confraternity members who commissioned it. Rosso himself left central Italy after the Sack of Rome in 1527 by Charles V, ultimately being lured to France to work for Francis I at his palace of Fontainebleau (see map 17.1 and Chapter 18).

Rosso's friend and contemporary Jacopo da Pontormo (1494–1556) developed his own version of the Mannerist style. The Capponi family hired Pontormo to transform their family chapel in the church of Santa Felicita in Florence (fig. **17.2**). The architecture of the chapel, built around 1420, is Brunelleschian in its simplicity, consisting of a dome over a square room, as in the Old Sacristy at San Lorenzo (see fig. 15.6). When Ludovico di Gino Capponi acquired its patronage in 1525, to be used as

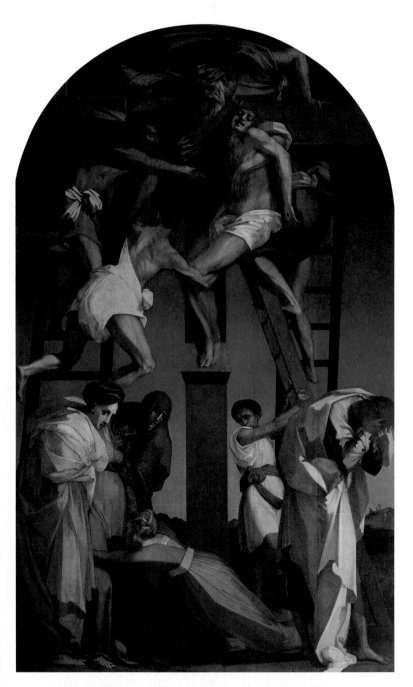

17.1 Rosso Fiorentino, *The Descent from the Cross*. 1521. Oil on panel, 13' × 6'6" (4 × 2 m). Commissioned for the Chapel of the Compagnia della Croce di Giorno in the church of San Francisco in Volterra. Pinacoteca Comunale, Volterra

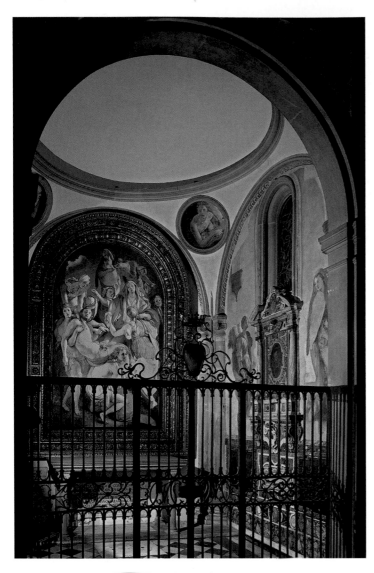

may have been inspired by the colors of the Sistine Chapel ceiling (see fig. 16.19). Although they seem to act together, the mourners are lost in a grief too personal to share with one another. In this hushed atmosphere, anguish is transformed into a lyrical expression of exquisite sensitivity. The entire scene is as haunted as Pontormo's self-portrait just to the right of the swooning Madonna. The body of Christ is held up for a viewer, much as the host is during the Mass, the image conveying to believers a sense of the tragic scale of Christ's sacrifice, which the Eucharist reenacts. Originally, the dome above the altarpiece depicted God the Father, to whom the body would be offered. Pontormo may have rejected the values of the High Renaissance, but he endows this image with deeply felt emotion.

17.2 Capponi Chapel, Santa Felicità, Florence.
Built by Filippo Brunelleschi, 1419–23.
Paintings by Pontormo, 1525–28.

a funerary chapel, he changed its dedication to the Pietà. He commissioned Pontormo to paint the altarpiece (fig. **17.3**) and frescoes on the walls and dome. The altarpiece, completed by 1528, remains in its original location in the chapel.

Pontormo's painting contrasts sharply with Rosso's *The Descent from the Cross*. It lacks a cross or any other indications of a specific narrative, so its subject is unclear, although the chapel's dedication points to the Pietà. The Virgin swoons as two androgynous figures hold up the body of Christ for a viewer's contemplation. Unlike Rosso's elongated forms, Pontormo's figures display an ideal beauty and sculptural solidity inspired by Michelangelo, yet Pontormo has squeezed them into an implausibly confined space.

In Pontormo's painting, everything is subordinated to the play of graceful rhythms created by the tightly interlocking forms. The colors are desaturated: pale blues, pinks, oranges, and greens that

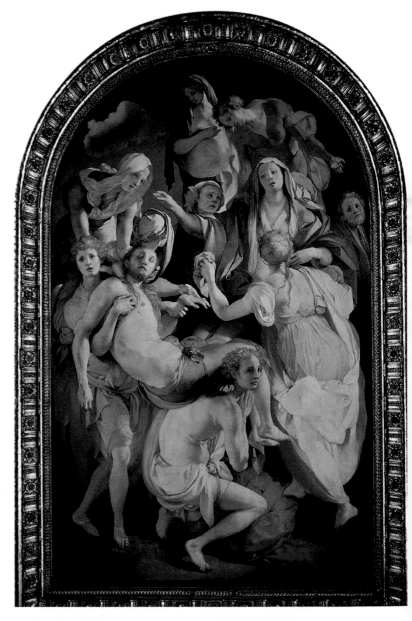

17.3 Jacopo da Pontormo, *Pietà*. ca. 1526–28. Oil on panel, 10'3" × 6'4" (3.1 × 1.9 m). Santa Felicita, Florence

The Medici in Florence: From Dynasty to Duchy

In the chaos after the Sack of Rome of 1527, the Medici were again ousted from Florence and the Republic of Florence was reinstated. But the restoration of relations between the pope and the Holy Roman emperor allowed the Medici to return to power by 1530. The Medici pope Clement VII (r. 1523–1534) promoted his family's interests, and worked to enhance their power as the rulers of Florence. Although he was an ardent republican, Michelangelo was continually employed by this court, executing works intended to glorify the Medici dynasty in Florence.

THE NEW SACRISTY OF SAN LORENZO Michelangelo's activities centered on the Medici church of San Lorenzo. A century after Brunelleschi's design for the sacristy of this church (see fig. 15.6), which held the tombs of an earlier generation of Medici,

Pope Leo X decided to build a matching structure, the New Sacristy. It was to house the tombs of Leo X's father, Lorenzo the Magnificent, Lorenzo's brother Giuliano, and two younger members of the family, also named Lorenzo and Giuliano. Aided by numerous assistants, Michelangelo worked on the project from 1519 to 1534 and managed to complete the architecture and two of the tombs, those for the later Lorenzo and Giuliano (fig. **17.4**); these tombs are nearly mirror images of each other. Michelangelo conceived of the New Sacristy as an architectural-sculptural ensemble.

Michelangelo's chapel starts from Brunelleschi's design for a square space covered by a dome, though he inserted another story above the architrave and below the supports for the dome. This gives the chapel greater verticality and brings in more light. The wall scheme also follows Brunelleschi, although the *pietra serena* pilasters and entablatures are bolder and taller than Brunelleschi's. Between the pilasters Michelangelo inserted blind windows

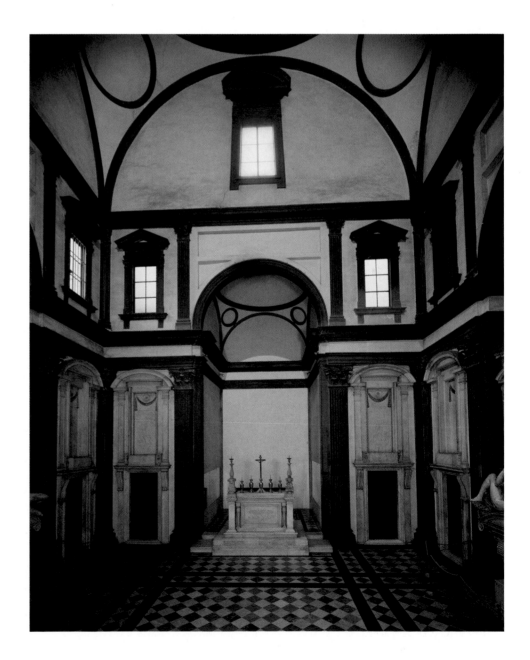

17.4 Michelangelo, New Sacristy, San Lorenzo, Florence. 1519–34

of verticals and horizontals hold the triangle of statues in place; their slender, sharp-edged forms contrast with the roundness and weight of the sculpture.

The design shows some kinship with such Early Renaissance tombs as Rossellino's tomb for Leonardo Bruni (see fig. 15.18), but the differences are marked. There is no outright Christian imagery, no inscription, and the effigy has been replaced by two allegorical figures—Day on the right and Night on the left. Some lines penned on one of Michelangelo's drawings suggest what these figures mean: "Day and Night speak, and say: We with our swift course have brought the Duke Giuliano to death....It is only just that the Duke takes revenge [for] he has taken the light from us; and with his closed eyes has locked ours shut, which no longer shine on earth." The reclining figures, themselves derived from ancient river-gods, contrast in mood: Day, whose face was left deliberately unfinished, seems to brood, while Night appears restless. Giuliano, the ideal image of the prince, wears classical military garb and bears no resemblance to the deceased. ("A thousand years from now, nobody will know what he looked like,"

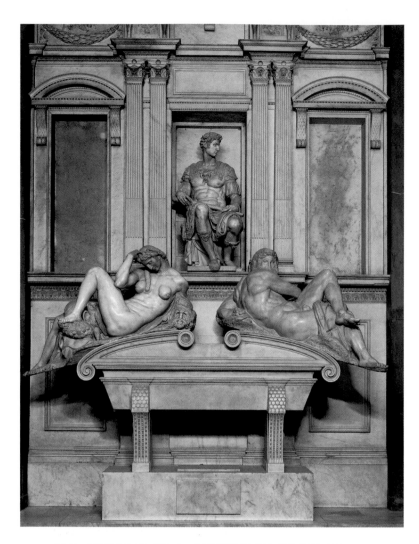

17.5 Michelangelo. Tomb of Giuliano de' Medici. 1519–34. Marble, height of central figure 5'11" (1.81 m). New Sacristy, San Lorenzo, Florence

topped by curved pediments. Such features activate the wall, leaving little blank surface; Michelangelo treated the walls themselves as sculptural forms in a way Brunelleschi never did.

The New Sacristy is the only one of the artist's works in which the statues remain in the setting originally intended for them, although their exact placement remains problematic. Michelangelo's plans for the Medici tombs underwent many changes while the work was under way. Other figures and reliefs for the project were designed but never executed. The present state of the Medici tombs can hardly be what Michelangelo ultimately intended, as the process was halted when the artist permanently left Florence for Rome in 1534.

The tomb of Giuliano (fig. 17.5) remains an imposing visual unit, composed of a sarcophagus structure supporting two sculpted nudes above which sits an armored figure, all framed by Michelangelo's inventive reimagining of Classical architecture. The central niche seems barely to accommodate the seated figure; paired pilasters flank the figure and support an entablature that breaks over them. The curving pediments over the blank windows on either side echo the shape of the sarcophagus below. A network

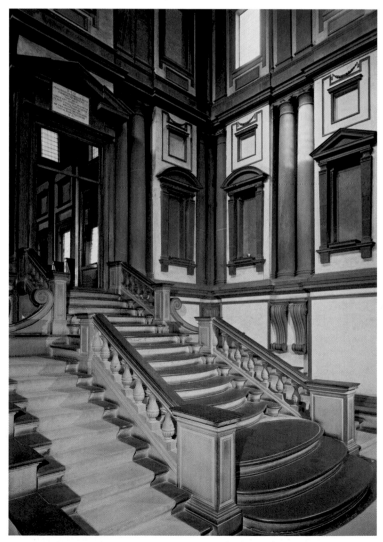

17.6 Michelangelo and Bartolommeo Ammanati. Vestibule of the Laurentian Library, Florence. Begun 1523; stairway designed 1558–59

Michelangelo is said to have remarked.) His beautifully proportioned figure seems ready for action, as he fidgets with his baton. His gaze was to be directed at the never-completed tomb of Lorenzo the Magnificent. Instead of a commemorative monument that looks retrospectively at the accomplishments of the deceased, the tomb of Giuliano and the New Sacristy as a whole were to express the triumph of the Medici family over time.

Michelangelo's reimagining of Brunelleschi at the New Sacristy inspired Vasari to write that "all artists are under a great and permanent obligation to Michelangelo, seeing that he broke the bonds and chains that had previously confined them to the creation of traditional forms." However, Michelangelo's full powers as a creator of architectural forms are only really displayed for the first time in the vestibule to the Laurentian Library, which adjoins San Lorenzo.

THE LAURENTIAN LIBRARY Clement VII commissioned this library (fig. **17.6**) in 1523 to house, for the public, the huge collection of books and manuscripts belonging to the Medici family. Such projects display the Medici beneficence to the city and their encouragement of learning. The Laurentian Library is a long narrow hall that is preceded by the imposing vestibule, begun in 1523 but not completed until much later.

Judged by the standards of Bramante or Vitruvius, everything in the vestibule is wrong. The pediment above the door is broken. The pilasters defining the blank niches taper downward, and the columns belong to no recognizable order. The scroll brackets sustain nothing. Most paradoxical of all are the recessed columns. This feature flies in the face of convention. In the classical post-and-lintel system, the columns (or pilasters) and entablature must

project from the wall in order to stress their separate identities, as they do in the Roman Temple of Portunus (see fig. 7.2). Michelangelo dared to defy the classical system by inserting columns into the wall. In the confined space of the entryway, the columns give the wall a monumental dignity without intruding into the vestibule. The grand staircase, designed later by Michelangelo and built by Bartolommeo Ammanati, activates the space through its cascading forms.

THE UFFIZI, PALAZZO PITTI AND BOBOLI GARDENS

In concentrating their patronage at San Lorenzo, this generation of Medici followed the patterns of the fifteenth century. But the Medici dukes were not content to live in the Palazzo Medici built by Michelozzo. The family of Cosimo I de' Medici moved into the Palazzo della Signoria in the center of the city in 1540 (see fig. 13.15). Where earlier generations of Medici rulers separated their private residence from the seat of government, the new Medici dukes did what they could to unite them. Consequently, they had the interior of the former town hall remodeled to create a residential space, and they built new areas for both court and government.

To this end, Cosimo I de' Medici commissioned a new building to house the bureaucracies of his court in 1559. This project was assigned to Giorgio Vasari (1511–1574), the painter, historian, and architect. The building of the Uffizi, finished around 1580, consists of two long wings that face each other across a narrow court and are linked at one end by a loggia (fig. **17.7**). Situated between the Palazzo della Signoria and the Arno River, it served to restructure both the city space and the widely dispersed Florentine ministries. Numerous windows and architectural moldings enliven the façades. Colonnades interrupted by piers at

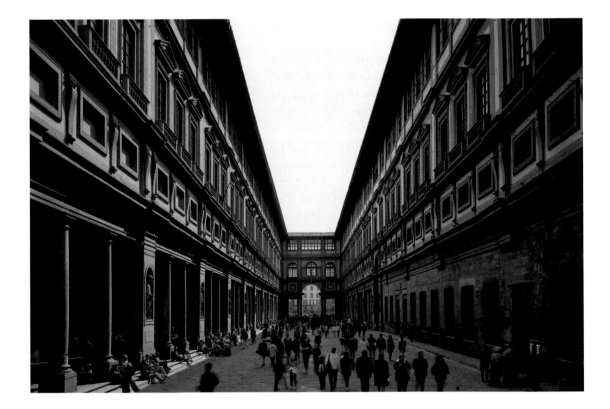

17.7 Giorgio Vasari. Courtyard of Uffizi, Florence. Begun 1560

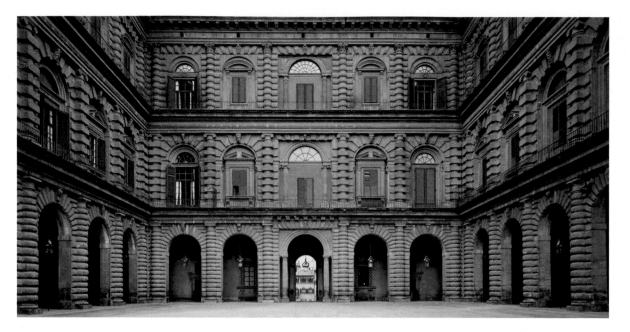

regular intervals define the long façade at left; these units define spaces allotted for different bureaucracies. Although strongly marked by Michelangelo's architecture at San Lorenzo, the courtyard also makes reference to the Roman Forum and thus links Cosimo to Roman emperors.

In their search for appropriate settings for the court, the Medici acquired the Palazzo Pitti, across the Arno River from the Uffizi, which had been built in the fifteenth century. The sculptor Bartolommeo Ammanati (1511–1592) enlarged the fifteenth-century palazzo with a courtyard between 1558 and 1570 (fig. **17.8**). Like Michelozzo's Medici palace (see fig. 15.32), this courtyard enframes a space that is both utilitarian and ceremonial; but

where the fifteenth-century palace seems ornate and delicate, this courtyard has a fortresslike character. The three-story scheme of superimposed orders, derived from the Roman Colosseum (fig. 7.20), has been overlaid with an extravagant pattern of rustication that "imprisons" the columns and reduces them to a passive role, despite the display of muscularity. The creative combination of a classical vocabulary with the unorthodox treatment of the rustication creates a raw expression of power. The Palazzo Pitti functions today as a museum displaying many of the works collected by the Medici family.

In addition to the new palace, the ducal family purchased a large area around it that they transformed into a carefully

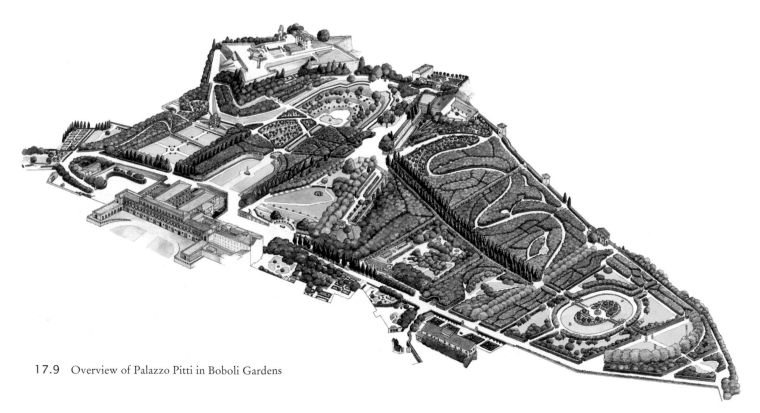

17.9 Overview of Palazzo Pitti in Boboli Gardens

landscaped park, called the Boboli Gardens (fig. **17.9**). Begun around 1549, this continued to grow and change down to the nineteenth century. The architect Nicolo Triboli (1500–1550) laid out the original plan; he imposed a regular geometry on an uneven site, including long walkways lined by foliage, fountains and pools of water, and artificial grottoes. Later in the century, other artists, including Vasari and Ammanati, adjusted and altered the design. The dukes commissioned numerous sculptures for the gardens, too, often of mythological beings or Greek gods. The gardens provided scenic vistas for the residents of the palace, but also a grand stage setting for ducal events.

PORTRAITURE AND ALLEGORY The Medici court had refined tastes and a good sense of how to use the visual arts to express their new status. As in the fifteenth century, the new generation of Medici patrons used portraiture as a means to this end. The *Portrait of Eleanora of Toledo and Her Son Giovanni de' Medici* (fig. **17.10**) by Agnolo Bronzino (1503–1572) exemplifies a new type of court portrait. This is a highly idealized painting of the wife of Cosimo I, who actually had blond hair (here darkened) and whose features have been perfected in the portrait. The portrait presents her as an ideal of beauty, just as her husband was admired for his virile good looks and courage.

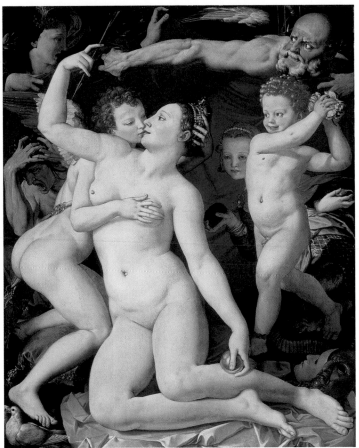

17.11   Agnolo Bronzino, *Allegory of Venus*. ca. 1546. Oil on panel, 57½ × 45⅝" (146.1 × 116.2 cm). The National Gallery, London

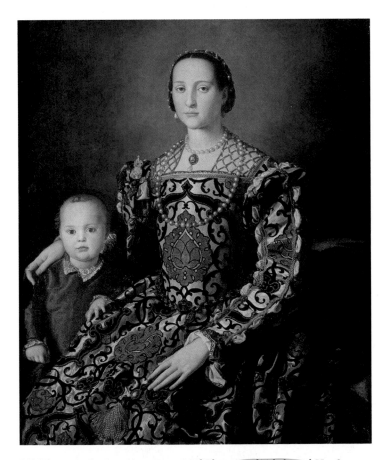

17.10   Agnolo Bronzino, *Portrait of Eleanora of Toledo and Her Son Giovanni de' Medici*. ca. 1550. Oil on panel, 45¼ × 37¾" (115 × 96 cm). Galleria degli Uffizi, Florence

An important message of the work is the continuity of the Medici dynasty, as Eleanora's arm enframes the male heir, Giovanni (born in 1543), who, however, would not outlive her. (She bore 11 children, including eight sons, before her death from tuberculosis in 1562 at about the age of 43.) This dynastic message is delivered by means of the formality of the portrait, with its frozen poses and aloof glances. Eleanora sits rigidly, with her arm resting on her silent, staring child; she wears a complicated brocaded dress and jewelry that demonstrates her wealth and status. Bronzino depicts the pair almost like a Madonna and Child, subtly comparing Eleanora to the Virgin: This reference may account for the lightening of the blue background around Eleanora's face that suggests a halo. The image contains a complex set of allusions as flattering as the improvements to her looks. Bronzino's painting describes the sitter as a member of an exalted social class, not as an individual personality. This kind of formal, distant, and allusive court portrait quickly became the ideal of court portraiture throughout Europe. (See, for example, fig. 18.26.)

Bronzino was Eleanora's preferred painter and held a court appointment. His passion for drawing and his gift for poetry came together in many of his works. Nowhere is this better seen than in his *Allegory of Venus* (fig. **17.11**), which Duke Cosimo presented to Francis I of France. From these different sources,

Benvenuto Cellini (1500–1571)

From *The Autobiography*

The Florentine sculptor wrote his autobiography between 1558 and 1566. Cellini's book retells the story of his early life, training, and artistic triumphs. It was not published until the eighteenth century. This excerpt focuses on the design and reception of the saltcellar of Francis I (see fig. 17.12). Cellini took the advice of several courtiers in approaching the project, but ultimately made his own decision about what to render in the model.

I made an oval shape the size of more than half an arm's length—in fact, almost two thirds of an arm's length—and on it, as if to show the Sea embracing the Land, I placed two nicely executed figures larger than a palm in size, seated with their legs intertwined in the same fashion as certain long-branched arms of the sea can be seen running into the land; and in the hand of the male figure of the Sea I placed a lavishly wrought ship, within which a great deal of salt could easily and well be accommodated; underneath this figure I placed four seahorses, and in the hand of this figure of the Sea I placed his

Trident. The Land I had represented as a woman whose beautiful figure was as full of as much loveliness and grace as I was able and knew how to produce, in whose hand I had placed a rich and lavishly decorated temple which rested upon the ground, and she was leaning on it with her hand; I had created the temple in order to hold the Pepper. I had placed a Horn of Plenty adorned with all the beautiful things I knew to exist in the world. Under this goddess and in the part that portrayed the earth, I had arranged all the most beautiful animals that the earth produces. Under the part devoted to the sea god I represented all the beautiful kinds of fishes and small snails that tiny space could contain; in the widest part of the oval space I created many extremely rich decorations. ... I uncovered the model [before the King], and, amazed, the King said: "This is something a hundred times more divine than anything I might have imagined. This is a magnificent piece of work by this man. He should never stop working." Then he turned to me with an expression full of delight, and told me that this was a work that pleased him enormously and that he wanted me to execute it in gold.

Source: Benvenuto Cellini, *My Life (Vita)*, tr. Julia Conaway Bondanella and Peter Bondanella (NY: Oxford University Press, 2002)

Bronzino creates a complex allegory whose meanings art historians are still probing.

Into a narrow plane close to the surface of the painting, Bronzino crowds a number of figures who have been identified only tentatively: The bald Father Time tears back the curtain from Fraud, the figure in the upper left-hand corner, to reveal Venus and Cupid in an incestuous embrace, much to the delight of the child Folly, who is armed with roses, and to the dismay of a figure tearing his hair, who has been identified as either Jealousy or Pain; on the right, Pleasure, half woman and half snake, offers a honeycomb. The moral of Bronzino's image may be that folly and pleasure blind one to the jealousy and fraud of sensual love, which time reveals.

With its extreme stylization, Bronzino's painting proclaims a refined erotic ideal that reduces passion to a genteel exchange of gestures between figures as polished and rigid as marble. The literary quality of the allegory reflects Bronzino's skill as a poet. The complexity of the conceit matches the complexity of the composition; the high quality of the technique matches the cleverness of the content. In Bronzino, the Medici found an artist whose technical virtuosity, complex imagery, and inventive compositions perfectly accorded with their taste and exemplify the Mannerist style. Cosimo's gift of a painting of such erudite imagery and accomplished technique to the king of France demonstrated his realm's achievements in the literary and visual arts.

Such complex and learned treatments occur also in the work of Benvenuto Cellini (1500–1571), a Florentine goldsmith and sculptor who owes much of his fame to his colorful autobiography. His gold saltcellar (fig. **17.12**), made for the same king, Francis I, between 1540 and 1543, is his only important work in precious metal to survive. The main function of this lavish object

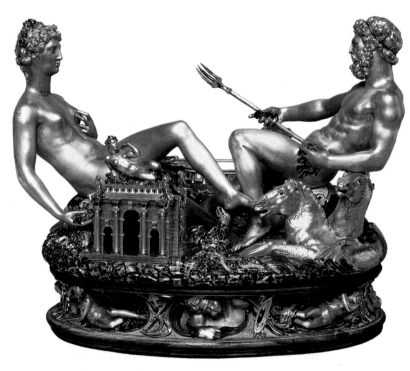

17.12   Benvenuto Cellini. Saltcellar of Francis I. 1540–43. Gold with enamel, 10¼ × 13⅛" (26 × 33.3 cm). Kunsthistorisches Museum, Vienna

is clearly as a conversation piece. Because salt comes from the sea and pepper from the earth, the boat-shaped salt container is protected by Neptune. The pepper, in a tiny triumphal arch, is watched over by a personification of Earth who, in another context, might be the god's consort Amphitrite. On the base are figures representing the four seasons and the four parts of the day. Such references remind the viewer of the Medici tombs, as does the figure personifying Earth. Cellini wants to impress with his ingenuity and skill. In his autobiography (see *Primary Source*, page 600), he explained how he came to design the model for the saltcellar and its **iconography**. He had imagined the figure of the Earth as "a woman whose beautiful figure was as full of as much loveliness and grace as I was able and knew how to produce." In true Mannerist fashion, the allegorical significance of the design is simply a pretext for this display of virtuosity. Cellini then modestly reports the reaction of Francis I to his design: "This is a magnificent piece of work by this man. He should never stop working."

THE ACCADEMIA DEL DISEGNO One of the aims of the duke was to promote the arts in Tuscany, a goal shared by Giorgio Vasari, who had dedicated his collection of biographies, first published in 1550, to Cosimo I. Cosimo sponsored the establishment of the Accademia del Disegno (Academy of Design) in 1563, intended to improve the training of artists and to enhance the status of the arts. Bronzino and Giorgio Vasari were founding members. Training in the academy stressed drawing and the study of the human figure, which was deepened not only by life drawing but also by dissections. Both nature and the ancients were esteemed, and the art of Michelangelo was held to be the highest achievement of the moderns. The academy emphasized the study of history and literature as well as the skills of the artist. The specifically Tuscan emphasis on drawing (*disegno*) reflected the allegiances of the founders, who stressed art as an intellectual activity, not mere craft.

To the academy came Jean Bologne (1529–1608), a gifted sculptor from Douai in northern France, who had encountered Italian styles at the court of Francis I. He found employment at the ducal court and, under the Italianized name of Giovanni Bologna, became the most important sculptor in Florence during the last third of the sixteenth century. To demonstrate his skill, he chose to sculpt what seemed to him a most difficult feat: three contrasting figures united in a single action. When creating the group, Bologna had no specific theme in mind, but when it was finished a member of the Florentine academy proposed the title *The Rape of the Sabine Woman* (fig. **17.13**), which the artist accepted. The duke admired the work so much he had it installed near the Palazzo della Signoria.

The subject proposed was drawn from the legends of ancient Rome. According to the story, the city's founders, an adventurous band of men from across the sea, tried in vain to find wives among their neighbors, the Sabines. Finally, they resorted to a trick. Having invited the entire Sabine tribe into Rome for a festival, they attacked them, took the women away by force, and thus

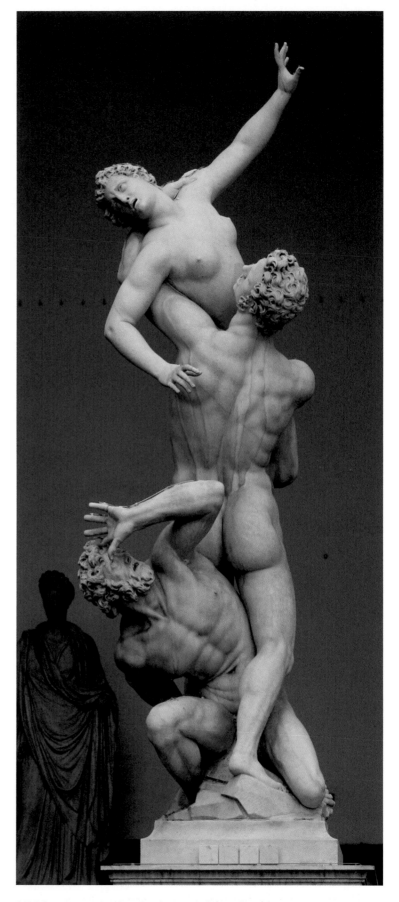

17.13 Giovanni Bologna, *The Rape of the Sabine Woman*. Completed 1583. Marble, height 13'6" (4.1 m). Loggia dei Lanzi, Florence

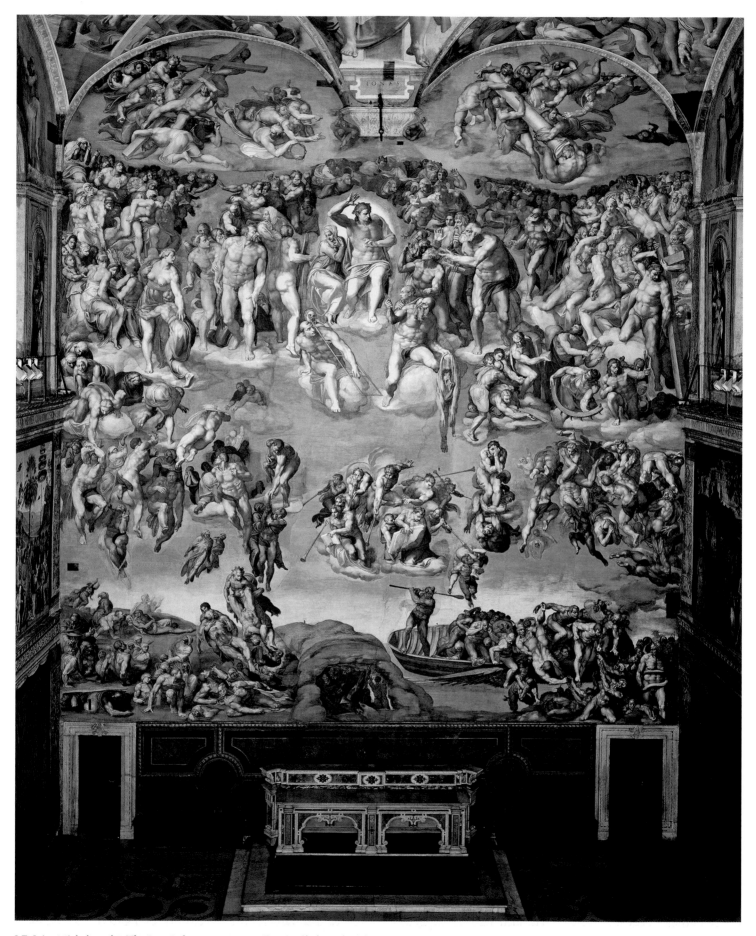

17.14 Michelangelo, *The Last Judgment*. 1534–41. Fresco. Sistine Chapel, Vatican City

Michelangelo the Poet

Michelangelo's prodigious creativity was manifested in many different art forms: sculpture, painting, architecture, and poetry. Allusive and dense with imagery, his poems do not explain his works in visual mediums, but they do sometimes treat parallel themes. This poem uses metaphors that appear visually in the Sistine Chapel's The Last Judgment. *It was a gift to his friend and reported lover Tommaso Cavalieri, a Roman nobleman.*

The smith when forging iron uses fire
to match the beauty shaped within his mind;
and fire alone will help the artist find

a way so to transmute base metal higher
to turn it gold; the phoenix seeks its pyre
to be reborn; just so I leave mankind
but hope to rise resplendent, new refined,
with souls whom death and time will never tire.
And this transforming fire good fortune brings
by burning out my life to make me new
although among the dead I then be counted.
True to its element the fire wings
its way to heaven, and to me is true
by taking me aloft where love is mounted.

Source: Michelangelo Buonarotti, *Life, Letters and Poetry*, ed. and tr. G. Bull (Oxford: Oxford University Press, 1987)

---

ensured the future of their race. Bologna's sculpture sanitizes what is an act of raw power and violence as the figures spiral upward in carefully rehearsed movements. Bologna wished to display his virtuosity and saw his task only in formal terms: to carve in marble, on a massive scale, a sculptural composition that was to be seen from all sides. The contrast between form and content that the Mannerist tendency encouraged could not be clearer.

ROME REFORMED

While the Medici were consolidating their power in Florence, in Rome, popes Julius II and Leo X sought to join their religious authority with secular power. Naturally, conflicts arose between the papacy and the princes of Europe: The contest between the papacy and the Holy Roman Empire resulted in the Sack of Rome in 1527 by Habsburg troops. Pope Leo X's cousin Clement VII fled, and much destruction ensued. Despite this shock to both the dignity of the city and the papacy, Clement ultimately crowned Charles V as emperor, and returned, once again, to his project of promoting the Medici family. When Clement died in 1534, the cardinals turned to a reform-minded member of a distinguished Roman family to restore the papacy's reputation and power. They chose Alessandro Farnese, a childhood friend of Leo X who had been educated in the palace of Lorenzo the Magnificent. As Pope Paul III, he encouraged Charles V's efforts to bring German princes back to the Roman Church, while at the same time trying to reassure Charles's enemy, Francis I, that Germany would not overpower France.

Paul III was very concerned by the spiritual crisis presented by the Reformation. Martin Luther had challenged both the doctrine and the authority of the Church, and his reformed version of Christianity had taken wide hold in northern Europe (see Chapter 18). To respond to the challenge of the Protestant Reformation, Paul III called the Council of Trent, which began its work in 1545 and issued its regulations in 1564. The council reaffirmed traditional Catholic doctrine and recommended reforms of liturgy, Church practices, and works of art. (See www.myartslab.com.)

The Catholic Church's most far-reaching and powerful weapon for combating what it considered heresy was the Inquisition, established in Italy in 1562 to investigate unapproved or suspect religious activities. Those found guilty of engaging in such heresies (deviations from religious orthodoxy) could be imprisoned or executed. To further control the spread of unorthodoxy, the Church compiled an Index of Prohibited Books in 1557. Texts by suspect authors or on subjects deemed unhealthful could be seized or denied publication.

Michelangelo in Rome

Like his predecessors, Paul III saw the value in commissioning large-scale projects from the leading artists of his day. Thus, he recalled Michelangelo to Rome to execute several key projects for him. Rome remained Michelangelo's home for the rest of his life. The new mood after the Sack of 1527 and during the Catholic Reformation may be reflected in the subject chosen for a major project in the Sistine Chapel. Beginning in 1534, Michelangelo painted for Paul III a powerful vision of The Last Judgment (fig. **17.14**). It took six years to complete the fresco, which was unveiled in 1541.

To represent the theme of the Last Judgment (Matthew 24:29–31) on the altar wall of the Sistine Chapel, Michelangelo had to remove not only the fifteenth-century frescoes commissioned by Sixtus IV but also parts of his own ceiling program in the upper lunettes. Traditional representations such as Giotto's at the Arena Chapel in Padua (see fig. 13.18) depict Hell as a place of physical torment. In envisioning his fresco, Michelangelo must have looked partly to Luca Signorelli's work at Orvieto Cathedral (see fig. 15.56), with its vigorous muscular nudes. Michelangelo replaces physical torments with spiritual agony expressed through violent contortions of the human body within a turbulent atmosphere. As angelic trumpeters signal the end of time, the figure of Christ sits at the fulcrum of a wheel of action: As he raises his arm, the dead rise from the earth at the lower left to yearn toward Heaven where the assembly of saints crowds about him. The damned plunge from Heaven toward Charon,

parallel ideas and metaphors may be seen in a poem he composed around 1532. (See *Primary Source*, page 603.)

These concerns also appear in a new version of the *Pietà*, begun around 1546 (fig. **17.16**). Here Michelangelo used his own features again, this time for the hooded figure—probably Nicodemus, who holds the broken body of Christ. He intended this sculptural group for his own tomb. By casting himself as a disciple tending the body of Christ, Michelangelo gives form to a conception of personal, unmediated access to the divine. The Catholic Church may have found such an idea threatening during the Catholic Reformation, when the authority of the Roman Church was being reaffirmed as Protestantism spread throughout Europe. For whatever reason, Michelangelo smashed the statue in 1555, and left it unfinished. Compared with his 1499 *Pietà*

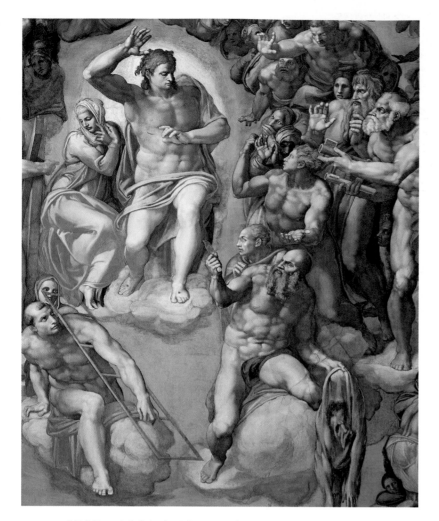

17.15   Michelangelo, *The Last Judgment* (detail, with self-portrait)

who ferries them to the underworld. (Some contemporary viewers complained about the inclusion of a pagan character in a sacred subject.) Throughout the fresco, human figures bend, twist, climb, fall, or gaze at Christ, their forms almost superhuman in their muscular power. The nudity of the figures, which expresses Michelangelo's belief in the sanctity of the human body, disturbed his contemporaries, and shortly after he died in 1564 one of his assistants was commissioned to add bits of clothing to the fresco to mask the nudity. The fresco was cleaned in 1994, bringing out the brilliant colors, the compressed space, and dramatic composition. These features link the work to the Mannerist style, though Michelangelo defies such labels.

That the fresco expresses Michelangelo's personal vision of the end of days is suggested by one detail: Straddling a cloud just below the Lord is the apostle Bartholomew, holding a human skin to represent his martyrdom by flaying (fig. **17.15**). The face on that skin, however, is not the saint's, but Michelangelo's. In this grim self-portrait, so well hidden that it was recognized only in modern times, the artist represents himself as unworthy to be resurrected in the flesh, which is a key theme of the image. Already in his sixties, Michelangelo frequently meditated on death and salvation in his poetry as well as in his art of the period. Some

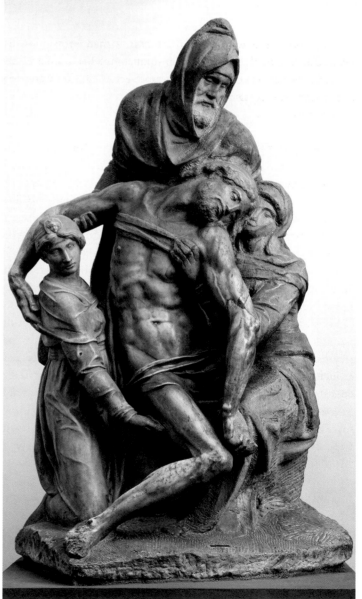

17.16   Michelangelo, *Pietà*. ca. 1546. Marble, height 7'8" (2.34 m). Museo del Opera del Duomo, Florence

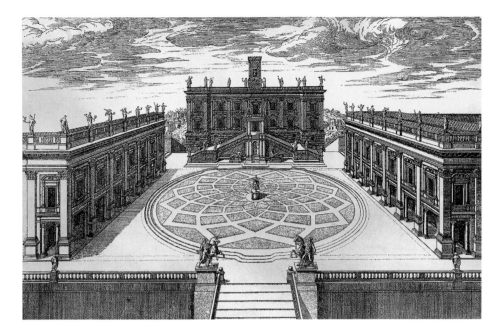

17.17 Michelangelo. Campidoglio, Rome (engraving by Étienne Dupérac, 1569)

(see fig. 16.12), this work is more expressive than conventionally beautiful, as though the ideals of his youth had been replaced by a greater seriousness of spiritual purpose. Many of Michelangelo's last sculptures remained unfinished as his efforts turned to architecture.

RESHAPING THE CAMPIDOGLIO While in Rome during the last 30 years of his life, Michelangelo's main pursuit was architecture. Among his activities were several public works projects. In 1537–39, he received the most ambitious commission of his career: to reshape the Campidoglio, the top of Rome's Capitoline Hill, into a piazza and frame it with a monumental architectural ensemble worthy of the site, which once had been the symbolic center of the ancient city. This was an opportunity to plan on a grand scale. Pope Paul III worked with the civilian authorities in Rome (the Conservators) to renovate this site and made Michelangelo its designer. Although not completed until long after his death, the project was carried out essentially as Michelangelo designed it. The Campidoglio has since served as a model for many other civic centers. Pope Paul III transferred the equestrian monument of Marcus Aurelius (see fig. 7.33) from the Lateran Palace to the Campidoglio and had it installed on a base that Michelangelo designed. Placed at the top of a gently rising oval mound that defines the space, the statue became the focal point of the entire scheme. (The sculpture was recently removed to an interior space to protect it.) Since the sculpted figure was thought to represent Constantine, the first Roman emperor to promote Christianity and the source of the papacy's claim to temporal power, by placing it at the center of the seat of secular government, the pope asserted papal authority in civic affairs.

Palace façades define three sides of the piazza. An engraving based on Michelangelo's design (fig. **17.17**), conveys the effect, albeit imperfectly, of the space created by the façades. The print shows the symmetry of the scheme and the sense of progression along the main axis toward the Senators' Palace, opposite the staircase that gives entry to the piazza. However, the shape of the piazza is not a rectangle but a trapezoid, a peculiarity dictated by the site. The Senators' Palace and the Conservators' Palace on the right were older buildings that had to be preserved behind new exteriors, but they were placed at an angle of 80 instead of 90 degrees. Michelangelo turned this problem into an asset. By adding the "New Palace" on the left, which complements the Conservators' Palace in style and placement, he makes the Senators' Palace look larger than it is, so that it dominates the piazza.

The whole conception has the appearance of a stage set. All three buildings are long but relatively narrow, like a show front with little behind it. However, these are not shallow screens but three-dimensional structures (fig. **17.18**). The "New Palace" and its twin, the Conservators' Palace, combine voids and solids, horizontals and verticals with a plasticity not found in any piece of architecture since Roman antiquity. The open porticoes in each structure further link the piazza and façades, just as a courtyard is related to the arcades of a **cloister**.

The columns and beams of the porticoes are contained in a colossal order of pilasters that supports a heavy cornice topped by a balustrade. Alberti had experimented with the colossal order at Sant'Andrea in Mantua (see fig. 15.45), but Michelangelo fully exploited this device. For the Senators' Palace he used a colossal order and balustrade above a tall base, which emphasizes the massiveness of the building. The single entrance at the top of the double-ramped stairway (see fig. 17.17) seems to gather all the spatial forces set in motion by the oval mound and the flanking structures. It thus provides a dramatic climax to the piazza. Brunelleschi's design for the façade of the Innocenti in Florence (see fig. 15.4), with its slim Tuscan columns and rhythmic arcade, seems a delicate frame for a piazza compared with the mass and energy of the Campidoglio. Michelangelo's powerful example of molding urban spaces was important for subsequent city planners throughout Europe.

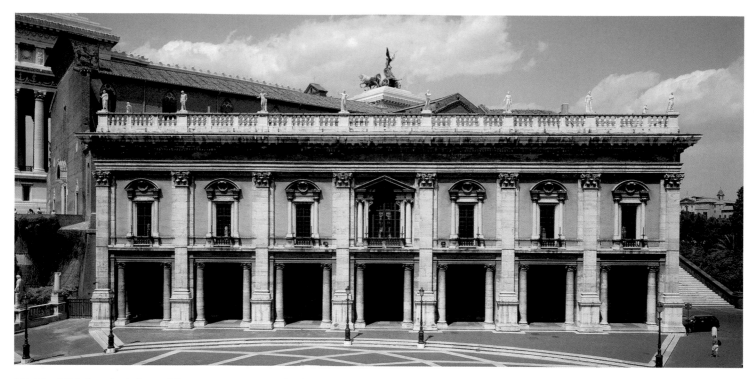

17.18   Michelangelo. Palazzo dei Conservatori, Campidoglio, Rome. Designed ca. 1545

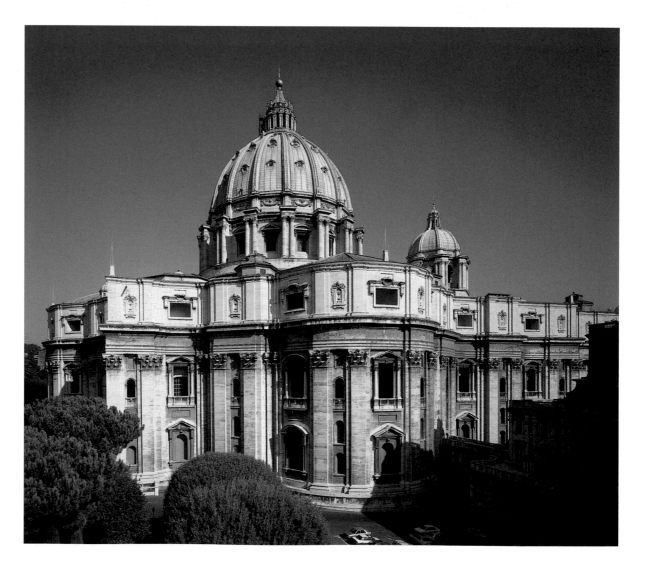

17.19   Michelangelo. St. Peter's, Rome, seen from the west. 1546–64; dome completed by Giacomo della Porta, 1590

ST. PETER'S Michelangelo used the colossal order again on the exterior of St. Peter's (fig. **17.19**). Several architects had taken on the project after Bramante's death in 1514. Michelangelo took over the design of the church in 1546 upon the death of the previous architect, Antonio da Sangallo the Younger, whose work he completely recast. Returning to a centrally focused plan, he adapted the system of the Conservators' Palace to the curving contours of the church, but with windows instead of open loggias and an attic instead of the balustrade.

Unlike Bramante's many-layered elevation (see fig. 16.11), Michelangelo uses a colossal order of pilasters to emphasize the compact body of the structure, thus setting off the dome more dramatically. The same desire for compactness and organic unity led him to simplify the interior spaces (fig. 17.20). He brought the complex spatial sequences of Bramante's plan (see fig. 16.10) into one cross and square, held in check by the huge piers that support the central dome. He further defined its main axis by modifying the eastern apse and adding a portico to it, although this part of his design was never carried out. The dome, however, reflects

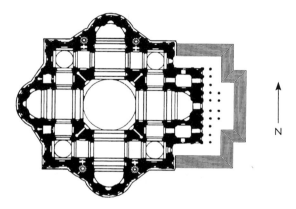

17.20 Michelangelo. Plan for St. Peter's

N

Michelangelo's ideas in every important respect, even though it was built after his death and has a steeper pitch than he intended.

Bramante had planned his dome as a stepped hemisphere above a narrow drum, which would have seemed to press down on the church. Michelangelo's, in contrast, has a powerful thrust that draws energy upward from the main body of the structure. Michelangelo borrowed not only the double-shell construction but also the Gothic profile from the Florence Cathedral dome (see fig. 15.3 and *Materials and Techniques*, page 512), yet the effect is very different. The smooth planes of Brunelleschi's dome give no hint of the internal stresses. Michelangelo, however, gives sculptured shape to these forces and visually links them to the rest of the building. The double columns of the high drum take up the vertical impetus of the colossal pilasters. This upward momentum continues in the ribs and the raised curve of the cupola, and then culminates in the tall lantern. The logic of this design is so persuasive that almost all domes built between 1600 and 1900 were influenced by it.

The Catholic Reformation and Il Gesù

Despite its visual logic and powerful design, Michelangelo's centralized plan at St. Peter's served as a model for few other churches in the era of the Catholic Reformation. As the Council of Trent finished its deliberations in 1564, the Church reasserted its traditions and reformed its liturgies. The council decreed that believers should see the elevation of the Host at the heart of the Mass, which was best accomplished in the long nave of a basilica with an unencumbered view of the altar. Despite its symbolic attractions, the centralized plan did not achieve this goal.

Another result of the reform movement within the Catholic Church was the establishment of new religious orders. One of the most ambitious and energetic was the Society of Jesus, or Jesuits, founded by Ignatius of Loyola and promoted by Pope Paul III. He approved the order in 1540; by 1550, the Jesuits were planning their own church, Il Gesù in Rome. Michelangelo once promised a design for this project, though he apparently never furnished it; the plan that the order adopted came from one of Michelangelo's assistants, Giacomo Vignola (1507–1573) in 1568. For Vignola's plan Giacomo della Porta (ca. 1540–1602) designed the façade. It was not completed until 1584. As the mother church of the Jesuits, its design must have been closely supervised so as to conform to the aims of the order. The Jesuits were at once intellectuals, mystics, and missionaries, whose charge was to fight heresy in Europe and spread Christianity to Asia and America. They required churches that adhered to the precepts of the Council of Trent—churches that would have impressive grand-eur while avoiding excessive ornament. Il Gesù may be seen as the architectural embodiment of the spirit of the Catholic Reformation.

Il Gesù is a compact basilica dominated by its mighty nave (fig. **17.21**). Chapels have replaced side aisles, thus assembling the congregation in one large, hall-like space directly in view of the altar. The attention of the audience is strongly directed toward altar and pulpit, as a representation of the interior shows

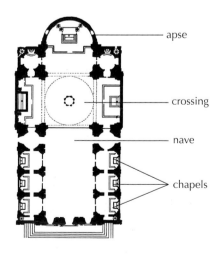

apse

crossing

nave

chapels

17.21 Giacomo Vignola. Plan of Il Gesù, Rome. 1568

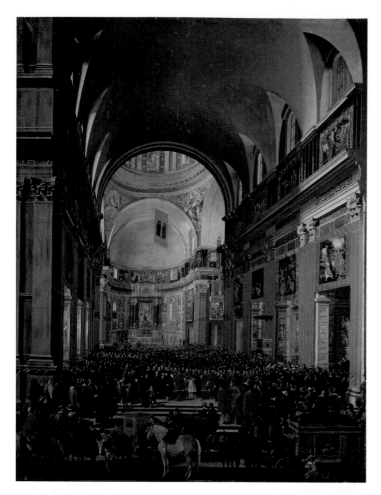

(fig. **17.22**). (The painting depicts how the church would look from the street if the center part of the façade were removed. For the later decoration of the nave vault, see fig. 19.12.) The painting also depicts a feature that the ground plan cannot show: the dramatic contrast between the dim nave and the amply lighted eastern part of the church, thanks to the large windows in the drum of the dome. Light has been consciously exploited for its expressive possibilities—a novel device, theatrical in the best sense of the term—to give Il Gesù a stronger emotional focus than we have as yet found in a church interior.

The façade by Giacomo della Porta (fig. **17.23**) is as bold as the plan. It is divided into two stories by a strongly projecting entablature that is supported by paired pilasters that clearly derive from Michelangelo, with whom Della Porta had worked. The same pattern recurs in the upper story on a somewhat smaller scale, with four instead of six pairs of supports. To bridge the difference in width and hide the roof line, Della Porta inserted two scroll-shaped buttresses. This device, taken from the façade of Santa Maria Novella in Florence by Alberti (see fig. 15.9), forms a graceful transition to the large pediment crowning the façade, which retains the classic proportions of Renaissance architecture: The height equals the width.

Della Porta has masterfully integrated all the parts of the façade into a single whole: Both stories share the same vertical rhythm, which even the horizontal members obey. (Note the way the broken entablature **responds** to the pilasters.) In turn, the

17.22 Andrea Sacchi and Jan Miel, *Urban VIII Visiting Il Gesù*. 1639–41. Oil on canvas. Galleria Nazionale d'Arte Antica, Rome

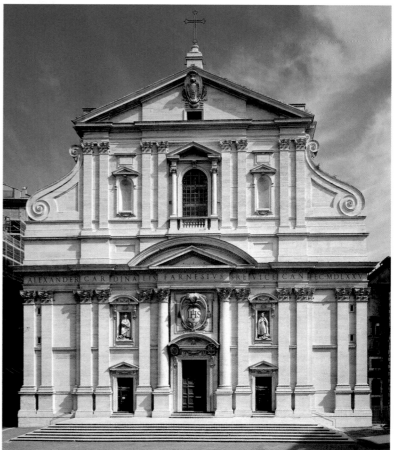

17.23 Giacomo della Porta. Façade of Il Gesù, Rome. ca. 1575–84

horizontal divisions determine the size of the vertical members, so there is no colossal order. Michelangelo inspired the sculptural treatment of the façade, which places greater emphasis on the main portal. Its double frame—two pediments resting on coupled pilasters and columns—projects beyond the rest of the façade and gives strong focus to the entire design. Not since Gothic architecture has the entrance to a church received such a dramatic concentration of features. This façade, and the freedom to add movement and plastic dimension to it, set an important precedent for church architecture by the Jesuits and others during ensuing centuries.

NORTHERN ITALY: DUCAL COURTS AND URBAN CENTERS

Northern Italy was divided into a number of principalities that were smaller than the Grand Duchy of Tuscany or the Papal States. One of the most stable of these principalities was Mantua, where the Gonzaga family retained the title of marquis into the sixteenth century. Mantua was host to major artists in the fifteenth century, including Alberti and Mantegna. The family's traditions of patronage extended to women as well as men, as Isabella d'Este, the wife of Francesco II Gonzaga, was one of the most active patrons of the early sixteenth century. Her son, Federico, became marquis in 1519, a title he held until Charles V named him duke in 1530. To impress the emperor, Federico displayed his wealth and taste expressed through the arts.

The Palazzo del Te

As part of his display, Federico II Gonzaga commissioned Giulio Romano (ca. 1499–1546) to design a villa for him outside the city itself, called the Palazzo del Te, where he could house his mistress and receive the emperor. Giulio had been Raphael's chief assistant in Rome, but came to Mantua to follow in the footsteps of Mantegna and Alberti in 1524.

He designed the Palazzo del Te as a low structure appropriate to the flat landscape. For the courtyard façade (fig. **17.24**), Giulio used a vocabulary familiar to patrons of villas and palaces, such as the rusticated blocks and the smooth Tuscan order of engaged columns that support the projecting entablature. As Michelangelo did at the Laurentian Library, Giulio subverts the conventions of traditional classical architecture. The massive keystones of the blank windows appear ready to burst the triangular lintels above them. The only true arch spans the central doorway, but a pediment surmounts it—a violation of the classical **canon**. The triglyph midway between each pair of columns "slips" downward in defiance of all logic and accepted practice, thereby creating a sense that the frieze might collapse before our eyes. In a Mannerist display, Giulio broke the rules of accepted practice as if to say that the rules did not apply to him, or to his patron.

What is merely a possibility on the exterior of the Palazzo del Te seems to be fully realized in the interior, where Giulio painted a series of rooms with illusionistic frescoes on themes drawn from antiquity. Unlike the frescoes of Raphael in Rome, these are not images of a distant and beautiful Golden Age, but vivid and dramatic expressions of power. In the Sala dei Giganti (Room of the Giants) (fig. **17.25**), Giulio painted a fresco of the gods expelling the giants from Mount Olympus as a cataclysm of falling bodies and columns. A viewer seems to see an entire temple collapsing. Figures of the winds in the upper corners of the wall appear to topple architectural elements onto the huge figures of giants, crushing them. As if witnessing the power of the new Olympian gods, a viewer feels transported into the terror

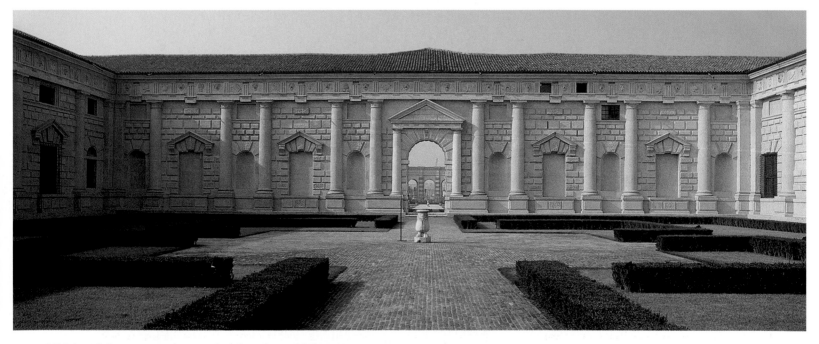

17.24 Giulio Romano. Courtyard of the Palazzo del Te, Mantua. ca. 1527–34

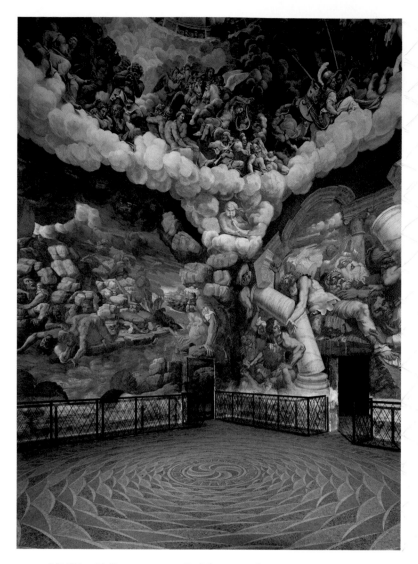

17.25 Giulio Romano, *Fall of the Giants from Mount Olympus*, from the Sala dei Giganti. ca. 1530–32. Palazzo del Te, Mantua

of the event. Of course, the duke himself was imagined as Zeus (Jupiter) in this conceit, so the whole illusion speaks to the power of Duke Federico.

This conceit was also applied to paintings for the same duke's palace in Mantua, which he commissioned from Antonio Allegri da Correggio (1489/94–1534), called Correggio, about the same time. This gifted northern Italian painter, who spent most of his brief career in Parma, absorbed the influences of Leonardo, the Venetians, Michelangelo, and Raphael into a distinctive and sensual style. Duke Federico commissioned a series of the Loves of Jupiter, among which is the *Jupiter and Io* (fig. **17.26**). As Ovid recounts, Jupiter changed his shape numerous times to seduce his lovers; here, the nymph Io, swoons in the embrace of a cloudlike Jupiter. The use of Leonardesque sfumato, combined with a Venetian sense of color and texture, produces a frank sensuality that exceeds even Titian's *Bacchanal* (see fig. 16.31). Correggio renders the vaporous form of the god with a remarkable degree of illusionism. The eroticism of the image reflects a taste shared by

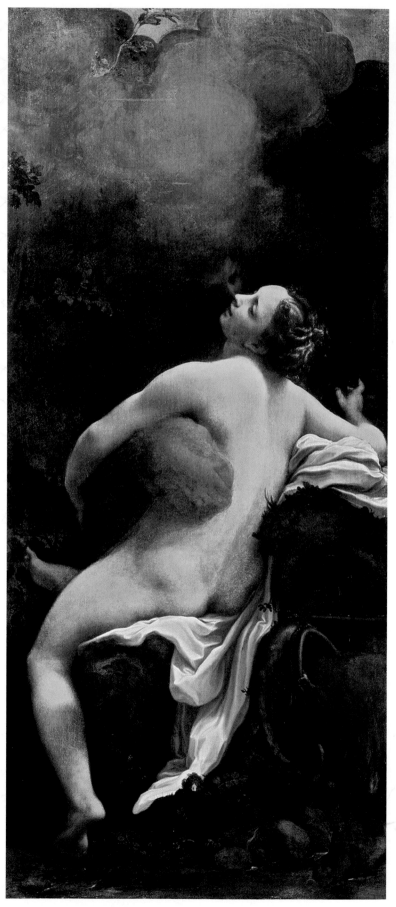

17.26 Correggio, *Jupiter and Io*. ca. 1532. Oil on canvas, 64½ × 27¾" (163.8 × 70.5 cm). Kunsthistorisches Museum, Vienna

many of the courts of Europe, visible in Bronzino's *Allegory of Venus* (see fig. 17.11) and Titian's *Rape of Europa* (see fig. 17.36).

PARMA AND CREMONA

The larger political entities in Italy aimed to swallow up the smaller ones. The Papal States expanded to include cities like Bologna and Parma, while the Duchy of Milan gobbled up the city of Cremona. Forms of art and patronage established by courts in Rome, Florence, and Milan were emulated by the citizens of these cities.

Correggio and Parmigianino in Parma

Correggio spent much of his career in the city of Parma, which had recently been absorbed into the Papal States. This new affiliation brought the city new wealth and inspired local patrons of art and architecture; more than once Correggio was the artist chosen for their projects. He put his skills to work in the dome of Parma Cathedral where he painted the fresco of *The Assumption of the Virgin* between 1522 and 1530 (fig. **17.27**). The surfaces of the dome are painted away by Correggio's illusionistic perspective. A viewer standing below the dome is transported into the heavens, as the sky opens to receive the body of the Virgin rising into the light.

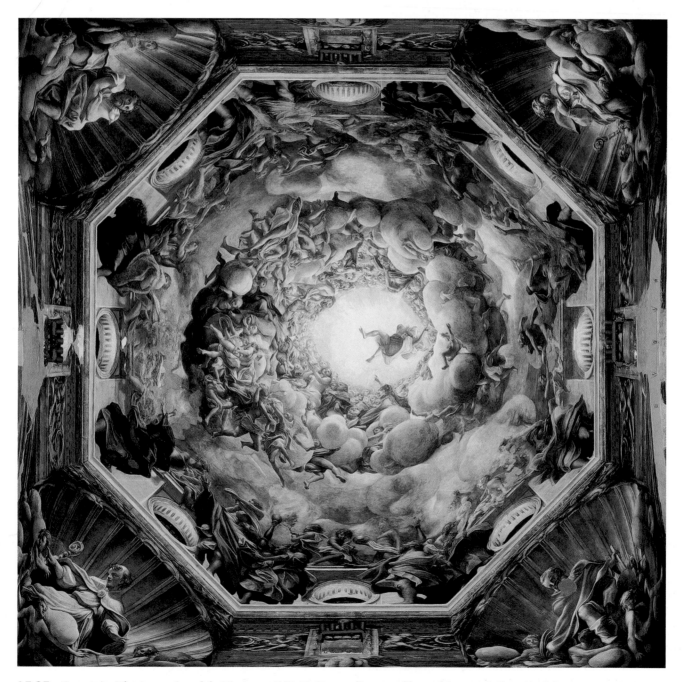

<u>17.27</u> Correggio, *The Assumption of the Virgin*. ca. 1522–30. Fresco, diameter of base of dome 35'10" × 37'11" (10.93 × 11.56 m). Dome of cathedral, Parma, Italy

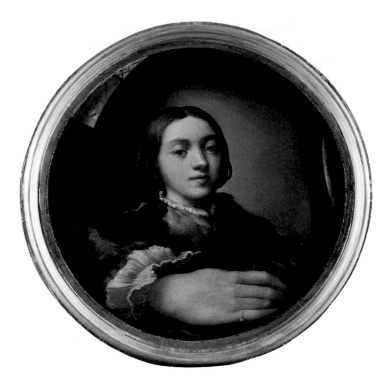

17.28 Parmigianino, *Self-Portrait*. 1524. Oil on panel, diameter 9⅝" (24.7 cm). Kunsthistorisches Museum, Vienna

Parmigianino's skill is evident in his most famous work, *The Madonna with the Long Neck* (fig. **17.29**), commissioned in 1535 by a noblewoman of Parma for a family chapel in the church of Santa Maria dei Servi. Despite his deep study of Raphael and Correggio, Parmigianino has a different ideal of beauty, which he establishes with the large amphora offered by the figure at the left. In his painting, the perfect oval of Mary's head rests on a swanlike neck, while her body swells only to taper to her feet, which mimics the shape of the amphora. By contrast, Raphael's *La Belle Jardinière* (see fig. 16.22) seems all circles and cubes, and her features are sweet rather than haughty. Nor does Parmigianino attempt to replicate Raphael's stable compositions. Here, the

Correggio here initiates a new kind of visionary representation in which Heaven and earth are joined visually and spiritually through the magic of perspective and the artist's skill. Not since Mantegna's *Camera Picta* in Mantua (see fig. 15.50) has a ceiling been so totally replaced by a painted illusion; the concept would reverberate in the works of other artists in the seventeenth century, when ceilings would disappear through illusionistic devices, as can be seen in the work of Pietro da Cortona (scc fig. 19.11) and Giovanni Battista Gaulli (see fig. 19.12). Correggio also gave the figures themselves the ability to move with such exhilarating ease that the force of gravity seems not to exist for them, and they frankly delight in their weightless condition. Reflecting the influence of Titian, these are healthy, energetic beings of flesh and blood, which makes the Assumption appear that much more miraculous.

Parma was the birthplace of yet another gifted painter, Girolamo Francesco Maria Mazzola (1503–1540), known as Parmigianino. Precocious and intelligent, Parmigianino had made his reputation as a painter in Rome, Florence, and elsewhere before returning to Parma in 1530. His *Self-Portrait* (fig. **17.28**), done as a demonstration piece, suggests his self-confidence. The artist's appearance is bland and well groomed. The features, painted with Raphael's smooth perfection, are veiled by a delicate sfumato. The picture records what Parmigianino saw as he gazed at his reflection in a convex mirror, including the fishbowl distortions in his hand. Parmigianino substitutes his painting for the mirror itself, even using a specially prepared convex panel. The painting demonstrates his skill at recording what the eye sees, yet at the same time it shows off his learning by a subtle allusion to the myth of Narcissus, who, according to Greek legend, looked in a pool of water and fell in love with his own reflection.

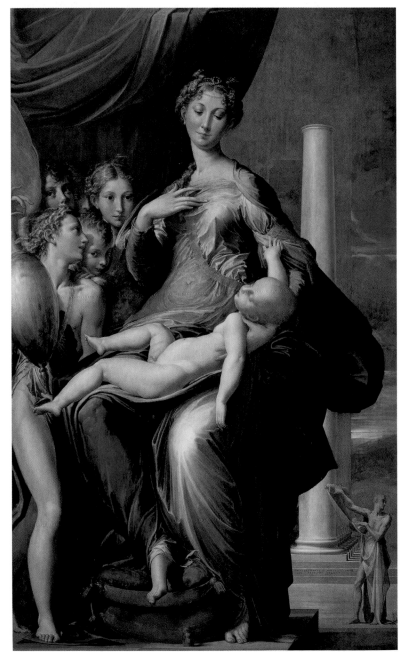

17.29 Parmigianino, *The Madonna with the Long Neck*. ca. 1535. Oil on panel, 7'1" × 4'4" (2.2 × 1.3 m). Galleria degli Uffizi, Florence

sleeping Christ Child balances precariously on the Madonna's lap, as she lifts a boneless hand to her breast. The composition is as unbalanced as the postures: heavily weighted to the left, open and distant to the right. All the figures have elongated limbs and ivory-smooth features, and the space is compressed. In typical Mannerist fashion, these elements draw attention to the artist's skill and his inversion of Raphael's ideals.

These choices may reflect the meaning of the image. The large Christ Child in his mother's lap recalls the theme of the Pietà, which implies that Jesus is already aware of his fate. Nor is the setting as arbitrary as it may seem. The gigantic column is a symbol often associated with the Madonna as the gateway to Heaven and eternal life, as well as the Immaculate Conception. At the same time it may also refer to the column on which Jesus endured the flagellation during the Passion, which the tiny figure of a prophet foretells on his scroll. *The Madonna with the Long Neck*, with its cold and memorable elegance, offers a vision of unearthly perfection.

Cremona

The Mannerist elegance that Correggio and Parmigianino achieved was but one stylistic option that artists and patrons of northern Italy could select. The work of Sofonisba Anguissola

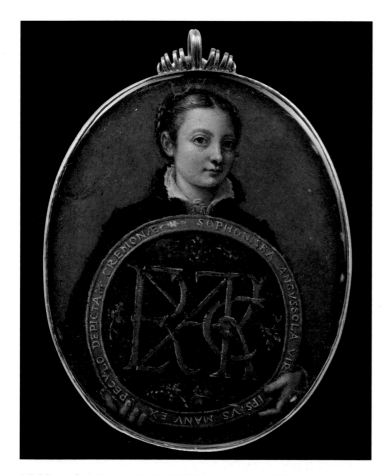

17.30   Sofonisba Anguissola, *Self-Portrait*. c. 1556. Oil on parchment, 3¼ × 2½" (8.3 × 6.4 cm). Museum of Fine Arts, Boston. Emma F. Munroe Fund, 1960. 60.155

(1532–1625) of Cremona represents a different approach. The daughter of a nobleman in that north Italian city, Sofonisba received her training in painting as a professional. This was a very unusual circumstance, as most women artists of the Renaissance learned their craft at home as the daughters of artists. Sofonisba became famous in Italy as a painter, communicating with artists all over the peninsula, including Michelangelo and Vasari. Her fame was such that Philip II of Spain hired her as his court artist. She moved to Spain in 1559 where she executed mostly portraits of imperial family members. She remained there until she married in 1573 and returned to Italy.

The reasons for her fame become clear in examining her self-portrait of about 1556 (fig. **17.30**). Executed as a miniature, the portrait was probably a gift. In the image, the 24-year-old artist represents herself staring out at the spectator wearing sober black costume and with respectably plaited hair. Sofonisba does not attempt the showy distortions that appear in Parmigianino's comparable self-portrait, done in 1524 (see fig. 17.28), preferring a straightforward naturalism to Mannerist display. She holds a medallion with a still mysterious monogram. (It may be an anagram of her father's name, although this is not certain.) Around the medallion she claims the image as a work "by her hand done with the aid of a mirror." In the miniature, Sofonisba has wittily placed her hands next to the words "by whose hand" (*ipsius manu ex*), so stressing the skill of her hands.

VENICE: THE SERENE REPUBLIC

Despite the attacks it endured at the beginning of the sixteenth century, Venice regained much of its territory and wealth by 1529. Its aristocracy reasserted its political and cultural power throughout the century, contributing to a distinctive situation for artists and for patrons. Instead of a court, Venice remained a nominal republic, controlled by ancient families, such as the Loredan, the Vendramin, and the Barbaro. In addition to religious works of art, these families commissioned works for their homes in town and for their villas in the country, so artists had a wide variety of themes to depict. The city itself expressed its status through public works projects commissioned by the civic fathers and intended to beautify the Most Serene Republic (*Serenissima*). One example of this is the refashioning of the heart of the city—the piazzetta between the cathedral of San Marco and the Canal of San Marco—with a pair of buildings in the 1530s.

Sansovino in Venice

The Council of Ten, who controlled the city, held a competition in 1535 to design a new home for the state mint (fig. **17.31**, left). They selected Jacopo Sansovino (1486–1570), a Florentine sculptor who left Rome for Venice after the Sack of Rome in 1527 and established himself as the city's chief architect. Not surprisingly, his buildings are sculptural in character. In the spirit of earlier Venetian structures such as the Ca' d'Oro (see fig. 15.51) and the

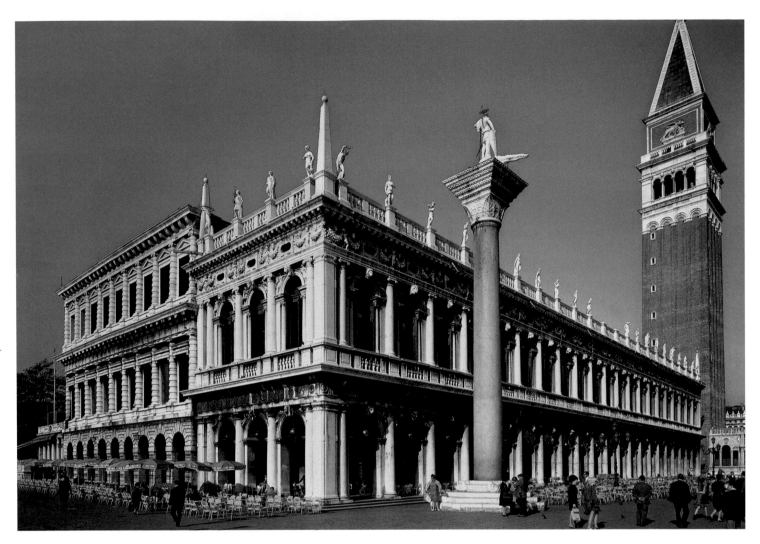

17.31 Jacopo Sansovino. Mint (left) and Library of St. Mark's, Venice. Begun ca. 1535–37

Doge's Palace (see fig. 13.32) nearby, Sansovino composed the façade to have numerous openings formed by arches and huge windows. The supporting arches and columns, however, are given greater stress by means of the rustication used throughout, which adds to the imposing effect of the building. (The top story was added around 1560.)

The Procurators of San Marco then hired Sansovino to build the Library of San Marco (see fig. 17.31, right) as a public library and repository for a rich collection of Greek and Latin manuscripts. Situated next to the mint, the library uses a much more elegant architectural vocabulary. It is a long, two-storied structure, composed as a series of arcades supporting heavy cornices. The street-level arcade is enframed by a Roman Doric order inspired by the Colosseum, while the upper story shows an elaborate treatment of the Ionic order (including triple engaged columns) surmounted by a garlanded entablature. A balustrade caps off the structure, with life-size statues over every column cluster and obelisks at each corner. The extravagant ornamentation of both structures creates an effect of opulence that proclaims the Venetian republic as a new Rome.

Andrea Palladio and Late Renaissance Architecture

Venice built many churches as well as civic buildings. The commission for San Giorgio Maggiore was awarded to one of the most influential architects of the Renaissance, Andrea Palladio (1508–1580), in 1565. Although Palladio's career centered on his native Vicenza, a town near Venice, his buildings and theoretical writings brought him international renown. Palladio believed that architecture should be governed by reason and by rules exemplified by the buildings of the ancients. He shared Leon Battista Alberti's faith in the significance of proportion. (See *Primary Source*, page 616.) The two architects differed in how they related theory to practice, however. With Alberti, the relationship had been flexible, whereas Palladio believed quite literally in practicing what he preached. This view stemmed in part from his earlier career as a stonemason and sculptor before entering the humanist circles of Count Giangiorgio Trissino of Vicenza, where he studied Vitruvius and other ancient authors and was introduced to elite patrons of the Veneto.

His first great project in Venice itself was the Benedictine church of San Giorgio Maggiore (fig. **17.32**), begun in 1565. Like his predecessors, Palladio declared that round temples are ideal because the circle is a symbol of uniformity and eternity; yet he and his patrons chose a basilican plan as the only one appropriate for Christian worship. The plan for San Giorgio Maggiore (fig. **17.33**) reflects the church's twofold purpose of serving a Benedictine monastery and a lay congregation. The main body of the church is strongly centralized—the transept is as long as the nave and a dome marks the crossing—but the longitudinal axis reasserts itself in the separate compartments for the main altar and the large choir beyond, where the monks worshiped. On the façade, Palladio wished to express the dignity of the church by using the architectural language of the ancients. He designed a flattened-out temple porch for the entrance on the grounds that "Temples ought to have ample porticos, and with larger columns than other buildings require; and it is proper that they should be great and magnificent…and built with large and beautiful proportions. They must be made of the most excellent and the most precious material, that the divinity may be honored as much as possible." To achieve this end, Palladio superimposed a tall, narrow temple front on another low, wide one to reflect the different heights of nave and aisles in the basilica itself. The interlocking design is held together by the four gigantic columns, which function as a variant of Alberti's colossal order.

Much of Palladio's architecture consists of town houses and country villas. The Villa Rotonda (fig. **17.34**), one of Palladio's finest buildings, exemplifies his interpretation of the ancients. This country residence, built near Vicenza, beginning in 1567, for the humanist cleric Paolo Almerico, consists of a square block surmounted by a dome, with identical porches in the shape of temple fronts on all four sides. Alberti had defined the ideal church as a symmetrical, centralized design of this sort; Palladio adapted the same principles for the ideal country house. He was convinced, on the basis of his reading of Vitruvius and Pliny, that Roman private houses had porticoes like these. (Excavations have since proved him mistaken.) Palladio's use of the temple front here is more than an expression of his regard for antiquity; he considered this feature both legitimate and essential for decorum—namely, appropriateness, beauty, **harmony**, and utility—befitting the houses of "great men." This concept was embedded in the social outlook of the later sixteenth century, which required

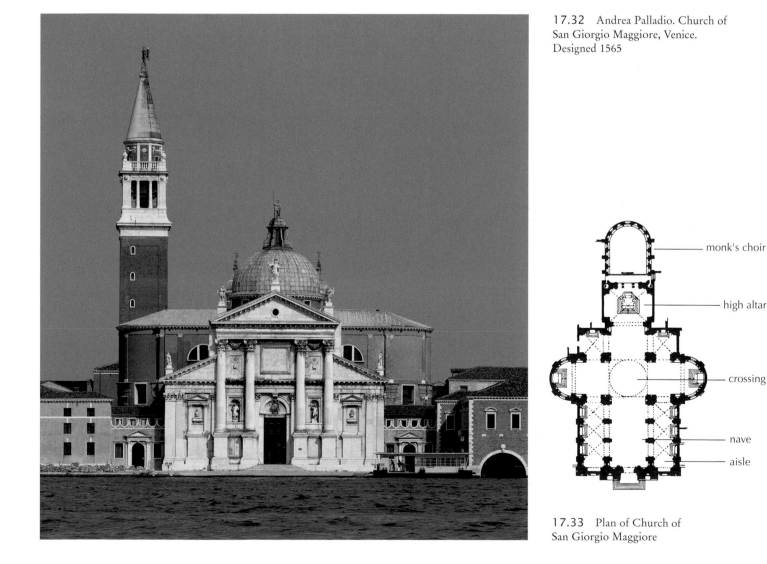

17.32   Andrea Palladio. Church of San Giorgio Maggiore, Venice. Designed 1565

17.33   Plan of Church of San Giorgio Maggiore

monk's choir

high altar

crossing

nave

aisle

Andrea Palladio (1508–1580)

From *The Four Books on Architecture*

Published in 1570, Palladio's Four Books on Architecture *made an enormous impression on his European contemporaries, providing the basis for much French and English architecture of the seventeenth and eighteenth centuries.*

One must describe as suitable a house which will be appropriate to the status of the person who will have to live in it and of which the parts will correspond to the whole and to each other. But above all the architect must observe that (as Vitruvius says in Books I and VI), for great men and especially those in public office, houses with loggias and spacious, ornate halls will be required, so that those waiting to greet the master of the house or to ask him for some help or a favor can spend their time pleasantly in such spaces; similarly, smaller buildings of lesser expense and ornament will be appropriate for men of lower status. One must build in the same way for judges and lawyers ... Merchants' houses should have places for storing their goods which face north and are so arranged that the owners have no fear of burglars. A building will also have decorum, if the parts correspond to the whole ...

So we read that when building temples the ancients used every ingenuity to maintain decorum, which is one of the most beautiful aspects of architecture. Therefore, to maintain decorum in the shapes of our temples, we too, who have no false gods, should choose the most perfect and excellent one; and because the round form would be just that, as it alone amongst all the plans is simple, uniform, equal, strong, and capacious, let us build temples round; this form is far and away the most appropriate for them, because it is enclosed by only one boundary in which the beginning and the end ... cannot be found ... and since at every point the outer edge is equidistant from the center, it is perfectly adapted to demonstrate the unity, the infinite existence, the consistency and the justice of God. ... recommended too are churches that are made in the shape of a cross ... because ... they represent, in the eyes of onlookers, that wood from which our Salvation was hung.

Source: Andrea Palladio, *The Four Books on Architecture*, tr. Robert Tavernor and Richard Schofield (Cambridge, MA: The MIT Press, 1997)

the display of great wealth and taste to assert status. Palladio's design also takes advantage of the pleasing views offered in every direction by the site. Beautifully correlated with the walls behind and the surrounding vistas, the porches of the Villa Rotonda give the structure an air of serene dignity and festive grace that is enhanced by the sculptures on the façades.

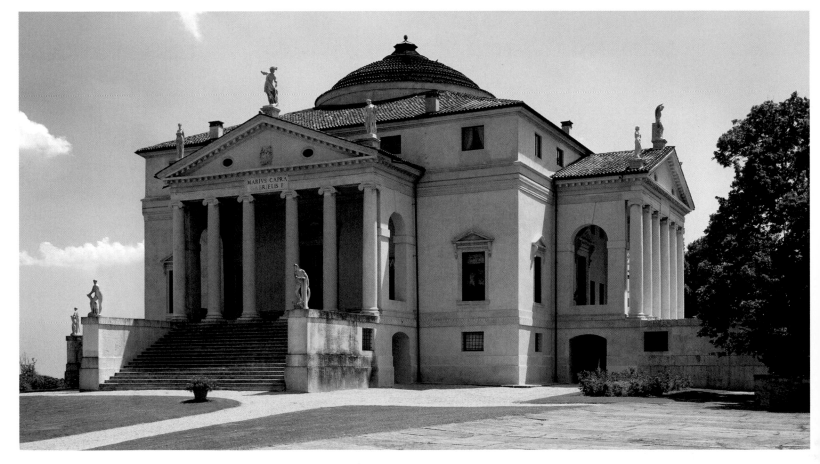

17.34   Andrea Palladio. Villa Rotonda, Vicenza. ca. 1567–70

His buildings alone would make Palladio an important figure in the history of art, but his influence extended beyond Italy, indeed beyond Europe, through his publications. Palladio's most important work in this field was his 1570 work, *The Four Books on Architecture* (excerpted in the *Primary Source*, page 616). While several architects, including Alberti, had written treatises in the fifteenth century, sixteenth-century printed books on architecture by Sebastiano Serlio and Palladio became bestsellers. Palladio's treatise was more practical than Alberti's, which may account for its great popularity among architects, and his many buildings are linked more directly with his theories. Some have claimed that Palladio designed only what was, in his view, sanctioned by ancient precedent. Indeed, the usual term for both Palladio's work and theoretical attitude is classicizing. This term denotes a conscious striving for qualities found in ancient art, although the results may not look like ancient works. Whenever later architects sought to express ideas through ancient forms, they consulted Palladio's *Four Books*. Thomas Jefferson, for instance, once referred to it as "the bible" and based several of his designs for buildings on its examples (see fig. 24.33). Such treatises, with their rules for designing beautiful buildings, formulas for correct proportion, and extensive drawings, including ground plans and elevations in woodcut, were a treasure trove for architects elsewhere in Europe and later throughout the world.

Titian

Titian (1485–1576) dominated painting in Venice throughout the sixteenth century. Like Michelangelo, he lived a long life, and he had numerous pupils to spread his ideas and techniques. His fame was such that by the 1530s his work was sought by the most elite patrons of Europe. For example, in 1538, Titian was commissioned by the duke of Urbino, Guidobaldo II della Rovere, to execute the so-called *Venus of Urbino* (fig. **17.35**). The painting, based on models by Giorgione, depicts a nude young woman lying on a bed in a well-furnished chamber. In the background, two women search in a cassone (or wedding chest) for something, perhaps for a garment. Details such as the presence of the cassone and the little dog have led some scholars to suggest that this may have been an image intended to celebrate a marriage (the dog representing faithfulness). However, the owner referred to the picture only as "the naked woman." Titian's use of color records the sensuous textures of the woman's body, which has been placed on display for a viewer whose gaze she meets. It may have been intended as an erotic image, not a classical theme.

Whether or not this is Venus, the sensuously depicted female nude became a staple product of Titian's workshop, which was supported by the patronage of other powerful men. For Phillip II of Spain (the son of Charles V), whom he met in 1548, Titian

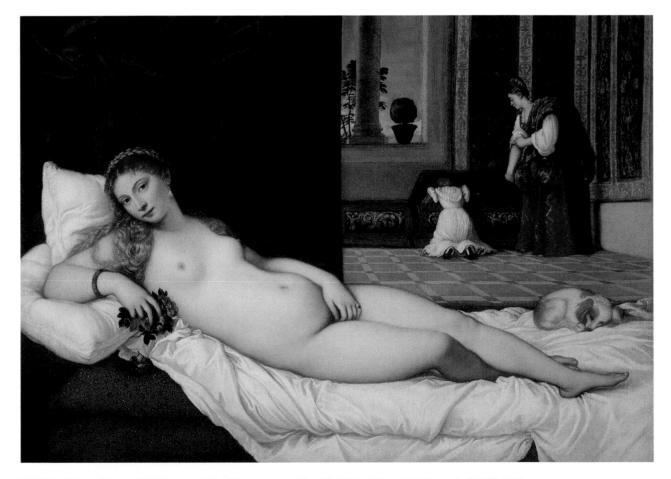

17.35 Titian, *Venus of Urbino*. ca. 1538. Oil on canvas, 47 × 65" (119 × 165 cm). Gallerie degli Uffizi, Florence

Oil on Canvas

For much of the Middle Ages and Renaissance, painters worked either directly on walls or on solid wood supports. Wood panels were formed of planks that had to be attached together, so seams are sometimes visible. While durable, wood is also heavy and susceptible to warping. In the fifteenth century, some artists both in Italy and in northern Europe painted on cloth supports, usually canvas or linen, as a less expensive substitute for wood. Canvas is also lighter, and more easily portable. Painted canvases from Flanders, called *panni dipinti*, were imported in good numbers to Italy.

In the humid climate of Venice, where neither fresco nor wood panels would easily survive, artists preferred to work on canvas supports, especially on large-scale projects. By the middle of the sixteenth century, canvas began to replace wood as the support of choice. By 1600, most patrons, who were not commissioning frescoes, preferred oil on canvas. Once the canvas itself had been stretched on a wooden framework, the artist would cover it with a gluelike material to seal the fibers. Then several priming coats would be applied and allowed to dry before painting commenced.

Working on a large scale also inspired Venetian painters to experiment with the oil medium itself. Instead of building up layers of tinted glazes over large surfaces, artists loaded the brush with more opaque color and laid it on with broad strokes. Sometimes the thick paint looked pastelike, a technique called impasto. In such cases, the surface does not have a mirrorlike smoothness, but is rough and catches the light unevenly. Titian is one of the innovators of this technique. His example was the inspiration for the painterly artists of the Baroque, including Rubens, Rembrandt, and Velázquez.

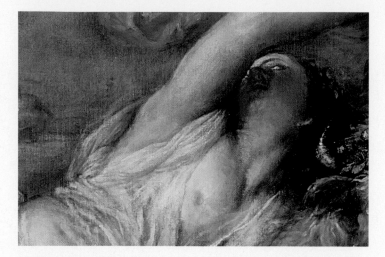

Detail of Titian, *Rape of Europa*

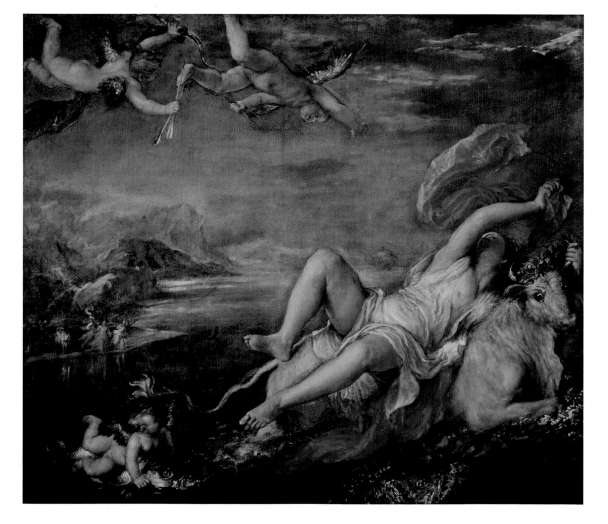

17.36 Titian, *Rape of Europa*. 1559–62. Oil on canvas, 6'1⅛" × 6'8⅔" (185 × 205 cm). Isabella Stewart Gardner Museum, Boston

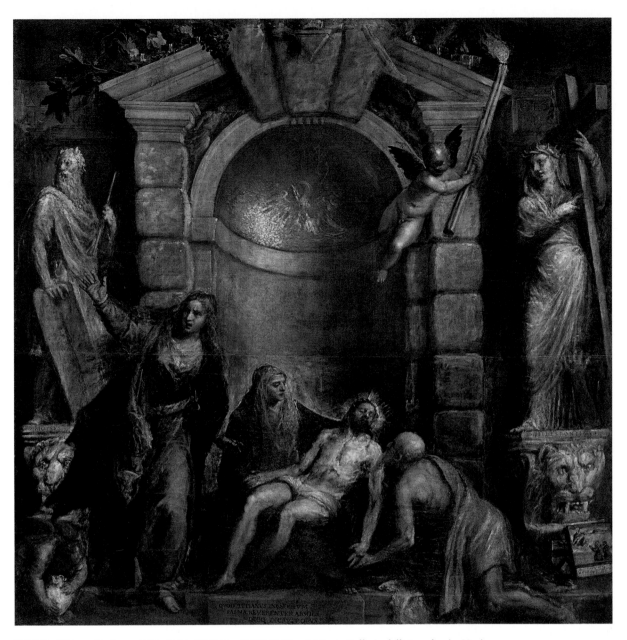

17.37 Titian, *Pietà*. ca. 1576. Canvas, 11'6" × 12'9" (3.51 × 3.89 m). Gallerie dell'Accademia, Venice

made a series of images of the Loves of Jupiter based on the Roman poet Ovid's *Metamorphoses*. There, Ovid recounted the story of the princess beguiled by Jupiter who had taken the shape of a white bull to avoid his wife's jealous gaze; this tale inspired Titian's *Rape of Europa*, finished by 1562 (fig. **17.36**). The poet says that the young woman admired the bull, whom she encountered on the seashore. When she climbed onto the beast, the god swam away with her, her veil fluttering behind her as she clung to his horn. Titian's painting takes up the story at its climax, as the bull moves away from land, leaving Europa's companions to wave ineffectually on the shore.

In Titian's painting, Europa can barely hold on to the energetic animal. Titian uses rich colors and swirling movement to heighten the sensuous forms and to create an atmospheric setting for the events. His brushwork is very free, to the point that the forms are barely defined. This effect is enhanced by his use of the impasto technique. (See *Materials and Techniques*, page 618.) The sharp disjunction between foreground and background emphasizes the main figures' distance from land and adds drama. Such images of sensuous interaction between gods and mortals offered artists like Titian an opportunity to compete with poets. Contemporaries called these images *poesie*, just as they did the works of Giorgione (see page 584).

Titian experimented with many different forms, including prints, but his most enduring innovations were in the technique of painting on canvas. His late works demonstrate his freest brushwork. Titian intended the *Pietà* (fig. **17.37**) for his own tomb in the Franciscan church of Santa Maria Gloriosa dei Frari; incomplete at his death in 1576, it was finished by one of his students. Like Michelangelo's late *Pietà* (see fig. 17.16), Titian depicts the

From a Session of the Inquisition Tribunal in Venice of Paolo Veronese

Because of the liberal religious atmosphere of Venice, Veronese was never required to make the various changes to his painting of the Last Supper (see fig. 17.38) asked for by the tribunal of the Inquisition in this interrogation. All parties seem to have been satisfied with a mere change of title to The Feast in the House of Levi.

Today, Saturday, the 18th of the month of July, 1573, having been asked by the Holy Office to appear before the Holy Tribunal, Paolo Caliari of Verona questioned about his profession:

A: I paint and compose figures.

Q: Do you know the reason why you have been summoned?

A: No, sir.

Q: Can you imagine it?

A: I can well imagine.

Q: Say what you think the reason is.

A: According to what the Reverend Father, the Prior of the Convent of SS. Giovanni e Paolo, told me, he had been here and Your Lordships had ordered him to have painted [in the picture] a Magdalen in place of a dog. I answered him by saying I would gladly do everything necessary for my honor and for that of my painting, but that I did not understand how a figure of Magdalen would be suitable there.

Q: What picture is this of which you have spoken?

A: This is a picture of the Last Supper that Jesus Christ took with His Apostles in the house of Simon.

Q: At this Supper of Our Lord have you painted other figures?

A: Yes, milords.

Q: Tell us how many people and describe the gestures of each.

A: There is the owner of the inn, Simon; besides this figure I have made a steward, who, I imagined, had come there for his own pleasure to see how things were going at the table. There are many figures there which I cannot recall, as I painted the picture some time ago.

Q: In this Supper which you made for SS. Giovanni e Paolo what is the significance of the man whose nose is bleeding?

A: I intended to represent a servant whose nose was bleeding because of some accident.

Q: What is the significance of those armed men dressed as Germans, each with a halberd in his hand?

A: We painters take the same license the poets and the jesters take and I have represented these two halberdiers, one drinking and the other eating nearby on the stairs. They are placed there so that they might be of service because it seemed to me fitting, according to what I have been told, that the master of the house, who was great and rich, should have such servants.

Q: And that man dressed as a buffoon with a parrot on his wrist, for what purpose did you paint him on that canvas?

A: For ornament, as is customary.

Q: Who are at the table of Our Lord?

A: The Twelve Apostles.

Q: What is St. Peter, the first one, doing?

A: Carving the lamb in order to pass it to the other end of the table.

Q: What is the Apostle next to him doing?

A: He is holding a dish in order to receive what St. Peter will give him.

Q: Tell us what the one next to this one is doing.

A: He has a toothpick and cleans his teeth.

Q: Did anyone commission you to paint Germans, buffoons, and similar things in that picture?

A: No, milords, but I received the commission to decorate the picture as I saw fit. It is large and, it seemed to me, it could hold many figures.

Q: Are not the decorations which you painters are accustomed to add to paintings or pictures supposed to be suitable and proper to the subject and the principal figures or are they for pleasure—simply what comes to your imagination without any discretion or judiciousness?

A: I paint pictures as I see fit and as well as my talent permits.

Q: Does it seem fitting at the Last Supper of the Lord to paint buffoons, drunkards, Germans, dwarfs, and similar vulgarities?

A: No, milords.

Q: Do you not know that in Germany and in other places infected with heresy it is customary with various pictures full of scurrilousness and similar inventions to mock, vituperate, and scorn the things of the Holy Catholic Church in order to teach bad doctrines to foolish and ignorant people?

A: Yes, that is wrong.

After these things had been said, the judges announced that the above named Paolo would be obliged to improve and change his painting within a period of three months from the day of this admonition and that according to the opinion and decision of the Holy Tribunal all the corrections should be made at the expense of the painter and that if he did not correct the picture he would be liable to the penalties imposed by the Holy Tribunal. Thus they decreed in the best manner possible.

Source: *A Documentary History of Art*, vol. 2, ed. Elizabeth Gilmore Holt (Princeton, NJ: Princeton University Press, 1982)

body of Christ in his mother's arms as friends and followers mourn. Moses and a sibyl flank a heavily rusticated niche reminiscent of the façade of Sansovino's mint (see fig. 17.31). This large canvas owes its power not only to its large scale and dramatic composition, although these are contributing factors, but also to Titian's technique. The forms emerging from the semidarkness seem to consist wholly of light and color. The artist applies the color in thick masses of paint, yet despite this heavy impasto, the surfaces have lost every trace of material solidity. The gesture of Mary Magdalen and the sorrow in the features of the Virgin add poignancy to the scene. A kneeling figure, possibly St. Jerome, stands in for Titian himself and reaches over to touch the body of Christ in reverence. The quiet, almost resigned mood is enhanced by the painting's ethereal forms.

Titian's Legacy

Titian's creative output and reputation drew many artists to work in his workshop, but he had a tremendous influence even on those who did not. From the island of Crete (then controlled by Venice), the young Domenikos Theotokopoulos, called El Greco, came to study in Titian's shop before heading to Spain (see Chapter 18). The two leading painters in Venice after Titian, Veronese and Tintoretto, developed in different directions. Where Veronese made images that depended on early Titian works such as the *Pesaro Madonna* (see fig. 16.32) and aimed for naturalism, Tintoretto exploited the drama and fluid brushwork of Titian's later work, like the *Pietà*.

PAOLO VERONESE The paintings of Paolo Cagliari (1528–1588), called Paolo Veronese, who was born and trained in Verona, start from the naturalism inherent in Titian's style, but add an interest in details of everyday reality, as seen in animals, textiles, and foodstuffs—and in grand architectural frameworks.

In his huge canvas *The Feast in the House of Levi* (fig. **17.38**), Veronese avoids any reference to the mystical. His symmetrical composition harks back to paintings by Leonardo and Raphael, while the festive mood of the scene reflects examples by Titian of the 1520s, so that at first glance the picture looks like a High Renaissance work born 50 years too late. Veronese, however, is less interested than Leonardo in conveying spiritual or psychological depth. Originally commissioned for the refectory of a Dominican monastery, the painting depicts a sumptuous banquet, a true feast for the eyes. As with his contemporaries elsewhere in Italy, Veronese was deliberately vague about which event from the life of Jesus he originally meant to depict. He gave the painting its present title only after he had been summoned by the religious tribunal of the Inquisition on the charge of filling his picture with "buffoons, drunkards, Germans, dwarfs, and similar vulgarities" unsuited to its theme. The account of the trial shows that the tribunal thought any such representation of the Last Supper irreverent. (See *Primary Source*, page 620.) In the face of their questions, Veronese therefore settled on a different title—*The Feast in the House of Levi*—which permitted him to leave the offending incidents in place. He argued that they were no more objectionable than the nudity of Jesus and the Heavenly Host in Michelangelo's *Last Judgment*. Nevertheless, the tribunal failed to see the analogy, on the grounds that "in the Last Judgment it was not necessary to paint garments, and there is nothing in those figures that is not spiritual." Like many of his contemporaries, Veronese claimed the privilege to "paint pictures as I see fit."

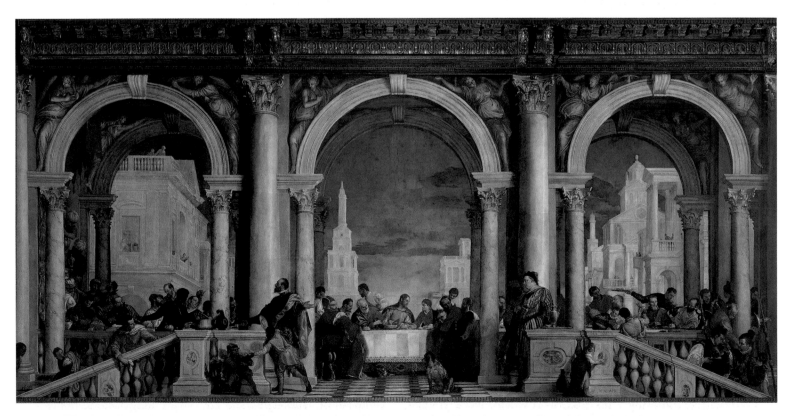

17.38 Paolo Veronese, *The Feast in the House of Levi*. 1573. Oil on canvas, 18'2" × 42' (5.5 × 12.8 m). Gallerie dell'Accademia, Venice

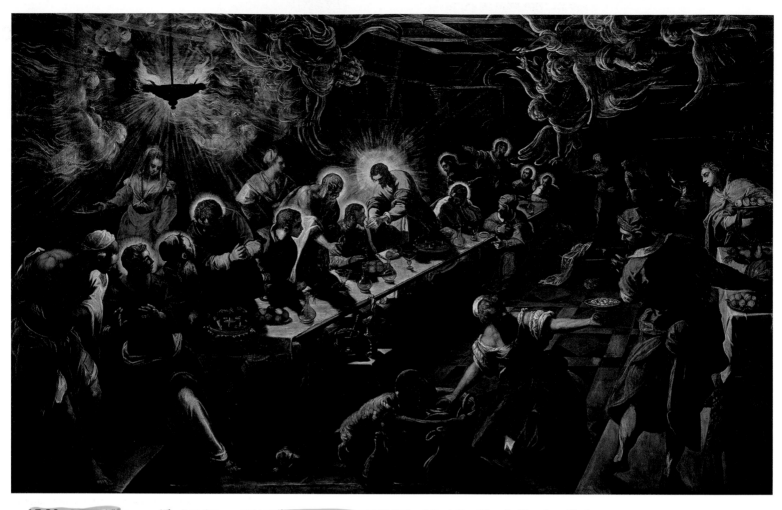

17.39 Jacopo Tintoretto, *The Last Supper*. 1594. Oil on canvas, 12' × 18'8" (3.7 × 5.7 m). San Giorgio Maggiore, Venice

TINTORETTO Jacopo Robusti (1519–1594), called Tintoretto, took a less worldly attitude. He reportedly wanted "to paint like Titian and to design like Michelangelo." He did not imitate the High Renaissance phases of those artists' careers, however, but absorbed their later styles, which are more expressive and less realistic in their effects. In a number of large-scale paintings for Venetian confraternities, groups of laypeople organized for religious activities, he assimilated the visionary effects of Titian's late paintings and the energetic compositions of the late Michelangelo. Tintoretto's final major work, *The Last Supper*, finished in 1594, is spectacular (fig. **17.39**). It seems to deny in every possible way the balance and clarity of Leonardo's version of the theme painted almost exactly a century before (see fig. 16.6), which nonetheless underlies Veronese's picture. Jesus, to be sure, is at the center of the composition, but his small figure in the middle distance is distinguished mainly by his brilliant halo. Tintoretto barely hints at the human drama of Judas' betrayal, so important to Leonardo. Judas can be seen isolated on the near side of the table across from Jesus (as Castagno had arranged him in his fresco in Sant'Apollonia, see fig. 15.29), but his role is so insignificant that he could almost be mistaken for an attendant. The table is now placed at a sharp angle to the picture plane in exaggerated perspective. This arrangement had a purpose. Tintoretto designed it to relate the scene to the space of the **chancel** of San Giorgio Maggiore in Venice, designed by Palladio (see fig. 17.33), for which it was commissioned. When the Benedictine friars knelt at the altar rail to receive communion, they could see the scene at a less acute angle, as if the painted space continued their own.

Tintoretto gives the event an everyday setting, cluttering the scene with attendants, containers of food and drink, and domestic animals. There are also celestial attendants who converge upon Jesus as he offers his body and blood, in the form of bread and wine, to the disciples. The smoke from the blazing oil lamp miraculously turns into clouds of angels, blurring the distinction between the natural and the supernatural and turning the scene into a magnificently orchestrated vision. The artist's main concern is to make visible the miracle of the Eucharist—the Transubstantiation of earthly into divine food—in both real and symbolic terms. The central importance of this sacrament to Catholic doctrine was forcefully reasserted during the Catholic Counter-Reformation. The painting was especially appropriate for its location in San Giorgio Maggiore, which played a prominent role in the reform movement that would have broad repercussions for the arts in Europe in subsequent centuries.

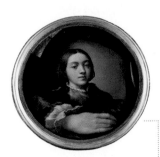

1524 Parmigianino,
Self-Portrait

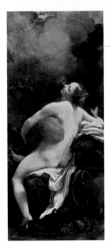

1532 Correggio,
Jupiter and Io

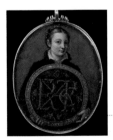

1556 Sofonisba
Anguissola,
Self-Portrait

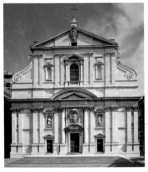

1575 Façade of Il Gesù in Rome

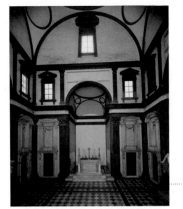

1519–34 Michelangelo's New
Sacristy at San Lorenzo in Florence

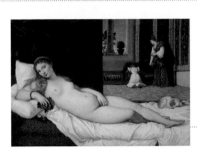

1538 Titian, *Venus of Urbino*

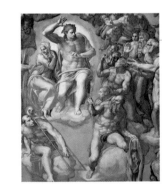

1541 Michelangelo's *Last
Judgment* in the Sistine Chapel

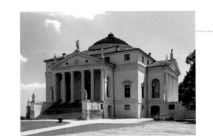

1570 Palladio's *Four Books on
Architecture* published

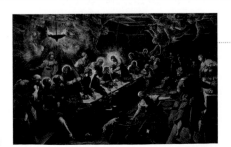

1594 Tintoretto's
Last Supper
at San Giorgio Maggiore

The Late Renaissance and Mannerism in Sixteenth-Century Italy

1500

1510

1520

1530

1540

1550

1560

1570

1580

1590

1600

ca. 1505 Bosch's *Garden of Earthly Delights*

◀ 1520 Death of Raphael
◀ 1521 Luther condemned at Diet of Worms

◀ 1527 Habsburg army sacks Rome; Giulio Romano
in Mantua

◀ 1537 Cosimo I ruler in Florence

◀ 1540 Ignatius of Loyola founds Society of Jesus
(Jesuits)

◀ 1545 Council of Trent opens; Catholic Reformation
begins

◀ 1563 Founding of Florence's Accademia del
Disegno

◀ 1571 Venetian and Spanish navies defeat Turkish
fleet at Lepanto

◀ 1582 Pope Gregory XIII reforms the calendar

◀ 1597 Annibale Carracci in Rome

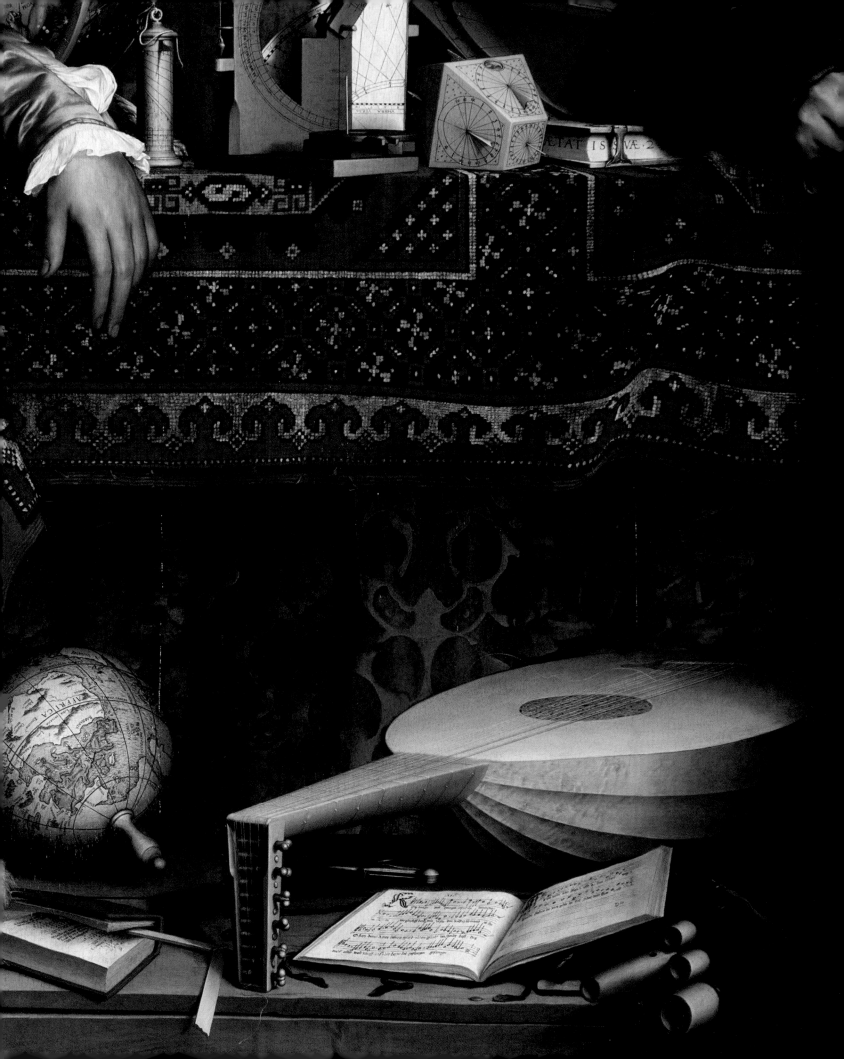

Renaissance and Reformation in Sixteenth-Century Northern Europe

CHAPTER 18

MANY OF THE KEY EVENTS THAT OCCURRED DURING THE HIGH
Renaissance brought important changes throughout Europe, as well as
in Italy. In addition to the religious challenge of the Reformation
fomented by Luther and the new cultural expressions of the Italian
Renaissance, northern Europeans witnessed significant changes: the growing power

of large centralized states in France, England, Spain, and the Holy
Roman Empire; the expansion of Europe's economic reach around
the globe; and the rapid dissemination of new ideas and styles. As
northern Europe experienced the birth pangs of the modern era,
artists reconciled local traditions with these new conditions.

The challenge of the Reformation to the Roman Catholic
Church would fundamentally change the map of Europe (map
18.1). Proponents of religious reform including Luther, Ulrich
Zwingli, John Calvin, and others attracted many adherents, and
whole communities, cities, and even states were converted, frac-
turing the religious unity of Europe. Catholic Europe faced off
against Protestant Europe, with great loss of life. While France and
Spain remained loyal to the Roman Catholic Church, Germany,
England, and the Netherlands were divided by religious sectarian-
ism. The more radical reformed faiths deplored the Catholic
tradition of religious images and relics, and encouraged the
destruction of images in the areas that converted to their beliefs.

Under such conditions, artists had to find new ways to pursue
their craft and new markets for their products. Those markets
would continue the trends established in the fifteenth century. A
growing capitalist economy brought wealth and an increasing
population to the cities. Manufacturing and trade grew, especially

with the new Atlantic trade routes and colonial settlements in the
Americas and Asia. Even as the cities developed in economic and
social importance, increasingly authoritarian rulers asserted
control over their domains.

These pressures affected the character of the arts in northern
Europe. In part because of the Protestant reformers' suspicion of
sculptural expression, the medium of painting increased in importance in the sixteenth century. As religious patronage waned,
artists turned to secular themes, which appealed to patrons in the
cities and in the courts. To compete in the open market, artists
began to specialize in particular subjects or themes. The achievements of the Italian Renaissance also challenged northern artists,
who absorbed Italian compositions, ideal figure types, and an
admiration of antiquity. Patrons in the courts found Italian style
particularly useful for expressing their power, as they built monumental palaces. Catholic rulers often used Italianate forms to
affirm their faith.

FRANCE: COURTLY TASTES FOR ITALIAN FORMS

France was fertile ground for the importation of Italian ideas.
French kings had been intervening in Italy for centuries, which
brought them into contact with developments in Italian art and
architecture. Charles VII of France had invaded Milan in 1499,

Detail of figure 18.23, Hans Holbein the Younger, Jean de Dinteville and Georges de Selve

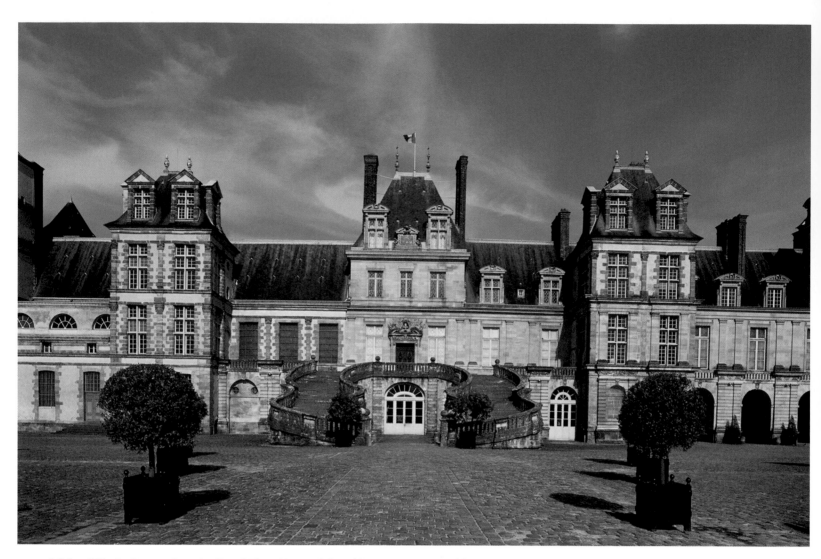

18.1   Gilles Le Breton. Cour du Cheval Blanc (Court of the White Horse), Fontainebleau. 1528–40

and his successors continued to meddle in the Italian peninsula. Francis I (r. 1515–1547) showed his admiration for Italian art by inviting Leonardo da Vinci to work for him in the Loire Valley. Leonardo had provided designs for a never-constructed chateau for the king before dying in Amboise in 1519. Francis's appreciation for Italian art and his propensity for spending money made his court a magnet for artists from Italy and elsewhere in Europe. Rosso Fiorentino, Francesco Primaticcio, Benvenuto Cellini, and others found work there. French traditions were maintained, too, as local architects interpreted Italian ideas for royal structures.

Chateaux and Palaces: Translating Italian Architecture

During the Renaissance, French castles lost their fortified aspect and became palaces for enjoying country life. The influence of Italian architectural design came into play in the design of many of these structures, especially in the chateau that Francis I built south of Paris amid the forest of Fontainebleau (fig. 18.1). In 1528,

he decided to expand the medieval hunting lodge that was once the haunt of King Louis IX. What began as a modest enlargement soon developed into a sprawling palace. The original design, much altered over the years, was largely the work of the stone-mason Gilles Le Breton (d. 1553), whose father, Jean (d. 1543/44), had helped design Chambord. Fontainebleau set a fashion for French translations of Italianate architecture that was followed for nearly all French chateaux for the next 250 years.

The Cour du Cheval Blanc (Court of the White Horse) is typical of the project as a whole. The design must have evolved in an organic fashion, with new generations of patrons and architects adding to it over time. (The Italianate staircase that now dominates the courtyard was built by Jean Androuet du Cerceau in 1634.) Rectangular pavilions at regular intervals define the units of the façade. The façade employs a vocabulary from Italian architecture: pilasters mark each story, entablatures tie the whole façade together horizontally, and the lowest level uses rusticated pilasters such as those used by Sansovino at the Mint in Venice (see fig. 17.31). These elements are blended with vertical proportions, especially in the windows and along the roofline. Such

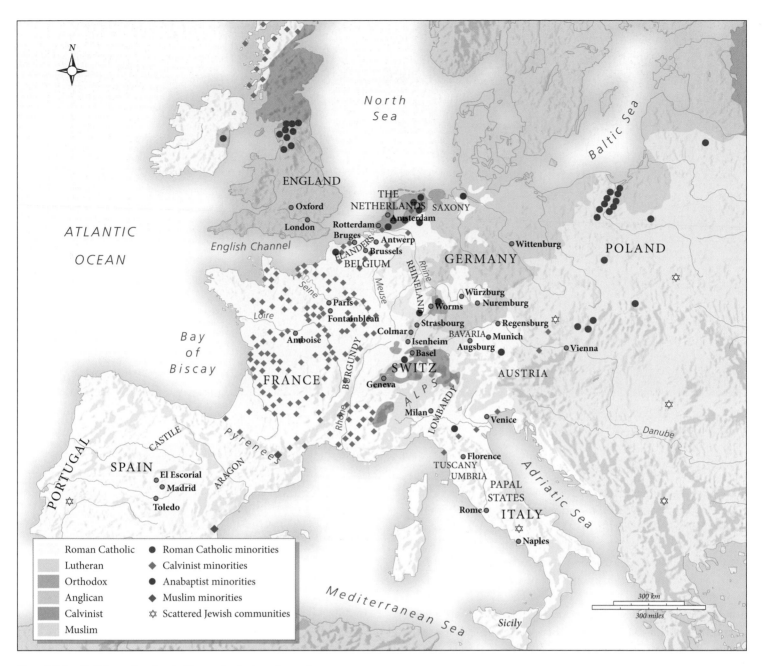

Map 18.1   Religious situation in Europe in the late sixteenth century

vertical massing of forms reflects traditional castle design and the Gothic proportions that French patrons preferred to the more horizontal Italianate models.

THE LOUVRE Despite a variety of wars and other entanglements, Francis I had a great appetite for commissioning large-scale projects. In 1546, he decided to replace the Gothic royal castle in Paris, the Louvre, with a new palace on the old site. The project had barely begun at the time of his death, but his architect, Pierre Lescot (ca. 1515–1578), continued and enlarged it under his successor, Henry II. This scheme was not completed for more than a century. Lescot built the southern half of the court's west side (fig. **18.2**) in a more thoroughly Italianate style than was seen at Fontainebleau.

The design represents a genuine synthesis of the traditional French chateau with the Italian palazzo. The superimposed classical orders, the pedimented window frames, and the arcade on the ground floor stem from Italy. Three projecting pavilions, however, have replaced the chateau turrets to interrupt the continuity of the façade. The high-pitched roof is also French. The vertical accents, and the tall, narrow windows counteract and balance the horizontal elements. The whole effect is symmetrical and well organized; it is made sumptuous by the ornate carvings of the pilasters and their capitals and the relief sculpture that covers nearly all of the wall surface of the third story. These reliefs, beautifully adapted to the architecture, are by Jean Goujon (ca. 1510–1565), a French sculptor of the mid-sixteenth century with whom Lescot often collaborated.

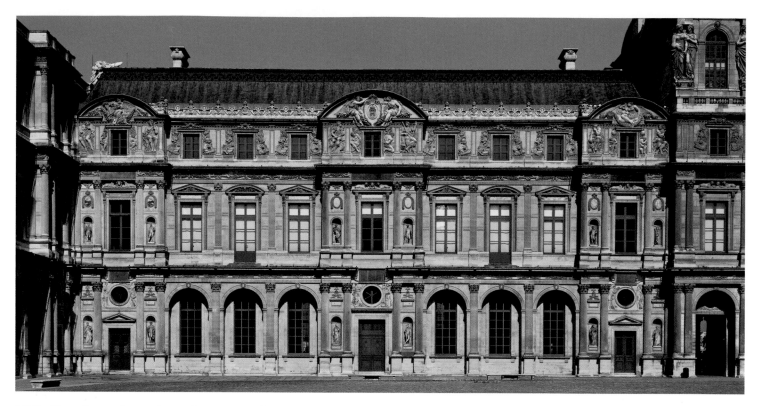

18.2   Pierre Lescot. Square Court, the Louvre, Paris. Begun 1546

Art for Castle Interiors

If the king showed a preference for Italian style, some members of the French court continued to commission works of art following the patterns established during the Middle Ages. Long after the invention of the printing press, French aristocrats continued to commission lavish books of hours and other illuminated books. French church architecture took the possibilities of the Gothic style to new heights (see fig. 12.44). Stained-glass windows remained an important medium for elite patrons, as did tapestry. The walls of their dwellings were lined with sets of these woven hangings, often depicting secular or allegorical themes. Tapestry weaving was an important industry in the Netherlands and in France. (See *Materials and Techniques*, page 629.)

A famous survival of this art form is the set of the *Unicorn Tapestries* that depict the Hunt for the Unicorn, woven around 1500 in the Southern Netherlands or northern France. *The Unicorn in Captivity* (fig. **18.3**) is the culmination of a series of images describing the hunt for, death of, and resurrection of the unicorn, the mythical one-horned equine beast who could only be captured by a virgin. The theme depicts the courtly pastime of hunting, but the unicorn itself has been read as symbolizing Christ (details in the imagery suggest this) and as a secular bridegroom. This panel, which is just over 12 by 8 feet, shows the

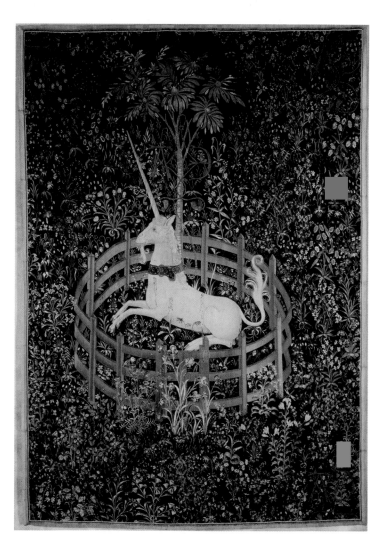

18.3   *The Unicorn in Captivity*, from the *Unicorn Tapestries*. South Netherlandish or French. ca. 1500. Wool warp, wool, silk, silver, and gilt wefts, 12'1" × 8'3" (3.68 × 2.52 m). Metropolitan Museum of Art, New York. Gift of John D. Rockefeller, Jr. 1937. 37.80.6

Making and Conserving Renaissance Tapestries

Tapestries—woven images hung on walls—were a major art form from the Middle Ages through the Baroque period. Elite patrons of Europe commissioned and purchased them to decorate the stone walls of their palaces and chateaux. In Flanders, the principal tapestry-making centers were in Arras, Tournai, and Brussels. In France, Louis XIV cemented the association of royalty with tapestry making by establishing the Royal Workshop of Gobelins in Paris, which dominated French tapestry production until the eighteenth century.

The textiles were woven on looms, such as the one pictured in the Penelope tapestry in figure 14.19. Before the weaving could begin, the patron and the master of the workshop would choose a design, which was worked up into a cartoon, a full-scale drawing for the weaver to follow.

To weave the textile, the weaver stretched supporting threads, called the warp, across the frame of a loom to the size desired. These warp threads are made of strong fibers, usually wool or linen. Colored threads of wool, silk, or spun metals are used to produce the design; these threads, called the weft, are then interwoven with the warp on the loom.

Renaissance tapestries are designated "high warp" and "low warp" according to the arrangement of the loom: The high-warp technique stretches the warp threads vertically on the loom, while the low-warp technique stretches the threads horizontally. The figure of Penelope uses a small low-warp loom, as was common in Flanders.

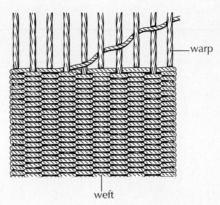

The weaver intertwines the horizontal threads (weft) with vertical threads (warp)

Once the warp threads are stretched on the loom, the cartoon is placed below the loom. The weaver pushes the weft threads through the warp threads, alternating colors to create the design, and then tamps the weft threads into place to form a tight weave. Because the weaver works on the back side of the tapestry as he follows the cartoon, so that different colors may be joined and threads knotted, the front (or visible side) of the tapestry reproduces the cartoon design in reverse.

Increasingly from the fifteenth century, the designs for tapestries came from painters, and as the pictorial ambitions of the painters grew, so did the techniques of the weavers to match them. The increasing illusionism in the cartoons inspired weavers to work with finer threads to make the tapestries more complex. Woven of wool, silk, and gilt threads, *The Unicorn in Captivity* (see fig. 18.3) displays tremendously detailed images of flowers, foliage, and animals. One scholar estimates that it took one hour per square inch to weave these dense designs; at this rate, a team of weavers would have been able to complete only one tapestry per year.

Conservators worked on the *Unicorn Tapestries* recently, replacing their linen backings. This made it possible to see the back of the tapestry, revealing the incredibly rich colors with which it was woven, but which have faded with the passage of time on the front. The tapestries were then immersed in purified water to be cleaned, before being allowed to dry. A new backing was then sewn into place.

---

unicorn fenced in below a pomegranate tree against a verdant background enlivened by numerous flowering plants. Specific elements such as the plants and flowers are wonderfully detailed and naturalistic, with the tapestry as a whole creating a sumptuous two-dimensional effect. The brilliant white body of the unicorn itself is the focal point at the center of the field of flowers. Details like the pomegranates—a symbol of fertility and of eternity—combine with the numerous plants and animals to suggest the theme of Christian salvation, but may also refer to marriage and procreation. Some scholars have suggested that these tapestries were created to celebrate a marriage, perhaps of the individuals whose initials (A and a backward E) intertwine in the tree branches. Despite exhaustive research, their identification remains uncertain. Tapestries continued to be an important art form in France, given an important boost by the establishment of the royal factory of Gobelins in the seventeenth century.

THE SCHOOL OF FONTAINEBLEAU Francis I's preference for Italian art is apparent throughout the chateau at Fontainebleau. The king called upon Italian artists, most of them

working in a Mannerist style, to work there, and these artists initiated the so-called School of Fontainebleau. To decorate the Gallery of Francis I, the king summoned Rosso Fiorentino from Italy (see page 593). Between 1531 and 1540, Rosso executed frescoes framed by stucco *putti*. The combination of painting and sculpted imagery inspired another Italian émigré, Francesco Primaticcio (1504–1570), who replaced Rosso as the chief designer at the royal chateau. The influence of Parmigianino is clear in Primaticcio's most important surviving work, the decorations for the room of the king's mistress, the Duchesse d'Étampes (fig. **18.4**). Primaticcio follows Rosso's general scheme of embedding paintings in a luxuriously sculptured stucco framework, which nearly swallows them. However, the figures are subtly elongated in the style of Parmigianino (see fig. 17.29). The four females in this detail have no specific allegorical significance, although their role recalls the nudes of the Sistine Chapel ceiling. These willowy figures (reminiscent of the caryatids in ancient Greek architecture) enframe paintings devoted to Alexander the Great that were executed by assistants from Primaticcio's designs.

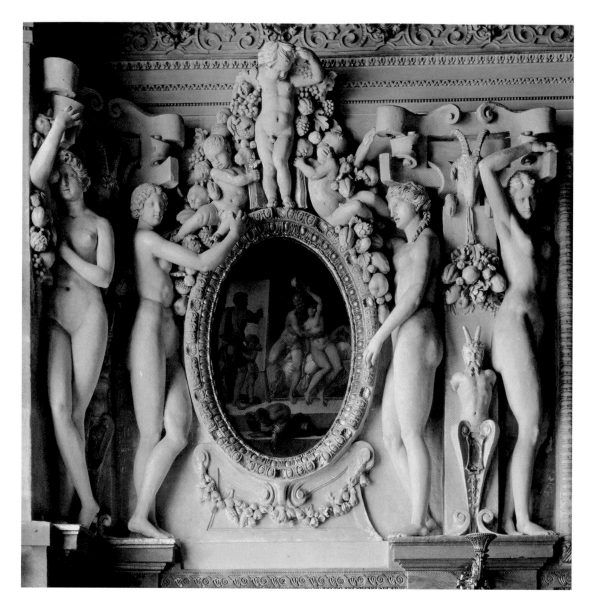

18.4 Francesco Primaticcio. Stucco figures. ca. 1541–45. Gallery of Francis I, designed for the Room of the Duchesse d'Étampes, Chateau of Fontainebleau

The scene in figure 18.4 shows Apelles painting the abduction of Campaspe by Alexander the Great. According to the story, Alexander gave his favorite concubine to the artist when he fell in love with her. Roman texts of this subject characterized this gift as a mark of Alexander's great respect for his court artist. Such mixtures of violence and eroticism appealed greatly to the courtly audience for which Primaticcio worked. The picture draws a parallel between Alexander and Francis I, and between Campaspe and the duchess, the king's mistress, who had taken Primaticcio under her protection. The artist may have seen himself in the role of Apelles.

ROYAL TOMBS AT SAINT-DENIS The presence of so many Italian artists at Fontainebleau made the chateau a laboratory of Italian style, which many French artists absorbed. For example, Germain Pilon (ca. 1535–1590) created monumental sculpture that is informed not only by the elegance of the School of Fontainebleau, but also by elements taken from ancient sculpture, the Gothic tradition, and Michelangelo. His main works are tombs,

such as the *Tomb of Henry II and Catherine de' Medici* (fig. **18.5**) commissioned by Catherine de' Medici and executed for the French royal pantheon at Saint-Denis. Primaticcio designed the architectural framework, a free-standing chapel on a platform decorated with bronze and marble reliefs. He also designed the corner figures of virtues as elegant young women. Pilon executed the sculpture. On the top of the tomb are the bronze figures of the king and queen kneeling in prayer, while inside the chapel the couple reappear as marble **gisants**, or recumbent effigies of the deceased. Gisants expressed the transient nature of the flesh, usually by showing the body in an advanced stage of decay, sometimes with vermin crawling through their open cavities. Pilon inverts this concept: Instead of portraying decaying flesh, his gisants are idealized nudes. While the likenesses of the royal couple kneeling atop the structure record their features in life, the gisants represent them as beautiful beings in death: The queen is in the pose of a classical Venus and the king is represented similarly to the dead Christ. They evoke neither horror nor pity. Instead, they have the pathos of a beauty that continues even in death.

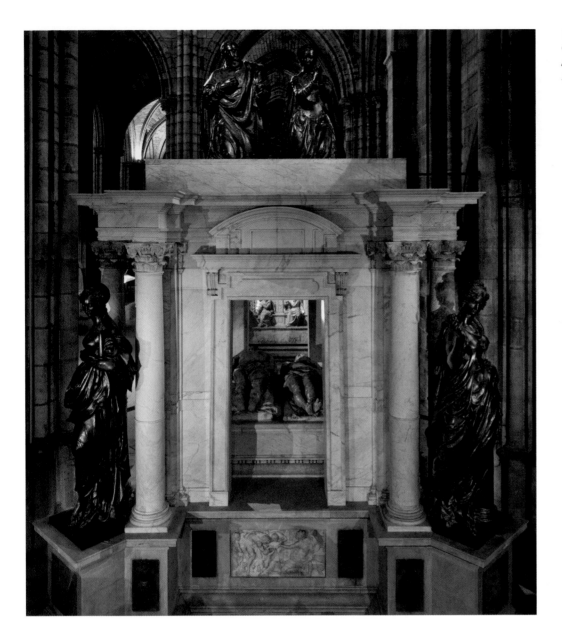

Henry II's death in 1559 left his young son—still a minor—to inherit the throne, so his widow, Catherine de' Medici, acted as regent during a troubled period. Increasing conflicts between Catholic and Protestant groups, called Huguenots, erupted into massacres and warfare between 1562 and 1598, when a policy of official toleration was announced by Henry IV.

SPAIN: GLOBAL POWER AND RELIGIOUS ORTHODOXY

Several events came together in the early sixteenth century to increase the status and influence of Spain in Europe. In 1500, Charles V was born to the son of Maximilian of Habsburg and the daughter of Ferdinand and Isabella. With this parentage, he became heir to the thrones of Spain, Aragon, and the Burgundian territories, as well as the title of Holy Roman emperor. Charles also asserted a Spanish claim to rule the Kingdom of Naples in southern Italy. Spain was thus integrated more fully into European power struggles than it had been in previous centuries. At the same time, the colonization of the lands Columbus had claimed in the Americas brought massive wealth into Spanish hands. Charles V's efforts to promote and rule his vast holdings so exhausted him that in 1556 he divided his territory in half and abdicated in favor of his son Philip and his brother Ferdinand. Ferdinand took control of the traditional Habsburg territories in Central Europe. Reigning as king of Spain, the Netherlands, and New Spain in the Americas from 1556 to 1598, Philip inherited the problems that had bedeviled his father. Having succeeded in preventing the Turkish advance into Europe in 1571, he turned his attention to the religious upheavals that the Reformation had brought to Christian Europe. Pious and ardent in his orthodoxy, he tried to quash the rebellion of the Calvinist Northern Netherlands, and unsuccessfully attempted to invade England in 1588, when the Spanish Armada suffered a disastrous defeat in the English Channel.

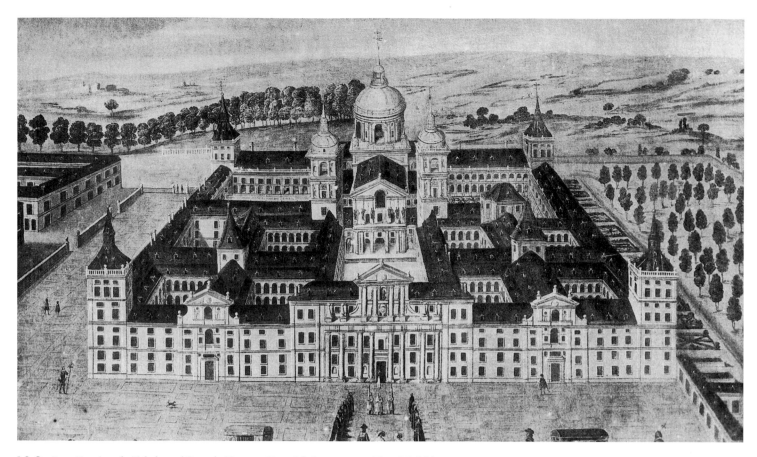

18.6 Juan Bautista de Toledo and Juan de Herrera. Escorial. Begun 1563. Near Madrid

The Escorial

Philip also inherited a taste for collecting works of art from his forebears. He invited Sophonisba Anguissola to become one of his court artists; he commissioned works from Titian and other Italian artists; he not only hired Netherlandish artists to work for him, he sought out fifteenth-century Flemish works, especially paintings by Bosch. In this effort, he acquired *The Garden of Earthly Delights* (see fig. 14.22) and many other objects, which were brought to his new palace and monastery complex outside Madrid, called the Escorial. Built to commemorate Philip's victory over the French in 1557, this massive complex (fig. **18.6**) was begun in 1563 by Juan Bautista de Toledo (d. 1567), who had worked with Michelangelo in Rome. The symmetrical massing of the buildings and the focus on the church of San Lorenzo at the center reflect Italian Renaissance models, but the scale and the simplicity of the façades were dictated by King Philip. In consultation with leading Italian architects, including Palladio and Vignola, Juan Bautista de Toledo's successor at the Escorial, Juan de Herrera, expanded the design and introduced classicizing details such as the temple fronts on the façades of the main portal and the Church of San Lorenzo (fig. **18.7**). These, however, use a very plain Doric order and the whole façade exhibits a severity and seriousness that may express Philip's commitment to the ideals of the Catholic Reformation. The complex includes a monastery and church, a palace, a seminary, a library, and a

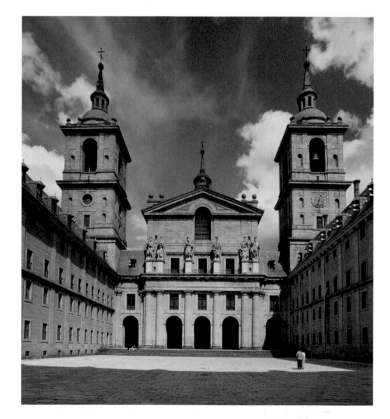

18.7 Juan Bautista de Toledo and Juan de Herrera. Escorial, façade of main church

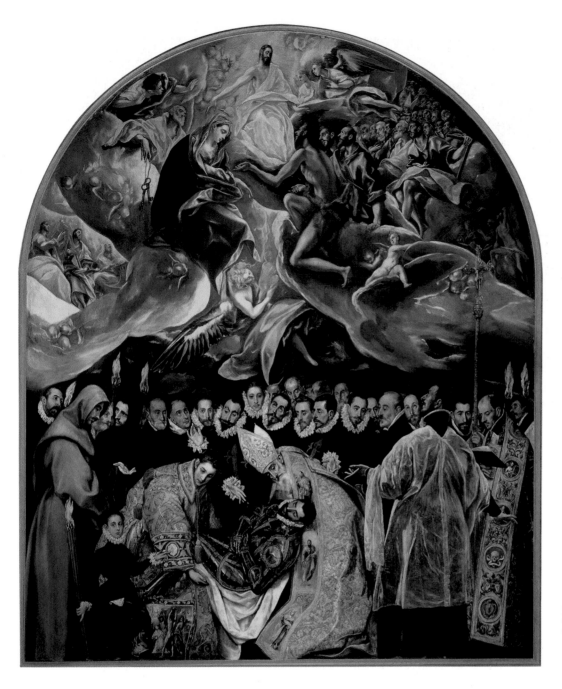

18.8 El Greco, *The Burial of Count Orgaz*. 1586. Oil on canvas, 16' × 11'10" (4.9 × 3.6 m). Santo Tomé, Toledo, Spain

burial chapel for the Spanish kings. Philip himself spent his last years here.

El Greco and Religious Painting in Spain

Philip's strong commitment to Catholic orthodoxy led him to support the work of many new orders and institutions that arose during the Catholic Reformation. The Spanish Inquisition, for example, fervently pursued the work of rooting out heresy. The Spanish-born Ignatius of Loyola's followers, the Jesuits, had a strong presence in Spain, as did the Carmelite order, whose most famous member was the nun and reformer Teresa of Ávila. Both the Jesuits and the Carmelites encouraged meditation among the faithful. Loyola wrote a treatise, *The Spiritual Exercises*, to teach believers to meditate in steps so that they might achieve visions so real that they would seem to appear before their very eyes. The spiritual writings of Teresa of Ávila, informed by her visions, urge prayer to achieve closer union with God (see fig. 19.31).

In this atmosphere, the best-known painter of sixteenth-century Spain, Domenikos Theotokopoulos (1541–1614), called El Greco, found a home. Born on Crete, which was then under Venetian rule, he probably trained there to become an icon painter. At some point before 1568, he arrived in Venice and quickly absorbed the lessons of Titian and Tintoretto, but he also knew the art of Raphael, Michelangelo, and the Italian Mannerists. He went to Spain in 1576–77 and settled in Toledo for the rest of his life. El Greco joined the leading intellectual circles of the city, then a major center of learning, as well as the seat of Catholic reform in Spain. El Greco's painting exhibits an exalted emotionalism informed by his varied artistic sources.

Among the most impressive of El Greco's commissions is *The Burial of Count Orgaz* (fig. 18.8), executed in 1586 in the church

share stylistic features with Italian Mannerist works such as Rosso's *The Descent from the Cross* (see fig. 17.1).

Only when the work is seen in its original setting (fig. **18.9**) does its full meaning become clear. The painting fills one entire wall of its chapel, like a huge window. In the shallow space of the chapel a viewer must stand close and look sharply upward to see the upper half of the picture. The violent foreshortening is calculated to achieve an illusion of boundless space in the upper portion of the painting, while the figures in the lower foreground appear as if on a stage. The large stone plaque set into the wall also belongs to the ensemble. It represents the front of the sarcophagus into which the two saints lower the body of the count, which explains the action in the picture. A viewer, then, perceives three levels of reality. The first is the grave itself, supposedly set into the wall at eye level and closed by an actual stone slab; the second is the reenactment of the miraculous burial; and the third is the vision of celestial glory witnessed by some of the participants. This step-by-step movement into the world of the picture may be linked to meditative practices of the era. Working in steps to achieve such a vision could only be achieved through the kind of strenuous devotion and commitment to mysticism encouraged by Loyola and Teresa of Ávila. El Greco's work mirrors the intensity of such deep spiritual struggle.

CENTRAL EUROPE: THE REFORMATION AND ART

While Italy, France, and Spain adhered to the Catholic faith, elsewhere in Europe the religious and artistic situation became more volatile. In addition to Spain, Charles V had inherited the many different political units that comprised what is now Germany, Austria, Hungary, and the Czech Republic. Governing such disparate regions posed many challenges, which were passed along to Charles's brother Ferdinand when Charles stepped down as ruler in 1556. Though linked in many cases by language and cultural ties, as well as by trade, these were independent regions only nominally under control of the Holy Roman emperor. What unity they may have had suffered another blow after 1517, when religious unity was fractured by the Protestant Reformation.

In October 1517, Martin Luther, a former Augustinian friar who had become professor of theology at the University of Wittenberg, issued a public challenge to both the theology and the institutional practices of the Catholic Church. In his famous *Ninety-five Theses*, which he posted on the church door at Wittenberg Castle, Luther complained about the Catholic practice of selling indulgences—promises of redemption of sins; he argued, too, against the veneration of Mary and the saints. Most fundamental to his critique of Catholicism, Luther claimed that the Bible and natural reason were the sole bases of religious authority, and that the intervention of clerics and saints was unnecessary for salvation, which was freely given by God. It followed from this that religious authority was transferred from the pope to the individual conscience of each believer. The Catholic

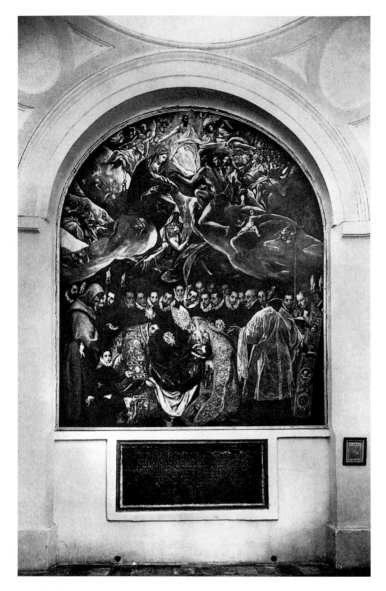

18.9 Chapel with *The Burial of Count Orgaz*. 1586. Santo Tomé, Toledo, Spain

of Santo Tomé in Toledo. The program, which was dictated in the commission, emphasizes the Roman Catholic position that good works are required to achieve salvation and that saints serve as intercessors with Heaven. This huge canvas honors a medieval benefactor so pious that St. Stephen and St. Augustine miraculously appeared at his funeral and lowered his body into its grave. Although the burial took place in 1323, El Greco presents it as a contemporary event; he even portrays many of the local nobility and clergy of his time among the attendants. The display of color and texture in the armor and vestments reflects El Greco's Venetian training. Above, the count's soul (a small, cloudlike figure like the angels in Tintoretto's *Last Supper*, see fig. 17.39) is carried to Heaven by an angel. The celestial assembly in the upper half of the picture is painted very differently from the group in the lower half: Every form—clouds, limbs, draperies—takes part in the sweeping, flamelike movement toward the figure of Christ. El Greco's compressed space, unearthly light, and weightless bodies

Church responded by condemning Luther in 1521. But many Christians in Europe accepted his critique, which eventually fueled political instability, rebellions, and wars. Many areas of northern Germany converted to the reformed faith, while southern regions, such as Bavaria, remained Catholic. In rethinking these basic issues of faith, Luther was joined by other religious reformers (see map 18.1).

Protestant thinkers following Luther aimed to eliminate the abuses they perceived in the Catholic Church. The Swiss pastor Ulrich Zwingli wanted to reduce religion to its essentials by stressing individual access to Scripture. As a result of his literal reading of the Bible, he denounced not only the sale of indulgences, but the visual arts as well. Zwingli interpreted the Eucharist as a symbolic, rather than actual, communion of bread and wine; his theology led to a split with Luther that was never healed. What concerned the reformers above all were the twin issues of grace and free will in attaining faith and salvation. By the time of Zwingli's death at the hands of the Catholic forces in 1531, the main elements of Protestant theology had been defined. John Calvin of Geneva codified these tenets around midcentury; Calvin's vision of a moral life based on a literal reading of Scripture was to prove very influential. The spread of the reformed faiths led to decades of violence, including a Peasants' Revolt in 1525 and wars in regions that were converting to Protestantism. From 1546, German principalities fought with the emperor Charles V, until the Peace of Augsburg in 1555. By this compromise, the rulers of individual regions of Germany chose the faith for their own inhabitants. This furthered the spread of the reformed faiths, but also fostered the political divisions of the area.

The repercussions for art were equally dramatic. Luther's own attitudes toward the visual arts, expressed in his writings, veered between warning of the danger of idolatry and seeing the value of art as a tool for teaching. (See www.myartslab.com.) Some of the more radical reformers saw the many forms of medieval and Renaissance religious art as nothing short of idolatry that needed to be cleansed. Inspired by reformers' zeal, civic leaders, artisans, and workers attacked religious images in the cities. Several waves of image destruction, called **iconoclasm**, resulted in great losses of works of art from earlier periods. And as large areas of Central Europe converted to the new faiths, art forms that had been the bread and butter for artists disappeared, as churches were whitewashed and religious commissions dried up. Artists in many mediums had to find new styles, new subjects, and new markets for their work.

Humanism and the new technology of printing played a vital role in the Reformation. The humanist spirit of inquiry and respect for original texts inspired the writings of famous intellectuals and teachers, such as Desiderius Erasmus in Rotterdam, Philip Melancthon in Germany, and Thomas More in England. Published Latin texts spread new ideas all over Europe. As a result, the printing press became an important factor in both the development and the dispersion of Reformation thought. Individual access to Scripture was a fundamental tenet of the

reformers, so they wanted to make available good texts of the Bible as well as translations of it into vernacular languages. Luther himself translated the Bible into German. Printed images contributed to the spread of Reformation ideas; inexpensive woodcuts satirized the Catholic hierarchy while making heroes of the reformers. Prints also illustrated the tenets of the new faiths.

Catholic Contexts: The Isenheim Altarpiece

Yet not all regions of German-speaking Europe converted to the reformed faiths, and it was not until the 1520s that the Reformation took wide hold. As such, some traditional objects were created in the sixteenth century to serve Catholic patrons. One such object is an altarpiece executed by the painter Matthias Gothart Nithart, who was known for centuries only as Grünewald (ca. 1475–1528). This nickname was given to him by a seventeenth-century author; when German artists in the modern period began searching for roots, they discovered the artist through his nickname and it has stuck. Grünewald was born in Würzburg in central Germany and worked for the archbishop of nearby Mainz. His most famous work is a transforming triptych called the *Isenheim Altarpiece*, similar in structure to the *St. Wolfgang Altarpiece* by Pacher (see fig. 14.28). It was painted between 1509–10 and 1515 for the monastery church of the Order of St. Anthony at Isenheim, in Alsace, not far from the former abbey that now houses it in the city of Colmar.

This church served the monks and the patients of the hospital attached to their monastery. The monks specialized in tending people who suffered from a disease called St. Anthony's Fire, which was a disorder caused by eating spoiled rye. This disease produced painful symptoms, including intestinal disorders, gangrenous limbs, and hallucinations. Treatment consisted mostly of soothing baths and in some cases the amputation of limbs. Grünewald's altarpiece stood on the high altar of the monastery church, where both the sick in the hospital and the monks who served them could see it. This extraordinary altarpiece encases a huge shrine carved in wood by Nicolas Hagenau around 1505. Enclosing the carved central section are nine panels organized in two sets of movable wings. These open in three stages or "views." The first of these views, when all the wings are closed, shows the Crucifixion in the center panel (fig. **18.10**). This is the view that was visible during the week. The wings depict St. Sebastian (left), who was invoked against the plague (see fig. 15.48) and St. Anthony Abbot (right), who was revered as a healer. The central image of the Crucifixion draws on the late medieval tradition of the Andachtsbild (see fig. 12.60) to emphasize the suffering of Christ and the grief of his mother. The figure of Christ, with its twisted limbs, its many wounds, its streams of blood, matches the vision of the fourteenth-century mystic St. Bridget as described in her book of *Revelations*, which had been published in a German edition in 1501–02.

Grünewald renders the body on the Cross on a heroic scale, so that it dominates the other figures and the landscape. The

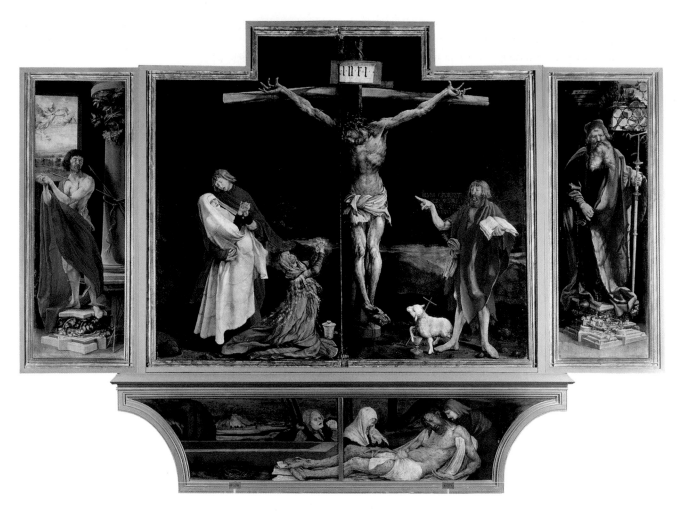

18.10 Matthias Grünewald, *St. Sebastian*; *The Crucifixion*; *St. Anthony Abbot*; predella: *Lamentation*. *Isenheim Altarpiece* (closed). ca. 1509/10–15. Oil on panel, main body 9'9½" × 10'9" (2.97 × 3.28 m), predella 2'5½" × 11'2" (0.75 × 3.4 m). Musée d'Unterlinden, Colmar, France

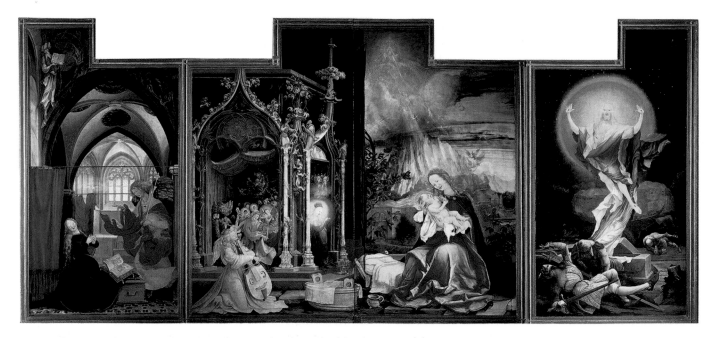

18.11 Matthias Grünewald, *The Annunciation*; *Madonna and Child with Angels*; *The Resurrection*. Second view of the *Isenheim Altarpiece*. ca. 1509/10–15. Oil on panel, each wing 8'10" × 4'8" (2.69 × 1.42 m), center panel 8'10" × 11'2½" (2.69 × 3.41 m). Musée d'Unterlinden, Colmar, France

Crucifixion, lifted from its familiar setting, becomes a lonely event silhouetted against a ghostly landscape and a blue-black sky. Despite the darkness of the landscape, an eerie light bathes the foreground figures to heighten awareness of them. On the left, Mary's white garment enfolds her as she swoons at the sight of her tortured son; the red of St. John's robe accents her paleness. Below the Cross, Mary Magdalen, identified by her ointment jar, kneels in grief to lament. On the right, John the Baptist points to the Crucified Christ with the words, "He must increase, and I must decrease," indicating the significance of Christ's sacrifice. Behind him a body of water recalls the healing power of baptism. The lamb at John's feet bleeds into a chalice, as does the lamb in the central panel of the *Ghent Altarpiece* (see fig. 14.10). The bleeding lamb is a reminder of the sacrament of the Eucharist, celebrated before the altarpiece. In the predella below, a tomb awaits the tormented body while his mother and friends bid him farewell. The predella slides apart at Christ's knees: Victims of amputation may have seen their own suffering reflected in this image.

On Sundays and feast days the outer wings were opened and the mood of the *Isenheim Altarpiece* changed dramatically (fig. **18.11**). All three scenes in this second view—*The Annunciation*, the *Madonna and Child with Angels*, and *The Resurrection* (fig. **18.12**)—celebrate events that are as jubilant as the Crucifixion is somber. Depicting the cycle of salvation, from the Incarnation to the Resurrection, this view of the altarpiece offered the afflicted a form of spiritual medicine while reminding them of the promise of Heaven. Throughout these panels, Grünewald depicts forms of therapy recommended for sufferers at the hospital: music, herbs, baths, and light. The contrast of the body of the dead Jesus in the predella with the Resurrected Christ in the right panel offers consolation to the dying.

Grünewald links the panels through color and composition. Reds and pinks in The Annunciation panel on the left are carried through the central panels to reach a climax with the brilliant colors surrounding the risen figure of Christ on the right. The figure of the dead Jesus held by his mother and friends in the predella adds poignancy to the figure of the child Jesus in his mother's arms in the central panel. The simple Gothic chapel in which the Annunciation takes place gives way in the next panel to a fanciful tabernacle housing choirs of angels who play stringed instruments and sing. Beneath that tabernacle appears a figure of the Virgin, crowned and glowing like a lit candle. The aureole surrounding this figure anticipates the brilliant figure of the Resurrected Christ in the right-hand panel, whose body seems to dissolve into light. The central image of the Madonna holding her child in a tender embrace gives way to a vision of Heaven, also made of pure light.

These elements lead the eye to the right panel, where the body of Christ appears to float above his stone sarcophagus. The guards set to watch the tomb are knocked senseless by the miracle. Their figures, carefully arranged in a perspectival display, contrast to the weightless and transfigured body of Christ. As he holds his hands up, the shroud falls to reveal the wounds he suffered in death,

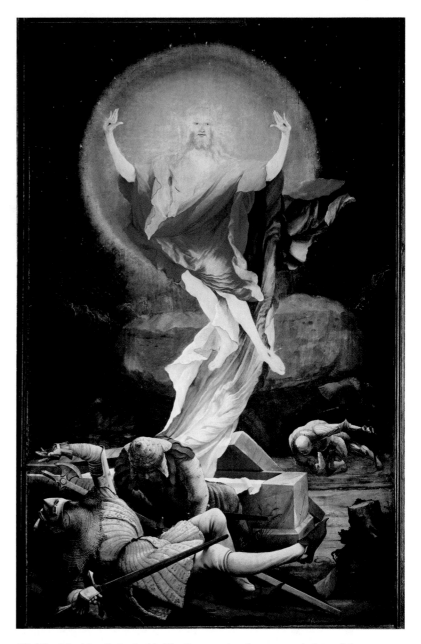

18.12 Matthias Grünewald, *The Resurrection*, from second view of the *Isenheim Altarpiece*. Musée d'Unterlinden, Colmar, France

now as brilliant as the halo that engulfs his body. This figure differs dramatically from the figure on the Cross; his body bears no scars and the proportions are closer to the Italian ideal seen in Piero della Francesca's *Resurrection* (see fig. 15.43).

Grünewald's strikingly individual approach to form is based on the traditions of the northern European Renaissance established in the fifteenth century. His oil technique, his brilliant use of color, and the detailed rendering of objects draw from that tradition, but he must have learned from the Italian Renaissance too. The low horizon lines suggest a deep space for his figures and the rendering of the tomb from which Christ rises is a study in perspective. Yet Grünewald does not try to convince the viewer of the weight and substance of his figures; his aim is to create an emotional response with the impact of a vision.

Albrecht Dürer and the Northern Renaissance

The crucial figure for the Renaissance in Germany is Grünewald's contemporary Albrecht Dürer (1471–1528). Dürer's style was formed in the tradition of northern European naturalism (which we explored in Chapter 14), but he delved deeply into the innovations and possibilities of Italian art. After training as a painter and printmaker in his native Nuremberg, Dürer traveled in northern Europe and Venice in 1494–95 before returning home to start his career. His travels not only expanded his visual repertoire, but changed his view of the world and the artist's place in it. (He returned to Italy in 1505.) Dürer adopted the ideal of the artist as a gentleman and humanistic scholar, and took the Italian view that the fine arts belonged among the liberal arts, as artists like Mantegna and Alberti had argued (see Chapter 15). By cultivating his artistic and intellectual interests, Dürer incorporated into his work an unprecedented variety of subjects and techniques. His painting technique owes much to the Flemish masters, but making copies of Italian works taught him many of the lessons of the Italian Renaissance. He was able to synthesize these traditions in his paintings and prints. As the greatest printmaker of the time, he had a wide influence on sixteenth-century art through his woodcuts and engravings, which circulated all over Europe. His prints made him famous and wealthy—so much so that he complained about the relatively poor reward he earned for his paintings.

Dürer's debt to the legacy of Jan van Eyck and Rogier van der Weyden is clear in the many drawings and watercolors he made in

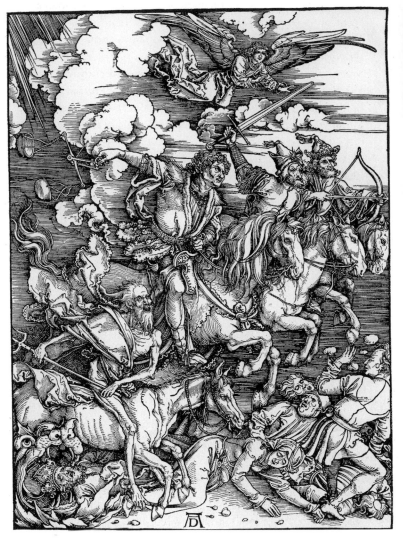

18.14   Albrecht Dürer, *The Four Horsemen of the Apocalypse*. 1498. Woodcut, 15½ × 11⅛" (39.3 × 28.3 cm). Metropolitan Museum of Art, New York. Gift of Junius S. Morgan, 1919. 19.73.209

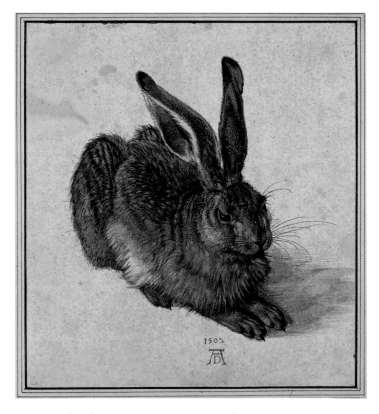

18.13   Albrecht Dürer, *Hare*. 1502. Watercolor, 9⅞ × 8⅞" (25.1 × 22.5 cm). Albertina, Vienna

preparation for his works. The watercolor of a hare he made in 1502 (fig. **18.13**) demonstrates the clarity of his vision and the sureness of his rendering. Dürer treated this small representative of the natural world with the dignity due to nature herself, much as Van Eyck had painted the small dog in the foreground of *The "Arnolfini Portrait"* (see fig. 14.14). Dürer uses the watercolor technique to render each hair of the fur, the curve of the ears, the sheen on the eyes. His monogram at the base of the page identifies Dürer as the creator of this image; this monogram was the signature he used on his mature prints.

Dürer's ability as a draftsman also informed his work as a printmaker. Having been trained in both woodcut and engraving, he pushed the limits of both mediums. As a mass medium, prints were not commissioned by individual patrons, but were made for the open market, so Dürer had to invest his own materials and unpaid time in these projects. This entrepreneurial spirit served him well, as his prints sold widely and quickly, in part because of his astute choice of subject matter. Signs and portents, such as the threat of invasion by the Turks and the birth of malformed animals, worried Europeans as they awaited the approach of the year 1500. As this year drew near, many people believed that the Second Coming of Christ was imminent, and prepared for the Millennium. Thus, with an eye to the market for things pertaining to popular fears about the end of time, Dürer produced a woodcut series illustrating the Apocalypse in 1498. This series was his most ambitious graphic work in the years following his return from Italy. *The Four Horsemen of the Apocalypse* (fig. **18.14**) offers the viewer a frightening visualization of the text of the book of Revelation. The image depicts War, Conquest, Famine, and Death overrunning the earth. During his trip to Italy in 1494, Dürer had encountered prints by Mantegna, which he carefully copied. He especially admired the sculptural quality Mantegna achieved in paintings such as the St. Sebastian (see fig. 15.48). The physical energy and full-bodied volume of the figures in the Apocalypse series is partly owed to Dürer's experience of Italian art, although he eliminates logical space in favor of an otherworldly flatness. Dürer has redefined his medium—the woodcut—by enriching it with the linear devices of engraving. Instead of the broad contours

and occasional hatchings used to define form in earlier woodcuts, Dürer's wide range of hatching marks, varied width of lines, and strong contrasts of black and white produce ambitious pictorial effects. (Compare, for example, the *Buxheim St. Christopher* of 1423 shown in fig. 14.29). He set a standard that soon transformed the technique of woodcuts all over Europe.

Dürer's fusion of northern European and Italian traditions is apparent in his engraving entitled *Adam and Eve* of 1504 (fig. **18.15**), for which the watercolor *Hare* was a preliminary study. Here the biblical subject allows him to depict the first parents as two ideal nudes: Apollo and Venus stand in a densely wooded forest. Unlike the picturesque setting and the animals in it, Adam and Eve are not observed from life; they are constructed according to what Dürer believed to be the perfect proportions based on Vitruvius. (See www.myartslab.com.) Once again, Dürer enlarged the vocabulary of descriptive marks an engraver could use: The lines taper and swell; they intersect at varying angles; marks start and stop and dissolve into dots, called **stipples**. The result is a monochrome image with a great tonal and textural range. The animals that populate the Garden of Eden are very deliberately chosen: Scholars have interpreted the cat, rabbit, ox, and elk as symbols of the medieval theory that bodily fluids, called humors, controlled personality. The cat represents the choleric humor, quick to anger; the ox the phlegmatic humor, lethargic and slow; the elk stands for the melancholic humor, sad and serious; and the rabbit for the sanguine, energetic and sensual. In this moment before the Fall, the humors coexist in balance and the humans retain an ideal beauty. The composition itself is balanced and unified by the tonal effects. Dürer's print, which he signed prominently on the plaque by Adam's head, was enormously influential. His ideal male and female figures became models in their own right for countless other artists.

IMAGES ABOUT ARTISTRY Although best known for his prints, Dürer was also a gifted draftsman and skilled painter. One of his earliest works, a drawing made at 13, is a self-portrait that foreshadowed his fascination with his own image throughout his career. Most impressive, and very revealing, is the painted *Self-Portrait* of 1500 (fig. 18.16). In pictorial terms, it belongs to the Flemish tradition of Jan van Eyck's *Man in a Red Turban* (see fig. 14.13), but the solemn pose and the idealization of the features have an authority not found in most portraits up to this time. Instead of a conventional three-quarter pose, Dürer places himself frontally in the composition, a pose usually reserved for images of the divine. The panel looks, in fact, like a secularized icon, for it is patterned after images of Christ. It reflects both Dürer's deep piety and the seriousness with which he viewed his mission as an artist and intellectual.

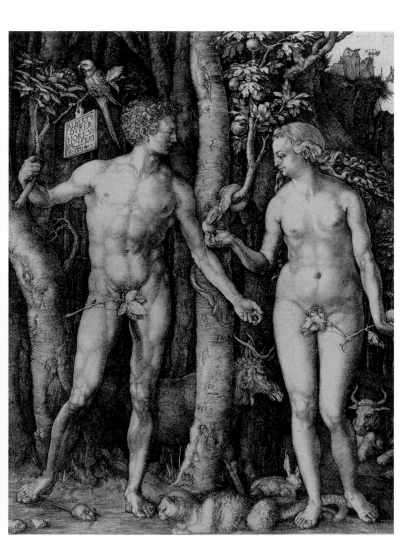

18.15   Albrecht Dürer, *Adam and Eve*. 1504. Engraving, 9⅞ × 7⅝" (25.2 × 19.4 cm). Museum of Fine Arts, Boston. Centennial gift of Landon T. Clay. 1968. 68.187

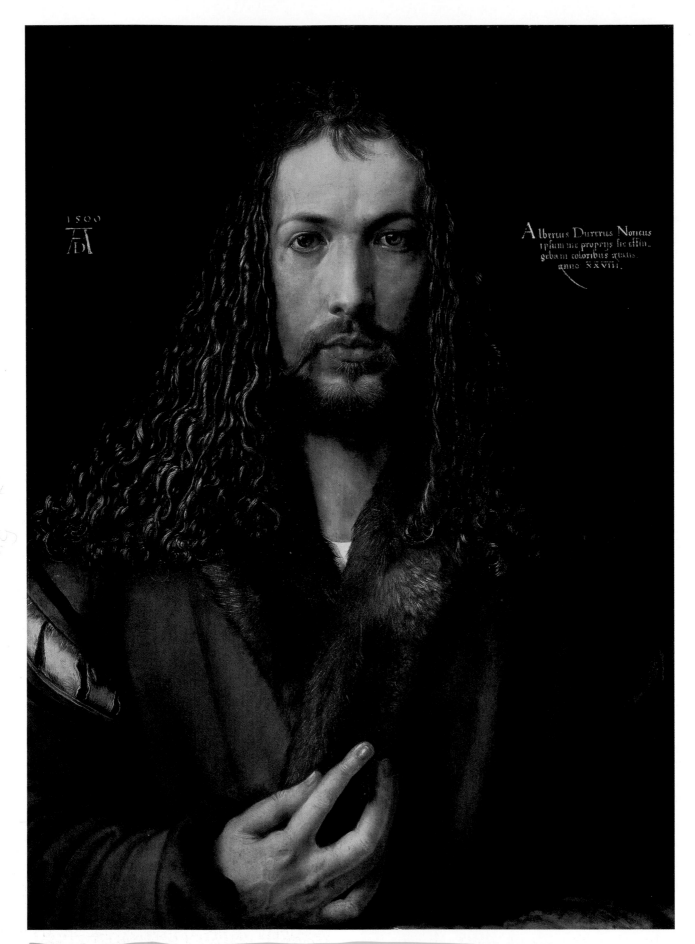

1500

ᴀᴅ

Albertus Durerus Noricus
ipsum me proprijs sic effin.
gebam coloribus aetatis.
anno XXVIII.

18.16 Albrecht Dürer, *Self-Portrait*. 1500. Oil on panel, 26¼ × 19¼" (66.3 × 49 cm). Alte Pinakothek, Munich

PRIMARY SOURCE

Albrecht Dürer (1471–1528)

From the journal of his trip to the Netherlands, 1521

Dürer traveled to Aachen and the Netherlands in 1521 to witness the investiture of the new emperor, Charles V. He kept a diary during this journey, which offers many insights into his finances, friends, and intellectual interests. While in Antwerp he heard a false rumor that Martin Luther had been taken prisoner. In response to this news, Dürer wrote the following lament which reveals his thinking about religious issues of the moment.

On Friday before Whitsunday in the year 1521 [May 17, 1521] the news came to me in Antwerp that Martin Luther had been so treacherously taken prisoner; ... there came 10 horsemen and they treacherously carried off the pious man, betrayed into their hands, a man enlightened by the Holy Ghost, a follower of Christ and the true Christian faith. And whether he is still alive, or whether they have murdered him, which I know not, he has suffered this for the sake of Christian truth and because he rebuked the unchristian Papacy. ...

Ach, God of Heaven, pity us! O Lord Jesus Christ, pray for Thy people! ...

And if we have lost this man, who has written more clearly than any that has lived for 140 years, and to whom Thou has given such a spirit of the Gospel, we pray Thee, O Heavenly Father, that Thou wouldst again give Thy Holy Spirit to another, that he may gather Thy church anew everywhere together, that we may again live united and in Christian manner, and so, by our good works, all unbelievers as Turks, Heathen and Calicuts, may of themselves turn to us and embrace the Christian faith. ...

May every man who reads Dr. Martin Luther's books see how clear and transparent his teaching is when he sets forth the Holy Gospel. Wherefore his books are to be held in great honor and not to be burned. ... Ach, God, what might he not still have written for us in ten or twenty years? O all ye Christian men, help me to weep without ceasing for this man, inspired of God, and to pray him to send us another such enlightened man. O Erasmus of Rotterdam, where will you stand? ... O Erasmus, take your stand here, so that God himself may be your praise.

Source: Jane Campbell Hutchison, *Albrecht Dürer, a Biography* (Princeton, NJ: Princeton University Press, 1990)

The status of the artist may also be the theme of one of Dürer's most famous and puzzling prints. This is an engraving labeled *Melencolia I* (fig. **18.17**), one of a trio of prints that Dürer sold or gave away together. Dated 1514, the image represents a winged female holding a compass, surrounded by the tools of the mathematician and the artist. She holds the tools of geometry, yet is surrounded by chaos. The figure is probably a personification, though her identity is controversial: She has been identified as Melancholy, as Geometry, and as Genius. Her face in shadow, she sits in a pose long associated with melancholy, which contemporaries connected with intellectual activity and creative genius. Compare her pose to Raphael's depiction of Michelangelo as Heraclitus in *The School of Athens* (see fig. 16.24). Like Raphael, Dürer shrouds the figure's face in shadow, as though she is lost in thought. Dürer's figure thinks but cannot act, while the infant scrawling on the slate, symbolizing practical knowledge, can act but not think. Dürer appears to be making a statement here about the artistic temperament and its relationship to the melancholic humor.

Renaissance philosophers, like the Italian humanist Marsilio Ficino, viewed melancholia as the source of divine inspiration. The notion of the melancholic genius was widespread in Dürer's time. This print seems to claim for the visual artist (and perhaps for Dürer himself?) the status of divinely inspired, if melancholic, genius.

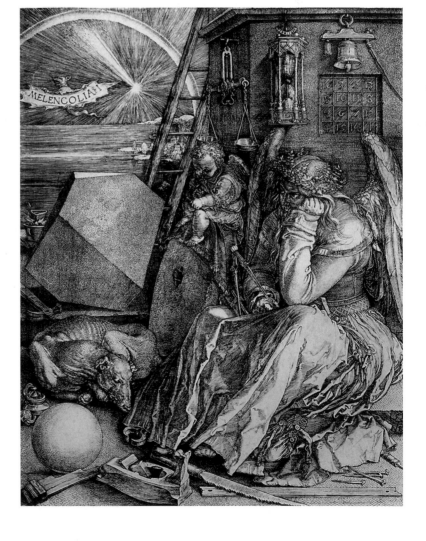

18.17 Albrecht Dürer, *Melencolia I*. 1514. Engraving, 9⅜ × 7½" (23.8 × 18.9 cm). The British Museum, London

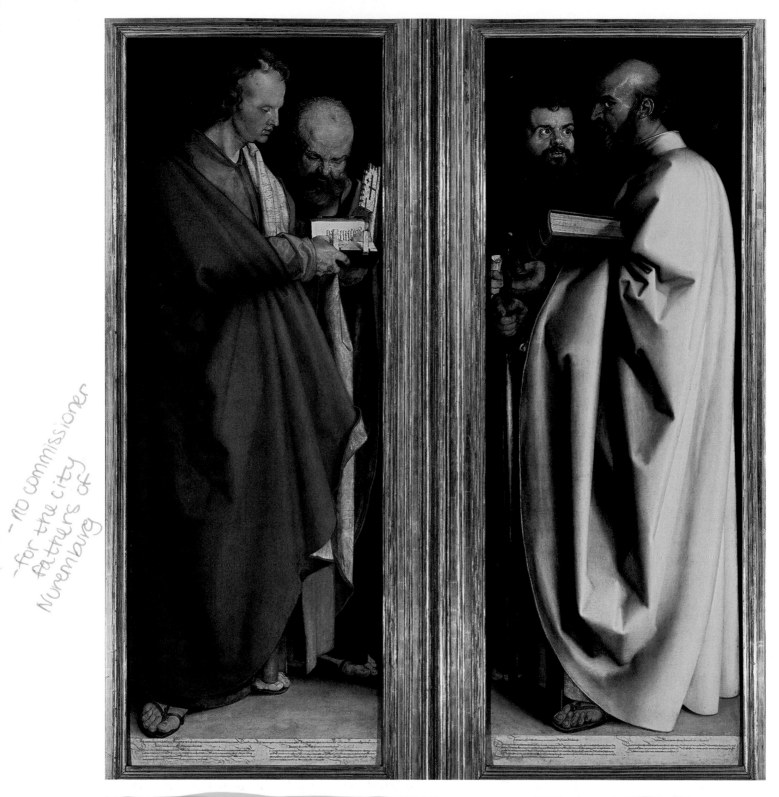

— no commissioner for the city fathers of Nuremberg

18.18 Albrecht Dürer, *The Four Apostles*. 1523–26. Oil on panel, each 7'1" × 2'6" (2.16 × 76 m). Alte Pinakothek, Munich

A REFORMATION ARTIST Dürer became an early and enthusiastic follower of Martin Luther, although, like Grünewald, he continued to work for Catholic patrons. His new faith can be sensed in the growing austerity of style and subject in his religious works after 1520, as well as in his admiration of Martin Luther, expressed in the journal he kept on a journey to the Netherlands

in 1521. (See *Primary Source*, page 641.) The climax of this trend is represented by *The Four Apostles* (fig. **18.18**). These paired panels have rightly been termed Dürer's artistic testament. He presented them in 1526 to the city of Nuremberg, which had joined the Lutheran camp the year before. These four men are fundamental to Protestant doctrine. John and Paul, Luther's

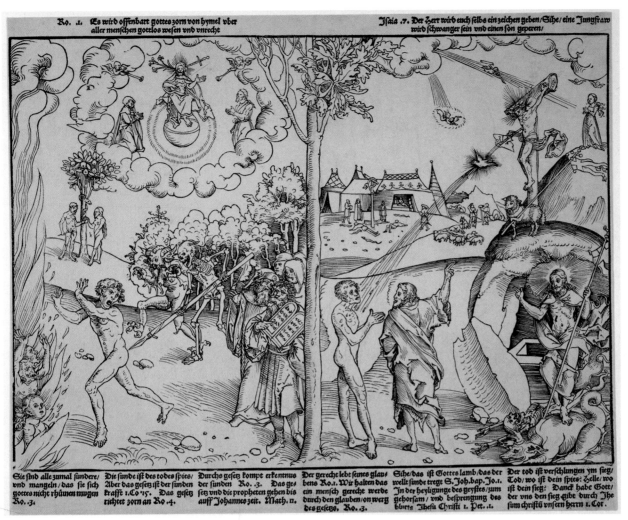

18.19 Lucas Cranach the Elder, *An Allegory of Law and Grace*. ca. 1530. Woodcut, 10⅝ × 12¾" (27 × 32.4 cm). The British Museum, London

favorite authors of Scripture, face one another in the foreground, with Peter and Mark behind. Quotations from their writings, inscribed below in Luther's translation, warn the city not to mistake human error and pretense for the will of God. They plead against Catholics and Protestant radicals alike. But in another, more universal sense, the figures represent the Four Temperaments and, by implication, the other cosmic quartets—the seasons, the elements, the times of day, and the ages of life. The apostles have a sculptural solidity that brings to mind Nanni di Banco's *Quattro Coronati* (see fig. 15.10). The heavily draped figures have the weight and presence of Raphael's figures in the tapestry cartoon *St. Paul Preaching at Athens* (see fig. 16.26), which Dürer probably saw on his trip to the Netherlands in 1521. Through the power of his paintings, the portable medium of prints, and his workshop, Dürer was the most influential artist of sixteenth-century Germany.

Religious and Courtly Images in the Era of Reform

The realignment of German culture and society produced by the Reformation required artists to adapt their styles and subject matter for the reformed faiths. The mass medium of prints was an important tool for spreading the tenets of the Protestant confessions. For courtly patrons, artists made images on classicizing themes, for which they used local visual traditions that emphasized detail, texture, and the natural world.

In Reformation Germany, painters had to contend with the Protestant leaders' ambivalence toward religious images. When a faith places the Word above the Image, image becomes subordinate to text; though Luther himself tolerated images (see www.myartslab.com), the works that most deliberately address Lutheran themes are often literal illustrations of texts.

LUCAS CRANACH: REFORMER AND COURT ARTIST

Lucas Cranach the Elder (1472–1553), a close friend of Martin Luther, attempted to solve the problem of casting Luther's doctrines into visual form. Cranach made numerous prints and paintings to express the tenets of the reformer. A woodcut of around 1530 entitled *An Allegory of Law and Grace* (fig. **18.19**) contrasts the difference between the fate of a Catholic and a Lutheran. The left side depicts the Catholic doctrine that the children of Adam and Eve, stained by Original Sin, must perform specific deeds according to the Law of Moses; yet when this is unsuccessful, the soul is consigned to Hell at the Last Judgment. The right side depicts Luther's position: the believer is washed in the blood of

Christ's Crucifixion, because faith in Christ alone assures salvation. Compared to Dürer's woodcuts, this image is rather simple and straightforward, without complex tonalities, illusions of space, or an emphasis on textures. Cranach makes the image as legible and accessible as the text, subordinating artistic effects to clarity.

In addition to images with Lutheran content, Cranach excelled in portraits and mythological scenes painted for aristocratic patrons, both Catholic and Protestant, in Saxony and elsewhere in Germany. In *The Judgment of Paris* (fig. **18.**20) of about 1528, Cranach retells a story from Greek mythology in which the Trojan prince Paris selects the most beautiful goddess of Olympus. He depicts Paris as a German knight clad in the fashionable armor of the nobles at the court of Saxony. The sinewy figures of the goddesses are displayed for the judgment of the prince, who confides his choice to Mercury, also dressed in armor.

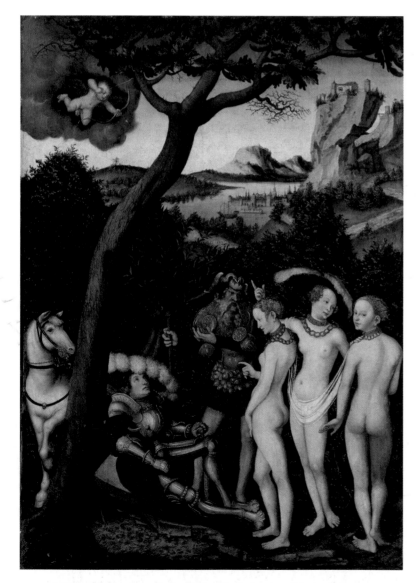

18.20 Lucas Cranach the Elder, *The Judgment of Paris*. ca. 1528. Oil on panel, 40⅛ × 28" (101.9 × 71.1 cm). Metropolitan Museum of Art, New York. Rogers Fund, 1928. 28.221

Like many of his Italian contemporaries working for aristocratic patrons, Cranach gives his classical subject an overtly erotic appeal, inviting a viewer to identify with Paris as the privileged observer of the female nudes. Yet the detailed, miniaturistic technique and the weightless bodies of the women are distinctive to Cranach. One of the most striking features here is the landscape, whose lush vegetation recalls Dürer's *Adam and Eve* (see fig. 18.15); through the thick hedge of trees in the foreground a viewer sees a distant view, featuring a body of water and a city, perhaps Troy.

ALTDORFER'S *BATTLE OF ISSOS* Both Cranach and Dürer played a critical role in the development of the Danube School of landscape painting, which appeared in southern Germany and Austria in the first half of the sixteenth century. The key figure in this school, however, was Albrecht Altdorfer (ca. 1480–1538), a slightly younger artist who spent most of his career in Bavaria. Altdorfer made prints and paintings on a variety of themes, though his primary subject is landscape, which he uses to great expressive effect. His most famous work is *The Battle of Issos* (fig. **18.21**). The painting, made in 1529, is one of a series of images depicting the exploits of historic heroes, commissioned for the Munich palace of William IV, duke of Bavaria. In a sweeping landscape, Altdorfer depicts Alexander the Great's victory over Darius of Persia, which took place in 333 BCE at Issos. This victory was the subject of a composition attributed to the Greek painter Apelles, preserved in a mosaic at Pompeii (see fig. 5.78). To make the subject clear, Altdorfer provided an explanatory text on the tablet suspended in the sky, inscriptions on the banners (probably written by the Regensburg court humanist Aventinus), and a label on Darius' fleeing chariot. The artist has tried to follow ancient descriptions of the actual number and kind of combatants in the battle and to record the geography of the Mediterranean accurately.

Altdorfer adopts an omniscient point of view, as if looking down on the action from a great height, to fit everything into the picture. From this planetary perspective, a viewer must search to find the two leaders lost in the antlike mass of their own armies. The drama of nature is more carefully elaborated than that of the human actors: One can almost feel the rotation of the globe as the sun sets in the distance and the moon rises. The curve of the earth, the drama of the clouds, the craggy mountain peaks overwhelm the mass of humanity. Such details suggest that the events portrayed have an earth-shaking importance, which was arguably the case with this historical event. However, the soldiers' armor and the fortified town in the distance are unmistakably of the sixteenth century, which encourages us to look for contemporary significance. The work was executed at the moment the Ottoman Turks were trying to invade Vienna after gaining control over much of eastern Europe. (Though the imperial forces repelled the Turks this time, they were to threaten Europe repeatedly for another 250 years.) Altdorfer's image suggests that the contemporary battle between Europeans and Turks has the same global significance as Alexander's battle with Darius.

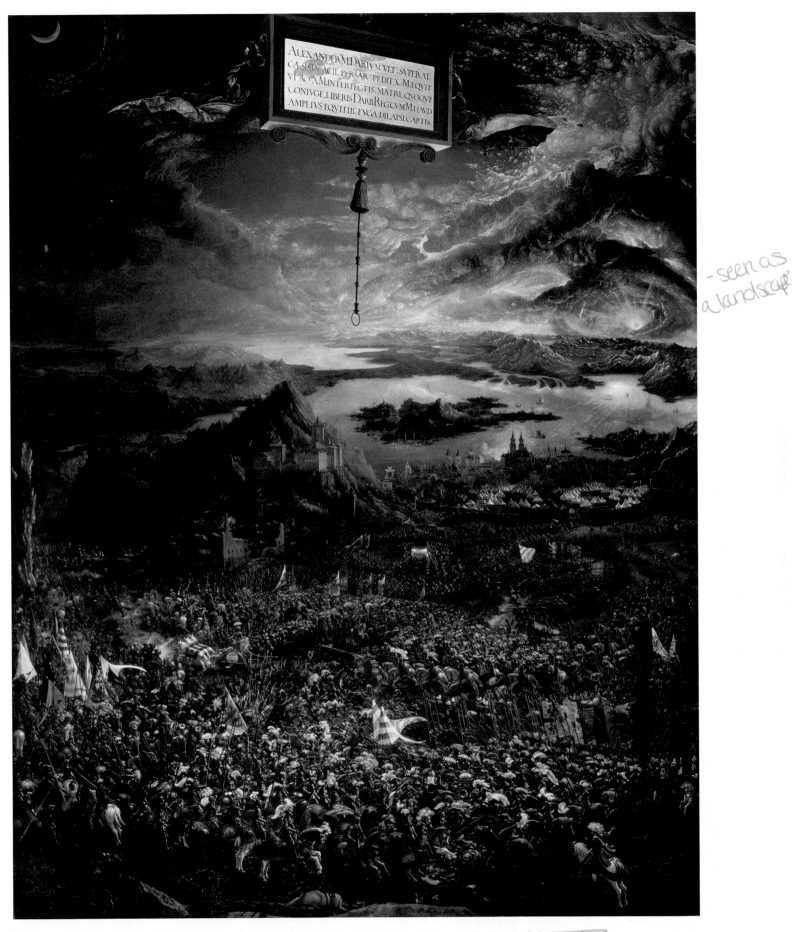

— seen as a landscape

18.21 Albrecht Altdorfer, *The Battle of Issos*. 1529. Oil on panel, 62 × 47" (157.5 × 119.5 cm). Alte Pinakothek, Munich

Painting in the Cities: Humanist Themes and Religious Turmoil

Cities along the Rhine River, especially Strasbourg and Basel, were centers of commerce, publishing, and humanism. The ancient city of Strasbourg's commercial success was due to its location and its industry. Further down the Rhine, Basel had a university as well as an early printing press. It was in Basel that Sebastian Brant's *Ship of Fools* was published in 1494 (see fig. 14.32). As elsewhere, the spread of Reformation and humanist ideas to these cities profoundly affected the arts, as seen especially in the work of Hans Baldung Grien and Hans Holbein.

THE DARK SIDE OF HUMANISM: HANS BALDUNG GRIEN'S *BEWITCHED GROOM* The impact of humanism on German artists may be seen in the work of the painter and print-maker Hans Baldung Grien (1484/85–1545). This former apprentice

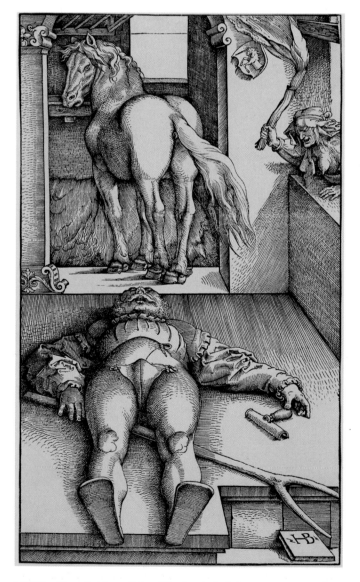

18.22 Hans Baldung Grien, *The Bewitched Groom*. ca. 1544. Woodcut on paper, 13⅓ × 7⅛" (34.2 × 20.1 cm). Art Institute of Chicago. John H. Wrenn Memorial Fund, 1937.136

of Dürer spent much of his career in Strasbourg. Although he made some religious works, Baldung Grien made numerous secular images that explore themes of witchcraft, magic, and death. A characteristic example is his woodcut usually called *The Bewitched Groom* (fig. **18.22**) and dated 1544. The print depicts a man lying on the floor of a stable, a grooming tool near his hand, while a woman waving a torch leans into the space. Having spent time in Dürer's workshop, Baldung has mastered the woodcut technique and the lessons of Italian art. He uses a variety of marks to define form and to suggest textures, but he also organizes the space using perspective and foreshortening of both man and beast. He puts these skills to use in an image of the occult; most scholars see the woman with the torch as a witch, who has either stunned the man or controlled the horse to do it for her. The pitchfork beneath the groom may be her goal, as witches were reputed to use such tools to ride across the sky. Her fearsome image reflects a fear of witchcraft that took hold in Europe in the turbulent sixteenth century, even in humanist circles.

HANS HOLBEIN, FROM BASEL TO LONDON The son of a painter, Hans Holbein the Younger (1497–1543) was born and raised in Augsburg, but he initially sought to make his career in Basel. By 1520, Holbein was established there as a painter and a designer of woodcuts. He had also become a member of the humanist circle that included the writer Desiderius Erasmus (1466–1536). Yet the spread of the Reformation disrupted humanist activities in Basel. By 1525, followers of Zwingli preached the sole authority of Scripture, while more radical reformers preached that images were idols. To escape this climate, Holbein sought employment elsewhere. He had traveled to France in 1523–24, perhaps intending to offer his services to Francis I. Hoping for commissions at the court of Henry VIII, Holbein went to England in 1527, in possession of a letter from Erasmus recommending him to the humanist and royal advisor, Thomas More. In that letter, Erasmus wrote: "Here [in Basel] the arts are out in the cold." By 1528, when Holbein returned to Basel, violence had replaced rhetoric. He witnessed Protestant mobs destroying religious images, a scene Erasmus described in a letter: "Not a statue has been left in the churches or in the monasteries; all the frescoes have been whitewashed over. Everything which would burn has been set on fire, everything else hacked into little pieces. Neither value nor artistry prevailed to save anything." Holbein resolved to return to London, which he did in 1532.

Back in England, Holbein found his first patrons among merchants and diplomats, who were often also humanists. One of his largest works (fig. **18.23**) depicts two ambassadors from France, Jean de Dinteville and Georges de Selve. Painted in 1533, when the English court was in turmoil because of the king's impending break with Rome, the image reflects Holbein's artistic origins and his gifts as a portraitist. The two men were friends, and Holbein represents them in full length standing in a draped room with a tall double-tiered table between them. Jean de Dinteville, on the left, wears an elaborate fur-lined tunic over his velvet garment, as well as a chain identifying him as a member of the Order of St. Michael,

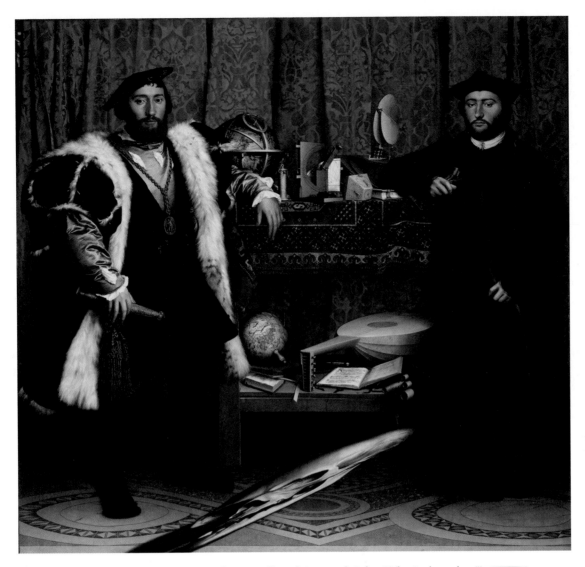

18.23 Hans Holbein the Younger, *Jean de Dinteville and Georges de Selve* ("The Ambassadors"). 1533. Oil on panel, 6'9½" × 6'10¼" (2.07 × 2.09 m). The National Gallery, London

a French chivalric order. Opposite him stands Bishop Georges de Selve, in his cleric's collar, and covered in a warm gown. He bears no weapon or baton of office, as his friend does, but rests his arm on the Bible placed on the upper tier of the table. Holbein distinguishes each man's features and social station in the portrait. His rendering of textures, surfaces, and details harks back to Jan van Eyck, as in fact the standing double portrait does (see fig. 14.14).

Nonetheless, the setting is as important as the two figures here. On the table between them, Holbein places a series of objects reflecting the interests of the two men. The bishop was a great patron of music, an enthusiasm alluded to in the presence of a lute (see page 624). The objects seem to have been chosen with care to add to the meaning of the image. Below the lute is an open book featuring hymns written by Martin Luther. The lute itself has a broken string—it is an emblem of discord. Instruments that measure time (a sundial) or that track the constellations sit on the upper tier. Two globes—a celestial globe above and a terrestrial one below—appear closer to de Dinteville. (His own town is

marked on the terrestrial globe.) These objects contrast the study of earthly and heavenly subjects, with the implication that discord and division rule the earthly sphere. Before all looms an **anamorphic** representation of a skull: It is set into a dramatically exaggerated perspective so that its form is only clearly readable from an acute angle. The skull serves as a **vanitas**, a reminder that the things of this world are fleeting. Holbein's success in recording the interests and concerns of these two men likely brought him to the notice of the rest of the court.

ENGLAND: REFORMATION AND POWER

Holbein's principal patron in England was the ambitious Henry VIII, who reigned from 1509 to 1547. Henry wanted England to be a powerbroker in the conflicts between Francis I of France and the Holy Roman emperor Charles V, although his personal

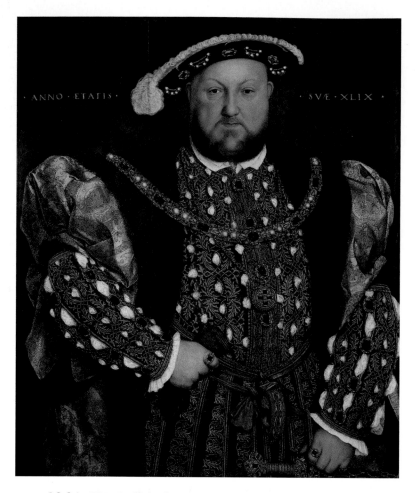

18.24 Hans Holbein the Younger, *Henry VIII*. 1540. Oil on panel, 32½ × 29" (82.6 × 74.5 cm). Galleria Nazionale d'Arte Antica, Rome

Henry's daughter Elizabeth came to the throne in 1558 at the age of 25, and through her shrewdness and luck ruled until 1603. She managed to unite a country that had been bitterly divided by religious differences, and increased the wealth and status of England through her diplomacy, her perspicacious choice of advisors and admirals, and her daring. Her most important victory was the defeat of the Spanish Armada, sent to invade England in 1588; but the Elizabethan age is also rightly famous for its music and literary arts.

The influence of Elizabethan poetry may be seen in a miniature portrait by the English painter Nicholas Hilliard (1547–1619), usually called *A Young Man Among Roses* (fig. **18.25**). Inspired by ancient **cameos** (small medallions in relief), these portable portraits on parchment were tiny keepsakes often worn as jewelry. Hilliard's style reveals the influence of Holbein in the even lighting and careful detail. However, the tall, slender proportions, elegant costume, and languorous grace may reflect the impact of Italian Mannerism, probably by way of Fontainebleau; compare the courtier's stance to that of Primaticcio's stucco figures from the French palace (see fig. 18.4). In tremendous detail on a very small scale (this miniature is just over 5 inches high), Hilliard records the costume and features of the young man and the tree and flowers that surround him. An inscription suggests that he is suffering for his love. Other details—the black and white costume, the type of rose—imply that Elizabeth herself is his beloved, inspiring speculation about the man's identity. The image may represent Robert Devereaux,

situation complicated these efforts. Married to Catherine of Aragon in 1509, 20 years later Henry was seeking to annul their union, for they had failed to produce a male heir to the throne. Thwarted in his desire by the Catholic Church, he established himself as the head of the breakaway Church of England in 1534. His desire for a male heir led Henry into a number of marriages, most of which ended either in divorce or in the execution of his wife. He had three children, who succeeded him as Edward VI, Mary I, and Elizabeth I.

Holbein had come to the notice of the king by 1536, and by 1537 was serving as the king's painter, his primary assignment being to make portraits of the king and his court. His *Henry VIII* (fig. **18.24**) of 1540 captures the supreme self-confidence of the king. He uses the rigid frontality that Dürer had chosen for his self-portrait to convey the almost divine authority of this absolute ruler. The king's physical bulk creates an overpowering sense of his ruthless, commanding personality. The portrait shares with Bronzino's *Eleanora of Toledo* (see fig. 17.10) its immobile pose, air of unapproachability, and precisely rendered costume and jewels. Holbein fashioned for Henry VIII a memorable public image of strength and power. Holbein's portraits of the king and his courtiers molded British taste in aristocratic portraiture for decades.

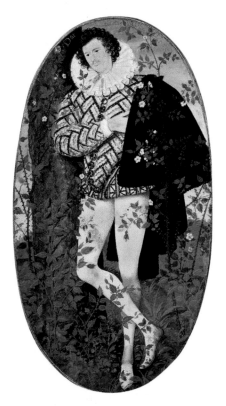

18.25 Nicholas Hilliard, *A Young Man Among Roses*. ca. 1588. Oil on parchment, 5⅜ × 2¾" (13.7 × 7 cm). Victoria & Albert Museum, London

Elizabethan Imagery

The poets and playwrights of Elizabethan England produced some of the most memorable literature in the English language. The sonnet, given authority as a poetic form by Petrarch, was used by both Edmund Spenser and William Shakespeare for their own love poetry. Spenser (ca. 1552–1599) is best known for his epic poem The Faerie Queen, *an allegory in part about Elizabeth I. Though best known for his plays, William Shakespeare (1564–1616) wrote many sonnets whose imagery is as vivid as that in the paintings of Nicholas Hilliard.*

Edmund Spenser, Sonnet Sixty-four, from the *Amoretti* (1595)

Coming to kiss her lips, such grace I found
Me seemed I smelt a garden of sweet flowers
That dainty odours from them threw around
For damzels fit to deck their lovers' bowers:
Her lips did smell like unto gillyflowers;
Her ruddy cheeks like unto roses red;
Her snowy brows like budded bellamours
Her lovely eyes like pinks but newly spread;
Her goodly bosom like a strawberry bed;
Her neck like to a bunch of columbines;
Her breast like lilies, ere their leaves be shed;
Her nipples like young blossomed jessamines:
Such fragrant flowers do give most odorous smell,
But her sweet odour did them all excel.

William Shakespeare, *Sonnet Eighteen*, from The Sonnets (published in 1609, though often dated to the 1590s)

Shall I compare thee to a summer's day?
Thou art more lovely and more temperate:
Rough winds do shake the darling buds of May,
And summer's lease hath all too short a date:
Sometime too hot the eye of heaven shines,
And often is his gold complexion dimmed;
And every fair from fair sometime declines,
By chance, or nature's changing course, untrimmed:
But thy eternal summer shall not fade,
Nor lose possession of that fair thou ow'st;
Nor shall Death brag thou wand'rest in his shade,
When in eternal lines to time thou grow'st.
So long as men can breathe or eyes can see,
So long lives this, and this gives life to thee.

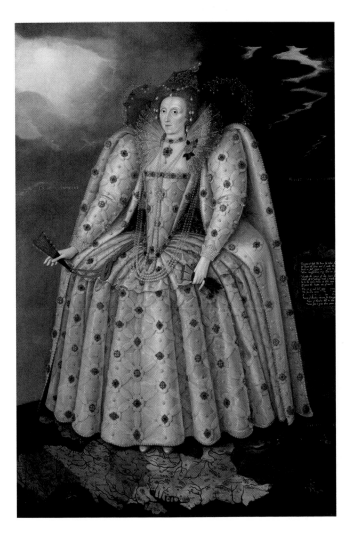

earl of Essex, Elizabeth's one-time favorite. The floral imagery and the lovesick poet are frequent motifs in Elizabethan sonnets, such as those of Edmund Spenser or William Shakespeare. Many images from the Elizabethan era carry texts or symbols that have parallels in Elizabethan court rituals and literature. (See *Primary Source*, above.)

Like her father, Henry VIII, Queen Elizabeth had a gift for managing her image. She had no Holbein in her employ to dominate the artistic life of her court, but she still managed to dictate to the many artists around her how she should be represented. She even imprisoned people for making unsanctioned images of her. A portrait by the Flemish artist Marcus Gheeraerts the Younger (fig. **18.26**) exemplifies her carefully controlled iconography. The portrait represents Elizabeth standing on a map of her realm, which she dominates by her size and frontality. Sir Henry Lee, one of Elizabeth's courtiers, probably commissioned this portrait, often called *The Ditcheley Portrait*; Ditcheley was his estate near Oxford. Elizabeth wears one of the elaborate dresses that she favored, significantly in white, the color of virginity; Elizabeth steadfastly refused to marry, claiming that she was married to England. One side of the background is dark and gloomy: A storm has just passed and the sun shines again. A fragmentary sonnet expresses thanks for a grace given. The whole image is one of supreme and serene authority.

18.26 Marcus Gheeraerts the Younger, *Portrait of Elizabeth I* (*The Ditcheley Portrait*). ca. 1592. Oil on canvas, 97'11" × 5' (2.41 × 1.52 m). The National Portrait Gallery, London

THE NETHERLANDS: WORLD MARKETPLACE

Such displays of aristocratic power found less favor in the sixteenth-century Netherlands. This region, comprising present-day Holland and Belgium, had the most turbulent history of any country north of the Alps. United under Burgundian rulers in the fifteenth century, the Netherlands passed to Habsburg control through the marriage of Mary of Burgundy (see fig. 14.18) to Maximilian I. When the Reformation began, it was part of the empire under their grandson, Charles V, who also inherited the crown of Spain. Protestantism quickly gained adherents in the Northern Netherlands, and attempts to suppress the spread of reform led to a revolt there against Spanish rule that resulted in the provinces of the Northern Netherlands declaring their independence in 1579. After a bloody struggle, the Northern Provinces (present-day Holland) emerged at the end of the century as an independent state in all but name.

The Southern Provinces (roughly corresponding to present-day Belgium) remained in Spanish hands and committed to Roman Catholicism. To govern the Netherlands, both Charles V and Philip II of Spain appointed regents who established courts in the southern cities. Economic changes accompanied the momentous changes in the political and religious situation. In the Southern Netherlands, the once-thriving port of Bruges silted up and was replaced as a commercial center by Antwerp, with its deep harbor and strategic location. Antwerp became the commercial and artistic capital of the Southern Netherlands. In the Northern Netherlands the city of Amsterdam became a center of international trade.

One byproduct of the religious strife was the destruction of works of art in waves of iconoclasm, inspired by the reformers' suspicion of images. In both the Northern and Southern Netherlands, vast numbers of medieval and earlier Renaissance works of art were lost, especially religious works and sculptures, as zealous reformers confiscated or burned images they considered idolatrous. The market for sculpture in the Netherlands was effectively destroyed for the rest of the early modern period, as painting and other two-dimensional art forms came to dominate artistic production. Although some reformers allowed painted or printed images that taught the faithful about doctrine, the Catholic practice of commissioning large-scale sculptures of saints or of the Virgin to install in churches was eliminated. Artists' practices changed under these conditions; as religious commissions dried up, especially in the Northern Netherlands, artists no longer waited for patrons to hire them, but made works of art to sell in the open market instead. (See *The Art Historian's*

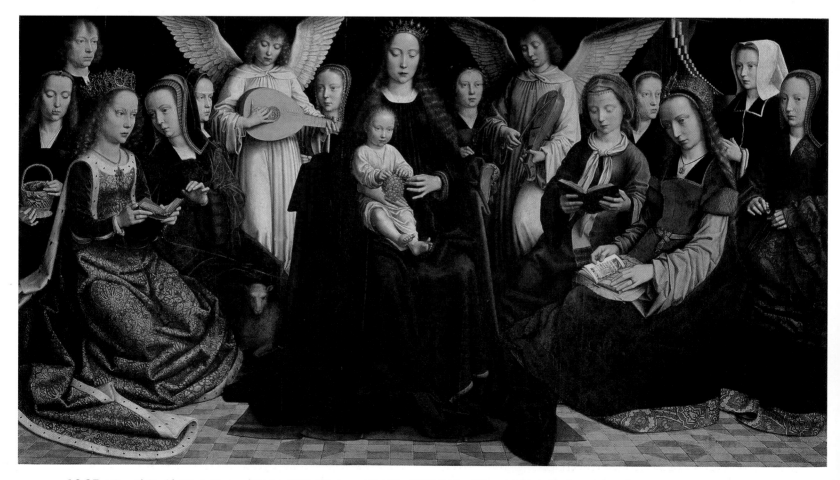

18.27 Gerard David, *Virgin Among Virgins*. 1509. Oil on panel, 46⅞ × 83½" (119 × 212 cm). Musée des Beaux-Arts, Rouen

The Economics of Art

As trade, specialization, and a money economy came to dominate northern Europe after the Middle Ages, the business of making and selling art changed. The patron–artist relationship, where a contract specified the work to be produced and the money to be paid, gave way to the modern market system, with artists beginning to make their goods for sale on the open market. In recent years, art historians have been researching and writing about this change in the economics of art, focusing on centers such as Bruges, Antwerp, Delft, Haarlem, and Amsterdam.

Scholars have used documents, such as chronicles, receipts, and contracts and the works themselves to explore the institutions that arose in response to these economic changes. The study of guilds and their regulation of the art trade illuminates one facet of the economics of art: Since the Middle Ages, these organizations had regulated the training of artists and their commercial activity and had controlled competition in their locales. The new technology of prints allowed artists to mass-produce images that were not regulated by the guilds; prints were available for purchase at trade fairs along with other commodities, sometimes by monks and nuns who sold them to support their monasteries. Dürer financed his trip from Nuremberg to Antwerp in 1521 by selling prints along the way.

By tracking the fluctuations in prices of works of art in the early modern period, scholars have been able to compare them to other commodities and to examine the impact of economic changes in the art trade on the artists themselves. Researchers have also explored the records and the physical arrangements of the marketplaces and neighborhoods where the artists displayed their work for buyers to examine and purchase them. Along with economic changes in the art trade a new player entered the art market—the dealer, who served as the middleman between the artist and the purchaser.

For art historians, an important issue is how these new economic changes and circumstances for making and selling art would affect the artworks themselves. Evidence indicates that artists and workshops standardized their production techniques, subcontracted specific elements of projects, and specialized in particular forms or subjects. The choices made for subject matter in works of art responded to economic changes, too; images such as Aertsen's *The Meat Stall* (see fig. 18.31) represent and comment on the market itself.

Lens, above.) One result was the development of new genres of art that would supplement, and eventually replace, traditional religious subjects.

To these challenges concerning subject matter and patronage should be added the challenge represented by the new Italianate style, which quickly gained favor in the courts. Responses to Italian style varied. Some artists saw no reason to change the northern European visual tradition they had inherited; some grafted Italianate decorative forms to their traditional compositions and techniques; and others dove deeply into Italian style. The latter were inspired by the example of Dürer, by works of Michelangelo and Raphael they had seen in the Netherlands, and by their own experience of Italy.

The City and the Court: David and Gossaert

The city of Bruges in the Catholic Southern Netherlands remained an important center for commerce into the sixteenth century, though much of its trade and prosperity transferred to Antwerp early in the period. Gerard David (ca. 1460–1523) carried on the distinguished tradition of Bruges painting established in the work of Van Eyck and Memling. David's workshop dominated the city to the middle of the sixteenth century. His style may be examined in a work he gave to the Carmelite nunnery in Bruges in 1509. This painting (fig. **18.27**) depicts the Virgin and Child surrounded by virgin saints; two angels serenade this assembly of women, while portraits of David and his wife, Cornelia Cnoop, appear in the corners. In traditional Flemish fashion, the forms exhibit detailed renderings of textures, layers of colors that create brilliant effects, and symbolic forms to enhance the meaning, such as the grapes held by the Christ Child and the attributes of the saints. Yet David's cool colors and soft modeling endow these figures with a calm dignity that is enhanced by the balanced composition. These silent virgins gather around the mother and son as the nuns of the convent would gather for prayer.

David worked for both individual patrons and the open market, but some of his contemporaries found employment in the aristocratic courts of the Netherlands, including Jan Gossaert (ca. 1478–1532), nicknamed "Mabuse," for his hometown of Maubeuge. His early career was spent in Antwerp, but in 1508 he accompanied Admiral Philip of Burgundy to Italy, where the Italian Renaissance and antiquity made a deep impression on him. He also worked for the regent of the Netherlands, Margaret of Austria. His paintings fuse the lessons of Italian monumentality with the detailed technique of the Netherlandish tradition.

For the castle of his patron Philip of Burgundy he made images of mythological subjects, including the *Neptune and Amphitrite* (fig. **18.28**), signed and dated by Gossaert in 1516. The painting displays the painter's fascination with antiquity and Italianate perspective, as well as his skill at rendering textures, details, and rich color, in the Netherlandish tradition. Gossaert here depicts the god and his consort as nudes, basing their postures on Dürer's 1504 *Adam and Eve* (see fig. 18.15). Gossaert endows these figures with bulky proportions that derive from his study in Rome of Hellenistic statues like the *Laocoön* (see page 183). The architecture, too, stems from ancient models, but it has a severity and a simplicity that are indebted to Bramante (see fig. 16.8). Gossaert places his figures in a templelike structure, but he gives them an impossible scale: Neptune stands as tall as the

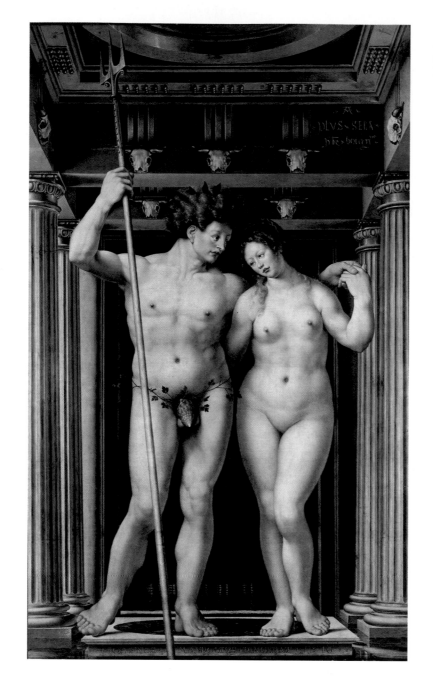

18.28 Jan Gossaert, *Neptune and Amphitrite*. 1516. Oil on panel, 6'2" × 4'⅕" (188 × 124 cm). Staatliche Museen, Berlin

columns. Either they are ancient cult statues come to life, or a viewer witnesses an epiphany (sudden appearance) of the pagan divinities. This subject, the god of the sea, clearly reflects Admiral Philip's interests. Gossaert brings Italianate forms to the service of his Netherlandish audience in a hybrid of the two traditions.

Antwerp: Merchants, Markets, and Morality

Bruges' decline as a center for commerce occurred as Antwerp rose to prominence, which brought it new wealth and the desire for a new form of expression of that wealth. As in earlier Netherlandish cities, the town hall was the most important civic structure, and in midcentury, the city held a competition for a new design. Cornelis Floris (1514–1575), a local sculptor and architect, won the commission and began work in 1561. Floris

had traveled to Italy and had studied both ancient and contemporary Italian architecture. In the design for the Antwerp town hall, he combined the precepts of Italian Renaissance architecture with northern European traditions to create the large and imposing structure (fig. **18.29**). The building uses Italian devices: The base is a rusticated arcade, like Ammanati's Palazzo Pitti (see fig. 17.8); the three stories above are articulated with Doric, Ionic, and Corinthian columns, like the Colosseum in Rome (see fig. 7.20); a central pavilion mixes sculpture and architecture, like a Roman triumphal arch (see fig. 7.70). Yet the proportions are vertical, the roofline more in keeping with Netherlandish practice, and rich carvings on the central pavilion add a focal point at the tall mass of this section of the façade. The building integrates Italian ideas differently from the way those ideas would be expressed in France or Spain (see figs. 18.2 and 18.6). Antwerp had become a global

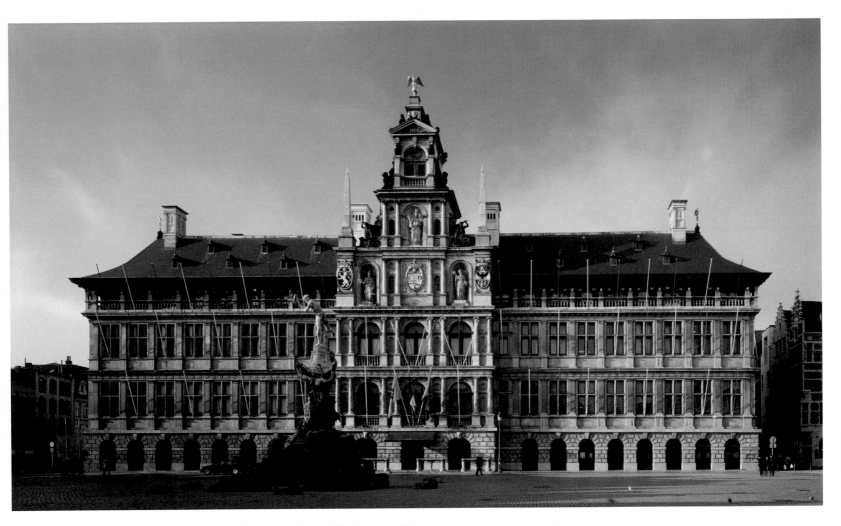

18.29 Cornelis Floris and Willem van den Broek. Town Hall, Antwerp. 1561–66

marketplace by this point, trading a variety of goods, from textiles to foodstuffs, all over the world, including the Americas and Asia. The visual arts participated in this market in a variety of ways. Tapestries were exported through Antwerp; there was a thriving market in prints; and the Plantin-Moretus Press produced editions of books that were sent all over the world. Painters in particular developed new genres of art to tap into this expanding market. Still-life, landscape, and **genre paintings** (images of daily life) had been explored by Flemish artists since the rise of the International Gothic Style and had become even more important during the fifteenth century as backdrops for religious themes. Some Antwerp artists of the sixteenth century specialized in these themes as subjects in themselves, perhaps in response to the loss of religious patronage, or maybe as a way to gain market share. These images often carry multiple meanings, at once depicting the pleasures of the world, while warning about those same pleasures.

PATINIR: THE WORLD LANDSCAPE Joachim Patinir (ca. 1480–1524) was an early specialist in landscape, whose work Dürer had seen and praised when he visited Antwerp in 1521. *The Penitence of St. Jerome* (fig. **18.30**) of about 1518 demonstrates Patinir's connection to the traditions of Flemish art while

updating that tradition. He has altered the triptych form to give it curved shapes along the top; this form became the fashion for triptychs in early sixteenth-century Antwerp. The three wings of the triptych depict three different saints, with Jerome in the wilderness at the center, and John the Baptist and St. Anthony Abbot in the wings; all three were venerated as hermit saints. Their figures appear in the foreground, while the continuous landscape behind them unites all three panels. The landscape is the true subject of Patinir's work. Any narrative is completely subordinate to the deep vista of the earth, whose fields, forests, mountains, seas, and sky fill most of the panel. The human presence is very small in this landscape. Tiny figures wander through this world, while villages, cities, even ships can be distinguished in the distance.

This kind of landscape, which became very popular among European collectors in the sixteenth century, has been called a "world landscape," because of the focus on deep vistas into the distance. Like Altdorfer, Patinir uses a high viewpoint to allow for the distant view, yet he also provides a shelf of space in the foreground for the figures. Creating a smooth relationship between the foreground and the distance is of less interest to Patinir than describing the craggy blue mountains and the verdant forests. How viewers interpreted such landscapes in Patinir's time is not

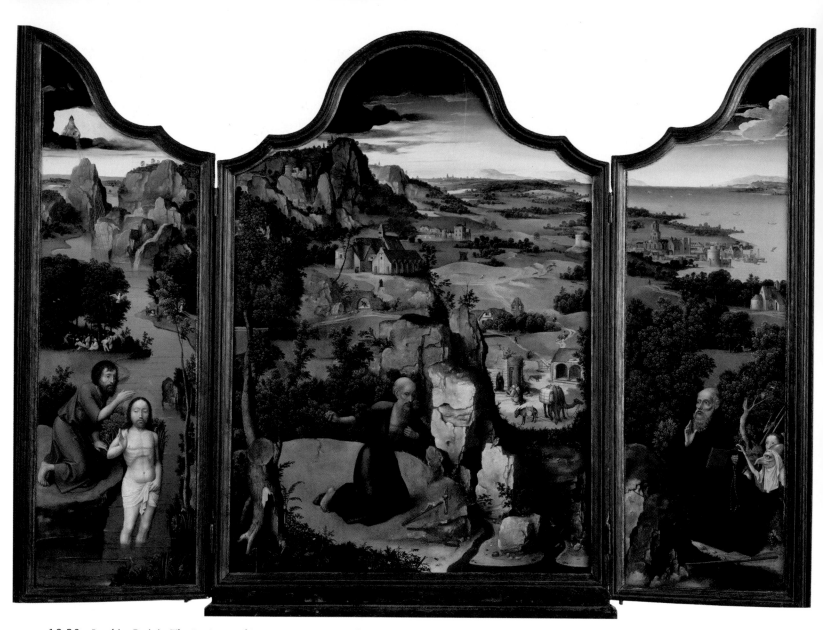

18.30 Joachim Patinir, *The Penitence of St. Jerome*. ca. 1518. Oil on panel, 47¼ × 14⅛" (120 × 36 cm).
Metropolitan Museum of Art, New York. Fletcher Fund, 1936, 36.14a–c

entirely clear. On the one hand, the vista itself invites careful perusal, and viewers could study the picture and imagine the distant lands then being explored instead of traveling there themselves. At the same time, the painting has a religious subject that may have a moralizing message. Perhaps Patinir was commenting on the dangers of life in the world compared with the hermit saints' rejection of worldly things.

AERTSEN'S *THE MEAT STALL* Scholars have also ascribed a moralizing meaning to the still lifes painted by the North Netherlandish painter Pieter Aertsen (1507/08–1575). He spent his early career in Antwerp, then returned to Amsterdam in 1557, where he saw first hand the destruction of religious images by iconoclasts in 1566. *The Meat Stall* (fig. **18.31**), done in 1551 while the artist was still in Antwerp, seems at first glance to be a purely secular picture. In the foreground, we see the products for sale in a butcher's shop in overwhelming detail, with tiny human figures

in the background almost blotted out by the food. A sign to the upper right also advertises a farm for sale, so the power of the market economy is reflected in the imagery.

The still-life imagery so dominates the picture that it seems independent of the religious subject in the background. But in the distance to the left we see Mary and Jesus on the Flight into Egypt giving bread to the poor, who are ignored by the worshipers lined up for church. To the right is a tavern scene where the excesses of the senses are for sale. (Oysters were recognized as an aphrodisiac.) The eye meanders over the objects on display: some of them items of gluttony; some, like the pretzels, eaten during Lent. Some of the products may be read as Christian symbols, such as the two pairs of crossed fish signifying the Crucifixion. The two background scenes suggest different choices a viewer could make: a life of dissipation or a life of almsgiving. The foreground with its emphasis on items for sale may implicate Antwerp's principal economic activity in these choices.

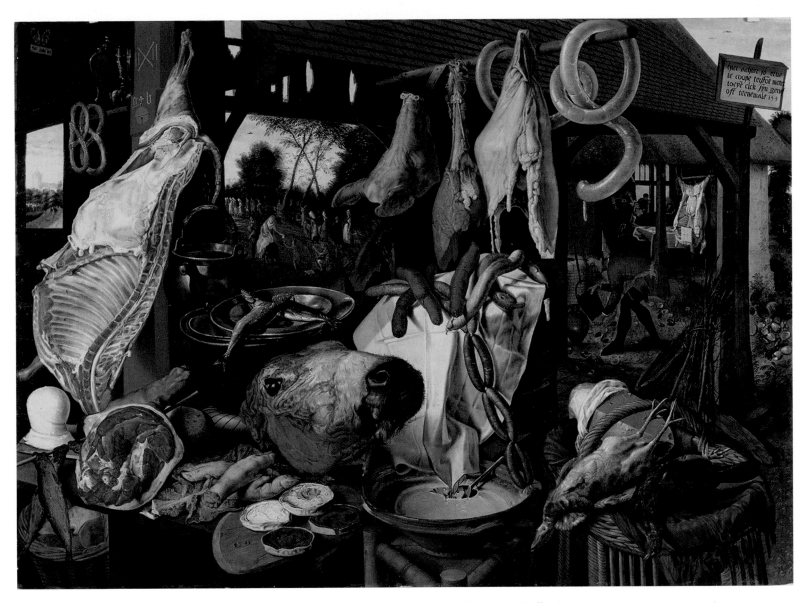

18.31 Pieter Aertsen, *The Meat Stall*. 1551. Oil on panel, 48½ × 59" (123.3 × 150 cm). University Art Collections, Uppsala University, Sweden

PIETER BRUEGEL THE ELDER Aertsen's younger contemporary and fellow Antwerp resident, Pieter Bruegel the Elder (1525/30–1569) used this same device of **inverted perspective**—putting the apparent subject of the picture in the background of many of his images. He explored landscape, peasant life, and moral allegory in his paintings. Although Bruegel spent his career in Antwerp and Brussels, he may have been born near 's-Hertogenbosch, the home of Hieronymus Bosch. Certainly Bosch's paintings impressed him deeply, and his work is similarly ambiguous in its messages. Bruegel's contemporaries admired his wit and his ability to mimic nature, though solid personal information about Bruegel is scarce.

Working as a painter and a designer of prints, he made pictures that demonstrate his interest in folk customs and the daily life of humble people. Bruegel himself was highly educated and the friend of humanists, who, with wealthy merchants, were his main clients: Urban elites collected images of the country and the people who worked the land. He also made images that many scholars have seen as offering a political commentary on the Habsburg rule over the Southern Netherlands. Members of the Habsburg court also collected his work, but during the turbulent climate of the 1560s when Philip II of Spain attempted to quash the Protestant rebellion in the Netherlands, Bruegel became fearful that his politically barbed imagery might cause trouble for his family. (See *Primary Source*, page 656.)

Like his contemporaries who followed Dürer's example, Bruegel traveled to Italy in 1552–53, visiting Rome, Naples, and Sicily. The famous monuments admired and sketched by other northern European artists, however, seem not to have interested him. He returned instead with a sheaf of magnificent landscape drawings, especially Alpine views. Out of this experience came the sweeping landscapes of Bruegel's mature style. *The Return of*

Karel van Mander Writes About Pieter Bruegel the Elder

From *The Painter's Treatise (Het Schilder Boeck)*, 1604

Van Mander's biography of Pieter Bruegel the Elder remains an important source of information about the artist, whose talent he appreciated fully.

On his journeys Bruegel did many views from nature so that it was said of him, when he traveled through the Alps, that he had swallowed all the mountains and rocks and spat them out again, after his return, on to his canvases and panels, so closely was he able to follow nature here and in her other works. ...

He did a great deal of work [in Antwerp] for a merchant, Hans Franckert, a noble and upright man, who found pleasure in Bruegel's company and met him every day. With this Franckert, Bruegel often went out into the country to see peasants at their fairs and weddings. Disguised as peasants they brought gifts like the other guests, claiming relationship or kinship with the bride or groom. Here Bruegel delighted in observing the droll behavior of the peasants, how they ate, drank, danced, capered, or made love, all of which he was well able to reproduce cleverly and pleasantly. ... He represented the peasants—men and women of the Campine and elsewhere—naturally, as they really were, betraying their boorishness in the way they walked, danced, stood still, or moved.

... An art lover in Amsterdam, Sieur Herman Pilgrims, owns a *Peasant Wedding* painted in oils, which is most beautiful. The peasants' faces and the limbs, where they are bare are yellow and brown, sunburnt; their skins are ugly, different from those of town dwellers. ...

... Many of his compositions of comical subjects, strange and full of meaning, can be seen engraved; but he made many more works of this kind in careful and beautifully finished drawings to which he had added inscriptions. But as some of them were too biting and sharp, he had them burnt by his wife when he was on his deathbed, from remorse or fear that she might get into trouble and have to answer for them.

Source: Karel van Mander, *Dutch and Flemish Painters*, tr. Constant van de Wall (Manchester, NH: Ayer Company Publishers, 1978)

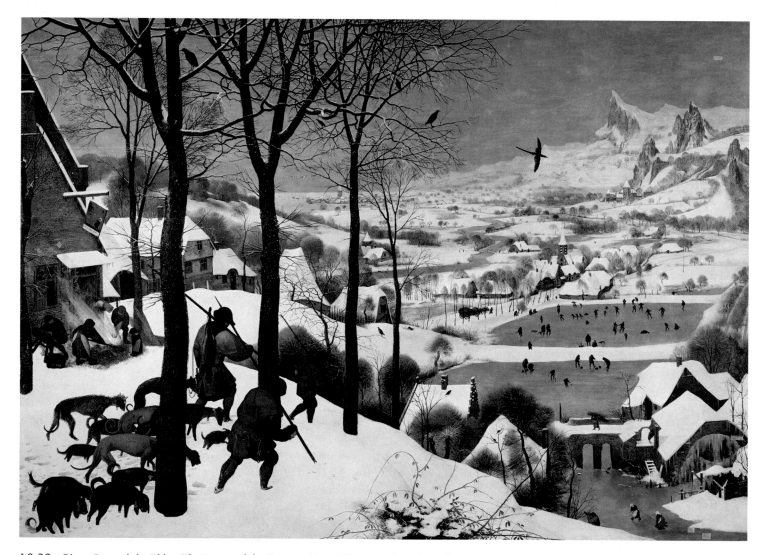

18.32   Pieter Bruegel the Elder, *The Return of the Hunters*. 1565. Oil on panel, 46½ × 63¾" (117 × 162 cm). Kunsthistorisches Museum, Vienna

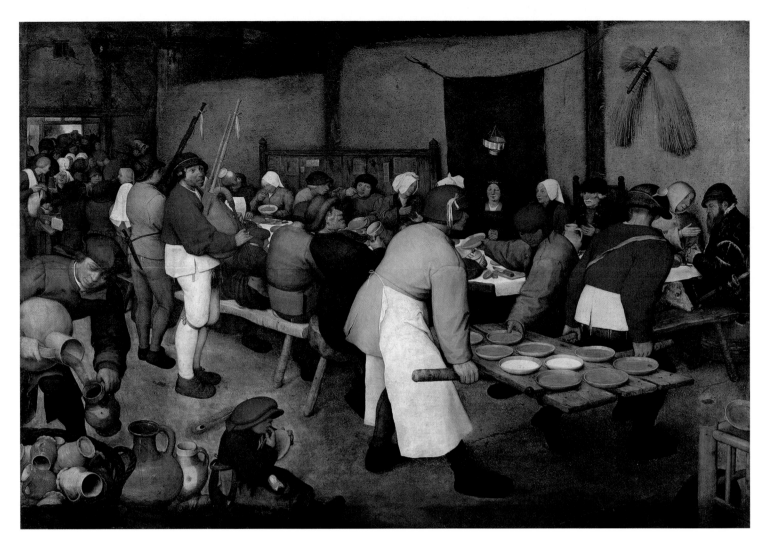

18.33 Pieter Bruegel the Elder, *Peasant Wedding*. ca. 1568. Oil on panel, 44⅞ × 64" (114 × 162.5 cm). Kunsthistorisches Museum, Vienna

the Hunters (fig. **18.32**) is one of a set of paintings depicting the months. (He often composed in series; those in this group were owned in 1565, a year after they were painted, by Niclaes Jonghelink, an Antwerp merchant.) Such scenes had their origin in medieval calendar illustrations, such as those in the *Très Riches Heures du Duc de Berry* (see fig. 14.4). In Bruegel's work, however, nature is more than a setting for human activities. It is the main subject of the picture.

Like Patinir, in *The Return of the Hunters* Bruegel provides a shelf of space in the foreground that moves precipitously into the distance toward a far horizon. In the snow-covered landscape, human and canine members of a hunting party return to their village with their skimpy catch in the gray of a northern winter. They move down a hill toward a village, where the water has frozen and become a place of recreation and where people rush to get back indoors. Human activity is fully integrated into the natural landscape in Bruegel's image.

The *Peasant Wedding* (fig. **18.33**), dated around 1568, is one of Bruegel's most memorable scenes of peasant life. His biographer, Karel van Mander, reported that Bruegel and his patron Hans

Franckert often disguised themselves as peasants and joined in their revelries so Bruegel could observe and sketch them. (See *Primary Source*, page 656.) In this painting Bruegel depicts a gathering of rustic people in a barn that has been decorated for a wedding. He has totally mastered Italian perspective, so the viewer enters a capacious room dominated by the table at which the wedding guests are gathered. The bride sits before a green curtain to distinguish her, though it is more difficult to identify the groom. Food is being distributed in the foreground, while the many empty jugs in the lower left suggest that much liquid has already been consumed. A far cry from the varieties of meats and fish depicted in Aertsen's *The Meat Stall*, the only food here is simple porridge. Bagpipers stand ready to play, but the noise level already seems high with so many figures talking amid the clattering of pottery. Bruegel's technique is as precise and detailed as that of many of his Flemish predecessors, and his figures have a weight and solidity that adds to the impression of reality.

Bruegel's images of peasants have presented challenges to art historians. Some scholars have seen Bruegel's peasant pictures as brutal caricatures of rural folk for the consumption of town

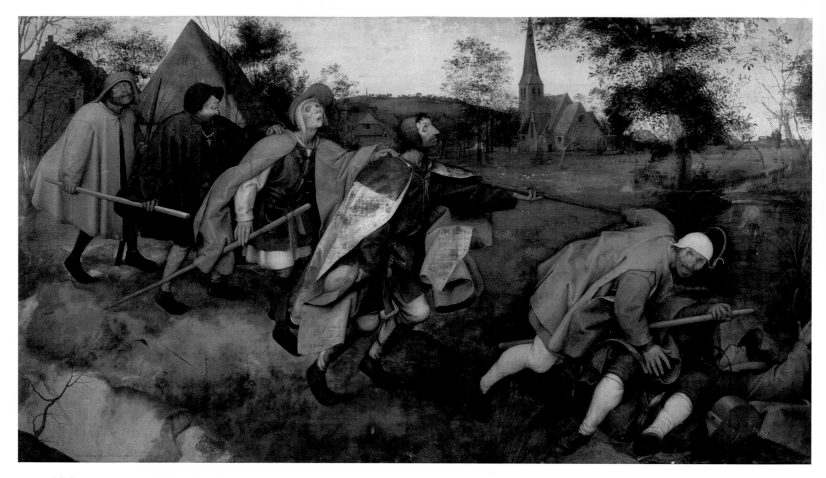

18.34   Pieter Bruegel the Elder, *The Blind Leading the Blind*. ca. 1568. Oil on panel, 34½ × 60⅝" (85 × 154 cm).
Museo e Gallerie di Capodimonte, Naples

dwellers; by this reading, urbane townsfolk could use them to chuckle at the foibles of their country cousins. Still, Bruegel treats this country wedding as a serious event, and if he records the peasants' rough manners, he also records their fellowship. He treats the least of the least, like the child licking a bowl in the foreground, as worthy of observation and remembrance. For Bruegel, the common man occupies an important place in the scheme of things.

Many of Bruegel's pictures offer ambivalent lessons, some of them based on the proverbial wisdom that permeates Netherlandish literature. One of his last pictures, *The Blind Leading the Blind* (fig. 18.34), presents just such a visual interpretation of verbal wisdom. Its source is the Gospels (Matthew 15:12–19). Jesus, speaking of the Pharisees, says, "And if the blind lead the blind, both shall fall into the ditch." This parable recurs in humanistic as well as popular literature, and it appears in at least one earlier work by Bruegel. However, the tragic depth of Bruegel's image gives urgency to the theme. He uses the detailed rendering of the Netherlandish tradition to record the infirmities

and the poverty of the blind beggars who march across this village landscape. The pose of each figure as a viewer's eye proceeds along the downward diagonal is less stable than the last one, leaving little doubt that everyone will end up in the ditch with the leader. Above the gap between the two groups, Bruegel places a village church, suggesting to some critics that the blindness is linked to the ecclesiastical establishment. But other readings are possible. For example, the church could be seen as the antidote to the men's spiritual blindness. Perhaps Bruegel found the meaning of the parable especially appropriate to his time, which was marked by religious and political fanaticism. The ambiguity of Bruegel's pictures has inspired critics and artists for centuries.

Bruegel's images offer criticism of the events of his day in a style derived from the Netherlandish past. In his time, traditional certainties about the world and man's place in it gave way to new faiths, new ideas, new political and social orders, and an expanding globe. These changes would have an important impact on subsequent centuries.

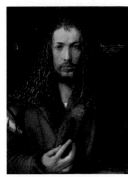

1500 Albrecht Dürer,
Self-Portrait

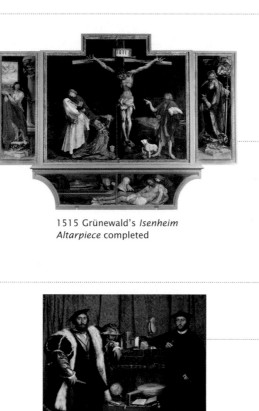

1515 Grünewald's *Isenheim
Altarpiece* completed

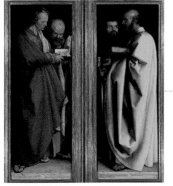

1526 Albrecht Dürer gives *The
Four Apostles* to the City of
Nuremberg

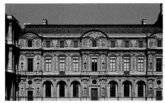

1533 Holbein's *Jean de Dinteville
and Georges de Selve* ("The
Ambassadors")

1546 Pierre Lescot, Square Court
of Louvre

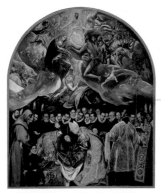

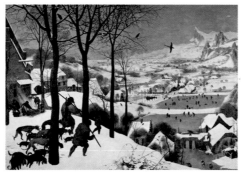

1565 Pieter Bruegel the Elder's *The Return
of the Hunters*

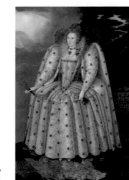

1586 El Greco, *The Burial of
Count Orgaz*

ca. 1592 *The Ditcheley
Portrait* of Elizabeth I

1500

1510

1520

1530

1540

1550

1560

1570

1580

1590

1600

Renaissance and Reformation in Sixteenth-Century Northern Europe

ca. 1503 Leonardo da Vinci, *Mona Lisa*

1506 Bramante's plan for new St. Peter's at the
Vatican

◄ 1521 Luther condemned by Catholic Church at
Diet of Worms

◄ 1525 Peasants' War ignited by Reformation

◄ 1527 Sack of Rome by German forces

◄ 1534 England breaks with Roman Church

◄ 1536 John Calvin publishes the *Institutes of the
Christian Religion*

ca. 1540 Cellini's saltcellar for Francis I

◄ 1556 Charles V abdicates in favor of Philip II of
Spain

◄ 1558 Elizabeth I accedes to English throne

◄ 1562 Wars of Religion in France

◄ 1564 Birth of William Shakespeare

◄ 1573 Veronese defends his work before the
Inquisition

◄ 1579 Establishment of the Dutch Republic

1583 Giovanni Bologna, *Rape of the Sabine
Woman*

◄ 1588 Philip II of Spain sends the Armada against
England

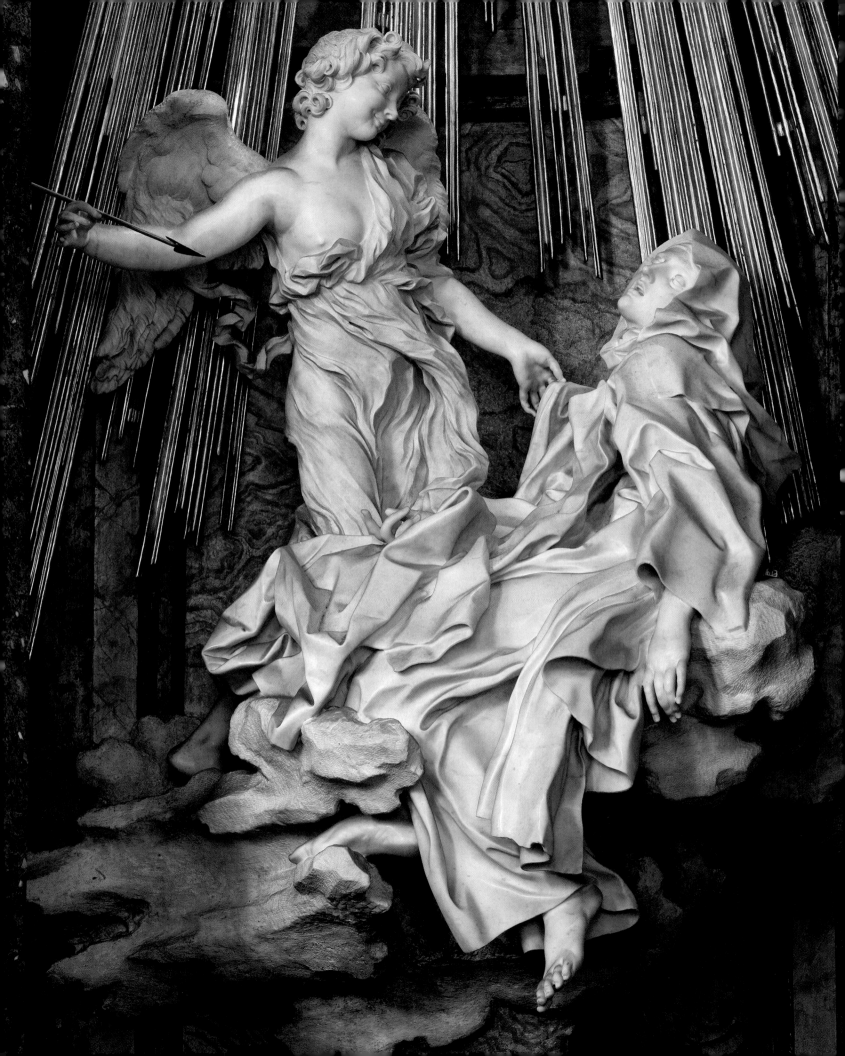

CHAPTER 19

The Baroque in Italy and Spain

BAROQUE ART IS THE EXUBERANT, EXPRESSIVE STYLE MOST CLOSELY associated with the seventeenth century. The term itself may come from the Portuguese word *barroco*, referring to an irregular pearl; it means contorted, even grotesque, and was intended as a disparaging description of the grand, turbulent, dynamic, overwhelming style of seventeenth-century art. Art

historians remain divided over its application. Should the term Baroque only be used for the dominant style of the seventeenth century, or should it include other tendencies, such as classicism, to which it bears a complex relationship? Should the time frame also include the period 1700 to 1750, known as the **Rococo**? More important, is the Baroque distinct from both the Renaissance and the modern eras? Although a good case can be made for viewing the Baroque as the final phase of the Renaissance, we shall treat it as a distinct era. It is the beginning of the early modern period, as so many of the concerns that characterize the latter era—issues of gender, class, and sexuality—are first explored in it. The desire to evoke emotional states by appealing to the senses and to persuade, often in dramatic ways, underlies Baroque art. Some of the qualities that characterize the Baroque are grandeur, sensual richness, emotional exuberance, tension, movement, and the successful unification of the various arts.

The expansive, expressive quality of the Baroque paralleled the true expansion of European influence—geographical, political and religious—throughout the seventeenth century. The exploration of the New World that began in the sixteenth century, mobilized primarily by Spain, Portugal, and England (map **19.1**), developed in the seventeenth century into colonization, first of

the eastern coasts of North and South America, and then of Polynesia and Asia. The Dutch East India Company developed trade with the East and was headquartered in Indonesia. Jesuit missionaries traveled to Japan, China, and India, and settled in areas of North and South America. In style and spirit, the reach of the Baroque was global.

The Baroque has been called a style of persuasion, as the Catholic Church attempted to use art to speak to the faithful and to express the spirit of the Counter-Reformation. In the sixteenth century, the Church tried to halt the spread of Protestantism in Europe; by the seventeenth century, it had declared this effort a success and was celebrating its triumph. Private influential families, some of whom would later claim a pope as a member, other private patrons, and ecclesiastical orders (Jesuits, Theatines, Carmelites, and Oratorians), each built new and often large churches in Rome in the seventeenth century. And the largest building program of the Renaissance—the rebuilding of St. Peter's—would finally come to an end, its elaborate decoration profoundly reflecting the new glory of the Roman Church.

This reinvigoration of the Catholic Church began a wave of canonizations that lasted through the mid-eighteenth century. The religious heroes of the Counter-Reformation—Ignatius of Loyola, Francis Xavier (both Jesuits), Teresa of Ávila, and Filippo Neri—were named saints. (Carlo Borromeo had already been made one in 1610.) In contrast to the piety and good deeds of these reformers, the new princes of the Church were vigorous

Detail of figure 19.31, Gianlorenzo Bernini, *The Ecstasy of St. Teresa*

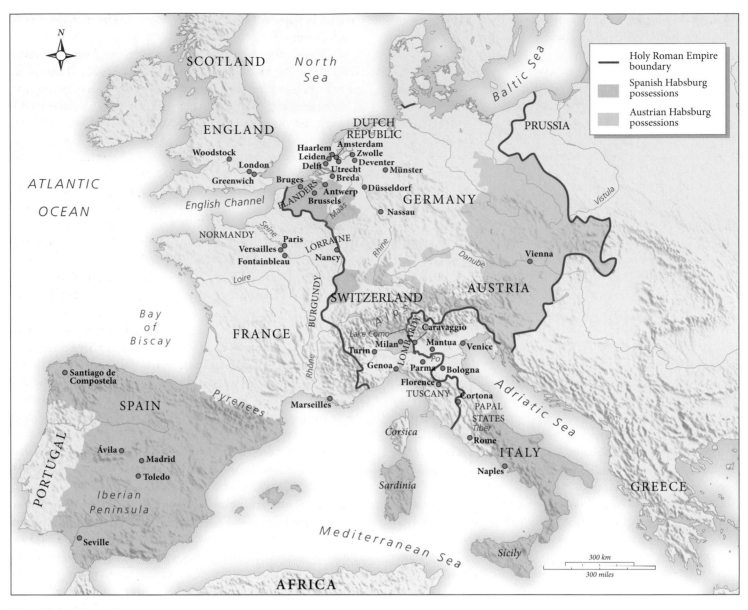

Map 19.1   Western Europe ca. 1648

patrons of the arts, both seeking glory for the Church and posthumous fame for their own families.

During the first half of the seventeenth century, Europe was torn by almost continuous warfare, which involved almost every European nation in a complex web of shifting alliances. The Thirty Years' War (1618–1648) was fueled by the ambitions of the kings of France, who sought to dominate Europe, and the Habsburgs, who ruled not only Austria and Spain but also the Southern Netherlands, Bohemia, and Hungary. Although fought largely in Germany, the war eventually engulfed nearly all of Europe. After the Treaty of Westphalia in 1648 ended the war and formally granted their freedom, the United Provinces—or the Dutch Republic as the independent Netherlands were now known—entered into a series of battles with England and France that lasted until 1679. Yet, other than in Germany, which was fragmented into over 300 little states, many in financial ruin, there

is little correlation between these rivalries and the art of the period. In fact, the seventeenth century has been called the Golden Age of Painting in France, Spain, and both the Dutch Republic and the Southern Netherlands.

The Baroque has also been identified as "the style of absolutism," reflecting the centralized state ruled by an autocrat of unlimited powers. In the latter half of the seventeenth century, Baroque palaces were built on an increasingly monumental scale to display the power and grandeur of their owners. Architecture emphasized massiveness, dramatic spaces and lighting, rich interior decoration from floor to ceiling, and luxurious materials; and it was meant as a reflection of political and economic power. Absolutism reached its climax during the reign of the French king Louis XIV in the late seventeenth century, and is seen in his palace at Versailles, with its grandiose combination of architecture, painting, decoration, and extensive gardens. But we can also associate absolutism with the Vatican, the power of the pope and his claim of authority won and reestablished through the Counter-Reformation. The power of absolutism suggests a style that will overwhelm and inspire awe in the spectator. The new style was not specifically Italian, even though it was born in Rome during the final years of the sixteenth century. Nor was it confined to religious art. Baroque elements of dramatic lighting and sweeping gestures entered the vocabulary of northern European art. The introduction of new subject matter was a vital addition. Still life, the genre scene, and the landscape quickly entered the art world of the Protestant north through etchings and paintings. Still-life paintings and landscapes were informed by the scientific observation of nature.

A recognition of the subtle relationship between Baroque art and science is essential to an understanding of the age. The complex metaphysics of the humanists, which gave everything religious meaning, was replaced by a new physics. The change began with Nicolaus Copernicus, Johannes Kepler, and Galileo Galilei, and culminated in René Descartes and Isaac Newton. Their cosmology brought scientific understanding to sensory perception. By placing the sun, not the earth (and humanity), at the center of the universe, it contradicted what our eyes (and common sense) tell us: that the sun revolves around the earth. Not only was the seventeenth century's worldview fundamentally different from the Renaissance's, but its understanding of visual reality was forever changed by the new science, thanks to advances in optical physics and physiology. These scientists knew or corresponded with each other and with the artists of their time, and their views and discoveries were known to the larger intellectual and artistic community. Newton's mathematics were known to Sir Christopher Wren and were possibly used in his rebuilding both of London and St. Paul's cathedral (see Chapter 21). Vermeer, who experimented with optical effects (see Chapter 20), would have known the developer of the microscope, Antonie van Leeuwenhoek, and the philosopher and scientist Descartes had his portrait painted by Frans Hals. Descartes postponed the publication of his own controversial work *The World* until after his death, as he had learned of Galileo's imprisonment and was also concerned for his own eternal soul, for he, too, was a Catholic and feared excommunication. Galileo's scientific and religious adversaries, the Jesuits, considered his views to be the antithesis of the Church's teachings; also opposing Galileo was Pope Urban VIII (Barberini), the same pope who envisioned a new Rome, and who was the most significant patron of Bernini. Seventeenth-century ceiling paintings, filled with astronomical and astrological figures so prominent in the Baroque, were executed to convey the all-encompassing power of the patron, who by implication controlled the very heavens above.

The rise of science also had the effect of displacing natural magic, a precursor of modern science that included both astrology and alchemy. Unlike the new science, natural magic tried to control the world through prediction and manipulation; it did so by uncovering nature's "secrets" instead of its physical laws. Yet, because it was linked to religion and morality, natural magic lived on in popular literature and folklore well beyond the seventeenth century.

Folklore, literature, and contemporary theater became subjects for the visual arts in the Baroque, usually depicted in genre scenes—scenes from everyday life—which became popular in the seventeenth century. These genre paintings include scenes of men and women in domestic situations, eating, drinking, smoking, and playing board games and musical instruments. Sometimes they illustrate proverbs and the senses. But they should not be confused with "reality" as they are artistic inventions. The paintings are often moralizing; that is, they often warn against the very things they are depicting! Such paintings were already being executed in the sixteenth century (see fig. 18.34), but in the seventeenth century they develop into a major force, along with landscape and still-life painting, in nearly every European country—in Italy, Spain, Flanders, the Dutch Republic, and France. Paintings of foodstuffs—plain and exotic—and landscapes of rural, urban, or far-off places were popular. Turkish carpets, African elephants and lions, Brazilian parrots, Chinese Ming vases, and peoples from Africa, India, and South America can be found in seventeenth-century art. If this sounds like a list of "exotica"—that is because the exotic was a major part of the seventeenth-century experience, as people, many of them artists, began to travel to faraway places. Paintings provide us with a gateway into the Baroque world.

In the end, Baroque art was not simply the result of religious, political, intellectual, or social developments: The strengthened Catholic faith, the absolutist state, the new science, and the beginnings of the modern world combined in a volatile mixture that gave the Baroque era its fascinating variety. What ultimately unites this complex era is a reevaluation of humanity and its relation to the universe. Philosophers gave greater prominence to the human passions, which encompassed a wider range of emotions and social levels than before. The scientific revolution leading up to Newton's unified mechanics in physics responded to this same new view of humanity, which presumes a more active role for people through their ability to understand and affect the world around them. Remarkably, the early modern period remained an age of great religious faith, however divided people may have been in their loyalties. The interplay of passions, intellect, and spirituality may be seen as forming a dialogue that has never been truly resolved.

PAINTING IN ITALY

Around 1600, Rome became the fountainhead of the Baroque, as it had of the High Renaissance a century before, by attracting artists from other regions. The papacy and many of the new Church orders (Jesuits, Theatines, and Oratorians), as well as numerous private patrons from wealthy and influential families (Farnese, Barberini, and Pamphili), commissioned art on a large scale, with the aim of promoting themselves and making Rome the most beautiful city in the Christian world "for the greater glory of God and the Church." This campaign had begun as early as 1585 (indeed, we may even date this revitalization to the reign of Julius II); by the opening of the seventeenth century, Rome had attracted hosts of ambitious young artists, especially from northern Italy. It was they who created the new style.

Caravaggio and the New Style

Foremost among the young artists was the revolutionary painter Michelangelo Merisi (1571–1610), called Caravaggio after his family's hometown near Milan. After his training, begun at age 13, under a minor Milanese painter, he came to Rome in 1592 or 1593 and worked as an assistant to various artists before setting out on his own. His style of painting, his new subjects, his use of lighting, and his concept of naturalism were to change the world of painting.

According to contemporary accounts, Caravaggio painted directly on the canvas, and he worked from live models. He depicted the world he knew, so that his canvases are filled with ordinary people. They are not idealized as High Renaissance figures, nor given classical bodies, clean clothes, and perfect features. But neither are they distorted, elongated, or overtly elegant as in Mannerism. This was an entirely new

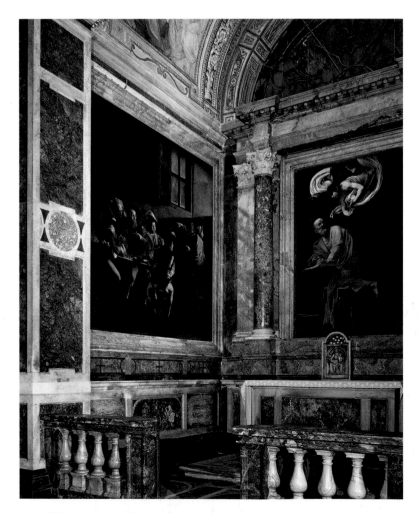

19.1 Contarelli Chapel, San Luigi dei Francesi, Rome

conception that was raw, immediate, and palpable. Caravaggio's style initiated the Baroque and caused a stir in the art world. (See www.myartslab.com.) He had numerous followers and imitators, and critics, both Italian and northern European, wrote of his work, so Caravaggio and his paintings became internationally known almost immediately.

Caravaggio's first important public commission was a series of three monumental canvases devoted to St. Matthew that he painted for the Contarelli Chapel in the church of San Luigi dei Francesi between 1599 and 1602 (fig. 19.1). This church for the French ("dei Francesi") in Rome, founded in 1518 by Cardinal Giulio de' Medici (later Pope Clement VII) and designed by Giacomo della Porta, was finished in 1589. The Chapel of St. Louis (Luigi) was endowed by the French cardinal Mathieu Contrel (Contarelli) in 1565, but the decoration was not completed at the time. More than 30 years later, Caravaggio received the commission to finish the work through the intervention of his patron, Cardinal del Monte.

As decorations, the three Contarelli paintings perform the same function that fresco cycles had in the Renaissance—each complements the others to fill out the narrative. In the chapel view, we see *St. Matthew and the Angel*, in which the tax collector Matthew turns dramatically for inspiration to the angel who dictates the gospel. The main image on the left in the chapel is *The Calling of St. Matthew* (fig. 19.2) which depicts the moment Matthew is chosen by Christ. The third canvas (on the right, but not seen here) is devoted to the saint's martyrdom.

The Calling of St. Matthew displays a naturalism that is both new and radical. Naturalism was not an end in itself for Caravaggio, but a means of conveying profoundly spiritual content. Never before have we seen a sacred subject depicted so entirely in terms of contemporary lowlife. Matthew, the well-dressed tax collector, sits with some armed men, who must be his agents, in a common, sparse room. The setting and costumes must have been very familiar to Caravaggio. Two figures approach from the right. The arrival's bare feet and simple biblical garb contrast strongly with the colorful costumes of Matthew and his companions.

Why do we sense a religious quality in this scene and not mistake it for an everyday event? What identifies one of the figures on the right as Christ, who has come to Matthew and says "Follow me"? It is surely not his halo, the only supernatural feature in the picture, which is a thin gold band that we might easily overlook. Our eyes fasten instead on his commanding gesture, borrowed from Michelangelo's Adam in *The Creation of Adam* (see fig. 16.21), which bridges the gap between the two groups of people and is echoed by Matthew, who points questioningly at himself.

The men on our left at the table seem not to be engaged in the unfolding drama, as they concentrate on the money being counted. In shadow, they are blind to the entrance of Christ—one even wears eyeglasses. Caravaggio uses the piercing light in this scene to announce Christ's presence, as Christ himself brought light: "I am the light of the world; he that followeth me shall not walk in darkness, but shall have the light of life" (John 8:12.)

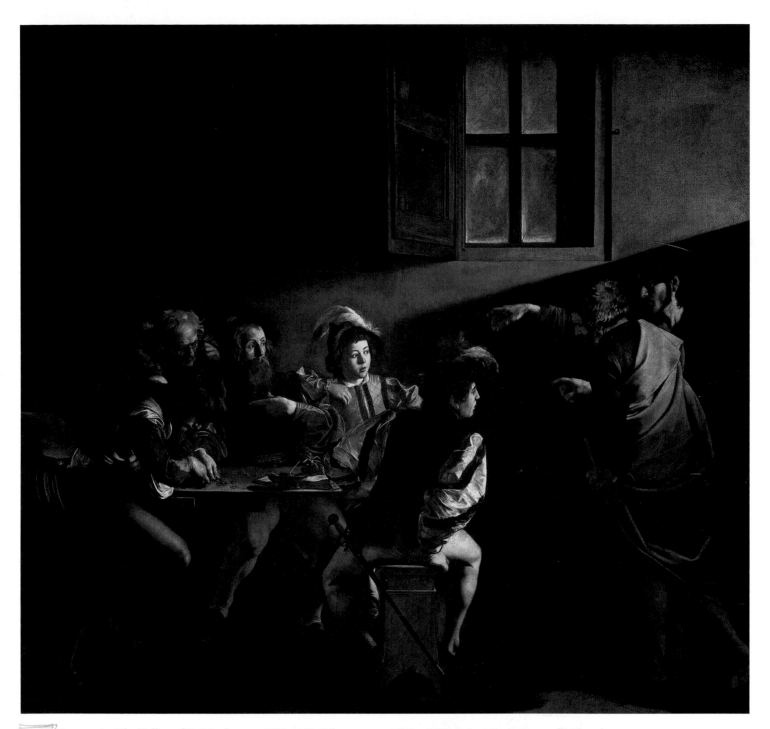

Caravaggio, *The Calling of St. Matthew*. ca. 1599–1600. Oil on canvas, 11'1" × 11'5" (3.4 × 3.5 m). Contarelli Chapel, San Luigi dei Francesi, Rome

The beam of sunlight in the darkness above Jesus is most decisive in determining the work's meaning and style. This strong beam of light against the dark background is known as a tenebristic effect, or **tenebrism**, a style that uses strong contrasts of light and dark. Caravaggio illuminates Christ's face and hand in the gloomy interior so that we see the precise *moment* of his calling to Matthew and witness a critical piece of religious history and personal conversion. Without this light, so natural yet so charged with meaning, the picture would lose its power to make us aware of the divine presence. Caravaggio gives direct expression to an

attitude shared by certain saints of the Counter-Reformation: that the mysteries of faith are revealed not by speculation but through an inner experience that is open to all people.

Caravaggio's paintings have a quality of "lay Christianity" that spoke powerfully to both Catholics and Protestants. Without the painting's religious context, the men seated at the table might seem like figures in a genre scene. Indeed, Caravaggio's painting became a source for secular scenes: Fanciful costumes, with slashed sleeves and feathered berets, will appear in the works of Caravaggio's followers. Figures seen in half-length (showing only the upper half of their bodies) will also be a common element in other works by Caravaggio and his followers (see fig. 20.15).

This intense, vivid tenebrism, the cornerstone of Caravaggio's style, can be seen again in his *The Conversion of St. Paul* (fig. **19.3**). He employed it to heighten the drama and to suggest divine light at the same time. The painting is one of a pair (the other is *The Crucifixion of St. Peter*) in Santa Maria del Popolo in Rome, placed to the left and right of the rich, colorful altarpiece of *The Assumption of the Virgin* by Annibale Carracci, which Caravaggio would have seen before he executed his own work. In contrast to

that altarpiece, Caravaggio employs muted tones and a nearly black background. He uses neither color nor line (indeed, there are no known drawings by him) to better indicate the narrative. Rather, he uses light to focus, even shock a viewer. A fallen Saul (to become St. Paul at his conversion) lies on his back; we view him foreshortened, and helpless, as he is struck by the light of God. The light also reveals the flank and mane of his huge horse, which takes up most of the space. The intense raking light from an unseen source at the left is used to model forms and create textures. The figures are nearly too big for the space.

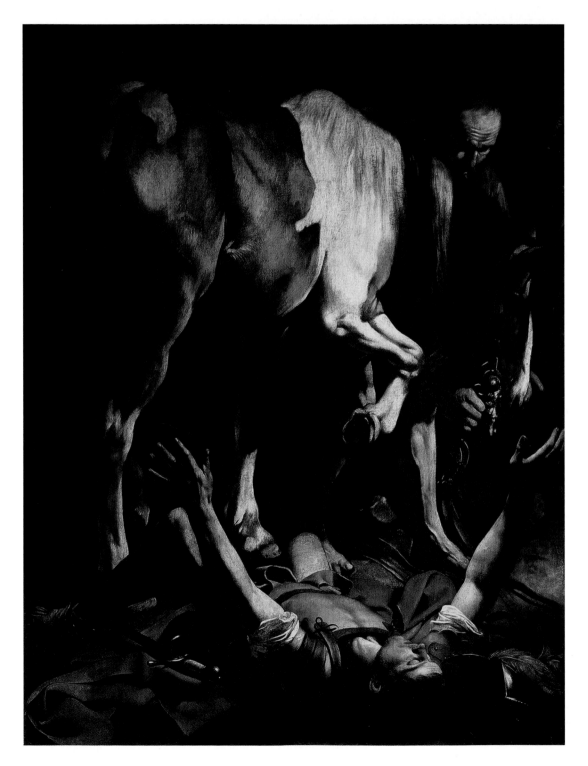

19.3 Caravaggio, *The Conversion of St. Paul.* ca. 1601. Oil on canvas, 7'6" × 5'7" (2.3 × 1.75 m). Cerasi Chapel, Santa Maria del Popolo, Rome

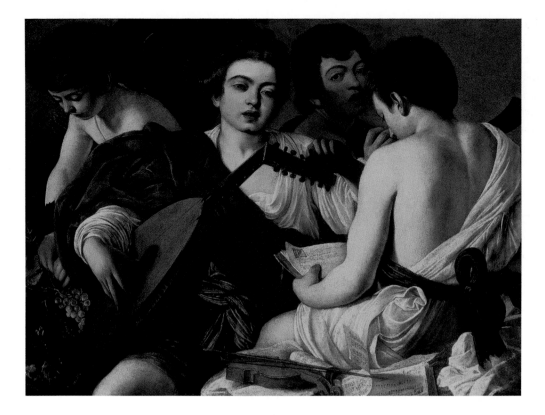

19.4 Caravaggio, *The Musicians*.
ca. 1595. Oil on canvas, 36¼ × 46⅝"
(92.1 × 118.4 cm). Metropolitan Museum
of Art, New York.
Rogers Fund, 1952. 52.81

They overwhelm us as we imagine them larger and only partly revealed by the light. The selective highlighting endows the life-size figures with a startling presence and theatricality typical of the Baroque.

Another aspect of Caravaggio's work is his focus on the sensual and erotic nature of both music and young men, who are depicted as seducing and soliciting. We see these elements in *The Musicians* (fig. **19.4**), with its four androgynous, seminude youths. Actually, it has been suggested that the painting shows two youths seen from two points of view. The musicians are half-length, but life-size; their blushed cheeks and full lips suggest erotic, sensual pleasures, enjoyed with each other and offered to a particular viewer. That viewer (the patron) was Cardinal del Monte, the influential, cultured patron and art collector, who arranged the *St. Matthew* commission for Caravaggio and who commissioned other homoerotic paintings from him. The lute, violin, horn (at back right), and the music sheets surrounding or being used by these half-draped men, and even the grapes being plucked at the left, suggest a contemporary bacchanal. The erotic undertones are part of the sensuality and passion that will be explored in the Baroque and frequently imitated in later works of art by other artists.

Highly argumentative, Caravaggio carried a sword and was often in trouble with the law for fighting. When he killed a friend in a duel over a game, Caravaggio fled Rome and spent the rest of his short life on the run. He first went to Naples, then Malta, then returned briefly to Naples. These trips account for both his work in these cities and his lasting influence there. He died traveling back to Rome, where he hoped to gain a pardon. In Italy, Caravaggio's work was praised by artists and connoisseurs—and also criticized. Conservatives regarded Caravaggio and his work as lacking decorum: the propriety and reverence that religious subjects demanded. But many who did not like Caravaggio as a man were nevertheless influenced by his work and had to concede that his style was pervasive. The power of his style and imagery lasted into the 1630s, when it was absorbed into other Baroque tendencies.

Artemisia Gentileschi

Born in Rome, Artemisia Gentileschi (1593–ca. 1653) was the daughter of Caravaggio's friend, follower, and rival Orazio Gentileschi, and grew up in this artistic milieu. She became one of the major painters of her day and was the first woman to be admitted to the Accademia del Disegno in Florence. Nonetheless, it was difficult for a woman artist to make her way professionally. In a letter of 1649 (see *Primary Source*, page 669), she wrote that "people have cheated me" after she had submitted a drawing to a patron only to have him commission "another painter to do the painting using my work. If I were a man, I can't imagine it would have turned out this way." Her best-known subjects are biblical heroines: Bathsheba, the tragic object of King David's passion, and Judith, who saved her people by beheading Holofernes. Both themes (see fig. 20.25) were popular during the Baroque era, which delighted in erotic and violent scenes. Artemisia's frequent depictions of these women (she often portrayed herself in the lead role) suggest an ambivalence toward men that was rooted in her turbulent life. (Artemisia was raped by her teacher, Agostino Tassi [see fig. 19.10], who was tried and sentenced to banishment from Rome.)

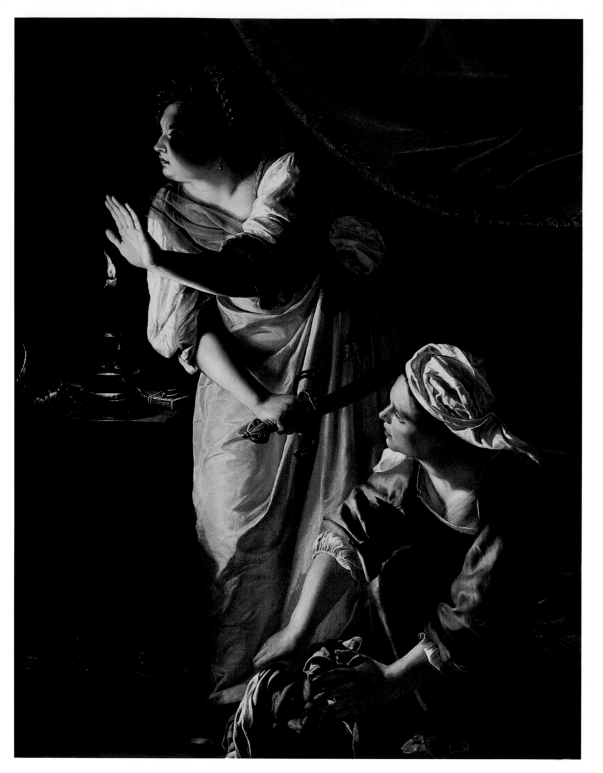

19.5 Artemisia Gentileschi, *Judith and Her Maidservant with the Head of Holofernes.* ca. 1625. Oil on Canvas, 6'½" × 4'7" (1.84 × 1.41 m). The Detroit Institute of Arts. Gift of Leslie H. Green. 52.253

Artemisia's *Judith and Her Maidservant with the Head of Holofernes* (fig. **19.5**) is a fully mature, independent, dramatic, and large work, no less powerful for its restraint. The theme is the apocryphal story of the Jewish widow Judith, who saved her people by traveling with her maid to the tent of the Assyrian general Holofernes (who was about to lead an attack on the Jews), got him drunk, and then cut off his head with his own sword. It yields parallels to the story of David and Goliath—might conquered by virtue and innocence. However, in the case of Judith slaying

Holofernes, the victor was not always seen positively, but with some suspicion since her triumph was one of deceit: Having entered his tent and offered him drink, Judith then killed her foe. The unspoken promise of sexual activity was never realized. Here, rather than the beheading itself, the artist shows the instant after. Momentarily distracted, Judith gestures theatrically as her servant stuffs Holofernes's head into a sack. The object of their attention remains hidden from view, heightening the air of suspense and intrigue. The hushed, candlelit atmosphere—tenebrism

Artemisia Gentileschi (1593–ca. 1653)

From a letter to Don Antonio Ruffo

Artemisia Gentileschi's letter of November 13, 1649 reveals the relationship of the painter to her patron and casts light on issues of originality, of price, and of working with models. Throughout, the letter discloses Artemisia's acute awareness and even contempt for those who treated her less fairly because she was a woman.

I have received a letter of October 26th, which I deeply appreciated, particularly noting how my master always concerns himself with favoring me, contrary to my merit. In it, you tell me about that gentleman who wishes to have some paintings by me, that he would like a Galatea and a Judgment of Paris, and that the Galatea should be different from the one that Your Most Illustrious Lordship owns. There was no need for you to urge me to do this, since by the grace of God and the Most Holy Virgin, they [clients] come to a woman with this kind of talent, that is, to vary the subjects in my painting; never has anyone found in my pictures any repetition of invention, not even of one hand.

As for the fact that this gentleman wishes to know the price before the work is done ... I do it most unwillingly ... I never quote a price for my works until they are done. However, since Your Most Illustrious Lordship wants me to do this, I will do what you command. Tell this gentleman that I want five hundred ducats for both; he can show them to the whole world and, should he find anyone who does not think the paintings are worth two hundred scudi more, I won't ask him to pay me the agreed price. I assure Your Most Illustrious Lordship that these are paintings with nude figures requiring very expensive female models, which is a big headache. When I find good ones they fleece me, and at other times, one must suffer [their] pettiness with the patience of Job.

As for my doing a drawing and sending it, I have made a solemn vow never to send my drawings because people have cheated me. In particular, just today I found ... that, having done a drawing of souls in Purgatory for the Bishop of St. Gata, he, in order to spend less, commissioned another painter to do the painting using my work. If I were a man, I can't imagine it would have turned out this way. ...

I must caution Your Most Illustrious Lordship that when I ask a price, I don't follow the custom in Naples, where they ask thirty and then give it for four. I am Roman, and therefore I shall act always in the Roman manner.

Source: *The Voices of Women Artists*, ed. Wendy Slatkin (Englewood Cliffs, NJ: Prentice Hall, 1993)

---

made intimate—creates a mood of mystery that conveys Judith's complex emotions with unsurpassed understanding. Gentileschi's rich palette, seen here, was to have a strong influence on painting in Naples, where she settled in 1630.

We know that, possibly for a few years (ca. 1638–40), Artemisia also worked in London where her father had been court painter to Charles I of England from 1626 to 1639. Indeed, several of her paintings were recorded in the king's inventory after his execution, and father and daughter may have worked together on a project in Greenwich. Among her most daring and creative works is *Self-Portrait as the Allegory of Painting* (fig. **19.6**), one of the most innovative self-portraits of the Baroque period.

Artemisia was able to do here what no male artist could: She depicted herself as the allegorical female figure of Painting, *La Pittura*. The dress and activity of the subject conforms to Cesare Ripa's description of *La Pittura* in his popular *Iconologia* (1593), a book of allegories and symbolic emblems for artists. There, the allegorical figure of Painting is described, in part, as a beautiful woman, with disheveled black hair, wearing a gold chain which hangs from her neck, and holding a brush in one hand and a **palette** in the other. Thus, the painting asserts Artemisia's unique role as a woman painter—representing not just herself, but all of Painting and reflecting the new, elevated status of artists.

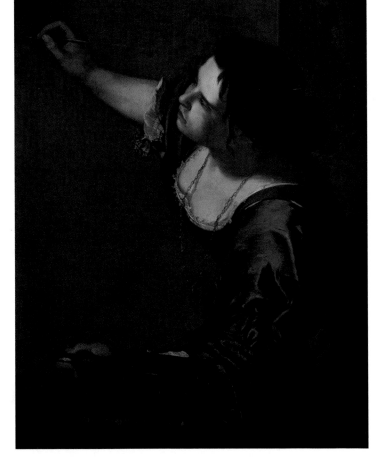

19.6 Artemisia Gentileschi, *Self-Portrait as the Allegory of Painting (La Pittura)*. ca. 1638–39. Oil on canvas, 38⅞ × 29⅝" (98.6 × 75.2 cm). The Royal Collection

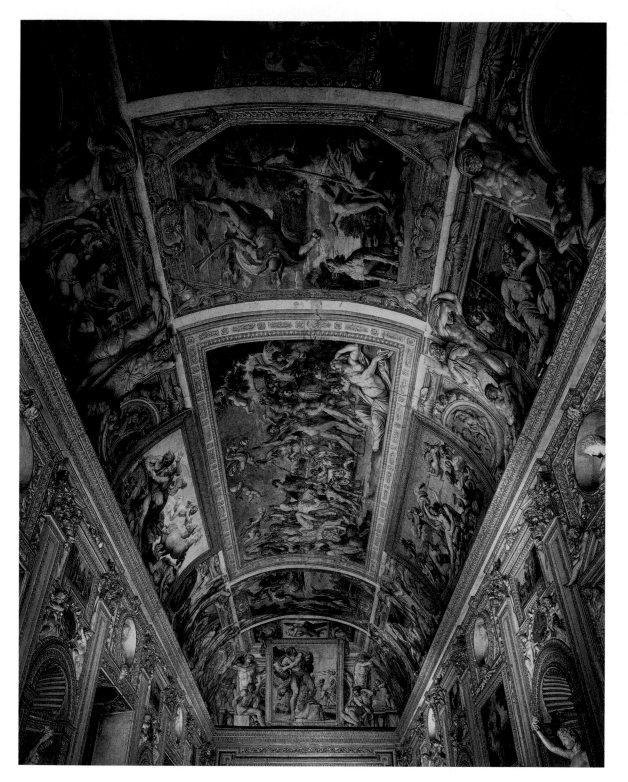

Ceiling Painting and Annibale Carracci

The conservative tastes of many Italian patrons were met by artists who were less radical than Caravaggio, and who continued a more classical tradition steeped in High Renaissance ideals. They took their lead from Annibale Carracci (1560–1609), who arrived in Rome in 1595. Annibale came from Bologna where, in the 1580s, he and two other members of his family formed an "Academy" (also see Vasari, page 601, and Goltzius, page 713) and

evolved an anti-Mannerist style based on northern Italian realism and Venetian art. He was a reformer rather than a revolutionary. Although we do not know completely what this "Academy" entailed, it seems to have incorporated drawing live models and ancient sculpture. As with Caravaggio, his experience of Roman classicism transformed his art. He, too, felt that painting must return to nature, but his approach emphasized a revival of the classics, which to him meant the art of antiquity. Annibale also sought to emulate Raphael, Michelangelo, Titian, and Correggio. In his best work, he was able to fuse these diverse elements.

Between 1597 and 1601 Annibale produced a ceiling fresco, *Loves of the Gods*, in the **gallery** of the Farnese Palace (fig. **19.7**), his most ambitious work, which soon became so famous that it ranked behind only the murals of Michelangelo and Raphael. Although we have seen ceiling painting in the Renaissance—from the fifteenth through the sixteenth centuries, with works by Mantegna, Correggio, and of course Michelangelo, whose painting of the ceiling of the Sistine Chapel would become the work against which all others would be judged—it is the Baroque period which is most associated with this form of painting.

Executed in chapels, churches, and private residences—in entranceways, hallways, and dining rooms—ceiling painting was meant to convey the power, domination, or even extravagance of the patron. One could not enter such a painted room without feeling a little awe. The styles of such works becomes increasingly extravagant from the beginning of the seventeenth century to the end and rivals even the majesty of Michelangelo. The Farnese Palace ceiling, commissioned to celebrate a family wedding, displays a humanist subject, the loves of the classical gods. As on the Sistine Chapel ceiling, the narrative scenes are surrounded by painted architecture, simulated sculpture, and nude youths, carefully foreshortened and lit from below so that they appear real. But the fresco does not rely solely on Michelangelo's masterpiece for inspiration. The main panels are presented as easel pictures, a solution adopted from Raphael. Although the ceiling is painted in fresco, these paintings are given "frames" to appear as easel paintings transported to the ceiling. This device is known as *quadri*

riportati (singular is *quadro riportato*). The ceiling "easel paintings," "medallions" and "sculpture" are painted as trompe-l'oeil. There is no regard for the spectator's point of view here. (When the viewpoint of the spectator is considered, then the artist is using "*di sotto in su*"—literally, "from below to above"; see figs. 15.50 and 17.27.) This imagery on the ceiling reflects the collection of the Farnese—paintings, medallions, sculpture—on display in the room and elsewhere. The figure of Polyphemus, hurling the stone in the "easel painting" on the short wall, is based on the *Farnese Hercules*, a Hellenistic sculpture owned by the family and displayed in the courtyard. (This same sculpture is the subject of fig. 20.14.) The ceiling is held together by an illusionistic scheme that reflects Annibale's knowledge of Correggio (see fig. 17.27) and Veronese (see fig. 17.38). Each level of reality is handled with consummate skill, and the entire ceiling has an exuberance that sets it apart from both Mannerism and High Renaissance art.

The sculptured precision of the Farnese ceiling shows us only one side of Annibale Carracci's style. Another important aspect is seen in his landscapes, such as the *Landscape with the Flight into Egypt* (fig. **19.8**). Its pastoral mood and soft light and atmosphere hark back to Giorgione and Titian (see figs. 16.29 and 16.30). The figures play a minor role here: They are as small and incidental in the manner of a northern European landscape (see fig. 18.30). The painting only hints at the biblical theme of the Flight into Egypt (there are some camels on the hillside). Indeed, the landscape would be equally suitable as a backdrop for almost any story. The old castle, the roads and fields, the flock of sheep, the ferryman with his boat—all show that this "civilized," hospitable countryside has been inhabited for a long time. Hence the figures,

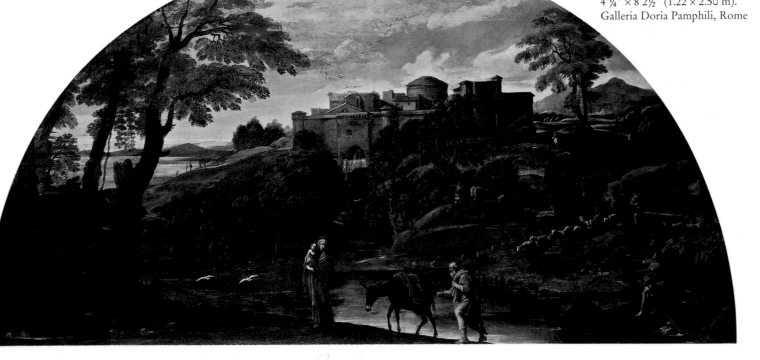

19.8 Annibale Carracci, *Landscape with the Flight into Egypt*. ca. 1603. Oil on canvas, 4'1¼" × 8'2½" (1.22 × 2.50 m). Galleria Doria Pamphili, Rome

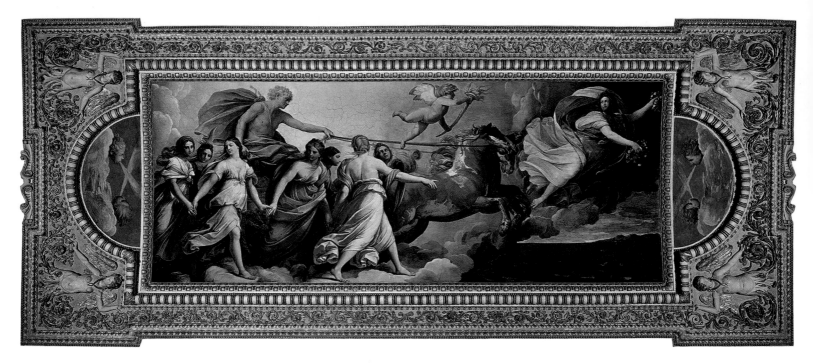

19.9   Guido Reni, *Aurora*. 1613. Ceiling fresco, approx. 9'2" × 22'11" (2.8 × 7m). Casino dell'Aurora, Palazzo Rospigliosi-Pallavinci, Rome

however tiny, do not appear lost or dwarfed. This firmly con-structed "ideal landscape" evokes a vision of nature that is gentle yet austere, grand but not awesome.

GUIDO RENI AND GUERCINO Baroque ceilings, which began with Annibale Carracci's illusionistic ceiling for the Farnese Palace, continued in Rome with Annibale's Bolognese followers Guido Reni (1575–1642) and Giovanni Francesco Barbieri (1591–1666), called Guercino. Guercino was the leader of the Bolognese School of painting, but both he and Reni worked in Rome and executed ceilings in the second and third decades of the seventeenth century.

Annibale's Farnese Gallery seemed to offer two alternatives to them and others inspired by it. Adopting the Raphaelesque style of the mythological panels, they could arrive at a deliberate, offi-cial classicism of *quadro riportato*; or they could take their cue instead from the illusionism of the framework. Approaches varied according to personal style and the specific site. Among the earli-est examples of the first alternative is Reni's *quadro riportato* ceil-ing fresco *Aurora* (fig. **19.9**), which shows Apollo in his chariot (the sun) led by Aurora (the dawn). Here, elegantly drawn grace becomes the pursuit of perfect beauty. The relieflike design with its glowing colors and dramatic light gives the painting an emotional force that the figures alone could never achieve. This style is called Baroque classicism to distinguish it from earlier forms of classicism.

Another *Aurora* ceiling (fig. **19.10**), painted less than ten years later by Guercino, is the very opposite of Reni's. Here (in the 1622 painting), architectural illusionistic framework (painted by Agostino Tassi), known as *quadratura*, combined with the picto-rial illusionism of Correggio (see fig. 17.27) and the intense light

and color of Titian, converts the entire surface into one limitless space, in which the figures sweep past as if driven by the winds. Rather than viewing Aurora in profile as in Reni's ceiling, we are clearly positioned below, looking up, seeing the underbelly of the horses as they gallop over our heads. With this work, Guercino continued and expanded the ceiling painting tradition descended from Correggio and started what became a flood of similar visions by other artists. The dynamic fulfillment of this style became known as the High Baroque, after 1630.

PIETRO DA CORTONA AND THE BARBERINI CEILING
The most overpowering of these illusionistic ceilings is the fresco by Pietro da Cortona (1596–1669) in the great hall of the Barberini Palace in Rome (fig. **19.11**). This enormous painting combines all three illusionistic systems—*quadratura* in its painted architectural framework, *quadri riportati* in the scenes on the sides, and *di sotto in su* in setting our point of view (as in our image here) to fully understand the ceiling. This work, a complex allegory, glorifies the reign of the Barberini pope Urban VIII.

The allegorical female figure of Divine Providence, its central theme, dominates the ceiling, proclaiming that the pope was chosen by her and not by political favor. Indeed, a swarm of bees (part of the Barberini coat of arms featured prominently in the ceiling) was said to have descended on the Vatican just prior to his election by the new secret ballot system in the College of Cardinals. Allegorical figures in the ceiling emphasize the pope's divine position: The Barberini bees are surrounded by the Theological Virtues, Faith, Hope, and Charity, while the papal tiara is carried by Rome and the keys of St. Peter by Religion. As in the Farnese Gallery, the ceiling area is subdivided by a painted framework that simulates architecture and sculpture, but beyond

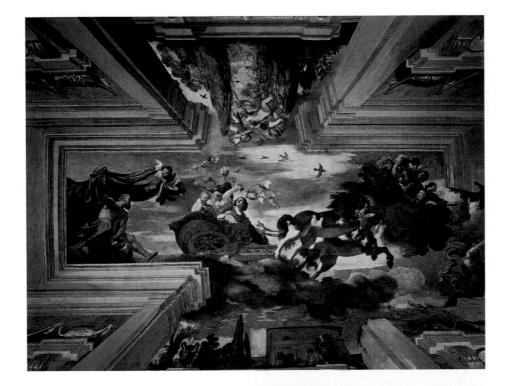

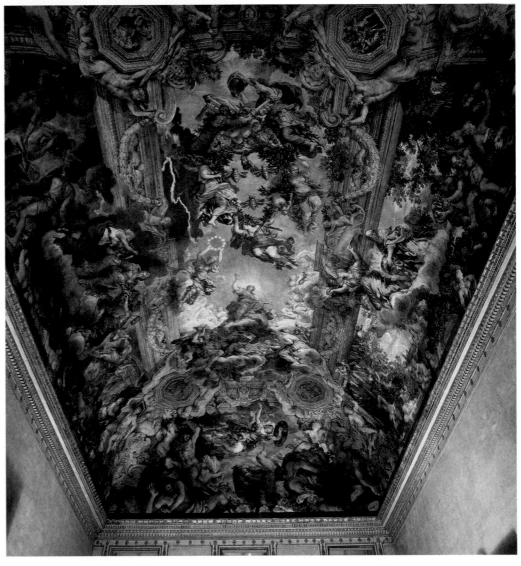

19.11 Pietro da Cortona, *Allegory of Divine Providence*. 1633–39. Ceiling fresco from intended viewpoint. Palazzo Barberini, Rome

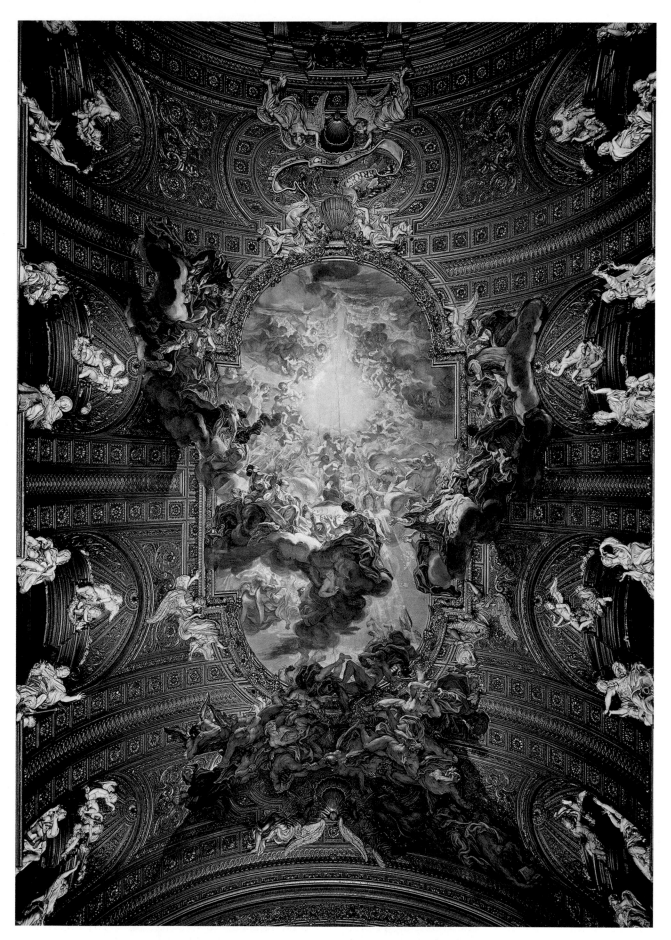

19.12 Giovanni Battista Gaulli, *Triumph of the Name of Jesus*. 1672–79. Ceiling fresco. Il Gesù, Rome

it we now see the limitless sky, as in Guercino's *Aurora*. Clusters of figures, perched on clouds or soaring freely, swirl above as well as below this framework. They create a dual illusion: Some figures appear to hover inside the hall, close to us, while others recede into the distance.

Cortona's frescoes were the focal point for the rift between the High Baroque, the exaggerated, triumphal style of the age, and the Baroque classicism that grew out of the Farnese Gallery ceiling. The classicists insisted that art served a moral purpose and should observe the principles of clarity, unity, and decorum. And, supported by a tradition based on Horace's adage *ut pictura poesis* ("as is painting, so is poetry"), they maintained that painting should follow the example of tragic poetry in conveying meaning through a minimum of figures whose movements, gestures, and expressions can be easily read. Cortona, while not anti-Classical, presented the case instead for art as epic poetry, with many actors and episodes that expand on the central theme and create a magnificent effect. He was also the first to argue that art has a sensuous appeal which exists as an end in itself. Although it took place largely on a theoretical level, the debate over illusionistic ceiling painting was about more than opposing approaches to telling a story and expressing ideas in art. The core issue here lies at the very heart of the Baroque. Illusionism allowed artists to fuse separate levels of reality into a pictorial unity of such overwhelming grandeur as to sweep aside any differences between them. Despite the intensity of the controversy, in practice the two sides rarely came into conflict over easel paintings, where the differences between Cortona's and Annibale's followers were not always so clear-cut. Surprisingly, Cortona found inspiration in classical art and Raphael throughout his career. The leader of the reaction against the "excesses" of the High Baroque was neither a fresco painter nor an Italian, but a French artist living in Rome: Nicolas Poussin, who moved early on in the same antiquarian circle as Cortona but drew very different lessons from it.

GIOVANNI BATTISTA GAULLI AND IL GESÙ It is a strange fact that few ceiling frescoes were painted after Cortona finished his *Allegory of Divine Providence*. Ironically, the new style of architecture fostered by Francesco Borromini and Guarino Guarini (see pages 679–83) provided few opportunities for decoration. But, after 1670, such frescoes enjoyed a revival in older buildings which reached its peak in the interior of Il Gesù (fig. **19.12**), the mother church for the Jesuit order. At the suggestion of Gianlorenzo Bernini, the greatest sculptor-architect of the century, the commission for the ceiling frescoes went to his young protégé Giovanni Battista Gaulli (1639–1709). A talented assistant, Antonio Raggi (1624–1686), made the stucco sculpture. The program, which proved extraordinarily influential, shows Bernini and Gaulli's imaginative daring. As in the Cornaro Chapel (see fig. 19.31), the ceiling is treated as a single unit that evokes a mystical vision. The nave fresco, with its contrasts of light and dark and sharply foreshortened figures, spills dramatically over its frame, then turns into sculptured figures, combining painting, sculpture, and architecture. Here, Baroque illusionism achieves its

ultimate expression. The subject of the ceiling painting is the illuminated name of Jesus—the IHS derived from the first three letters of the Greek name of Jesus—in the center of the golden light. It is a stirring reference both to the Jesuit order, dedicated to the Name of Jesus and to the concept that Christ is the Light of the World. The impact of his light and holiness then creates the overflowing turbulence that tumbles out of the sky at the end of days and spreads the word of the Jesuit missionaries: "That at the name of Jesus, every knee should bow…" (Epistle of St. Paul to the Philippians 2:10).

ARCHITECTURE IN ITALY

The Baroque style in architecture, like that of painting, began in Rome, which was a vast construction site from the end of the sixteenth through the middle of the seventeenth century. The goals of the Counter-Reformation caused the Church to embark on a major building campaign. New churches were constructed and the new St. Peter's was finally completed. Although many of these building projects began during Renaissance, they developed distinctly different characteristics as they were completed during the Baroque. Some architects continued to use a classical vocabulary but expanded or stretched it. For instance, the idea of perfection was no longer represented by a circle, but an oval or ellipse (a new concept that was frequently the object of astronomical discussions). They incorporated domes based on Michelangelo's (see fig. 17.19) but which had a steeper profile to suggest greater drama in punctuating the sky; others designed buildings based on amorphous shapes that used classical ornamentations but not its principles.

The Completion of St. Peter's and Carlo Maderno

Carlo Maderno (ca. 1556–1629) was the most talented young architect to emerge in the midst of the vast ecclesiastical building program that commenced in Rome toward the end of the sixteenth century. In 1603, he was given the task of completing, at long last, the church of St. Peter's (fig. **19.13**). Pope Clement VIII had decided to add a nave and narthex to the west end of Michelangelo's building, thereby converting it into a basilica plan. This change, which had already been proposed by Raphael in 1514, made it possible to link St. Peter's with the Vatican Palace to the right of the church (fig. **19.14**).

Maderno's design for the façade follows the pattern established by Michelangelo for the exterior of the church. It consists of a colossal order supporting an attic, but with a dramatic emphasis on the portals. The effect can only be described as a crescendo that builds from the corners toward the center. The spacing of the supports becomes closer, the pilasters turn into columns, and the façade wall projects step by step. This quickened rhythm had been hinted at a generation earlier in Giacomo della Porta's façade for Il Gesù (see fig. 17.23). Maderno made it the dominant principle of his façade designs, not only for St. Peter's

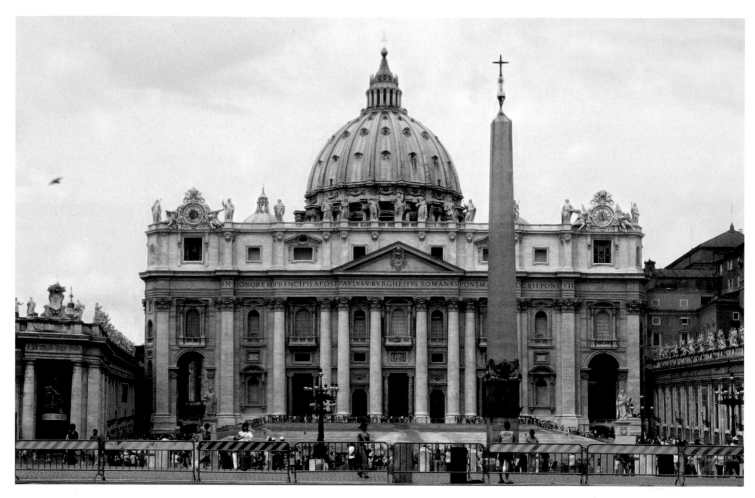

19.13 Carlo Maderno. Façade of St. Peter's, Rome. 1607–12

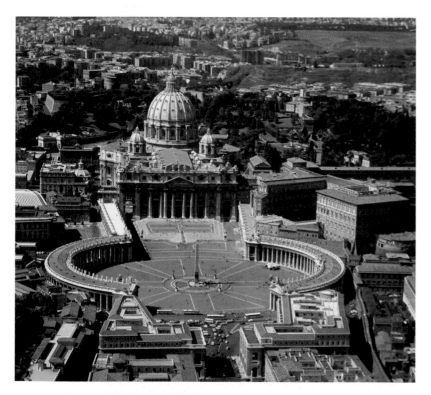

19.14 Aerial view of St. Peter's, Rome. Nave and façade by Carlo Maderno, 1607–12; colonnade by Gianlorenzo Bernini, designed 1657

but for smaller churches as well. In the process, he replaced the traditional concept of the church façade as one continuous wall surface, with the "façade-in-depth" becoming dynamically related to the open space before it. The possibilities of this new treatment, which derives from Michelangelo's Palazzo dei Conservatori (see fig. 17.18), were not to be exhausted until 150 years later. Recent cleaning of the façade of St. Peter's revealed it to be of a warm cream color, which emphasized its sculptural qualities.

Bernini and St. Peter's

After Maderno's death in 1629, his assistant Gianlorenzo Bernini (1598–1680) assumed the title "architect of St. Peter's." Considering himself Michelangelo's successor as both architect and sculptor, Bernini directed the building campaign and coordinated the decoration and sculpture within the church as well. Given these tasks, the enormous size of St. Peter's posed equal challenges for anyone seeking to integrate architecture and sculpture. How could its vastness be related to the human scale and given a measure of emotional warmth? Once the nave was extended following Maderno's design, Bernini realized that the vast interior needed an internal focal point. His response was to create the monumental sculptural/architectural composite form, known as the **Baldacchino** (fig. **19.15**), the "canopy" for the main altar of St. Peter's, at the very crossing of the transept and the

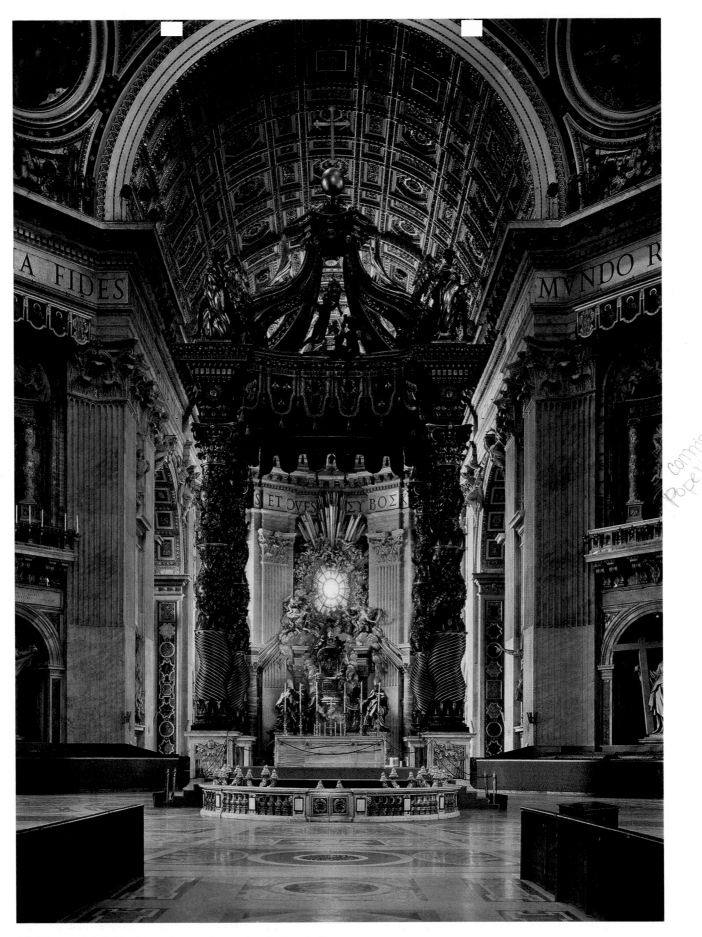

19.15   Bernini, *Baldacchino*. 1624–33. At crossing. St. Peter's, Rome

nave, directly under Michelangelo's dome (see fig. 17.19) and just above the actual **crypt** of St. Peter where the pope would celebrate Mass. This nearly 100-foot piece created mostly in bronze stripped from the ancient Pantheon (see fig. 7.23) stands on four twisted columns, reminiscent of those from the original St. Peter's (and thought, too, to replicate those of Solomon's Temple). Rather than an architectural entablature mounted between the columns, Bernini inventively suggests fabric hanging between them. He used actual leaves, vines, fruits, and even lizards and cast them in bronze for the decoration. The *Baldacchino* is a splendid fusion of sculpture and architecture. At its corners are statues of angels and vigorously curved scrolls, which raise a cross above a golden orb, the symbol of the triumph of Christianity throughout the world. The entire structure is so alive with expressive energy that it may be considered as the epitome of Baroque style. In a related tribute, we see through the columns of the *Baldacchino* to the sculptural reliquary of the throne of St. Peter, the *Cathedra Petri* in the apse of the church, also designed by Bernini.

The papal insignia—the triple crown and crossed keys of St. Peter—and the coat of arms of the pope under whose patronage this structure was created—the Barberini bees of Urban VIII—are significant elements of decoration in the *Baldacchino*. These same identifiers can also be seen in Cortona's Barberini ceiling (see fig. 19.11). Bernini's *Baldacchino* honors not just the power and majesty of God, but that of his emissary on earth, the pope. Bernini's relationship with the pope was one of the most successful in the history of patronage. Indeed, upon his elevation to the papacy, Urban VIII was said to have told the artist: "It is your great good luck, Cavaliere, to see Maffeo Barberini pope; but We are even luckier in that Cavaliere Bernini lives at the time of our pontificate." (However, the artistic aims of this pope drained the papal treasury and both the pope and, by association, Bernini were blamed for the excesses after Urban's death.) As Bernini directed our attention within the church, he also (later, under the patronage of Pope Alexander VII [r. 1655–1667] orchestrated our entrance into St. Peter's. Thus, he molded the open space in front of the façade into a magnificent oval piazza that is amazingly sculptural (see fig. 19.14). This "forecourt"—an immense keyhole-shaped colossal colonnade—imposed a degree of unity on the sprawling Vatican complex, while screening off the surrounding slums. This device, which Bernini himself likened to the motherly, all-embracing arms of the Church, was not new. What *was* novel was the idea of placing it at the main entrance to a building. Also unusual was the huge scale. For sheer impressiveness, this integration of architecture and grandiose setting can be compared only with the ancient Roman sanctuary at Palestrina (see fig. 7.5). Bernini's one major failure visually of St. Peter's was his inability to execute the bell towers that were initially planned by Bramante (see fig. 16.10). He began construction, but, much to Bernini's humiliation, cracks appeared, and although these could have been the result of normal foundation settling, an inquest was convened, and the towers were dismantled. This failure would haunt him, but would provide a competitive resource for his rivals: Borromini in Italy and later Wren in England.

Architectural Components in Decoration

The huge scale, the dynamic sculptural vitality, and the ornamentation of Baroque architecture were expressed in the decorative arts as well. The 5-foot-high clock seen in figure **19.16** is made of colorful marble, lapis lazuli, black ebony, and gilt bronze, and features an oil-on-copper painting.

Clocks in the seventeenth century were not yet accurate, certainly not silent, and rarely readable at night. The novel example shown here, however, was known as an *orologio della notte* (nocturnal clock)—a clock that would be useful even at night, thanks to an innovative design by Pier Tommaso Campani (active ca. 1650– 1700). Bernini had seen a nocturnal clock on his trip to France in 1665; it was considered a true marvel. This one was made for Pope Alexander VII, a known insomniac, who requested a clock that could display the time even in darkness and run without sound. The time here is expressed in Roman

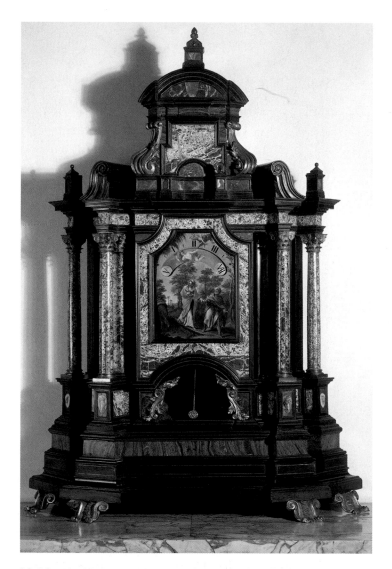

19.16   Pier Tommaso Campani and Francesco Trevisani, *Nocturnal Clock*. ca. 1680–90. Ebony and other types of hardwood, oil on copper, gilt bronze, colored stones, 63 × 45¼ × 18½" (160 × 115 × 47 cm). Pinacoteca Capitolini, Rome

numerals, pierced so that light from a hidden oil lamp could pass through them; a drum was used to quash the ticktocking sound of a pendulum.

The clock was encased in an elaborate architectural structure with paired columns and scrolled feet that resembles a tabernacle. It shows the influence of both Bernini and Borromini. The painting at its center, by Francesco Trevisani (1656–1746), is the *Flight into Egypt*. This theme is a pun on time—as time also flies. Trevisani was a well-known Roman painter, and this was no small commission. Indeed, we know that Gaulli, the painter of the ceiling of Il Gesù (see fig. 19.12), also executed paintings for such clocks.

A Baroque Alternative: Francesco Borromini

Bernini's greatest rival in architecture, Francesco Borromini (1599–1667), was a secretive and emotionally unstable artist who committed suicide. The contrast in temperament between these two architects would be evident from their works alone, even if we did not have the accounts written by their contemporaries. Bernini's church designs are dramatically simple and unified, while Borromini's structures are extravagantly complex. But where the surfaces of Bernini's interiors are extremely rich, Borromini's are surprisingly plain: They rely on the architect's phenomenal grasp of spatial geometry to achieve their spiritual effects. Bernini himself agreed with those who denounced Borromini for flagrantly disregarding the classical tradition, enshrined in Renaissance theory and practice, that architecture must reflect the proportions of the human body. Certainly, Bernini, even at the height of the Baroque, was more tied to a classical vocabulary. But perhaps his criticisms of Borromini were only an expression of all-too-human rivalries.

SAN CARLO ALLE QUATTRO FONTANE Borromini's first major project was the church of San Carlo alle Quattro Fontane (fig. **19.17**), a small structure on a difficult-to-fit corner. It is the syntax, not the vocabulary, that is new and disquieting here. The ceaseless play of concave and convex surfaces makes the entire structure seem elastic, as if pulled out of shape by pressures that no previous building could have withstood. The plan (fig. **19.18**) is a pinched oval that suggests a distended and half-melted Greek cross, yet it is a basically central-planned church. The inside of the coffered dome (fig. **19.19**), like the plan, looks "stretched": If the tension were relaxed, it would snap back to normal. Light coming from the windows, partially hidden at the base of the dome, and a honeycomb of fanciful coffers of decreasing size to create the illusion of greater height make the dome appear weightless. The symbol of the Trinity appears in the vault of the lantern in this church, built for the Trinitarians, an order dedicated to the mysteries of the Holy Trinity.

On the façade (see fig. 19.17), designed almost 30 years later, the pressures and counterpressures reach their maximum intensity. Borromini merges architecture and sculpture in a way that must have shocked Bernini. No such union had been

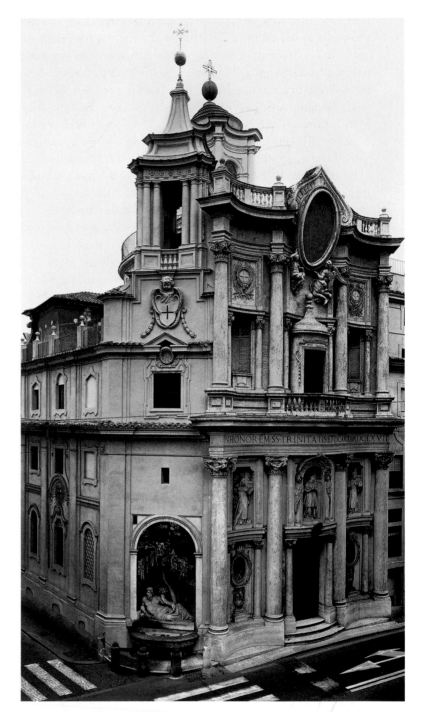

19.17 Francesco Borromini. Façade of San Carlo alle Quattro Fontane, Rome. ca. 1665–67

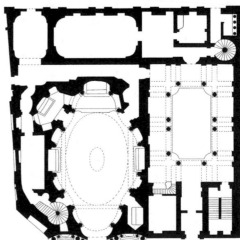

19.18 Plan of San Carlo alle Quattro Fontane. 1638–41

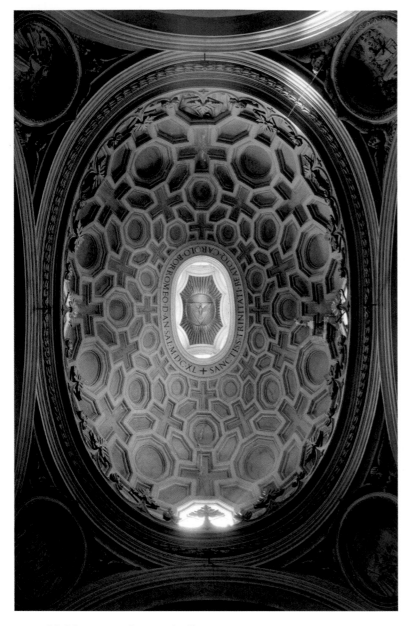

19.19 Dome of San Carlo alle Quattro Fontane. 1638–41

SANT'IVO Borromini's church of Sant'Ivo alla Sapienza (figs. **19.20** and **19.21**) was built at the end of an existing cloister for a university, which soon became the University of Rome. It is more compact than San Carlo, but equally daring. Sant'Ivo is a small, central-plan church based on a hexagonal star. The six-pointed plan represents Sapienza (wisdom), although as the church was first built under Pope Urban VIII (Barberini) it was suggested by contemporaries that the plan represented the Barberini bee, also seen in Bernini's *Baldacchino* and Cortona's ceiling (see figs. 19.15 and 19.11). In designing this unique church, Borromini may have been thinking of octagonal structures, such as San Vitale in

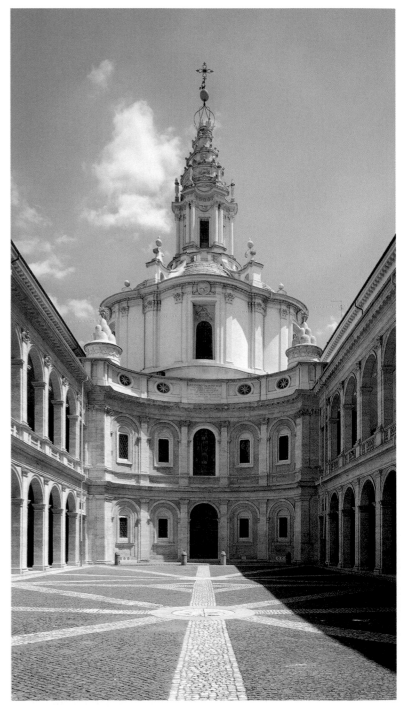

attempted since Gothic art. A study of the two entablatures of fluid concave and convex turns over the bays in a mix and match fashion provides an insight into his design methods. The statues above the entrance emerge like actors entering a stage from behind a thin screen. The sculptures, interestingly enough, are by Bernini's assistant Antonio Raggi, who also worked on the ceiling of Il Gesù (see fig. 19.12). San Carlo alle Quattro Fontane established Borromini's fame. "Nothing similar," wrote the head of the religious order for which the church was built, "can be found anywhere in the world. This is attested by the foreigners who…try to procure copies of the plan. We have been asked for them by Germans, Flemings, Frenchmen, Italians, Spaniards, and even Indians." Yet the design was also described by a contemporary, no doubt because of its seeming disregard of regular geometry, as "the corruption of architecture."

19.20 Francesco Borromini. Exterior of Sant'Ivo, Rome. Begun 1642

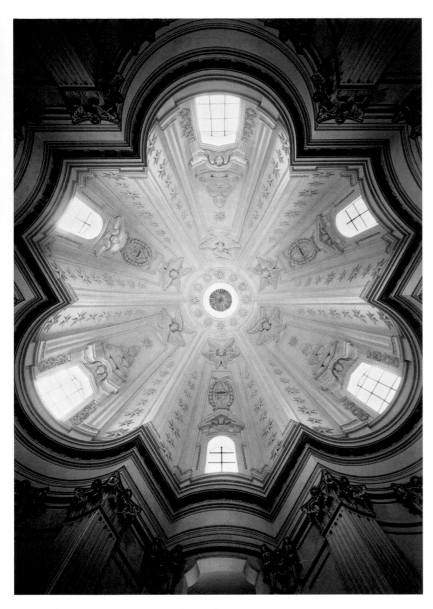

19.21 Interior view into dome of Sant'Ivo

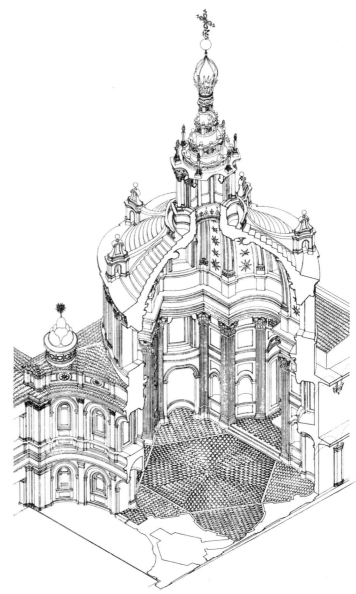

19.22 Cutaway plan of Francesco Borromini's Sant'Ivo (from Portoghesi)

Ravenna (fig. 8.21), but the result is completely novel. Inside (fig. **19.22**), it offers a single, unified, organic experience, as the walls extend the ground plan into the vault, culminating in Borromini's unique spiral lantern. The hexagonal star pattern is continued up to the circular base of the lantern. The stars on the wall refer to the Chigi family of Pope Alexander VII, who was in power when the building was completed.

SANT'AGNESE A third project by Borromini, the church of Sant'Agnese, is set on the Piazza Navona (fig. **19.23**), a grand ancient stadium space in which three sculptural Baroque fountains celebrate the new age. The central monument, topped by an Egyptian obelisk, is the *Four Rivers Fountain* by Bernini, and its location in front of Sant'Agnese demonstrates the rivalry between Borromini and Bernini: The latter fought for the church commission, but lost.

Sant'Agnese is of special interest as a critique of St. Peter's and each of its architects. There were two problems that Maderno had been unable to solve at St. Peter's. Although his façade forms an impressive unit with Michelangelo's dome when seen from a distance, the dome is gradually hidden by the new façade as we approach the church. It appears to "sink." Furthermore, the towers he planned for each end posed formidable structural difficulties. After Bernini's first attempt to overcome these problems failed, he proposed making the towers free-standing, but he was forced to abandon the plan when it was severely criticized. The façade of Sant'Agnese offers a brilliant solution to both of these difficulties. Borromini took over the project, which had been begun by another architect, Carlo Rainaldi (1611–1691), the year before, and completely recast it without, however, entirely abandoning the Greek-cross plan. The design is essentially a central-plan (fig. **19.24**), and the dome is

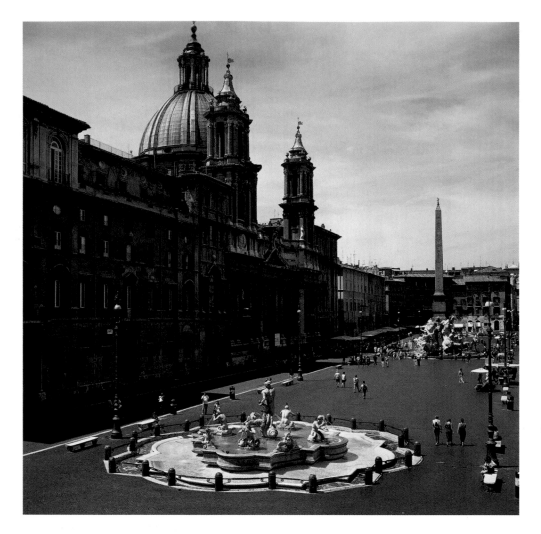

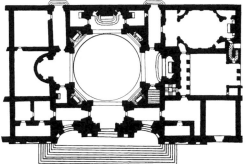

19.23 Piazza Navona, Rome, with Francesco Borromini, Sant'Agnese, center left, 1653–63, and Bernini's *Four Rivers Fountain*, center, 1648–52

19.24 Francesco Borromini. Plan of Sant'Agnese

not set back at all. The façade's lower part is adapted from the façade of St. Peter's, but it curves inward, so that the dome (a tall, slender version of Michelangelo's) functions as the upper part of the façade. As the dome is nearly at the entranceway, the problem of its apparent "sinking" is solved. The dramatic juxtaposition of concave and convex, so characteristic of Borromini, is emphasized by the two towers, which form a monumental group with the dome. Once again, Borromini joins Gothic and Renaissance features—the two-tower façade and the dome—into a remarkably elastic compound to tower over the ancient site.

The Baroque in Turin: Guarino Guarini

The new ideas introduced by Borromini were developed further not in Rome but in Turin, the capital of Piedmont, which became the creative center of Baroque architecture in Italy toward the end of the seventeenth century. In 1666, Guarino Guarini (1624–1683), Borromini's most brilliant successor, was called to Turin to work as an engineer and mathematician by Duke Carlo Emanuele II. Guarini was a Theatine priest whose genius was grounded in philosophy and mathematics. His design for the façade of the Palazzo Carignano (figs. **19.25** and **19.26**) repeats on a larger scale the undulating movement of San Carlo alle Quattro Fontane (see

fig. 19.17), using a highly individualized vocabulary. Incredibly, the exterior of the building, in the local tradition, is made almost entirely of brick, but was probably meant to be stuccoed in imitation marble.

Even more extraordinary is Guarini's dome for the Chapel of the Holy Shroud, a round structure attached to Turin cathedral (fig. **19.27**). The dome and the tall drum, with its alternating windows and niches, consists of familiar Borrominian motifs. Yet it ushers us into a realm of pure illusion completely unlike anything by the earlier architect. Here, the surface has disappeared in a

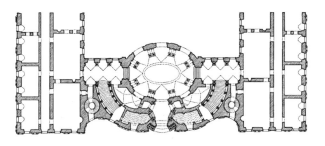

19.25 Plan of Palazzo Carignano

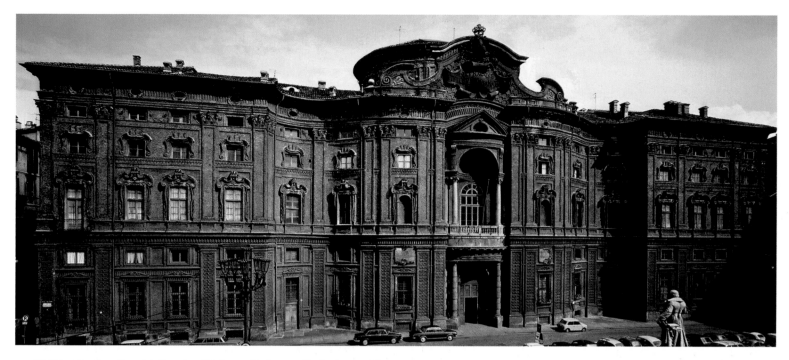

19.26 Guarino Guarini, Façade of Palazzo Carignano. Turin. Begun 1679

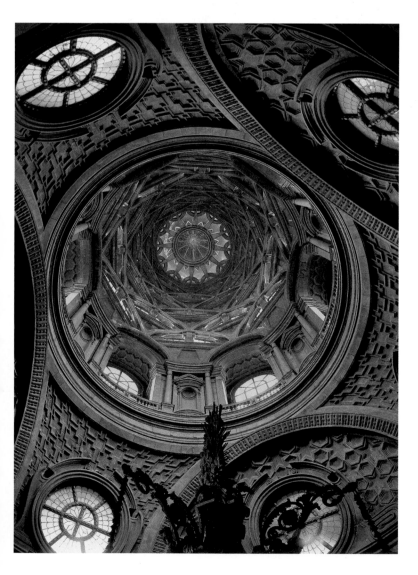

19.27 Guarino Guarini. Dome of the Chapel of the Holy Shroud, Turin cathedral. 1668–94

maze of ribs that is both unusual and exotic, created through the manipulation of repeated geometric forms. As a result, we find ourselves staring into a huge kaleidoscope. Above this seemingly infinite funnel of space hovers the dove of the Holy Spirit within a 12-point star inside the chapel, which holds one of the most precious relics of Christendom, the Shroud of Christ.

Guarini's dome retains the symbolic meaning of the dome of Heaven, and repeats architecturally what Correggio achieved in painting in his *Assumption of the Virgin* (see fig. 17.27). A concentric structure of alternating rings of light and shadow enhances the illusion of great depth and features brilliant light at its center; it also recalls the Passion of Christ. The objective harmony of the Renaissance has here become subjective, a compelling experience of the infinite, close to the Gothic mysticism of Abbot Suger's infinite (see page 391). If Borromini's style at times suggests a fusion of Gothic and Renaissance, Guarini takes the next step. In his writings, he contrasts the "muscular" architecture of the ancients with the effect of Gothic churches, which appear to stand only by means of some kind of miracle, and he expresses equal admiration for both. This attitude corresponds exactly to his own practice. Guarini and Borromini were obsessed with originality and were willing to break architectural rules to achieve it. By using the most advanced mathematical techniques of his day, Guarini accomplished wonders even greater than the seeming weightlessness of Gothic structures. The dome itself, for example, is on three pendentives instead of the usual four—a completely fresh approach to a traditional form.

The Baroque in Venice: Baldassare Longhena

The Republic of Venice commissioned a church at the head of the Grand Canal to show its gratitude to the Virgin for ending the plague of 1630—Santa Maria della Salute (fig. **19.28**; *salute* means "good health"). It was designed by Baldassare Longhena (1598–1682) in 1631 and as such may well be the first Baroque church, but it was not consecrated until 1687, after Longhena's death. It took the heart of the century to complete and rivals the masterpieces of Rome. The Salute's commission required that it be in "harmony with the site"; the structure dominates the Grand Canal and has become a focal point on the Venice skyline—unique, graceful, classical, yet ornate.

The most important aspect of the building is that its plan is that of a regular octagon whose distinctive form can be seen on its multiple façades, with a dome rising from its center. It is in the

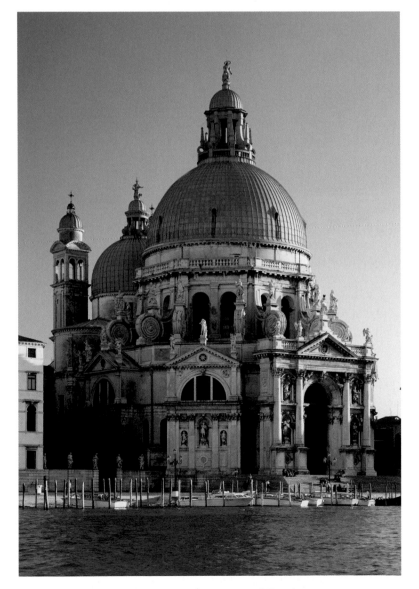

19.28 Baldassare Longhena, Santa Maria della Salute. Venice. 1631–87

shape of a crown, referring to its dedication to the Virgin, Queen of Heaven. Each face is a double-columned triumphal arch whose columns stand on high pedestals. The entablature is joined to the drum in a series of large sculptural volutes that are both elegant and distinctive. The details—drum, double columns, and octagonal shape—all have their sources in the early Church, and in works by Bramante and Palladio, but they became the hallmark of the Baroque in Venice.

SCULPTURE IN ITALY

Baroque sculpture, like Baroque painting, was vital, energized, and dynamic, suggesting action and deep emotion. The subject matter was intended to evoke an emotional response in the viewer. Sculpture was usually life-size, but with a sense of grandeur that suggested larger-than-life figures; and many figures were indeed monumental. Deeply cut, the facial expressions and clothing caught the light and cast shadows to create not just depth but drama.

Early Baroque Sculpture: Stefano Maderno

Baroque sculpture began with the delicate naturalism of the *Santa Cecilia* (fig. **19.29**) by Stefano Maderno (ca. 1576–1636). Rather than showing his subject standing as in life, as with almost all depictions of saints, Maderno depicted her as a recumbent dead body. This fifth-century saint's body had been found, uncorrupted, just a year before, in 1599, in the church of Santa Cecilia in Trastevere. The recovery of her body prompted numerous depictions during the Baroque period of Santa Cecilia, the patron saint of music, but always showing her young, alive, engaged, and often playing a musical instrument. Here, however, she lies on her right side, on a slab of marble, her dress pulled between her knees and down to her toes as if lying on a bed rather than a morgue slab. The cut in her neck and the twisting away of her head indicate that she is dead. (Indeed, she was martyred by decapitation, but her head did not actually separate from her body.) She lies vulnerable even in her death, evoking pathos. The poignancy of Maderno's depiction of his subject is one of the characteristics of the Baroque.

The Evolution of the Baroque: Gianlorenzo Bernini

Bernini was a sculptor as well as an architect, and sculpture and architecture are never far apart in his work as we have seen in the *Baldacchino* (see fig. 19.15). He was trained by his father, Pietro Bernini (1562–1629), a sculptor who worked in Florence, Naples, and Rome, but who was also influenced by Giovanni Bologna (see fig. 17.13). Bernini's style was thus a direct outgrowth of Mannerist sculpture in many ways, but this debt alone does not explain its revolutionary qualities, which emerged early in his career.

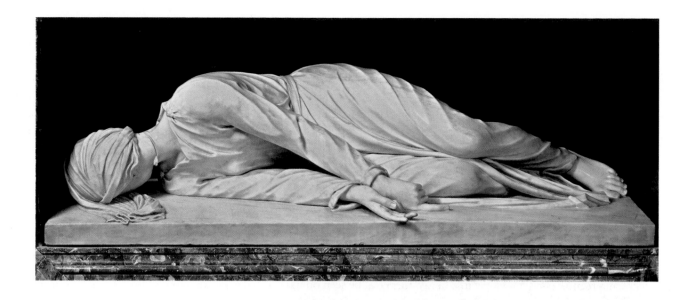

19.29 Stefano Maderno, *Santa Cecilia*. 1600. Marble, life-size. Santa Cecilia in Trastevere, Rome

DAVID As in the colonnade for St. Peter's (see fig. 19.14), we can often see a strong relationship between Bernini's sculpture and examples from antiquity. If we compare Bernini's *David* (fig. 19.30) with Michelangelo's (see fig. 16.13) and ask which is closer to the Pergamon frieze or the *Laocoön* (see fig. 5.73 and page 183), our vote must go to Bernini, whose sculpture shares with Hellenistic works that union of body and spirit, of motion and emotion, which Michelangelo so consciously tempers. This does not mean that Michelangelo is more classical than Bernini. It shows, rather, that the Baroque and the High Renaissance drew different lessons from ancient art.

Bernini's *David* has the fierceness of expression, movement, and dynamism of the *Laocoön*. In part, what makes it Baroque in character is the implied presence of Goliath. Unlike earlier statues of David, including Donatello's (see fig. 15.33), Bernini's is conceived not as a self-contained figure but as half of a pair, with his entire being focused on his (invisible) adversary. Bernini's *David* tells us clearly enough where he sees the enemy. Consequently, the space between David and his invisible opponent is charged with energy—it "belongs" to the statue. The intensity of his expression suggests his focused determination. It has come down to us that the *David*'s face is modeled on Bernini's own; he made this self-portrait by looking in a mirror held by his patron, Cardinal Barberini, who would become Pope Urban VIII. (See *Materials and Techniques*, page 688.)

Bernini's *David* shows us a distinctive feature of Baroque sculpture: its new, active relationship with the surrounding space. But it is meant to be seen, as is most other Baroque sculpture, from one primary point of view. Bernini presents us with "the moment" of action, not just the contemplation of the killing—as in Michelangelo's work—or the aftermath of it—as in Donatello's. Baroque sculpture often suggests a heightened vitality and energy. Because they so often present an "invisible complement" (like the

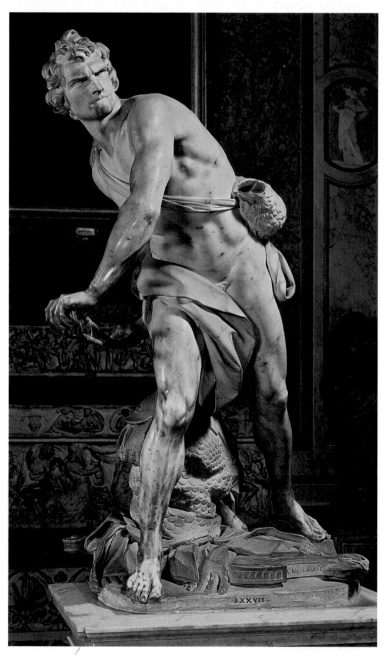

19.30 Gianlorenzo Bernini, *David*. 1623. Marble, life-size. Galleria Borghese, Rome

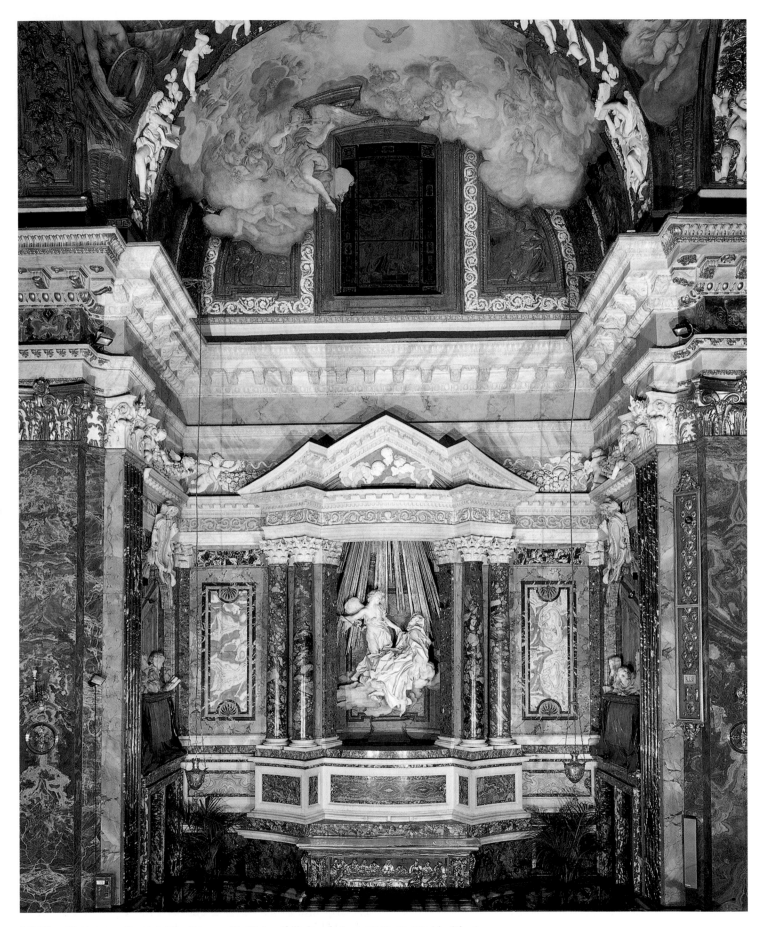

19.31 Gianlorenzo Bernini, *The Ecstasy of St. Teresa* (full chapel view). 1645–52. Marble, life-size.
Cornaro Chapel, Santa Maria della Vittoria, Rome

Goliath of Bernini's *David*), Baroque statues attempt pictorial effects that were traditionally outside the realm of monumental sculpture. Such a charging of space with energy is, in fact, a key feature of Baroque art. Caravaggio had achieved it in his *The Calling of St. Matthew* with the aid of a sharply focused beam of light (see fig. 19.2). And as we have seen in Gaulli's ceiling for Il Gesù (see fig. 19.12), both painting and sculpture may be combined with architecture to form a compound dramatic illusion—one that Bernini would explore in other works.

THE CORNARO CHAPEL: *THE ECSTASY OF ST. TERESA*

Bernini had a passionate interest in the theater and was an innovative scene designer. A contemporary wrote that he "gave a public opera wherein he painted the scenes, cut the statues, invented the engines, composed the music, writ the comedy, and built the theatre." Thus he was at his best when he could merge architecture, sculpture, and painting. (See www.myartslab.com.) His masterpiece in this vein is the Cornaro Chapel in the church of Santa Maria della Vittoria, which contains *The Ecstasy of St. Teresa* (fig. **19.31** and see page 660). Teresa of Ávila (1515–1582), one of the great saints of the Counter-Reformation, and director of the Reformed Order of the Discalced ("shoeless," as shown here) Carmelites was canonized in 1622. Known for her mystical visions, she had described how an angel pierced her heart with a flaming golden arrow: "The pain was so great that I screamed aloud; but at the same time I felt such infinite sweetness that I wished the pain to last forever. It was not physical but psychic pain, although it affected the body as well to some degree. It was the sweetest caressing of the soul by God."

Bernini has made Teresa's visionary experience as sensuously real as Correggio's *Jupiter and Io* (see fig. 17.26); her arm and leg are limp and the saint's rapture is obvious. (In a different context the angel could be Cupid.) The two figures on their floating cloud, which is hollow (so Bernini could hang this group rather than fasten it to the wall), are lit from a hidden window above, so that they seem almost dematerialized. A viewer thus experiences them as a vision. The "invisible complement" here, less specific than *David*'s but equally important, is the force that carries the figures—they levitate—toward Heaven and causes the turbulence of their drapery. Its divine nature is suggested by the golden rays (gilt wood) which come from a source high above the altar. In an illusionistic fresco by Guidobaldo Abbatini (ca.1600/05–1656) on the vault of the chapel, the glory of Heaven is revealed as a dazzling burst of light from which tumble clouds of jubilant angels. This celestial explosion gives force to the thrusts of the angel's arrow and makes the ecstasy of the saint fully believable.

To complete the illusion, Bernini even provides a built-in audience for his "stage." On the sides of the chapel are balconies resembling theater boxes that contain marble relief figures depicting members of the Cornaro family, who also witness the vision. Their space and ours are the same, and thus they are part of our reality, while the saint's ecstasy, which is framed in a niche, occupies a space that is real but beyond our reach, for it is intended as a divine realm.

Finally, the ceiling fresco represents the infinite space of Heaven. We may recall that *The Burial of Count Orgaz* and its setting also form a whole that includes three levels of reality (see figs. 18.8 and 18.9). Yet there is a fundamental difference between the two chapels. El Greco's Mannerism evokes an ethereal vision in which only the stone slab of the sarcophagus is "real," in contrast to Bernini's Baroque staging, where there are several levels of reality and the distinctions between them break down. It would be easy to dismiss *The Ecstasy of St. Teresa* as a theatrical display, but Bernini was also a devout Catholic who believed that he was inspired directly by God. Like the *Spiritual Exercises* of Ignatius of Loyola, which Bernini practiced, his religious sculpture is intended to help a viewer identify with miraculous events through a vivid appeal to the senses. Theatricality in the service of faith was basic to the Counter-Reformation, which often referred to the Church as the theater of human life: It took the Baroque to bring this ideal to life.

Bernini was steeped in Renaissance humanism. Central to his sculpture is the role of gesture and expression in arousing emotion. While these devices were also important to the Renaissance, Bernini uses them with a freedom that seems anti-Classical. However, he essentially followed the concept of decorum (which also explains why his *David* is not completely nude), and he planned his effects carefully by varying them in accordance with his subject. Unlike the Frenchman Nicolas Poussin, whom he respected, Bernini did this for the sake of expressive impact rather than conceptual clarity. The approaches of the two artists were diametrically opposed. For Bernini, antiquity served as no more than a point of departure for his own inventiveness, whereas for Poussin it was a standard of comparison (see Chapter 21). It is nevertheless characteristic of the Baroque that Bernini's theories were far more orthodox than his art. Thus, he often sided with the classicists against his fellow High Baroque artists, especially Pietro da Cortona, who, like Raphael before him, also made an important contribution to architecture and was a rival to Bernini in that sphere.

A Classical Alternative: Alessandro Algardi

It is no less ironic that Cortona was the closest friend of the sculptor Alessandro Algardi (1598–1654), who is regarded as the leading classical sculptor of the Italian Baroque. His main contribution is the great marble relief *The Meeting of Pope Leo I and Attila* (fig. **19.32**), done when he took over Bernini's role as principal sculptor at St. Peter's during the papacy of Innocent X. It introduces a new kind of high relief that soon became widely popular. Bernini avoided doing reliefs (when such projects were required, his studio executed them), but Algardi liked working in this more pictorial sculptural form.

The scene depicts the Huns under Attila being driven away after threatening an attack on Rome in 452, a fateful event in the early history of Christianity, when its very survival was at stake. (The actual event was very different: Leo persuaded the Huns not to attack, just as he did with the Vandals three years

Bernini's Sculptural Sketches

Small sketches in sculpture—for large-scale works of sculpture or architecture—serve as models, practice pieces, or presentation pieces for the artist to show a patron. These sculptural models are called *bozzetti* or *modelli*. *Bozzetto* (singular) means "sketch," and *bozzetti* are generally smaller and less finished than *modelli*, which may be closer to the final product, or in some other way "finished" so that a patron can see them before the completion of the project.

Artists may do several drawings as well as several *bozzetti* for a completed piece. And, indeed, Bernini did both drawings in pen and ink, in red or black chalk, or even in combinations of chalk and pen in preparation for a project, as well as making *bozzetti*. Bernini's *bozzetti* and *modelli* are made in clay (terra cotta), although the completed sculptures were executed in marble. This is not just a difference in medium, but in technique. Marble sculpture is created through a subtractive process—marble is chiseled away. But clay can be worked using both additive and subtractive methods, and we know that Bernini's work in clay was primarily additive.

We can see multiple methods and evidence of a variety of tools used by Bernini in his clay *bozzetto* of the life-size *Head of St. Jerome*, created for a full-length marble sculpture of the saint. Analysis of the clay sculpture has shown that this piece, like many others, was made from wedged clay—that is, fresh clay that is rolled, smashed, and rolled repeatedly to expel air, and then subsequently "worked." The clay is worked on by hand, using fingers (most probably the thumbs, index fingers, and middle fingers), with fingernails creating tracks, and tools that often have teeth.

The idea that the clay is worked on by the artist with his own hands—his own fingers—is a tantalizing one. Large-scale sculpture and complex sculptural and architectural projects may employ several assistants chiseling marble. But here in a *bozzetto* we may be looking at the handiwork—the very fingerprints—of the artist. Several of Bernini's *bozzetti* have been examined for fingerprints in the clay, and indeed many have been found. Of the fifteen Bernini *bozzetti* at the Fogg Art Museum (the largest single collection of his *bozzetti*), thirteen have fingerprints. Thirty-four fingerprints in total have been found and some of the same prints have been found in works executed years apart. Therefore, it is most likely that these prints are Bernini's own. He smoothed surfaces, added clay, created lines and edges with his nails, wiped and depressed the clay with his own fingers.

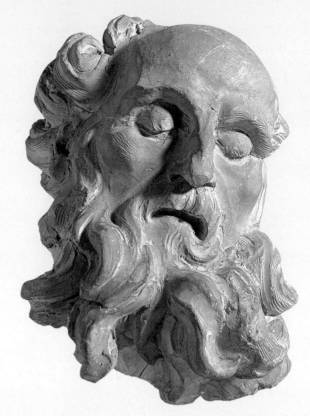

Gianlorenzo Bernini, *Head of St. Jerome*. ca. 1661. Terra cotta, height 14¼" (36.2 cm). Courtesy of the Fogg Art Museum, Harvard University Art Museum, Cambridge, MA. Alpheus Hyatt Purchasing and Friends of the Fogg Art Museum Funds, 1937.77

The *Head of St. Jerome* reveals Bernini's fingerprints, evidence of nail edging, and texturing from tined (fork-like) tools as he added more clay to represent the hair and nose. We know that the clay was hollowed out from the back, after being scooped out with fingers. As clay would be added to the face and hair, chances of cracking and breaking off increased. And we see much evidence of cracking in this *bozzetto*. It is apparent that areas were specifically smoothed over to prevent this. There is further evidence that a cloth was placed over the *Head* to keep the clay moist for continued work and to prevent further cracking.

The *Head of St. Jerome* is enormously expressive, looking tortured, with his deep-set eyes and hollow cheeks, but it is the textures in clay that make this gaunt face most memorable.

---

later. Both protagonists were on horseback, not on foot as seen here.) The subject revives a theme that is familiar to us from antiquity: the victory over barbarian forces. Now, however, it is the Church that triumphs; and the victory is spiritual rather than military.

A sculpture was commissioned since water condensation caused by its location in an old doorway of St. Peter's (and through most of the church) made paintings impossible to maintain in pristine condition. Never before had an Italian sculptor attempted such a large relief—it stands nearly 28 feet high (nearly twice the height of Ghiberti's bronze doors, see fig. 15.16).

The problems posed by translating a pictorial conception into a relief on this gigantic scale were formidable. If Algardi has not succeeded in resolving every detail, his achievement is stupendous nonetheless. By varying the depth of the carving, he nearly convinces us that the scene takes place in the same space as our own. The foreground figures are in such high relief that they seem detached from the background. They are modeled almost fully in the round. To emphasize the effect, the stage on which they are standing projects several feet beyond its surrounding niche. Thus, Attila seems to rush out toward us in fear and astonishment as he flees the vision of the two apostles defending the

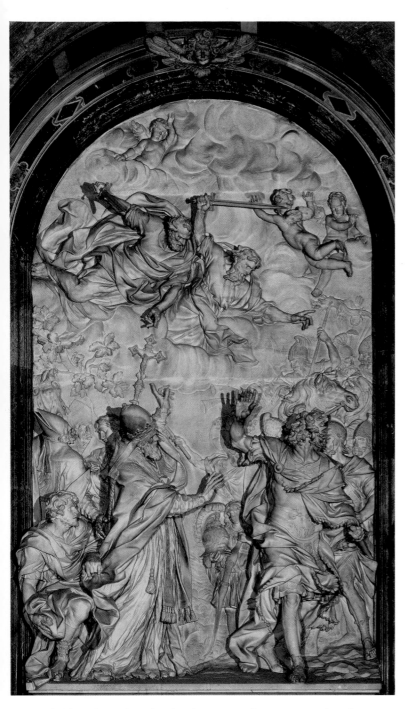

19.32 Alessandro Algardi, *The Meeting of Pope Leo I and Attila.* 1646–53. Marble, 28'1¾" × 16'2½" (8.5 × 4.9 m). St. Peter's, The Vatican, Rome

instead of continuously variable depth), his preference for frontal poses, and his restraint in dealing with the violent action can Algardi be called a classicist, and then purely in a relative sense. Clearly we must not draw the distinction between the High Baroque and Baroque classicism too sharply in sculpture, any more so than in painting.

PAINTING IN SPAIN

Spain may have been the most powerful political entity at the turn of the seventeenth century. It ruled the kingdoms of Portugal, Sicily, Naples, Milan, the North and South Netherlands, territories in North America (Florida) and South America (Chile and Argentina), the Philippines, the Canary Islands, and parts of Africa. This expansion during the sixteenth century brought it to the height of its political and economic power. Spain also produced great writers and influential saints. Indeed, the newly canonized saints of the early seventeenth century (1622)—Ignatius of Loyola, the founder of the Jesuit order, Francis Xavier, an early and influential Jesuit missionary, and Teresa of Ávila (see fig. 19.31)—were all Spanish.

Ironically, the Spanish court and most of the aristocracy held native artists in low esteem, and so preferred to employ foreign painters whenever possible. Thus, the main influences came from the Italian kingdoms and the Netherlands. Jan van Eyck visited Spain and inspired followers there, Titian worked for Charles V of Spain, and El Greco worked in Toledo from the late sixteenth into the seventeenth century; we also know that Rubens visited Spain at least twice and his work was much admired there. The patronage of the court in Madrid and its aggressive collecting, mostly by Philip IV, led to a deep appreciation of contemporary and Old Master foreign artists. The collection included works by Bosch, Raphael, Titian, Annibale, Carracci, Reni, Van Dyck, and Rubens.

Politics, art, and a common bond of loyalty to the Catholic Church connected Italy and Spain in the seventeenth century. Spain, still in the throes of the Inquisition (a medieval institution that was established separately in Spain in 1478 to enforce religious orthodoxy and revived in Italy in 1542), was staunchly conservative and unflinching; their king was titled "The Most Catholic Majesty." Spain restricted membership of the Church to only those subjects who professed their unaltering loyalty, and imprisoned, executed, or expelled those who did not, while the Vatican used its resources to bring Protestant reformers and the disaffected back to the Church. The Counter-Reformation, or Catholic Reform, began in Rome with a style—Baroque—intended to convince viewers of the dynamism and power of the Catholic Church, its patrons, and defenders. And, at the beginning of the seventeenth century, the largest city on the Italian mainland, Naples, was under the rulership of Spain, so the impact of Baroque Roman art on Neapolitan and Spanish art was profound. Spanish Baroque art was heavily influenced by the style and subject matter of Caravaggio—directly and via Naples—but had a greater

faith. The result is surprisingly persuasive in both visual and expressive terms.

Such illusionism is quintessentially Baroque. So is the intense drama, which is heightened by the twisting poses and theatrical gestures of the figures. Algardi was obviously touched by Bernini's genius. Strangely enough, the relief is partly a throwback to an *Assumption of the Virgin* of 1606–10 in Santa Maria Maggiore by Bernini's father, Pietro. Only in his observance of the three traditional levels of relief carving (low, middle, and high,

starkness. Spanish naturalism may throw a harsher, stronger light on its subjects, but it is ultimately at least as sympathetic.

Spanish Still Life: Juan Sánchez Cotán

Still-life painting was unknown as a separate form until the 1590s. Spanish artists, inspired by the example of Pieter Aertsen (see fig. 18.31) and other Netherlandish painters, were the first to explore this new theme, and Spanish connoisseurs acquired vast collections of the resulting works. We see the distinctive character that Spanish artists brought to this new subject in this example (fig. **19.33**) by Juan Sánchez Cotán (1561–1627). This minor religious artist, who became a Carthusian monk, is remembered today as one of the first and most remarkable members of the Toledo school of still-life painters. Sánchez Cotán's painting has a clear order and stark simplicity, qualities that are completely controlled by the artist, who hung the vegetables with a fine string at different levels to coordinate the design—although whether the thin string would hold that full head of cabbage is a tantalizing question. Other vegetables sit on a ledge or sill. A window frames the still life: This orchestration of subject matter in direct sunlight against impenetrable darkness is the hallmark of early Spanish still-life painting. The painstaking realism in this stark setting creates a memorable image of the humble fruits and vegetables.

Although he probably used northern Italian paintings as his point of departure, Sánchez Cotán's still lifes make one think of Caravaggio, whose full impact on Spanish art, however, is not felt until considerably later. We do not know exactly how Caravaggism was transmitted. The likeliest route was through Naples, where Caravaggio had fled to safety and which was under Spanish rule.

Naples and the Impact of Caravaggio: Jusepe de Ribera

Caravaggio's main disciple in Naples was the Spaniard Jusepe de Ribera (1591–1652). Ribera settled there after having seen Caravaggio's paintings in Rome. Especially popular were Ribera's paintings of saints, prophets, and ancient beggar-philosophers. Their asceticism appealed strongly to the otherworldliness of Spanish Catholicism. Such pictures also reflected the learned humanism of the Spanish nobility, who were the artist's main patrons. Most of Ribera's figures possess a unique blend of inner strength and intensity.

His *The Club-Footed Boy* (fig. **19.34**) smiles openly and endearingly out at us, with a dimpled cheek, although we may be somewhat discomforted by his peasant dress, his begging, and his

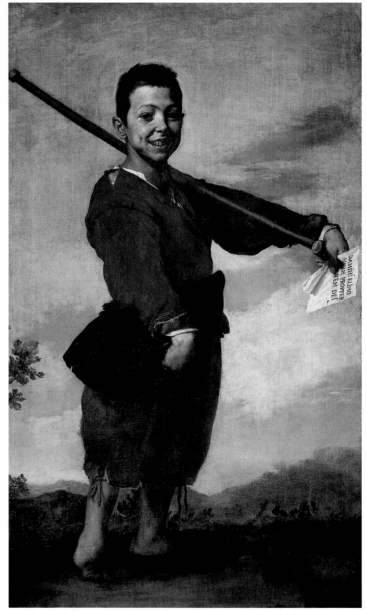

19.34   Jusepe de Ribera, *The Club-Footed Boy*. 1642. Oil on canvas, 64⅛ × 36⅝" (164 × 93 cm). Musée du Louvre, Paris

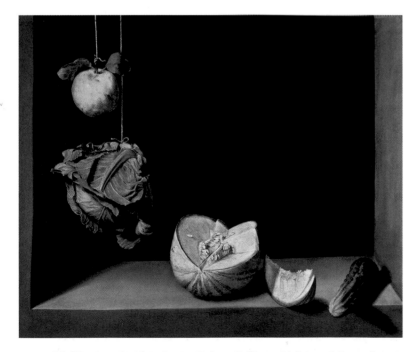

19.33   Juan Sánchez Cotán, *Quince, Cabbage, Melon, and Cucumber*. ca. 1602. Oil on canvas, 27⅛ × 33¼" (68.8 × 84.4 cm). San Diego Museum of Art. Gift of Anne R. and Amy Putnam. 1945:43

handicap. The words on the paper he holds state (in translation): "Give me alms for the love of God." This plea for charity alludes to the idea in Counter-Reformation theory that only through good works may the rich hope to attain salvation. The painting, indeed, was made for the viceroy of Naples, a wealthy collector who would have seen it as a testament to the importance of Christian charity and mercy to the poor. The boy seems almost monumental here as he stands against the broad sky with a low horizon line, like a musketeer; but instead of a weapon he holds a crutch across his shoulder. His deformed foot appears in shadow and one doesn't quite see it at first; but as the leg is lit, Ribera clearly directs our attention to it. The deformity may in fact not be a club foot but an indication of cerebral palsy. In either case, in the seventeenth century, such a deformity would have committed one to a life of begging.

Ribera executed other large paintings of beggars, of the poor, and of the blind. These were also the subjects of Pieter Bruegel the Elder (see fig. 18.34), who made prints and drawings of beggars using various crutches. As with Bruegel's works, *The Club-Footed Boy* is made with a moral purpose. The boy himself seems an embodiment of joy as he smiles, even laughs. This was considered a way for the subject to withstand misfortune, for he has the ability to dispense grace: He provides an opportunity for others to do good. Ribera's use of naturalism is a hallmark of Spanish and Neapolitan painting and etching, and it extends Caravaggio's impact. Caravaggism was felt especially in Seville, the home of the most influential Spanish Baroque painters before 1640: Diego Velázquez.

Diego Velázquez: From Seville to Court Painter

Diego Velázquez (1599–1660) painted in a Caravaggesque vein during his early years in Seville. His interests at that time centered on scenes of people eating and drinking rather than religious themes. Known as *bodegónes*, these grew out of the paintings of table-top displays brought to Spain by Flemish artists in the early seventeenth century. *The Water Carrier of Seville* (fig. **19.35**), which Velázquez painted at age 20 under the apparent influence of Ribera, already shows his genius. His powerful grasp of individual character and dignity gives this everyday scene the solemn spirit of a ritual. The scene is related to Giving Drink to the Thirsty, one of the Seven Acts of Mercy, a popular theme among Caravaggesque painters of the day. Velázquez's use of focused light and the revelation of shapes, textures, surfaces—from the glass of water to the sweat of water on the pottery jug—is extraordinary. He must have thought so, too, as he gave this painting to his sponsor, a royal chaplain from Seville, no doubt in hopes of gaining royal attention.

In the late 1620s, Velázquez was appointed court painter to Philip IV, whose reign from 1621 to 1665 was the great age of painting in Spain. Much of the credit for this must go to the duke of Olivares, who largely restored Spain's fortunes and supported an ambitious program of artistic patronage to proclaim the monarchy's greatness. Upon moving to Madrid, Velázquez

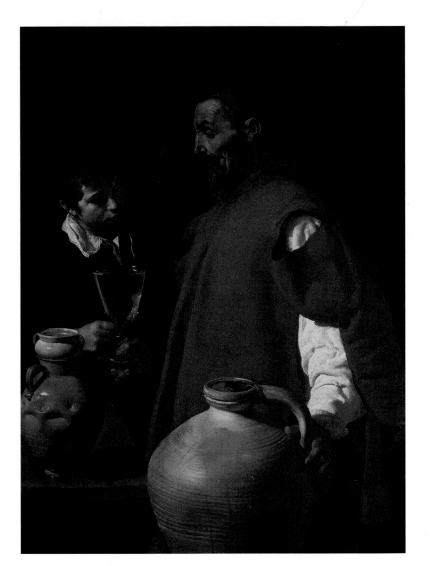

19.35 Diego Velázquez, *The Water Carrier of Seville*. ca. 1619. Oil on canvas, 41½ × 31½" (105.3 × 80 cm). Wellington Museum, London

quickly displaced the Florentines who had enjoyed the favor of Philip III and his chief minister, the duke of Lerma. A skilled courtier, the artist soon became a favorite of the king, whom he served as chamberlain. Velázquez spent most of the rest of his life in Madrid painting mainly portraits of the royal family. The earlier of these still have the strong division of light and dark and the clear outlines of his Seville period, but his work soon acquired a new fluency and richness.

SURRENDER AT BREDA During his visit to the Spanish court on a diplomatic mission in 1628, the Flemish painter Peter Paul Rubens helped Velázquez discover the beauty of the many Titians in the king's collection. We see this most immediately in Velázquez's *Surrender at Breda* (fig. **19.36**), a dramatic and lush painting with color as rich as Titian's. It, too, would have been in the royal collection, intended as part of a series for the king's Buen Retiro Palace. The subject is an interpretation of an event in the war between the United Provinces (the Northern Netherlands) and Spain which took place in 1625, just a few years before the

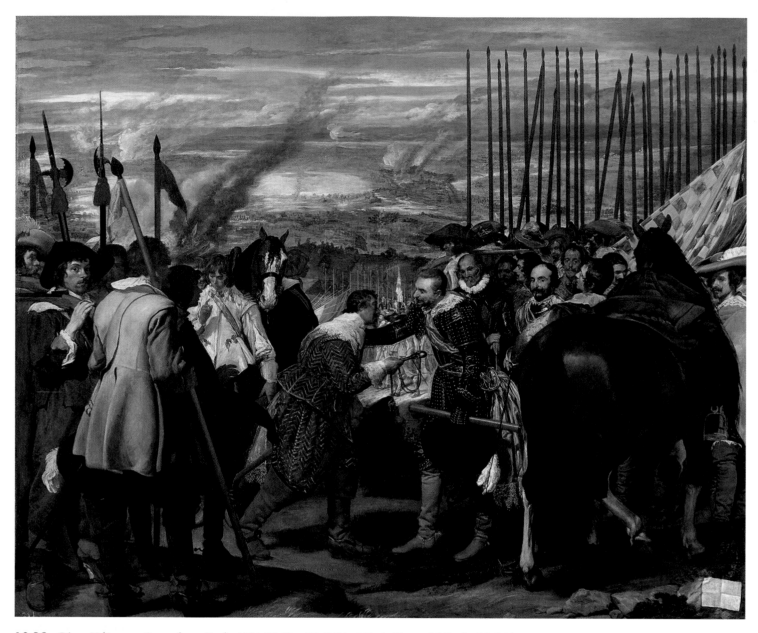

19.36 Diego Velázquez, *Surrender at Breda*. 1634–35. 10 × 12' (3.07 × 3.7 m). Museo del Prado, Madrid

painting's execution. Although the surrender did indeed occur, it certainly did not transpire in this elegant fashion. Here, the Dutch general, Justin of Nassau, on the left, bows to give the keys of the city to Spanish general, Ambrogio de Spinola, who has just gotten off his horse to meet his Dutch counterpart, even to comfort him: Note how he places his hand on the shoulder of the vanquished officer. Smoke comes from the left over the heads of the Dutch soldiers, who seem a bit dazed and forlorn, signaling the defeat of Breda. On the right are the Spanish troops who, by positioning themselves in front of the raised lances, seem to be standing more erect. Additional lances can be seen in the middle distance; one expects that the Spanish outnumbered the Dutch.

In truth, the Netherlands' revolt against Spain had ended by about 1585, with a truce in 1609, but conflicts (such as the one at Breda) continued to flare up. There were no keys to the city, and

the general probably did not get off his horse. By having the two generals confront each other not with hate but with acquiescence, Velázquez transforms a military drama into a human one. The scene Velázquez painted may in fact be derived from a contemporary play in which Spinola states: "Justin, I accept them [the keys] in full awareness of your valor; for the valor of the defeated confers fame upon the victor."

THE PORTRAIT OF JUAN DE PAREJA At court, Velázquez was famed as a portrait painter. As such, when Philip IV dispatched him to Rome in 1648 to purchase paintings and antique sculpture, he also gave permission for the artist to paint Pope Innocent X. But Velázquez's reputation seems not to have preceded him when he arrived in 1649, and he was left waiting for an interview with the pope. It was during this interlude that he

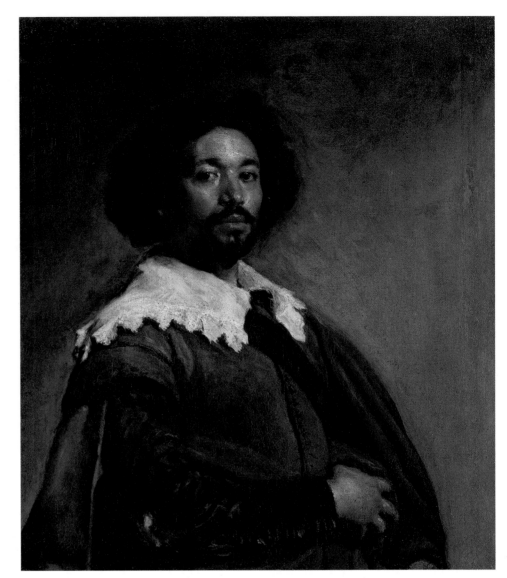

19.37 Diego Velázquez, *Juan de Pareja*. 1650. Oil on canvas, 32 × 27½" (81.3 × 69.9 cm). Metropolitan Museum of Art, New York. Purchase, Fletcher and Rogers Funds, and Bequest of Miss Adelaide Milton de Groot (1876–1967), by exchange, supplemented by gifts from Friends of the Museum, 1971. (1971.86)

painted the portrait of his Sevillian assistant and servant of Moorish descent, Juan de Pareja (ca. 1610–1670), who accompanied him to Rome and was an artist himself (fig. **19.37**). The portrait, stunningly lifelike, was acclaimed when it was exhibited at an annual art show in the Pantheon in Rome in March 1650. It was said that, of all the paintings, this one was "truth." Juan de Pareja is shown half-length, turned at a three-quarter view, but facing us—a triangular format developed by Raphael and Titian in the High Renaissance, simplifying the *Mona Lisa* (fig. 16.7), but still using it as their point of departure. As used here, the format rivets our attention to his face. The feathery lace collar, brilliantly painted, picks up the white highlights of the subject's face, creating a formidably sculptural visage. A white patch, a tear in his clothing at the elbow, reminds a viewer of his class, a device Velázquez had used earlier in *The Water Carrier of Seville*. The success of this portrait and Velázquez's sudden fame in Rome may have prompted the pope to sit for him, which he did, soon after.

THE MAIDS OF HONOR Velázquez's mature style is seen at its fullest in *The Maids of Honor* (fig. **19.38**). Both a group portrait

and a genre scene, it might be subtitled "the artist in his studio," for Velázquez depicts himself at work on a huge canvas. In the center is Princess Margarita, who has just posed for him, among her playmates and maids of honor. The faces of her parents, King Philip IV and Queen Maria Anna, appear in the mirror on the back wall. Their position also suggests a slightly different vantage point than ours, and indeed there are several viewpoints throughout the picture. In this way, the artist perhaps intended to include a viewer in the scene by implication, even though it was clearly painted for the king and hung in his summer quarters at the Alcázar Palace. Antonio Palomino, the first to discuss *The Maids of Honor*, wrote: "the name of Velázquez will live from century to century, as long as that of the most excellent and beautiful Margarita, in whose shadow his image is immortalized." Thanks to Palomino (see *Primary Source*, page 695), we know the identity of every person in the painting. Through the presence of the princess, king, and queen, the canvas commemorates Velázquez's position as royal painter and his aspiration to the Order of Santiago—a papal military order to which he gained admission only with great difficulty three years after the painting was

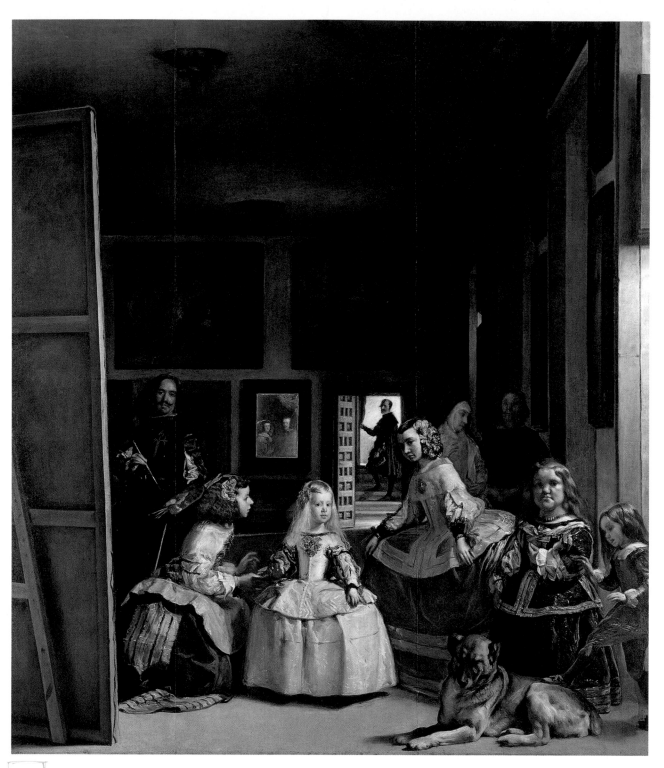

tenebrism

19.38 Diego Velázquez, *The Maids of Honor*. 1656. Oil on canvas, 10'5" × 9' (3.2 × 2.7 m). Museo del Prado, Madrid

executed. In the painting, he wears the red cross of the order, a detail added after his death.

Velázquez had struggled to establish his status at court. Even though the usual family investigations (almost 150 friends and relatives were interviewed) assisted his claim to nobility, the very nature of his profession worked against him. "Working with his hands" conveyed on Velázquez the very antithesis of noble status. Only by special papal dispensation was he eventually accepted into

the Order of Santiago. *The Maids of Honor*, then, is an expression of personal ambition; it is a claim for both the nobility of the act of painting and that of the artist himself. The presence of the king and queen affirm his status. The Spanish court had already honored Titian and Rubens (although not in the same way); as these artists were both held in high regard, they served as models for Velázquez and continued to have a significant impact on him. The painting reveals Velázquez's fascination with light as fundamental

Antonio Palomino (1655–1726)

From *El Museo Pictórica y Escala Óptica*: On Velázquez

In 1724, Palomino wrote a biography of Spanish artists with a special focus on Velázquez, whom he revered above others. The following is a description of Velázquez's The Maids of Honor, *identifying the figures and recording comments on its reception.*

Among the marvelous pictures done by Velázquez was a large canvas with the portrait of the Empress (then the Infanta of Spain), Margarita María of Austria, as a young child. ... Kneeling at her feet is María Agustina, maid of honor of the Queen, giving her water in a small vessel. On the other side is Isabel de Velasco, also a maid of honor, who seems to be speaking. In the foreground is a dog lying down and next to it Nicolas Pertusato, a dwarf, who is stepping on it to show that it is a gentle animal in spite of its ferocious appearance. These two figures are in shadow and impart great harmony to the composition. Behind is Mari-Bárbola, a formidable-looking dwarf, and slightly farther back and in darker colors are Marcela de Ulloa, attendant to the ladies-in-waiting, and a bodyguard. On the other side is Diego Velázquez painting; he holds the palette in his left hand and a brush in his right. Around his waist he wears the key to the King's Chamber and on his breast, the Cross of the Order of Santiago that was added at His Majesty's orders after Velázquez died, because Velázquez was not a member of this Order when the picture was painted. ...

The canvas on which he is painting is large, and nothing of what he paints can be seen because only the back part is visible.

Velázquez proved his great genius because of the clever way in which he reveals the subject of what he is painting. He makes use of the mirror at the rear of the gallery to show us the reflection of our Catholic kings, Philip and Mariana. In this gallery, which is called the Room of the Prince, where he used to paint, several pictures can be seen indistinctly on the walls. These are known to be by Rubens and represent stories from Ovid's *Metamorphoses*. This gallery has several windows that are shown in perspective to make the room seem large. The light comes from the [picture's] left but enters only through the front and rear windows. ... To the left of the mirror is an open door where stands Joseph Nieto, the Queen's Marshal. He can be clearly seen in spite of the distance and poor light. Between the figures there is atmosphere. The figure painting is superior, the conception new, and in short it is impossible to overrate this painting because it is truth, not painting. Velázquez finished it in 1656. ...

The painting was highly esteemed by His Majesty and he frequently went to look at it. It was placed in the King's lower suite, in the office, along with other excellent works. In our own day, Luca Giordano was asked by Charles the Second what he thought of it and he answered, "Sir, this is the theology of Painting."

Source: *Italian & Spanish Art, 1600–1750: Sources and Documents*, ed. Robert Enggass and Jonathan Brown (Evanston, IL: Northwestern University Press, 1999)

to vision. The artist challenges us to match the mirror image against the paintings on the same wall, and against the "picture" of the man in the open doorway. Although the side lighting and strong contrasts of light and dark still suggest the influence of Caravaggio, Velázquez's technique is far subtler. The glowing colors have a Venetian richness, but the brushwork is even freer and sketchier than Titian's. Velázquez explored the optical qualities of light more fully than any other painter of his time. His aim is to represent the movement of light itself and the infinite range of its effects on form and color. For Velázquez, as for Jan Vermeer in Delft (see pages 732–33), light *creates* the visible world.

Monastic Orders and Zurbarán

Francisco de Zurbarán (1598–1664) began his professional life as a painter, as did Velázquez, in Seville, and he stands out among his contemporaries for his quiet intensity. His most important works, done for monastic orders, are filled with an ascetic piety that is uniquely Spanish. *St. Serapion* (fig. **19.39**) shows an early member of the Mercedarians (Order of Mercy) who was brutally murdered by pirates in 1240 but canonized only 100 years after this

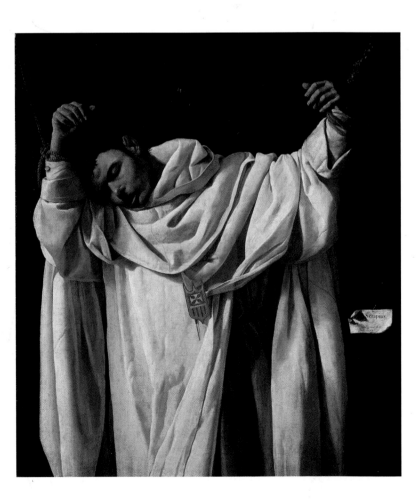

19.39 Francisco de Zurbarán, *St. Serapion*. 1628. Oil on canvas, 47½ × 41" (120.7 × 104.1 cm). Wadsworth Atheneum, Hartford, Connecticut. Ella Gallup Sumner and Mary Catlin Sumner Collection

picture was painted. The canvas was placed as a devotional image in the funerary chapel of the order, which was originally dedicated to self-sacrifice.

Zurbarán's painting reminds us of Caravaggio. Shown as a life-size, three-quarter-length figure, St. Serapion fills the picture plane: He is both a hero and a martyr. The contrast between the white habit and the dark background gives the figure a heightened visual and expressive presence, so that a viewer contemplates the slain monk with a mixture of compassion and awe. Here, pictorial purity and spiritual purity become one, and the stillness creates a reverential mood that complements the stark realism of the image. As a result, we identify with the strength of St. Serapion's faith rather than with his physical suffering. The absence of rhetorical pathos is what makes this image deeply moving.

Culmination in Devotion: Bartolomé Esteban Murillo

The work of Bartolomé Esteban Murillo (1617–1682), Zurbarán's (and, before him, Velázquez's) successor as the leading painter in Seville, is the most cosmopolitan, as well as the most accessible, of any of the Spanish Baroque artists. For that reason, he had countless followers, whose pale imitations obscure his real achievement. His many religious images, especially his depictions of the Virgin (fig. **19.40**), typified Spanish art's desire to promote the Virgin in the visual vocabulary of the seventeenth century, and they were much copied. The insistence on Virgin imagery defied the Protestant influence in much of Europe. The Immaculate Conception was controversial even among Catholics; the doctrine, promoted by Franciscans (Murillo was a lay member), says that the Virgin was conceived without Original Sin. Its detractors, led by the Dominicans, thought that she had been cleansed of sin in the womb after conception, but before birth. Paintings on this theme were used as propaganda to promote the Virgin's status so that the concept would, through art, become church dogma (accepted as true on the basis of faith); it was finally decreed as dogma in 1854. However, already in the seventeenth century there were spectacles of the "Immaculata" (processions carrying the image of the Immaculate Virgin) in Seville and papal declarations (notably by Alexander VII in 1661) that urged this change. Murillo was one of the major painters of this theme.

The haunting expressiveness of the Virgin's face and of the cherubs or angels has a gentle pathos that is more emotionally appealing than Zurbarán's austerity. This human warmth reflects a basic change in religious outlook. The Virgin's piety is shown

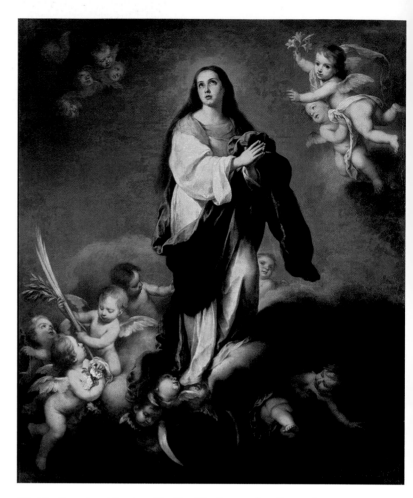

19.40 Bartolomé Esteban Murillo, *The Immaculate Conception*. ca. 1645–50. Oil on canvas, 7'8" × 6'5" (2.35 × 1.96 m). State Hermitage Museum, St. Petersburg, Russia

by her hands folded in prayer and upward glance to Heaven; she stands on a crescent moon, an attribute of the Immaculate Conception ("And there appeared a great wonder in Heaven: a woman clothed with the sun and the moon under her feet"—Revelation 12:1). The extraordinary sophistication of Murillo's brushwork and the subtlety of his color show the influence of Velázquez. Murillo succeeded so well that the vast majority of religious paintings in Spain and its South American colonies for the next 150 years were derived from his work. Although genre and still-life painting were also popular, the promotion of the Virgin in Spanish art defined Spain's Catholic and conservative art and its role in defying the Reformation of northern Europe.

The Baroque in Italy and Spain

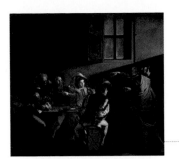

1599–1600 Caravaggio's
The Calling of St. Matthew

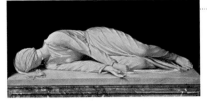

1600 Maderno's *Santa Cecilia*

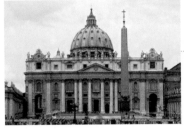

ca. 1602 Sánchez Cotán's
*Quince, Cabbage, Melon, and
Cucumber*

1607 Maderno begins completion of
St. Peter's Basilica

ca. 1638–39 Artemisia
Gentileschi's *Self-Portrait
as the Allegory of Painting*

1642 Borromini's
Sant'Ivo

1645 Bernini's
*The Ecstasy of
St. Teresa*

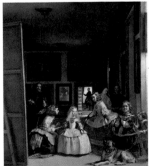

1656 Velázquez's *The Maids
of Honor*

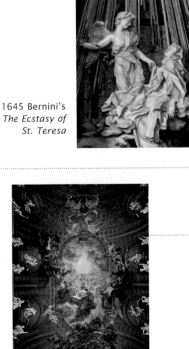

1672–79 Gaulli's *Triumph
of the Name of Jesus*

1590

1600

1610

1620

1630

1640

1650

1660

1670

1680

1690

1700

◄ 1594 Tintoretto dies

◄ 1605 Miguel de Cervantes writes *Don Quixote*
◄ 1607 First opera, *L'Orfeo* by Monteverdi, performed
◄ 1609 Galileo Galilei refines astronomical telescope

◄ 1614 El Greco dies

◄ 1621 Philip IV becomes king of Spain
◄ 1622 Ignatius of Loyola, founder of the Jesuit order,
Francis Xavier, Teresa of Ávila, and Filippo Neri, canonized
1623 Urban VIII assumes papal throne

◄ 1633 The Inquisition forces Galileo Galilei to recant

◄ 1644 Evangelista Torricelli invents barometer
1644 Innocent X assumes papal throne

◄ 1648 Treaty of Münster—Spain recognizes the
Netherlands

◄ 1653 Arcangelo Corelli, master of modern violin, born
◄ 1655 Alexander VII assumes papal throne

◄ 1678 Antonio Vivaldi, composer, born

◄ 1697 Treaty of Rijswijk between Spain and France
◄ ca. 1698–1709 Bartolomeo Cristofori invents the
modern piano

697

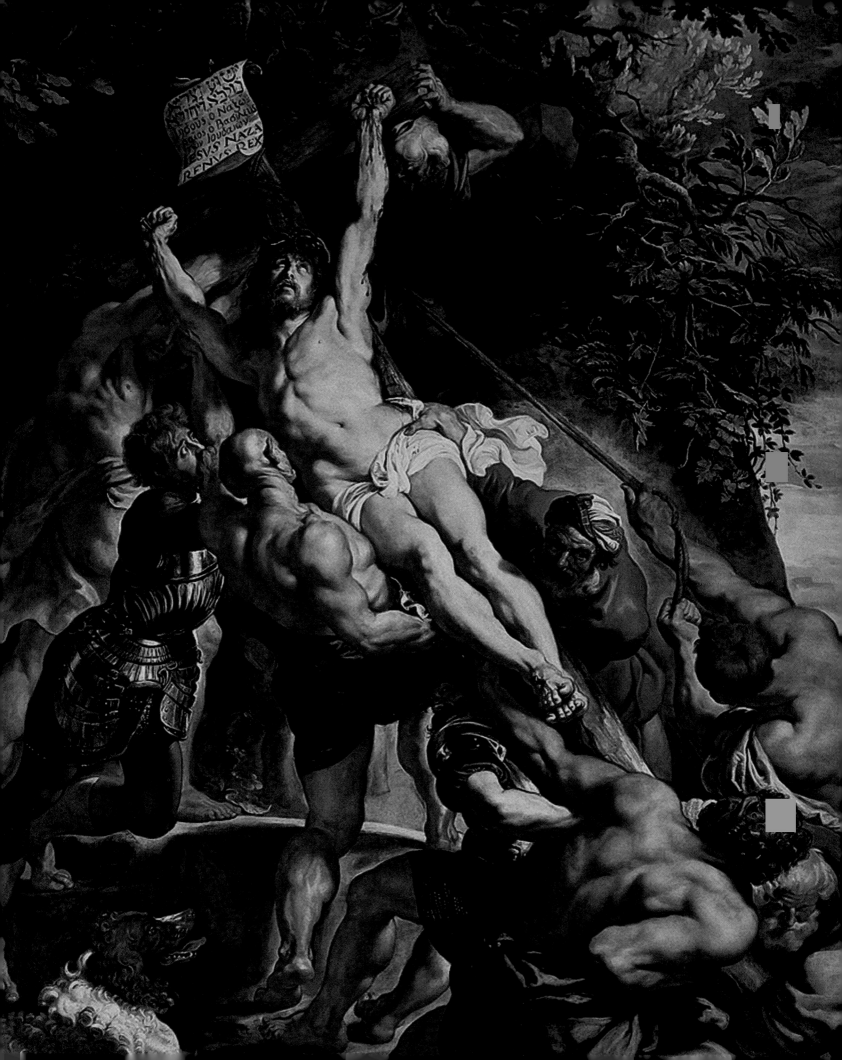

CHAPTER 20

The Baroque in the Netherlands

THE SEVENTEENTH CENTURY BROUGHT A DIVISION OF THE Netherlands into two parts: the Northern Netherlands (the present-day Netherlands) and the Southern Netherlands (present-day Belgium and part of France). Each is often known by the name of its most important province: Holland (North) and Flanders (South). The Catholic Spanish Habsburgs

had ruled the Netherlands in the sixteenth century, but Philip II's repressive measures against the Protestants and his attempts to curtail their autonomy led to a rebellion that lasted 15 years. In 1581, the northern provinces of the Netherlands, led by William the Silent of Nassau of the House of Orange, declared their independence from Spain. Spain soon recovered the Southern Netherlands in 1585, and Catholicism remained the official religion. After a long struggle, the seven major provinces of the North, whose inhabitants were predominantly of the Reformed Church, became the United Provinces and gained their autonomy, which was recognized by the truce declared in 1609. Although hostilities broke out once more in 1621, the freedom of the Dutch (i.e., the people of the North) was never again seriously in doubt. Their independence was finally ratified by the Treaty of Münster, which ended the Thirty Years' War in 1648. The Dutch Republic was formally recognized by the rest of Europe as an independent state.

The division of the Netherlands had very different consequences for the respective economies, social structures, cultures, and religions of the North and the South. At the same time, throughout the seventeenth century, people crossed back and forth between the two regions, so providing some social and

cultural fluidity. After being sacked by Spanish troops in 1576, Antwerp, the leading port of the Southern Netherlands, lost half its population: Many migrated to the Northern Netherlands. The city gradually regained its position as Flanders's commercial and artistic capital, although Brussels was the seat of government. As part of the Treaty of Münster, however, the Scheldt River leading to Antwerp's harbor was closed to shipping, thus crippling trade for the next two centuries. Because Flanders continued to be ruled by Spanish regents, the Habsburgs, who viewed themselves as the defenders of the "true" (i.e., Catholic) faith, its artists relied primarily on commissions from Church and State, but the aristocracy and wealthy merchants were also important patrons.

Holland, in contrast, was proud of its hard-won freedom. Although the predominant religion was the Reformed Church, the Dutch were notable for their religious tolerance. Even Catholicism continued to flourish there, and included many artists among its ranks, while Jews found a haven from persecution. While the cultural links with Flanders remained strong, several factors encouraged the quick development of specifically Dutch artistic traditions. Unlike Flanders, where most artistic activity radiated from Antwerp, Holland had a number of local schools of painting. Besides Amsterdam, the commercial capital, there were important artists in Haarlem, Utrecht, Leiden, Delft, and other towns who established local styles. Thus, Holland produced an almost bewildering variety of masters and styles.

Detail of figure 20.1, Peter Paul Rubens, *The Raising of the Cross*

The new nation was one of merchants, farmers, and seafarers, who may formerly have earned their living from local commerce such as the fishing trade, but who now had the opportunity to have more distant adventures with the development of the famous Dutch East India Company (known as the VOC from its Dutch initials), established in 1602, and its counterpart, established in 1621, the Dutch West India Company. These companies developed trade in East Asia (China, Japan, and Indonesia) and in the Americas, bringing home exotic wares (map 20.1, page 702), strange creatures, and fabulous flora and fauna, as well as engaging in exploration, map making, and the creation of colonial settlements. These adventures rippled though the economy: The sailors experienced them directly, but they also had a major impact on the directors and governors of the companies, who made their fortunes from these ventures. Even the townspeople who stayed home were able to purchase or at least see some of the wonders brought back from faraway places. From this time forward, the Dutch could never again be thought provincial; even those who did not travel could be considered, and would consider themselves, worldly.

As the Reformed Church was iconoclastic, Dutch artists rarely received the large-scale altarpiece commissions that were available throughout the Catholic world. While the House of Orange in The Hague and city governments and civic bodies such as militias provided a certain amount of artistic patronage, their demands were limited. As a result, private collectors became the painters' chief source of support. This was true before 1600, but the full effect of such patronage can be seen only after that date. There was no shrinkage of output. On the contrary, the public developed such an appetite for pictures that the whole country became gripped by a kind of collector's mania. During a visit to Holland in 1641, the English traveler John Evelyn noted in his diary that "tis an ordinary thing to find, a common Farmor lay out two, or 3000 pounds in this Commodity, their houses are full of them, and they vend them at their kermas'es [fairs] to very great gaines." Although it was unlikely farmers' houses were filled with paintings, or that Evelyn even visited them, there is no doubt paintings were not made only for the Church and the court. In the Northern Netherlands (as well as the Southern Netherlands), a new class of patron arose—the wealthy merchant.

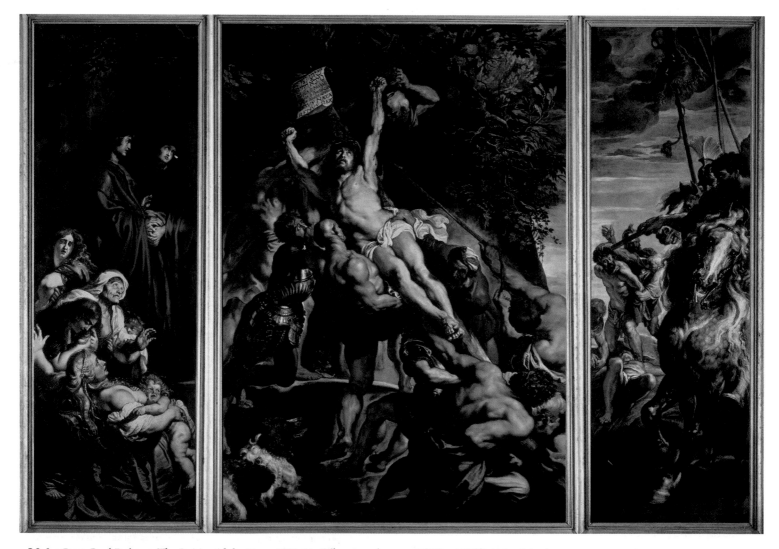

20.1 Peter Paul Rubens, *The Raising of the Cross*. 1610–11. Oil on panel, center 15'1" × 11'9⅝" (4.6 × 3.4 m), each wing 15' × 4'11" (4.57 × 1.52 m). Antwerp Cathedral, Belgium

FLANDERS

Art in seventeenth-century Flanders was defined by the art of Peter Paul Rubens. Rubens brought Flanders, really Antwerp, to international notice and the art of the Western world to Flanders. He did this through his own travels (bringing ideas back to Antwerp), his commissions, and his own extensive workshop.

Baroque art in Flanders was based on commissions. Its many churches could now, with the Truce of 1609 and hope of a sustained peace, be rebuilt and redecorated. The Habsburg archduke and archduchess, their family, and private patrons provided these commissions. Rubens's own interests were largely within the realm of painting, but his role in sculpture and sculptural decoration, architecture, costumes, and illustrated books (published by the famous Plantin Press in Antwerp) was still significant. All these art forms were directly affected by Rubens and his art.

The subjects of Flemish art, and of Rubens's paintings, were primarily religious—they were frequently large altarpieces with life-size figures, but portraits also accounted for many works. Although Rubens also executed landscapes, other artists, including Frans Snyders, Clara Peeters, Jan Davidsz. de Heem, and Jan Brueghel the Elder, frequently painted still lifes or "game pieces," sometimes in collaboration with Rubens. Rubens's one-time assistant Anthony van Dyck excelled in portraits and religious and mythological paintings, as did Jacob Jordaens, who also painted genre scenes. But all artistic efforts were influenced by Rubens.

Peter Paul Rubens and Defining the Baroque

Although the Baroque style was born in Rome, it soon became international. The great Flemish painter Peter Paul Rubens (1577–1640) played a role of unique importance in this process. He epitomized the Baroque ideal of the virtuoso artist, acting as diplomat and advisor, with an *entrée* to the courts of Europe. He was widely read and widely traveled, with a knowledge of classical literature and several languages. He was acclaimed for his intellect, and for a vitality that enabled him to unite the natural and supernatural and to attain a Baroque theatricality and drama that we have also seen in Bernini (see Chapter 19). He finished what Dürer had started 100 years earlier and Jan Gossaert had continued (see Chapter 18): the breakdown of the artistic barriers between Northern and Southern Europe. Rubens's father was a prominent Antwerp Protestant who had fled to Germany to escape Spanish persecution during the war of independence. The family had returned to Antwerp after his death, when Peter Paul was ten years old, and the boy had grown up a devout Catholic. Trained by local painters, Rubens became a master in Antwerp's Guild of St. Luke in 1598, but he only really developed a personal style when he went to Italy two years later.

During his eight years in Italy, in the art and patronage centers of Mantua, Genoa, Florence, and Rome, he absorbed the Italian tradition far more completely than had any northern European before him. He eagerly studied ancient sculpture, the masterpieces of the High Renaissance, and the work of Caravaggio and Annibale Carracci. In fact, Rubens competed on even terms with the best Italians of his day and could well have made his career in Italy: He received major commissions there for both portraits and altarpieces.

RUBENS AND THE ALTARPIECE *The Raising of the Cross* (fig. **20.1** and see page 698) was painted for the high altar of the church of St. Walburga (now destroyed). It was the first major altarpiece Rubens painted after his return to Antwerp in 1609. Its very subject (the *raising*) speaks to the dynamism of the Baroque and it shows how much he was indebted to his Italian experience. The muscular figures, modeled to show their physical power and passionate feeling, recall the antique Hellenistic sculpture that Rubens saw, drew, and collected (see *Primary Source*, page 704), and the figures from the Sistine Chapel ceiling that he also copied (fig. **20.2**). These works of art served as models for his heroic figures throughout his life. He also gathered inspiration from the Farnese Gallery, while the lighting suggests Caravaggio's work (see figs. 19.1–19.4 and 19.7). The composition of the altarpiece recalls that of Rosso's *The Descent from the Cross* (see fig.

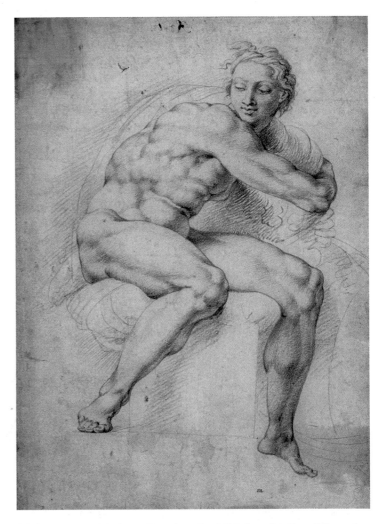

20.2 Peter Paul Rubens, *Drawing after Michelangelo's Ignudi from the Sistine Chapel Ceiling.* ca. 1601–02. Red chalk with touches of red wash, 15⅓ × 11" (38.9 × 27.8 cm). The British Museum, London

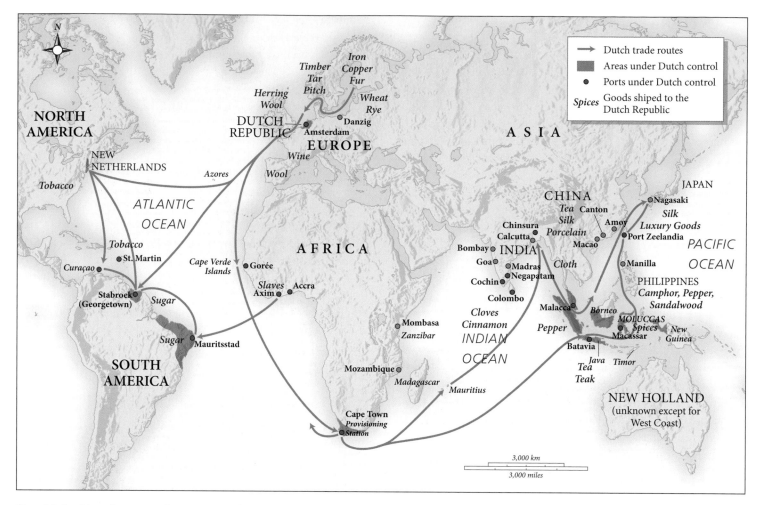

Map 20.1   Map of seventeenth-century Dutch trade routes

17.1), yet the painting is more heroic in scale and conception. Its rich color and luminosity, especially in the sky and background of the right wing, is ultimately indebted to the influence of Titian (see fig. 16.31). Thus, the altarpiece owes much of its success to Rubens's ability to combine Italian influences with Netherlandish ideas, thereby creating something entirely new. Rubens is also a Flemish realist in such details as the foliage, the armor of the soldier, and the curly-haired dog in the foreground. These varied elements are integrated into a composition of tremendous force. The unstable pyramid of bodies, swaying precariously under the strain of the dramatic action, bursts the limits of the frame in a typically Baroque way, making a viewer feel like a participant in the action.

Christ is shown parallel to the plane, so that we fully see him being raised to the crucifixion. The "raising" implies movement and action that is happening at that moment. Rubens extended the figure groups into both wings with an implied continuous landscape background. On the left are the Virgin and St. John, with horrified women; on the right are Roman soldiers; on the back of the wings (not shown here) are saints.

The altarpiece would have been 35 feet high in its final form—the main triptych was beneath a now-lost painting of God the Father, which explains Christ's heavenward imploring glance. He was surrounded by angels and a sculpted pelican (a symbol of God's sacrifice) topped the work. The painting was placed on the high altar at the top of 19 steps, so the entire altarpiece ensemble—dramatic, powerful, and monumental—would have towered above all else.

Rubens's epic canvases define the scope and style of High Baroque painting. They possess a seemingly boundless energy and inventiveness, which, like his heroic nudes, express life at its fullest. And his portraits were equally inventive and dramatic.

RUBENS AS PORTRAITIST   Rubens was one of the greatest and most influential portraitists of the seventeenth century, recording the vast wealth and stature of his often noble patrons. He painted several portraits while in Italy and maintained contacts with his Genoese patrons for years after he left. His resplendent portrait of Marchesa Brigida Spinola Doria (fig. **20.3**), a member of the ruling class of Genoese banking families, who invested in trade with Africa and the East, was painted in 1606, probably in celebration of her wedding at age 22.

Although still a large painting, it was even more monumental in the seventeenth century—perhaps 9 feet high—before being cut down on all four sides. A nineteenth-century lithograph of the painting shows that the Marchesa was originally full-length, and was shown striding from the terrace of her palazzo. She is

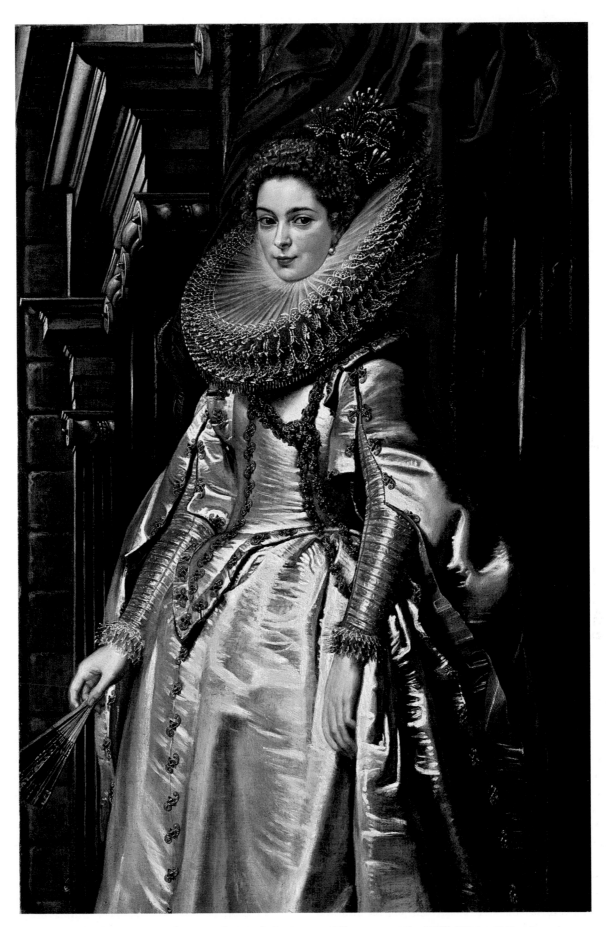

20.3   Peter Paul Rubens, *Marchesa Brigida Spinola Doria*. 1606. Oil on canvas, 5' × 3'2⅞" (152.2 × 98.7 cm).
The National Gallery of Art, Washington, D.C. Samuel H. Kress Collection. 1961.9.60.

Peter Paul Rubens (1577–1640)

From a Letter to Sir Dudley Carleton

In 1618, Rubens began a correspondence with Sir Dudley Carleton (1573–1632), the English ambassador to The Hague, in order to arrange an exchange of the Englishman's antique sculptures for his own paintings. Well-traveled and with diplomatic appointments to Paris and Venice (he was later made secretary of state), Carleton had acquired a notable collection of antique sculpture during his time in Italy (1610–15). Rubens, too, had a collection that he began to amass during his own stay in Italy (1600–1608). In his first letter, Rubens proposed an exchange for "pictures by my hand," and explains that the paintings he proposes to offer are the "flower of his stock," implying that many paintings by Rubens were not in fact executed for specific commissions but were kept by him (he lists 12 paintings in his house). The deal went through, and Rubens then had the greatest collection of antique sculpture in northern Europe, until he in turn sold part of it a few years later. In the end, 123 marbles from Carleton were exchanged for nine paintings by Rubens and three by Tintoretto, as well as a set of tapestries from Rubens's collection.

Most Excellent Sir:

By the advice of my agent, I have learned that Your Excellency is very much inclined to make some bargain with me concerning your antiquities; and it has made me hope well of this business, to see that you go about it seriously, having told him the exact price that they cost you. In regard to this, I wish to place my complete trust in your knightly word. ... Your Excellency may be assured that I shall put prices on my pictures, just as if I were negotiating to sell them for cash; and in this I beg you to rely upon the word of an honest man. I find that at present I have in the house the flower of my stock, particularly some pictures which I have kept for my own enjoyment; some I have even repurchased for more than I had sold them to others. But the whole shall be at the service of Your Excellency, because I like brief negotiations, where each party gives and receives his share at once. To tell the truth, I am so burdened with commissions, both public and private, that for some years to come I cannot commit myself. Nevertheless, in case we agree as I hope, I will not fail to finish as soon as possible all those pictures that are not yet entirely completed, even though named in the list here attached. [*In the margin:* The greater part are finished.] Those that are finished I would send immediately to Your Excellency. In short, if Your Excellency will resolve to place as much trust in me as I do in you, the matter is settled. I am content to offer Your Excellency of the pictures by my hand, enumerated below, to the value of 6,000 florins, at current cash prices, for all those antiquities in Your Excellency's house, of which I have not yet seen the list, nor do I even know the number, but in everything I trust your word. Those pictures which are finished I will consign immediately to Your Excellency, and for the others that remain in my hands to finish, I will furnish good security to Your Excellency, and finish them as soon as possible. ...

From Your Excellency's most affectionate servant,
Peter Paul Rubens

Antwerp, April 28, 1618

Source: *The Letters of Peter Paul Rubens*, ed. and tr. Ruth Saunders Magurn (Cambridge, MA: Harvard University Press, 1971)

---

sumptuously dressed in white satin, with a matching cape, bejeweled with a rope of gold set with gems of onyx and rubies. Her huge, multilayered ruff, typical of her time and class, frames her face, and her red hair is arranged with decorative combs of pearls and feathers. The vast flowing red cloth, which unfurls behind her, contrasts with her dress and heightens the color of her face. The diagonal movement of this drapery also suggests her forward stride. The size, full-length view, elements of movement, and color against her face are just a few of the aspects that influenced Rubens's student and assistant Anthony van Dyck (see figs. 20.7 and 20.8) in his portraits. Later stately portraits of the eighteenth and nineteenth centuries also reflect such influences.

OIL SKETCHES Rubens executed hundreds of oil sketches in preparation for his final works. They are small—small enough to hand to a patron—and represent the working art of preliminary concepts. An oil sketch for *The Raising of the Cross*, for example, suggests a less dynamic composition, changed in the final painting.

Four Studies of the Head of a Negro (fig. **20.4**) is not a sketch for any known larger piece, but we do know that Rubens used Africans in several of his paintings; studying the features and nuanced expressions of this man informed his work. It has been claimed that the four studies were done on separate occasions

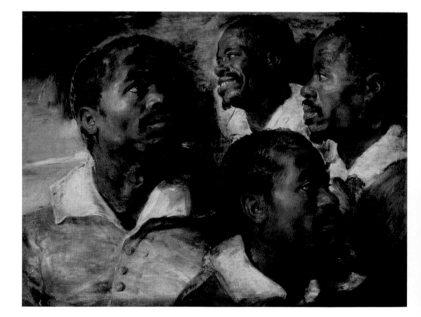

20.4   Peter Paul Rubens. *Four Studies of the Head of a Negro.* ca. 1613–15. Oil on panel transferred to canvas, 20 1/12 × 26" (51 × 66 cm). Musées Royaux des Beaux Arts de Belgique, Brussels, Belgium

over a few years, suggesting that this man was in Antwerp over an extended period—or left and returned. It is therefore likely that this African was a servant or a slave in a wealthy household. Rubens does not indicate his status; he is concerned only with his expressive sharply chiseled face.

MARIE DE' MEDICI CYCLE Rubens exhibited his virtuoso talent in portraits and monumental historical works in the 1620s with his famous cycle of paintings glorifying the career of Marie de' Medici, widow of Henry IV and mother of Louis XIII, in the Luxembourg Palace in Paris. The cycle consists of 21 paintings at least 13 feet high, with some as much as 28 feet wide. Rubens executed more than 35 sketches for these enormous paintings. Our

illustration shows one episode: the young queen landing in Marseille (fig. **20.5**). Rubens has turned an ordinary disembarkation into a spectacle of unparalleled splendor, combining reality and allegory. As Marie de' Medici walks down the gangplank to enter France; she has already married Henry IV by proxy in Florence, but is yet to meet her husband. Accompanied by her sister and aunt as the allegorical figure, Fame flies overhead sounding a triumphant blast on two trumpets; she is welcomed by the allegorical figure of France draped in a *fleur-de-lis* cape. Neptune and his fish-tailed crew, the Nereids, rise from the sea; having guarded the queen's journey, they rejoice at her arrival. Everything flows together here in swirling movement: Heaven and earth, history and allegory.

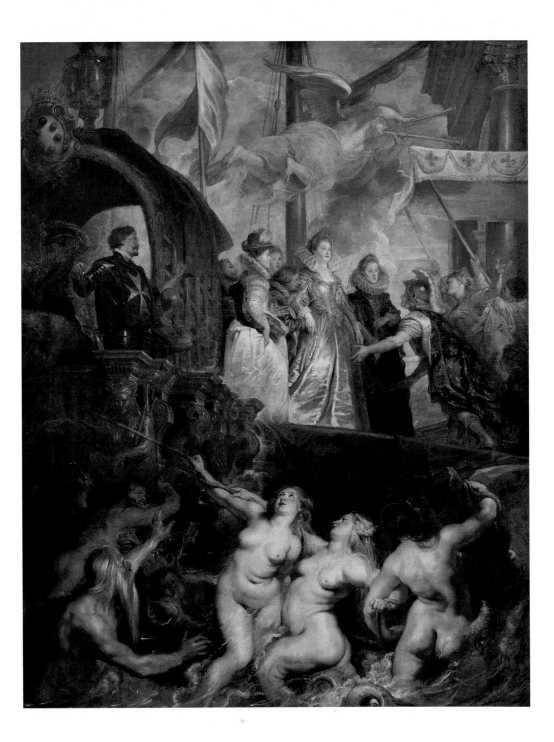

20.5   Peter Paul Rubens,
*Marie de' Medici, Queen of France,
Landing in Marseilles
(November 3, 1600).* 1622–25.
Oil on canvas, 12'11½" × 9'7"
(3.94 × 2.95 m).
Musée du Louvre, Paris

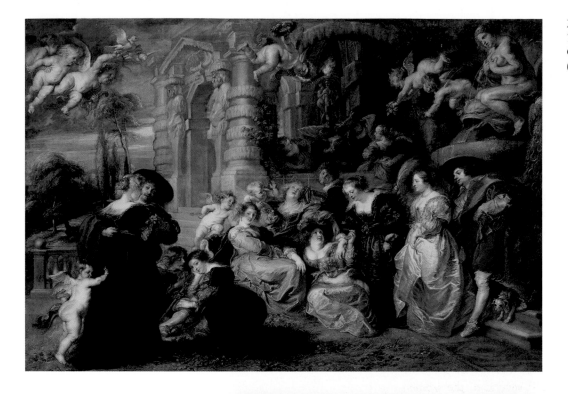

20.6 Peter Paul Rubens, *The Garden of Love.* ca. 1638. Oil on canvas, 6'6" × 9'3½" (2 × 2.8 m). Museo del Prado, Madrid

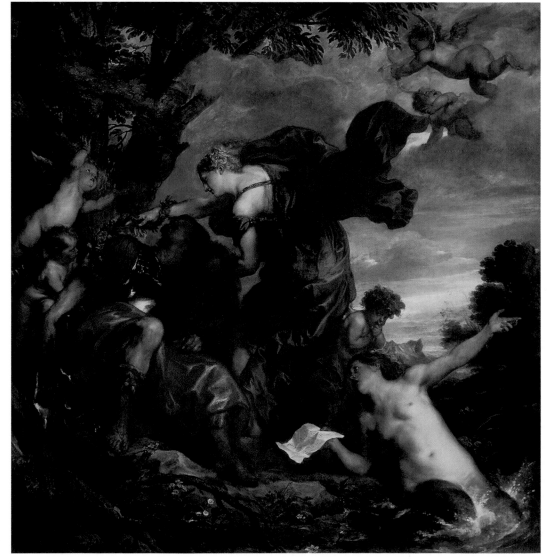

20.7 Anthony van Dyck, *Rinaldo and Armida*. 1629. Oil on canvas, 7'9" × 7'6" (2.36 × 2.24 m). The Baltimore Museum of Art, Baltimore, MD. The Jacob Epstein Collection. 1951.103

RUBENS'S WORKSHOP To produce these large paintings, painting cycles, ceilings, and altarpieces, Rubens needed a large workshop; most of the Flemish artists working in the early seventeenth century studied with him at some point. They often traveled with him, worked on paintings he had begun or sketched, or began paintings for him to complete.

Rubens worked as a painter and a royal emissary. Diplomatic errands gave him entry to the royal households of the major powers, where he received numerous commissions. His duties took him to Paris, London, and Madrid—having already been to Italy—and he went to the Northern Netherlands to find an engraver for his work. He was truly an international artist.

LATE RUBENS In the 1630s, after Rubens remarried at the age of 53, his art turned inward and he made many paintings of his beautiful young wife, home, and children. He even wrote of being "at home, very contented." Rubens's *The Garden of Love* (fig. **20.6**) is a glowing tribute to life's pleasures. It shows couples, cupids, and a lifelike statue of Venus (at the upper left) in a garden in front of a building, much like Rubens's own Italianate house in Antwerp. Suggestions have been made that the male figure on the left is actually Rubens, and several of the women (mostly, the center-seated one) look like his new wife, Hélène Fourment. Certainly, the sensuality of *The Garden of Love* parallels changes in his life. This painting and the Paris *Marie de' Medici Cycle* would influence eighteenth-century Rococo painting (see page 763).

Anthony van Dyck: History and Portraiture at the English Court

Besides Rubens, only one other Flemish Baroque artist won international acclaim: Anthony van Dyck (1599–1641). He was that rarity among painters: a child prodigy. Before he was 20, he had become Rubens's most valued assistant. Like Rubens, he developed his mature style only after a stay in Italy.

As a history painter, Van Dyck was at his best in lyrical scenes of mythological love. *Rinaldo and Armida* (fig. **20.7**) is taken from Torquato Tasso's immensely popular poem about the crusades, *Jerusalem Freed* (1581), which gave rise to a new courtly ideal throughout Europe and inspired numerous operas, as well as paintings (a popular subject of Tiepolo, see page 781). Men and women at court masques played the roles of Christian Knight and Bewitching Sorceress in acting out this love-and-adventure story. Van Dyck shows the Sorceress falling in love with the Christian Knight she had intended to slay. The canvas reflects the ideals of Charles I, the English monarch for whom it was painted, and who found parallels in his own life with Tasso's epic. The English monarch, nominally a Protestant, had married the Catholic Henrietta Maria, sister of his main rival, the king of France. Charles saw himself as the virtuous ruler of a peaceful realm much like the Fortunate Isle where Armida had brought Rinaldo. (Ironically, Charles's reign ended in civil war.) The artist tells his story of ideal love in the pictorial language of Titian and Veronese,

with an expressiveness and opulence that would have been the envy of any Venetian painter. The picture was so successful that it helped Van Dyck gain an appointment to the English court two years later.

Van Dyck's fame rests mainly on the portraits he painted in London between 1632 and 1641. The *Portrait of Charles I Hunting* (fig. **20.8**) shows the king standing near a horse and two grooms in a landscape. Representing the sovereign at ease, the painting might be called a "dismounted equestrian portrait," and it is vastly different in effect from Holbein's *Portrait of Henry VIII* (see fig. 18.24). It is less rigid than a formal state portrait, but hardly less grand, for the king remains in full command of the state, which is symbolized here by the horse, which bows its head toward its master. The fluid movement of the setting complements the self-conscious elegance of the king's pose, which continues the stylized grace of Hilliard's portraits (see fig. 18.25). Charles's political position, however, was less secure than his confidence here suggests. He was beheaded by his subjects in 1649. Charles was succeeded by the puritan leader Oliver Cromwell and his followers, known as the "Roundheads" in reference to

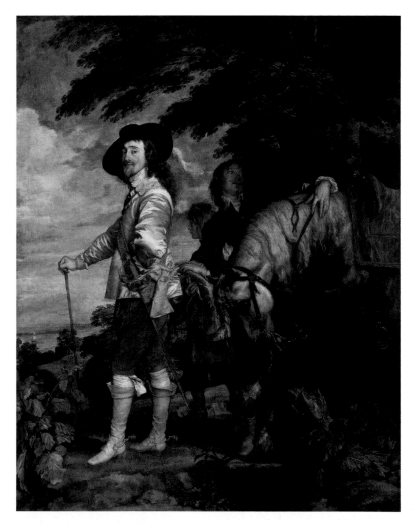

20.8 Anthony van Dyck, *Portrait of Charles I Hunting*. ca. 1635. Oil on canvas, 8'11" × 6'11½" (2.7 × 2.1 m). Musée du Louvre, Paris. Inv. 1236

their short-cropped hair. In contrast, note that in the painting Charles I's tresses drop below his shoulder in the French (Catholic) manner. However, despite Charles's execution, his son, Charles II, assumed the throne later in the period known as the Restoration.

Van Dyck has brought the court portrait up-to-date by using Rubens and Titian as his points of departure. He died eight years before the beheading of Charles I and so never had the chance to work for Charles's successors. But he created a new aristocratic portrait tradition that continued in England until the late eighteenth century and which had considerable influence on the Continent as well.

Local Flemish Art and Jacob Jordaens

Jacob Jordaens (1593–1678) was the successor to Rubens and Van Dyck as the leading artist in Flanders. Jordaens was quite prolific and is known for his paintings, drawings, watercolors, and designs for tapestries. Unlike his predecessors, he did not travel to Italy, although he received commissions from outside the country—

from the Northern Netherlands, as well as from the court of Sweden and a limited one from England. Although Jordaens was never formally a student of Rubens, he was a member of his workshop, and he collaborated with the older artist, turning to him for inspiration throughout his career.

Jordaens's most characteristic subjects are mythological themes and works depicting eating and drinking such as his *The King Drinks* (fig. **20.9**), one of several versions he executed of this popular subject marking the feast of the Epiphany or Three Kings, which in Flanders is celebrated on January 6th. Traditionally, on this date friends and family gather for a large dinner where a "king" is chosen, often by lot. But in Jordaens's paintings it is always the oldest man; usually, as is the case here, the appearance of the king is based on the features of his father-in-law and former teacher, Adam van Noordt (1562–1641), although we should not suppose this work to be a family portrait. Other roles—the queen, a musician, a jester (seen at top left)—are also assigned. Jordaens shows the most exuberant moment when all toast and shout: "The King drinks!" This is a particularly rowdy scene where the physician (identified from his cap) vomits

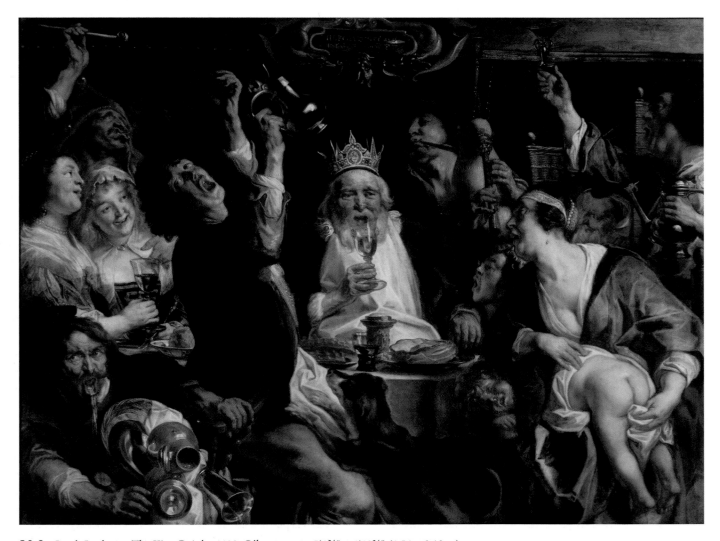

20.9 Jacob Jordaens, *The King Drinks*. 1638. Oil on canvas, 5'1⅖" × 6'10⅔" (1.56 × 2.10 m).
Musées Royaux des Beaux Arts, Brussels, Belgium

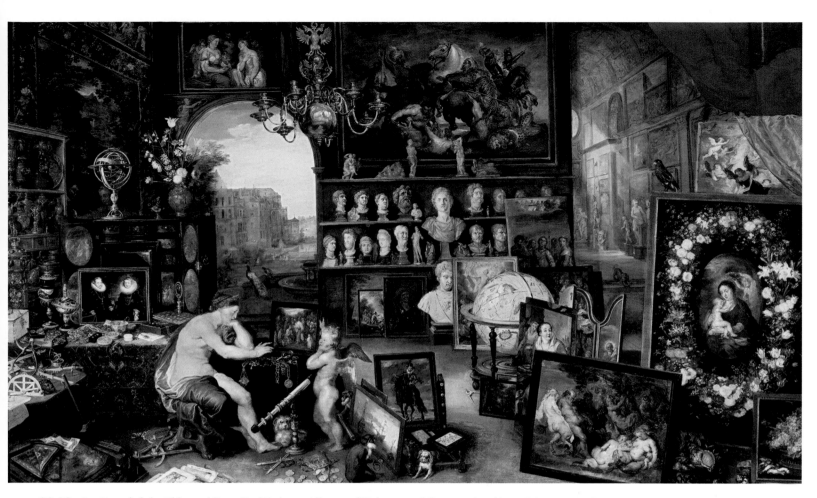

20.10 Jan Brueghel the Elder and Peter Paul Rubens, *Allegory of Sight*. 1617. Oil on panel, 25⅝ × 43" (65 × 109 cm). Museo del Prado, Madrid

on the left while a boy's bottom (not even an infant's!) is being wiped on the right—neither activity is suitable for a dinner table, but together they make a joyous painting. The painterly execution and figure types show a strong debt to Rubens, but Jordaen's figures are not idealized. There is a softness, roundness, and plainness to his life-size figures which distinguish his work. His paintings were purchased or commissioned by the newly prosperous middle class.

The Bruegel Tradition

Jan Brueghel the Elder (1568–1625) was the principal heir of the tradition of his illustrious father, Pieter Bruegel the Elder (see Chapter 18), whom he hardly knew but whose work he copied. Jan Brueghel was largely a still-life painter and one of the innovators of the "art collection" paintings that are unique to Flanders and that provide us with a view into the depth and variety of European "art collections" which developed in the princely quarters of Antwerp in the seventeenth century. These eclectic collections were known as *Kunstkammern* (literally "rooms of art") or *Wunderkammern* ("rooms of wonder"), and they give us a glimpse of the vast collections of exotica, from seashells, insects,

and rare flowers to scientific instruments and paintings, that were accumulated by the aristocracy and the wealthy at that time.

His *Allegory of Sight* (fig. **20.10**) from a set of *The Five Senses* (paintings illustrating the senses of touch, smell, hearing, taste, and sight), each of the same size, executed with Rubens, shows such a *Wunder-* or *Kunstkammer*. The *Allegory of Sight*, viewed in an art gallery and appreciated only by seeing, is, of course, meant as a visual pun. The art collection seen here is that of the Habsburg archduke and archduchess (Albert and Isabella), depicted in a double portrait on the left (by Rubens), and suggests the wealth and splendor of the court. A double-headed eagle—the symbol of the Habsburgs—tops the brass chandelier. Albert and Isabella were Catholic rulers who would have associated this homage to the visible world with spiritual insight (explaining the painting of the Virgin and Child in the foreground). We obviously only glimpse part of the collection in the foreground, as the background at right indicates other rooms with more items (at left is a view of their castle outside Brussels), but the collection of paintings is prime here. We see scientific instruments (telescopes, globes), a Persian carpet (suggesting the bounty of the world), Roman portrait busts, and large and small paintings: portraits, mythological scenes, and still lifes. Some of the paintings are recognizably by

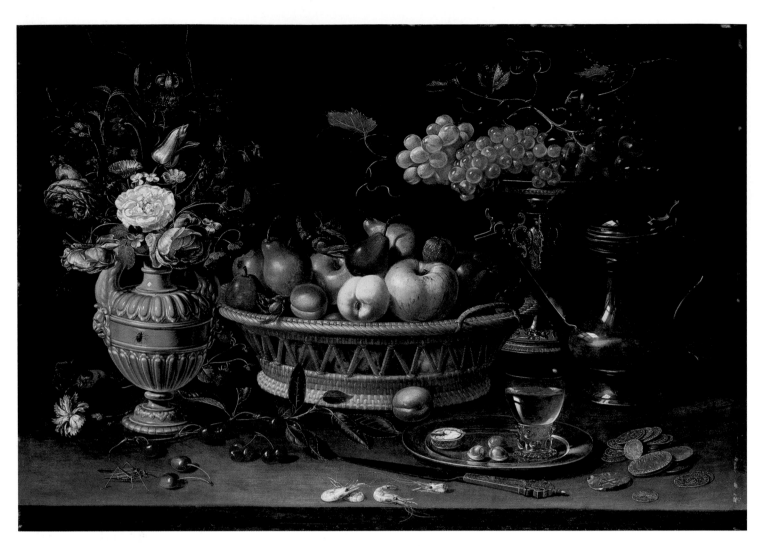

20.11 Clara Peeters, *Still Life with Fruit and Flowers.* ca. 1612. Oil on copper, 25⅛ × 35" (64 × 89 cm). Ashmolean Museum, Oxford

Rubens and indicate his wide range—from a mythological scene featuring Silenus at the lower right to a lion and tiger hunt at the top left. The large painting seen at right showing the Virgin and Child encircled by a wreath of flowers, like the *Allegory of Sight* itself, is a collaborative effort between Brueghel and Rubens. In any collaboration, Brueghel would have begun the work, leaving areas for Rubens to fill in later, and then Brueghel would have returned to add the finishing touches. Jan Brueghel also collaborated with other artists and was a noted flower painter.

Still-Life Painting

Still-life painting in seventeenth-century Flanders took many forms—paintings of flowers, game, food, and precious objects. Even Jan Brueghel's *Allegory of Sight* enters into this realm. We usually do not know who commissioned these works and presume they were for private patrons for their homes.

The century opens with predominantly simple paintings, but by midcentury this genre has begun to explore the elaborate and dramatic explosion of objects collected at that time.

EARLY STILL LIFE: CLARA PEETERS Probably born in Antwerp, and most closely associated with that city, Clara Peeters (active 1607–ca. 1621) may have also worked in Haarlem, in the Netherlands. Her name, however, is not listed in any archival record in these cities, even though their guilds began to admit women and the number of signed works by Peeters indicate that she was a professional artist. Little is known of her life, patrons, or teachers. Nevertheless, she created some of the earliest still-life paintings. *Still Life with Fruit and Flowers* (fig. **20.11**) is an early work that combines studies of both flowers and fruit and displays several different containers, exploring a variety of textures. In the center is a basket of fruit (apples, pears, plums, apricots, and filberts), flanked on the left by a bouquet of colorful flowers (roses, a tulip—a flower relatively new to western Europe, columbine, a marigold, a cornflower, borage, wild pansies, forget-me-nots, and lilies) in a white pottery vase. On the right is a pewter wine tankard (with a reflection of Peeters) and a silver *tazza* (an Italian-made plate) holding a bunch of grapes. Also on the right is a pewter plate with a glass of white wine and some nuts. Strewn across the wooden tabletop are prawns, a carnation, a plum, cherries, a grasshopper, a strawberry, some gold and silver coins, and a knife.

Although the natural life here is plentiful, it is the coins and knife that are particularly important for both dating and determining the possible use or meaning of the painting. The coins have been dated to the reign of the Archduke Albert and Archduchess Isabella (1598–1621), and, based on the painting's style, a date of 1612 has been suggested. The knife (with its matching fork not seen here) is quite special and is of a type given as a wedding or betrothal gift. The same knife appears in several of Peeters's paintings and was probably copied from an actual one. It is inscribed in Latin with the words "fidelity" and "temperance," and is illustrated with small allegorical figures with hearts and clasped hands. Such a knife would often be inscribed with the bride's name; here, it is inscribed "Clara Peeters." Thus, it has been suggested that she painted the work in celebration of her own wedding—and that all the fruits and flowers represent the bounty and hopefulness of this event. Such paintings were frequently hung in the dining rooms of houses and complemented the meals and festivities. Many of Clara Peeters's paintings still remain in private collections today.

GAME STILL LIFE: FRANS SNYDERS A frequent collaborator with Rubens, Frans Snyders (1579–1657) studied with Pieter Brueghel the Younger (1564–1638), a son of Pieter Bruegel the Elder (see figs. 18.32–18.34) and with Jan Brueghel the Elder (see fig. 20.10). His splendid *Still Life with Dead Game, Fruits, and Vegetables in a Market* (fig. **20.12**) is the first known "gamepiece" and is a masterpiece of its kind.

Large and small items of game are for sale, but unlike the wares in Pieter Aertsen's *The Meat Stall* (fig 18.31) these animals are whole and unbutchered. The sale of game was newly regulated (as of 1613) by laws detailing hours, location (in front of town halls as shown here), and season. Anyone who followed those rules could set up a stand and give the middle class—not just the privileged nobility—a legal and easily accessible way to purchase venison and other prized game.

The artist revels in the virtuoso application of paint to create the varied textures of the game. The youth picking the old man's pocket (he is greeting us, the middle-class customer, and not paying attention to what is going on around him) and the cocks fighting in the foreground, as a cat looks on from the shadows beneath the low bench, further enliven the scene. Snyders subordinates

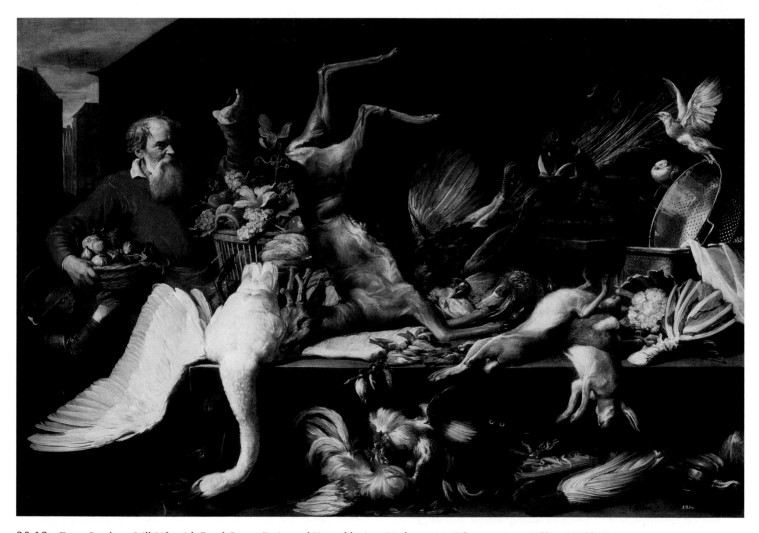

20.12 Frans Snyders, *Still Life with Dead Game, Fruits, and Vegetables in a Market*. 1614. Oil on canvas, 6'11⅞" × 10'3⅝" (2.1 × 3 m). The Art Institute of Chicago. Charles H. and Mary F. S. Worcester Fund, 1981.182

everything to the ensemble, which is characteristically Baroque in its lavishness and immediacy. The painting celebrates a time of peace and prosperity after the truce of 1609, when hunting was resumed in the replenished game preserves.

THE FLAMBOYANT STILL LIFE: JAN DAVIDSZ. DE HEEM

By midcentury, still-life paintings often presented lavish displays. These were known as **pronk** still lifes for their visual splendor, as *pronk* means "showy" or "ostentatious." This type reached its peak in the work of Jan Davidsz. de Heem (1606–1684). De Heem began his career in Holland but he soon moved to Antwerp, where he transformed the still life with his unique, flamboyant style. His *Still Life with Exotic Birds* (fig. **20.13**) is a spectacular example. He depicts sumptuous commodities—delicious food, exotic birds, and luxurious goods—from around the world (see map 20.1). The conch and nautilus shells are from the West Indies, the gray parrot is from Africa, the scarlet macaw is from Brazil, and the brilliant lobsters are probably from the New World; the Seville oranges, plums, figs, melons, oysters, gilt goblet, and silver ewer are all imported, commanding high prices in the marketplace. It is the whole world in one picture. And De Heem magnificently details the colors and textures of each of the objects.

The food is piled up on pewter platters that are unstable and suggest extravagance. Unlike in the even, horizontal compositions of Peeters (see fig. 20.11), the silver pitcher, pewter plate, Venetian glass, and gilt goblet are set in varying heights, building up to a climax with the exotic birds.

De Heem intends this display to be wondrous and theatrical, drawing back a curtain for us to see what is behind it. Even the column in the background is meant to suggest a heroic work. The result is a stunning, celebratory display that reveals the virtuosity of De Heem and defines the elements of the new style of *pronk* still life.

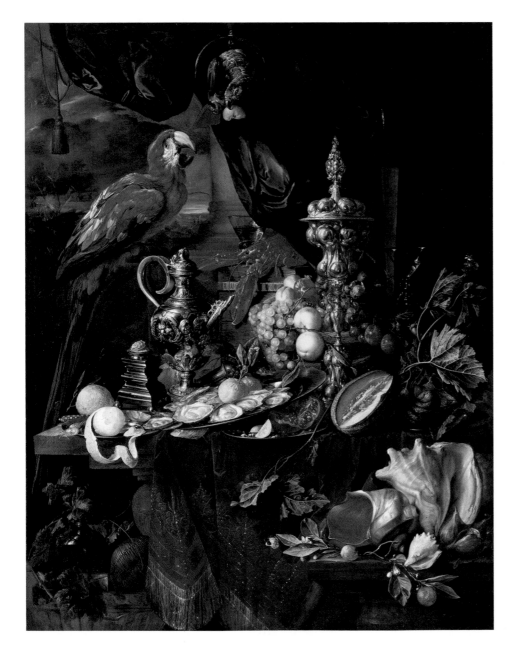

20.13 Jan Davidsz. de Heem, *Still Life with Exotic Birds*. Late 1640s. Oil on canvas, 59¼ × 45½" (150.5 × 115.5 cm). Collection of the John and Mable Ringling Museum of Art, the State Art Museum of Florida, Sarasota, Florida. Bequest of John Ringling, 1936, SN289

THE DUTCH REPUBLIC

Art in the Dutch Republic, unlike the art of Flanders, was not based largely on church or state commissions, but was one conducted primarily through private patronage and an open art market. Pictures became a commodity, and the trade in them followed the law of supply and demand. Many artists produced for the market rather than for individual patrons. Yet even the greatest masters were sometimes hard-pressed and could not fully support themselves with the money earned from their art. It was not unusual for an artist to keep an inn or run a small business on the side.

There were many artists—enough to form artistic communities—in Haarlem, Utrecht, Amsterdam, and Delft, to name but a few. Artists frequently traveled between these cities and may have known each other's work, but most artists are usually associated with only one place—Hendrick Goltzius, Frans Hals and Judith Leyster with Haarlem; Hendrick Terbrugghen with Utrecht; Rembrandt with Amsterdam; and Jan Vermeer with Delft. Some of the paintings were religious in nature, but most were not. There were individual portraits, group portraits commissioned by civic groups, landscapes, cityscapes, architectural paintings, still lifes, and genre paintings.

There were many types of paintings, and they ranged from large to small in size—small enough to hold in your hand or for ordinary people to hang on the walls of their homes.

The Haarlem Academy: Hendrick Goltzius

Like Rubens, Van Dyck, and even Jan Brueghel the Elder, many Dutch artists learned of the greatness of contemporary art in Rome and of its roots in antiquity by going there. And some, like Hendrick Goltzius (1558–1617), made numerous prints and drawings on their sojourn and brought them back for their own and others' use. Goltzius (with two other artists, Karel van Mander and Cornelis Cornelisz van Haarlem) created an "academy" in Haarlem in 1585. We know little about it, but copying from prints, from antiquity, and from each other was part of their program. The academy also produced teachers for the next generation and made the city of Haarlem a focal point for early Dutch painting, printmaking, and drawing.

The collaborative efforts of the academy seem to be limited to Goltzius's engravings of the works by his colleagues. He was a masterful engraver, whose injured hand (burned in a childhood accident) may have provided the force behind his deep curvilinear cuts in the metal. (See *Materials and Techniques*, page 501.) He also executed woodcuts and only began painting after 1600.

The engraving of the *Farnese Hercules* (fig. **20.14**) illustrates the back of the Hellenistic sculpture owned by the Farnese family, housed in their palace, and also immortalized in a painting on a ceiling there (see fig. 19.7). It is seen here in its monumental, heroic scale, being viewed by two Dutch men—probably Goltzius's two companions in Italy during his trip of 1590–91. In many ways, it is an allegory for the wide-eyed Dutch experience in Rome—awed by this city filled with ruins, architecture, and

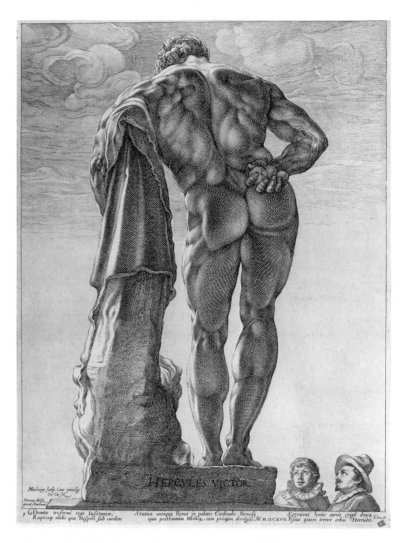

20.14 Hendrick Goltzius, *Farnese Hercules*. ca. 1597. Engraving, 16½ × 11¾" (418 × 301 cm). Metropolitan Museum of Art, New York. Gift of Henry Walters, 1917. (17.37.59)

sculpture of an ancient past. (Indeed, the Dutch would later decide to keep as ruins those buildings nearly destroyed by the Spanish so as to have their own ruins of a heroic past.) This *Hercules*, like others in the same series, is also a very large print—a Herculean effort. Goltzius's trip to Italy was taken before the appearance of Caravaggio and the Baroque, and thus it was the art of the past, rather than contemporary Italian works, that had an impact on him.

The Caravaggisti in Holland: Hendrick Terbrugghen

The Baroque style came to Holland from Antwerp through the work of Rubens, and from Rome through contact with Caravaggio's followers. Although most Dutch painters did not go to Italy, the majority of those who went in the early years of the century were from Utrecht, a town with strong Catholic traditions. One of those artists from Utrecht, Hendrick Terbrugghen (1588–1629), worked in Italy for several years and was one of the first

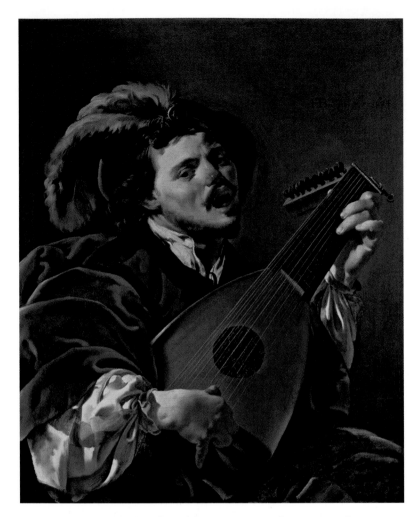

20.15 Hendrick Terbrugghen, *Singing Lute Player*. 1624. Oil on canvas, 39⅝ × 31" (100.5 × 78.7 cm). The National Gallery, London

"Caravaggisti" to return to the North. He adapted Caravaggio's style for religious paintings, but also for the single-figure genre painting. Terbrugghen's *Singing Lute Player* (fig. **20.15**) is inspired by Caravaggio's painting of the same subject, by his *Musicians* (see fig. 19.4) and by the young men in his *The Calling of St. Matthew* (see fig. 19.2), who wear slashed doublets and feathered berets. Such life-size, half-length single-figure portraits, filling the entire canvas, became common in Utrecht and grew popular elsewhere in Holland. The Utrecht School transmitted the style of Caravaggio to other Dutch masters, such as Frans Hals.

The Haarlem Community and Frans Hals

One of the first to profit from these new ideas permeating the Dutch Republic was Haarlem artist Frans Hals (ca. 1585–1666), who was born in Antwerp. Hals captured his contemporaries in both portraiture and genre painting, and he excelled at combining the two—animating his portraits and setting his subjects in somewhat relaxed or even casual stances. His genre painting, usually of single figures, portray characters that seem to be drawn from real life.

HALS AND THE CIVIC GUARD Hals's six group portraits of the Civic Guards allowed him to provide multiple enlivened, life-size portraits in single dynamic paintings. The Civic Guards, founded in the fourteenth century, were local voluntary militia groups that were instrumental in defending their cities through military service. They also had civic and religious duties, and they began having their portraits painted in the early sixteenth century. Although they had successfully defended their cities from the Spanish in the 1580s and, indeed, were proud of this accomplishment, with the truce of 1609, the Civic Guards became more like civic fraternities, with annual banquets, as seen in the *Banquet of the Officers of the St. George Civic Guard* (fig. **20.16**). The military aspects are indeed subordinated to the sense of general prosperity orchestrated in ritual. The captain in the center back wields a knife, but not as a military weapon; he is about to cut the roast. As was the custom, the colonel at the left raises his wine glass at the entrance of the standard-bearer with an unfurled banner. The highest-ranking officers are seated, while the men of lower rank and the servants stand at the back. The subjects arranged around a table laden with food on a white damask tablecloth, turn and face each other and the viewer. But 12 men around a table beg comparison with Leonardo's *The Last Supper* (see fig. 16.6). This is an undeniably secular painting, yet the event depicted is steeped in ceremony.

Although the painting vividly suggests a moment in time at an actual gathering, art historians do not believe that Hals here painted an actual event. The officers did not pose for this seating. The realism comes from the life-size scale, their gestures, the three-dimensional modeling created by paint applied "wet-in-wet" (while initial paint is still wet) with strokes of varied width and length. This modeling generated its own vibrancy, and thus the men appear as "speaking likenesses." The Civic Guard painting would become a staple in Haarlem and also in Amsterdam. Rembrandt's *The Night Watch* (see fig. 20.23) represents another form of this standard.

In Hals's painting, the black-and-white fashions offset with the red-and-white sashes nearly vibrate, creating a brilliant tableau. These men, the officers of the company, were wealthy citizens (in the case of Haarlem, they were brewers and merchants) who may have used their civic service to further their careers in government. Some even engaged Hals to execute individual portraits of themselves and family members; Hals himself became a member of the company in 1612.

A WEDDING PORTRAIT Hals's only double portrait, *Married Couple in a Garden* (fig. **20.17**), probably commemorates the wedding in 1622 of Isaac Massa (1586–1643) and his wife, Beatrix van der Laen (1592–1639). It combines the relaxed informal atmosphere of genre painting with the individual likenesses and formal attire of portraiture. This life-size couple modestly display their affection by sitting close together. Her arm is loped over his elbow, so displaying her rings (customary on the index finger); they smile broadly, their eyes twinkling, as they sit in a garden— an imaginary Garden of Love—surrounded by ivy, a symbol of steadfast love (as the ivy clings to the tree), faithfulness, and

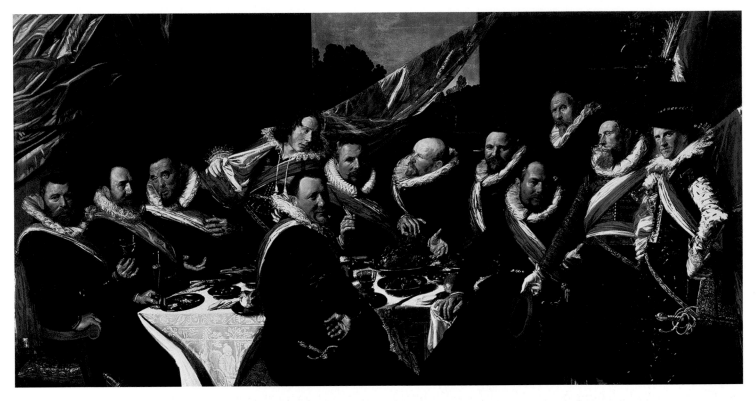

20.16 Frans Hals, *Banquet of the Officers of the St. George Civic Guard*. 1616. Oil on canvas, 5'9" × 10'7½" (175 × 324 cm). Frans Hals Museum, Haarlem

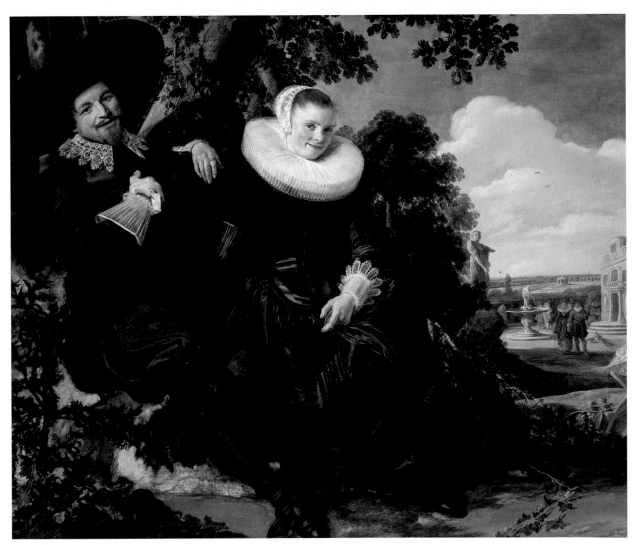

20.17 Frans Hals, *Married Couple in a Garden: Portrait of Isaac Massa and Beatrix van der Laen*. ca. 1622. Oil on canvas. 55 × 65½" (140 × 166.5 cm). Rijksmuseum, Amsterdam

fidelity. Indeed, they seem in love with each other. His right hand touches his chest (his heart) as a show of his intended affection. This painting makes a sharp contrast with Jan van Eyck's *The "Arnolfini Portrait"* (see fig. 14.14), and whether we interpret that earlier couple's presence as signaling a betrothal, wedding, or contract, we can see that the emotional tie between the Arnolfini couple was not Van Eyck's concern. This is more than a difference in personal artistic style; it is the difference between the Renaissance and the Baroque, developing over the course of 200 years. Between Van Eyck and Hals also stood Rubens, who had executed a wedding portrait of himself and his first wife that may have served as an example to Hals.

Ingeniously, Hals set the couple off-center, which adds to the spontaneity; there is also a sense that Massa, open-mouthed, is speaking to us. They wear expensive lace cuffs; his is the lace collar customary for men whereas she wears a millstone collar, with an embroidered and ribboned cap, usually worn indoors or under another hat. He wears a broad-brimmed hat in the new French fashion. Her skirt is of silk; her *vlieger* (bodice) of velvet with broad shoulders is of a kind worn only by married women, so it identifies her status.

Hals painted Massa, an important and wealthy diplomat, at least two more times as a single figure. Massa had an adventurous life: He was a geographer and a cartographer of Siberia. He traveled to Russia in 1600 and lived there for eight years, becoming fluent in the language. He was active in the fur trade and influential in establishing trade routes between the Netherlands and Russia. But his worldliness is only barely suggested in this wedding portrait set in his own garden.

HALS AND GENRE PAINTING Hals's mature style is seen in *The Jolly Toper* (fig. 20.18), which perhaps represents an allegory of taste, one of the Five Senses, which were among the most popular themes in the seventeenth century. The painting combines Rubens's robustness with a focus on the "dramatic moment" that Hals must have derived from Caravaggesque painters in Utrecht. Everything here conveys complete spontaneity: the twinkling eyes and half-open mouth, the raised hand, the teetering wineglass, and—most important of all—the painter's quick way of setting down the forms. Hals worked in dashing brushstrokes, each so clearly visible that we can almost count the total number of "touches." Thanks to this open, split-second technique, the completed picture has the immediacy of a sketch. The impression of a race against time is, of course, deceptive. Hals undoubtedly spent hours on this life-size canvas, but he maintains the illusion of having done it all in the blink of an eye.

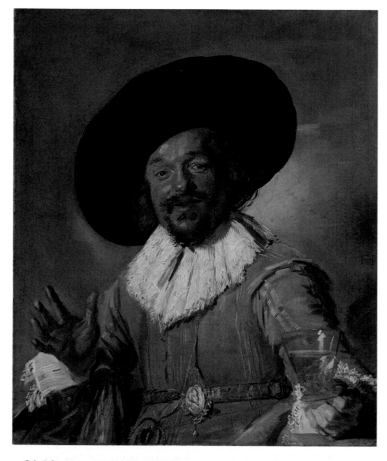

20.18   Frans Hals, *The Jolly Toper*. ca. 1628–30. Oil on canvas, 31⅞ × 26¼" (81 × 66.6 cm). Rijksmuseum, Amsterdam

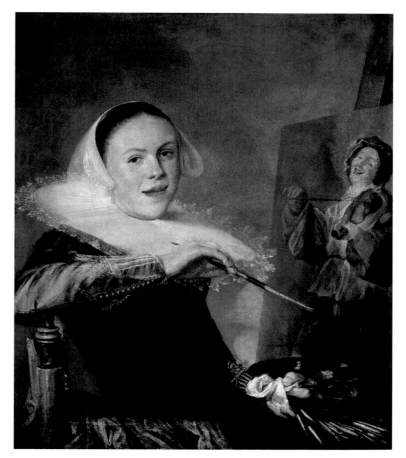

20.19   Judith Leyster, *Self-Portrait*. ca. 1633. Oil on canvas, 29⅜ × 25⅝" (72.3 × 65.3 cm). National Gallery of Art, Washington, D.C. Gift of Mr. and Mrs. Robert Woods Bliss. 1949.6.1

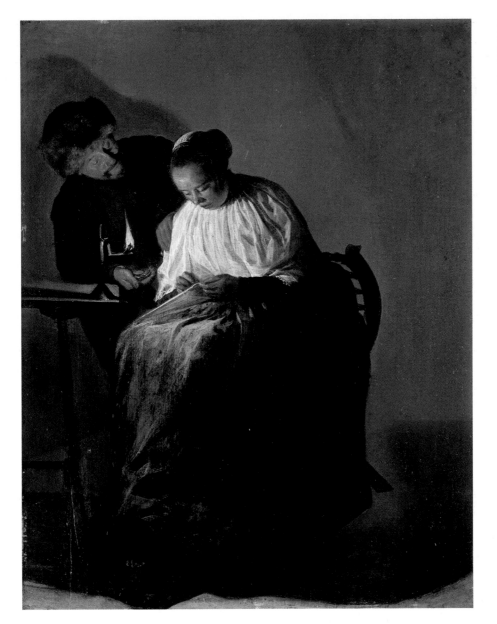

Hals, like Rembrandt van Rijn and Jan Vermeer, whom we will meet later in this chapter, is most closely identified with a period referred to as the Golden Age of Dutch Art. Individually these three artists took their northern heritage and developed from it the unique style of seventeenth-century Dutch art in Haarlem, Amsterdam, and Delft, respectively. Neither Hals, nor Rembrandt, nor Vermeer traveled to Italy.

The Next Generation in Haarlem: Judith Leyster

The most important follower of Hals was Judith Leyster (1609–1660), who was responsible for a number of works that once passed as Hals's own. She painted portraits and still lifes, but mostly genre paintings. Her *Self-Portrait* (fig. **20.19**) shows Leyster as both a portrait and genre painter, and was executed to show her mastery of both. It was probably her presentation piece to the Guild of St. Luke in Haarlem in 1633, when she became a

master and took on her own students. The painting on the easel is a detail of a popular work of hers; she uses this canvas to advertise her diverse talents. It also reveals her technical skill as she wields numerous brushes and a palette as she sits in her studio, open-mouthed, casually conversing with us. Many women artists, as Leyster does here, showed themselves painting—indicating their new professional status and their unique position. Indeed, Artemisia Gentileschi's *Self-Portrait as the Allegory of Painting* (*La Pittura*) (see fig. 19.6), executed about the same time, explores this same theme.

Leyster also explored the relationship between men and women in her work—and frequently used candlelight scenes to create mood and intimacy. Leyster's small lamplit *The Proposition* (fig. **20.20**) is one such painting. A man in a beaver hat (a foreigner) with coins in his hand approaches a woman who is diligently sewing. Is he offering to pay for her needlework? Clearly not. What are the clues to what he really wants? Leyster assigns the figures to a dark setting, whose lighting suggests intimacy. His

Authenticity and Workshops: Rubens and Rembrandt

Rubens and Rembrandt are among the many artists who ran workshops employing other artists. Anthony van Dyck, Frans Snyders, and Jan Brueghel the Elder worked with Rubens as well as independently. Frequently, paintings by Rubens will be attributed to "Rubens and Workshop." By contrast, the idea of collaboration with Rembrandt in a workshop has been slow to develop. The notion of Rembrandt as a solitary genius endured through the twentieth century and has only recently been more carefully scrutinized. Paintings found to be not wholly by Rembrandt have been "demoted" and attributed to an artist of his workshop instead. Art historians have thus begun to rethink workshop practices.

According to some art historians, Rembrandt's oeuvre (the number of paintings he produced) was almost a thousand; other historians thought he had produced a few hundred. In the 1960s, as exhibitions celebrating the 300th anniversary of his death were being organized (for 1969), it became clear that art historians had different views of who Rembrandt was and what he did. As such, in 1968, the Rembrandt Research Project was set up, establishing a team of art historians who would use scientific methods as well as connoisseurship to establish the authenticity of works attributed to Rembrandt. They would study the wood and canvas supports, date the wood

(a process called dendochronology), take x-rays, use infrared photography, examine paints and ground samples, and view the paintings in raking (strong) light. The researchers made their reports and jointly issued three volumes, *The Corpus of Rembrandt Paintings*, reporting on works painted in 1625–31, 1631–34, and 1635–42; a fourth volume is devoted to self-portraits. Because of deaths and retirements, the committee's personnel has since changed, but the project continues.

Although their deliberate and scientific examinations have been incredibly useful and have provided a model for others engaged in such endeavors, their analysis of the attributions of Rembrandt works into three categories, A, B, and C, has been controversial: "A" for authentic works by Rembrandt; "B" for paintings that cannot be either accepted or rejected as authentic (the "B" category has been sarcastically labeled by some as "Bothersome"); and "C" for works rejected as inauthentic and to be attributed to others, usually to named followers of Rembrandt. What is missing from this list, of course, is the notion of collaboration—the usual workshop method we have seen in the case of Rubens. Although Rembrandt and Rubens both had active workshops over the course of their careers, art historians have chosen to view the art from these workshops differently.

---

hand touches her shoulder. Indeed, in today's jargon, she is being "hit on" by the intruder. A copy of the painting, which introduces a wine glass, points to what is missing here—any inference that the woman is interested. Such proposition paintings were in fact common, but they usually differ from this example in that they are often jovial and larger, showing women as active participants in this exchange of sex for money. Many were painted by the Utrecht Caravaggisti whose works Leyster may have known through her family's stay near Utrecht. Her painting differs markedly from these, though, as the woman does not appear interested. This intriguingly different point of view has been attributed to the fact that the artist is a woman. The painting is signed with her monogram, a conjoined "J," "L," and star, punning on her name, which means "leading star." Indeed, Leyster was referred to and celebrated during her lifetime as a "leading star" in art.

After her marriage to a fellow student of Hals's, Jan Miense Molenaer (ca. 1610–1668), the couple moved from Haarlem to Amsterdam where Leyster continued to paint, although the main body of her oeuvre was executed in Haarlem. Leyster's exploration of domestic genre painting and the poetic quality of the light in her canvases means that her work bridges the generation gap between the Caravaggisti and Jan Vermeer (see figs. 20.34 and 20.35).

Rembrandt and the Art of Amsterdam

Like Hals and Leyster, Rembrandt van Rijn (1606–1669) was influenced indirectly by Caravaggio through the Utrecht School. Rivaling Rubens as the most famous artist of his age, Rembrandt is

perhaps the better-known of the two today. A painter, draftsman, and printmaker, he is equally significant in each medium. Rembrandt is known both for the intimacy and poignancy of his images which convey personal relationships and emotions (see www.myartslab.com)—an aspect seldom explored before—as well as for producing large group portraits and history pieces. He had an active workshop (see *The Art Historian's Lens*, above) for four decades and many of his followers became significant artists in his native Leiden or in Amsterdam, where he established himself.

REMBRANDT'S DRAWINGS The poignancy of his drawings can be seen in many of his studies "from life"—that is, made with the model before him. He drew in pen and ink, wash, red or black chalk, silverpoint, and combinations of these. Rembrandt's drawing of his wife, *Portrait of Saskia van Uylenburgh* (fig. **20.21**), upon their engagement, is executed in silverpoint, an unforgiving drawing tool (commonly used before the invention of the pencil) that requires precision and a sure hand, on parchment. It is clearly meant as a very special drawing to commemorate their betrothal. The inscription states (in Dutch): "This is drawn after my wife, when she was 21 years old, the third day of our betrothal, the 8th of June 1633." They were married a year later; the drawing shows a dreamy-eyed Saskia looking very much in love with the viewer (the artist). She wears a straw hat, usually associated with shepherdesses, country life, and pastoral, amorous scenes. The flowers in her hat and hands further embellish this idea. Saskia came from a well-to-do family and was the niece of Rembrandt's art dealer.

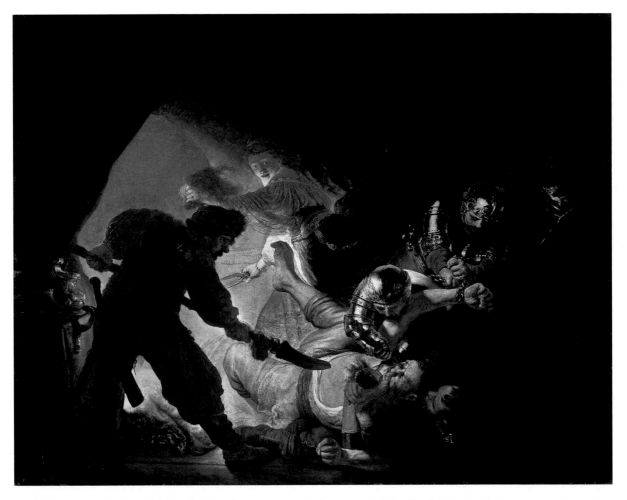

20.21 Rembrandt van Rijn, *Portrait of Saskia van Uylenburgh*. 1633. Silverpoint on white prepared parchment, arched at the top, 7¼ × 4" (18.5 × 10.7 cm). Staatliche Museen Preussischer Kulturbesitz, Kupferstichkabinett, Berlin. Inv. Kdz 1152

Her features appear in many of the paintings and studies for etchings he made before her death at the age of 30 in 1642.

REMBRANDT'S PAINTINGS Rembrandt's earliest paintings are small, sharply lit, and intensely realistic. Many deal with Hebrew Bible subjects, a lifelong preference on the part of the artist. (See www.myartslab.com; see also figs. 20.22 and 20.25.) They show both his greater realism and his new, more emotional attitude. Rembrandt and, indeed, many other seventeenth-century Protestants viewed the stories of the Hebrew Bible in much the same lay Christian spirit that governed Caravaggio's approach to the New Testament—as direct accounts of God's dealings with his human creations. Some of Rembrandt's biblical paintings were produced for the princely court in The Hague (despite the Reformation, the use of such images died hard), as well as for private patrons.

How strongly these stories affected him is clear in *The Blinding of Samson* (fig. **20.22**). Painted in the Baroque style he

20.22 Rembrandt van Rijn, *The Blinding of Samson*. 1636. Oil on canvas, 7'9" × 9'11" (2.4 × 3 m). Städelsches Kunstinstitut und Stadtische Galerie, Frankfurt

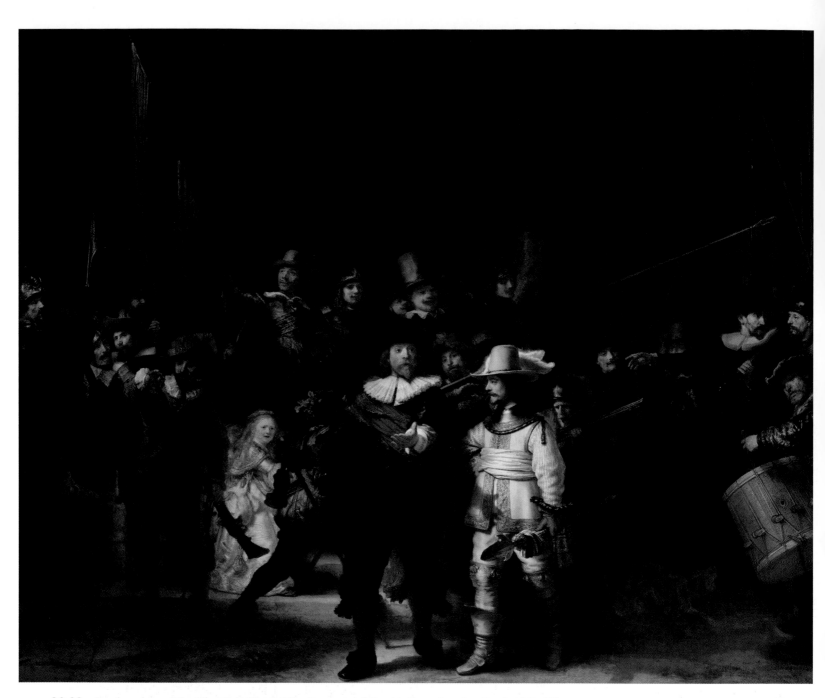

20.23 Rembrandt van Rijn, *The Night Watch* (*The Company of Captain Frans Banning Cocq*). 1642. Oil on canvas, 12'2" × 14'7" (3.8 × 4.4 m). Rijksmuseum, Amsterdam

developed in the 1630s after moving to Amsterdam, it shows Rembrandt as a master storyteller. The artist depicts the Hebrew Bible world as full of Oriental splendor and violence, and he is directly influenced by Caravaggio through the Utrecht Caravaggisti. The theatrical light pouring into the dark tent heightens the drama to the same pitch as *The Raising of the Cross* (see fig. 20.1) by Rubens, whose work Rembrandt sought to rival. But Rembrandt's decision not to travel to Italy to see the art of antiquity or the Renaissance for himself may have limited his opportunities to widen his experiences and to see contemporary art, as well. (See www.myartslab.com.) Instead, he

brought the outside world to himself. Rembrandt was an avid collector of Near Eastern objects, which often served as props in his pictures.

REMBRANDT AND THE CIVIC GUARD By the 1640s, Rembrandt had become Amsterdam's most sought-after portrait painter, and a man of considerable wealth. His famous group portrait (fig. **20.23**) known as *The Night Watch*, because of its old darkened varnish (now cleaned off), was painted in 1642. It shows a military company in the tradition of Frans Hals's Civic Guard groups (see fig. 20.16), possibly assembling for the visit of Marie de' Medici of France to Amsterdam. Although the members of the company had each contributed toward the cost of the huge canvas (originally it was much larger), Rembrandt did not give them equal weight pictorially. He wanted to avoid the mechanically regular designs of earlier group portraits—a problem only Frans Hals had solved successfully. Instead, he made the picture a virtuoso performance filled with movement and lighting, which captures the excitement of the moment and provides a unique sense of drama. The focus is on Captain Frans Banning Cocq, whose hand extends toward us and even creates a shadow across the yellow jacket of his lieutenant; other figures are plunged into shadow or hidden by overlapping. Legend has it that the people whose portraits Rembrandt had obscured were not satisfied with the painting, but there is no evidence for this claim. On the contrary, we know that the painting was much admired in its time, and Rembrandt continued to receive major public commissions in the 1650s and 1660s.

REMBRANDT AS PRINTMAKER Rembrandt's etchings show a new depth of feeling leant by the intimacy of the print medium. *The Hundred Guilder Print* (fig. **20.24**), which has been interpreted as a depiction of the entire nineteenth chapter of the Gospel of St. Matthew, combines various aspects of Christ's preachings, including the healing of the multitudes, and the gathering to him of children and those who had been forsaken. This is crystallized in the phrase which has been associated with the print from a contemporary poem: "The Son of God in a world of sorrow. …" The print is filled with pathos, revealing a humble world of bare feet and ragged clothes. The scene reveals Christ's deep compassion for the poor and outcast, who make up his audience in the print. Rembrandt had a special sympathy for the Jews, both as heirs of the biblical past and as victims of persecution, and they were often his models and also his patrons. The setting of this print suggests some corner in Amsterdam where the Jews had found a haven; they are used here to provide an "authentic" setting for Christ's teachings. Rembrandt incorporates observations of life from the drawings he made throughout his career; several of these drawings have been identified as studies for this work. Here, as in Caravaggio's *The Calling of St. Matthew* (see fig. 19.2), it is the magic of light and dark that gives the etching its spiritual significance.

The print derives its name from a story that 100 guilders was the great price paid for it at a contemporary auction. It is a

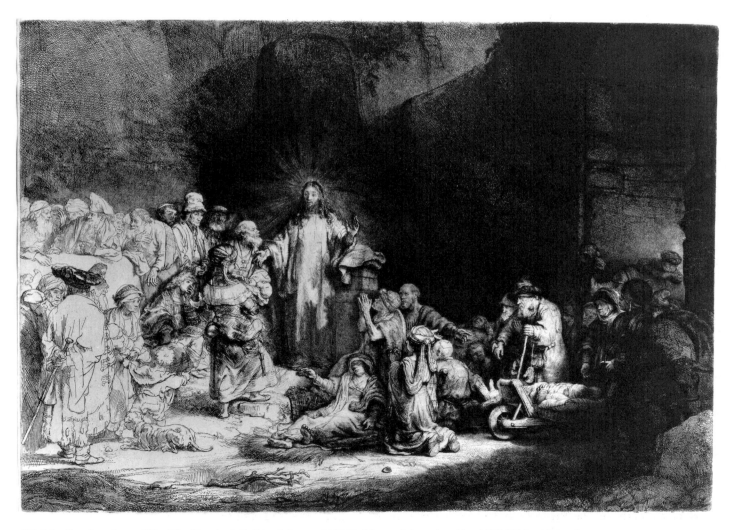

20.24   Rembrandt van Rijn, *The Hundred Guilder Print*. ca. 1647. Etching and drypoint, 11 × 12¾" (27.8 × 32.4 cm). Metropolitan Museum of Art, New York. H. O. Havemeyer Collection, Bequest of Mrs H. O. Havemeyer, 1929 (29.107.35)

Etching, Drypoint, and Selective Wiping

Etching is a form of intaglio printing. The modern technique calls for a metal plate to be cut by the artist using acid. The process begins with the metal plate initially being coated with a waxy substance. Instead of gouging grooves directly in the metal, the artist can lightly "draw" on the plate with a stylus, thereby removing the waxy coating and revealing the metal beneath. The plate is then placed in an acid bath, and the revealed metal will react with the acid, which will burn away the metal to create grooves. The plate is then removed, wiped off, and covered in ink. The excess ink is then wiped off, leaving ink only in the grooves. As with engraving, dampened paper is used to cover the plate. This is then rolled through a press. But because the acid continues to burn the metal, the etched lines may be uneven, and depending on the length of time spent in the acid bath, the grooves may be deeper. With etching, therefore, the actual creation is much like drawing (artists may even carry prepared plates with them), but the finished process also includes a component of chance.

The possibilities for creating greater tonal qualities increased with the introduction of different varieties of paper. In the seventeenth century, several printmakers, including Rembrandt, used papers ranging in quality and origin, from fine laid to a creamy, nubby oatmeal paper, to tan Chinese and Japanese papers, which seemed to make the blacks even blacker. Rembrandt also printed on vellum and even on pigskin.

The range of blacks was further extended by the use of **drypoint**. Drypoint is the process of picking out the metal on a plate with a fine, hard needle and leaving the burr, the metal filings, which will then gather up the ink. This process has the possibility of creating areas of higher black density, as in Rembrandt's *The Hundred Guilder Print* (see fig. 20.24). Drypoint is often used in combination with etching and engraving.

Another option for creating greater tonal range is not to wipe the plate completely clean. This is called **selective wiping**. It can achieve an overall dark tone, creating chiaroscuro effects. In some cases, Rembrandt seems to have hardly wiped the plate at all, keeping it mostly inked. This very selective wiping was used to create nocturnal tenebristic effects. Rembrandt's printed images created an enthusiasm for these dark etchings, and a new form of etching was developed in the late seventeenth century, called **mezzotint**. This is a process of creating many indentations in the metal so that almost the entire plate (called a "rocked" plate) will print dark and only a few areas, smoothed out by the artist, will print light. This process has recently been revived with the availability of prepared "rocked" plates.

In each of these processes, changes are possible. The initial print is called a state. In each case, after printing one example, the artist can make a change. The second printing, using the same plate or block, is called a second state. There can be many states for a single print. The block or plate is therefore quite valuable and can be used again many years later—even after the artist's death, thereby providing family members or others with income. The block or plate can be purchased, and those who make new prints can even produce new states. Sometimes the artist will deface a plate (called "striking" it) to prevent unauthorized people from using it.

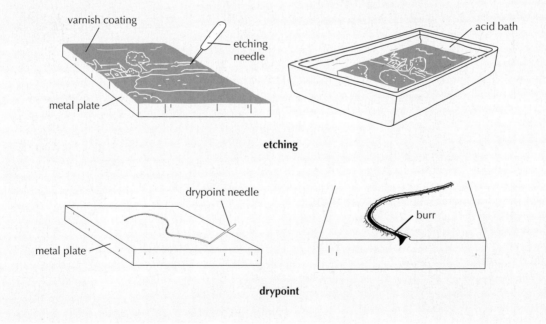

varnish coating

etching needle

metal plate

acid bath

etching

drypoint needle

metal plate

burr

drypoint

virtuoso combination of etching and drypoint (see *Materials and Techniques*, above), creating a velvety tone that can only be suggested in the reproduction here. Rembrandt's importance as a graphic artist is second only to Dürer's, although we get no more than a hint of his virtuosity from this single example.

MATURE WORK Both poignant and "from life," Rembrandt's monumental painting of *Bathsheba with King David's Letter* (fig. **20.25**) is a stunning work. We know nothing of its commissioning or later purchase. The subject of the painting, from 2 Samuel 11:2–27, would have been familiar to seventeenth-century viewers:

The biblical King David noticed the beautiful, but married, Bathsheba at her bath and summoned her. Thus began a series of events culminating in her pregnancy, the death of her husband, specifically sent to the front lines of battle to be killed, her marriage to King David, and the birth of her son who would be King Solomon. Although in the biblical account Bathsheba does not actually receive a letter, this prop became part of the visual tradition along with the attendant performing the pedicure at left.

The large nude, so close to our space, confronts us—even though she does not. Bathsheba with deep sadness and melancholy looks down at David's letter, contemplating its consequences and the loss of her own innocence. Indeed, Bathsheba, in the seventeenth century, was not considered innocent but complicit in allowing the king to see her body and therefore in betraying her marriage vows. The painting itself is not eroticized, but the sheer fleshiness and palpability of her body makes the sensual difficult to ignore. This work brings to mind the many

life-size nudes by Titian (see fig. 17.35), but our painting is of a flawed human, while Titian's is that of a goddess. Rembrandt's Bathsheba is formed of flesh and light in contrast to the color of Titian's subject. Bathsheba is not at all idealized and contemporary criticism faults Rembrandt for this. "Fat swollen belly, hanging breasts, garter marks" were descriptions associated with Rembrandt's nudes. We cannot escape her disturbing reality and get lost in the narrative of the painting—as there isn't one. The work remains an icon of vulnerability.

Because Hendrickje Stoffels, Rembrandt's wife (as she was known, although they were never officially married; Saskia had died 12 years before), was also pregnant in 1654 and because she was summoned in July of that year to appear before a church committee which censured her for living in sin with Rembrandt, it has been suggested—nearly unanimously—that Bathsheba is a portrait of Hendrickje, or that Hendrickje is shown in the guise of Bathsheba. As tantalizing as this association is, there is no

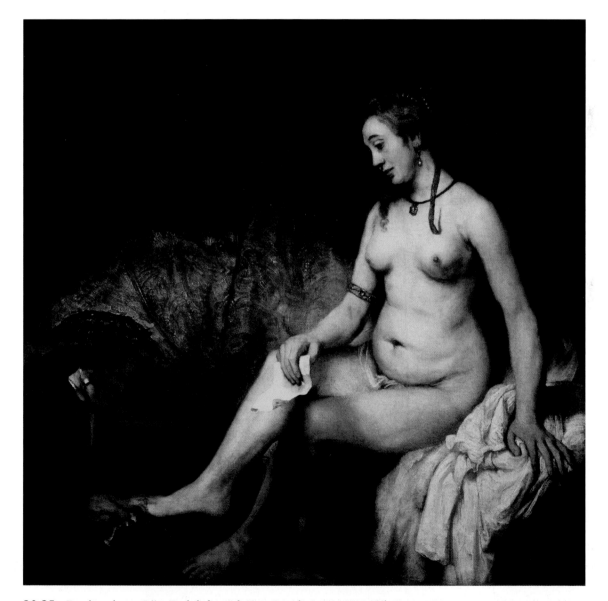

20.25 Rembrandt van Rijn, *Bathsheba with King David's Letter*. 1654. Oil on canvas, 55⅒ × 55⅒" (142 × 142 cm). Musée du Louvre, Paris

known image of Hendrickje, although many paintings have been called "Rembrandt's wife." But without knowing what Hendrickje looked like the connection with the *Bathsheba* is only speculation. The painting remains a poignant, powerful example of an aching drama. Creating a work of significant emotional impact was Rembrandt's forte in his mature years.

SELF-PORTRAITURE Although no likeness of Hendrickje is known, likenesses of Rembrandt are common, since he painted many self-portraits over his long career. They are experimental in the early Leiden years, theatrically disguised in the 1630s, and frank toward the end of his life. Many reasons for their execution have been suggested—as models for other paintings, as explorations of different expressions, and as possible advertisements for his craft. While our late example (fig. **20.26**) is partially indebted to frontally posed Venetian portraits, Rembrandt examines himself with a typically northern European candor. The bold pose and penetrating look bespeak a resigned but firm resolve that suggests princely nobility, which is materially underlined by his richly brocaded gold collar, fur mantle, and silver staff (sceptor?). A comparison with Holbein's *Henry VIII* (see fig. 18.24) suggests the similar concept of authority, but in the latter Holbein's interest in the detail of fabric and jewels dominates while Rembrandt uses chiaroscuro to suggest mood. There is also a marked difference in technique, as Rembrandt uses impasto, which is the layering of paints and glazes to achieve textured and atmospheric effects. Rembrandt painted several large self-portraits, including this one, toward the end of his life, and the acquisition of a "large mirror" (its breakage is documented) may have allowed him to do this.

Rembrandt and his school dominated Amsterdam. Rembrandt produced many history paintings, portraits, and etchings, and is known for his depictions of the inner person and for revealing the pathos in a scene or moment. His works are famous for their poignancy and came to represent the epitome of the Golden Age of Dutch Art.

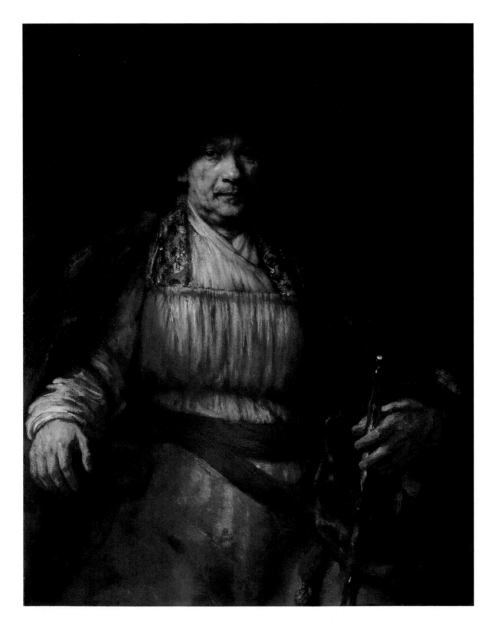

20.26 Rembrandt van Rijn, *Self-Portrait*. 1658. Oil on canvas, 52⅝ × 40⅞" (133.6 × 103.8 cm). Signed and dated on the arm of the chair at right: Rembrandt/f.1658. The Frick Collection, New York. Purchased in 1906. Acc #"06.1.97

THE MARKET: LANDSCAPE, STILL-LIFE, AND GENRE PAINTING

While Italian art was dominated by private patronage or that of the Church, art in northern Europe was largely made for the open market. Of course, portraits and group portraits, like those for the Civic Guards, were commissioned works, but a great number of paintings were also made "on spec"—that is, with the hope that they would be purchased on the open market from dealers, fairs, stores, and lotteries. We know (see *Primary Source*, page 704) that Rubens kept paintings in stock for his own use, and that these were not commissioned works. Perhaps with princely patrons in mind, Rubens painted many large works, but in Holland, paintings were often small, and featured subjects suitable for a middle-class home. Most art buyers in the Dutch Republic preferred images within their own experience: landscapes, architectural views, still lifes, and genre (everyday) scenes. These subjects, we recall, emerged in the latter half of the sixteenth century (see page 653). As the subjects became fully defined, artists began to specialize. Although this trend was not confined to Holland, Dutch painting became famous for both its volume and variety.

The richest of the newly developed "specialties" was landscape, both as a portrayal of familiar views and as an imaginative vision of nature. Landscapes—frequently with only small human figures or none at all—became a staple of seventeenth-century Dutch painting. We can see the beginnings of this in the work of Pieter Bruegel the Elder (see fig. 18.32) and in Italy as well, in such paintings as Carracci's *Landscape with the Flight into Egypt* (see fig. 19.8). But in the Netherlands, greater realism, almost a "portrait of the land," was common. A contemporary said of these landscapes: "nothing is lacking except the warmth of the sun and the movement caused by the gentle breeze."

Landscape Painting: Jan van Goyen

Jan van Goyen's (1596–1656) *Pelkus Gate Near Utrecht* (fig. 20.27), a seascape or marine painting, is the kind of landscape that enjoyed great popularity because its elements were so familiar: the distant town, with a low horizon line, under an overcast sky, seen through a moist atmosphere across an expanse of water. Van Goyen executed about a dozen paintings of this site, each featuring the fourteenth-century gate (which no longer exists). But we can see from his drawings of the site that the views are not exact, but a patchwork of reality and imaginary. The painting is characteristic of Van Goyen's ability to combine the familiar with the picturesque, creating a melancholic mood of these "nether lands," ever threatened by the sea, but also in need of it.

Like other early Dutch Baroque landscapists, Van Goyen frequently used only grays and browns, highlighted by green accents; but within this narrow range he achieved an almost infinite variety of effects. The tonal landscape style in Holland was accompanied by radically simplified compositions, and we see this effect in a monochromatic still-life painting (see fig. 20.31) of the same time. As he worked in several cities (Haarlem, Leiden, and The Hague), Van Goyen was especially influential and extremely prolific; he is credited with over 1,200 paintings and 800 drawings. His family is also evidence of the interrelationship of artists—his daughter married the genre painter Jan Steen (see page 730).

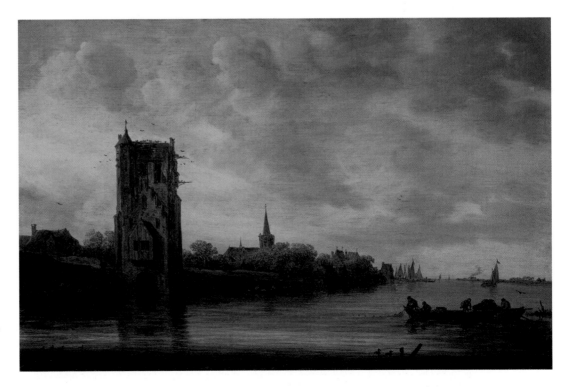

20.27 Jan van Goyen, *Pelkus Gate Near Utrecht*. 1646. Oil on wood, 14½ × 22½" (36.8 × 57.2 cm). Signed and dated (on boat): VG 1646. Metropolitan Museum of Art, New York. Gift of Francis Neilson, 1945 (45.146.3)

City Views: Jacob van Ruisdael

Identifiable city views—panoramic landscapes with their outlying countryside and picturesque sand dunes, showing Amsterdam, Haarlem, Deventer—became popular throughout the century. In the art of Jacob van Ruisdael (ca. 1628–1682), these views become testaments to the city skyline—and to the sky, which might occupy three-quarters of the painting, as it does in this painting of Haarlem (fig. **20.28**). Ruisdael did many paintings of Haarlem, known as *Haarlempjes* (little views of Haarlem). The church

spires, windmills, and ruins are all identifiable, as is the major church, the Grote Kerk (Big Church), known before the Reformation as St. Bavo (see fig. 20.30). In the foreground are the bleaching fields, where both domestic and foreign linen was washed and set out to be bleached by the sun. Haarlem water was well known for its purity and so the city was famous for its linen bleaching and beer production.

A heightened sense of drama is the core of Ruisdael's *The Jewish Cemetery* (fig. **20.29**). Natural forces dominate this wild scene, which is imaginary except for the tombs from the Jewish

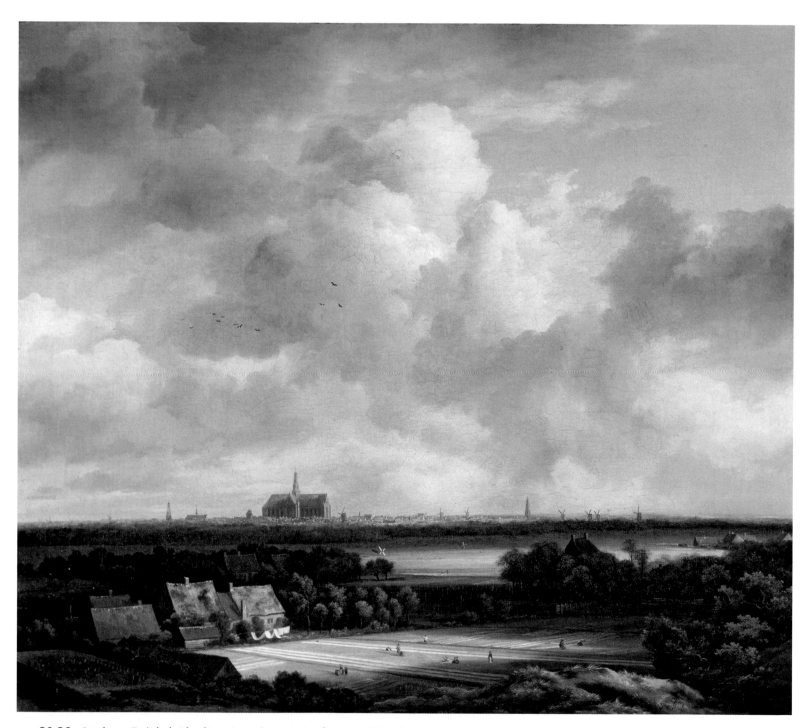

20.28   Jacob van Ruisdael, *Bleaching Grounds Near Haarlem*. ca. 1670. Oil on canvas, 21⅔ × 24½" (55.5 × 62 m). Royal Cabinet of Paintings, Mauritshuis, The Hague. Inv. 1.55

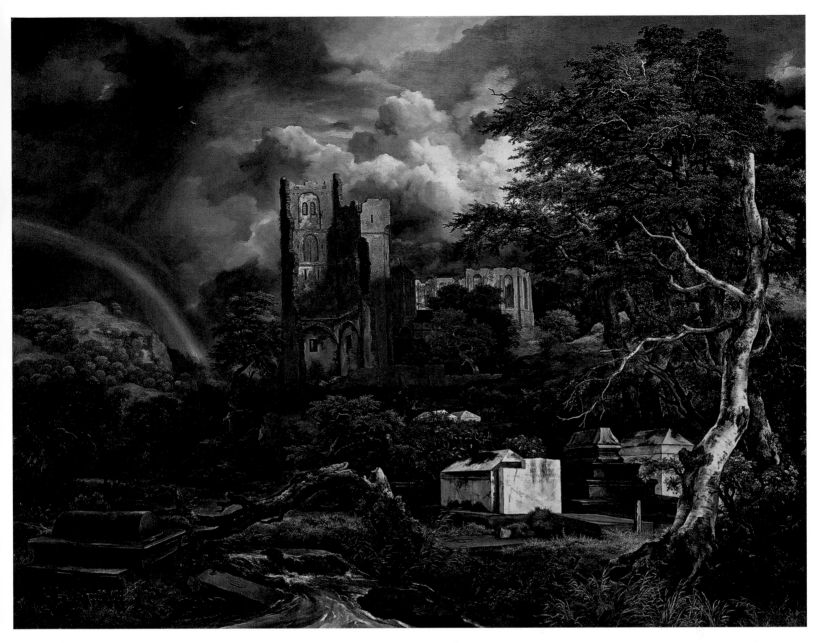

20.29 Jacob van Ruisdael, *The Jewish Cemetery*. 1655–70. Oil on canvas, 4'6" × 6'2½" (1.42 × 1.89 m). The Detroit Institute of Arts, Detroit, MI. Gift of Julius H. Haass in memory of his brother, Dr. Ernest W. Haass. 26.3

cemetery near Amsterdam. As we have seen in Rembrandt's work (see fig. 20.24), Jews had been living in Amsterdam through the seventeenth century—some, often poor, from Germany and eastern Europe, others, often more prosperous, newly arrived from Brazil, where they went to seek refuge from the Inquisition in Spain. The cemetery, called Bet Haim (House of Life), belonged to the latter group, the Sephardic or Portuguese and Spanish Jews. Each of the tombs has been identified, and, though appearing ancient, they were all erected in the seventeenth century. Several drawings of this site by Ruisdael exist, as do prints by other artists. Jews in Amsterdam were exotic—the "other"—and this may account for the theme's popularity. Foreigners who came to Amsterdam visited and wrote about this community with curiosity and even awe.

Ruisdael adds other nonrealistic elements to his imaginary wild scene: The ruined building in the background has been identified as Egmond Abbey (Catholic), which suggests a contrast between Jews and Catholics—or perhaps a complementary relationship—since both are superseded in the Dutch Republic by the Reformed Church. Thus, the theme of death—the cemetery, the tombs, the crumbling ruins of the abbey, and the dead trees—suggests the painting is a vanitas, a memorial to the brevity of life. The term comes from the biblical book of Ecclesiastes and its phrase "vanity of vanities." It is a text on the passage of time and on mortality, just as this painting is also a visual reminder of the shortness of life. Yet the cemetery is arched by a rainbow, a sign of God's promise of redemption. *The Jewish Cemetery* inspires that awe on which the Romantics, 150 years later, based their concept of the sublime.

Architectural Painting: Pieter Saenredam

In contrast to the dramatic mood and theatrical setting of *The Jewish Cemetery*, there are many examples, in paintings, prints, and drawings, of more realistic, descriptive images of the Sephardic synagogue and many of the austere Reformed churches. The *Interior of the Choir of St. Bavo's Church at Haarlem* (fig. **20.30**), painted by Pieter Saenredam (1597–1665),

one of 11 such views that he painted, is meant to serve as more than a mere record. It is, in fact, an impossible view, suggesting a greater sense of vastness in the medieval structure than actually exists. Saenredam went to great lengths to construct his paintings. First, he made both freehand sketches and measured drawings in the church. His next step was to combine the two in additional drawings. Finally, he would paint a representation of the church that utilized accurate details from his drawings but also included

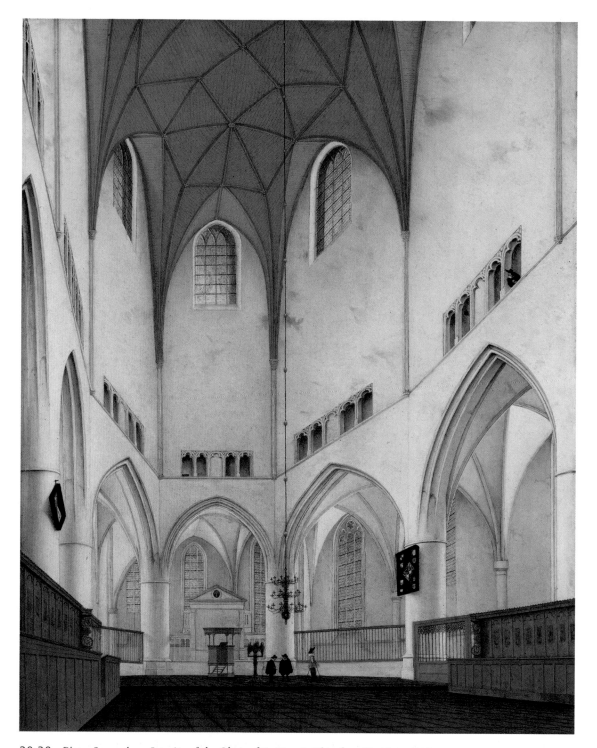

20.30 Pieter Saenredam, *Interior of the Choir of St. Bavo's Church at Haarlem*. 1660. Oil on panel, 27⅞ × 21⅝" (70.4 × 54.8 cm). Worcester Art Museum, Worcester, Massachusetts. Charlotte E. W. Buffington Fund. 1951.29

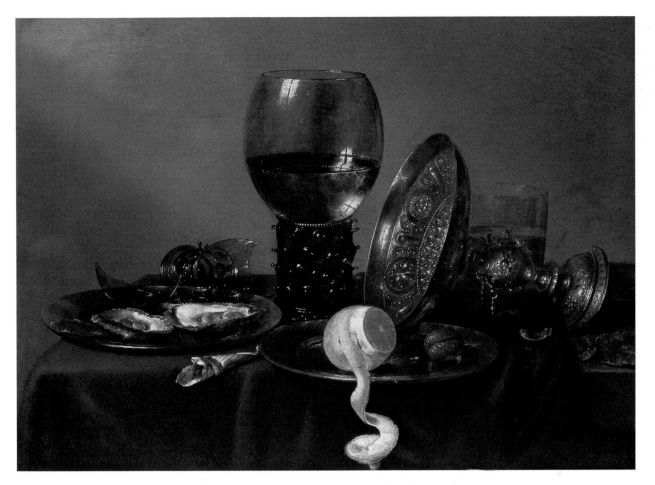

20.31   Willem Claesz, Heda. *Still Life with Oysters, a Roemer, a Lemon, and a Silver Bowl.* 1634.
Oil on panel, 16⅞ × 22⅞" (43 × 57 cm). Museum Boijmans-van Beuningen, Rotterdam, the Netherlands

exaggerated elements for effect. This is the same church that is the focus of Ruisdael's *Bleaching Grounds Near Haarlem* (see fig. 20.28). It is shown here stripped of all furnishings and white-washed under the Protestants, and it has acquired a crystalline purity that invites spiritual contemplation through the painting's quiet intensity. (Both Saenredam and Frans Hals would be buried here.) The tiny figures in the interior provide scale and often narrative. Note the fellow at right looking out of the **triforium**.

Still-life Painting: Willem Claesz. Heda

Dutch still lifes may show the remains of a meal—suggesting pleasure—and luxury objects, such as crystal goblets, glasses of different sizes, and silver dishes, chosen for their contrasting shapes, colors, and textures. Flowers, fruits, and seashells may also be shown. All are part of the world of still life. And these are not too different from the ingredients in a Flemish still life; many artists, such as Clara Peeters and Jan Davidsz. de Heem, traveled between both regions.

As seen here in his *Still Life with Oysters, a Roemer, a Lemon, and a Silver Bowl* (fig. **20.31**), the Haarlem artist Willem Claesz. Heda (1594–1680) was fascinated by surfaces and reflections—the rough edge of the lemon, the liquid, slimy quality of the oysters,

the engraving on the silver, the sparkling light on the roemer (wine glass), its multiple reflections of the window, and its *prunts* (glass drops). Heda is famous for such light effects, which are heightened by the tonal quality of the painting, which is largely monochromatic, much as in Jan van Goyen's landscape (see fig. 20.27), also of midcentury. These are in marked contrast to the colorful Flemish works of Clara Peeters and Jan Davidsz. de Heem (see figs. 20.11 and 20.13). The table is set with white wine, beer (back right), lemon, and a paper of pepper in a cone to use with the oysters, which were known to be aphrodisiacs. Yet the broken glass and overturned silver *tazza* suggest some upheaval on a narra-tive level. Whoever sat at this table was suddenly forced to leave the meal. The curtain that time has lowered on the scene, as it were, gives the objects a strange pathos. The unstable composition, with its signs of a hasty departure, suggests transience—a vanitas.

Flower Painting: Rachel Ruysch

The independent floral still life seems to have begun in Flanders, but it developed in both the Northern and Southern Netherlands. Rachel Ruysch (1664–1750) was one of the leading Dutch flower painters of the day, and was lauded as such in her lifetime. She had a long and prolific career and worked in Amsterdam, The Hague,

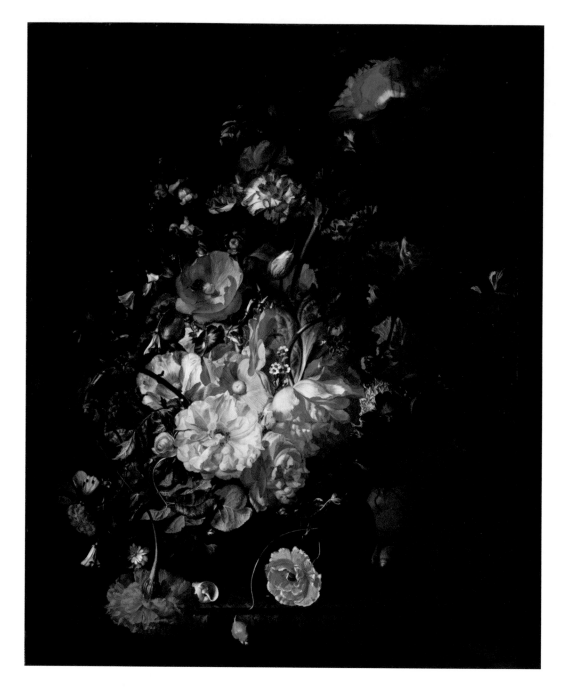

20.32 Rachel Ruysch, *Flower Still Life*. After 1700. Oil on canvas, 29¾ × 23⅞" (75.5 × 60.7 cm). The Toledo Museum of Art, Toledo, Ohio. Purchased with Funds from the Libbey Endowment, Gift of Edward Drummond Libbey. 1956.57

and Düsseldorf, where she and her husband, Juriaen Pool II (1665–1745), a portraitist, became court painters to the Elector Palatine until his death. One could say she was born to be a flower painter, as her father was a professor of anatomy and botany. Ruysch knew every blossom, every butterfly, moth, and snail that she put into a piece intimately. We know from the inclusion of flowers in earlier paintings, such as the lilies in a vase in the *Mérode Triptych* (see fig. 14.8), that flowers can have meaning beyond their beauty. The flowers in figure **20.32**, some with wild and impossibly long stems that stretch across the diagonal of the canvas, are arranged to create an extravaganza of color. Like the Heda *Still Life with Lemon and Oysters* (see fig. 20.31) with its broken glass, this still life features fallen, drooping flowers, and their near-death state again suggests a vanitas theme.

Genre Painting: Jan Steen

Many of the same themes continue to be featured in genre painting at the end of the seventeenth century, but the paintings now contain more complex narratives. Often, there are interior scenes of homes and taverns. The human figures are often no longer half-length; they are shown full length instead, even when the paintings are small, creating a further sense of intimacy. The paintings of Jan Steen, Jan Vermeer and Gerard ter Borch provide a range of subject matter, from the comical to the deeply introspective, while offering a glimpse of home, and family life, relationships, and even the fashions of the seventeenth century. A scene of both comical circumstance and family intimacy—much in the vein of Jordaens's *The King Drinks* (see fig. 20.9)—can be seen in *The Feast of St. Nicholas* (fig. **20.33**) by Jan Steen (1626–1679).

St. Nicholas has just paid his pre-Christmas visit to the household on 5 December, leaving toys, candy, and cake for the children. The little girl and boy are delighted with their presents. She holds a doll of St. John the Baptist and a bucket filled with sweets, while he plays with a golf club and ball. Everybody is jolly except their brother, on the left, who has received only a birch rod (held by the maidservant) for caning naughty children. Soon his tears will turn to joy, however: His grandmother, in the background, beckons him toward the bed, where a toy is hidden.

Steen tells the story with relish, embroidering it with many delightful details. Of all the Dutch painters of daily life, he was the sharpest and best-humored observer. To supplement his earnings, he kept an inn, which may explain his keen insight into human behavior. His sense of timing and his characterizations often remind us of Frans Hals (see figs. 20.16–20.18), while his storytelling stems from the tradition of Pieter Bruegel the Elder (see fig. 18.33). Steen was also a gifted history painter, and although portions of his work are indeed humorous, they usually convey a serious message as well. *The Feast of St. Nicholas* has just such content: The doll of St. John the Baptist is meant as a reminder of the importance of spiritual matters over worldly possessions, no matter how pleasurable the latter might be.

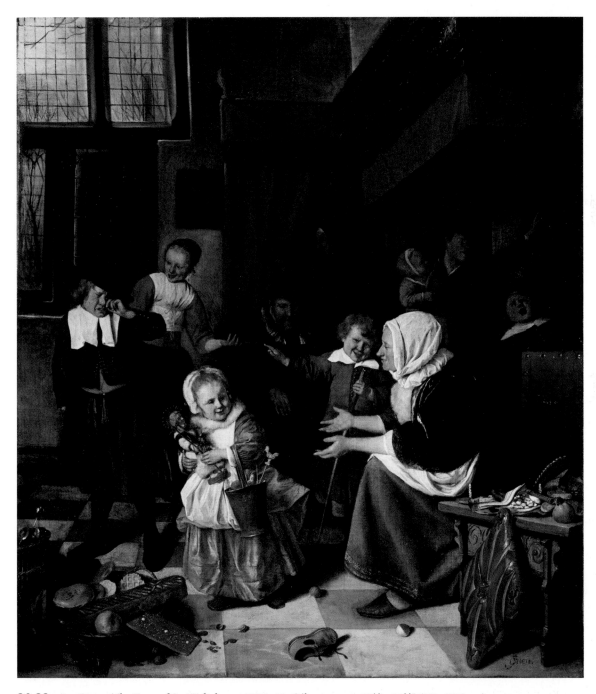

20.33 Jan Steen, *The Feast of St. Nicholas*. ca. 1660–65. Oil on canvas, 32¼ × 27¾" (82 × 70.5 cm). Rijksmuseum, Amsterdam

Intimate Genre Painting: Jan Vermeer

In the genre scenes of the Delft artist Jan Vermeer (1632–1675), by contrast, there is seldom a clear narrative. Vermeer's reputation rests on only a small number of paintings (about 35), but these are indeed quite special. Vermeer may have studied in Amsterdam and/or Utrecht, but he was certainly familiar with old and contemporary works as he, like his father, worked as an art dealer.

In an early work, *Officer and Laughing Girl* (fig. **20.34**), the figures are in a room infused by a nearly glowing light. The young woman sits beneath a large, contemporary map of the Netherlands (on its side), smiles cheerfully, and offers the man a glass of wine. We see only the silhouette of the man dressed in red, as light from the left-hand window pours in between them so that the entire painting seems to sparkle with light.

Vermeer's use of light, frequently coming from a window at the left and creating flecks of light on fabric and reflections, marks his work. To achieve these effects and create a perfectly balanced painting, he seems to have used techniques that are both old and new. Vermeer may have used a *camera obscura*, an experimental optical device (a forerunner of the photographic camera) that

created an image by means of a hole for light on the inside of a dark box. The hole acts as a primitive lens and a scene from outside the box can be seen, inverted, inside it. It is not suggested here that Vermeer copied such scenes, but he may have been inspired by them. *Camera obscura* scenes have a sparkling quality, often seen in parts of Vermeer's work (as seen here in the gold threads in the woman's dress). These sparkling areas are known as "discs of confusion." The *camera obscura* was well known, and there is considerable evidence that it was used by Dutch artists. Further, Anthonie van Leeuwenhoek, the inventor of the modern microscope, lived in Delft at the same time, which suggests a local interest in practical optics.

This new way of looking is paired in Vermeer's work with an old way—a one-point perspective view with a vanishing point. It has been shown that a hole (for a pin and string) was set in a number of Vermeer's paintings to create a one-point perspective system. And indeed a vanishing point with pinhole is also observable in an x-ray. The vanishing point in this painting is set between the two figures and as such we do not focus on either one of them, but we are drawn to the space in between instead—to the very seduction of the relationship. It is the wall we focus on, with

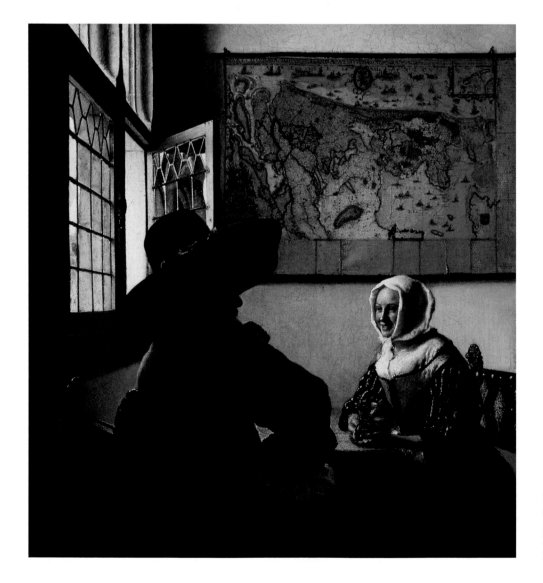

20.34 Jan Vermeer, *Officer and Laughing Girl*. ca. 1657. Oil on canvas (lined), 19⁷⁄₈ × 18⅛" (50.5 × 46 cm). The Frick Collection, New York, Henry Clay Frick Bequest. 1911.1.127

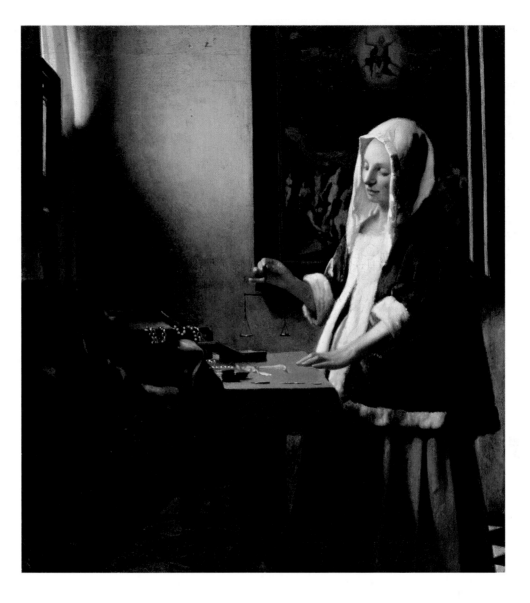

20.35 Jan Vermeer, *Woman Holding a Balance.* ca. 1664. Oil on canvas, 16¾ × 15" (42.5 × 38.1 cm). National Gallery of Art, Washington, D.C. Widener Collection. (1942.9.97)

its subtle and varying tones of gray, yellow, and blue on a seemingly white surface. These are the same colors used for the map. Vermeer created an unparalleled quality of light and texture.

Vermeer is best known for his single figures, usually women, seemingly engaged in everyday tasks at private moments. They exist in a timeless "still-life" world, as if becalmed by a spell. In *Woman Holding a Balance* (fig. **20.35**), a young woman, richly dressed in the at-home wear of the day, is contemplating the balance in her hand, with strings of pearls and gold coins spread out on the table before her. The painting gives a view into such a still-life world—with a table laden with pearls and gold, paintings and fur, all magically providing an eternal, yet momentary, glance into a private world where, in fact, our view is not acknowledged. The painting in the background depicts Christ at the Last Judgment, when every soul is weighed. This may refer to the soul of the pregnant woman's unborn child, and it parallels her own activity, now contemplating the future of her unborn child. The pans of the balance were once thought to contain gold or pearls but scientific analysis of the painting indicates that they actually contain nothing, only beads of light. The painting is intensely private,

quiet, yet also highly sensual, created with optical effects that make the surface shimmer. It is the light on the pan and the pearls that we see as "discs of confusion." The vanishing point in this painting, where a hole has punctured the canvas, is just to the left of the pinky finger that holds the balance. Our eye is drawn to this spot and is fascinated by this tentative gesture. It sets the balance of all elements of the painting.

Vermeer's mastery of light's expressive qualities raises his interest in the reality of appearances to the level of poetry. He is concerned with all of light's visual and symbolic possibilities. *Woman Holding a Balance* is also testimony to the artist's faith: He was a Catholic (as was Jan Steen) living in Protestant Holland, where his religion was officially banned, although worship in private houses was tolerated.

But all of these facts somehow do not get to the magical, hypnotic, truly original nature of his paintings. We do not know Vermeer's teachers or how he developed his unique style. No painter since Jan van Eyck *saw* as intensely as Vermeer. No other painter recorded his seeing in such an exact yet somehow personal way.

Exquisite Genre Painting: Gerard ter Borch

Perhaps the most elegant—even exquisite—Dutch genre paintings were executed by Gerard ter Borch (1617–1681), who worked in the small city of Zwolle, but traveled widely both within Holland (he worked in Amsterdam and briefly in Haarlem) and Europe. He came from a family of artists but little is known of his patrons or commissions. He painted both portraits and genre scenes; both types were often small (about the size of a notebook), but the figures were full-length and attired in the height of fashion. Such is the case in the *Lady at Her Toilet* (fig. **20.36**). She is, as are most of his women, dressed in satin, and Ter Borch was noted as an expert in recording this luxurious fabric. He did this by creating highly contrasting areas of light and dark, and by allowing the long satin skirts to reach the floor and buckle, creating even more shadows. The same dress is worn by another woman in a different painting by him,

and these repeated patterns suggest that Ter Borch made drawings that he could use over again. The figures stand in a seemingly contemporary, but possibly imaginary, late seventeenth-century room, with a marble, four-column fireplace, and with a canopied bed in the background. There is a Turkish-carpeted table and a page, magnificently dressed. (Pages or messengers similarly dressed also appear in paintings by other contemporary artists.) The simplicity of the room accentuates the high fashion of the woman. Her maid adjusts her dress. The mirror set in a contemporary gilt frame reflects the profile of the woman; in reality, she could not be seen from that angle. The theme of "at her toilet" can be seen in the work of Titian and Vouet (see figs. 17.35 and 21.3), and even in Rembrandt's *Bathsheba with King David's Letter* (see fig. 20.25), and the breathtaking beauty of Ter Borch's lady is reflected in all the trappings around her. The painting looks forward to the magnificence and opulence of the eighteenth century.

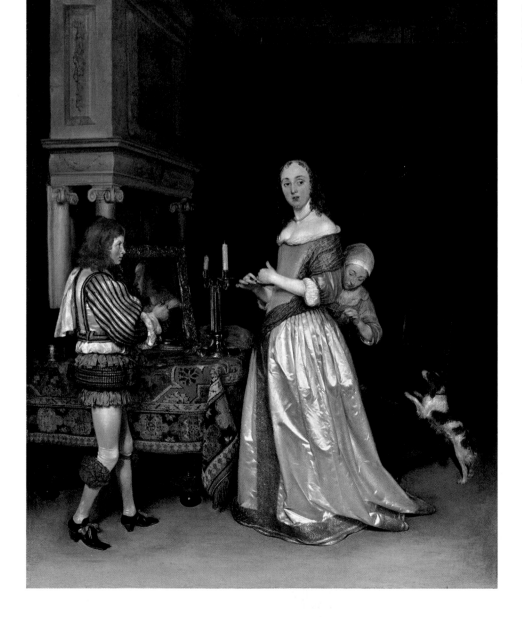

20.36 Gerard ter Borch, *Lady at Her Toilet*. ca. 1660. Oil on canvas, 30 × 23½" (76.2 × 59.7 cm). The Detroit Institute of Art, Detroit, MI. Founders Society Purchase, Eleanor Clay Ford Fund, General Membership Fund, Endowment Income Fund, and Special Activities Fund. 65.10

The Baroque in the Netherlands

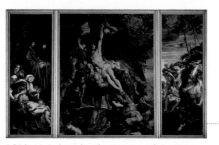

1610–11 Rubens's *The Raising of the Cross*

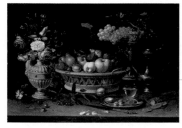

ca. 1612 Clara Peeters's *Still Life with Fruit and Flowers*

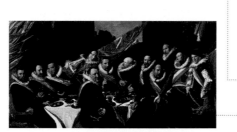

1616 Hals's *Banquet of the Officers of the St. George Civic Guard*

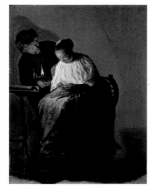

1631 Leyster's *The Proposition*

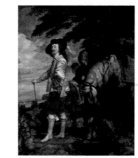

ca. 1635 Van Dyck's *Portrait of Charles I Hunting*

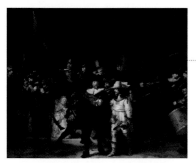

1642 Rembrandt's *The Night Watch*

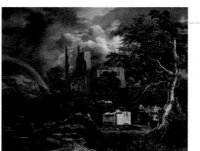

1655–70 Ruisdael's *The Jewish Cemetery*

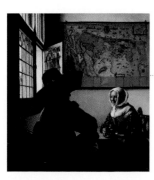

ca. 1657 Vermeer's *Officer and a Laughing Girl*

1590

1600

1610

1620

1630

1640

1650

1660

1670

1680

1597 Carracci's *Loves of the Gods*

◄ 1598 Albert and Isabella jointly rule the Spanish Netherlands

1599–1600 Caravaggio's *The Calling of St. Matthew*

◄ 1602 Dutch East India Company founded

ca. 1600 Sánchez Cotán's *Still Life with Quince, Cabbage, Melon, and Cucumber*

◄ 1626 New Amsterdam (New York City) founded by the Dutch West India Company

ca. 1638 Gentileschi's *Self-Portrait as the Allegory of Painting*

◄ 1639 Japan enforces policy of isolation from Europeans; permits a Dutch trading post

1645 Bernini's *The Ecstasy of St. Teresa*

◄ 1648 Treaty of Münster legally recognizes the Dutch Republic

1650 Velázquez's *The Maids of Honor*

◄ 1676 Anthonie van Leeuwenhoek first to record bacteria under a microscope

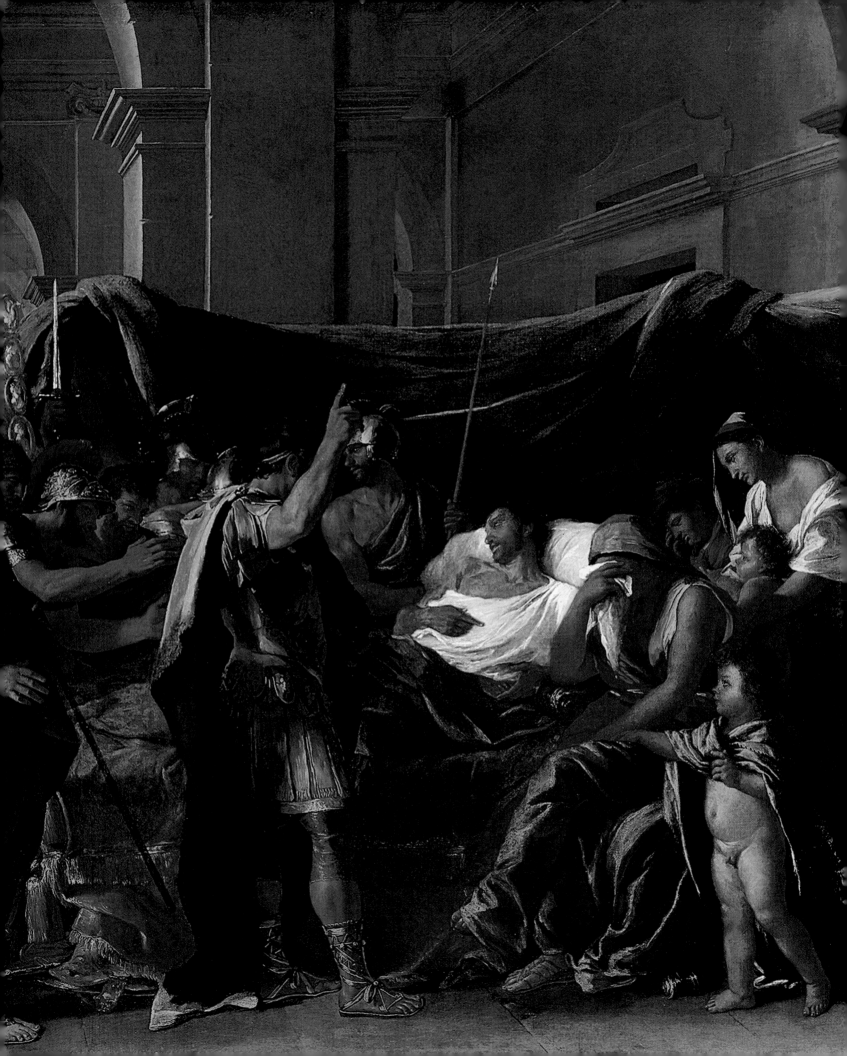

CHAPTER 21

The Baroque in France and England

DURING THE COURSE OF THE TUMULTUOUS SEVENTEENTH CENTURY, the great monarchies of France and England served as the greatest patrons of the arts. Expanding civic projects, notably in architecture, symbolized the wealth of each nation. France, led by an absolute ruler, and England, governed by a king who shared power with the Parliament, underwent

dramatic change. Devastated by the previous era's religious wars and dynastic struggles, both nations saw their treasuries sorely drained, their populations severely reduced, and their societies bitterly divided. The theological controversies that had characterized the earlier Reformation and Counter-Reformation continued in this period, with Catholicism becoming the dominant religion in France (ever since the public conversion of Henry IV in 1593 when he is reputed to have declared, "Paris is well worth a Mass") and Protestantism in England (since the establishment of the Church of England under Henry VIII). Each successive French and English monarch sought to strike a delicate balance between these competing religious forces while attempting to favor the religion of his choice. The same was true throughout Europe, where isolated skirmishes eventually coalesced into a conflict that encompassed nearly all nations—the Thirty Years' War (1618–48).

England faced still more upheavals (**map 21.1**) and its situation degenerated in 1642 into a civil war that led to the trial of King Charles I, who was convicted of treason and beheaded in 1649. With the abolishment of the monarchy, the puritan Oliver Cromwell was named head of state and Lord Protector. Although he restored political stability, upon his death in 1658 his government foundered. Two years later, in 1660, Parliament offered the throne to the son of the beheaded king, Charles II (r. 1660–1685),

Detail of figure 21.4, Nicolas Poussin, *The Death of Germanicus*

thus ushering in the period known as the Restoration. Unfortunately, old religious rivalries and economic crises persisted, and the reign of Charles II's successor, James II (r. 1685–1688), was soon in jeopardy. In the so-called Glorious Revolution of 1688, a relatively peaceful and bloodless event, members of the governing classes of Whigs and Tories proclaimed the prince of Orange, ruler of the Dutch Republic, as king of England; he reigned as William III from 1689 to 1702. The Bill of Rights (1689) established Parliament's supremacy, thus creating a unique form of government that would gradually influence nations worldwide, notably the British colonies in North America.

Waging war was an expensive undertaking and sovereigns throughout Europe realized the pressing need to consolidate the state's power and exert economic control. In France, which by midcentury had emerged as Europe's most powerful nation both militarily and culturally, this centralization was most successfully implemented by Louis XIV (r. 1643–1715). Louis evoked the age-old Divine Right of Kings—the idea that the monarch received his authority directly from God. He used this to increase the state's power over the nobility and over local authorities, amassing revenue through taxation. He relied on a form of royal government known as absolutism, which gave full power to the monarch. The absolute monarchy in France differed from England's post-Restoration constitutional monarchy, which divided power between the ruler and other institutions. In his quest to assert the preeminence of France, Louis XIV embarked

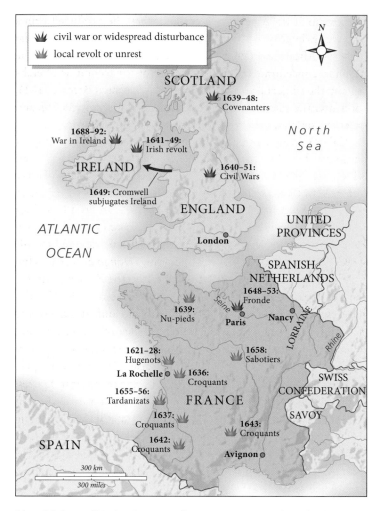

Map 21.1   Political resistance and unrest in France and England in the seventeenth century

on a series of military campaigns from 1688 to 1713 against his rivals, Spain, the Dutch Republic, Germany, and England. Despite eventual defeat, France remained a world power upon Louis's death in 1715.

The wars and social turmoil took perhaps their harshest toll on peasants and commoners, who reeled from continually increasing taxes as well as from devastating natural disasters and the ensuing food shortages, famine, and rising prices. Yet despite the abject poverty endured by some members of society, others enjoyed new wealth and prosperity. Both England and France reaped enormous profits from investments in their colonial empires, and established trade routes that delivered a wider range of goods and enhanced the lifestyles of many Europeans. The development of mercantilism and a worldwide marketplace brought about the rise of a class of increasingly wealthy urban merchants seeking art to furnish and decorate their homes.

Classicism is the style now associated with the art of these two nations. Through its use of a Classical vocabulary—from columns, capitals, and pediments in architecture to styles of dress in painting—it draws on the example of the ancient world to suggest authority, order, and enduring tradition by evoking the imperial grandeur of Rome. Although the Mannerist style of the later School of Fontainebleau persisted in France until about 1625 (see page 629), classicism soon became the hallmark of seventeenth-century French art. It was the official court style of painting between 1660 and 1685, the climactic phase of Louis XIV's reign. Classical principles also dominated architecture, with the new Louvre and Versailles palaces representing the most visible accomplishments in France.

In England, too, classicism dominated art and architecture, notably the hospitals, churches, and country houses designed by Inigo Jones and Sir Christopher Wren. In the wake of the Great Fire of London in 1666, architecture thrived as massive reconstruction projects were undertaken to rebuild the city. Yet England's most lasting artistic successes in the seventeenth century were in literature, including the works of William Shakespeare, John Donne, and John Milton as well as the royal committee's translation of what would become known as the King James Bible.

FRANCE: THE STYLE OF LOUIS XIV

By the late seventeenth century Paris was vying with Rome to become Europe's art center. The French kings Henry IV (r. 1589–1610), Louis XIII (r. 1610–1643), and Louis XIV (r. 1643–1715)—aided by ambitious and able ministers and advisors such as the duc de Sully, cardinals Richelieu and Mazarin, and Jean-Baptiste Colbert—created the climate for this exciting turn of events. The rulers and their officials recognized the power of art to convey the majesty and strength of the monarchy, and they set out on a massive program of patronage of all the arts and sciences—painting, sculpture, architecture, landscape design, decorative arts, theoretical and applied science, philosophy, and literature. Louis XIV especially manipulated art to serve as propaganda for his absolutist policies. He adopted the symbolic imagery of the sun as well as the Greek god of the sun, Apollo, and came to be called the Sun King. This symbolism provided an ancient lineage for Louis and his status as absolute ruler. The ideal of *gloire* (glory), seen in the portraits and architecture he commissioned, reflected his desire to give concrete form to the majesty of his rule, and of France too.

Because the Palace of Versailles (see figs. 21.12–21.15) and other vast building projects glorified the French king, we are tempted to think of French art in the age of Louis XIV as merely an expression of absolute rule. This perception perhaps holds true for the period 1660–85, but by that time seventeenth-century French painting and sculpture had already attained their distinctive Classical character. French historians are reluctant to call this style Baroque but refer to it instead as the "Style of Louis XIV" (art created during his reign). They also use this term to describe art created prior to Louis XIV, particularly that produced at the court of his father, Louis XIII. In addition, scholars often describe the period's art and literature as "classic." In this context, the word has three meanings. It is a synonym for "highest achievement," which suggests that the Style of Louis XIV is the equivalent of the High Renaissance in Italy or the age of Perikles in ancient Greece. It also refers to the imitation of the forms and subject matter of Classical antiquity. Finally, it suggests qualities of balance and restraint shared by ancient art and the Renaissance. The last two meanings describe what could more accurately be called Classicism. Because the Style of Louis XIV reflects Italian Baroque art, although in modified form, we may call it Baroque Classicism.

Painting and Printmaking in France

The many foreign artists working in France drew inspiration from that country's styles and traditions, whereas French artists often traveled to Italy and the Netherlands to work. In the hopes of creating a nucleus of artists who would shape the Baroque style in France, Louis XIII began to recall these artists to Paris. That is, French artists who were abroad were then required to come home. Among the summoned artists were painters Nicolas Poussin and Simon Vouet, who had been working in Rome, and the printmaker Jacques Callot, who returned from Florence to his home in northern France. The influences of foreign artists were significant.

JACQUES CALLOT: A TRANSITIONAL FIGURE One of the most important early seventeenth-century artists was Jacques Callot (1592/93–1635), an etcher and engraver whose small-scale prints recording actual events inspired his compatriot Georges de La Tour (discussed below) and the young Rembrandt (see page 718). Callot's exploitation of the medium's ability to produce stark tonal contrasts and intricate details reflects the tradition, dating from the fifteenth century, of using mass-produced prints to disseminate information. Yet his poignant representations of contemporary figures and events places him firmly in the art of his own time. Callot spent much of his early career at the court

of Cosimo II de' Medici in Florence, where he produced prints inspired primarily by the theater and especially the *commedia dell'arte*. After returning to his native town of Nancy in 1621, he began to concentrate almost exclusively on the technique of etching and the subject of his work changed. He visited Breda in 1626, soon after the surrender of Dutch troops there (see fig. 19.36), and executed six plates showing a large panorama of the site.

Callot's insight into the personal and political geography of battle can best be seen in the series *The Great Miseries of War*, which represents a distillation of his experience of the Thirty Years' War. (Scholars once thought Callot executed the series in 1633 but now consider it to be from 1629–32.) In the 18 etchings in the series, Callot reveals the misery, destruction, and poverty brought by the invading army. Several prints are devoted to soldiers' crimes, whereas others, including *Hangman's Tree* (fig. **21.1**), focus on the punishments dealt out to the French army for their own excesses. The inscription at the bottom reads: "Finally these thieves, sordid and forlorn, hanging like unfortunate pieces of fruit from this tree, experience the justice of Heaven sooner or later." Despite the work's small size (it measures only a few inches), nearly 50 figures inhabit the scene. The awkward perspective emphasizes the tiny, elongated, Mannerist-style figures; in the figures on the right, however, Callot shows a naturalism in costume and attitude that is characteristic of the new Baroque style. The bleak scene is as disturbing as Hieronymus Bosch's vision of Hell in *The Garden of Earthly Delights* (see fig. 14.22); indeed, it may be even more so, for it is based on the artist's own experience of the horrors of war.

GEORGES DE LA TOUR AND THE INFLUENCE OF CARAVAGGIO Many French painters in the early seventeenth century were influenced by Caravaggio, although how they came to be exposed to the Italian artist's style remains unclear. Besides being named a painter to King Louis XIII, Georges de La Tour (1593–1652) received important commissions from the governor

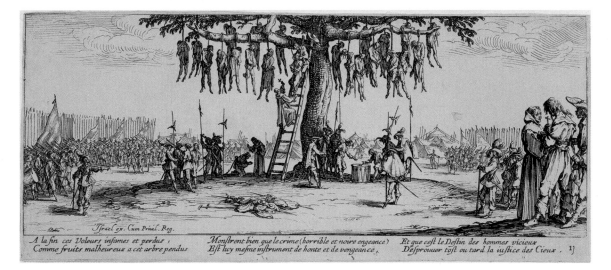

A la fin ces Voleurs infames et perdus ,
Comme fruits malheureux a cet arbre pendus

Monstrent bien que le crime (horrible et noire engeance)
Est luy mesme instrument de honte et de vengeance .

Et que c'est le Destin des hommes vicieux
Desprouuer tost ou tard la iustice des Cieux .

21.1 Jacques Callot, *Hangman's Tree*, from *The Great Miseries of War*. ca. 1629–32. Etching, 3½ × 9" (9 × 23 cm). The British Museum, London

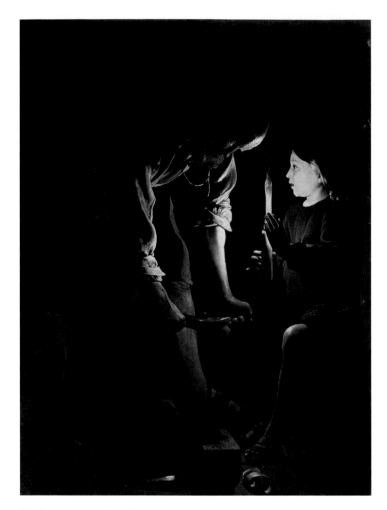

21.2 Georges de La Tour, *Joseph the Carpenter*. ca. 1642. Oil on canvas, 51⅛ × 39¾" (130 × 100 cm). Musée du Louvre, Paris

of Lorraine, his hometown in northeast France. His use of light and his reliance on detailed naturalism derived largely from Caravaggio's northern European followers (see page 664), whom he may have visited in the Dutch Republic.

La Tour's mature religious pictures effectively convey the complex mysteries of the Christian faith. With its carefully observed details and seemingly humble subject, *Joseph the Carpenter* (fig. **21.2**) might initially be mistaken for a genre scene, but its devotional spirit soon overwhelms us. The two figures are set in profile, thus yielding little by their expressions. La Tour lends maximum significance to each gesture, each look. The boy Jesus holds a candle, a favorite device of the artist, whose flame reinforces the devotional mood and imbues the scene with intimacy and tenderness. The painting has the power of Caravaggio's *The Calling of St. Matthew* (see fig. 19.2), but the simplified forms, warm palette, and arrested movement are characteristic of La Tour's restrained and focused vision.

SIMON VOUET AND THE DECORATIVE STYLE Although Simon Vouet (1590–1649) may be little known today, he was the most important French painter in the first third of the seventeenth century. He was the leader of the French Caravaggesque painters

in Rome, although he painted in many styles throughout his career. At an early age he accompanied his artist father to England and Constantinople, but his most significant foreign journey took him to Rome, where he lived from 1613 to 1627. There, he became an adherent of Caravaggio's style but was also later influenced by the Bolognese artist Annibale Carracci. Vouet was so well respected that he was elected president of the Academy of St. Luke in Rome. Officially recalled to France in 1627 by Louis XIII, he settled in Paris and became the leading painter of his day. Vouet quickly shed all traces of Caravaggio's manner and developed a colorful style, which won such acclaim that he was named first painter to the king. It is from Vouet's studio that the official style in France emanated in the 1630s and 1640s. His paintings, influenced by Venetian artists, were known for their rich colors and use of light and thus provided the interiors of royal residences and a growing number of French aristocratic houses with a new vibrant decorative style.

The Toilet of Venus (fig. **21.3**), possibly painted for one of the king's mistresses, is one of several on this theme that Vouet

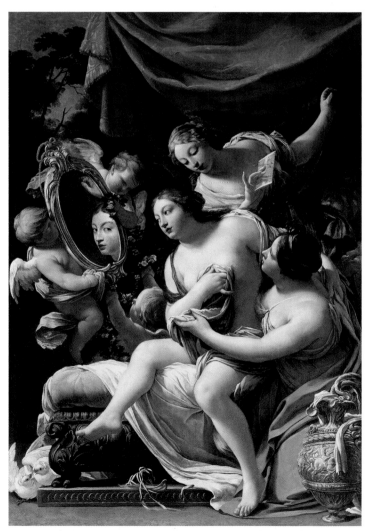

21.3 Simon Vouet, *The Toilet of Venus*. ca. 1640. Oil on canvas, 65¼ × 45" (165.7 × 114.3 cm). The Carnegie Museum of Art, Pittsburgh. Gift of Mrs. Horace Binney Hare (52.7)

executed. It depicts a subject popular in Venice, notably treated by Titian and Veronese, and also by Rubens (compare also the introspective toilet scene of Bathsheba by Rembrandt, see fig. 20.25). Vouet's central figure recalls Correggio's *Jupiter and Io* (see fig. 17.26) but lacks that work's frank eroticism. Instead, Vouet has imbued his Venus with an elegant sensuousness that is uniquely French. The continuous swirling circles, near-nudity, interest in fabric, and luminous colors only suggest the erotic, whose appeal would continue well into the eighteenth century and provide the basis for the Rococo style in painting. Vouet taught the next generation of artists, including those who worked on Louis XIV's palace at Versailles, the landscape designer and royal gardener André Le Nôtre, and Charles Le Brun, the royal painter who would later establish the French Royal Academy (from which he would exclude his teacher).

NICOLAS POUSSIN AND BAROQUE CLASSICISM Despite Vouet's earlier influence on painting, after the 1640s Classicism reigned supreme in France. The artist who contributed most to its rise was Nicolas Poussin (1594–1665), one of the most influential French painters of the century. Aside from an ill-fated two-year sojourn in Paris (he was "recalled" there by Louis XIII), Poussin spent his entire career in Rome. There, he hosted and taught visiting French artists, absorbing the lessons of Raphael's and Carracci's classically ordered paintings and developing his own style of rational classicism. Patrons brought Poussin's paintings back to Paris, where they influenced the royal court. Indeed,

when establishing the curriculum of the French Royal Academy in the 1660s, Jean-Baptiste Colbert, the king's chief advisor, and Charles Le Brun chose Poussin's classical style to serve as a model for French artists.

POUSSIN AND HISTORY PAINTING: ANCIENT THEMES IN THE GRAND MANNER Arriving in Rome via Venice in early 1624, Poussin studied perspective and anatomy and examined ancient sculpture, such as the *Laocoön* (see page 183), the *Belvedere Torso*, and the *Apollo Belvedere*, the reliefs on ancient sarcophagi and vases, and the paintings of Raphael. His *The Death of Germanicus* (fig. **21.4** and page 736) reflects these studies. The work served as a model for artistic depictions of heroic deathbed scenes for the next two centuries and may in fact be the first example of this subject in the history of art. In some respects a typical history painting, the work relates the powerful themes of death, loyalty, and revenge. The story comes from Tacitus and is set in the year 19 CE. Germanicus was a Roman general who had led campaigns against the Germanic tribes. At the urging of Tiberius, Germanicus' adoptive father, the ruler in Syria, poisoned the powerful general. Poussin depicts Germanicus on his deathbed; on the left his loyal soldiers are swearing revenge and on the right his mournful family weeps. The promise to avenge is set at the center, commanding attention, as figures gesture their grief, loyalty, and suffering. Framed by the two groups, Germanicus becomes the focus of the composition, which is based on antique scenes of the death of Meleager (see fig. 7.69).

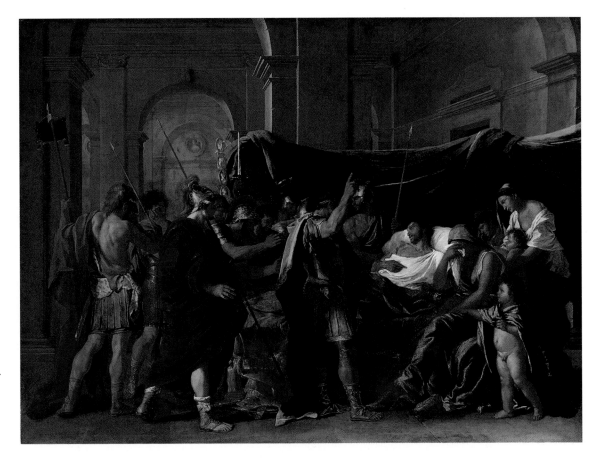

21.4 Nicolas Poussin, *The Death of Germanicus*. 1627–28. Oil on canvas, 4'10¼" × 6'6" (1.48 × 1.98 m). Minneapolis Institute of Art, Minneapolis, Minnesota. The William Hood Dunwoody Fund. 58.28

Nicolas Poussin (1594–1665)

From an undated manuscript

Poussin's ideas on art were central to the formation of the French Academy in 1648 and, because of the preeminence of that body, to the entire European academic movement of the seventeenth through the nineteenth centuries.

The magnificent manner consists of four things: subject, or topic, concept, structure and style. The first requirement, which is the basis for all the others, is that the subject or topic should be great, such as battles, heroic actions and divine matters. However, given the subject upon which the painter is engaged is great, he must first of all make every effort to avoid getting lost in minute detail, so as not to detract from the dignity of the story. He should describe the magnificent and great details with a bold brush and disregard anything that is vulgar and of little substance. Thus the painter should not only be skilled in formulating his subject matter, but wise enough to know it well and to choose something that lends itself naturally to embellishment and perfection. Those who choose vile topics take refuge in them on account of their own lack of ingenuity. Faintheartedness is therefore to be despised, as is baseness of subject matter for which any amount of artifice is useless. As for the concept, it is simply part of the spirit, which concentrates on things, like the concept realized by Homer and Phidias of Olympian Zeus who could make the Universe tremble with a nod of his head. The drawing of things should be such that it expresses the concept of the things themselves. The structure, or composition of the parts, should not be studiously researched, and not sought after or contrived with effort but should be as natural as possible. Style is a particular method of painting and drawing, carried out in an individual way, born of the singular talent at work in its application and in the use of ideas. This style, and the manner and taste emanate from nature and from the mind.

Source: Alain Merot, *Nicolas Poussin*, tr. Fabia Claris (London: Thames & Hudson, 1990)

The architecture sets the stage for the figures, which are arranged horizontally in a rectangular space, as in a Classical frieze. The curtain in the rear restricts the action to a shallow space, heightening the drama and creating a more intimate environment.

This early work by Poussin, painted just a few years after he arrived in Rome, was probably created for Cardinal Francesco Barberini's secretary, Cassiano dal Pozzo (1588–1657), a major patron of the arts. Its composition, setting, and heroic historical subject (see *Primary Source*, above), are typical of Poussin's classicism and his concept of the Grand Manner.

THE ABDUCTION OF THE SABINE WOMEN Demonstrating Poussin's allegiance to classicism, *The Abduction of the Sabine Women* (fig. **21.5**) displays the severe discipline of his intellectual

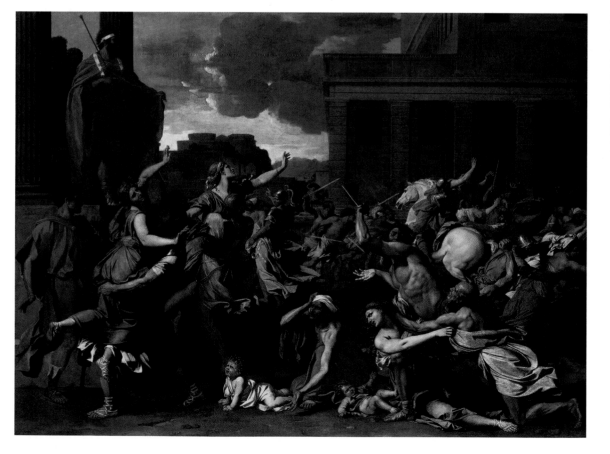

21.5 Nicolas Poussin, *The Abduction of the Sabine Women.* ca. 1633–34. Oil on canvas, 5'7⅞" × 6'10⅝" (1.54 × 2.09 m). Metropolitan Museum of Art, New York. Harris Brisbane Dick Fund, 1946 (46.160)

style, which developed in response to what he regarded as the excesses of the High Baroque. The strongly modeled figures are "frozen in action," like statues. Many are, in fact, derived from Hellenistic sculpture, but the main group is directly inspired by Giovanni Bologna's *The Rape of the Sabine Woman* (see fig. 17.13). Poussin has placed them before reconstructions of Roman architecture that he believed to be archaeologically correct.

Poussin thought the highest aim of painting was to represent noble and serious human actions. Emotion is abundantly displayed in the dramatic poses and expressions of the figures here, but there is a lack of spontaneity that perhaps causes it to fail to touch us. In part, this is due to their derivation from sculpture. The scene has a theatrical air, and for good reason. Before beginning the painting, Poussin, besides making preliminary drawings, arranged wax figurines on a miniature stage until he was satisfied with the composition.

Poussin believed that the viewer must be able to "read" the emotions of each figure as they related to the story. Such beliefs later proved influential to his student Charles Le Brun when establishing an approved court style for French painting. These ideas were not really new. We recall Horace's motto *Ut pictura poesis* ("As is painting, so is poetry"), and Leonardo's statement that the highest aim of painting is to depict "the intention of man's soul" (see page 564). Before Poussin, however, no artist had made the analogy between painting and literature so closely or put it into practice so singlemindedly.

The historical event portrayed in *The Abduction of the Sabine Women* was admired as an act of patriotism ensuring the future of Rome. According to the accounts of Livy and Plutarch, the Sabines were young women abducted by the Romans to become their wives; the women later acted as peacemakers between the two opposing sides. Clearly, in the painting the women do not go willingly as swords are drawn, babies are abandoned, and the elderly suffer. But Poussin's apparent detachment and lack of sympathy for those suffering has caused the work to be labeled "heroic." His work appeals to the mind, that is, to the larger view of history, rather than to the senses. Poussin suppresses color and instead stresses form and composition.

This method accounts for the visual rhetoric in *The Abduction of the Sabine Women* that makes the picture seem so remote. This preliminary drawing (fig. **21.6**) (made in fact for a different version of the painting) suggests how deliberate the artist's process was. Using pen and ink and wash, Poussin worked out many of his compositions beforehand, as did Rubens. We have already mentioned his employment of wax figurines. In this drawn example, he placed figures in the foreground and ancient architecture as a stage set in the background. Such studies con-trast sharply with the methods of Caravaggio and the Caravaggisti, who supported painting "from nature," that is, from living models and without the aid of preparatory drawings. Poussin, on the other hand, regarded history painting as more intellectual and as derived from the imagination; he reportedly told a contemporary that "Caravaggio had come into the world to destroy painting."

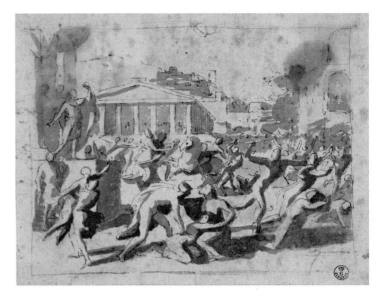

21.6 Nicolas Poussin,. *The Abduction of the Sabine Women*. ca. 1630. Brush drawing, 6¼ × 8⅛" (16.1 × 20.7 cm). Archivio del Gabinetto Disegni e Stampe, Galleria degli Uffizi, Florence

POUSSIN AND THE IDEAL LANDSCAPE The "ideal" landscape, serene and balanced, does not represent a particular locale but rather a generalized and often beautiful place. Poussin's ideal landscape is the opposite of those of his Dutch contemporaries (Van Goyen and Ruisdael, see figs. 20.27–20.29) and their topographical views. Indeed, because figures play only a minor role in landscapes, it is surprising that Poussin chose to explore this subject at all. The austere beauty and somber calm of Poussin's work can be seen in his *Landscape with St. John on Patmos* (fig. **21.7**), which continues the Classical landscape tradition of Annibale Carracci; with this work, Poussin is considered to have invented the ideal landscape. The brilliantly lit, ancient landscape strewn with architectural ruins suggests both the actual site and the concept of antiquity upon which early Christianity was founded. Trees on either side balance the composition, and many of the ruins are set parallel to the picture plane. A reclining St. John, who at the end of his life lived on the island of Patmos, reportedly in somewhat abject circumstances, is shown in profile facing left. Poussin's pendant (paired) painting, *Landscape with St. Matthew*, shows that saint facing right, yet the works were created independently. Poussin may have conceived the project as four paintings of the four Evangelists; if so, those featuring St. Luke and St. Mark were never executed. Both known paintings were made in Rome for the secretary to Pope Urban VIII. The composition suggests the physical, rational arrangement of a spiritual, eternal, ideal world—a concept well suited to and best explored by Baroque Classicism. Poussin's mythological landscapes show a similar blend of the physical, rational, and mythic.

CLAUDE LORRAIN AND THE IDYLLIC LANDSCAPE While Poussin developed the heroic qualities of the ideal landscape, the great French landscapist Claude Lorrain (Claude Gellée, also called Claude; 1604/05?–1682) brought its idyllic aspects of both

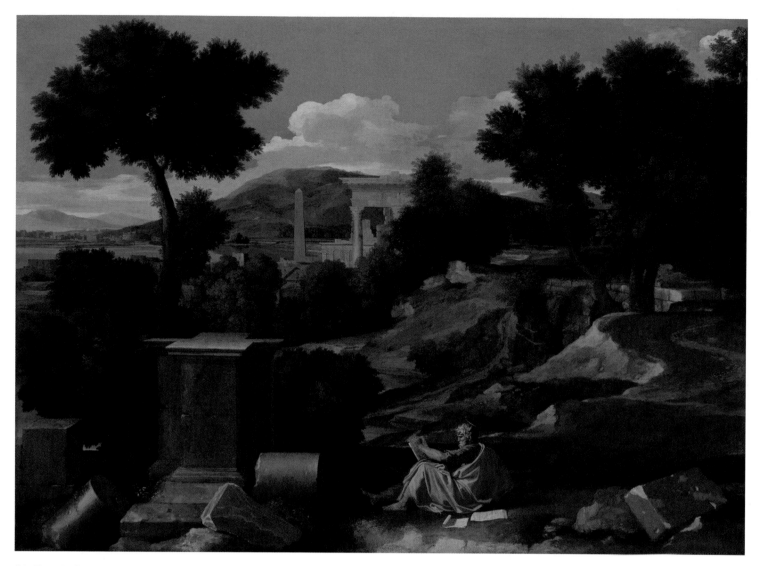

21.7   Nicolas Poussin. *Landscape with St. John on Patmos*. 1640. Oil on canvas, 39½ × 53¾" (100.3 × 136.4 cm).
Art Institute of Chicago. A. A. Munger Collection. (1930.500)

landscapes and seascapes. He, too, spent nearly his entire career in Rome, beginning as a pastry chef. From 1625 to 1627, however, he returned briefly to Nancy, where he was familiar with fellow resident Jacques Callot. He later copied Callot's etchings from *The Great Miseries of War* series (see fig. 21.1). Claude's family in Nancy had been victims of the Thirty Years' War and so the series may have had a particularly personal meaning for him. While in Rome, Claude worked with several artists and was a pupil and assistant to Agostino Tassi (see fig. 19.10). Like many northern Europeans, Claude thoroughly explored the surrounding countryside, the *campagna*, of Rome and his countless drawings made on site reveal his powers of observation. He is also the first artist known to have painted oil studies outdoors. Such sketches, however, were only the raw material for his landscapes. To guard against forgeries, about 1635 Claude began making drawings of his paintings, which he kept as a record in a book known as *Liber Veritatis* (*The Book of Truth*). (See *The Art Historian's Lens*, page 747.) It is from annotations made on the backs of these drawings that we have learned the subjects of his paintings known as

"pastorals," a literary genre that flourished in Venice in the six-teenth century in works by painters such as Giorgione and Titian (see figs. 16.29 and 16.30).

Claude's themes are often historical or pastoral, as in *A Pastoral Landscape* (fig. 21.8). He does not aim for topographic accuracy in his paintings but instead evokes the poetic essence of a countryside filled with echoes of antiquity. Many of Claude's paintings are visual narratives drawn from ancient texts, such as the epic tales and poetry of Vergil. Often, as in this painting, the compositions have the hazy, luminous atmosphere of early morning or late afternoon. One can refer to Claude as painting "into the light." That is, his sunlight (often sunsets) is at the center and at the horizon line of the painting so that the architecture and other elements in the foreground or middleground appear almost as silhouettes. This example is painted on copper, a material sev-enteenth-century artists frequently employed for small works. The surfaces of copper paintings are luminous. Here, the space expands serenely rather than receding step by step as in works by Poussin. An air of nostalgia, of past experience enhanced by memory, imbues the scene. It is this nostalgic mood founded in ancient literature that forms its subject.

Claude succeeded in elevating the landscape genre, which had traditionally been accorded only a very low status. Prevailing artistic theory had ranked the rendering of common nature at the bottom of the hierarchy of painting genres, with landscape only just above still life. Claude, encouraged by sophisticated patrons, progressively moved away from showing the daily activity of life at the ports, and embellished his seascapes and landscapes with historical, biblical, and mythological subjects, thereby raising the status of the genre.

CHARLES LE BRUN AND THE ESTABLISHMENT OF THE ROYAL ACADEMY In art as in life, the French monarchy sought to maintain strict control, and thus the Royal Academy of Painting and Sculpture was founded in Paris in 1648. One of the 12 founding members was artist Charles Le Brun (1619–1690), who helped reorganize the academy in the 1660s into a formal institution.

Although it came to be associated with the absolutism of Louis XIV's reign, at its inception the king was only ten years old, his mother Anne was regent, and Cardinal Mazarin effectively controlled affairs of state. Yet the ideology of academy and throne would increasingly coincide and strengthen each other in the ensuing years.

When Louis XIV assumed control of the government in 1661, Jean-Baptiste Colbert, his chief advisor, began to build an administrative apparatus capable of supporting the power of the absolute monarch. In this system, aimed at controlling the thoughts and actions of the nation, the task of the visual arts was to glorify the king. As in music and theater, which shared the same purpose, the official "royal style" was Classicism. Centralized control over the visual arts was exerted by Colbert and Le Brun, who became supervisor of all the king's artistic projects. As chief dispenser of royal artistic patronage, Le Brun's power was so great that for all practical purposes he acted as dictator of the arts in France.

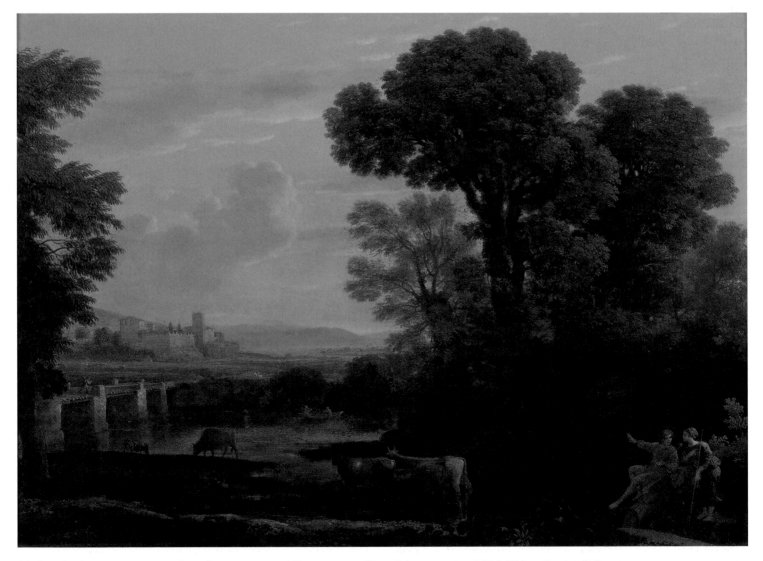

21.8   Claude Lorrain, *A Pastoral Landscape*. ca. 1648. Oil on copper, 15½ × 21" (39.3 × 53.3 cm). Yale University Art Gallery, New Haven, Connecticut. Leonard C. Hanna, Jr., B. A. 1913, Fund. 1959.47

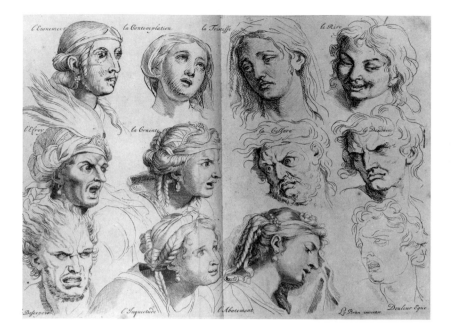

21.9 Henri Testelin after Charles Le Brun, *The Expressions*, 6th plate in Henri Testelin's *Sentiments des plus habiles peintres* (Paris, 1696). Etching (with later additions in ink), 13⅟₁₆ × 17¾" (33.1 × 45.1 cm). Metropolitan Museum of Art, Rogers Fund, 1968. (68.513.6(6))

Upon becoming the academy's director in 1663, Le Brun established a rigid curriculum of practical and theoretical instruction. He lectured extensively at the academy; several lectures were devoted to examining the art of Poussin, venerating the works of Raphael, and studying physiognomy (facial expressions). Probably about 1668, he codified facial expressions in a series of annotated drawings published posthumously as engravings (fig. **21.9**). His lectures documented the movements of eyes, eyebrows, and mouths to show passions and emotions such as fear, anger, and surprise, corresponding to those described in the *Passions of the Soul*, published in 1649 by Descartes. Le Brun's schemata were intended to be used as formulas by artists to establish narratives in their paintings that could be easily "read" by viewers.

Much of Le Brun's doctrine was derived from Poussin, with whom he had studied for several years in Rome. The academy also devised a method for assigning numerical grades to artists past and present in such categories as drawing, expression, and proportion. The ancients received the highest marks, followed by Raphael and his school, and then Poussin. Venetian artists, who "overemphasized" color, ranked low, while the Flemish and Dutch were placed lower still. Subjects were also classified: At the top was history (that is, narrative subjects, whether Classical, biblical, or mythological) and at the bottom was still life, with portraiture falling in between.

HYACINTHE RIGAUD AND THE SPLENDOR OF LOUIS XIV

The monumental *Portrait of Louis XIV* (fig. **21.10**) by Hyacinthe Rigaud (1659–1743) conveys the power, drama, and splendor of the absolutist ruler. The king is shown life-size and full-length, much like Charles I in Van Dyck's portrait (see fig. 20.8). The resemblance is intentional, and the work follows the formulaic nature of royal portraiture of the time to espouse power and authority through the use of the insignias of rulership and the symbols of the opulence of the monarch's reign. Louis is shown

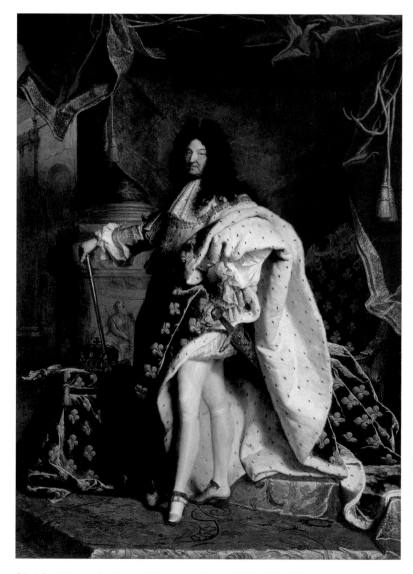

21.10 Hyacinthe Rigaud, *Portrait of Louis XIV*. 1701. Oil on canvas, 9'2" × 6'3" (2.8 × 1.9 m). Musée du Louvre, Paris. Inv. 7492

Forgeries and The Book of Truth

Art forgery—the deliberate copying or creation of a work of art without permission and with the intention to deceive—has long posed a serious threat to both artists and collectors. Art forgers have targeted jewelry, sculpture, painting, and prints, usually in the hopes of selling their fakes for personal gain.

Forgers may copy the works or styles of artists from either the past or present. In ancient times, reports surfaced of forgeries being made of the works of Myron and Praxiteles (see Chapter 5). We know, too, that Michelangelo made "antique" forgeries by burying sculpture to produce a patina imitating the effects of time and wear. To create the look of an older product, forgers may use materials such as old paper, homemade paints, previously used canvases, and wood that has been peppered with buckshot to resemble aged wood infested with wormholes.

Not only are artists deprived of monetary compensation by a forgery, but their reputation can also be jeopardized by art of lesser quality being passed off as theirs. Such was the case with Albrecht Dürer (see Chapter 18), who discovered upon his visit to Venice in 1506 that the well-known printmaker Marcantonio Raimondi (ca. 1480–ca. 1527) was selling engravings that he had created in the manner of Dürer's woodcuts and bearing Dürer's monogram. Dürer sued, and although Raimondi was allowed to continue producing the engravings, he could no longer include Dürer's signature on them.

Claude Lorrain experienced a similar problem, for which he developed a unique solution. We know from the writer Filippo Baldinucci (1625–1697) that Claude discovered that another artist, Sébastien Bourdon (1616–1671), was adept at imitating the light and tonal effects in Claude's paintings. In fact, Bourdon's skill in producing them was so great that, after visiting Claude's studio, he painted a landscape and sold it as a work purportedly by Claude. Other artists also found it easy to imitate Claude's techniques and compositions.

To safeguard against any such dishonest practices, around 1635 Claude decided to compile the *Liber Veritatis* (*The Book of Truth*), an album of drawings reproducing all of his paintings from that time on. On the verso, or back, he annotated each drawing with the name of the patron, buyer, or place to which the work was sent; he sometimes included the date and a reference to the work's subject as well. Collectors could consult the book and verify whether a painting was included—and thus foil any potential forger.

By the time of his death, Claude had made drawings of 195 of his paintings. He did not record paintings made before 1635, and therefore an estimated 50 works are missing from the album. Claude was a prolific draftsman—over 1,200 drawings by him are known, although the album records only drawings of his finished paintings (see Claude's drawing of *A Storm off the Coast*, above). The *Liber Veritatis*,

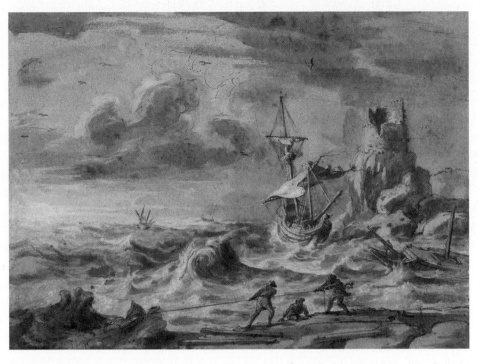

Claude Lorrain, *A Storm off the Coast*. ca. 1635. Pen and brown wash, heightened with white highlights on blue paper, 7¹¹⁄₁₆ × 10¼" (195 × 260 mm). The British Museum, London

now in the collection of the British Museum, consists of sheets measuring 7¹¹⁄₁₆ by 10¼ inches (195 × 260 mm) that are organized in groups of four white sheets alternating with four blue ones. Scholars have speculated that Claude chose these paper colors to reflect the light effects in his paintings. It also suggests that he probably did not execute the drawings in chronological order. To create them, he used pen and ink with brown and sometimes gray washes. He added highlights with white chalk and touches of gold. Such time-consuming details, especially evident in the book's later drawings, show that Claude began to use the album not just to reproduce paintings but also to create elaborate, finished drawings that stand on their own as accomplished works of art.

Dealers and collectors today often rely on a comparable type of book called a **catalogue raisonné**. Compiled by an expert after years of meticulous research, this publication describes and illustrates all the known, verified, and some attributed (but nonauthenticated) works by a particular artist as well as pertinent information about each object's dimensions, condition, and **provenance** (history of ownership). But perhaps most important in the fight against forgeries is the wide range of available technologies—from carbon dating to infrared spectroscopy—to analyze and date a work's materials and stages of creation. Still, even with these advanced detection methods, not all experts agree about the authenticity of a given work since these technologies can often only verify the time or place a work was produced and not the artist's hand. For that we still rely on connoisseurship and the experience and expertise of the art historian.

draped with his velvet coronation robes lined with ermine and trimmed with gold *fleurs-de-lis*. He appears self-assured, powerful, majestic—and also tall, an illusion created by the artist, for his subject actually measured only 5 feet 4 inches. The portrait proudly displays the king's shapely legs (emphasized by the high heels Louis himself designed to increase his height), which were his pride and joy as a dancer. Indeed, the king actively participated in the ballets of Jean-Baptiste Lully (1632–1687) from the 1650s until his coronation. All the arts, from the visual arts to the performing arts, fell under royal control—a fact exemplified in Rigaud's painting, which expresses Louis's dominance and unequaled stature as the center of the French state.

French Classical Architecture

Because they were large, ostentatious, and public, building projects, even more than paintings, transmitted the values of the royal court to a wide audience. In French architecture, the Classical style expressed the grandeur and authority of imperial Rome and confirmed the ideals of tradition, omnipotence, absolutism, strength, and permanence espoused by the monarchy. Mammoth scale and repetition of forms evoke these broad concepts, which were embodied in royal structures erected in the heart of Paris as well as outside the city, in the palace and gardens at Versailles.

In 1655, Louis XIV declared: "*L'état, c'est moi*" ("I am the state"). This statement was not just political but represented an artistic and aesthetic idea as well. Louis's projects for his palace and court took on colossal proportions and represented not a single individual, or even a single monarch, but the entirety of France. He began by renovating the Louvre, a project begun by his father, but that proved insufficient. Louis wanted to move his entire royal court to a more isolated location where he could control them more efficiently, and so he began construction on the palace and gardens at Versailles, located a few miles outside Paris. These complex building projects all share a single style—that of Baroque Classicism.

THE LOUVRE Work on the palace had proceeded intermittently for more than a century, following Pierre Lescot's original design under Francis I; what remained was to close the square court on the east side with an impressive façade. Colbert was dissatisfied with the proposals of French architects including François Mansart (1598–1666), who submitted designs not long before his death. Colbert then invited Bernini to Paris in the hope that the most famous artist of the Roman Baroque would do for the French king what he had done for the popes in Italy. Bernini spent several months in Paris in 1665 and submitted three innovative designs on a scale that would have dwarfed the existing palace. After much argument and intrigue, Louis XIV rejected them and turned the problem over to a committee: Charles Le Brun, his court painter; Louis Le Vau (1612–1670), his court architect who had already done much work on the Louvre (including the

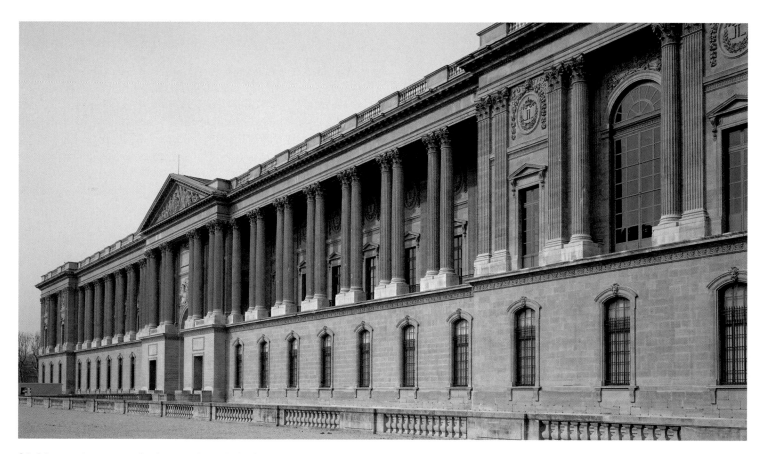

21.11   Louis Le Vau, Claude Perrault, and Charles Le Brun. East front of the Louvre, Paris. 1667–70

Gallery of Apollo, the Queen's Court, and the south façade); and Claude Perrault (1613–1688), an anatomist and student of ancient architecture. All three men were responsible for the structure of the new Louvre (fig. 21.11), but Perrault is rightly credited with the major share. Certainly his detractors at the time thought so, and he was often called upon to defend his design.

Perrault based the center pavilion on a Roman temple front, and the wings look like the sides of a temple folded outward. The colonnade was controversial because of its use of paired columns, but this treatment quickly became a characteristic of French Classicism in architecture.

The east front of the Louvre signaled the victory of French Classicism over the Italian Baroque as the royal style. It further proclaimed France as the new Rome, both politically and culturally, by linking Louis XIV with the glory of the Caesars. This revitalization of the antique, both in its conception and its details, was Perrault's main contribution.

Claude Perrault owed his position to his brother Charles (1628–1703), who, as Colbert's master of buildings under Louis XIV, had helped undermine Bernini during his stay at the French court. It is likely that Claude Perrault shared the views set forth some 20 years later in his brother's *Parallels Between the Ancients and Moderns* in which Charles claimed that "Homer and Vergil made countless mistakes which the moderns no longer make [because] the ancients did not have all our rules." The Louvre's east front presents not simply a Classical revival but a vigorous distillation of what Claude Perrault considered to be the eternal ideals of beauty, intended to surpass anything built by the Romans themselves. Indeed, Perrault annotated Vitruvius and wrote his own treatise on the Classical orders.

THE PALACE OF VERSAILLES Louis XIV's largest enterprise was the Palace of Versailles (fig. 21.12), located 11 miles (18 km) from the center of Paris. By forcing the aristocracy to live under royal scrutiny outside Paris, the king hoped to prevent a repeat of the civil rebellion known as the Fronde, which had occurred during his minority in 1648–53.

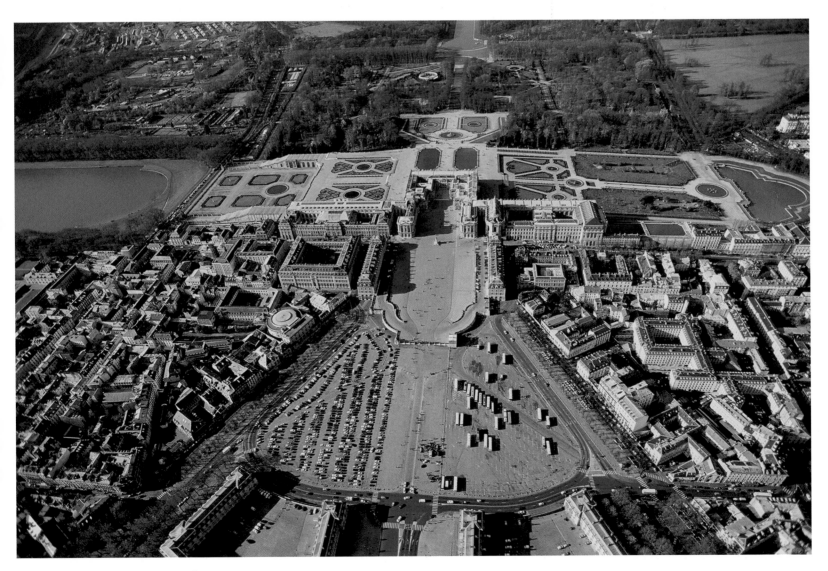

21.12 Aerial view of Versailles

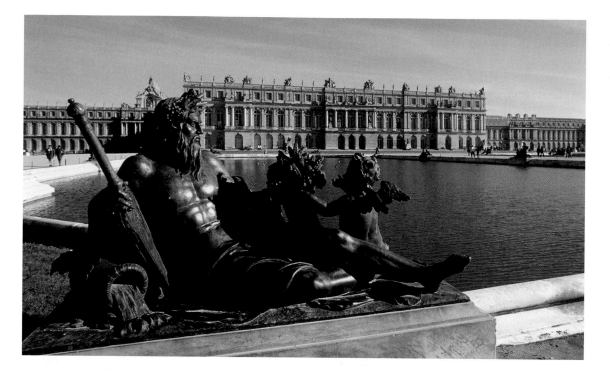

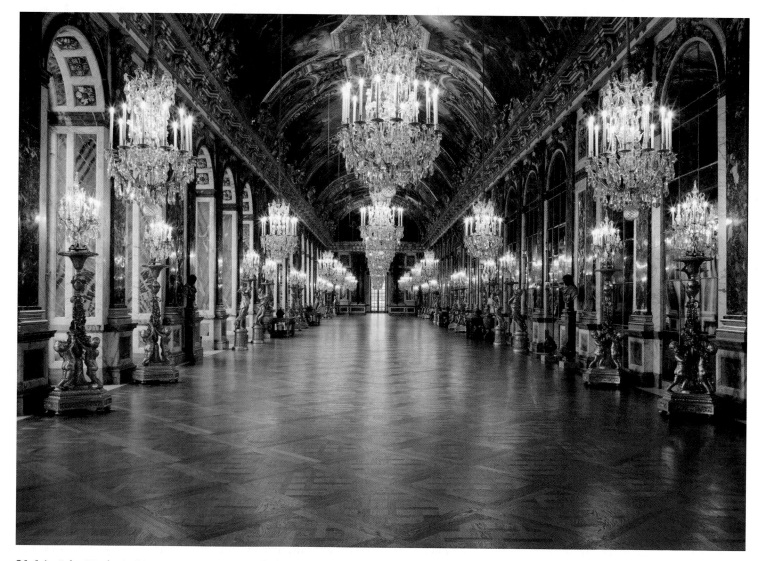

21.14 Jules Hardouin-Mansart, Louis Le Vau, and Charles Le Brun. Galerie des Glaces (Hall of Mirrors), Palace of Versailles. Begun 1678

The project was begun in 1669 by Le Vau, who designed the elevation of the garden front (fig. **21.13**); within a year of doing so he had died. Under the leadership of Jules Hardouin-Mansart (1646–1708), the structure was greatly expanded to accommodate the ever-growing royal household. The garden front, intended by Le Vau to be the main view of the palace, was stretched to an enormous length but with no change in the architectural elements. As a result, Le Vau's original façade design, a less severe variant of the Louvre's east front, now looks repetitious and out of scale. The center block contains a single room measuring 240 feet in length, the spectacular Galerie des Glaces, or Hall of Mirrors (fig. **21.14**). At either end are the Salon de la Guerre (Salon of War) and its counterpart, the Salon de la Paix (Salon of Peace). The sumptuous effect of the Galerie des Glaces recalls the gallery of Francis I at Fontainebleau, but the use of full-length mirrors was unique: They represented a great investment on the part of the monarchy. The art of large mirror-making was invented in Venice and brought to France by agents of Colbert. Such extravagant details were meant to reinforce the majesty of both Louis's reign and of France. The mirrors were placed in such a way as to reflect the gardens outside, making the room appear larger by day. At night, myriad reflections of candlelight illuminated the grand space. Whether by day or by night, the effect was impressive.

Baroque features, although not officially acknowledged by the architects, appeared inside the palace. This shift reflected the king's own taste. Louis XIV was interested less in architectural theory and monumental Classical exteriors than in the lavish interiors that would provide suitable settings for himself and his court. Thus, the man to whom he listened most often was not an architect but the painter Charles Le Brun, whose goal was to subordinate all the arts to the expression of the king's power. To achieve this aim, he drew freely on his memories of Rome; the great decorative schemes of the Italian Baroque must have impressed him. Although a disciple of Poussin, Le Brun had studied first with Vouet and became a superb decorator. At Versailles, he employed architects, sculptors, painters, and decorators to produce ensembles of unprecedented splendor. The Salon de la Guerre (fig. **21.15**), which includes a relief of *The Triumph of Louis XIV* by Antoine Coysevox (see page 753), is close in many ways to the theatricality and variety of mediums of Bernini's Cornaro Chapel (see fig. 19.31). Although Le Brun's ensemble is less adventurous than Bernini's, he has given greater emphasis to surface decoration. As in many Italian Baroque interiors, the separate components are less impressive than the effect of the whole.

THE GARDENS AT VERSAILLES Apart from its magnificent interior, the most impressive aspect of Versailles is its park designed by André Le Nôtre (1613–1700), who had become director of the gardens of Louis XIII in 1643 and whose family had served as royal gardeners for generations. Versailles and its gardens are vast: The completed palace and park covers almost 18,000 acres (the wall around it is 27 miles long). The type of formal gardens found at Versailles had their beginnings in Renaissance Florence but had never been attempted on the scale

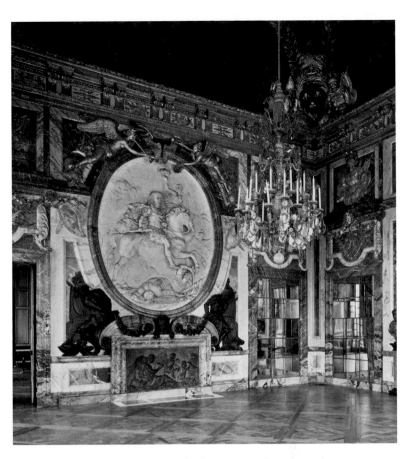

21.15 Jules Hardouin-Mansart, Charles Le Brun (the room and decoration), and Antoine Coysevox (for the relief, *The Triumph of Louis XIV*). Salon de la Guerre (Salon of War), Palace of Versailles. Begun 1678

achieved by Le Nôtre, who transformed an entire natural forest into a controlled park, a massive and expensive enterprise that reflected the grandeur of the king. The park follows its Grand Axis from east to west, intended to imply the course of the sun as it rises in the east over the king (the Sun King) in the palace and sets in the west at the farthest end of the gardens. Conceptually, the landscape is as significant as the palace—perhaps more so, for it suggests the king's dominion over nature. The landscape design is so strictly correlated with the plan of the palace that it in effect continues the architectural space. Like the interiors, the formal gardens were meant to provide a suitable setting for the king's public appearances. They form a series of "outdoor rooms" for the splendid fêtes and spectacles that were an integral part of Louis's court.

The spirit of absolutism is apparent in Le Nôtre's plan, which called for the taming of nature: Forests were thinned to create stately avenues, plants were shaped into manicured hedges, water was pumped into exuberant fountains and serene lakes. The formal gardens consist of a multitude of paths, terraces, basins, mazes, and parterres (designed flower beds) that create a unified geometric whole. Farther from the palace, the plan becomes less formal and incorporates the site's densely wooded areas and open meadows. Throughout, carefully planned vistas give rise to visual surprises. An especially important aspect of the landscape design was the program of sculpture, much of which incorporated images of Apollo, the sun-god, a favorite symbol of Louis XIV.

Versailles was called by a contemporary "pure harmony. Everything there is part of the unity of a perfect work of art." But the elaborate and expansive gardens had their detractors as well. From these critics we are able to ascertain what life was like at Versailles. The duc de Saint-Simon, a member of the court but no admirer of Louis, recorded in his diary:

> Versailles…the dullest of all places, without prospect, without wood, without water without soil; for the ground is all shifting sand or swamp, the air accordingly bad.…You are introduced [in the gardens] to the freshness of the shade only by a vast torrid zone.…The violence everywhere done to nature repels and wearies us despite ourselves. The abundance of water forced up and gathered together in all parts is rendered green thick and muddy; it disseminates humidity, unhealthy and evident; and an odor still more so. I might never finish upon the monstrous defects of a palace so immense.

Memoirs of Louis XIV and His Court and of the Regency by the Duke of Saint-Simon, II (New York: P. F. Collier and Son, 1910)

THE STYLE OF JULES HARDOUIN-MANSART Constrained at Versailles by the design of Le Vau, Jules Hardouin-Mansart's own style can be better appreciated in the church of the Invalides (fig. **21.16**), best known today for housing the tomb of Napoleon. Originally the structure formed part of a hospital that served as a hostel for the many disabled soldiers returning from Louis's continuous wars, gathering them off the streets of Paris where they might incite disorder. The complex consists of a series of dormitories, dining halls, infirmaries, and two chapels—a simple, unadorned one for the soldiers and an elaborate, domed space for the king, where he could be seen high above them during his visits. Hardouin-Mansart's design visually connected the sacrifice of the soldiers to their allegiance to the king and the absolute authority of the monarchy.

In plan, the Invalides consists of a Greek cross with four corner chapels (fig. **21.17**); it is based on Michelangelo's and Bramante's centralized plans for St. Peter's. The dome, too, reflects the influence of Michelangelo, but consists of three shells instead of the usual two. The façade breaks forward repeatedly in the crescendo effect introduced by Maderno (see fig. 19.13), and the façade and dome are as closely linked as at Borromini's Sant'Agnese in the Piazza Navona (see fig. 19.23). The dome itself is the most original, as well as the most Baroque, feature of Hardouin-Mansart's design. Tall and slender, it rises in a single continuous curve from the base of the drum to the spire atop the lantern. On the first drum rests a second, short drum. Its windows provide light for the paintings on the dome's interior. The windows are hidden behind a "pseudo-shell" with a large opening at the top so that the painted visions of heavenly glory seem to be mysteriously illuminated and suspended in space. The bold theatrical lighting of the Invalides places it firmly within the Baroque style.

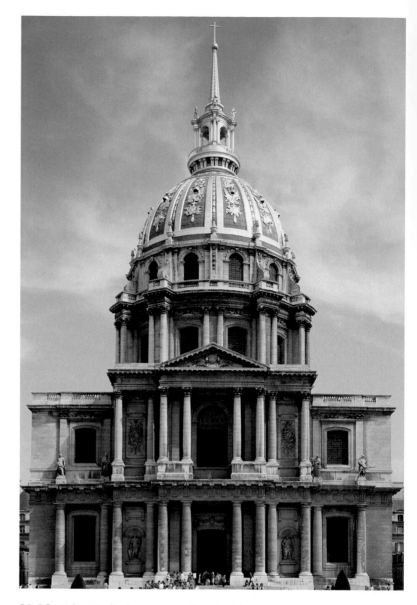

21.16 Jules Hardouin-Mansart. Church of the Invalides, Paris. 1677–91

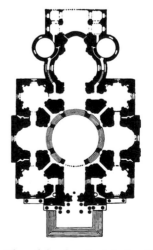

21.17 Plan of the church of the Invalides

Sculpture: The Impact of Bernini

Sculpture evolved into an official royal style in much the same way as architecture—through the influence of Rome and the impact of Bernini's visit to the royal court in 1665. While in Paris, Bernini carved a marble bust of Louis XIV. He was also commissioned to create an equestrian statue of the king, which he later executed in Rome and sent back to Paris, where it was reworked. It is now at Versailles.

ANTOINE COYSEVOX Bernini's influence can be seen in the work of Antoine Coysevox (1640–1720), the first in a long line of distinguished French portrait sculptors and one of the artists employed by Charles Le Brun at Versailles. The large stucco relief of the victorious Louis XIV that Coysevox made for the Salon de la Guerre (see fig. 21.16) retains the pose of Bernini's equestrian statue, although it has more restraint. In a vivacious terra-cotta portrait of the influential Le Brun (fig. **21.18**), Coysevox shows the artist with head turned to the side and slightly parted lips in a "speaking likeness" of the kind we have already seen in the paintings of Frans Hals (see fig. 20.17). The drapery folded over itself below the shoulder line recalls the general outline of Bernini's bust of Louis XIV. Le Brun's face, however, shows a naturalism and subtle characterization that are Coysevox's own.

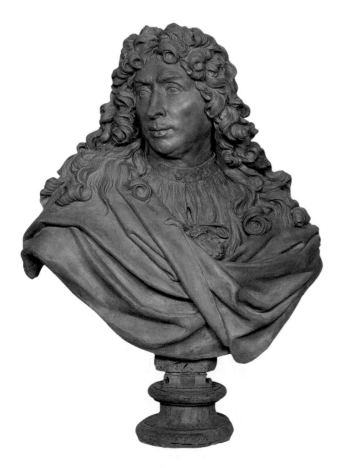

21.18   Antoine Coysevox, *Charles Le Brun*. 1676. Terra cotta, height 26" (66 cm). The Wallace Collection, London. Reproduced by Permission of the Trustees

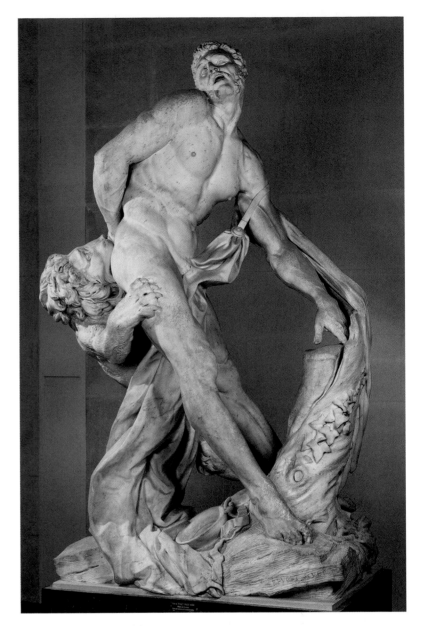

21.19   Pierre-Paul Puget, *Milo of Crotona*. 1671–82. Marble, height 8'10½" (2.7 m). Musée du Louvre, Paris

PIERRE-PAUL PUGET Of all the seventeenth-century French sculptors, Pierre-Paul Puget (1620–1694) best represents the High Baroque style. Puget had no success at court until after Colbert's death, when Le Brun's power began to decline. His finest statue, *Milo of Crotona* (fig. **21.19**), owes its fierceness and drama to the impact of Bernini's trip to Paris and benefits from a comparison with Bernini's *David* (see fig. 19.30). Although Puget's composition is more contained, he nevertheless successfully conveys the dramatic force of the hero as he is attacked by a lion while his hand is trapped in a tree stump. The creature attacks from behind and digs its claws deeply into the thigh of Milo, who twists painfully and cries out in agony. The violent action imbues the statue with an intensity that also recalls the *Laocoön* (see page 183). This reference to antiquity, one suspects, is what made the work acceptable to Louis XIV.

BAROQUE ARCHITECTURE IN ENGLAND

The English contribution to the Baroque came mostly in the form of architecture since in painting it was artists from Italy, Flanders, and the Dutch Republic (Orazio and Artemisia Gentileschi, Anthony van Dyck and Peter Paul Rubens—the latter two were knighted during their stays—who dominated the English royal court through the century. Orazio Gentileschi and Rubens worked for James I, while Charles I's court painter Van Dyck executed both portraits and allegorical paintings (see figs. 20.7 and 20.8). After Van Dyck's death, many artists continued his style of portraiture for wealthy patrons, initiating little in the visual arts until the Restoration of Charles II in 1660. After the Great Fire of London in 1666, the rebuilding of the city gave priority to architecture, which thereafter represented the most important English artistic achievement.

Inigo Jones and the Impact of Palladio

The first significant English architect was Inigo Jones (1573–1652), architect to James I and Charles I as well as the era's leading English theatrical designer. Jones's style developed from the country-house tradition of large private mansions in parklike settings. Jones took two lengthy trips to Italy in 1597–1603 and 1613–14, with an interlude in Paris in 1609. Upon returning from his second trip to Italy, he was appointed surveyor of the king's works, a post he held until 1643. Jones was now an affirmed disciple of Andrea Palladio, whose work he saw in Venice and whose treatises (along with those of Alberti) he owned and annotated. Before Jones, English architecture was a pastiche of medieval and Renaissance forms; its high point was the English Gothic cathedral (see figs. 12.49–12.54). Jones is responsible for introducing Palladio's Renaissance Classicism to England, although the style took root only in the early decades of the eighteenth century, when a building boom resulted in the trend called the Palladian Revival.

The Banqueting House Jones built at Whitehall Palace in London (fig. 21.20) conforms to the principles set out in Palladio's treatises, although it does not copy any specific Palladian project. It was originally intended to be used for court ceremonies and performances called masques (a spectacle combining dance, theater, and music), although evening entertainments were halted after 1635 because smoke from torchlights was damaging Rubens's ceiling painting, the *Apotheosis of James I*. The Banqueting House is essentially a Vitruvian "basilica," a double cube with an apse for the king's throne, which Jones has treated as a Palladian villa. It is more like a Renaissance palazzo than any other building north of the Alps that had been designed at that time. Jones uses an ordered, Classical vocabulary and the rules of proportion to compose the building in three parts. The Ionic and composite orders of the pilasters add an understated elegance, and alternating segmental and triangular pediments over the first-floor windows create a rhythmic effect. The sculpted garland below the roofline and the balustrade above decoratively enhance the overall structure. The building is perhaps starker than originally conceived; it bore colored stones for each of the stories before the façade was resurfaced. Jones's spare style stood as a beacon of Classicist orthodoxy in England for 200 years.

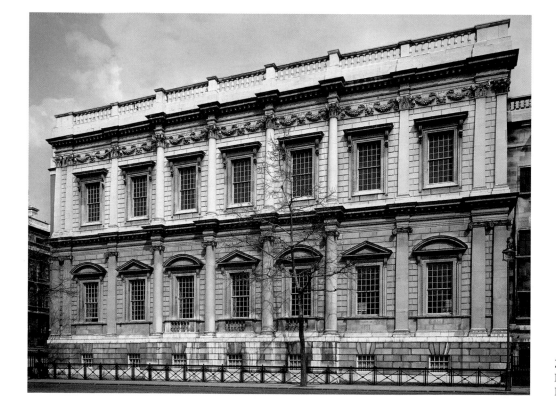

21.20 Inigo Jones. West front of the Banqueting House, Whitehall Palace, London. 1619–22

Sir Christopher Wren

But for the destruction caused by the Great Fire of London of 1666, Sir Christopher Wren (1632–1723), the most important English architect of the late seventeenth century, might have remained an amateur. Wren may be considered the Baroque counterpart of the Renaissance artist-scientist. An intellectual prodigy, he first studied anatomy and then physics, mathematics, and astronomy, and he was highly esteemed by Sir Isaac Newton for his understanding of geometry. Early in his career, Wren held the position of chair in the astronomy department at Gresham College, London, and then professor of mathematics at Oxford University. His interest in architecture did not surface until he was about 30 years old. His technical knowledge may have affected the shape of his buildings; certainly, no previous architect had gone to such lengths to conceal a building's structural supports. Only an architect thoroughly grounded in geometry and mathematics could have achieved such results, and the technical proficiency of Wren's structures has continually confounded his critics.

THE GREAT FIRE OF LONDON In early September 1666, the city of London was devastated by a catastrophic, uncontrollable fire covering 373 acres; four-fifths of the city was razed; 400 streets smoked and over 100,000 people made homeless. One observer famously wrote: "London was, but is no more." Within a few days, Wren had already planned a new London: The burned areas would be cleared and the builders would start anew. His drawing of September 11, 1666 has been translated three-dimensionally here (fig. **21.21**) and shows the influence of the planning of Renaissance Rome, known to him through engravings, and of Paris, a city he had only recently visited. The plan includes wide avenues and focal points punctuated by church steeples he would design (see fig. 21.24); the focal point (in the detail) is Wren's Monument to the Great Fire of London, which was erected between 1671 and 1677. Although his plan proved too radical for the crown to adopt, Wren was named to the short-lived royal commission to reconstruct the city (see www.myartslab.com) and many of his ideas were incorporated into the new urban planning: for example, concern about materials (limitations on the use of wood), and provisions for pavements and treatment of sewage.

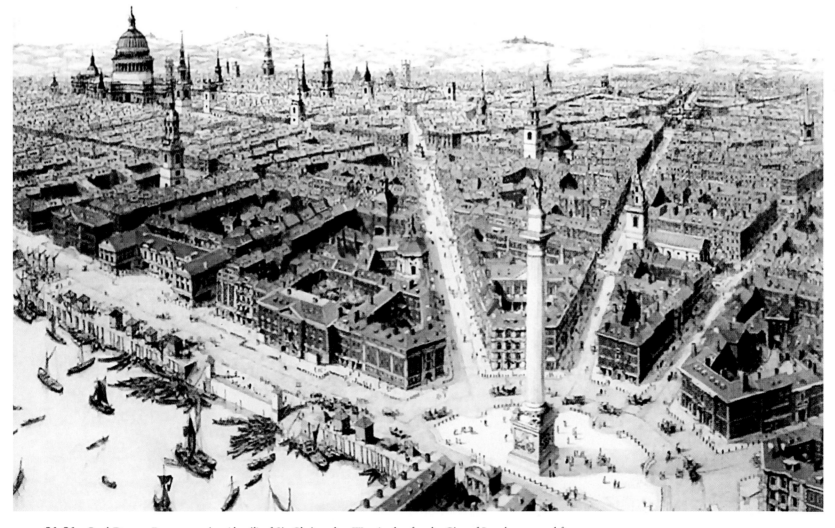

21.21 Paul Draper. Reconstruction (detail) of Sir Christopher Wren's plan for the City of London created from Wren's September 11, 1666 drawing after the Great Fire

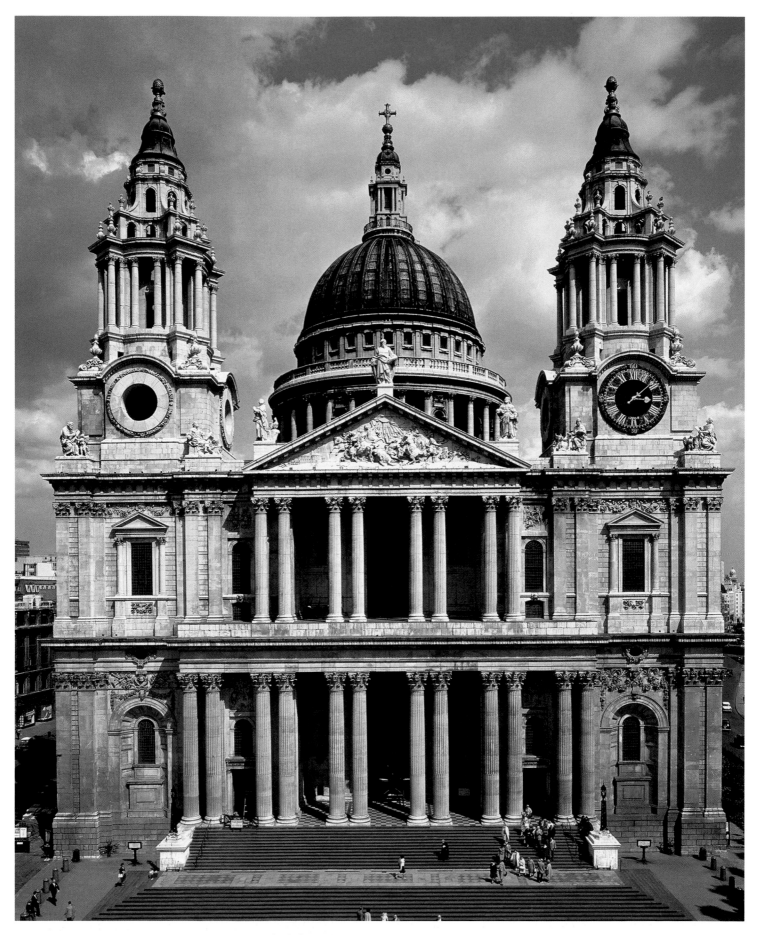

21.22   Sir Christopher Wren. Façade of St. Paul's cathedral, London. 1675–1710

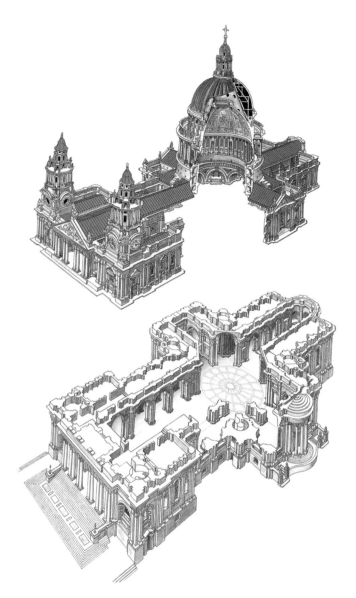

21.23 Cutaway 3D reconstruction of St. Paul's cathedral

The Great Fire of London provided Wren with the opportunity to rebuild and reframe the city and its skyline.

A few years later he began his designs for the rebuilding of the almost totally destroyed St. Paul's cathedral (figs. **21.22**). Wren favored central-plan churches and originally conceived of St. Paul's in the shape of a Greek cross with a huge domed crossing, based on Michelangelo's plan of St. Peter's. This idea was also inspired by a previous design by Inigo Jones, who had been involved with the restoration of the original Gothic structure of St. Paul's earlier in the century. Wren's proposal was rejected by the church authorities, however, who favored a conventional basilica. In the end, the plan is that of a Latin cross (as can be seen in the cut-away reconstruction fig. **21.23**), the same followed for most Catholic churches, including St. Peter's. This was an ironic outcome given that the building program could have provided an opportunity to create a new vocabulary for the Protestant Church of England.

On his only journey abroad in 1665–66, Wren visited France and met with Bernini, who was in Paris at the invitation of Louis

XIV to design and complete the Louvre. The influence of this trip can be seen on the façade of St. Paul's (as well as in Wren's new street plans for London), where the impact of contemporary architecture in Paris can be discerned—the double columns of the Louvre and the three-part dome of Hardouin-Mansart's church of the Invalides. Unlike St. Peter's, St. Paul's dome (see fig. 21.22) rises high above the main body of the building and dominates the façade. It looks like a much-enlarged version of Bramante's Tempietto (see fig. 16.8). St. Paul's is an up-to-date Baroque design that reflects Wren's thorough knowledge of the Italian and French architecture of the day. Indeed, Wren believed that Paris provided "the best school of architecture in Europe," and he was equally affected by the Roman Baroque. The lantern and upper part of the bell towers suggest that he knew Borromini's Sant'Agnese in Piazza Navona (see fig. 19.23), probably from drawings or engravings. The present structure reflects not only the complex evolution of the design but also later changes made by the commission overseeing construction, which dismissed Wren in 1718.

For Wren as for Newton (who was appointed a commissioner of St. Paul's in 1697), mathematics and geometry were central to the new understanding of the universe and humanity's place in it. In Wren's *Five Tracts*, written toward the end of his life and presented by his son to the Royal Society in 1740, he stated that architecture must conform to "natural reason," which is the basis of eternal Beauty. In other words, architecture must use rational (that is, abstract) geometrical forms, such as the square and the

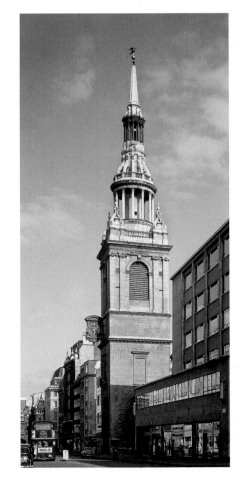

21.24 Sir Christopher Wren. Steeple of church of St. Mary-le-Bow, London. 1680

circle, as well as proportion, perspective, and harmony—but it must not sacrifice variety. Such rationality and diversity are clearly evident in Wren's design for St. Paul's.

Besides St. Paul's, Wren worked on 52 of the 87 damaged or destroyed churches, designing distinctive steeples for many of them. The steeple of the church of St. Mary-le-Bow (fig. 21.24) provides us with the most famous example. (It should be noted that many of these churches, including this one, were damaged during the bombing of London in World War II and have been reconstructed.) The steeple is exceptionally tall (225 feet high) and even today soars over surrounding buildings. The height is achieved through an unusual stacking of components: a two-story base (with arched entrance), plain attic, bell housing with paired pilasters, and a colonnaded temple surmounted by buttresses that support a lantern and obelisklike pinnacle as seen in the church of the Invalides. To indicate the church's dedication, Wren designed 12 "bows"—actually inverted brackets—at the base of the round temple. The result is an elaborate, multistoried steeple, Gothic in its verticality yet based on Classical motifs. Nothing like it had ever been seen before. Wren's innovations in this church and the others built after the Great Fire gave English Baroque church architecture its distinctive character.

John Vanbrugh and Nicholas Hawksmoor

The marriage of English, French, and Italian Baroque elements is still more evident in Blenheim Palace (fig. 21.25), a grandiose structure designed by Sir John Vanbrugh (1664–1726), a gifted amateur, with the aid of Nicholas Hawksmoor (1661–1736), Wren's most talented pupil. Although Blenheim is considered to be Vanbrugh's greatest work, the building was in fact completed by Hawksmoor; yet the architecture is seamless. Blenheim skillfully combines the massing of an English castle with the breadth of a country house, the rambling character of a French chateau such as Fontainebleau (see fig. 18.1), and a façade inspired by Sir Christopher Wren, Vanbrugh's rival. However, when Blenheim and its framing colonnade are compared with the piazza of St. Peter's (see fig. 19.14), Vanbrugh's design reveals itself to be even closer to Bernini. The main block uses a colossal Corinthian order to wed a temple portico with a Renaissance palace, while the wings rely on a low-slung Doric order. Such an eclectic approach, extreme even by the relaxed standards of the period, is maintained in the details. Vanbrugh, like Inigo Jones, had a strong interest in the theater and was a popular playwright. Blenheim's theatricality and massiveness make it a symbol of English power, a fitting, but more modest, counterpart to Versailles in both its structure and its grounds. Designed mainly for show and entertainment, it was presented by a grateful nation to the duke of Marlborough for his victories over French and German forces at the Battle of Blenheim in 1704, during the War of Spanish Succession.

The power and massiveness of Baroque architecture from Bernini to Blenheim changed the look of western Europe in the seventeenth century. It also provided the foundation for the art and architecture of the Rococo—both in continuation and in contrast.

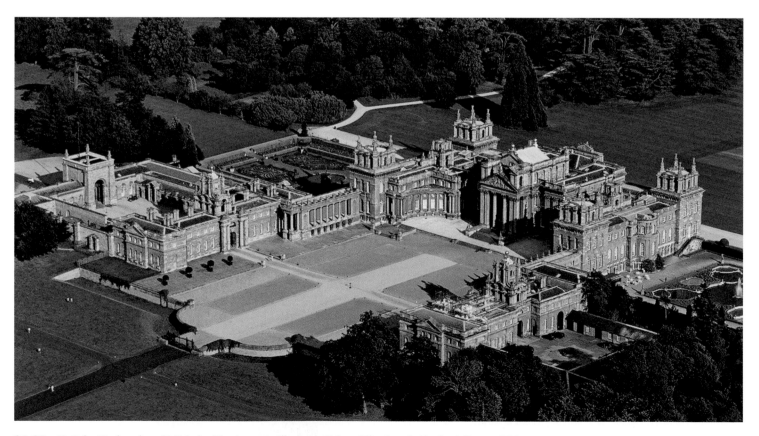

21.25   Sir John Vanbrugh and Nicholas Hawksmoor. Blenheim Palace, Woodstock, England. Begun 1705

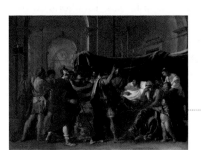

1619–22 Inigo Jones, Banqueting House, Westminster

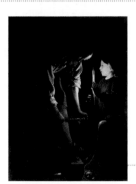

1627–28 Poussin's *Death of Germanicus*

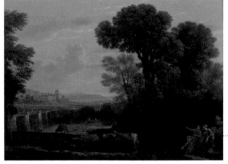

1648 Claude's *A Pastoral Landscape*

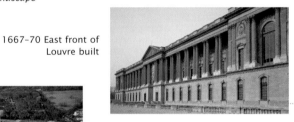

1667–70 East front of Louvre built

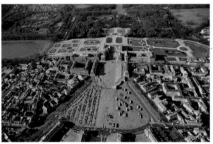

1669–85 Palace of Versailles built

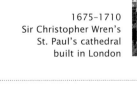

ca. 1642 La Tour, *Joseph the Carpenter*

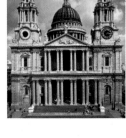

1675–1710 Sir Christopher Wren's St. Paul's cathedral built in London

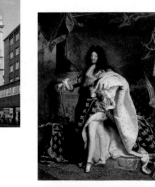

1680 Wren's steeple for Mary-le-Bow

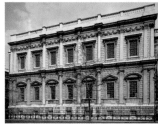

1701 Rigaud's *Portrait of Louis XIV*

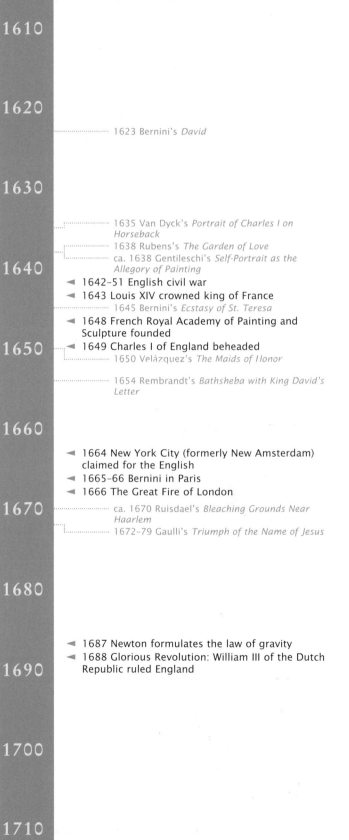

1610

1620

1623 Bernini's *David*

1630

1635 Van Dyck's *Portrait of Charles I on Horseback*
1638 Rubens's *The Garden of Love*
ca. 1638 Gentileschi's *Self-Portrait as the Allegory of Painting*

1640

◄ 1642–51 English civil war
◄ 1643 Louis XIV crowned king of France
1645 Bernini's *Ecstasy of St. Teresa*
◄ 1648 French Royal Academy of Painting and Sculpture founded
◄ 1649 Charles I of England beheaded
1650 Velázquez's *The Maids of Honor*

1650

1654 Rembrandt's *Bathsheba with King David's Letter*

1660

◄ 1664 New York City (formerly New Amsterdam) claimed for the English
◄ 1665–66 Bernini in Paris
◄ 1666 The Great Fire of London

1670

ca. 1670 Ruisdael's *Bleaching Grounds Near Haarlem*
1672–79 Gaulli's *Triumph of the Name of Jesus*

1680

◄ 1687 Newton formulates the law of gravity
◄ 1688 Glorious Revolution: William III of the Dutch Republic ruled England

1690

1700

1710

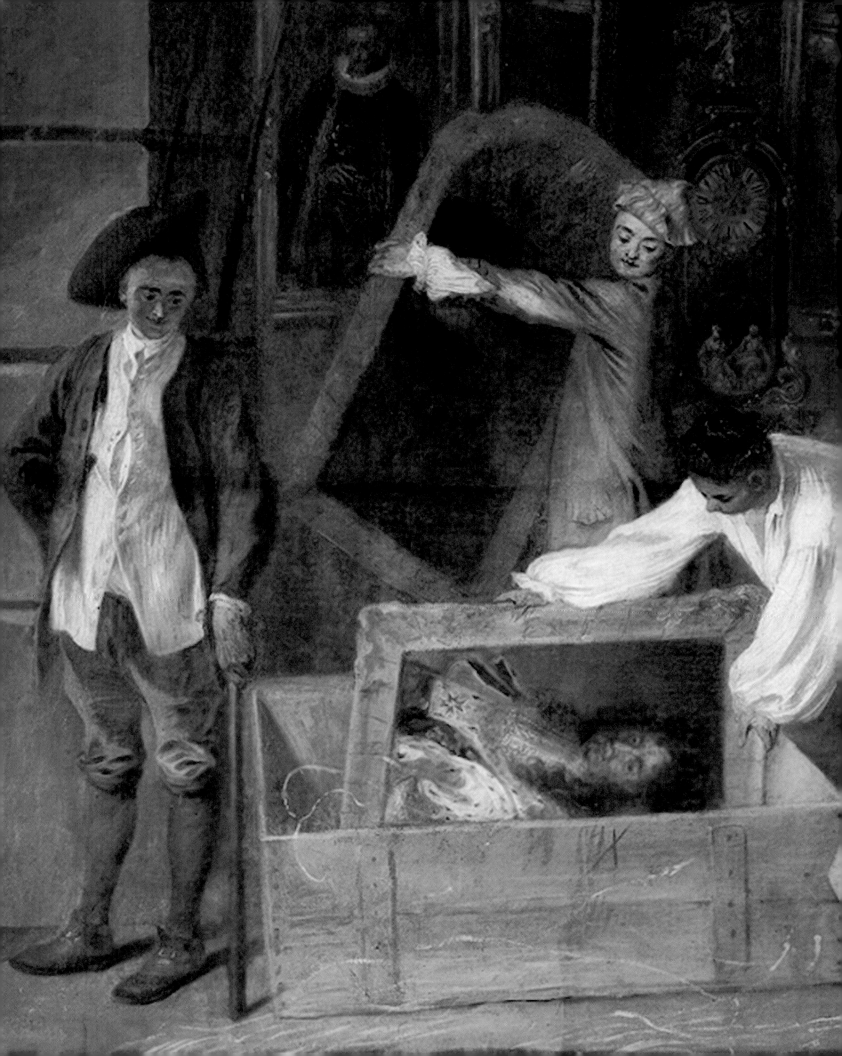

CHAPTER 22

The Rococo

N FRANCE THE ROCOCO STYLE IS LINKED WITH LOUIS XV (1710–1774) because it corresponds roughly to his lifetime—the heart of the eighteenth century. But the first signs of the Rococo style had appeared as much as 50 years before Louis's birth, at the height of the late seventeenth-century Baroque style, and it continued on through the excesses of the reign of Louis XVI (r. 1774–1792)

and his wife, Marie Antoinette, to the French Revolution of 1789. As noted by the philosopher François-Marie Arouet, better known by his pen name, Voltaire (1694–1778), the eighteenth century lived indebted to the past. In art, Poussin and Rubens cast long shadows over the period. The controversy between their followers, in turn, goes back much further to the debate between the supporters of Michelangelo and those of Titian over the merits of *disegno* (expressed through drawing or line) versus color (see page 584). In this sense, the Rococo, like the Baroque, still belongs to the Renaissance world.

Despite similarities between the Baroque and Rococo, a fundamental difference exists between the two styles. In a word, it is fantasy. If the Baroque presents theater on a grand scale, the Rococo stage is smaller and more intimate. Its artifice evokes an enchanted realm that presents a diversion from real life. In some ways, the Rococo in France manifests a shift in taste among aristocrats, who reasserted their power as patrons and began to favor stylized motifs drawn from nature and a more domestic art—private rather than public—with which to decorate their new homes in Paris.

The word Rococo fits well, for it implies both a natural quality and a sense of ornamentation well suited to court life. It was coined in the nineteenth century as a disparaging term, taken from the French word *rocaille* (meaning "pebble") and the Portuguese *barocco* ("**baroque**"), to refer to what were then perceived as the excessively ornate tastes of the early eighteenth century. The word Rococo, then, in the first place refers to the playful, irregular pebbles, stones, and shells that decorated grottoes of Italian gardens and became the principal motifs of French interior designs.

Although sometimes viewed as the final phase of the Baroque, the Rococo asserted its own stylistic traits and represents a period of independent intense creative and intellectual activity. French artists continued to be trained in the tradition of the Royal Academy of Painting and Sculpture, which stressed working from live models, studying anatomy, and practicing perspective and proportion—lessons supplemented by lectures on the art of Raphael and Poussin. Yet artists also began exploring new subjects and treating old themes in new ways. The interest in the poetic genre of the pastoral, as practiced by Baroque artists including Claude (see pages 743–44), with subjects of love and loss, romantic trysts, and poetic musings took on growing importance in the eighteenth century. Patrons were increasingly taken with the notion of the "simple man" existing in an idealized nature. By way of response, the French Academy even established a new category to reflect this new interest, called the *fête galante*, a type of painting introduced by Jean-Antoine Watteau. The style celebrated the tradition of love and eroticism in art, and broadened the range of human emotion depicted there.

Although most directly associated with France, the Rococo exerted a wide geographical influence and affected the arts in most

Detail of figure 22.4, Jean-Antoine Watteau, *Gersaint's Signboard*

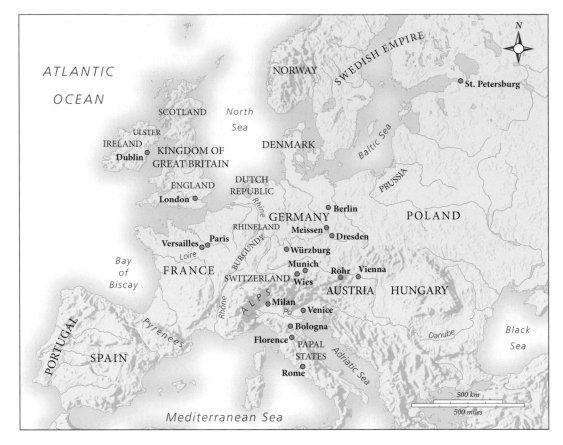

Map 22.1   Map of western Europe in the eighteenth century

of western and central Europe (map **22.1**). In Germany and Austria, the devastation of the Thirty Years' War (1618–1648) was followed in the eighteenth century by a period of rebuilding and a growth in the number of pilgrimage churches, whose architecture and decoration reflected both the transformation of the Baroque and the new Rococo style. Italian artists such as Tiepolo, with his assistants, painted ceiling frescoes in central European churches and palaces in this new elaborate and elegant style and produced similar works for their native city of Venice as well. There, Canaletto painted *vedute*, or scenes of the city, which provided foreign visitors with souvenirs of their Venetian stay.

European colonization of the New World continued in the eighteenth century. Armies battled to secure these distant lands, depleting their nations' treasuries but succeeding in sending back to their homelands exotic objects, including feathers, jewels, and metals that collectors coveted and artists used in the creation of new art. In the performing arts, the Venetian composer Antonio Vivaldi (1678–1741) and the German composer Johann Sebastian Bach (1685–1750) produced extraordinary music, and London became home to established theater, notably in Haymarket, Drury Lane, and Covent Garden.

FRANCE: THE RISE OF THE ROCOCO

After the death of Louis XIV in 1715, the nobility, formerly attached to the court at Versailles, found themselves freer from royal control. Louis XV, only two years old at Louis XIV's death, would not be crowned until 1723. This early period of the Rococo—between 1715 and 1723—is known as the Regency, so-called because France was governed by Louis's cousin Philip, duke of Orléans, who was acting as regent. With a nobleman in power, the aristocracy regained much of their former authority, and they abandoned the strict, demanding court life of Versailles. Rather than returning to their chateaux in the provinces, many chose to live in Paris, where they built elegant town houses with small intimate rooms. These *hotels particuliers* developed into social centers, known as **salons**, for intellectual gatherings. The rooms were decorated with paintings, porcelain, and small sculptures that created a lavish, light-hearted mood. Paintings, therefore, were just one element in the creation of an ambiance of refinement that permeated pre-revolutionary France. These paintings, as well as interior designs, would influence the decor of western and central Europe throughout the century.

Painting: Poussinistes versus Rubénistes

Toward the end of the seventeenth century, a dispute arose among the members of the French Academy, who formed themselves into two factions: the Poussinistes and the Rubénistes. Neither Poussin nor Rubens was still alive at the time of this debate, which focused on the issue of drawing versus color. French artists were familiar with Poussin's paintings, which had been sent from Rome back to Paris throughout his career, and they knew Rubens's work from the *Marie de' Medici Cycle* (see fig. 20.5) in the Luxembourg Palace. The conservative **Poussinistes** defended Poussin's view that line, which appealed to the mind, was superior to color, which appealed to the senses. The **Rubénistes** (many of whom were of Flemish descent) favored color, rather than drawing, as being truer to nature. They also pointed out that drawing, while admittedly based on reason, appealed only to the expert few, whereas color appealed to everyone. This argument had important implications. It suggested that the layperson should be the judge of artistic values, which challenged the Renaissance notion that painting, as a liberal art, could be appreciated only by the educated mind. The colorists eventually won the day, due in part to the popularity of painter Jean-Antoine Watteau.

JEAN-ANTOINE WATTEAU The greatest of the Rubénistes was Jean-Antoine Watteau (1684–1721). Born in Valenciennes, which until a few years before his birth had still been part of the Southern Netherlands, Watteau showed an affinity for the work of Rubens, the region's greatest artist. After moving to Paris in 1702, he made many drawings styled after Rubens's French works, including the *Marie de' Medici Cycle* (see fig. 20.5). Watteau was a significant contributor to the new Rococo style as well as to the new subjects associated with it. His painted visions show idyllic images of aristocratic life, with elegant figures luxuriously dressed in shimmering pastel colors and set in dreamlike outdoor settings. He often seamlessly interweaves theater and real life in his works, incorporating well-known characters from the *commedia dell'arte* (a type of improvisational Italian theater) and creating stagelike settings that serve as backdrops for his actors. The carefully posed figures evoke forlorn love, regret, or nostalgia, and imbue the scenes with an air of melancholy. Such works became increasingly sought after by collectors in France, and the popularity of such themes soon spread throughout Europe.

Because Watteau's fantasies had little historical or mythological basis, his paintings broke many academic rules and did not conform to any established category. In order to be able to admit Watteau as a member, the French Academy had to create a new classification of painting, *fêtes galantes* (meaning "elegant fêtes" or "outdoor entertainments"). This category joined the hierarchy of genres that had been established in the seventeenth century by academy member André Félibien (1619–1695). The premier category was history painting, considered to be the highest form of art because it was thought to require the most imagination and was therefore the most difficult to execute. Next came portraits, landscapes, and finally still lifes. Watteau's reception piece for the French Academy, required when he became a member in 1712, was not delivered until five years later. The work, *A Pilgrimage to Cythera* (fig. 22.1), is an evocation of love and includes elements of classical mythology. Cythera, which came to be viewed as an

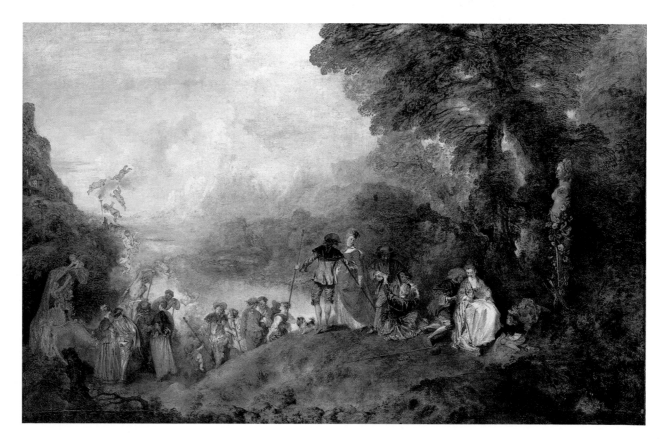

22.1 Jean-Antoine Watteau, *A Pilgrimage to Cythera*. 1717. Oil on canvas, 4'3" × 6'4½" (1.3 × 1.9 m). Musée du Louvre, Paris

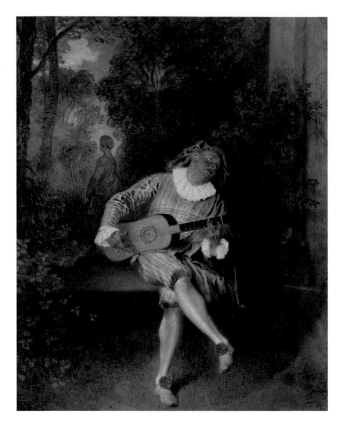

22.2 Jean-Antoine Watteau, *Mezzetin*. ca. 1718. Oil on canvas, 21¾ × 17" (55.3 × 43.2 cm). Metropolitan Museum of Art, New York. Munsey Fund, 1934 (34.138)

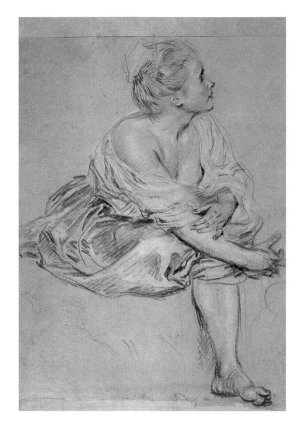

22.3 Jean-Antoine Watteau, *Seated Young Woman*. ca. 1716. Red, black, and white chalks on cream paper, 10 × 6¾" (25.5 × 17.1 cm). The Pierpont Morgan Library, New York

island of love, was one of the settings for the Greek myth of the birth of Aphrodite (Venus), who rose from the foam of the sea. The title suggests this traditional subject, but the painting was described in the French Academy records as a *fête galante*, perhaps the first use of this term.

Watteau has created a delightful yet slightly melancholic scene. It is unclear whether the couples are arriving at or leaving the island. The action unfolds in the foreground from right to left like a continuous narrative, which suggests that the figures may be about to board the boat. Two lovers remain engaged in their amorous tryst; behind them, another couple rises to follow a third pair down the hill as the reluctant young woman casts a longing look back at the goddess's sacred grove. Young couples, accompanied by swarms of cupids, pay homage to Venus, whose garlanded sculpture appears on the far right. The delicate colors—pale greens, blues, pinks, and roses—suggest the gentle nature of the lovers' relationships. The subtle gradations of tone showed Watteau's debt to Rubens and helped establish the supremacy of the Rubénistes.

As a fashionable conversation piece, the scene recalls the elegant figures in the courtly scenes of the Limbourg brothers' illuminations and those in Rubens's *The Garden of Love* (see figs. 14.3 and 20.6), but Watteau has altered the scale and added a touch of poignancy reminiscent of Giorgione and Titian. Watteau's figures are slim, graceful, and small in scale; they appear even

more so when compared with most Baroque imagery. The landscape does not overwhelm the scene but echoes its idyllic and somewhat elegiac mood. Watteau produces a sense of nostalgia, with its implications of longing and unrealized passion. This is achieved not only through the figures and their gentle touching and hesitancy, but also through the sympathetic parallel found in his landscape and the sculptures in it.

A similarly nostalgic atmosphere is evoked in Watteau's *Mezzetin* (fig. **22.2**), a painting of a stock figure from the *commedia dell'arte*, whose name means "half-measure" and who played the role of an amorous suitor. He sings a pleading love song while playing his guitar in a parklike setting decorated with a statue of a woman in the background. Scholars presume that he is playing his music to her. It has been suggested that the painting, which was owned by Watteau's friend Jean de Jullienne (the author of a biography of the artist; see *Primary Source*, page 766), may have related to Jean's courtship of his wife. The wistful musician strains to look up to the right, out of the picture. Yet the fantastical, delicately striped costume of rose, pale blue, and white, paired with yellow shoes and rose beret and cape, transforms the scene from melancholic to magical. The small, single figure in pastel colors, set amid this pale verdant setting, is typical of the Rococo in terms of spirit, figure type, and color of costume and setting.

As already stated, Watteau's use of color planted him firmly in the Rubéniste camp. However, his innovations and creativity as a

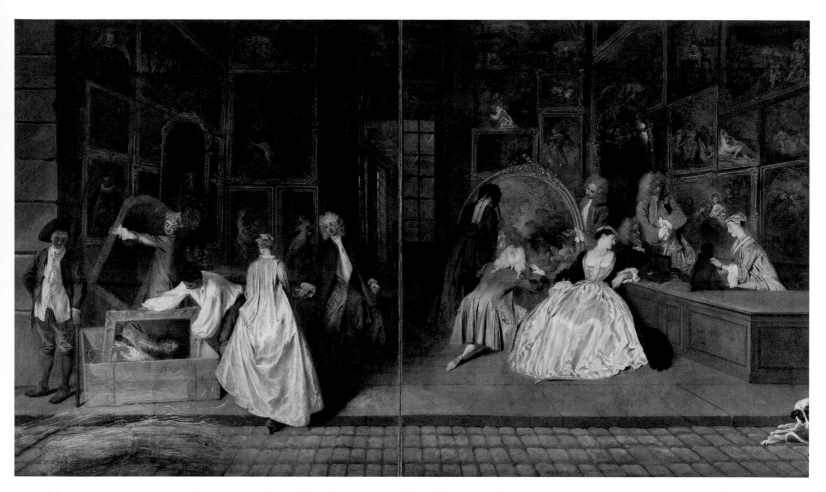

22.4   Jean-Antoine Watteau, *Gersaint's Signboard*. 1721. Oil on canvas, 5'5¼" × 10' (1.63 × 3.08 m). (Later cut in two pieces and then rejoined.) Schloss Charlottenburg, Staatliche Schlösser und Gärten, Berlin

draftsman (which would have implied a Poussiniste status) combined both color and line. (See *Materials and Techniques*, page 769.) Although previous artists, including Rubens, may have drawn with red or black chalk heightened with white, Watteau excelled in this technique, known as **trois crayons**. In *Seated Young Woman* (fig. **22.3**), he uses the three chalks to best effect, so that the red color that defines her body—legs, hands, parts of her face (lips, tip of nose), nape, breast—suggests a vivacious quality when contrasted against the black and white of her clothing, eyebrows, and upswept hair. The colors enliven and add a spontaneity to this life drawing. In numerous sketches, Watteau worked out poses, movements, gestures, and expressions, many of which (although apparently not this drawing) served as studies for figures in his paintings.

The same informality can be seen in one of Watteau's best-known works, *Gersaint's Signboard* or *The Shop Sign* (fig. **22.4** and page 760). Created to advertise the wares of his friend and art dealer Edmé Gersaint, the sign does not in fact show Gersaint's gallery. Gersaint wrote about this commission and indicated that it was made at Watteau's suggestion to allow him to "stretch his fingers" after he had returned from a trip to London. Watteau had been ill (he would die soon after of tuberculosis), and the implication was that the artist used this work as part of his hoped-for

convalescence. This account has since been disputed, but the work remains Watteau's last. The painting (originally arched at top) reportedly took only eight mornings to complete. It was meant to be exhibited outside but was shown for only 15 days (perhaps due to the weather or because it sold quickly). Gersaint reported that the painting attracted many artists as well as passersby who admired the natural, elegant poses of the figures—traits still admired today. The voluminous rose satin dress of the woman on the left, seen from the back, draws the eye; this figure is balanced by the languidly leaning woman on the right. Sophisticated and comfortable in the setting, the women are attended to by a solicitous staff as they admire paintings in the shop, arranged three to four high on the walls. Scholars do not believe these are copies of actual paintings but rather variants on Flemish and Venetian works, a theory that seems plausible when this work is compared with Jan Brueghel the Elder's *Allegory of Sight* and its real painting gallery (see fig. 20.10). The shop's stock also includes a variety of clocks and mirrors, which create an atmosphere of opulence and would remind the viewer of the world of the *ancien régime*. This association is supported by a portrait of Louis XIV based on Rigaud's (see fig. 21.10), seen on the left, which is being placed in a crate. Although on one level the presence of the king's image suggests the departure of the old (he had

PRIMARY SOURCE

Jean de Jullienne (1686–1767)

A Summary of the Life of Antoine Watteau, 1684–1721

Jullienne, a dyer and later the director of the Gobelin tapestry manufactory, was a lifelong friend of Watteau's and a collector of his works. At Watteau's death, he had all of the artist's drawings engraved and later did the same with his paintings, after buying many of them. His biography of the artist was first published in two volumes in 1726–28, along with 350 engravings after Watteau's paintings and drawings. Another two volumes followed.

Watteau, inclined more and more to study, and excited by the beauties of the gallery of this palace [the Luxembourg Palace] painted by Rubens, often went to study the color and the composition of this great master. This in a short time gave him a taste much more natural and very different from that which he had acquired with Gillot. …

Watteau was of medium height and weak constitution. He had a quick and penetrating mind and elevated sensibilities. He spoke little but well, and wrote likewise. He almost always meditated. A great admirer of nature and of all the masters who have copied her, assiduous work had made him a little melancholy. Cold and awkward in demeanor, which sometimes made him difficult to his friends and often to himself, he had no other fault than that of indifference and of a liking for change. It can be said that no painter ever had more fame than he during his life as well as after his death. His paintings which have risen to a very high price are today still eagerly sought after. They may be seen in Spain, in England, in Germany, in Prussia, in Italy, and in many places in France, especially in Paris. Also one must concede that there are no more agreeable pictures for small collections than his. They incorporate the correctness of drawing, truth of color and an inimitable delicacy of brushwork. He not only excelled in *gallant* and rustic compositions, but also in subjects of the army, of marches, and bivouacs of soldiers, whose simple and natural character makes this sort of pictures very precious. He even left a few historical pieces whose excellent taste shows well enough that he would have been equally successful in this genre if he had made it his principal objective.

Although Watteau's life was very short, the great number of his works could make one think that it was very long, whereas it only shows that he was very industrious. Indeed, even his hours of recreation and walking were never spent without his studying nature and drawing her in the situations in which she seemed to him most admirable.

The quantity of drawings produced by his study and which have been chose to be engraved and to form a separate work is a proof of this truth.

Source: *A Documentary History of Art*, II, ed. Elizabeth Gilmore Holt (Princeton, NJ: Princeton University Press, 1982)

died only a few years before in 1715), it is actually a pun on the name of the shop, Au Grand Monarque. Watteau's extraordinary abilities as a painter are apparent as he transforms this commercial venture into a sensitive work of sophistication and tender beauty.

FRANÇOIS BOUCHER Following the untimely death of Watteau in 1721, François Boucher (1703–1770) rose to prominence in French painting. Boucher built his reputation on his imaginative compositions, pastoral landscapes, and scenes of bourgeois daily life. He served as court painter to Madame de Pompadour (1721–1764), who has been called the "godmother of the Rococo." She was Louis XV's mistress, as well as his frequent political advisor and a major patron of the arts.

Boucher painted her portrait numerous times and with his 1756 life-size painting: *Portrait of Madame de Pompadour* (fig. **22.5**) he established—even orchestrated—her self-fashioning as a *femme-savante*—an educated, cultured, accomplished woman who was also elegant, beautiful, and sophisticated. Born Jeanne-Antoinette Poisson, she became the Royal Mistress (an actual title) in 1746. She had come from a nonaristocratic family, but because of her relationship with the king had been made a duchess, a marquis, and in the year this painting was done (when she was 35 years old and no longer his mistress, but lifelong confidante), she was named Lady-in-Waiting to the Queen, the highest nonroyal title at court. It has even been suggested that the background clock indicates the actual time she was given this title (although 8:20 is often the time set on old clocks for display purposes).

Madame de Pompadour is shown amid luxurious surroundings wearing a dress that signals opulence. The voluminous nature of the shimmering fabric, its turquoise blue color, and the intricacy of its bows and sewn roses also show off her small, narrow waist. She sits in her boudoir/library, which reflects the range of her accomplishments. The rosewood writing table set with pen, ink, and envelopes and the well-used book in her hand as well as the many in the cabinet and on the floor (truly an overflow) further confirm—even define—her level of literacy and qualify her as an educated woman. She also identified herself with Venus. The cupid by the clock, the roses on her dress and at her feet, and the pearl bracelets (pearls from the sea in which Venus was born) are each attributes that suggest her affinity with the love-goddess. She doesn't just sit on the day bed (*chaise longue*), but leans on its pillows, much like the languid female customer in Watteau's *Gersaint's Signboard* (see fig. 22.4). It suggests a relaxed, casual mood—the nonchalance of the leisurely aristocracy.

We can also compare the portrait to Rubens's life-size *Marchesa Brigida Spinola Doria* (see fig. 20.3), who strides from her palazzo. The Rococo portrait uses the play of diagonals (in her posture) and verticals (the pilasters, bookcase, and mirror's gilt frame) in much the same way Rubens uses these design elements. But the pastel colors, detail, and opulence anchor Boucher's painting in the Rococo world. The painting mirrors the luxurious and exuberant lifestyles of Madame de Pompadour, and the French aristocracy, for whom Boucher's works held great appeal.

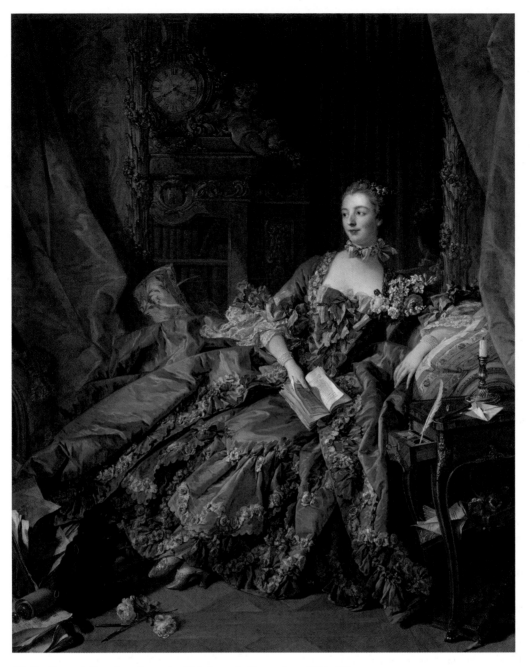

22.5 François Boucher, *Portrait of Madame de Pompadour*. 1756. Oil on canvas, 6'7⅛" × 5'1⅞" (2.01 × 1.57 m). Alte Pinakothek, Munich

JEAN-HONORÉ FRAGONARD Transforming fantasy into reality in paint was the forte of Jean-Honoré Fragonard (1732–1806)—or at least that was the reputation of this star pupil of Boucher. Also a brilliant colorist, Fragonard won the distinguished Rome Prize in 1752 and spent five years in Rome, beginning in 1756. Upon his return to Paris, he worked mostly for private collectors. Fantasy, flirtation, and licentiousness—in short, the spirit of the Rococo and the tradition that began with Watteau—coalesce in his painting *The Swing* (fig. **22.6**). An anecdote provides an interpretation of the painting. According to the story, another artist, Gabriel-François Doyen, was approached by the baron de Saint-Julien to paint his mistress "on a swing which a bishop is setting in motion. You will place me in a position in

which I can see the legs of the lovely child and even more if you wish to enliven the picture." Doyen declined the commission but directed it to Fragonard.

The painting, an example of an "intrigue," suggests a collusion in erotic fantasy between the artist and patron, with the clergy as their unwitting dupe. This "boudoir painting" (on the subject of sexual intimacy) offers the thrill of sexual opportunity and voyeurism but translated to a stagelike outdoor setting. The innocence of the public arena heightens the teasing quality of the motion of the swing toward the patron-viewer. The painted sculpture of a cupid to the left, holding a finger to his lips, suggests the conspiracy in the erotic escapade in which we as viewers are now participants. Fragonard used painted sculpture in many

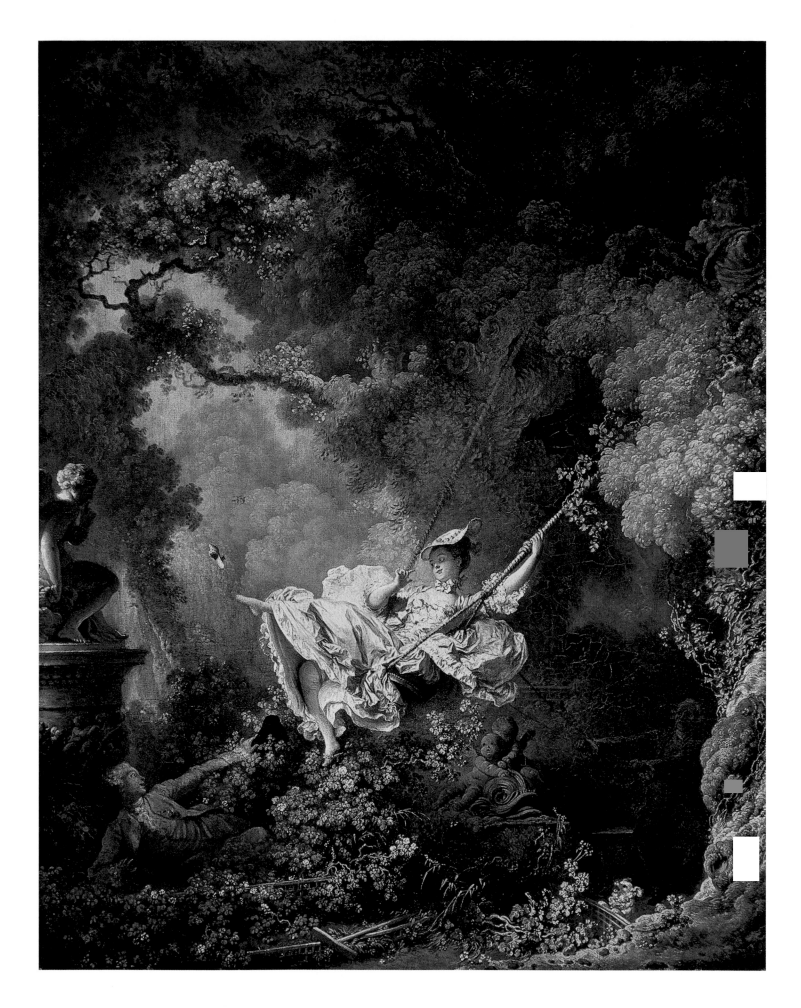

Pastel Painting

Pastels are a form of colored chalks or powders that are mixed (or filtered) with glue, juice, gum arabic, or whey and then rolled into a cylindrical tube. They are made and sold today in much the same way as they were in the Rococo era. The fillers and water enable the pastels to be applied smoothly. Pastels can be soft or hard, but they must be dried out to be packaged as pastel crayons.

Leonardo worked with pastels in the late fifteenth century (for his portrait of Isabella d'Este, 1499), but they really gained popularity among artists in the sixteenth century. Yet artists used them only to execute preparatory drawings, not to create finished works. In the eighteenth century, however, artists realized the possibilities of the medium and began making pastel paintings as finished works. Pastels, as well as the popular trois crayons technique (see fig. 22.3), had the advantage of suggesting both line and color at the same time. Since much debate arose in the late seventeenth and early eighteenth centuries about drawing (i.e., line) versus color, and since critics lauded artists such as Raphael who could combine both, the use of pastels may be considered a response to this issue. The lines could be smudged, built on each other, or hatched so that a single line could become an area of color and several together could create an even more vibrant patch.

Artists chose pastels primarily to make portraits, applying flicks of color to suggest animation, emotion, or expression and thus giving the sitter a more vivid and lifelike appearance. One of the greatest pastel portraitists is Rosalba Carriera (1675–1757), a Venetian artist known for revealing the psychological intensity of her sitters. Carriera was famous in her own time and had an international clientele of British, French, German, and Polish patrons. She became a member of the Academy of St. Luke of Rome in 1705, the Academy Clementina of Bologna in 1720, and the French Academy in 1721. Upon traveling to Paris in 1720–21, she was hailed by both the French court and French artists including Hyacinthe Rigaud (see Chapter 21) and Watteau (see pages 763–66), who made several drawings of her. The intimacy and

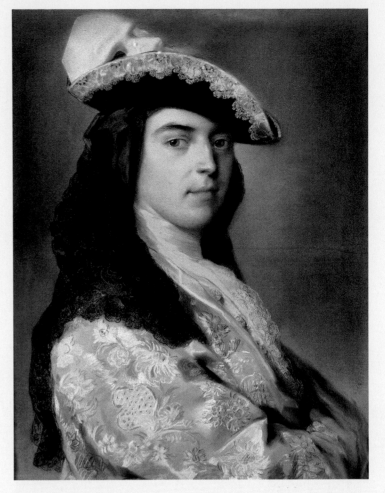

Rosalba Carriera, *Charles Sackville, Second Duke of Dorset*. ca. 1730. Pastel on paper, 25 × 19" (63.5 × 48.3 cm). Private collection

immediacy of her technique, combined with the indistinct, even hazy, quality of the resulting images, suggest a tantalizingly allusive sensuality, as seen in this portrait of the second duke of Dorset.

of his works to echo or reinforce their themes. Set in a lush arbor, this scene encapsulates the secluded "place of love" that provides secrecy for this erotic encounter. The dense and overgrown landscape, lit by radiant sunlight, suggests the warmth of spring or summer and their overtones of sexuality and fertility. The glowing pastel colors create an otherworldly haze that enhances the sensuality of this fantasy spun by Fragonard.

Fragonard epitomized the sensuality of the Rococo, and his works are marked by an extraordinary virtuosity in their use of color. His paintings range from erotic fantasies to intimate studies and pastoral landscapes, subjects that provided a distraction for his wealthy patrons.

JEAN-SIMÉON CHARDIN Raised in a bourgeois household, Jean-Siméon Chardin (1699–1779) rose to become treasurer of the French Academy as well as its *tapissier*, responsible for installing the paintings at its exhibitions. Chardin's expertise in still life as well as in genre painting was indebted to the many Dutch and Flemish seventeenth-century paintings then in France (many of these small, highly portable paintings were sold at auction). Indeed, some of Chardin's own patrons were important collectors of seventeenth-century Dutch and Flemish art.

To Chardin's patrons, members of the rising bourgeoisie in France, such genre scenes and domestic still lifes proclaimed the virtues of hard work, frugality, honesty, and devotion to family. Chardin's quiet household scenes struck a chord with his sophisticated patrons, and demand for them was so high that he often painted copies of his most popular subjects. His paintings were also reproduced as prints, making them affordable to those who lacked the means to buy an original work.

22.6 Jean-Honoré Fragonard, *The Swing*. 1767. Oil on canvas, 32⅝ × 26" (82.9 × 66.0 cm). Wallace Collection, London

Soap Bubbles (fig. **22.7**) is very much an outgrowth of Dutch genre painting and the vanitas symbols frequently seen in the still-life tradition. The bubble, intact only for a moment, symbolizes the brevity of life, which serves as one of the painting's underlying themes. However, Chardin has chosen a charming, endearing way to send his message to a viewer. He presents two children: an older boy who is possibly instructing a younger one, who eagerly looks on—play was a common theme in Chardin's work. Unlike most Rococo painting, the figures in this work are half-length, life-size rather than diminutive, and their scale affects our understanding of the reality, reinforcing the possibility that we could encounter a similar scene in our own world.

Back from the Market (fig. **22.8**) shows life in a Parisian bourgeois household. We see the large room but cannot ignore the potentially amorous scene taking place outside on the left. The maid's posture, leaning to her left with her shoes pointed to the right, suggests informality (we have seen this leaning in figs. 22.4 and 22.5). The beauty hidden in everyday life and a clear sense of spatial order beg comparison with the Dutch artist Jan Vermeer (see fig. 20.35). However, Chardin's brushwork is soft at the edges and suggests objects rather than defines them. In the still-life

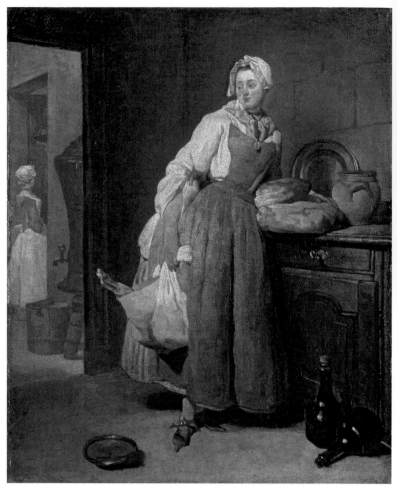

22.8 Jean-Siméon Chardin, *Back from the Market*. 1739. Oil on canvas, 18½ × 14¾" (47 × 37.5 cm). Musée du Louvre, Paris

elements in the painting (the floured loaves of bread are especially notable), he summarizes forms and subtly alters their appearance and texture. Thus, one can understand the appeal of pastel painting (see *Materials and Techniques*, page 769) as Chardin often turned to this medium late in life, when his eyes were failing him.

Still-life painting was important to Chardin (see page 769) as it was as a still-life artist (considered the lowest rank of painting) that he was admitted to the French Academy. But he raised this form of painting in its simplicity and elegance to a newly appreciated level. *The Brioche* (*The Dessert*), named for the center roll, displays a variety of textures set on a ledge that we view at eye level (fig. **22.9**). We can compare Chardin's painting to Heda's *Still Life with Oysters, Roemer, a Lemon, and a Silver Bowl* (see fig. 20.31). Texture in the Dutch work is created by the defined, sparkling edges of the broken glass, the shine of the silver, and the distinct reflections in the roemer. In Chardin's work, we are mostly impressed by the blurring of the edges: on the brioche topped with an orange branch, in the difficult-to-discern facets of the glass liqueur bottle on the right, and in the gilt-edged Meissen tureen on the left. Chardin used contemporary ceramics and porcelain in his paintings: German Meissen porcelain (celebrated French Sèvres would be its rival later in the century) was produced

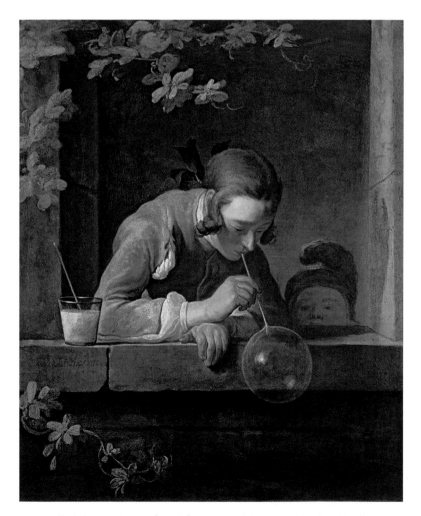

22.7 Jean-Siméon Chardin, *Soap Bubbles*. ca. 1733. Oil on canvas, 36⅝ × 29⅜" (93 × 74.6 cm). The National Gallery of Art, Washington, D.C. Gift of Mrs. John W. Simpson (1942.5.1)

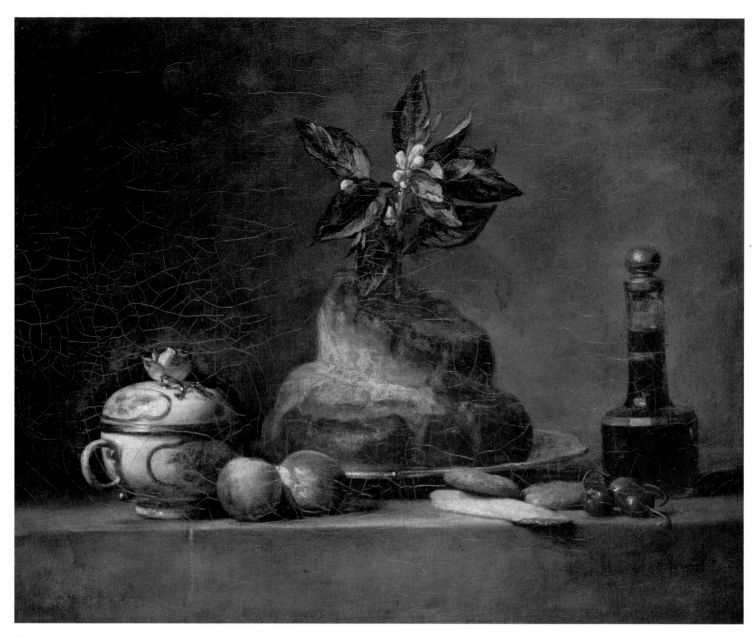

22.9 Jean-Siméon Chardin, *The Brioche (The Dessert)*. 1763. Oil on canvas, 18½ × 22" (47 × 56 cm). Museé du Louvre, Paris

in imitation of Chinese porcelain. In fact, in the eighteenth century, the tureen in the painting was described as Chinese (although, as is clear from the painted images on it, it is not).

Chinoiserie

Chinese wares—in the Netherlands spurred on by the Dutch East India Company (see page 700), in France, and throughout Europe—were wildly popular. As such, the Chinese also began making pieces for export to fulfill the desires of the European market, and European manufacturers developed products and designs in imitation of the Chinese. These items in Chinese style were known as **Chinoiserie** (*chinois* means "Chinese" in French) and belonged mostly to the decorative arts: silk, furniture (desks, cabinets), screens, garden décor, lacquerware, and of course,

porcelain. But perhaps the most significant Chinese export to Europe was tea, which first came to Europe through the Dutch East India Company in 1610.

Drinking tea changed both the daily routines of individuals and the economies of nations. It was only in the eighteenth century that tea sets (teapots, cups and saucers, sugar bowls, creamers and the utensils for them) in a variety of materials (porcelain, silver, pewter) were first created. Jean-Étienne Liotard's (1702–1789) *Still Life Tea Set* (fig. **22.10**) is an example of several levels of Chinoiserie—the tea, the porcelain Chinese-style tea set with images of Chinese figures and decoration (an example of Chinese export ware), all assembled on a lacquer tray.

Both Watteau and Boucher created designs in Chinoiserie for various patrons in prints, lacquerware and tapestry designs. Nicolas Pineau (see fig. 22.11), who designed salon interiors, also

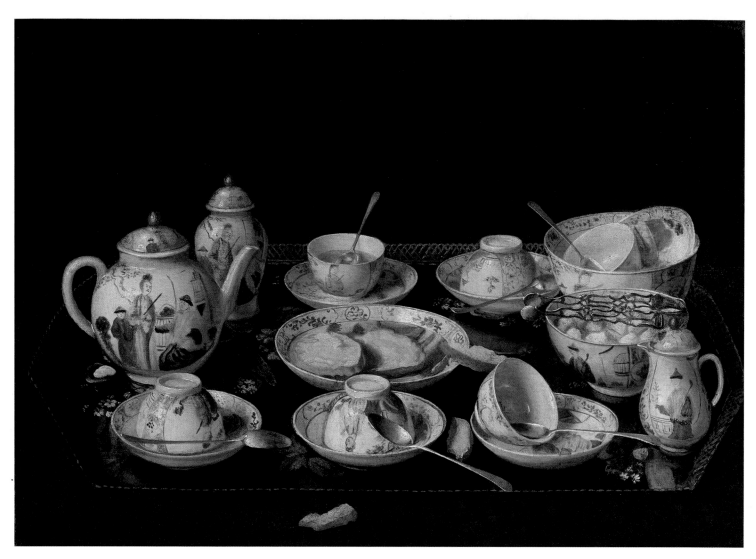

22.10 Jean-Étienne Liotard, *Still-Life: Tea Set*. ca. 1781–83. Oil on canvas mounted on board, 14⅞ × 20⅓" (37.8 × 51.6 cm). The J. Paul Getty Museum, Los Angeles

used Chinoiserie elements in his work. This was a style that artists could adapt to their own ends.

The French Rococo Interior

It is in the intimate spaces of early eighteenth-century interiors that the full elegance and charm of the Rococo are shown. The Parisian *hôtels* of the dispersed nobility soon developed into social centers. The field of "design for private living" took on new importance at this time. Because these city sites were usually cramped and irregular, they offered few opportunities for impressive exteriors. Hence, the layout and décor of the rooms became the architects' main concern. The *hôtels* demanded an intimate style of interior decoration that gave full scope to individual fancy, uninhibited by the classicism seen in the monumentality of Versailles.

Crucial to the development of French décor was the new importance assigned to interior designers. Their engravings established new standards of design that were expected to be followed by artisans, who thereby lost much of their independence. Designers also collaborated with architects, who became more involved in interior decoration. Along with sculptors, who often created the architectural ornamentation, and painters, architects helped to raise the decorative arts to the level of the fine arts, thus establishing a tradition that continues today. The decorative and fine arts were most clearly joined in furniture. Gilt, metals, and enamels were often applied to interior décor to create the feathery ornamentation associated with the Rococo. Many of these artisans came originally from the Netherlands, Germany, and Italy.

The decorative arts played a unique role during the Rococo. *Hôtel* interiors were more than collections of objects: They were total environments assembled with extraordinary care by discerning collectors and the talented architects, sculptors, decorators, and dealers who catered to their exacting taste. A room, like an item of furniture, could require the services of a wide variety of artisans: cabinetmakers, wood carvers, gold- and silversmiths, upholsterers, and porcelain makers. The products of these artisans were set in white rooms decorated with gilt molding and pastel-colored Rococo paintings, the overall effect being enhanced by mirrors and lighting. The artisans involved were dedicated to producing an ensemble, even though each craft was, by tradition, a separate specialty subject to strict regulations. Together they fueled the insatiable hunger for novelty that swept the aristocracy and haute bourgeoisie of Europe.

NICOLAS PINEAU Few of these Rococo rooms survive intact; the vast majority have been destroyed or greatly changed, or the objects and decorations have been dispersed. Even so, we can get a good idea of their appearance through the reconstruction of one such room (perhaps from the ground floor behind the garden elevation) from the Hôtel de Varengeville, Paris (fig. **22.11**), designed about 1735 by Nicolas Pineau (1684–1754) for the duchesse de Villars. Pineau had spent 14 years in Russia collaborating with other French craftsmen on Peter the Great's elaborate new city of

St. Petersburg. His room for the duchess incorporates many contemporary Rococo features. To create a sumptuous effect, the white walls are encrusted with gilded stucco ornamentation in arabesques, C-scallops, S-scrolls, fantastic birds, bat's wings, and acanthus foliage sprays. The elaborately carved furniture is embellished with gilt bronze. Everything swims in a sea of swirling patterns united by perhaps the most sophisticated sense of design and materials the world has ever known. No clear distinction exists between decoration and function in the richly designed fireplace and the opulent chandelier. The paintings, too, have been completely integrated into the decorative scheme, with works by Boucher set over two of the doors (such paintings even established a new type of work called "overdoors"). Similarly elaborate, gilt-decorated white walls became the hallmark of the Rococo, not only in its private spaces, but in church and palace decoration as well, especially in central Europe (see pages 776–77).

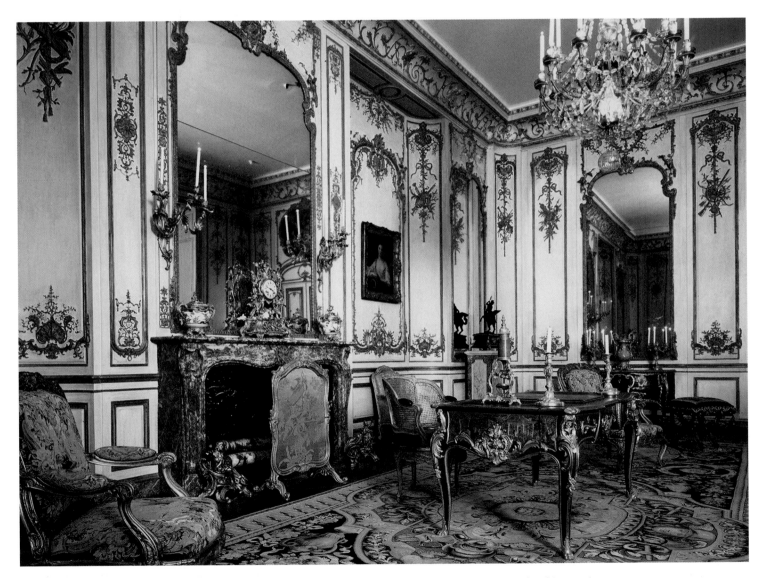

22.11   Nicolas Pineau. Room in the Hôtel de Varengeville, 217 Boulevard St.-Germain, Paris. ca. 1735. (The chimneypiece on the wall at left is not original to room.) Original paneling probably commissioned by Pineau. Carved, painted, and gilded oak, 18'3¾" × 40'6½" × 23'½" (5.58 × 12.35 × 7.07 m). Photographed about 1995. Metropolitan Museum of Art, New York. Purchase, Mr. and Mrs. Charles Wrightsman Gift, 1963. (63.228.1)

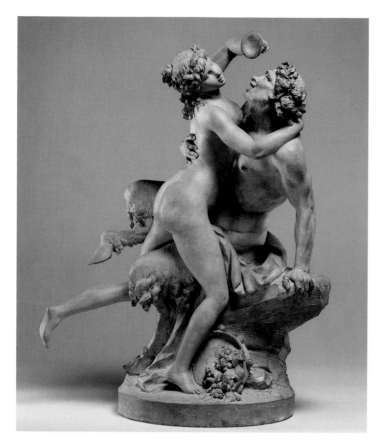

22.12 Clodion, *Nymph and Satyr Carousing*. ca. 1780. Terra cotta, height 23¼" (59 cm). Metropolitan Museum of Art, New York. Bequest of Benjamin Altman, 1913. (14.40.687)

CLODION AND FRENCH ROCOCO SCULPTURE Used to adorn interiors, French Rococo sculpture took many forms and was designed to be viewed at close range. A typical example is the small *Nymph and Satyr Carousing* (fig. **22.12**) by Claude Michel (1738–1814), known as Clodion, a successful sculptor of the Rococo period who later effectively adapted his style to the more austere Neoclassical manner. Clodion began his studies at Versailles and won the prestigious Rome Prize. His greatest contribution to the Rococo was transforming the fantasies of Boucher and Fragonard into three-dimensional works of coquettish eroticism. The open and airy composition of this sculpture is related to a work by Bernini, but its miniature scale produces a more intimate and sensual effect. Although Clodion undertook several large sculptural cycles in marble, he reigned supreme in the more intimate medium of terra cotta.

THE ROCOCO IN WESTERN EUROPE OUTSIDE OF FRANCE

The French Rococo exerted a major influence across the English Channel. There, foreign artists—Holbein, Gentileschi, Rubens, Van Dyck—had flourished for generations, and the works of Dutch and Italian artists were widely collected. Although foreign artists still reigned supreme, the Rococo helped to bring about the first school of English painting since the Middle Ages that had more than local importance. As we have seen with the works of Chardin and Rubens, among others, printmaking was used not just to create new compositions but to disseminate painted works, giving them a larger audience and broader appeal. This medium proved most beneficial for genre paintings and landscapes, areas of great interest to, and increasingly collected by, the British public.

William Hogarth and the Narrative

William Hogarth (1697–1764) was the first major native English artist since Nicholas Hilliard (see fig. 18.25). He began his career as an engraver and soon took up painting. Although he must have learned lessons about color and brushwork from Venetian and French examples, as well as from Van Dyck, his work is entirely original. He made his mark in the 1730s with a new kind of painting, which he described as "modern moral subjects … similar to representations on the stage." Hogarth's work is in the same vein as John Gay's *The Beggar's Opera* of 1728, a biting social and political stage satire that Hogarth illustrated in one of his paintings. Hogarth's morality paintings teach, by bad example, solid middle-class virtues and reflect the desire for a return to simpler times and values. They proved enormously popular among the newly prosperous middle class in England.

In the scene reproduced here both as a painting and an engraving (figs. **22.13** and **22.14**), taken from his *The Rake's Progress* series, the artist shows a young man, Tom Rakewell, who has just received an inheritance and is now spending his fortune by overindulging in wine and women. He is seen disheveled and drunk. (Later in the series, the rogue enters into a marriage of convenience, is arrested for debt, turns to gambling, goes to debtors' prison, and dies in Bedlam, the London insane asylum.) This scene is set in a famous London brothel, The Rose Tavern. The young woman adjusting her shoe in the foreground is a stripper preparing for a vulgar dance involving the mirrorlike silver plate and the candle behind her; to the left, a chamber pot spills its foul contents over a chicken dish; and in the background, a singer holds sheet music for a bawdy song of the day. A candle held to a map on the back wall indicates that Tom's world will burn—as did Nero's, the only Roman emperor whose image is not defaced in the paintings in the room. The scene is full of witty visual clues to its overall meaning, which the viewer would discover little by little, adding a comic element to this satire of social evils.

Hogarth combines Watteau's sparkling color with Jacob Jordaens's or Jan Steen's emphasis on narrative (see figs. 22.1, 20.9, and 20.33). Hogarth's moral narratives are so entertaining and popular that viewers can enjoy his sermon without being overwhelmed by the stern message. Of course, the "progress" of the rake was really his downfall. This series was the counterpart to Hogarth's earlier set, *The Harlot's Progress* (1731), where an innocent girl, Molly Hackabout, upon comes to the city and is tricked into becoming a prostitute, which leads to her demise.

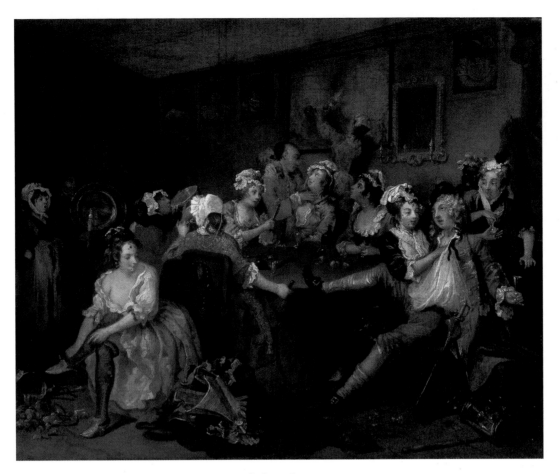

22.13　William Hogarth, *The Orgy*, scene III of *The Rake's Progress*. ca. 1734.
Oil on canvas, 24½ × 29½" (62.2 × 74.9 cm). Sir John Soane's Museum, London

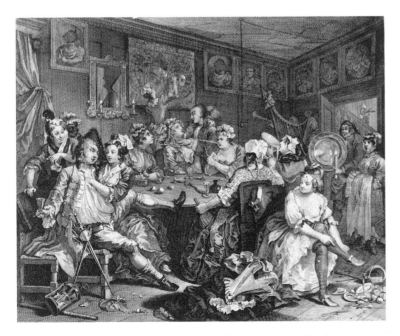

22.14　William Hogarth, *He Revels (The Orgy)*, scene III of
The Rake's Progress. 1735. Engraving. Metropolitan Museum of Art, New
York. Harris Brisbane Dick Fund, 1932. (32.35(30))

After executing the paintings, Hogarth made prints to sell
to the public. For *The Rake's Progress*, he made the prints only
after the passing of the Engraver's Copyright Act of 1735 which
provided protection from the many imitators who sought to
copy his works (see *The Art Historian's Lens*, page 747 for other
artists' concerns about counterfeiters). Prints made Hogarth a
wealthy man.

Canaletto

The paintings of the Venetian artist Canaletto (Giovanni Antonio
Canal, 1697–1768), known for his *vedute* (meaning "view" paintings) were especially popular with the British, particularly young
men on the Grand Tour (planned trips through western Europe to
complete their education) after their formal schooling. They
brought these scenes of Venice (and elsewhere) home as souvenirs.
This new form of subject can be traced back to the seventeenth
century, when many foreign artists, such as Claude Lorrain (see
fig. 21.8), specialized in depicting the Roman countryside, or to
the *Haarlempjes*, the local Dutch landscapes of Ruisdael (see fig.
20.28). After 1720, however, *vedute* took on a specifically urban
identity, focusing more narrowly on buildings or cityscapes.
During the eighteenth century, landscape painting in Italy evolved
into a new form in keeping with the character of the Rococo.

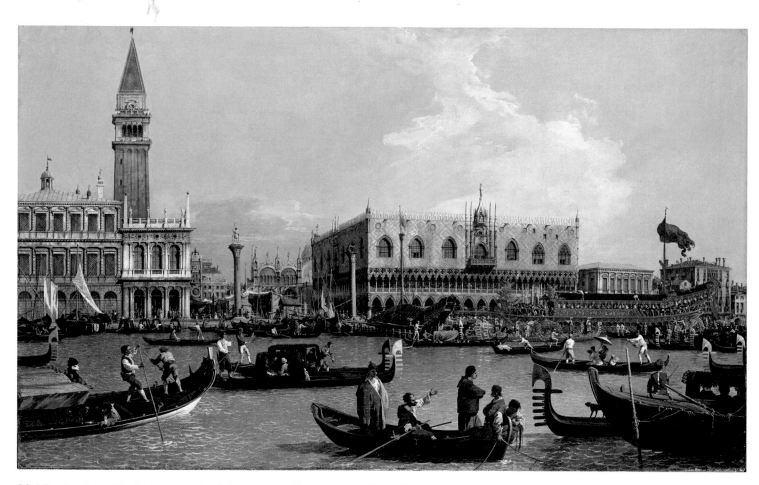

22.15 Canaletto, *The Bucintoro at the Molo*. ca. 1732. Oil on canvas, 30¼ × 49½" (77 × 126 cm).
The Royal Collection, copyright Her Majesty Queen Elizabeth II

The Bucintoro at the Molo (fig. **22.15**) is one of a series of paintings of Venice commissioned by Joseph Smith, an English entrepreneur (later named British consul to Venice) living there. Smith then issued the paintings as a suite of etchings to meet the demand for mementos of Venice from those who could not afford an original canvas by the artist. This work shows a favorite subject: the Doge returning on his magnificent barge to the Piazza San Marco from the Lido (the city's island beach) on Ascension Day after celebrating the Marriage of the Sea. Canaletto has captured the pageantry of this great public festival, which is presented as a brilliant theatrical display.

Canaletto's landscapes are, for the most part, topographically accurate. However, he usually made slight adjustments for the sake of the composition, and sometimes treated scenes with greater freedom or created composite views. He may have used a mechanical or optical device, perhaps a *camera obscura*, a forerunner of the photographic camera (see page 732), to render some of his views. The liveliness and sparkle of his pictures, as well as his sure sense of composition, sprang in large part from his training as a scenographer (a painter of stage sets for operas—including those by Antonio Vivaldi, 1678–1741). As in our example, Canaletto often included vignettes of daily life in Venice that lend greater human interest to his scenes and make them fascinating cultural documents as well.

Canaletto later became one of several Venetian artists to spend long sojourns in London, where he created views of the city's new skyline dotted with the church towers of Wren (see page 755). Other Venetian artists, such as Giovanni Battista Tiepolo (see page 781) and painters from his workshop had significant careers outside of Italy, in Germany and Austria, where the Rococo flourished.

THE ROCOCO IN CENTRAL EUROPE

Rococo architecture was a refinement in miniature of the curvilinear, "elastic" Baroque of Borromini and Guarini. It was readily united with the architecture of central Europe, where the Italian Baroque had firmly taken root. It is not surprising that the Italian style received such a warm response there. In Austria and southern Germany, ravaged by the Thirty Years' War, patronage for the arts was limited and the number of new buildings remained small until near the end of the seventeenth century. The Baroque here was an imported style, practiced mainly by visiting Italian artists. Not until the 1690s did native architects come to the fore. By the eighteenth century, however, these countries, especially the Catholic parts, were beginning to rebuild on a larger scale. A period of intense building activity in the first half of the

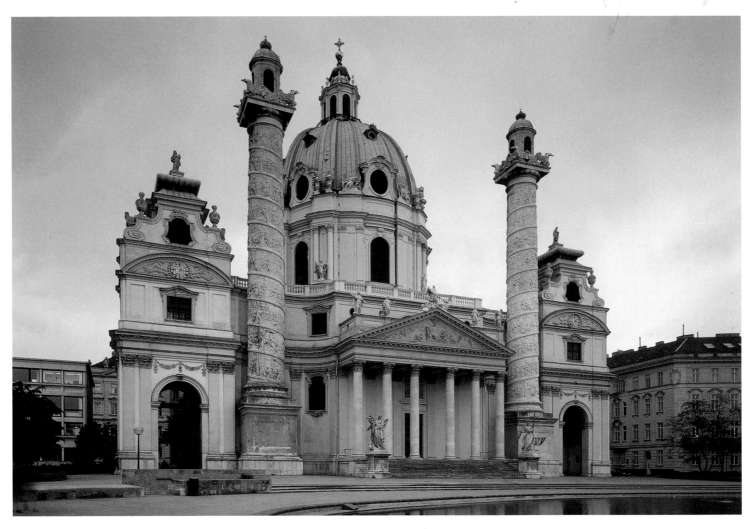

22.16 Johann Fischer von Erlach. Façade of the Karlskirche (church of St. Charles Borromeo), Vienna. 1716–37

eighteenth century gave rise to some of the most imaginative creations in the history of architecture. These monuments were built to glorify princes and prelates, who are generally remembered now only as lavish patrons of the arts. Rococo architecture in central Europe is larger in scale and more exuberant than that in France. Moreover, painting and sculpture are more closely linked with their settings. Palaces and churches are decorated with ceiling frescoes and sculpture unsuited to domestic interiors, however lavish, although they reflect the same taste that produced the Rococo French *hôtels*.

Johann Fischer von Erlach

The Austrian Johann Fischer von Erlach (1656–1723), the first important architect of the Rococo in central Europe, studied in Rome and was closely linked to the Italian tradition. His work represents the decisive shift of the center of architecture from Italy to north of the Alps. He is best known for the Karlskirche (the church of St. Charles Borromeo, literally "Charles's church") in Vienna (figs. **22.16** and **22.17**), built in thanks for the ending of the plague of 1713, much like the church of Santa Maria della

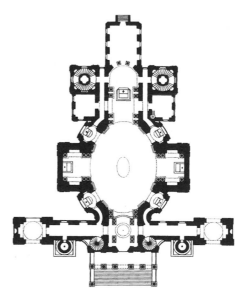

22.17 Plan of the Karlskirche

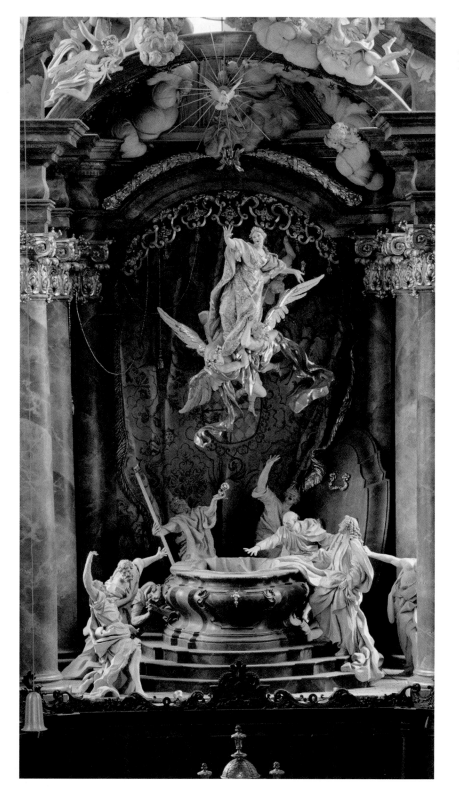

Salute in Venice in the previous century (see fig. 19.28). It was dedicated to the Counter-Reformation saint Charles Borromeo, for whom Emperor Charles VI was named and whose life is celebrated throughout the building. Fischer von Erlach uses several Italian and French architectural features to new effect, combining the façade of Borromini's Sant'Agnese and the Pantheon portico (see figs. 19.23 and 7.23). He added a pair of huge columns, derived from the Column of Trajan (see fig. 7.39) and decorated

with scenes from the life of the saint. The two columns symbolize the Pillars of Hercules—the Straits of Gibraltar—a reference to Charles VI's claim to the throne of Spain. They also take the place of towers, which have become corner pavilions reminiscent of Lescot's Louvre court façade (see fig. 18.2). The church proclaims the emperor Charles VI as a Christian ruler and assures us of his domination over the Turks, who repeatedly menaced Austria and Hungary. They had been defeated only recently—at the Siege of

Vienna in 1683—but only with the aid of John III of Poland. The Turks remained a serious threat as late as 1718.

Fischer von Erlach uses aspects of major works of the canon of Western architecture here to create an entirely new work that brings with it all the grandeur and esteem of the old traditions. The extraordinary breadth of this architectural ensemble is due to the site itself (see fig. 22.16), which obscures the equally long main body of the church. With the inflexible elements of Roman imperial art embedded into the elastic curves of his church, Fischer von Erlach expresses, more boldly than any Italian architect of the time, the power of the Christian faith to transform the art of antiquity.

Egid Quirin Asam

The Rococo made stirring claims in the heart of southern Germany—Bavaria—where new buildings or renovations of old ones transformed churches into extravagant liturgical stage sets. Egid Quirin Asam (1692–1750) and his brother, Cosmas Damian Asam (1686–1739), were responsible for the complete design and decoration of several churches and palaces in Bavaria. The brothers traveled to Rome (1711–13) where they studied the works of Bernini and his influence in their work is palpable.

Egid Quirin Asam's magnificent contribution to the renovation of the Benedictine abbey at Rohr (his brother was to execute paintings here, but they were never completed) reveals a clear debt to the Roman Baroque master. The original Romanesque church had been remodeled several times before the eighteenth century, but Asam completely transformed the interior. The main altar is set as a stage with larger than life-size stucco figures depicting *The Assumption of the Virgin* (fig. 22.18). The Virgin with the help of angels ascends into the golden heavens (the dome lit by windows), welcomed by the Trinity in the clouds as the white stuccoed apostles who surround her open sarcophagus (the huge lid is standing on the right) gesticulate wildly in amazement at this miracle. Their grand, broad gestures fill the space and are mirrored by the Virgin's own outstretched arms and fluttering fabrics. The scene is set before a flowing blue-gold curtain and framed by four columns. It is as if Bernini's *Ecstasy of St. Teresa* (see fig. 19.31) has met his *Baldacchino* and *Cathedra Petri* (see fig. 19.15). The lightness of the stucco (rather than marble) allowed for the use of wires and supports to raise the Virgin and to support the extended arms of the saints. The ensemble of exaggerated drama from the tomb to the golden heavens is an extravagant fulfillment of the Baroque in the eighteenth century.

Dominikus Zimmermann

Dominikus Zimmermann (1685–1766) created what may be the finest architectural design of the mid-eighteenth century: the rural Bavarian pilgrimage church nicknamed "*Die Wies*" ("The Meadow"). The exterior is so plain that by comparison the interior seems overwhelming (figs. 22.19 and 22.20). This richness reflects the fact that the architect and his brother, Johann Baptist

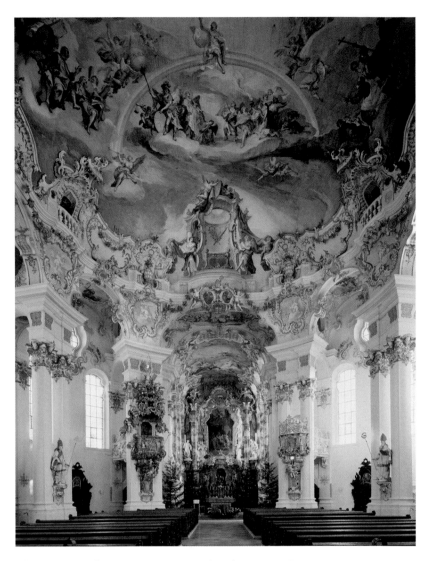

22.19 Dominikus Zimmermann. Interior of "*Die Wies*," Upper Bavaria. 1757

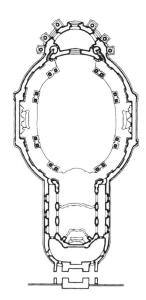

22.20 Plan of "*Die Wies*"

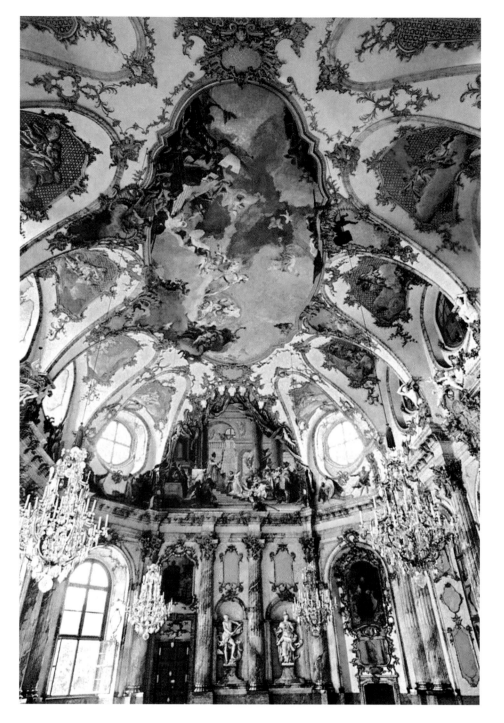

22.21 Balthasar Neumann. Kaisersaal, Residenz, Würzburg. 1719–44. Frescoes by Giovanni Battista Tiepolo, 1751–52

Zimmermann (1680–1758), who was responsible for the frescoes, trained initially as stucco workers. The interior design includes a combination of sculptural painted stucco decoration and painting. Like Fischer von Erlach's Karlskirche, the church's basic shape is oval. Yet because the ceiling rests on paired, free-standing supports, the space is more fluid and complex, recalling a German Gothic *Hallenkirche* (hall church). Even the way the Rococo décor tends to break up the ceiling recalls the webbed vaults of the Gothic Heiligenkreuz in Schwäbisch-Gmünd (see fig. 12.56). Here Guarini's prophetic reevaluation of Gothic architecture has become reality.

Balthasar Neumann

The work of Balthasar Neumann (1687–1753), a contemporary of Zimmerman's who designed buildings exuding lightness and elegance, represents one of the high points of the Rococo in central Europe. Trained as a military engineer, he was named a surveyor for the Residenz (Episcopal Palace) in Würzburg after his return from a visit to Milan in 1720. Although the basic plan was already established, Neumann was required to consult the leading architects of Paris and Vienna in 1723 before he made his extensive modifications. The final result is a skillful blend of the latest German, French, and Italian ideas. The breathtaking Kaisersaal (fig. **22.21**)

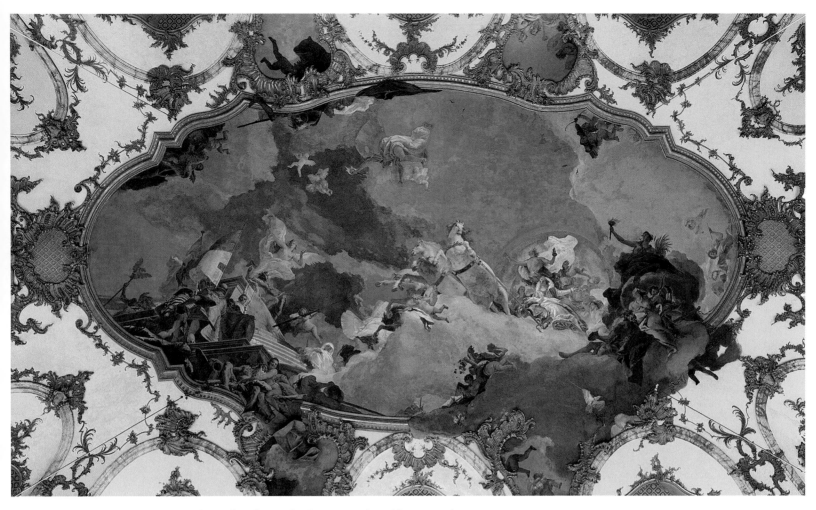

22.22 Giovanni Battista Tiepolo. Ceiling fresco (detail), Kaisersaal, Residenz, Würzburg. 1751

is a great oval hall decorated in the favorite color scheme of the mid-eighteenth century: white, gold, and pastel shades. The structural importance of the columns, pilasters, and architraves has been minimized in favor of their decorative role. Windows and vault segments are framed by continuous, ribbonlike moldings, and the white surfaces are covered with irregular ornamental designs. These lacy, curling motifs, the hallmark of the French style (see fig. 22.11), are happily combined with German Rococo architecture. (The basic design recalls an early interior by Fischer von Erlach.) But it is the painted decoration that completes the rich organic structure. The abundant daylight, the play of curves and countercurves, and the weightless grace of the stucco sculpture give the Kaisersaal an airy lightness far removed from the Roman Baroque. The vaults and walls seem thin and pliable, like membranes easily punctured by the expansive power of space.

Giovanni Battista Tiepolo and Illusionistic Ceiling Decoration

Central European Rococo churches and palaces required paintings to complement the architecture and achieve the full effect of extensive, overwhelming, yet light decoration (through the use of white, gold trim, and pastel colors). Venetian colorists with a revived appreciation of Veronese's colorism and pageantry, but with an airy sensibility that is new, were skilled in the Baroque illusionism of the previous century and were able to adapt it to Rococo architecture. They were active in every major center throughout Europe, especially in London, Dresden, and Madrid. And the most sought-after of these Venetian artists—both in Venice and throughout central Europe in the eighteenth century—was Giovanni Battista Tiepolo (1696–1770).

The last and most refined stage of Italian illusionistic ceiling decoration can be seen in the works of Tiepolo, who spent most of his life in Venice, where his works defined the Rococo style. Tiepolo spent two years in Germany, and in the last years of his life he worked for Charles III in Spain. His mastery of light and color, his grace and masterful touch, and his power of invention made him famous far beyond his home territory. When Tiepolo painted the Würzburg frescoes (figs. **22.22** and **22.23**), his powers were at their height. The tissuelike ceiling gives way so often to illusionistic openings, both painted and sculpted, that it no longer feels like a spatial boundary. Unlike Baroque ceilings (see figs. 19.11 and 19.12), these openings do not reveal avalanches of figures propelled by dramatic bursts of light. Rather, pale blue skies

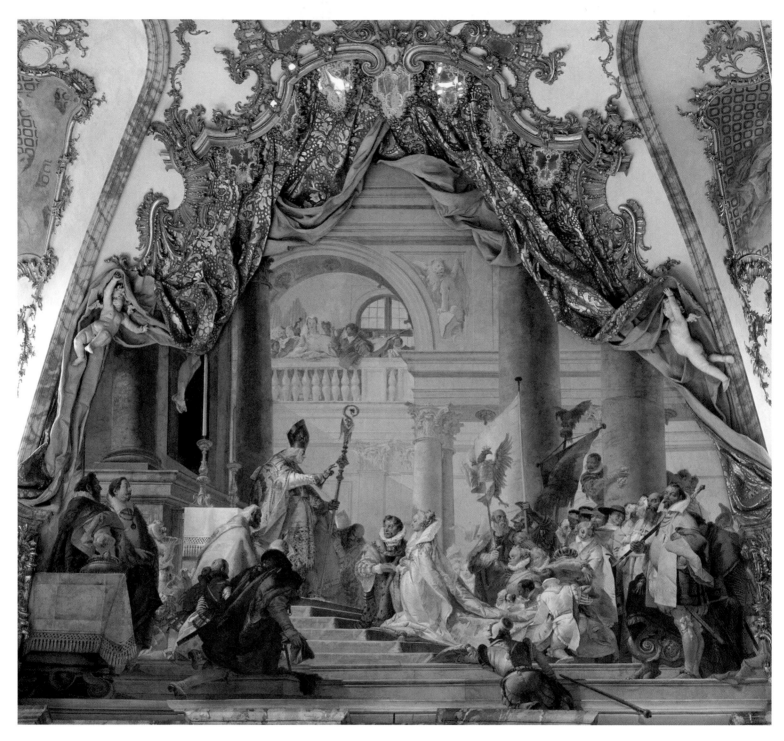

22.23   Giovanni Battista Tiepolo, *The Marriage of Frederick Barbarossa* (partial view), Kaisersaal, Residenz, Würzburg. 1752. Fresco

and sunlit clouds are dotted with an occasional winged creature soaring in the limitless expanse. Only along the edges of the ceiling do solid clusters of figures appear.

At one end, replacing a window, is *The Marriage of Frederick Barbarossa* (see fig. 22.23). As a public spectacle, it is as festive as *The Feast in the House of Levi* by Veronese (see fig. 17.38). The artist has followed Veronese's example by putting the event, which took place in the twelfth century, in a contemporary setting. Its allegorical fantasy is "revealed" by the carved putti opening a gilt-stucco curtain onto the wedding ceremony in a display

of theatrical illusionism worthy of Bernini. Indeed, it parallels the drama orchestrated by Egid Quirin Asam at Rohr (see fig. 22.18). Unexpected in this festive procession is the element of classicism, which gives an air of noble restraint to the main figures, in keeping with the solemnity of the occasion.

Tiepolo later became the last in the long line of Italian artists who were invited to work at the Royal Court in Madrid where he worked for Charles III. There, he encountered the German painter Anton Raphael Mengs, a champion of the classical revival, whose presence signaled the end of the Rococo.

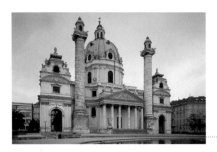

1716-37 Fischer von Erlach's Karlskirche
built in Vienna

The Rococo

1685 Versailles Palace completed

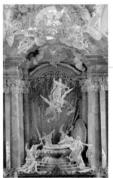

1717-23 Asam's
Assumption of the Virgin

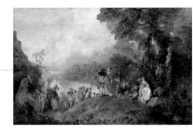

1717 Watteau's *A Pilgrimage to Cythera*

1710

◄ 1710 Meissen porcelain factory established

◄ 1715 Louis XIV dies

1720

◄ 1723 Louis XV crowned king of France

◄ 1725 Antonio Vivaldi writes *Four Seasons* concerto

◄ 1728 John Gay, *The Beggar's Opera*

1730

◄ 1732 Theatre Royal in Covent Garden, London
opens

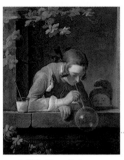

ca. 1733 Chardin's
Soap Bubbles

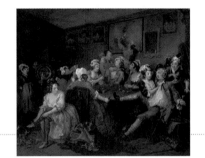

1733-35 Hogarth's
The Rake's Progress

1740

◄ 1741 Johann Sebastian Bach publishes *"Goldberg"
Variations*

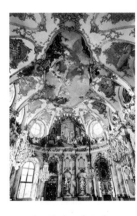

ca. 1751-52
Neumann's
Kaisersaal and
Tiepolo's frescoes
within

1750

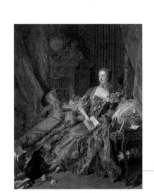

1760

◄ 1759 Louis XV becomes sole owner of Sèvres
porcelain factory

1756 Boucher's *Portrait of
Madame de Pompadour*

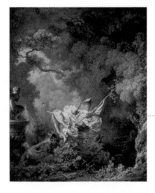

1770

1767 Fragonard's *The Swing*

Glossary

ABACUS. A slab of stone at the top of a Classical capital just beneath the architrave.

ABBEY. (1) A religious community headed by an abbot or abbess. (2) The buildings that house the community. An abbey church often has an especially large choir to provide space for the monks or nuns.

ACROTERION (pl. **ACROTERIA**). Decorative ornaments placed at the apex and the corners of a pediment.

ACTION PAINTING. In Abstract art, the spontaneous and uninhibited application of paint, as practiced by the avant-garde from the 1930s through the 1950s.

AEDICULA. A small shrine or altar that dates to ancient Rome.

AEOLIC. An early style of Greek architecture, found in northwestern Asia Minor. The Aeolic style is often considered a precursor to the Ionic style.

AISLE. The passageway or corridor of a church that runs parallel to the length of the building. It often flanks the nave of the church but is sometimes set off from it by rows of piers or columns.

ALABASTRON. A perfume container, similar to an aryballos, crafted by Greek vase-painters and often imported into Etruria.

ALBUMEN PRINT. A process in photography that uses the proteins found in eggs to produce a photographic plate.

ALLEGORY. A representation in which figures or events stand for ideas beyond themselves as symbols or metaphors, to create a moral or message for the viewer.

ALLOVER PAINTING. A painting in which the texture tends to be consistent throughout and which has no traditional compositional structure with a dominant focus of interest but, rather, even stresses throughout the image, as in Jackson Pollock's Abstract Expressionist action paintings.

ALTAR. A mound or structure on which sacrifices or offerings are made in the worship of a deity. In a Catholic church, a tablelike structure used in celebrating the Mass.

ALTARPIECE. A painted or carved work of art placed behind and above the altar of a Christian church. It may be a single panel or a *triptych* or a *polytych*, both having hinged wings painted on both sides. Also called a reredos or retablo.

AMBULATORY. A covered walkway. (1) In a basilican church, the semicircular passage around the apse. (2) In a central-plan church, the ring-shaped aisle around the central space. (3) In a cloister, the covered colonnaded or arcaded walk around the open courtyard.

ANAMORPHIC. Refers to a special form of perspective, which represents an object from an unusual or extreme viewpoint, so that it can only be understood from that viewpoint, or with the aid of a special device or mirror.

ANDACHTSBILD. German for "devotional image." A picture or sculpture with imagery intended for private devotion. It was first developed in Northern Europe.

ANIMAL STYLE. A style that appears to have originated in ancient Iran and is characterized by stylized or abstracted images of animals.

ANNULAR. From the Latin word for "ring." Signifies a ring-shaped form, especially an annular barrel vault.

APOTROPAIC DEVICE. An object deployed as a means of warding off evil. Often a figural image (such as a Medusa head) or a composite image (like a Near Eastern lamassu), inserted into an architectural setting.

APSE. A semicircular or polygonal niche terminating one or both ends of the nave in a Roman basilica. In a Christian church, it is usually placed at the east end of the nave beyond the transept or choir. It is also sometimes used at the end of transept arms.

APSIDIOLE. A small apse or chapel connected to the main apse of a church.

ARCADE. A series of arches supported by piers or columns. When attached to a wall, these form a blind arcade.

ARCH. A curved structure used to span an opening. Masonry arches are generally built of wedge-shaped blocks, called *voussoirs*, set with their narrow sides toward the opening so that they lock together. The topmost *voussoir* is called the *keystone*. Arches may take different shapes, such as the pointed Gothic arch or the rounded Classical arch.

ARCHAIC SMILE. A fixed, unnaturalistic smile characteristic of many archaic Greek sculpted images. Artists ceased to depict figures smiling in this way once they began to explore greater naturalism.

ARCHITRAVE. The lowermost member of a classical entablature, such as a series of stone blocks that rest directly on the columns.

ARCHIVOLT. A molded band framing an arch, or a series of such bands framing a tympanum, often decorated with sculpture.

ARCUATION. The use of arches or a series of arches in building.

ART BRUT. Meaning "raw art" in French, *art brut* is the direct and highly emotional art of children and the mentally ill that served as an inspiration for some artistic movements in Modern art.

ARYBALLOS. A perfume jar, generally small in size, and often minutely decorated. This was a favorite type of vessel for Corinthian vase-painters.

ASHLAR MASONRY. Carefully finished stone that is set in fine joints to create an even surface.

ASSOCIATIONISM. A 20th-century art historical term that refers to the concept that architecture and landscape design can have motifs or aspects that associate them with earlier architecture, art, history, or literature.

ATMOSPHERIC PERSPECTIVE. Creates the illusion of depth by reducing the local color and clarity of objects in the distance, to imply a layer of atmosphere between the viewer and the horizon.

ATRIUM. (1) The central court or open entrance court of a Roman house. (2) An open court, sometimes colonnaded or arcaded, in front of a church.

AVANT-GARDE. Meaning "advance force" in French, the artists of the avant-garde in 19th- and 20th-century Europe led the way in innovation in both subject matter and technique, rebelling against the established conventions of the art world.

BALDACCHINO. A canopy usually built over an altar. The most important one is Bernini's construction for St. Peter's in Rome.

BAROQUE. A style of Hellenistic Greek sculpture, characterized by extreme emotions and extravagant gestures, as seen on the Great Altar of Zeus at Pergamon. The term is usually used to describe a style of 17th-century CE art, and scholars of ancient art coin it in recognition of similarities of style.

BARREL VAULT. A vault formed by a continuous semicircular arch so that it is shaped like a half-cylinder.

BAR TRACERY. A style of tracery in which glass is held in place by relatively thin membranes.

BAS-DE-PAGE. Literally "bottom of the page." An illustration or decoration that is placed below a block of text in an illuminated manuscript.

BASILICA. (1) In ancient Roman architecture, a large, oblong building used as a public meeting place and hall of justice. It generally includes a nave, side aisles, and one or more apses. (2) In Christian architecture, a longitudinal church derived from the Roman basilica and having a nave, an apse, two or four side aisles or side chapels, and sometimes a narthex. (3) Any one of the seven original churches of Rome or other churches accorded the same religious privileges.

BATTLEMENT. A parapet consisting of alternating solid parts and open spaces designed originally for defense and later used for decoration. See *crenelated*.

BAY. A subdivision of the interior space of a building. Usually a series of bays is formed by consecutive architectural supports.

BELVEDERE. A structure made for the purpose of viewing the surroundings, either above the roof of a building or free-standing in a garden or other natural setting.

BLACK-FIGURED. A style of ancient Greek pottery decoration characterized by black figures against a red background. The black-figured style preceded the red-figured style.

BLIND ARCADE. An arcade with no openings. The arches and supports are attached decoratively to the surface of a wall.

BLOCK BOOKS. Books, often religious, of the 15th century containing woodcut prints in which picture and text were usually cut into the same block.

BOOK OF HOURS. A private prayer book containing the devotions for the seven canonical hours of the Roman Catholic church (matins, vespers, etc.), liturgies for local saints, and sometimes a calendar. They were often elaborately illuminated for persons of high rank, whose names are attached to certain extant examples.

BUON FRESCO. See *fresco*.

BURIN. A pointed metal tool with a wedged-shaped tip used for engraving.

BUTTRESS. A projecting support built against an external wall, usually to counteract the lateral thrust of a vault or arch within. In Gothic church architecture, a *flying buttress* is an arched bridge above the aisle roof that extends from the upper nave wall, where the lateral thrust of the main vault is greatest, down to a solid pier.

CALOTYPE. Invented in the 1830s, calotype was the first photographic process to use negatives and positive prints on paper.

CAMEO. A low relief carving made on agate, seashell, or other multilayered material in which the subject, often in profile view, is rendered in one color while the background appears in another, darker color.

CAMES. Strips of lead in stained-glass windows that hold the pieces of glass together.

CAMPANILE. From the Italian word *campana*, meaning "bell." A bell tower that is either round or square and is sometimes free-standing.

CANON. A law, rule, or standard.

CAPITAL. The uppermost member of a column or pillar supporting the architrave.

CARAVANSARAY. A wayside inn along the main caravan routes linking the cities of Asia Minor, usually containing a warehouse, stables, and a courtyard.

CARTE-DE-VISITE. A photographic portrait mounted on thicker card stock measuring 2½ x 4 inches (6 x 10 cm) that people commissioned and distributed to friends and acquaintances. They were developed in 1854 by the French photographer Adolphe-Eugène Disdéri, and by the end of the decade were so popular that they were widely collected in Europe and America, a phenomenon called "cardomania."

CARTOON. From the Italian word *cartone*, meaning "large paper." (1) A full-scale drawing for a picture or design intended to be transferred to a wall, panel, tapestry, etc. (2) A drawing or print, usually humorous or satirical, calling attention to some action or person of popular interest.

CARYATID. A sculptured female figure used in place of a column as an architectural support. A similar male figure is an *atlas* (pl. *atlantes*).

CASEMATE. A chamber or compartment within a fortified wall, usually used for the storage of artillery and munitions.

CASSONE (pl. **CASSONI**). An Italian dowry chest often highly decorated with carvings, paintings, inlaid designs, and gilt embellishments.

CATACOMBS. The underground burial places of the early Christians, consisting of passages with niches for tombs and small chapels for commemorative services.

CATALOGUE RAISONNÉ. A complete list of an artist's works of art, with a comprehensive chronology and a discussion of the artist's style.

CATHEDRAL. The church of a bishop; his administrative headquarters. The location of his *cathedra* or throne.

CAVEA. The seating area in an ancient theater. In a Greek theater, it was just over semicircular; in a Roman theater, it was semicircular. Access corridors divided the seating into wedges (*cunei*).

CELLA. (1) The principal enclosed room of a temple used to house an image. Also called the *naos*. (2) The entire body of a temple as distinct from its external parts.

CENOTAPH. A memorial monument to honor a person or persons whose remains lie elsewhere.

CENTERING. A wooden framework built to support an arch, vault, or dome during its construction.

CHAMPLEVÉ. An enameling method in which hollows are etched into a metal surface and filled with enamel.

CHANCEL. The area of a church around the altar, sometimes set off by a screen. It is used by the clergy and the choir.

CHIAROSCURO. Italian word for "light and dark." In painting, a method of modeling form primarily by the use of light and shade.

CHIASTIC POSE. From the Greek letter chi: an asymmetrical stance, where the body carries the weight on one leg (and often bears a weight with the opposite arm). Also described as *contrapposto*.

CHINOISERIE. Objects, usually in the decorative arts (screens, furniture, lacquerware) made in a Chinese or pseudo-Chinese style, most popular in the 18th century.

CHITON. A woman's garment made out of a rectangle of fabric draped and fastened at the shoulders by pins. The garment is worn by some Archaic Greek *korai*, where it provides a decorative effect.

CHRYSELEPHANTINE. Usually referring to a sculpture in Classical Greece, signifying that it is made of gold and ivory. Pheidias' cult statues of Athena in the Parthenon, and Zeus at Olympia, were chryselephantine.

CLASSICISM. Art or architecture that harkens back to and relies upon the style and canons of the art and architecture of ancient Greece or Rome, which emphasize certain standards of balance, order, and beauty.

CLASSICIZING. To refer to the forms and ideals of the Classical world, principally Greece and Rome.

CLERESTORY. A row of windows in the upper part of a wall that rises above an adjoining roof. Its purpose is to provide direct lighting, as in a basilica or church.

CLOISONNÉ. An enameling method in which the hollows created by wires joined to a metal plate are filled with enamel to create a design.

CLOISTER. (1) A place of religious seclusion such as a monastery or nunnery. (2) An open court attached to a church or monastery and surrounded by an ambulatory. Used for study, meditation, and exercise.

COFFER. (1) A small chest or casket. (2) A recessed, geometrically shaped panel in a ceiling. A ceiling decorated with these panels is said to be coffered.

COLONNETTE. A small, often decorative, column that is connected to a wall or pier.

COLOPHON. (1) The production information given at the end of a book. (2) The printed emblem of a book's publisher.

COLOR-FIELD PAINTING. A technique of Abstract painting in which thinned paints are spread onto an unprimed canvas and allowed to soak in with minimal control by the artist.

COLOSSAL ORDER. Columns, piers, or pilasters in the shape of the Greek or Roman orders but that extend through two or more stories rather than following the Classical proportions.

COMBINES. The label the American artist Robert Rauschenberg gave to his paintings of the mid-1950s that combined painting, sculpture, collage, and found objects.

COMPOSITE CAPITAL. A capital that combines the volutes of an Ionic capital with the acanthus leaves of the Corinthian capital. Roman architects developed the style as a substitute for the Ionic style, for use on secular buildings.

COMPOSITE IMAGE. An image formed by combining different images or different views of the subject.

COMPOUND PIER. A pier with attached pilasters or shafts.

CONSTRUCTION. A type of sculpture, developed by Picasso and Braque toward 1912, and popularized by the Russian Constructivists later in the decade. It is made by assembling such materials as metal or wood.

CONTINUOUS NARRATION. Portrayal of the same figure or character at different stages in a story that is depicted in a single artistic space.

CONTRAPPOSTO. Italian word for "set against." A composition developed by the Greeks to represent movement in a figure. The parts of the body are placed asymmetrically in opposition to each other around a central axis, and careful attention is paid to the distribution of weight.

CORBEL. (1) A bracket that projects from a wall to aid in supporting weight. (2) The projection of one course, or horizontal row, of a building material beyond the course below it.

CORBEL VAULT. A vault formed by progressively projecting courses of stone or brick, which eventually meet to form the highest point of the vault.

CORINTHIAN CAPITAL. A column capital ornamented with acanthus leaves, introduced in Greece in the late fifth century BCE, and used by Roman architects throughout the Empire.

CORNICE. (1) The projecting, framing members of a classical pediment, including the horizontal one beneath and the two sloping or "raking" ones above. (2) Any projecting, horizontal element surmounting a wall or other structure or dividing it horizontally for decorative purposes.

CORPUS. In carved medieval altarpieces, the corpus is the central section which usually holds a sculpted figure or design.

COURT STYLE. See *Rayonnant*.

CRENELATIONS. A sequence of solid parts, and the intervals between them, along the top of a parapet, allowing for defense and to facilitate firing weapons. The effect is of a notched termination of a wall. Generally used in military architecture.

CROSSING. The area in a church where the transept crosses the nave, frequently emphasized by a dome or crossing tower.

CRYPT. A space, usually vaulted, in a church that sometimes causes the floor of the choir to be raised above that of the nave; often used as a place for tombs and small chapels.

CUBICULUM (pl. **CUBICULA**) A bedroom in a Roman house. A cubiculum usually opened onto the atrium. Most were small; some contained wall-paintings.

CUNEUS (pl. **CUNEI**). A wedgelike group of seats in a Greek or Roman theater.

CUNEIFORM. The wedge-shaped characters made in clay by the ancient Mesopotamians as a writing system.

CURTAIN WALL. A wall of a modern building that does not support the building; the building is supported by an underlying steel structure rather than by the wall itself, which serves the purpose of a façade.

DADO. The lower part of an interior wall. In a Roman house, the dado was often decorated with paintings imitating costly marbles.

DAGUERREOTYPE. Originally, a photograph on a silver-plated sheet of copper, which had been treated with fumes of iodine to form silver iodide on its surface and then after exposure developed by fumes of mercury. The process, invented by L. J. M. Daguerre and made public in 1839, was modified and accelerated as daguerreotypes gained popularity.

DEËSIS. From the Greek word for "entreaty." The representation of Christ enthroned between the Virgin Mary and St. John the Baptist, frequent in Byzantine mosaics and depictions of the Last Judgment. It refers to the roles of the Virgin Mary and St. John the Baptist as intercessors for humankind.

DIKKA. An elevated, flat-topped platform in a mosque used by the muezzin or cantor.

DIPTERAL. Term used to describe a Greek or Roman building—often a temple or a stoa—with a double colonnade.

DIPTYCH. (1) Originally a hinged, two-leaved tablet used for writing. (2) A pair of ivory carvings or panel paintings, usually hinged together.

DOLMEN. A structure formed by two or more large, upright stones capped by a horizontal slab. Thought to be a prehistoric tomb.

DOME. A true dome is a vaulted roof of circular, polygonal, or elliptical plan, formed with hemispherical or ovoidal curvature. May be supported by a circular wall or drum and by pendentives or related constructions. Domical coverings of many other sorts have been devised.

DOMUS. Latin word for "house." A detached, one-family Roman house with rooms frequently grouped around two open courts. The first court, called the *atrium*, was used for entertaining and conducting business. The second court, usually with a garden and surrounded by a *peristyle* or colonnade, was for the private use of the family.

DORIC COLUMN. A column characterized by a simple cushionlike abacus and the absence of a base. One of three styles of column consistently used by Greek and Roman architects.

DRÔLERIES. French word for "jests." Used to describe the lively animals and small figures in the margins of late medieval manuscripts and in wood carvings on furniture.

DROMOS. A pathway, found, for instance, in Bronze Age, Aegean and Etruscan tomb structures.

DRUM. (1) A section of the shaft of a column. (2) A circular-shaped wall supporting a dome.

DRYPOINT. A type of *intaglio* printmaking in which a sharp metal needle is use to carve lines and a design into a (usually) copper plate. The act of drawing pushes up a burr of metal filings, and so, when the plate is inked, ink will be retained by the burr to create a soft and deep tone that will be unique to each print. The burr can only last for a few printings. Both the print and the process are called drypoint.

EARLY ENGLISH STYLE. A term used to describe Gothic architecture in England during the early- and mid-13th century. The style demonstrates the influence of architectural features developed during the Early Gothic period in France, which are combined with Anglo-Norman Romanesque features.

EARTHWORKS. Usually very large scale, outdoor artwork that is produced by altering the natural environment.

ECHINUS. In the Doric or Tuscan Order, the round, cushionlike element between the top of the shaft and the abacus.

ENCAUSTIC. A technique of painting with pigments dissolved in hot wax.

ENGAGED COLUMN. A column that is joined to a wall, usually appearing as a half-rounded vertical shape.

ENGRAVING. (1) A means of embellishing metal surfaces or gemstones by incising a design on the surface. (2) A print made by cutting a design into a metal plate (usually copper) with a pointed steel tool known as a burin. The burr raised on either side of the incised line is removed. Ink is then rubbed into the V-shaped grooves and wiped off the surface. The plate, covered with a damp sheet of paper, is run through a heavy press. The image on the paper is the reverse of that on the plate. When a fine steel needle is used instead of a burin and the burr is retained, a drypoint engraving results, characterized by a softer line. These techniques are called, respectively, engraving and drypoint.

ENNEASTYLE. A term used to describe the façade of a Greek or Roman temple, meaning that it has nine columns.

ENTABLATURE. (1) In a classical order, the entire structure above the columns; this usually includes architrave, frieze, and cornice. (2) The same structure in any building of a classical style.

ENTASIS. A swelling of the shaft of a column.

ENVIRONMENT. In art, environment refers to the Earth itself as a stage for Environmental art, works that can be enormously large yet very minimal and abstract. These works can be permanent or transitory. The term Earth art is also used to describe these artworks.

EVENTS. A term first used by John Cage in the early 1950s to refer to his multimedia events at Black Mount College in North Carolina that included dance, painting, music, and sculpture. The term was appropriated by the conceptual artist George Brecht in 1959 for his performance projects, and shortly thereafter by the conceptual and performance group Fluxus, which included Brecht.

EXEDRA (pl. **EXEDRAE**). In Classical architecture, an alcove, often semicircular, and often defined with columns. Sometimes, exedrae framed sculptures.

FAIENCE. (1) A glass paste fired to a shiny opaque finish, used in Egypt and the Aegean. (2) A type of earthenware that is covered with a colorful opaque glaze and is often decorated with elaborate designs.

FIBULA. A clasp, buckle, or brooch, often ornamented.

FILIGREE. Delicate decorative work made of intertwining wires.

FLAMBOYANT. Literally meaning "flamelike" in French, describes a late phase of Gothic architecture where undulating curves and reverse curves were a main feature.

FLUTES. The vertical channels or grooves in Classical column shafts, sometimes thought to imitate the faceting of a hewn log.

FLYING BUTTRESS. An arch or series of arches on the exterior of a building, connecting the building to detached pier buttresses so that the thrust from the roof vaults is offset. See also *Buttress*

FOLIO. A leaf of a manuscript or a book, identified so that the front and the back have the same number, the front being labeled *recto* and the back *verso*.

FORESHORTENING. A method of reducing or distorting the parts of a represented object that are not parallel to the picture plane in order to convey the impression of three dimensions as perceived by the human eye.

FRESCO. Italian word for "fresh." Fresco is the technique of painting on plaster with pigments ground in water so that the paint is absorbed by the plaster and becomes part of the wall itself. *Buon fresco* is the technique of painting on wet plaster; *fresco secco* is the technique of painting on dry plaster.

FRIEZE. (1) A continuous band of painted or sculptured decoration. (2) In a Classical building, the part of the entablature between the architrave and the cornice. A Doric frieze consists of alternating triglyphs and metopes, the latter often sculptured. An Ionic frieze is usually decorated with continuous relief sculpture.

FRONTALITY. Representation of a subject in a full frontal view.

FROTTAGE. The technique of rubbing a drawing medium, such as a crayon, over paper that is placed over a textured surface in order to transfer the underlying pattern to the paper.

GABLE. (1) The triangular area framed by the cornice or eaves of a building and the sloping sides of a pitched roof. In Classical architecture, it is called a *pediment*. (2) A decorative element of similar shape, such as the triangular structures above the portals of a Gothic church and sometimes at the top of a Gothic picture frame.

GALLERY. A second story placed over the side aisles of a church and below the clerestory. In a church with a four-part elevation, it is placed below the triforium and above the nave arcade.

GEISON. A projecting horizontal cornice. On a Greek or Roman temple, the geison will often be decorated.

GENRE PAINTING. Based on the French word for type or kind, the term sometimes refers to a category of style or subject matter. But it usually refers to depictions of common activities performed by contemporary people, often of the lower or middle classes. This contrasts with grand historical themes or mythologies, narratives or portraits.

GEOMETRIC ARABESQUE. Complex patterns and designs usually composed of polygonal geometric forms, rather than organic flowing shapes; often used as ornamentation in Islamic art.

GESTURE PAINTING. A technique in painting and drawing where the actual physical movement of the artist is reflected in the brushstroke or line as it is seen in the artwork. The artist Jackson Pollock is particularly associated with this technique.

GISANT. In a tomb sculpture, a recumbent effigy or representation of the deceased. At times, the gisant may be represented in a state of decay.

GLAZE. (1) A thin layer of translucent oil color applied to a painted surface or to parts of it in order to modify the tone. (2) A glassy coating applied to a piece of ceramic work before firing in the kiln as a protective seal and often as decoration.

GLAZED BRICK. Brick that is baked in a kiln after being painted.

GOTHIC. A style of art developed in France during the 12th century that spread throughout Europe. The style is characterized by daring architectural achievements, for example, the opening up of wall surfaces and the reaching of great heights, particularly in cathedral construction. Pointed arches and ribbed groin vaults allow for a lightness of construction that permits maximum light to enter buildings through stained-glass windows. Increasing naturalism and elegance characterize Gothic sculpture and painting.

GRANULATION. A technique of decoration in which metal granules, or tiny metal balls, are fused to a metal surface.

GRATTAGE. A technique in painting whereby an image is produced by scraping off paint from a canvas that has been placed over a textured surface.

GREEK CROSS. A cross with four arms of equal length arranged at right angles.

GRISAILLE. A monochrome drawing or painting in which only values of black, gray, and white are used.

GRISAILLE GLASS. White glass painted with gray designs.

GROIN VAULT. A vault formed by the intersection of two barrel vaults at right angles to each other. A groin is the ridge resulting from the intersection of two vaults.

GUILLOCHE PATTERN. A repeating pattern made up of two ribbons spiraling around a series of central points. A guilloche pattern is often used as a decorative device in Classical vase-painting.

GUILDS. Economic and social organizations that control the making and marketing of given products in a medieval city. To work as a painter or sculptor in a city, an individual had to belong to a guild, which established standards for the craft. First mentioned on p.211. Emboldened entry on p.258

GUTTAE. In a Doric entablature, small peglike projections above the frieze; possibly derived from pegs originally used in wooden construction.

HALL CHURCH. See *hallenkirche*.

HALLENKIRCHE. German word for "hall church." A church in which the nave and the side aisles are of the same height. The type was developed in Romanesque architecture and occurs especially frequently in German Gothic churches.

HAN. In Turkish, an establishment where travelers can procure lodging, food, and drink. Also called a *caravansaray*.

HAPPENING. A type of art that involves visual images, audience participation, and improvised performance, usually in a public setting and under the loose direction of an artist.

HARMONY. In medieval architecture, the perfect relationship among parts in terms of mathematical proportions or ratios. Thought to be the source of all beauty, since it exemplifies the laws by which divine reason made the universe.

HATAYI. A style of ornament originated by the Ottomans and characterized by curved leaves and complex floral palmettes linked by vines, sometimes embellished with birds or animals.

HATCHING. A series of parallel lines used as shading in prints and drawings. When two sets of crossing parallel lines are used, it is called *crosshatching*.

HERALDIC POSE. A pose where two figures are mirror images of one another, sometimes flanking a central object, as in the relieving triangle above the Lioness Gate at Mycenae.

HEROÖN. The center of a hero cult, where Classical Greeks venerated mythological or historical heroes.

HEXASTYLE. A term used to describe the façade of a Greek or Roman temple, meaning that it has six columns.

HIERATIC SCALE. An artistic technique in which the importance of figures is indicated by size, so that the most important figure is depicted as the largest.

HIEROGLYPH. A symbol, often based on a figure, animal, or object, standing for a word, syllable, or sound. These symbols form the early Egyptian writing system, and are found on ancient Egyptian monuments as well as in Egyptian written records.

HOUSE CHURCH. A place for private worship within a house; the first Christian churches were located in private homes that were modified for religious ceremonies.

HUMANISM. A philosophy emphasizing the worth of the individual, the rational abilities of humankind, and the human potential for good. During the Italian Renaissance, humanism was part of a movement that encouraged study of the classical cultures of Greece and Rome; often it came into conflict with the doctrines of the Catholic church.

HYDRIA. A type of jar used by ancient Greeks to carry water. Some examples were highly decorated.

HYPOSTYLE. A hall whose roof is supported by columns.

ICON. From the Greek word for "image." A panel painting of one or more sacred personages, such as Christ, the Virgin, or a saint, particularly venerated in the Orthodox Christian church.

ICONOCLASM. The doctrine of the Christian church in the 8th and 9th centuries that forbade the worship or production of religious images. This doctrine led to the destruction of many works of art. The iconoclastic controversy over the validity of this doctrine led to a division of the church. Protestant churches of the 16th and 17th centuries also practiced iconoclasm.

ICONOGRAPHY. (1) The depicting of images in art in order to convey certain meanings. (2) The study of the meaning of images depicted in art, whether they be inanimate objects, events, or personages. (3) The content or subject matter of a work of art.

IMPASTO. From the Italian word meaning "to make into a paste"; it describes paint, usually oil paint, applied very thickly.

IMPLUVIUM. A shallow pool in a Roman house, for collecting rain water. The impluvium was usually in the atrium, and stood beneath a large opening in the roof, known as a compluvium.

INFRARED LIGHT. Light on the spectrum beyond the comprehension of the naked eye is referred to as infrared. Special filters are needed to perceive it.

INFRARED REFLECTOGRAPHY. A technique for scientifically examining works of art. Special cameras equipped with infrared filters can look below the top layer of paintings to record the darker materials, such as carbon, which artists used to create drawings on panels or other supports.

INLAID NIELLO. See *niello*.

INSULA (pl. **INSULAE**). Latin word for "island." (1) An ancient Roman city block. (2) A Roman "apartment house": a concrete and brick building or chain of buildings around a central court, up to five stories high. The ground floor had shops, and above were living quarters.

INTAGLIO. A printing technique in which the design is formed from ink-filled lines cut into a surface. Engraving, etching, and drypoint are examples of intaglio.

INTERCOLUMNIATION. The space between two columns, measured from the edge of the column shafts. The term is often used in describing Greek and Roman temples.

INVERTED PERSPECTIVE. The technique, in some 16th- and 17th-century paintings, of placing the main theme or narrative of a work in the background and placing a still life or other representation in the foreground.

IONIC COLUMN. A column characterized by a base and a capital with two volutes. One of three styles of column consistently used by Greek and Roman architects.

IWAN. A vaulted chamber in a mosque or other Islamic structure, open on one side and usually opening onto an interior courtyard.

JAMBS. The vertical sides of an opening. In Romanesque and Gothic churches, the jambs of doors and windows are often cut on a slant outward, or "splayed," thus providing a broader surface for sculptural decoration.

JAPONISME. In 19th-century French and American art, a style of painting and drawing that reflected the influence of the Japanese artworks, particularly prints, that were then reaching the West.

JASPERWARE. A durable, unglazed porcelain developed by the firm of Josiah Wedgwood in the 18th century. It is decorated with Classically inspired bas relief or cameo figures, and ornamented in white relief on a colored ground, especially blue and sage green.

KORE (pl. **KORAI**). Greek word for "maiden." An Archaic Greek statue of a standing, draped female.

KOUROS (pl. **KOUROI**). Greek word for "male youth." An Archaic Greek statue of a standing, nude youth.

KRATER. A Greek vessel, of assorted shapes, in which wine and water are mixed. A *calyx krater* is a bell-shaped vessel with handles near the base; a *volute krater* is a vessel with handles shaped like scrolls.

KUFIC. One of the first general forms of Arabic script to be developed, distinguished by its angularity; distinctive variants occur in various parts of the Islamic worlds.

KYLIX. In Greek and Roman antiquity, a shallow drinking cup with two horizontal handles, often set on a stem terminating in a foot.

LAMASSU. An ancient Near Eastern guardian of a palace; often shown in sculpture as a human-headed bull or lion with wings.

LANCET. A tall, pointed window common in Gothic architecture.

LANTERN. A relatively small structure crowning a dome, roof, or tower, frequently open to admit light to an enclosed area below.

LATIN CROSS. A cross in which three arms are of equal length and one arm is longer.

LEKYTHOS (pl. **LEKYTHOI**). A Greek oil jug with an ellipsoidal body, a narrow neck, a flanged mouth, a curved handle extending from below the lip to the shoulder, and a narrow base terminating in a foot. It was used chiefly for ointments and funerary offerings.

LIGHT WELLS. Open shafts that allow light to penetrate into a building from the roof. These were a major source of light and ventilation in Minoan "palaces."

LIMINAL SPACE. A transitional area, such as a doorway or archway. In Roman architecture, liminal spaces were often decorated with apotropaic devices.

LINEARITY. A term used to refer to images that have a strong sense of line that provides sharp contours to figures and objects.

LITURGY. A body of rites or rituals prescribed for public worship.

LOGGIA. A covered gallery or arcade open to the air on at least one side. It may stand alone or be part of a building.

LUNETTE. (1) A semicircular or pointed wall area, as under a vault, or above a door or window. When it is above the portal of a medieval church, it is called a *tympanum*. (2) A painting, relief sculpture, or window of the same shape.

LUSTER. A metallic pigment fired over glazed ceramic, which creates an iridescent effect.

MACHICOLATIONS. A gallery projecting from the walls of a castle or tower with holes in the floor in order to allow liquid, stones, or other projectiles to be dropped on an enemy.

MAIDAN. In parts of the Near East and Asia a large open space or square.

MANDORLA. A representation of light surrounding the body of a holy figure.

MANUSCRIPT ILLUMINATION. Decoration of handwritten documents, scrolls, or books with drawings or paintings. Illuminated manuscripts were often produced during the Middle Ages.

MAQSURA. A screened enclosure, reserved for the ruler, often located before the *mihrab* in certain important royal Islamic mosques.

MARTYRIUM (pl. **MARTYRIA**). A church, chapel, or shrine built over the grave of a Christian martyr or at the site of an important miracle.

MASTABA. An ancient Egyptian tomb, rectangular in shape, with sloping sides and a flat roof. It covered a chapel for offerings and a shaft to the burial chamber.

MATRIX. (1) A mold or die used for shaping a ceramic object before casting. (2) In printmaking, any surface on which an image is incised, carved, or applied and from which a print may be pulled.

MEANDER PATTERN. A decorative motif of intricate, rectilinear character applied to architecture and sculpture.

MEGALITH. From the Greek *mega*, meaning "big," and *lithos*, meaning "stone." A huge stone such as those used in cromlechs and dolmens.

MEGARON (pl. **MEGARONS** or **MEGARA**). From the Greek word for "large." The central audience hall in a Minoan or Mycenaean palace or home.

MENHIR. A megalithic upright slab of stone, sometimes placed in rows by prehistoric peoples.

METOPE. The element of a Doric frieze between two consecutive triglyphs, sometimes left plain but often decorated with paint or relief sculpture.

MEZZOTINT. Printmaking technique developed in the late 17th century where the plate is roughened or "rocked" to better retain the ink and create dark images.

MIHRAB. A niche, often highly decorated, usually found in the center of the *qibla* wall of a mosque, indicating the direction of prayer toward Mecca.

MINA'I. From the Persian meaning "enameled," polychrome overglaze-decorated ceramic ware produced in Iran.

MINARET. A tower on or near a mosque, varying extensively in form throughout the Islamic world, from which the faithful are called to prayer five times a day.

MINBAR. A type of staircase pulpit, found in more important mosques to the right of the mihrab, from which the Sabbath sermon is given on Fridays after the noonday prayer.

MINIATURIST. An artist trained in the painting of miniature figures or scenes to decorate manuscripts.

MODULE. (1) A segment of a pattern. (2) A basic unit, such as the measure of an architectural member. Multiples of the basic unit are used to determine proportionate construction of other parts of a building.

MONOTYPE. A unique print made from a copper plate or other type of plate from which no other copies of the artwork are made.

MOSQUE. A building used as a center for community prayers in Islamic worship; it often serves other functions including religious education and public assembly.

MOZARAB. Term used for the Spanish Christian culture of the Middle Ages that developed while Muslims were the dominant culture and political power on the Iberian peninsula.

MUQARNAS. A distinctive type of Islamic decoration consisting of multiple nichelike forms usually arranged in superimposed rows, often used in zones of architectural transition.

NAOS. See *cella*.

NARTHEX. The transverse entrance hall of a church, sometimes enclosed but often open on one side to a preceding atrium.

NATURALISM. A style of art that aims to depict the natural world as it appears.

NAVE. (1) The central aisle of a Roman basilica, as distinguished from the side aisles. (2) The same section of a Christian basilican church extending from the entrance to the apse or transept.

NECROPOLIS. Greek for "city of the dead." A burial ground or cemetery.

NEMES HEADDRESS. The striped cloth headdress worn by Egyptian kings, and frequently represented in their sculpted and painted images.

NEOCLASSICISM. An 18th-century style that emphasizes Classical themes, sometimes with strong moral overtones, executed in a way that places a strong emphasis on line, with figures and objects running parallel to the picture plane. Paintings and drawings are typically executed with sharp clarity, by way of tight handling of paint and clearly defined line and light.

NIELLO. Dark metal alloys applied to the engraved lines in a precious metal plate (usually made of gold or silver) to create a design.

NIKE. The ancient Greek goddess of victory, often identified with Athena and by the Romans with Victoria. She is usually represented as a winged woman with windblown draperies.

NOCTURNE. A painting that depicts a nighttime scene, often emphasizing the effects of artificial light.

NOMAD'S GEAR. Portable objects, including weaponry, tackle for horses, jewelry and vessels, crafted by nomadic groups such as the tribes of early Iran, and sometimes buried with their dead.

OBELISK. A tall, tapering, four-sided stone shaft with a pyramidal top. First constructed as *megaliths* in ancient Egypt, certain examples have since been exported to other countries.

OCTASTYLE. A term used to describe the façade of a Greek or Roman temple, meaning that it has eight columns.

OCULUS. The Latin word for "eye." (1) A circular opening at the top of a dome used to admit light. (2) A round window.

OPISTHONAOS. A rear chamber in a Greek temple, often mirroring the porch at the front. The opisthonaos was sometimes used to house valuable objects. Access to the chamber was usually from the peristyle rather than the cella.

OPTICAL IMAGES. An image created from what the eye sees, rather than from memory.

ORANT. A standing figure with arms upraised in a gesture of prayer.

ORCHESTRA. (1) In an ancient Greek theater, the round space in front of the stage and below the tiers of seats, reserved for the chorus. (2) In a Roman theater, a similar space reserved for important guests.

ORIEL. A bay window that projects from a wall.

ORIENTALISM. The fascination of Western culture, especially as expressed in art and literature, with Eastern cultures. In the 19th-century, this fascination was especially focused on North Africa and the Near East, that is, the Arab world.

ORTHOGONAL. In a perspective construction, an imagined line in a painting that runs perpendicular to the picture plane and recedes to a vanishing point.

ORTHOSTATS. Upright slabs of stone constituting or lining the lowest courses of a wall, often in order to protect a vulnerable material such as mud-brick.

POUSSINISTES. Those artists of the French Academy at the end of the 17th century and the beginning of the 18th century who favored "drawing," which they believed appealed to the mind rather than the senses. The term derived from admiration for the French artist Nicolas Poussin. See *Rubénistes*.

PALETTE. (1) A thin, usually oval or oblong board with a thumbhole at one end, used by painters to hold and mix their colors. (2) The range of colors used by a particular painter. (3) In Egyptian art, a slate slab, usually decorated with sculpture in low relief. The

small ones with a recessed circular area on one side are thought to have been used for eye makeup. The larger ones were commemorative objects.

PARCHMENT. From Pergamon, the name of a Greek city in Asia Minor where parchment was invented in the 2nd century BCE. (1) A paperlike material made from bleached animal hides used extensively in the Middle Ages for manuscripts. Vellum is a superior type of parchment made from calfskin. (2) A document or miniature on this material.

PEDIMENT. (1) In Classical architecture, a low gable, typically triangular, framed by a horizontal cornice below and two raking cornices above; frequently filled with sculpture. (2) A similar architectural member used over a door, window, or niche. When pieces of the cornice are either turned at an angle or interrupted, it is called a *broken pediment*.

PENDENTIVE. One of the concave triangles that achieves the transition from a square or polygonal opening to the round base of a dome or the supporting drum.

PERFORMANCE ART. A type of art in which performance by actors or artists, often interacting with the audience in an improvisational manner, is the primary aim over a certain time period. These artworks are transitory, perhaps with only a photographic record of some of the events.

PERIPTERAL TEMPLE. In Classical architecture, a temple with a single colonnade on all sides, providing shelter.

PERISTYLE. (1) In a Roman house or *domus*, an open garden court surrounded by a colonnade. (2) A colonnade around a building or court.

PERPENDICULAR GOTHIC STYLE. Describes Late Gothic architecture in England, characterized by dominant vertical accents.

PERSPECTIVE. A system for representing spatial relationships and three-dimensional objects on a flat two-dimensional surface so as to produce an effect similar to that perceived by the human eye. In *atmospheric* or *aerial* perspective, this is accomplished by a gradual decrease in the intensity of color and value and in the contrast of light and dark as objects are depicted as farther and farther away in the picture. In color artwork, as objects recede into the distance, all colors tend toward a light bluish-gray tone. In *scientific* or *linear* perspective, developed in Italy in the 15th century, a mathematical system is used based on orthogonals receding to vanishing points on the horizon. Transversals intersect the orthogonals at right angles at distances derived mathematically. Since this presupposes an absolutely stationary viewer and imposes rigid restrictions on the artist, it is seldom applied with complete consistency. Although traditionally ascribed to Brunelleschi, the first theoretical text on perspective was Leon Battista Alberti's *On Painting* (1435).

PHOTOGRAM. A shadowlike photograph made without a camera by placing objects on light-sensitive paper and exposing them to a light source.

PHOTOMONTAGE. A photograph in which prints in whole or in part are combined to form a new image. A technique much practiced by the Dada group in the 1920s.

PICTOGRAPH. A pictorial representation of a concept or object, frequently used by Egyptian artists, sometimes in conjunction with hieroglyphs.

PICTURESQUE. Visually interesting or pleasing, as if resembling a picture.

PIER. An upright architectural support, usually rectangular and sometimes with capital and base. When columns, pilasters, or shafts are attached to it, as in many Romanesque and Gothic churches, it is called a compound pier.

PIETÀ. Italian word for both "pity" and "piety." A representation of the Virgin grieving over the dead Christ. When used in a scene recording a specific moment after the Crucifixion, it is usually called a Lamentation.

PILE CARPET. A weaving made on a loom in which rows of individual knots of colored wool are tied so that the ends of each knot protrude to form a thick pile surface.

PILGRIMAGE PLAN. The general design used in Christian churches that were stops on the pilgrimage routes throughout medieval Europe, characterized by having side aisles that allowed pilgrims to ambulate around the church. See *pilgrimage choir*.

PILOTIS. Pillars that are constructed from *reinforced concrete (ferroconcrete)*.

PINAKOTHEKE. A museum for paintings. The first known example may have been in the Propylaia on the Athenian Akropolis.

PINNACLE. A small, decorative structure capping a tower, pier, buttress, or other architectural member. It is used especially in Gothic buildings.

PISÉ. A construction material consisting of packed earth, similar to wattle and daub. Etruscan architects used pisé for houses, with the result that little survives of them.

PLANARITY. A term used to described a composition where figures and objects are arranged parallel to the picture plane.

PLATE TRACERY. A style of tracery in which pierced openings in an otherwise solid wall of stonework are filled with glass.

PLEIN-AIR. Sketching outdoors, often using paints, in order to capture the immediate effects of light on landscape and other subjects. Much encouraged by the Impressionists, their *plein-air* sketches were often taken back to the studio to produce finished paintings, but many *plein-air* sketches are considered masterworks.

POCHADES. Small outdoor oil paintings made by landscape painters, serving as models for large-scale pictures that would be developed in the artist's studio.

POLIS. A city-state, in the Classical Greek world. City-states began to develop in the course of the 7th and 6th centuries BCE, and were governed in a variety of different ways, including monarchy and oligarchy.

POLYPTYCH. An altarpiece or devotional work of art made of several panels joined together, often hinged.

PORTRAIT BUST. A sculpted representation of an individual which includes not only the head but some portion of the upper torso. Popular during the Roman period, it was revived during the Renaissance.

POST AND LINTEL. A basic system of construction in which two or more uprights, the posts, support a horizontal member, the lintel. The lintel may be the topmost element or support a wall or roof.

POUNCING. A technique for transferring a drawing from a cartoon to a wall or other surface by pricking holes along the principal lines of the drawing and forcing fine charcoal powder through them onto the surface of the wall, thus reproducing the design on the wall.

PREDELLA. The base of an altarpiece, often decorated with small scenes that are related in subject to that of the main panel or panels.

PREFIGURATION. The representation of Old Testament figures and stories as forerunners and foreshadowers of those in the New Testament.

PRIMITIVISM. The appropriation of non-Western (e.g., African, tribal, Polynesian) art styles, forms, and techniques by Modern era artists as part of innovative

and avant-garde artistic movements; other sources were also used, including the work of children and the mentally ill.

PROCESS ART. Art in which the process is the art, as when Richard Serra hurled molten lead where a wall meets the floor, or Hans Haacke put water in a hermetic acrylic cube, which resulted in condensation forming on it.

PRONAOS. In a Greek or Roman temple, an open vestibule in front of the *cella*.

PRONK. A word meaning ostentatious or sumptuous; it is used to refer to a still life of luxurious objects.

PROPYLON. A monumental gateway, often leading into a citadel or a precinct, such as the Akropolis of Mycenae or Athens.

PROTOME. A decorative, protruding attachment, often on a vessel. Greek bronze-workers attached griffin-shaped protomes to tripod cauldrons in the 7th century BCE.

PROVENANCE. The place of origin of a work of art and related information.

PSALTER. (1) The book of Psalms in the Old Testament, thought to have been written in part by David, king of ancient Israel. (2) A copy of the Psalms, sometimes arranged for liturgical or devotional use and often richly illuminated.

PYLON. Greek word for "gateway." (1) The monumental entrance building to an Egyptian temple or forecourt consisting either of a massive wall with sloping sides pierced by a doorway or of two such walls flanking a central gateway. (2) A tall structure at either side of a gate, bridge, or avenue marking an approach or entrance.

PYXIS. A lidded box, often made of ivory, to hold jewelry or cosmetics in daily life, and, in the context of the Christian church, used on altars to contain the Host (Communion wafer).

QIBLA. The direction toward Mecca, which Muslims face during prayer. The qibla wall in a mosque identifies this direction.

QUADRANT VAULT. A half-barrel vault designed so that instead of being semicircular in cross-section, the arch is one-quarter of a circle.

QUATREFOIL. An ornamental element composed of four lobes radiating from a common center.

RAYONNANT. The style of Gothic architecture, described as "radiant," developed at the Parisian court of Louis IX in the mid-13th century. Also referred to as *court style*.

READYMADE. An ordinary object that, when an artist gives it a new context and title, is transformed into an art object. Readymades were important features of the Dada and Surrealism movements of the early 20th century.

RED-FIGURED. A style of ancient Greek ceramic decoration characterized by red figures against a black background. This style of decoration developed toward the end of the 6th century BCE and replaced the earlier *black-figured* style.

REGISTER. A horizontal band containing decoration, such as a relief sculpture or a fresco painting. When multiple horizontal layers are used, registers are useful in distinguishing between different visual planes and different time periods in visual narration.

RELIEF. (1) The projection of a figure or part of a design from the background or plane on which it is carved or modeled. Sculpture done in this manner is described as "high relief" or "low relief" depending on the height of the projection. When it is very shallow, it is called *schiacciato*, the Italian word for "flattened out." (2) The apparent projection of forms represented in a painting or drawing. (3) A category of printmaking in which lines raised from the surface are inked and printed.

RELIEVING TRIANGLE. A space left open above a lintel to relieve it of the weight of masonry. This device was used by Bronze Age architects in gate and tomb construction.

RELIQUARY. A container used for storing or displaying relics.

RENAISSANCE. Literally, rebirth. During the 14th and 15th centuries, Italian writers, artists, and intellectuals aimed to revive the arts of the ancient world. From their accomplishments, the term has been applied to the period, and is used generally to refer to a cultural flowering.

REPOUSSÉ. A metalworking technique where a design is hammered onto an object from the wrong side. Sasanian craftsmen used this techniques for silver vessels.

RESPOND. (1) A half-pier, pilaster, or similar element projecting from a wall to support a lintel or an arch whose other side is supported by a free-standing column or pier, as at the end of an arcade. (2) One of several pilasters on a wall behind a colonnade that echoes or "responds to" the columns but is largely decorative. (3) One of the slender shafts of a compound pier in a medieval church that seems to carry the weight of the vault.

RHYTON. An ancient drinking or pouring vessel made from pottery, metal, or stone, and sometimes designed in a human or animal form.

RIBBED GROIN VAULTS. A vault is a stone or brick roof. Groin vaults result from the intersection of two barrel vaults; the places where the arched surfaces meet is called the groin. Adding ribs or thickenings of the groins increases the strength of the roof.

RIBBED VAULT. A style of vault in which projecting surface arches, known as ribs, are raised along the intersections of segments of the vault. Ribs may provide architectural support as well as decoration to the vault's surface.

ROCOCO. The ornate, elegant style most associated with the early-18th-century in France, and which later spread throughout Europe, generally using pastel colors and the decorative arts to emphasize the notion of fantasy.

ROMANESQUE. (1) The style of medieval architecture from the 11th to the 13th centuries that was based upon the Roman model and that used the Roman rounded arch, thick walls for structural support, and relatively small windows. (2) Any culture or its artifacts that are "Roman-like."

ROMANTICISM. A cultural movement that surfaced in the second half of the 18th century and peaked in the first half of the 19th century. The movement was based on a belief in individual genius and originality and the expression of powerful emotions, as well as preference for exotic themes and the omnipotent force of nature, often viewed as manifestation of God.

ROSE WINDOW. A large, circular window with stained glass and stone tracery, frequently used on façades and at the ends of transepts in Gothic churches.

ROSTRUM (pl. ROSTRA). (1) A beaklike projection from the prow of an ancient warship used for ramming the enemy. (2) In the Roman forum, the raised platform decorated with the beaks of captured ships from which speeches were delivered. (3) A platform, stage, or the like used for public speaking.

ROTULUS (pl. ROTULI). The Latin word for scroll, a rolled written text.

RUBÉNISTES. Those artists of the French Academy at the end of the 17th century and the beginning of the 18th century who favored "color" in painting because it appealed to the senses and was thought to be true to nature. The term derived from admiration for the work of the Flemish artist Peter Paul Rubens. See *Poussinistes*.

RUSTICATION. A masonry technique of laying rough-faced stones with sharply indented joints.

SALON. (1) A large, elegant drawing or reception room in a palace or a private house. (2) Official government-sponsored exhibition of paintings and sculpture by living artists held at the Louvre in Paris, first biennially, then annually. (3) Any large public exhibition patterned after the Paris Salon.

SARCOPHAGUS (pl. **SARCOPHAGI**). A large coffin, generally of stone, and often decorated with sculpture or inscriptions. The term is derived from two Greek words meaning "flesh" and "eating."

SAZ. Meaning literally "enchanted forest," this term describes the sinuous leaves and twining stems that are a major component of the *hatayi* style under the Ottoman Turks.

SCHIACCIATO. Italian for "flattened out." Describes low relief sculpture used by Donatello and some of his contemporaries.

SCHOLASTICISM. A school of medieval thought that tries to reconcile faith and reason by combining ancient philosophy with Christian theology.

SCIENTIFIC PERSPECTIVE. See *perspective*.

SCRIPTORIUM (pl. **SCRIPTORIA**). A workroom in a monastery reserved for copying and illustrating manuscripts.

SECTION. An architectural drawing presenting a building as if cut across the vertical plane at right angles to the horizontal plane. A *cross section* is a cut along the transverse axis. A *longitudinal section* is a cut along the longitudinal axis.

SELECTIVE WIPING. The planned removal of certain areas of ink during the etching process to produce changes in value on the finished print.

SEPTPARTITE VAULT. A type of vault divided into seven sections.

SERDAB. In Egyptian architecture, an enclosed room without an entrance, often found in a funerary context. A sculpture of the dead king might be enclosed within it, as at Saqqara.

SEXPARTITE VAULT. See *vault*.

SFUMATO. Italian word meaning "smoky." Used to describe very delicate gradations of light and shade in the modeling of figures. It is applied especially to the work of Leonardo da Vinci.

SGRAFFITO ORNAMENT. A decorative technique in which a design is made by scratching away the surface layer of a material to produce a form in contrasting colors.

SHADING. The modulation of volume by means of contrasting light and shade. Prehistoric cave-painters used this device, as did Greek tomb-painters in the Hellenistic period.

SILKSCREEN PRINTING. A technique of printing in which paint or ink is pressed through a stencil and specially prepared cloth to produce a previously designed image. Also called serigraphy.

SILVERPOINT. A drawing instrument (stylus) of the 14th and 15th centuries made from silver; it produced a fine line and maintained a sharp point.

SIMULTANEOUS CONTRAST. The theory, first expressed by Michel-Eugène Chevreul (1786–1889), that complementary colors, when placed next to one another, increase the intensity of each other (e.g., red becoming more red and green more green.)

SITE-SPECIFIC ART. Art that is produced in only one location, a location that is an integral part of the work and essential to its production and meaning.

SKENE. A building erected on a Greek or Roman stage, as a backdrop against which some of the action took place. It usually consisted of a screen of columns, arranged in several storeys.

SOCLE. A portion of the foundation of a building that projects outward as a base for a column or some other device.

SPANDREL. The area between the exterior curves of two adjoining arches or, in the case of a single arch, the area around its outside curve from its springing to its keystone.

SPATIAL PERSPECTIVE. The exploration of the spatial relationships between objects. Painters were especially interested in spatial perspective in the Hellenistic period in Greece.

SPIRE. A tall tower that rises high above a roof. Spires are commonly associated with church architecture and are frequently found on Gothic structures.

SPOLIA. Latin for "hide stripped from an animal." Term used for (1) spoils of war and (2) fragments of architecture or sculpture reused in a secondary context.

SPRINGING. The part of an arch in contact with its base.

SQUINCHES. Arches set diagonally at the corners of a square or rectangle to establish a transition to the round shape of the dome above.

STAIN PAINTING. A type of painting where the artist works on unprimed canvas, allowing the paint to seep into the canvas, thus staining it.

STELE. From the Greek word for "standing block." An upright stone slab or pillar, sometimes with a carved design or inscription.

STEREOBATE. The substructure of a Classical building, especially a Greek temple.

STEREOCARDS. Side-by-side photographs of the same image taken by a camera with two lenses, replicating human binocular vision. When put into a special viewer, the twin flat pictures appear as a single three-dimensional image.

STILL LIFE. A term used to describe paintings (and sometimes sculpture) that depict familiar objects such as household items and food.

STIPPLES. In drawing or printmaking, stippling is a technique to create tone or shading in an image with small dots rather than lines.

STREET PHOTOGRAPHY. A term applied to American documentary photographers such as Walker Evans, who emerged in the 1930s, and Robert Frank, who surfaced in the 1950s, who took to the streets to find their subject matter, often traveling extensively.

STYLOBATE. A platform or masonry floor above the stereobate forming the foundation for the columns of a Greek temple.

SUBLIME. In 19th-century art, the ideal and goal that art should inspire awe in a viewer and engender feelings of high religious, moral, ethical, and intellectual purpose.

SUNKEN RELIEF. Relief sculpture in which the figures or designs are modeled beneath the surface of the stone, within a sharp outline.

SYMPOSIUM. In ancient Greece, a gathering, sometimes of intellectuals and philosophers to discuss ideas, often in an informal social setting, such as at a dinner party.

SYNCRETISM. The act of bringing together disparate customs or beliefs. Historians usually describe Roman culture as syncretistic, because Romans embraced many of the the practices of those they conquered.

SYNOPTIC NARRATIVE. A narrative with different moments presented simultaneously, in order to encapsulate the entire story in a single scene. The device appears in early Greek pediment sculpture.

TEMPERA. Medium for painting in which pigments are suspended in egg yolk tempered with water or chemicals; this mixture dries quickly, reducing the possibility of changes in the finished painting.

TENEBRISM. The intense contrast of light and dark in painting.

TESSERA (pl. **TESSERAE**). A small piece of colored stone, marble, glass, or gold-backed glass used in a mosaic.

THOLOS. A building with a circular plan, often with a sacred nature.

TONDO. A circular painting or relief sculpture.

TRANSEPT. A cross arm in a basilican church placed at right angles to the nave and usually separating it from the choir or apse.

TRANSVERSALS. In a perspective construction, transversals are the lines parallel to the picture plane (horizontally) that denote distances. They intersect orthogonals to make a grid that guides the arrangement of elements to suggest space.

TRIBUNE. A platform or walkway in a church constructed overlooking the *aisle* and above the *nave*.

TRIFORIUM. The section of a nave wall above the arcade and below the clerestory. It frequently consists of a blind arcade with three openings in each bay. When the gallery is also present, a four-story elevation results, the triforium being between the gallery and clerestory. It may also occur in the transept and the choir walls.

TRIGLYPH. The element of a Doric frieze separating two consecutive metopes and divided by grooves into three sections.

TRILITHIC. A form of construction using three stones—two uprights and a lintel—found frequently in Neolithic tomb and ritual architecture.

TRIPTYCH. An altarpiece or devotional picture, either carved or painted, with one central panel and two hinged wings.

TRIUMPHAL ARCH. (1) A monumental arch, sometimes a combination of three arches, erected by a Roman emperor in commemoration of his military exploits and usually decorated with scenes of these deeds in relief sculpture. (2) The great transverse arch at the eastern end of a church that frames altar and apse and separates them from the main body of the church. It is frequently decorated with mosaics or mural paintings.

TROIS CRAYONS. The use of three colors, usually red, black, and white, in a drawing; a technique popular in the 17th and 18th centuries.

TROMPE L'OEIL. Meaning "trick of the eye" in French, it is a work of art designed to deceive a viewer into believing that the work of art is reality, an actual three-dimensional object or scene in space.

TRUMEAU. A central post supporting the lintel of a large doorway, as in a Romanesque or Gothic portal, where it is frequently decorated with sculpture.

TRUSS. A triangular wooden or metal support for a roof that may be left exposed in the interior or be covered by a ceiling.

TUMULUS (pl. **TUMULI**) A monumental earth mound, often raised over a tomb. Etruscan builders constructed tumuli with internal chambers for burials.

TURRET. (1) A small tower that is part of a larger structure. (2) A small tower at a corner of a building, often beginning some distance from the ground.

TUSCAN STYLE. An architectural style typical of ancient Italy. The style is similar to the Doric style, but the column shafts have bases.

TUSCHE. An inklike liquid containing crayon that is used to produce solid black (or solid color) areas in prints.

TYMPANUM. (1) In Classical architecture, a recessed, usually triangular area often decorated with sculpture. Also called a pediment. (2) In medieval architecture, an arched area between an arch and the lintel of a door or window, frequently carved with relief sculpture.

TYPOLOGY. The matching or pairing of pre-Christian figures, persons, and symbols with their Christian counterparts.

VANISHING POINT. The point at which the orthogonals meet and disappear in a composition done with scientific perspective.

VANITAS. The term derives from the book of Ecclesiastes I:2 ("Vanities of vanities, …") that refers to the passing of time and the notion of life's brevity and the inevitability of death. The vanitas theme found expression especially in the Northern European art of the 17th century.

VAULT. An arched roof or ceiling usually made of stone, brick, or concrete. Several distinct varieties have been developed; all need buttressing at the point where the lateral thrust is concentrated. (1) A barrel vault is a semicircular structure made up of successive arches. It may be straight or annular in plan. (2) A groin vault is the result of the intersection of two barrel vaults of equal size that produces a bay of four compartments with sharp edges, or groins, where the two meet. (3) A ribbed groin vault is one in which ribs are added to the groins for structural strength and for decoration. When the diagonal ribs are constructed as half-circles, the resulting form is a domical ribbed vault. (4) A sexpartite vault is a ribbed groin vault in which each bay is divided into six compartments by the addition of a transverse rib across the center. (5) The normal Gothic vault is quadripartite with all the arches pointed to some degree. (6) A fan vault is an elaboration of a ribbed groin vault, with elements of tracery using conelike forms. It was developed by the English in the 15th century and was employed for decorative purposes.

VELLUM. See *parchment*.

VERISTIC. From the Latin *verus*, meaning "true." Describes a hyperrealistic style of portraiture that emphasizes individual characteristics.

VIGNETTE. A decorative design often used in manuscripts or books to separate sections or to decorate borders.

VOLUTE. A spiraling architectural element found notably on Ionic and Composite capitals but also used decoratively on building façades and interiors.

VOUSSOIR. A wedge-shaped piece of stone used in arch construction.

WARP. The vertical threads used in a weaver's loom through which the weft is woven.

WEBS. Masonry construction of brick, concrete, stone, etc. that is used to fill in the spaces between groin vault ribs.

WEFT. The horizontal threads that are interlaced through the vertical threads (the warp) in a woven fabric. Weft yarns run perpendicular to the warp.

WESTWORK. From the German word *Westwerk*. In Carolingian, Ottonian, and German Romanesque architecture, a monumental western front of a church, treated as a tower or combination of towers and containing an entrance and vestibule below and a chapel and galleries above. Later examples often added a transept and a crossing tower.

WET-COLLODION PROCESS. A 19th-century photographic technique that uses a very sensitive emulsion called collodion (gun-cotton dissolved in alcohol ether), that reduces exposure time to under a second and produces a sharp, easily reproducible negative.

WHITE-GROUND. Vase-painting technique in which artists painted a wide range of colors onto a white background. This was a favorite technique for decorating lekythoi (vases used in a funerary context in ancient Greece.)

WOODCUT. A print made by carving out a design on a wooden block cut along the grain, applying ink to the raised surfaces that remain, and printing from those.

X-RADIOGRAPHIC. Using a form of electromagnetic radiation called X-rays, researchers can examine the layers of paint or other materials used by artists to construct works of art.

ZIGGURAT. From the Assyrian word *ziqquratu*, meaning "mountaintop" or "height." In ancient Assyria and Babylonia, a pyramidal mound or tower built of mud-brick forming the base for a temple. It was often either stepped or had a broad ascent winding around it, which gave it the appearance of being stepped.

Books for Further Reading

This list is intended to be as practical as possible. It is therefore limited to books of general interest that were printed over the past 20 years or have been generally available recently. However, certain indispensable volumes that have yet to be superseded are retained. This restriction means omitting numerous classics long out of print, as well as much specialized material of interest to the serious student. The reader is thus referred to the many specialized bibliographies noted below.

REFERENCE RESOURCES IN ART HISTORY

1. BIBLIOGRAPHIES AND RESEARCH GUIDES

Arntzen, E., and R. Rainwater. *Guide to the Literature of Art History*. Chicago: American Library, 1980.
Barnet, S. *A Short Guide to Writing About Art*. 8th ed. New York: Longman, 2005.
Ehresmann, D. *Architecture: A Bibliographical Guide to Basic Reference Works, Histories, and Handbooks*. Littleton, CO: Libraries Unlimited, 1984.
———. *Fine Arts: A Bibliographical Guide to Basic Reference Works, Histories, and Handbooks*. 3d ed. Littleton, CO: Libraries Unlimited, 1990.
Freitag, W. *Art Books: A Basic Bibliography of Monographs on Artists*. 2d ed. New York: Garland, 1997.
Goldman, B. *Reading and Writing in the Arts: A Handbook*. Detroit, MI: Wayne State Press, 1972.
Kleinbauer, W., and T. Slavens. *Research Guide to the History of Western Art*. Chicago: American Library, 1982.
Marmor, M., and A. Ross, eds. *Guide to the Literature of Art History 2*. Chicago: American Library, 2005.
Sayre, H. M. *Writing About Art*. New ed. Upper Saddle River, NJ: Pearson Prentice Hall, 2000.

2. DICTIONARIES AND ENCYCLOPEDIAS

Aghion, I. *Gods and Heroes of Classical Antiquity*. Flammarion Iconographic Guides. New York: Flammarion, 1996.
Boström, A., ed. *Encyclopedia of Sculpture*. 3 vols. New York: Fitzroy Dearborn, 2004.
Brigstocke, H., ed. *The Oxford Companion to Western Art*. New York: Oxford University Press, 2001.
Burden, E. *Illustrated Dictionary of Architecture*. New York: McGraw-Hill, 2002.
Carr-Gomm, S. *The Hutchinson Dictionary of Symbols in Art*. Oxford: Helicon, 1995.
Chilvers, I., et al., eds. *The Oxford Dictionary of Art*. 3d ed. New York: Oxford University Press, 2004.
Congdon, K. G. *Artists from Latin American Cultures: A Biographical Dictionary*. Westport, CT: Greenwood Press, 2002.
Cumming, R. *Art: A Field Guide*. New York: Alfred A. Knopf, 2001.
Curl, J. *A Dictionary of Architecture*. New York: Oxford University Press, 1999.
The Dictionary of Art. 34 vols. New York: Grove's Dictionaries, 1996.
Duchet-Suchaux, G., and M. Pastoureau. *The Bible and the Saints*. Flammarion Iconographic Guides. New York: Flammarion, 1994.
Encyclopedia of World Art. 14 vols., with index and supplements. New York: McGraw-Hill, 1959–1968.
Fleming, J., and H. Honour. *The Penguin Dictionary of Architecture and Landscape Architecture*. 5th ed. New York: Penguin, 1998.
———. *The Penguin Dictionary of Decorative Arts*. New ed. London: Viking, 1989.
Gascoigne, B. *How to Identify Prints: A Complete Guide to Manual and Mechanical Processes from Woodcut to Inkjet*. New York: Thames & Hudson, 2004.
Hall, J. *Dictionary of Subjects and Symbols in Art*. Rev. ed. London: J. Murray, 1996.
———. *Illustrated Dictionary of Symbols in Eastern and Western Art*. New York: HarperCollins, 1995.
International Dictionary of Architects and Architecture. 2 vols. Detroit, MI: St. James Press, 1993.
Langmuir, E. *Yale Dictionary of Art and Artists*. New Haven: Yale University Press, 2000.
Lever, J., and J. Harris. *Illustrated Dictionary of Architecture, 800–1914*. 2d ed. Boston: Faber & Faber, 1993.
Lucie-Smith, E. *The Thames & Hudson Dictionary of Art Terms*. New York: Thames & Hudson, 2004.
Mayer, R. *The Artist's Handbook of Materials and Techniques*. 5th ed. New York: Viking, 1991.
———. *The HarperCollins Dictionary of Art Terms & Techniques*. 2d ed. New York: HarperCollins, 1991.
Murray, P., and L. Murray. *A Dictionary of Art and Artists*. 7th ed. New York: Penguin, 1998.
———. *A Dictionary of Christian Art*. New York: Oxford University Press, 2004, © 1996.
Nelson, R. S., and R. Shiff, eds. *Critical Terms for Art History*. Chicago: University of Chicago Press, 2003.
Pierce, J. S. *From Abacus to Zeus: A Handbook of Art History*. 7th ed. Englewood Cliffs, NJ: Pearson Prentice Hall, 2004.
Reid, J. D., ed. *The Oxford Guide to Classical Mythology in the Arts 1300–1990*. 2 vols. New York: Oxford University Press, 1993.
Shoemaker, C., ed. *Encyclopedia of Gardens: History and Design*. Chicago: Fitzroy Dearborn, 2001.
Steer, J. *Atlas of Western Art History: Artists, Sites, and Movements from Ancient Greece to the Modern Age*. New York: Facts on File, 1994.
West, S., ed. *The Bulfinch Guide to Art History*. Boston: Little, Brown, 1996.
———. *Portraiture*. Oxford History of Art. New York: Oxford University Press, 2004.

3. INDEXES, PRINTED AND ELECTRONIC

ARTbibliographies Modern. 1969 to present. A semiannual publication indexing and annotating more than 300 art periodicals, as well as books, exhibition catalogues, and dissertations. Data since 1974 also available electronically.
Art Index. 1929 to present. A standard quarterly index to more than 200 art periodicals. Also available electronically.
Avery Index to Architectural Periodicals. 1934 to present. 15 vols., with supplementary vols. Boston: G. K. Hall, 1973. Also available electronically.
BHA: Bibliography of the History of Art. 1991 to present. The merger of two standard indexes: *RILA* (*Répertoire International de la Littérature de l'Art/ International Repertory of the Literature of Art*, vol. 1. 1975) and *Répertoire d'Art et d'Archéologie* (vol. 1. 1910). Data since 1973 also available electronically.
Index Islamicus. 1665 to present. Multiple publishers. Data since 1994 also available electronically.
The Perseus Project: An Evolving Digital Library on Ancient Greece and Rome. Medford, MA: Tufts University, Classics Department, 1994.

4. WORLDWIDE WEBSITES

Visit the following websites for reproductions and information regarding artists, periods, movements, and many more subjects. The art history departments and libraries of many universities and colleges also maintain websites where you can get reading lists and links to other websites, such as those of museums, libraries, and periodicals.

http://www.aah.org.uk/welcome.html Association of Art Historians
http://www.amico.org Art Museum Image Consortium
http://www.archaeological.org Archaeological Institute of America
http://archnet.asu.edu/archnet Virtual Library for Archaeology
http://www.artchive.com
http://www.art-design.umich.edu/mother/ Mother of all Art History links pages, maintained by the Department of the History of Art at the University of Michigan
http://www.arthistory.net Art History Network
http://artlibrary.vassar.edu/ifla-idal International Directory of Art Libraries
http://www.bbk.ac.uk/lib/hasubject.html Collection of resources maintained by the History of Art Department of Birkbeck College, University of London
http://classics.mit.edu The Internet Classics Archive
http://www.collegeart.org College Art Association
http://www.constable.net
http://www.cr.nps.gov/habshaer Historic American Buildings Survey
http://www.getty.edu Including museum, five institutes, and library
http://www.harmsen.net/ahrc/ Art History Research Centre
http://icom.museum/ International Council of Museums
http://www.icomos.org International Council on Monuments and Sites
http://www.ilpi.com/artsource
http://www.siris.si.edu Smithsonian Institution Research Information System
http://whc.unesco.org/ World Heritage Center

5. GENERAL SOURCES ON ART HISTORY, METHOD, AND THEORY

Andrews, M. *Landscape and Western Art*. Oxford History of Art. New York: Oxford University Press, 1999.
Barasch, M. *Modern Theories of Art: Vol. 1, From Winckelmann to Baudelaire. Vol. 2, From Impressionism to Kandinsky*. New York: 1990–1998.
———. *Theories of Art: From Plato to Winckelmann*. New York: Routledge, 2000.
Battistini, M. *Symbols and Allegories in Art*. Los Angeles: J. Paul Getty Museum, 2005.
Baxandall, M. *Patterns of Intention: On the Historical Explanation of Pictures*. New Haven: Yale University Press, 1985.
Bois, Y.-A. *Painting as Model*. Cambridge, MA: MIT Press, 1993.
Broude, N., and M. Garrard. *The Expanding Discourse: Feminism and Art History*. New York: Harper & Row, 1992.
———, eds. *Feminism and Art History: Questioning the Litany*. New York: Harper & Row, 1982.
Bryson, N., ed. *Vision and Painting: The Logic of the Gaze*. New Haven: Yale University Press, 1983.

———., et al., eds. *Visual Theory: Painting and Interpretation*. New York: Cambridge University Press, 1991.

Chadwick, W. *Women, Art, and Society*. 3d ed. New York: Thames & Hudson, 2002.

D'Alleva, A. *Methods & Theories of Art History*. London: Laurence King, 2005.

Freedberg, D. *The Power of Images: Studies in the History and Theory of Response*. Chicago: University of Chicago Press, 1989.

Gage, J. *Color and Culture: Practice and Meaning from Antiquity to Abstraction*. Berkeley: University of California Press, 1999.

Garland Library of the History of Art. New York: Garland, 1976. Collections of essays on specific periods.

Goldwater, R., and M. Treves, eds. *Artists on Art, from the Fourteenth to the Twentieth Century*. 3d ed. New York: Pantheon, 1974.

Gombrich, E. H. *Art and Illusion*. 6th ed. New York: Phaidon, 2002.

Harris, A. S., and L. Nochlin. *Women Artists, 1550–1950*. New York: Random House, 1999.

Holly, M. A. *Panofsky and the Foundations of Art History*. Ithaca, NY: Cornell University Press, 1984.

Holt, E. G., ed. *A Documentary History of Art: Vol. 1, The Middle Ages and the Renaissance. Vol. 2, Michelangelo and the Mannerists. The Baroque and the Eighteenth Century. Vol. 3, From the Classicists to the Impressionists*. 2d ed. Princeton, NJ: Princeton University Press, 1981. Anthologies of primary sources on specific periods.

Johnson, P. *Art: A New History*. New York: HarperCollins, 2003.

Kemal, S., and I. Gaskell. *The Language of Art History*. Cambridge Studies in Philosophy and the Arts. New York: Cambridge University Press, 1991.

Kemp, M., ed. *The Oxford History of Western Art*. New York: Oxford University Press, 2000.

Kleinbauer, W. E. *Modern Perspectives in Western Art History: An Anthology of Twentieth-Century Writings on the Visual Arts*. Reprint of 1971 ed. Toronto: University of Toronto Press, 1989.

Kostof, S. A. *History of Architecture: Settings and Rituals*. 2d ed. New York: Oxford University Press, 1995.

Kruft, H. W. *A History of Architectural Theory from Vitruvius to the Present*. Princeton, NJ: Princeton Architectural Press, 1994.

Kultermann, U. *The History of Art History*. New York: Abaris Books, 1993.

Langer, C. *Feminist Art Criticism: An Annotated Bibliography*. Boston: G. K. Hall, 1993.

Laver, J. *Costume and Fashion: A Concise History*. 4th ed. The World of Art. London: Thames & Hudson, 2002.

Lavin, I., ed. *Meaning in the Visual Arts: Views from the Outside: A Centennial Commemoration of Erwin Panofsky (1892–1968)*. Princeton, NJ: Institute for Advanced Study, 1995.

Minor, V. H. *Art History's History*. Upper Saddle River, NJ: Pearson Prentice Hall, 2001.

Nochlin, L. *Women, Art, and Power, and Other Essays*. New York: HarperCollins, 1989.

Pächt, O. *The Practice of Art History: Reflections on Method*. London: Harvey Miller, 1999.

Panofsky, E. *Meaning in the Visual Arts*. Reprint of 1955 ed. Chicago: University of Chicago Press, 1982.

Penny, N. *The Materials of Sculpture*. New Haven: Yale University Press, 1993.

Pevsner, N. *A History of Building Types*. Princeton, NJ: Princeton University Press, 1976.

Podro, M. *The Critical Historians of Art*. New Haven: Yale University Press, 1982.

Pollock, G. *Differencing the Canon: Feminist Desire and the Writing of Art's Histories*. New York: Routledge, 1999.

———. *Vision and Difference: Femininity, Feminism, and the Histories of Art*. New York: Routledge, 1988.

Prettejohn, E. *Beauty and Art 1750–2000*. Oxford: Oxford University Press, 2005.

Preziosi, D., ed. *The Art of Art History: A Critical Anthology*. New York: Oxford University Press, 1998.

Rees, A. L., and F. Borzello. *The New Art History*. Atlantic Highlands, NJ: Humanities Press International, 1986.

Roth, L. *Understanding Architecture: Its Elements, History, and Meaning*. New York: Harper & Row, 1993.

Sedlmayr, H. *Framing Formalism: Riegl's Work*. Amsterdam: G+B Arts International, © 2001.

Smith, P., and C. Wilde, eds. *A Companion to Art Theory*. Oxford: Blackwell, 2002.

Sources and Documents in the History of Art Series. General ed. H. W. Janson. Englewood Cliffs, NJ: Prentice Hall. Anthologies of primary sources on specific periods.

Sutton, I. *Western Architecture*. New York: Thames & Hudson, 1999.

Tagg, J. *Grounds of Dispute: Art History, Cultural Politics, and the Discursive Field*. Minneapolis: University of Minnesota Press, 1992.

Trachtenberg, M., and I. Hyman. *Architecture: From Prehistory to Post-Modernism*. 2d ed. New York: Harry N. Abrams, 2002.

Watkin, D. *The Rise of Architectural History*. Chicago: University of Chicago Press, 1980.

Wolff, J. *The Social Production of Art*. 2d ed. New York: New York University Press, 1993.

Wölfflin, H. *Principles of Art History: The Problem of the Development of Style in Later Art*. Various eds. New York: Dover.

Wollheim, R. *Art and Its Objects*. 2d ed. New York: Cambridge University Press, 1992.

PART ONE: THE ANCIENT WORLD

GENERAL REFERENCES

Baines, J., ed. *Civilizations of the Ancient Near East*. 4 vols. New York: Scribner, 1995.

Boardman, J., ed. *The Oxford History of Classical Art*. New York: Oxford University Press, 2001.

De Grummond, N., ed. *An Encyclopedia of the History of Classical Archaeology*. Westport, CT: Greenwood, 1996.

Fine, S. *Art and Judaism in the Greco-Roman World: Toward a New Jewish Archaeology*. New York: Cambridge University Press, 2005.

Holliday, P. J. *Narrative and Event in Ancient Art*. New York: Cambridge University Press, 1993.

Redford, D. B., ed. *The Oxford Encyclopedia of Ancient Egypt*. 3 vols. New York: Oxford University Press, 2001.

Stillwell, R. *The Princeton Encyclopedia of Classical Sites*. Princeton, NJ: Princeton University Press, 1976.

Tadgell, C. *Origins: Egypt, West Asia and the Aegean*. New York: Whitney Library of Design, 1998.

Van Keuren, F. *Guide to Research in Classical Art and Mythology*. Chicago: American Library Association, 1991.

Wharton, A. J. *Refiguring the Post-Classical City: Dura Europos, Jerash, Jerusalem, and Ravenna*. New York: Cambridge University Press, 1995.

Winckelmann, J. J. *Essays on the Philosophy and History of Art*. 3 vols. Bristol, England: Thoemmes, 2001.

Wolf, W. *The Origins of Western Art: Egypt, Mesopotamia, the Aegean*. New York: Universe Books, 1989.

Yegül, F. K. *Baths and Bathing in Classical Antiquity*. Architectural History Foundation. Cambridge, MA: MIT Press, 1992.

CHAPTER 1. PREHISTORIC ART

Bahn, P. G. *The Cambridge Illustrated History of Prehistoric Art*. New York: Cambridge University Press, 1988.

Chauvet, J.-M., É. B. Deschamps, and C. Hilaire. *Dawn of Art: The Chauvet Cave*. New York: Harry N. Abrams, 1995.

Clottes, J. *Chauvet Cave*. Salt Lake City: University of Utah Press, 2003.

———. *The Shamans of Prehistory: Trance and Magic in the Painted Caves*. New York: Harry N. Abrams, 1998.

Cunliffe, B., ed. *The Oxford Illustrated Prehistory of Europe*. New York: Oxford University Press, 1994.

Fitton, J. L. *Cycladic Art*. London: British Museum Press, 1999.

Fowler, P. *Images of Prehistory*. New York: Cambridge University Press, 1990.

Leroi-Gourhan, A. *The Dawn of European Art: An Introduction to Paleolithic Cave Painting*. New York: Cambridge University Press, 1982.

McCold, C. H., and L. D. McDermott. *Toward Decolonizing Gender: Female Vision in the Upper Palaeolithic*. American Anthropologist 98, 1996.

Ruspoli, M. *The Cave of Lascaux: The Final Photographs*. New York: Harry N. Abrams, 1987.

Sandars, N. *Prehistoric Art in Europe*. 2d ed. New Haven: Yale University Press, 1992.

Saura Ramos, P. A. *The Cave of Altamira*. New York: Harry N. Abrams, 1999.

Twohig, E. S. *The Megalithic Art of Western Europe*. New York: Oxford University Press, 1981.

White, R. *Prehistoric Art: The Symbolic Journey of Mankind*. New York: Harry N. Abrams, 2003.

CHAPTER 2. ANCIENT NEAR EASTERN ART

Amiet, P. *Art of the Ancient Near East*. New York: Harry N. Abrams, 1980.

Aruz, J., ed. *Art of the First Cities: The Third Millennium B.C. from the Mediterranean to the Indus*. Exh. cat. New York: Metropolitan Museum of Art; Yale University Press, 2003.

Collon, D. *Ancient Near Eastern Art*. Berkeley: University of California Press, 1995.

———. *First Impressions: Cylinder Seals in the Ancient Near East*. Chicago: University of Chicago Press, 1987.

Crawford, H. *The Architecture of Iraq in the Third Millennium B.C.* Copenhagen: Akademisk Forlag, 1977.

Curtis, J., and N. Tallis. *Forgotten Empire: The World of Ancient Persia*. Exh. cat. London: British Museum, 2005.

Frankfort, H. *The Art and Architecture of the Ancient Orient*. 5th ed. Pelican History of Art. New Haven: Yale University Press, 1997.

Goldman, B. *The Ancient Arts of Western and Central Asia: A Guide to the Literature*. Ames: Iowa State University Press, 1991.

Harper, P. O., ed. *The Royal City of Susa: Ancient Near Eastern Treasures in the Louvre*. New York: Metropolitan Museum of Art; Dist. by Harry N. Abrams, 1992.

Leick, G. *A Dictionary of Ancient Near Eastern Architecture*. New York: Routledge, 1988.

Lloyd, S. *The Archaeology of Mesopotamia: From the Old Stone Age to the Persian Conquest*. Rev. ed. New York: Thames & Hudson, 1984.

Moscati, S. *The Phoenicians*. New York: Abbeville Press, 1988.

Oates, J. *Babylon*. Rev. ed. London: Thames & Hudson, 1986.

Reade, J. *Mesopotamia*. 2d ed. London: Published for the Trustees of the British Museum by the British Museum Press, 2000.

Zettler, R., and L. Horne, eds. *Treasures from the Royal Tombs of Ur*. Exh. cat. Philadelphia: University of Pennsylvania, Museum of Archaeology and Anthropology, 1998.

CHAPTER 3. EGYPTIAN ART

Aldred, C. *The Development of Ancient Egyptian Art, from 3200 to 1315 B.C.* 3 vols. in 1. London: Academy Editions, 1972.

———. *Egyptian Art*. London: Thames & Hudson, 1985.

Arnold, D., and C. Ziegler. *Building in Egypt: Pharaonic Stone Masonry*. New York: Oxford University Press, 1991.

———. *Egyptian Art in the Age of the Pyramids*. New York: Harry N. Abrams, 1999.

Bothmer, B. V. *Egyptian Art: Selected Writings of Bernard V. Bothmer*. New York: Oxford University Press, 2004.

Davis, W. *The Canonical Tradition in Ancient Egyptian Art*. New York: Cambridge University Press, 1989.

Edwards, I. E. S. *The Pyramids of Egypt*. Rev. ed. Harmondsworth, England: Penguin, 1991.

Egyptian Art in the Age of the Pyramids. New York: Metropolitan Museum of Art; Dist. by Harry N. Abrams, 1999.

Grimal, N. *A History of Ancient Egypt*. London: Blackwell, 1992.

Mahdy, C., ed. *The World of the Pharaohs: A Complete Guide to Ancient Egypt*. London: Thames & Hudson, 1990.

Malek, J. *Egypt: 4000 Years of Art*. London: Phaidon, 2003.

———. *Egyptian Art. Art & Ideas*. London: Phaidon, 1999.

Mendelssohn, K. *The Riddle of the Pyramids*. New York: Thames & Hudson, 1986.

Parry, D. *Engineering the Pyramids*. Stroud, England: Sutton, 2004.

Robins, G. *The Art of Ancient Egypt*. Cambridge, MA: Harvard University Press, 1997.

Schaefer, H. *Principles of Egyptian Art*. Oxford: Clarendon Press, 1986.

Schulz, R., and M. Seidel. *Egypt: The World of the Pharaohs*. Cologne: Könemann, 1998.

Smith, W., and W. Simpson. *The Art and Architecture of Ancient Egypt*. Rev. ed. Pelican History of Art. New Haven: Yale University Press, 1999.

Tiradritti, F. *Ancient Egypt: Art, Architecture and History*. London: British Museum Press, 2002.

Walker, S. and P. Higgs, eds. *Cleopatra of Egypt: From History to Myth*. Exh. cat. Princeton, NJ: Princeton University Press, 2001.

Wilkinson, R. *Reading Egyptian Art: A Hieroglyphic Guide to Ancient Egyptian Painting and Sculpture*. New York: Thames & Hudson, 1992.

CHAPTER 4. AEGEAN ART

Akurgal, E. *The Aegean, Birthplace of Western Civilization: History of East Greek Art and Culture, 1050–333 B.C.* Izmir, Turkey: Metropolitan Municipality of Izmir, 2000.

Barber, R. *The Cyclades in the Bronze Age*. Iowa City: University of Iowa Press, 1987.

Dickinson, O. T. P. K. *The Aegean Bronze Age*. New York: Cambridge University Press, 1994.

Elytis, O. *The Aegean: The Epicenter of Greek Civilization*. Athens: Melissa, 1997.

German, S. C. *Performance, Power and the Art of the Aegean Bronze Age*. Oxford: Archaeopress, 2005.

Getz-Preziosi, P. *Sculptors of the Cyclades*. Ann Arbor: University of Michigan Press, 1987.

Graham, J. *The Palaces of Crete*. Rev. ed. Princeton, NJ: Princeton University Press, 1987.

Hampe, R., and E. Simon. *The Birth of Greek Art from the Mycenean to the Archaic Period*. New York: Oxford University Press, 1981.

Higgins, R. *Minoan and Mycenaean Art*. Rev. ed. The World of Art. New York: Oxford University Press, 1981.

Hood, S. *The Arts in Prehistoric Greece*. Pelican History of Art. New Haven: Yale University Press, 1992.

———. *The Minoans: The Story of Bronze Age Crete*. New York: Praeger, 1981.

Hurwit, J. *The Art and Culture of Early Greece, 1100–480 B.C.* Ithaca, NY: Cornell University Press, 1985.

McDonald, W. *Progress into the Past: The Rediscovery of Mycenaean Civilization*. 2d ed. Bloomington: Indiana University Press, 1990.

Preziosi, D., and L. Hitchcock. *Aegean Art and Architecture*. New York: Oxford University Press, 1999.

Renfrew, C. *The Cycladic Spirit: Masterpieces from the Nicholas P. Goulandris Collection*. London: Thames & Hudson, 1991.

Vermeule, E. *Greece in the Bronze Age*. Chicago: University of Chicago Press, 1972.

CHAPTER 5. GREEK ART

Beard, M. *The Parthenon*. Cambridge, MA: Harvard University Press, 2003.

Beazley, J. D. *Athenian Red Figure Vases: The Archaic Period: A Handbook*. The World of Art. New York: Thames & Hudson, 1991.

———. *Athenian Red Figure Vases: The Classical Period: A Handbook*. The World of Art. New York: Thames & Hudson, 1989.

———. *The Development of Attic Black-Figure*. Rev. ed. Berkeley: University of California Press, 1986.

———. *Greek Vases: Lectures*. Oxford and New York: Clarendon Press and Oxford University Press, 1989.

Boardman, J. *The Archaeology of Nostalgia: How the Greeks Re-created Their Mythical Past*. London: Thames & Hudson, 2002.

———. *Athenian Black Figure Vases: A Handbook*. Corrected ed. The World of Art. New York: Thames & Hudson, 1991.

———. *Early Greek Vase Painting: 11th–6th Centuries B.C.: A Handbook*. The World of Art. New York: Thames & Hudson, 1998.

———. *Greek Art*. 4th ed., rev. and expanded. The World of Art. New York: Thames & Hudson, 1996.

———. *Greek Sculpture: The Archaic Period: A Handbook*. Corrected ed. The World of Art. New York: Thames & Hudson, 1991.

———. *Greek Sculpture: The Classical Period: A Handbook*. Corrected ed. New York: Thames & Hudson, 1991.

———. *The History of Greek Vases: Potters, Painters, and Pictures*. New York: Thames & Hudson, 2001.

Burn, L. *Hellenistic Art: From Alexander the Great to Augustus*. London: The British Museum, 2004.

Carpenter, T. H. *Art and Myth in Ancient Greece: A Handbook*. The World of Art. New York: Thames & Hudson, 1991.

Carratelli, G. P., ed. *The Greek World: Art and Civilization in Magna Graecia and Sicily*. Exh. cat. New York: Rizzoli, 1996.

Fullerton, M. D. *Greek Art*. New York: Cambridge University Press, 2000.

Hampe, R., and E. Simon. *The Birth of Greek Art*. Oxford: Oxford University Press, 1981.

Haynes, D. E. L. *The Technique of Greek Bronze Statuary*. Mainz am Rhein: P. von Zabern, 1992.

Himmelmann, N. *Reading Greek Art: Essays*. Princeton, NJ: Princeton University Press, 1998.

Hurwit, J. M. *The Acropolis in the Age of Pericles*. New York: Cambridge University Press, 2004.

———. *The Art & Culture of Early Greece, 1100–480 B.C.* Ithaca, NY: Cornell University Press, 1985.

Lawrence, A. *Greek Architecture*. Rev. 5th ed. Pelican History of Art. New Haven: Yale University Press, 1996.

L'Empereur, J. *Alexandria Rediscovered*. London: British Museum Press, 1998.

Osborne, R. *Archaic and Classical Greek Art*. New York: Oxford University Press, 1998.

Papaioannou, K. *The Art of Greece*. New York: Harry N. Abrams, 1989.

Pedley, J. *Greek Art and Archaeology*. 2d ed. New York: Harry N. Abrams, 1997.

Pollitt, J. *The Ancient View of Greek Art: Criticism, History, and Terminology*. New Haven: Yale University Press, 1974.

———. *Art in the Hellenistic Age*. New York: Cambridge University Press, 1986.

———, ed. *Art of Ancient Greece: Sources and Documents*. New York: Cambridge University Press, 1990.

Potts, A. *Flesh and the Ideal: Winckelmann and the Origins of Art History*. New Haven: Yale University Press, 1994.

Rhodes, R. F. *Architecture and Meaning on the Athenian Acropolis*. New York: Cambridge University Press, 1995.

———, ed. *The Acquisition and Exhibition of Classical Antiquities: Professional, Legal, and Ethical Perspectives*. Notre Dame, IN: University of Notre Dame Press, 2007.

Richter, G. M. A. *A Handbook of Greek Art*. 9th ed. New York: Da Capo, 1987.

———. *Portraits of the Greeks*. Ed. R. Smith. New York: Oxford University Press, 1984.

Ridgway, B. S. *Hellenistic Sculpture: Vol. 1, The Styles of ca. 331–200 B.C.* Bristol, England: Bristol Classical Press, 1990.

Robertson, M. *The Art of Vase Painting in Classical Athens*. New York: Cambridge University Press, 1992.

Rolley, C. *Greek Bronzes*. New York: Philip Wilson for Sotheby's Publications; Dist. by Harper & Row, 1986.

Schefold, K. *Gods and Heroes in Late Archaic Greek Art*. New York: Cambridge University Press, 1992.

Smith, R. *Hellenistic Sculpture*. The World of Art. New York: Thames & Hudson, 1991.

Spivey, N. *Greek Art*. London: Phaidon, 1997.

Stafford, E. *Life, Myth, and Art in Ancient Greece*. Los Angeles: J. Paul Getty Museum, 2004.

Stansbury-O'Donnell, M. *Pictorial Narrative in Ancient Greek Art*. New York: Cambridge University Press, 1999.

Stewart, A. F. *Greek Sculpture: An Exploration*. New Haven: Yale University Press, 1990.

Whitley, J. *The Archaeology of Ancient Greece*. New York: Cambridge University Press, 2001.

CHAPTER 6. ETRUSCAN ART

Boethius, A. *Etruscan and Early Roman Architecture*. 2d ed. Pelican History of Art. New Haven: Yale University Press, 1992.

Bonfante, L., ed. *Etruscan Life and Afterlife: A Handbook of Etruscan Studies*. Detroit, MI: Wayne State University, 1986.

Borrelli, F. *The Etruscans: Art, Architecture, and History*. Los Angeles: J. Paul Getty Museum, 2004.

Brendel, O. *Etruscan Art*. Pelican History of Art. New Haven: Yale University Press, 1995.

Hall, J. F., ed. *Etruscan Italy: Etruscan Influences on the Civilizations of Italy from Antiquity to the Modern Era*. Provo, UT: Museum of Art, Brigham Young University, 1996.

Haynes, Sybille. *Etruscan Civilization: A Cultural History*. Los Angeles: J. Paul Getty Museum, 2000.

Richardson, E. *The Etruscans: Their Art and Civilization*. Reprint of 1964 ed., with corrections. Chicago: University of Chicago Press, 1976.

Spivey, N. *Etruscan Art*. The World of Art. New York: Thames & Hudson, 1997.

Sprenger, M., G. Bartoloni, and M. Hirmer. *The Etruscans: Their History, Art, and Architecture*. New York: Harry N. Abrams, 1983.

Steingräber, S., ed. *Etruscan Painting: Catalogue Raisonné of Etruscan Wall Paintings*. New York: Johnson Reprint, 1986.

Torelli, M., ed. *The Etruscans*. Exh. cat. Milan: Bompiani, 2000.

CHAPTER 7. ROMAN ART

Allan, T. *Life, Myth and Art in Ancient Rome*. Los Angeles: J. Paul Getty Museum, 2005.

Andreae, B. *The Art of Rome*. New York: Harry N. Abrams, 1977.

Beard, M., and J. Henderson. *Classical Art: From Greece to Rome*. New York: Oxford University Press, 2001.

Bowe, P. *Gardens of the Roman World*. Los Angeles: J. Paul Getty Museum, 2004.

Brilliant, R. *Commentaries on Roman Art: Selected Studies*. London: Pindar Press, 1994.

———. *My Laocoon: Alternative Claims in the Interpretation of Artworks*. University of California Press, 2000.

Claridge, A. *Rome: An Oxford Archaeological Guide*. New York: Oxford University Press, 1998.

D'Ambra, E. *Roman Art*. New York: Cambridge University Press, 1998.

———, comp. *Roman Art in Context: An Anthology*. Englewood Cliffs, NJ: Prentice Hall, 1993.

Davies, P. *Death and the Emperor: Roman Imperial Funerary Monuments from Augustus to Marcus Aurelius*. Austin: University of Texas Press, 2004.

Dunbabin, K. M. D. *Mosaics of the Greek and Roman World*. New York: Cambridge University Press, 1999.

Elsner, J. *Imperial Rome and Christian Triumph: The Art of the Roman Empire, A.D. 100–450*. New York: Oxford University Press, 1998.

Gazda, E. K. *Roman Art in the Private Sphere: New Perspectives on the Architecture and Decor of the Domus, Villa, and Insula*. Ann Arbor: University of Michigan Press, 1991.

Jenkyns, R., ed. *The Legacy of Rome: A New Appraisal*. New York: Oxford University Press, 1992.

Kleiner, D. *Roman Sculpture*. New Haven: Yale University Press, 1992.

———, and S. B. Matheson, eds. *I, Claudia: Women in Ancient Rome*. New Haven: Yale University Art Gallery, 1996.

Ling, R. *Ancient Mosaics*. London: British Museum Press, 1998.

———. *Roman Painting*. New York: Cambridge University Press, 1991.

Nash, E. *Pictorial Dictionary of Ancient Rome*. 2 vols. Reprint of 1968 2d ed. New York: Hacker, 1981.

Pollitt, J. J. *The Art of Rome, c. 753 B.C.– A.D. 337: Sources and Documents*. New York: Cambridge University Press, 1983.

Ramage, N., and A. Ramage. *The Cambridge Illustrated History of Roman Art*. Cambridge: Cambridge University Press, 1991.

———. *Roman Art: Romulus to Constantine*. 4th ed. Upper Saddle River, NJ: Pearson Prentice Hall, 2005.

Richardson, L. *A New Topographical Dictionary of Ancient Rome*. Baltimore, MD: Johns Hopkins University Press, 1992.

Rockwell, P. *The Art of Stoneworking: A Reference Guide*. Cambridge: Cambridge University Press, 1993.

Strong, D. E. *Roman Art*. 2d ed. Pelican History of Art. New Haven: Yale University Press, 1992.

Vitruvius. *The Ten Books on Architecture*. Trans. I. Rowland. Cambridge: Cambridge University Press, 1999.

Ward-Perkins, J. B. *Roman Imperial Architecture*. Reprint of 1981 ed. Pelican History of Art. New York: Penguin, 1992.

Zanker, P. *The Power of Images in the Age of Augustus*. Ann Arbor: University of Michigan Press, 1988.

PART TWO: THE MIDDLE AGES

GENERAL REFERENCES

Alexander, J. J. G. *Medieval Illuminators and Their Methods of Work*. New Haven: Yale University Press, 1992.

———., ed. *A Survey of Manuscripts Illuminated in the British Isles*. 6 vols. London: Harvey Miller, 1975–1996.

Avril, F., and J. J. G. Alexander, eds. *A Survey of Manuscripts Illuminated in France*. London: Harvey Miller, 1996.

Bartlett, R., ed. *Medieval Panorama*. Los Angeles: J. Paul Getty Museum, 2001.

Cahn, W. *Studies in Medieval Art and Interpretation*. London: Pindar Press, 2000.

Calkins, R. G. *Medieval Architecture in Western Europe: From A.D. 300 to 1500*. New York: Oxford University Press, 1998.

Cassidy, B., ed. *Iconography at the Crossroads*. Princeton, NJ: Princeton University Press, 1993.

Coldstream, N. *Medieval Architecture*. Oxford History of Art. New York: Oxford University Press, 2002.

De Hamel, C. *The British Library Guide to Manuscript Illumination: History and Techniques*. Toronto: University of Toronto Press, 2001.

———. *A History of Illuminated Manuscripts*. Rev. and enl. 2d ed. London: Phaidon Press, 1994.

Duby, G. *Art and Society in the Middle Ages*. Polity Press; Malden, MA: Blackwell Publishers, 2000.

Hamburger, J. *Nuns as Artists: The Visual Culture of a Medieval Convent*. Berkeley: University of California Press, 1997.

Katzenellenbogen, A. *Allegories of the Virtues and Vices in Medieval Art*. Reprint of 1939 ed. Toronto: University of Toronto Press, 1989.

Kazhdan, A. P. *The Oxford Dictionary of Byzantium*. 3 vols. New York: Oxford University Press, 1991.

Kessler, H. L. *Seeing Medieval Art*. Peterborough, Ont. and Orchard Park, NY: Broadview Press, 2004.

Luttikhuizen, H., and D. Verkerk. *Snyder's Medieval Art*. 2d ed. Upper Saddle River, NJ: Prentice Hall, 2006.

Pächt, O. *Book Illumination in the Middle Ages: An Introduction*. London: Harvey Miller, 1986.

Pelikan, J. *Mary Through the Centuries: Her Place in the History of Culture*. New Haven: Yale University Press, 1996.

Ross, L. *Artists of the Middle Ages*. Westport, CT: Greenwood Press, 2003.

———. *Medieval Art: A Topical Dictionary*. Westport, CT: Greenwood Press, 1996.

Schütz, B. *Great Cathedrals*. New York: Harry N. Abrams, 2002.

Sears, E., and T. K. Thomas, eds. *Reading Medieval Images: The Art Historian and the Object*. Ann Arbor: University of Michigan Press, 2002.

Sekules, V. *Medieval Art*. New York: Oxford University Press, 2001.

Stokstad, M. *Medieval Art*. Boulder, CO: Westview Press, 2004.

Tasker, E. *Encyclopedia of Medieval Church Art*. London: Batsford, 1993.

Watson, R. *Illuminated Manuscripts and Their Makers: An Account Based on the Collection of the Victoria and Albert Museum*. London and New York: V & A Publications; Dist. by Harry N. Abrams, 2003.

Wieck, R. S. *Painted Prayers: The Book of Hours in Medieval and Renaissance Art*. New York: George Braziller in association with the Pierpont Morgan Library, 1997.

Wixom, W. D. *Mirror of the Medieval World*. Exh. cat. New York: Metropolitan Museum of Art; Dist. by Harry N. Abrams, 1999.

CHAPTER 8. EARLY JEWISH, EARLY CHRISTIAN, AND BYZANTINE ART

Beckwith, J. *Studies in Byzantine and Medieval Western Art*. London: Pindar Press, 1989.

Bowersock, G. W., ed. *Late Antiquity: A Guide to the Postclassical World*. Cambridge, MA: Belknap Press of Harvard University Press, 1999.

Cormack, R. *Icons*. London: British Museum Press, 2007.

Demus, O. *Studies in Byzantium, Venice and the West*. 2 vols. London: Pindar Press, 1998.

Drury, J. *Painting the Word: Christian Pictures and Their Meanings*. New Haven and London: Yale University Press in association with National Gallery Publications, 1999.

Durand, J. *Byzantine Art*. Paris: Terrail, 1999.

Evans, H. C., ed. *Byzantium: Faith and Power, 1261–1557*. Exh. cat. New York: Metropolitan Museum of Art; New Haven: Yale University Press, 2004.

Evans, H. C., and W. D. Wixom, eds. *The Glory of Byzantium: Art and Culture of the Middle Byzantine Era, A. D. 843–1261*. Exh. cat. New York: Metropolitan Museum of Art; New Haven: Yale University Press, 1997.

Galavaris, G. *Colours, Symbols, Worship: The Mission of the Byzantine Artist*. London: Pindar, 2005.

Grabar, A. *Christian Iconography: A Study of Its Origins*. Princeton, NJ: Princeton University Press, 1968.

Henderson, G. *Vision and Image in Early Christian England*. New York: Cambridge University Press, 1999.

Kalavrezou, I. *Byzantine Women and Their World*. Exh. cat. Cambridge, MA and New Haven: Harvard University Art Museums; Yale University Press, © 2003.

Kleinbauer, W. *Early Christian and Byzantine Architecture: An Annotated Bibliography and Historiography*. Boston: G. K. Hall, 1993.

Krautheimer, R., and S. Curcic. *Early Christian and Byzantine Architecture*. 4th ed. Pelican History of Art. New Haven: Yale University Press, 1992.

Lowden, J. *Early Christian and Byzantine Art*. London: Phaidon Press, 1997.

Maguire, H. *Art and Eloquence in Byzantium*. Princeton, NJ: Princeton University Press, 1981.

Mango, C. *The Art of the Byzantine Empire, 312–1453: Sources and Documents*. Reprint of 1972 ed. Toronto: University of Toronto Press, 1986.

Mark, R., and A. S. Çakmak, eds. *Hagia Sophia from the Age of Justinian to the Present*. New York: Cambridge University Press, 1992.

Matthews, T. *Byzantium from Antiquity to the Renaissance*. New York: Harry N. Abrams, 1998.

———. *The Clash of Gods: A Reinterpretation of Early Christian Art*. Princeton, NJ: Princeton University Press, 1993.

Milburn, R. *Early Christian Art and Architecture*. Berkeley: University of California Press, 1988.

Rodley, L. *Byzantine Art and Architecture: An Introduction*. New York: Cambridge University Press, 1994.

Simson, O. G. von. *Sacred Fortress: Byzantine Art and Statecraft in Ravenna*. Reprint of 1948 ed. Princeton, NJ: Princeton University Press, 1987.

Webster, L., and M. Brown, eds. *The Transformation of the Roman World A.D. 400–900*. Berkeley: University of California Press, 1997.

Weitzmann, K. *Late Antique and Early Christian Book Illumination*. New York: Braziller, 1977.

CHAPTER 9. ISLAMIC ART

Asher, C. E. B. *Architecture of Mughal India*. New Cambridge History of India, Cambridge, England. New York: Cambridge University Press, 1992.

Atil, E. *The Age of Sultan Süleyman the Magnificent*. Exh. cat. Washington, DC: National Gallery of Art; New York: Harry N. Abrams, 1987.

———. *Renaissance of Islam: Art of the Mamluks*. Exh. cat. Washington, DC: Smithsonian Institution Press, 1981.

Behrens-Abouseif, D. *Beauty in Arabic Culture*. Princeton, NJ: Markus Wiener, 1998.

Bierman, I., ed. *The Experience of Islamic Art on the Margins of Islam*. Reading, England: Ithaca Press, 2005.

Blair, S., and J. Bloom. *The Art and Architecture of Islam 1250–1800*. Pelican History of Art. New Haven: Yale University Press, 1996.

Brookes, J. *Gardens of Paradise: The History and Design of the Great Islamic Gardens*. New York: New Amsterdam, 1987.

Burckhardt, T. *Art of Islam: Language and Meaning*. London: World of Islam Festival, 1976.

Creswell, K. A. C. *A Bibliography of the Architecture, Arts, and Crafts of Islam*. Cairo: American University in Cairo Press, 1984.

Denny, W. B. *The Classical Tradition in Anatolian Carpets*. Washington, DC: Textile Museum, 2002.

Dodds, J. D., ed. *al-Andalus: The Art of Islamic Spain*. Exh. cat. New York: Metropolitan Museum of Art; Dist. by Harry N. Abrams, 1992.

Erdmann, K. *Oriental Carpets: An Essay on Their History*. Fishguard, Wales: Crosby Press, 1976, © 1960.

Ettinghausen, R., O. Grabar, and M. Jenkins-Madina. *Islamic Art and Architecture, 650–1250*. 2d ed. Pelican History of Art. New Haven: Yale University Press, 2002.

Frishman, M., and H. Khan. *The Mosque: History, Architectural Development and Regional Diversity*. London: Thames & Hudson, 2002, © 1994.

Goodwin, G. *A History of Ottoman Architecture*. New York: Thames & Hudson, 2003, © 1971.

Grabar, O. *The Formation of Islamic Art*. Rev. and enl. ed. New Haven: Yale University Press, 1987.

Hillenbrand, R. *Islamic Architecture: Form, Function, and Meaning*. New ed. New York: Columbia University Press, 2004.

Komaroff, L., and S. Carboni, eds. *The Legacy of Genghis Khan: Courtly Art and Culture in Western Asia, 1256–1353*. Exh. cat. New York: Metropolitan Museum of Art; New Haven: Yale University Press, 2002.

Lentz, T., and G. Lowry. *Timur and the Princely Vision: Persian Art and Culture in the Fifteenth Century*. Exh. cat. Los Angeles: Los Angeles County Museum of Art; Washington, DC: Arthur M. Sackler Gallery; Smithsonian Institution Press, 1989.

Lings, M. *The Quranic Art of Calligraphy and Illumination*. 1st American ed. New York: Interlink Books, 1987, © 1976.

Necipolu, G. *The Age of Sinan: Architectural Culture in the Ottoman Empire*. Princeton, NJ: Princeton University Press, 2005.

———. *The Topkapı Scroll: Geometry and Ornament in Islamic Architecture*. Topkapı Palace Museum Library MS H. 1956. Santa Monica, CA: Getty Center for the History of Art and the Humanities, 1995.

Pope, A. U. *Persian Architecture: The Triumph of Form and Color*. New York: Braziller, 1965.

Robinson, F. *Atlas of the Islamic World Since 1500*. New York: Facts on File, 1982.

Ruggles, D. F. *Gardens, Landscape, and Vision in the Palaces of Islamic Spain*. University Park: Pennsylvania State University Press, 2000.

———., ed. *Women, Patronage, and Self-Representation in Islamic Societies*. Albany: State University of New York Press, 2000.

Tabbaa, Y. *The Transformation of Islamic Art During the Sunni Revival*. Seattle: University of Washington Press, 2001.

Thompson, J., ed. *Hunt for Paradise: Court Arts of Safavid Iran, 1501–1576.* Milan: Skira; New York: Dist. in North America and Latin America by Rizzoli, 2003.

———. *Oriental Carpets from the Tents, Cottages, and Workshops of Asia.* New York: Dutton, 1988.

Vernoit, S., ed. *Discovering Islamic Art: Scholars, Collectors and Collections, 1850–1950.* London and New York: I. B. Tauris; Dist. by St. Martin's Press, 2000.

Welch, S. C. *Imperial Mughal Painting.* New York: Braziller, 1978.

———. *A King's Book of Kings: The Shah-nameh of Shah Tahmasp.* New York: Metropolitan Museum of Art; Dist. by New York Graphic Society, 1972.

CHAPTER 10. EARLY MEDIEVAL ART

Backhouse, J. *The Golden Age of Anglo-Saxon Art, 966–1066.* Bloomington: Indiana University Press, 1984.

———. *The Lindisfarne Gospels: A Masterpiece of Book Painting.* London: British Library, 1995.

Barral i Altet, X. *The Early Middle Ages: From Late Antiquity to A.D. 1000.* Taschen's World Architecture. Köln and New York: Taschen, © 1997.

Conant, K. *Carolingian and Romanesque Architecture, 800–1200.* 4th ed. Pelican History of Art. New Haven: Yale University Press, 1992.

Davis-Weyer, C. *Early Medieval Art, 300–1150: Sources and Documents.* Reprint of 1971 ed. Toronto: University of Toronto Press, 1986.

Diebold, W. J. *Word and Image: An Introduction to Early Medieval Art.* Boulder, CO: Westview Press, 2000.

Dodwell, C. R. *Anglo-Saxon Art: A New Perspective.* Ithaca, NY: Cornell University Press, 1982.

———. *The Pictorial Arts of the West, 800–1200.* New ed. Pelican History of Art. New Haven: Yale University Press, 1993.

Graham-Campbell, J. *The Viking-age Gold and Silver of Scotland, A.D. 850–1100.* Exh. cat. Edinburgh: National Museums of Scotland, 1995.

Harbison, P. *The Golden Age of Irish Art: The Medieval Achievement, 600–1200.* New York: Thames & Hudson, 1999.

Henderson, G. *The Art of the Picts: Sculpture and Metalwork in Early Medieval Scotland.* New York: Thames & Hudson, 2004.

Kitzinger, E. *Early Medieval Art, with Illustrations from the British Museum.* Rev. ed. Bloomington: Indiana University Press, 1983.

Lasko, P. *Ars Sacra, 800–1200.* 2d ed. Pelican History of Art. New Haven: Yale University Press, 1995.

Mayr-Harting, M. *Ottonian Book Illumination: An Historical Study.* 2 vols. London: Harvey Miller, 1991–1993.

Megaw, M. R. *Celtic Art: From Its Beginnings to the Book of Kells.* New York: Thames & Hudson, 2001.

Mosacati, S., ed. *The Celts.* Exh. cat. New York: Rizzoli, 1999.

Nees, L. *Early Medieval Art.* Oxford History of Art. New York: Oxford University Press, 2002.

Ohlgren, T. H., comp. *Insular and Anglo-Saxon Illuminated Manuscripts: An Iconographic Catalogue, c. A.D. 625 to 1100.* New York: Garland, 1986.

Rickert, M. *Painting in Britain: The Middle Ages.* 2d ed. Pelican History of Art. Harmondsworth, England: Penguin, 1965.

Stalley, R. A. *Early Medieval Architecture.* Oxford History of Art. New York: Oxford University Press, 1999.

Stone, L. *Sculpture in Britain: The Middle Ages.* 2d ed. Pelican History of Art. Harmondsworth, England: Penguin, 1972.

Webster, L., and J. Backhouse, eds. *The Making of England: Anglo-Saxon Art and Culture, A.D. 600–900.* Exh. cat. London: Published for the Trustees of the British Museum and the British Library Board by British Museum Press, 1991.

CHAPTER 11. ROMANESQUE ART

Barral i. Altet, X. *The Romanesque: Towns, Cathedrals, and Monasteries.* Cologne: Taschen, 1998.

Bizzarro, T. *Romanesque Architectural Criticism: A Prehistory.* New York: Cambridge University Press, 1992.

Boase, T. S. R. *English Art, 1100–1216.* Oxford History of English Art. Oxford: Clarendon Press, 1953.

Cahn, W. *Romanesque Bible Illumination.* Ithaca, NY: Cornell University Press, 1982.

Davies, M. *Romanesque Architecture: A Bibliography.* Boston: G. K. Hall, 1993.

Focillon, H. *The Art of the West in the Middle Ages.* Ed. J. Bony. 2 vols. Reprint of 1963 ed. Ithaca, NY: Cornell University Press, 1980.

Hearn, M. F. *Romanesque Sculpture: The Revival of Monumental Stone Sculpture.* Ithaca, NY: Cornell University Press, 1981.

Mâle, E. *Religious Art in France, the Twelfth Century: A Study of the Origins of Medieval Iconography.* Bollingen series, 90:1. Princeton, NJ: Princeton University Press, 1978.

Minne-Sève, V. *Romanesque and Gothic France: Architecture and Sculpture.* New York: Harry N. Abrams, 2000.

Nichols, S. *Romanesque Signs: Early Medieval Narrative and Iconography.* New Haven: Yale University Press, 1983.

O'Keeffe, T. *Romanesque Ireland: Architecture and Ideology in the Twelfth Century.* Dublin and Portland, OR: Four Courts, 2003.

Petzold, A. *Romanesque Art.* Perspectives. Upper Saddle River, NJ: Prentice Hall, 1996.

Platt, C. *The Architecture of Medieval Britain: A Social History.* New Haven: Yale University Press, 1990.

Sauerländer, W. *Romanesque Art: Problems and Monuments.* 2 vols. London: Pindar, 2004.

Schapiro, M. *Romanesque Art.* New York: Braziller, 1977.

Stoddard, W. *Art and Architecture in Medieval France.* New York: Harper & Row, 1972, © 1966.

Stones, A., J. Krochalis, P. Gerson, and A. Shaver-Crandell. *The Pilgrim's Guide to Santiago de Compostela: A Critical Edition.* 2 vols. London: Harvey Miller, 1998.

Toman, R., and A. Bednorz. *Romanesque Architecture, Sculpture, Painting.* Cologne: Könemann, 2008.

Zarnecki, G. *Further Studies in Romanesque Sculpture.* London: Pindar, 1992.

CHAPTER 12. GOTHIC ART

Barnes, C. F. *Villard de Honnecourt, the Artist and His Drawings: A Critical Bibliography.* Boston: G. K. Hall, 1982.

Belting, H. *The Image and Its Public: Form and Function of Early Paintings of the Passion.* New Rochelle, NY: Caratzas, 1990.

Blum, P. *Early Gothic Saint-Denis: Restorations and Survivals.* Berkeley: University of California Press, 1992.

Bony, J. *French Gothic Architecture of the Twelfth and Thirteenth Centuries.* Berkeley: University of California Press, 1983.

Camille, M. *Gothic Art: Glorious Visions.* Perspectives. New York: Harry N. Abrams, 1997.

———. *The Gothic Idol: Ideology and Image Making in Medieval Art.* New York: Cambridge University Press, 1989.

———. *Sumptuous Arts at the Royal Abbeys of Reims and Braine.* Princeton, NJ: Princeton University Press, 1990.

Cennini, C. *The Craftsman's Handbook (Il Libro dell'Arte).* New York: Dover, 1954.

Coldstream, N. *Medieval Architecture.* Oxford History of Art. New York: Oxford University Press, 2002.

Erlande-Brandenburg, A. *Gothic Art.* New York: Harry N. Abrams, 1989.

Frankl, P. *Gothic Architecture.* Rev. by P. Crossley. Pelican History of Art. New Haven, CT: Yale University Press, 2001.

Frisch, T. G. *Gothic Art, 1140–c. 1450: Sources and Documents.* Reprint of 1971 ed. Toronto: University of Toronto Press, 1987.

Grodecki, L. *Gothic Architecture.* New York: Electa/Rizzoli, 1985.

———. *Gothic Stained Glass, 1200–1300.* Ithaca, NY: Cornell University Press, 1985.

Hamburger, J. F. *The Visual and the Visionary: Art and Female Spirituality in Late Medieval Germany.* Zone Books. Cambridge, MA: MIT Press, 1998.

Jantzen, H. *High Gothic: The Classic Cathedrals of Chartres, Reims, Amiens.* Reprint of 1962 ed. Princeton, NJ: Princeton University Press, 1984.

Kemp, W. *The Narratives of Gothic Stained Glass.* New York: Cambridge University Press, 1997.

Limentani Virdis, C. *Great Altarpieces: Gothic and Renaissance.* New York: Vendome Press; Dist. by Rizzoli, 2002.

Mâle, E. *Religious Art in France, the Thirteenth Century: A Study of Medieval Iconography and Its Sources.* Ed. H. Bober. Princeton, NJ: Princeton University Press, 1984.

Marks, R., and P. Williamson, eds. *Gothic: Art for England 1400–1547.* Exh. cat. London and New York: Victoria & Albert Museum; Dist. by Harry N. Abrams, 2003.

Murray, S. *Beauvais Cathedral: Architecture of Transcendence.* Princeton, NJ: Princeton University Press, 1989.

Panofsky, E. ed. and trans. *Abbot Suger on the Abbey Church of Saint-Denis and Its Art Treasures.* 2d ed. Princeton, NJ: Princeton University Press, 1979.

———. *Gothic Architecture and Scholasticism.* Reprint of 1951 ed. New York: New American Library, 1985.

Parnet, P., ed. *Images in Ivory: Precious Objects of the Gothic Age.* Exh. cat. Detroit, MI: Detroit Institute of Arts, © 1997.

Sandler, L. *Gothic Manuscripts, 1285–1385.* Survey of Manuscripts Illuminated in the British Isles. London: Harvey Miller, 1986.

Scott, R. A. *The Gothic Enterprise: A Guide to Understanding the Medieval Cathedral.* Berkeley: University of California Press, 2003.

Simson, O. von. *The Gothic Cathedral: Origins of Gothic Architecture and the Medieval Concept of Order.* 3d ed. Princeton, NJ: Princeton University Press, 1988.

Toman, R., and A. Bednorz. *The Art of Gothic: Architecture, Sculpture, Painting.* Cologne: Könemann, 1999.

Williamson, P. *Gothic Sculpture, 1140–1300.* New Haven: Yale University Press, 1995.

Wilson, C. *The Gothic Cathedral: The Architecture of the Great Church, 1130–1530.* 2d rev. ed. London: Thames & Hudson, 2005.

PART THREE: THE RENAISSANCE THROUGH THE ROCOCO

GENERAL REFERENCES AND SOURCES

Campbell, L. *Renaissance Portraits: European Portrait-Painting in the 14th, 15th, and 16th Centuries.* New Haven: Yale University Press, 1990.

Chastel, A., et al. *The Renaissance: Essays in Interpretation.* London: Methuen, 1982.

Cloulas, I. *Treasures of the French Renaissance.* New York: Harry N. Abrams, 1998.

Cole, A. *Art of the Italian Renaissance Courts: Virtue and Magnificence.* London: Weidenfeld & Nicolson, 1995.

Gascoigne, B. *How to Identify Prints: A Complete Guide to Manual and Mechanical Processes from Woodcut to Inkjet.* New York: Thames & Hudson, 2004.

Grendler, P. F., ed. *Encyclopedia of the Renaissance.* 6 vols. New York: Scribner's, published in association with the Renaissance Society of America, 1999.

Gruber, A., ed. *The History of Decorative Arts: Vol. 1, The Renaissance and Mannerism in Europe. Vol. 2, Classicism and the Baroque in Europe.* New York: Abbeville Press, 1994.

Harbison, C. *The Mirror of the Artist: Northern Renaissance Art in its Historical Context.* New York: Harry N. Abrams, 1995.

Harris, A. S. *Seventeenth-Century Art and Architecture.* 2d ed. Upper Saddle River, NJ: Pearson Education, 2008.

Hartt, F., and D. Wilkins. *History of Italian Renaissance Art.* 6th ed. Upper Saddle River, NJ: Pearson Prentice Hall, 2007.

Hopkins, A. *Italian Architecture: from Michelangelo to Borromini.* World of Art. New York: Thames & Hudson, 2002.

Hults, L. *The Print in the Western World.* Madison: University of Wisconsin Press, 1996.

Impey, O., and A. MacGregor, eds. *The Origins of Museums: The Cabinet of Curiosities in Sixteenth- and Seventeenth-Century Europe.* New York: Clarendon Press, 1985.

Ivins, W. M., Jr. *How Prints Look: Photographs with a Commentary*. Boston: Beacon Press, 1987.

Landau, D., and P. Parshall. *The Renaissance Print*. New Haven: Yale University Press, 1994.

Lincoln, E. *The Invention of the Italian Renaissance Printmaker*. New Haven: Yale University Press, 2000.

Martin, J. R. *Baroque*. Harmondsworth, England: Penguin, 1989.

Millon, H. A., ed. *The Triumph of the Baroque: Architecture in Europe, 1600–1750*. New York: Rizzoli, 1999.

Minor, V. H. *Baroque & Rococo: Art & Culture*. New York: Harry N. Abrams, 1999.

Norberg-Schultz, C. *Late Baroque and Rococo Architecture*. New York: Harry N. Abrams, 1983.

Olson, R. J. M. *Italian Renaissance Sculpture*. The World of Art. New York: Thames & Hudson, 1992.

Paoletti, J., and G. Radke. *Art in Renaissance Italy*. 3d ed. Upper Saddle River, NJ: Pearson Prentice Hall, 2006.

Payne, A. *Antiquity and Its Interpreters*. New York: Cambridge University Press, 2000.

Pope-Hennessy, J. *An Introduction to Italian Sculpture: Vol. 1, Italian Gothic Sculpture. Vol. 2, Italian Renaissance Sculpture. Vol. 3, Italian High Renaissance and Baroque Sculpture*. 4th ed. London: Phaidon Press, 1996.

Richardson, C. M., K. W. Woods, and M. W. Franklin, eds. *Renaissance Art Reconsidered: An Anthology of Primary Sources*. Wiley-Blackwell, 2007.

Smith, J. C. *The Northern Renaissance*. Art & Ideas. London: Phaidon Press, 2004.

Snyder, J. *Northern Renaissance Art: Painting, Sculpture, the Graphic Arts, from 1350–1575*. 2d ed. New York: Harry N. Abrams, 2005.

Strinati, E., and J. Pomeroy. *Italian Women Artists of the Renaissance and Baroque*. Exh. cat. Washington, DC: National Museum of Women in the Arts; New York: Rizzoli, 2007.

Tomlinson, J. *From El Greco to Goya: Painting in Spain 1561–1828*. Perspectives. New York: Harry N. Abrams, 1997.

Turner, J. *Encyclopedia of Italian Renaissance & Mannerist Art*. 2 vols. New York: Grove's Dictionaries, 2000.

Vasari, G. *The Lives of the Artists*. Trans. with an introduction and notes by J. C. Bondanella and P. Bondanella. New York: Oxford University Press, 1998.

Welch, E. *Art in Renaissance Italy, 1350–1500*. New ed. Oxford: Oxford University Press, 2000.

Wiebenson, D., ed. *Architectural Theory and Practice from Alberti to Ledoux*. 2d ed. Chicago: University of Chicago Press, 1983.

Wittkower, R. *Architectural Principles in the Age of Humanism*. 5th ed. New York: St. Martin's Press, 1998.

CHAPTER 13. ART IN THIRTEENTH- AND FOURTEENTH-CENTURY ITALY

Bellosi, L. *Duccio, the Maestà*. New York: Thames & Hudson, 1999.

Bomford, D. *Art in the Making: Italian Painting Before 1400*. Exh. cat. London: National Gallery of Art, 1989.

Christiansen, K. *Duccio and the Origins of Western Painting*. New York: Metropolitan Museum of Art and Yale University Press, 2009.

Derbes, A. *The Cambridge Companion to Giotto*. New York: Cambridge University Press, 2004.

———., and M. Sandona. *The Usurer's Heart: Giotto, Enrico Scrovegni, and the Arena Chapel in Padua*. University Park: Pennsylvania State University Press, 2008.

Kemp, M. *Behind the Picture: Art and Evidence in the Italian Renaissance*. New Haven: Yale University Press, 1997.

Maginnis, H. B. J. *The World of the Early Sienese Painter*. With a translation of the Sienese Breve dell'Arte del pittori by Gabriele Erasmi. University Park: Pennsylvania State University Press, 2001.

Meiss, M. *Painting in Florence and Siena after the Black Death: The Arts, Religion, and Society in the Mid-Fourteenth Century*. Princeton, NJ: Princeton University Press, 1978, © 1951.

Nevola, F. *Siena: Constructing the Renaissance City*. New Haven and London: Yale University Press, 2008.

Norman, D., ed. *Siena, Florence, and Padua: Art, Society, and Religion 1280–1400*. New Haven: Yale University Press in association with the Open University, 1995.

Schmidt, V., ed. *Italian Panel Painting of the Duecento and Trecento*. Washington, DC: National Gallery of Art; New Haven: Dist. by Yale University Press, 2002.

Stubblebine, J. H. *Assisi and the Rise of Vernacular Art*. New York: Harper & Row, 1985.

———. *Dugento Painting: An Annotated Bibliography*. Boston: G. K. Hall, 1983.

Trachtenberg, M. *Dominion of the Eye: Urbanism, Art, and Power in Early Modern Florence*. New York: Cambridge University Press, 2008.

White, J. *Art and Architecture in Italy, 1250–1400*. 3d ed. Pelican History of Art. New Haven: Yale University Press, 1993.

CHAPTER 14. ARTISTIC INNOVATIONS IN FIFTEENTH-CENTURY NORTHERN EUROPE

Ainsworth, M. W., and K. Christiansen. *From Van Eyck to Bruegel: Early Netherlandish Painting in the Metropolitan Museum of Art*. New York: Metropolitan Museum of Art, 1998.

Borchert, T., ed. *The Age of van Eyck: the Mediterranean World and Early Netherlandish Painting, 1430–1530*. New York: Thames & Hudson, 2002.

Chapuis, J., ed. *Tilman Riemenschneider, Master Sculptor of the Late Middle Ages*. Washington, DC: National Gallery of Art; New York: Metropolitan Museum of Art; New Haven: Dist. by Yale University Press, 1999.

Cuttler, C. *Northern Painting from Pucelle to Bruegel*. Fort Worth: Holt, Rinehart & Winston, 1991, © 1972.

De Vos, D. *Rogier van der Weyden: The Complete Works*. New York: Harry N. Abrams, 1999.

Dhanens, E. *Hubert and Jan van Eyck*. New York: Alpine Fine Arts Collection, 1980.

Dixon, L. *Bosch*. Art & Ideas. London: Phaidon Press, 2003.

Friedländer, M. *Early Netherlandish Painting*. 14 vols. New York: Praeger, 1967–1973.

Hand, J. O., C. Metzger, and R. Spronk. *Prayers and Portraits: Unfolding the Netherlandish Diptych*. Exh. cat. Washington DC, National Gallery of Art; New Haven: Yale University Press, 2006.

Koldeweij, J., ed. *Hieronymus Bosch: New Insights into His Life and Work*. Rotterdam: Museum Boijmans Van Beuningen: NAi; Ghent: Ludion, 2001.

Muller, T. *Sculpture in the Netherlands, Germany, France, and Spain, 1400–1500*. Pelican History of Art. Harmondsworth, England: Penguin, 1966.

Nuttall, P. *From Flanders to Florence: The Impact of Netherlandish Painting, 1400–1500*. New Haven: Yale University Press, 2004.

Pächt, O. *Van Eyck and the Founders of Early Netherlandish Painting*. London: Harvey Miller, 1994.

Panofsky, E. *Early Netherlandish Painting*. 2 vols. New York: Harper & Row, 1971. Orig. published Cambridge, MA: Harvard University Press, 1958.

Rothstein, B. L. *Sight and Spirituality in Early Netherlandish Painting*. Cambridge: Cambridge University Press, 2005.

Van der Velden, H. *The Donor's Image: Gérard Loyet and the Votive Portraits of Charles the Bold*. Turnhout: Brepols, 2000.

Williamson, P. *Netherlandish Sculpture 1450–1550*. London: V & A; New York: Dist. by Harry N. Abrams, 2002.

CHAPTER 15. THE EARLY RENAISSANCE IN ITALY

Ahl, D. C. *The Cambridge Companion to Masaccio*. New York: Cambridge University Press, 2002.

Aikema, B. *Renaissance Venice and the North: Crosscurrents in the Time of Bellini, Dürer and Titian*. Exh. cat. Milan: Bompiani, 2000.

Ajmar-Wollheim, M., and F. Dennis, eds. *At Home in Renaissance Italy*. Exh. cat. London: Victoria & Albert Museum; V&A Publications, 2006.

Alberti, L. B. *On Painting*. Trans. C. Grayson, introduction and notes M. Kemp. New York: Penguin, 1991.

———. *On the Art of Building, in Ten Books*. Trans. J. Rykwert, et al. Cambridge, MA: MIT Press, 1991.

Ames-Lewis, F. *Drawing in Early Renaissance Italy*. 2d ed. New Haven: Yale University Press, 2000.

Baxandall, M. *Painting and Experience in Fifteenth-Century Italy: A Primer in the Social History of Pictorial Style*. 2d ed. New York: Oxford University Press, 1988.

Blunt, A. *Artistic Theory in Italy, 1450–1600*. Reprint of 1940 ed. New York: Oxford University Press, 1983.

Bober, P., and R. Rubinstein. *Renaissance Artists and Antique Sculpture: A Handbook of Sources*. New York: Oxford University Press, 1986.

Borsook, E. *The Mural Painters of Tuscany: From Cimabue to Andrea del Sarto*. 2d ed. New York: Oxford University Press, 1980.

Cole, B. *The Renaissance Artist at Work: From Pisano to Titian*. New York: Harper & Row, © 1983.

Fejfer, J. *The Rediscovery of Antiquity: The Role of the Artist*. Copenhagen: Museum Tusculanum Press, University of Copenhagen, 2003.

Gilbert, C. E. *Italian Art, 1400–1500: Sources and Documents*. Englewood Cliffs, NJ: Prentice Hall, 1980.

Goldthwaite, R. *Wealth and the Demand for Art in Italy, 1300–1600*. Baltimore, MD: Johns Hopkins University Press, 1993.

Gombrich, E. H. *New Light on Old Masters*. New ed. London: Phaidon Press, 1994.

Heydenreich, L., and W. Lotz. *Architecture in Italy, 1400–1500*: Rev. ed. Pelican History of Art. New Haven: Yale University Press, 1996.

Humfreys, P., and M. Kemp, eds. *The Altarpiece in the Renaissance*. New York: Cambridge University Press, 1990.

———., ed. *The Cambridge Companion to Giovanni Bellini*. New York: Cambridge University Press, 2004.

Huse, N., and W. Wolters. *The Art of Renaissance Venice: Architecture, Sculpture, and Painting, 1460–1590*. Chicago: University of Chicago Press, 1990.

Janson, H. W. *The Sculpture of Donatello*. 2 vols. Princeton, NJ: Princeton University Press, 1979.

Kempers, B. *Painting, Power, and Patronage: The Rise of the Professional Artist in the Italian Renaissance*. New York: Penguin, 1992.

Kent, D. V. *Cosimo de' Medici and the Florentine Renaissance: The Patron's Oeuvre*. New Haven: Yale University Press, © 2000.

Krautheimer, R., and T. Krautheimer-Hess. *Lorenzo Ghiberti*. Princeton, NJ: Princeton University Press, 1982.

Lavin, M. A. *Piero della Francesca*. Art & Ideas. New York: Phaidon Press, 2002.

Murray, P. *The Architecture of the Italian Renaissance*. New rev. ed. The World of Art. New York: Random House, 1997.

Musacchio, J. M. *Art, Marriage, and Family in the Florentine Renaissance Palace*. New Haven: Yale University Press, 2009.

Pächt, O. *Venetian Painting in the 15th Century: Jacopo, Gentile and Giovanni Bellini and Andrea Mantegna*. London: Harvey Miller, 2003.

Panofsky, E. *Perspective as Symbolic Form*. New York: Zone Books, 1997.

———. *Renaissance and Renascences in Western Art*. Trans. C. S. Wood. New York: Humanities Press, 1970.

Pope-Hennessy, J. *Italian Renaissance Sculpture*. 4th ed. London: Phaidon Press, 2000.

Randolph, A. *Engaging Symbols: Gender, Politics, and Public Art in Fifteenth-Century Florence*. New Haven: Yale University Press, 2002.

Saalman, H. *Filippo Brunelleschi: The Buildings*. University Park: Pennsylvania State University Press, 1993.

Seymour, C. *Sculpture in Italy, 1400–1500*. Pelican History of Art. Harmondsworth, England: Penguin, 1966.

Turner, A. R. *Renaissance Florence*. Perspectives. New York: Harry N. Abrams, 1997.

Wackernagel, M. *The World of the Florentine Renaissance Artist: Projects and Patrons, Workshop and Art Market*. Princeton, NJ: Princeton University Press, 1981.

Wood, J. M., ed. *The Cambridge Companion to Piero della Francesca*. New York: Cambridge University Press, 2002.

CHAPTER 16. THE HIGH RENAISSANCE IN ITALY, 1495–1520

Ackerman, J., *The Architecture of Michelangelo*. 2d ed. Chicago: University of Chicago Press, 1986.

Beck, J. H. *Three Worlds of Michelangelo*. New York: W. W. Norton, 1999.

Boase, T. S. R. *Giorgio Vasari: The Man and the Book*. Princeton, NJ: Princeton University Press, 1979.

Brown, P. F. *Art and Life in Renaissance Venice*. Perspectives. New York: Harry N. Abrams, 1997.

———. *Venice and Antiquity: The Venetian Sense of the Past*. New Haven: Yale University Press, 1997.

Chapman, H. *Raphael: From Urbino to Rome*. London: National Gallery; New Haven: Dist. by Yale University Press, 2004.

Clark, K. *Leonardo da Vinci*. Rev. and introduced by M. Kemp. New York: Penguin, 1993, © 1988.

Cole, A. *Virtue and Magnificence: Art of the Italian Renaissance Courts*. Perspectives. New York: Harry N. Abrams, 1995.

De Tolnay, C. *Michelangelo*. 5 vols. Some vols. rev. Princeton, NJ: Princeton University Press, 1969–1971.

Freedberg, S. *Painting in Italy, 1500–1600*. 3d ed. Pelican History of Art. New Haven: Yale University Press, 1993.

———. *Painting of the High Renaissance in Rome and Florence*. 2 vols. New rev. ed. New York: Hacker Art Books, 1985.

Goffen, R. *Renaissance Rivals: Michelangelo, Leonardo, Raphael, Titian*. New Haven: Yale University Press, 2002.

Hall, M. B. *The Cambridge Companion to Raphael*. New York: Cambridge University Press, 2005.

Hersey, G. L. *High Renaissance Art in St. Peter's and the Vatican: An Interpretive Guide*. Chicago: University of Chicago Press, 1993.

Hibbard, H. *Michelangelo*. 2d ed. Boulder, CO: Westview Press, 1998, © 1974.

Kemp, M. *Leonardo*. New York: Oxford University Press, 2004.

———., ed. *Leonardo on Painting: An Anthology of Writings*. New Haven: Yale University Press, 1989.

Nicholl, C. *Leonardo da Vinci: Flights of the Mind*. New York: Viking Penguin, 2004.

Panofsky, E. *Studies in Iconology: Humanist Themes in the Art of the Renaissance*. New York: Harper & Row, 1972.

Partridge, L. *The Art of Renaissance Rome*. Perspectives. New York: Harry N. Abrams, 1996.

Rowland, I. *The Culture of the High Renaissance: Ancients and Moderns in Sixteenth Century Rome*. Cambridge: 1998.

Rubin, P. L. *Giorgio Vasari: Art and History*. New Haven: Yale University Press, 1995.

Steinberg, L. *Leonardo's Incessant Last Supper*. New York: Zone Books, 2001.

Wallace, W. *Michelangelo: The Complete Sculpture, Painting, Architecture*. Southport, CT: Hugh Lauter Levin, 1998.

Wölfflin, H. *Classic Art: An Introduction to the High Renaissance*. 5th ed. London: Phaidon Press, 1994.

CHAPTER 17. THE LATE RENAISSANCE AND MANNERISM

Ackerman, J. *Palladio*. Reprint of the 2d ed. Harmondsworth, England: Penguin, 1991, © 1966.

Barkan, L. *Unearthing the Past: Archaeology and Aesthetics in the Making of Renaissance Culture*. New Haven: Yale University Press, 1999.

Beltramini, G., and A. Padoan. *Andrea Palladio: The Complete Illustrated Works*. New York: Universe; Dist. by St. Martin's Press, 2001.

Cole, M., ed. *Sixteenth-Century Italian Art*. Oxford: Blackwell, 2006.

Ekserdjian, D. *Correggio*. New Haven: Yale University Press, 1997.

Fortini Bown, P. *Private Lives in Renaissance Venice: Art, Architecture, and the Family*. New Haven: Yale University Press, 2004.

Friedlaender, W. *Mannerism and Anti-Mannerism in Italian Painting*. Reprint of 1957 ed. Interpretations in Art. New York: Columbia University Press, 1990.

Furlotti, B., and G. Rebecchini. *The Art and Architecture of Mantua: Eight Centuries of Patronage and Collecting*. London: Thames & Hudson, 2008.

Goffen, R. *Titian's Women*. New Haven: Yale University Press, 1997.

Jacobs, F. H. *Defining the Renaissance "Virtuosa": Women Artists and the Language of Art History and Criticism*. New York: Cambridge University Press, 1997.

Klein, R., and H. Zerner. *Italian Art, 1500–1600: Sources and Documents*. Reprint of 1966 ed. Evanston, IL: Northwestern University Press, 1989.

Kliemann, J., and M. Rohlmann. *Italian Frescoes: High Renaissance and Mannerism, 1510–1600*. New York: Abbeville Press, 2004.

Partridge, L. *Michelangelo—The Last Judgment: A Glorious Restoration*. New York: Harry N. Abrams, 1997.

Rearick, W. R. *The Art of Paolo Veronese, 1528–1588*. Cambridge: Cambridge University Press, 1988.

Rosand, D. *Painting in Sixteenth-Century Venice: Titian, Veronese, Tintoretto*. New York: Cambridge University Press, 1997.

Shearman, J. K. G. *Mannerism*. New York: Penguin Books, 1990, © 1967.

Smyth, C. H. *Mannerism and Maniera*. 2d ed. Bibliotheca artibus et historiae. Vienna: IRSA, 1992.

Tavernor, R. *Palladio and Palladianism*. The World of Art. New York: Thames & Hudson, 1991.

Valcanover, F., and T. Pignatti. *Tintoretto*. New York: Harry N. Abrams, 1984.

Wundram, M. *Palladio: The Complete Buildings*. Köln and London: Taschen, 2004.

CHAPTER 18. EUROPEAN ART OF THE SIXTEENTH CENTURY: RENAISSANCE AND REFORMATION

Bartrum, G. *Albrecht Dürer and His Legacy: The Graphic Work of a Renaissance Artist*. Princeton, NJ: Princeton University Press, 2002.

Baxandall, M. *The Limewood Sculptors of Renaissance Germany*. New Haven: Yale University Press, 1980.

Campbell, T. P. *Tapestry in the Renaissance: Art and Magnificence*. Exh. cat. New York: Metropolitan Museum of Art; New Haven: Yale University Press, 2006.

Eichberger, D., ed. *Durer and His Culture*. New York: Cambridge University Press, 1998.

Hayum, A. *The Isenheim Altarpiece: God's Medicine and the Painter's Vision*. Princeton, NJ: Princeton University Press, 1989.

Hitchcock, H.-R. *German Renaissance Architecture*. Princeton, NJ: Princeton University Press, 1981.

Honig, E. A. *Painting and the Market in Early Modern Antwerp*. New Haven: Yale University Press, 1998.

Hulse, C. *Elizabeth I: Ruler and Legend*. Urbana: Published for the Newberry Library by the University of Illinois Press, 2003.

Hutchison, J. C. *Albrecht Dürer: A Biography*. Princeton, NJ: Princeton University Press, 1990.

Jopek, N. *German Sculpture, 1430–1540: A Catalogue of the Collection in the Victoria and Albert Museum*. London: V & A, 2002.

Kavaler, E. M. *Pieter Bruegel: Parables of Order and Enterprise*. New York: Cambridge University Press, 1999.

Koerner, J. *The Moment of Self-Portraiture in German Renaissance Art*. Chicago: University of Chicago Press, 1993.

———. *The Reformation of the Image*. Chicago: University of Chicago Press, 2004.

Mann, R. *El Greco and His Patrons: Three Major Projects*. New York: Cambridge University Press, 1986.

Melion, W. *Shaping the Netherlandish Canon: Karel van Mander's Schilder-Boeck*. Chicago: University of Chicago Press, 1991.

Moxey, K. *Peasants, Warriors, and Wives: Popular Imagery in the Reformation*. Chicago: University of Chicago Press, 1989.

Osten, G. von der, and H. Vey. *Painting and Sculpture in Germany and the Netherlands, 1500–1600*. Pelican History of Art. Harmondsworth, England: Penguin, 1969.

Panofsky, E. *The Life and Art of Albrecht Dürer*. 4th ed. Princeton, NJ: Princeton University Press, 1971.

Smith, J. C. *Nuremberg: A Renaissance City, 1500–1618*. Austin: Published for the Archer M. Huntington Art Gallery by the University of Texas Press, 1983.

Stechow, W. *Northern Renaissance Art, 1400–1600: Sources and Documents*. Evanston, IL: Northwestern University Press, 1989, © 1966.

Van Mander, K. *Lives of the Illustrious Netherlandish and German Painters*. Ed. H. Miedema. 6 vols. Doornspijk, Netherlands: Davaco, 1993–1999.

Wood, C. *Albrecht Altdorfer and the Origins of Landscape*. Chicago: University of Chicago Press, 1993.

Zerner, H. *Renaissance Art in France: The Invention of Classicism*. Paris: Flammarion; London: Thames & Hudson, 2003.

CHAPTER 19. THE BAROQUE IN ITALY AND SPAIN

Avery, C. *Bernini: Genius of the Baroque*. London: Thames & Hudson, 1997.

Bissell, R. W. *Masters of Italian Baroque Painting: The Detroit Institute of Arts*. Detroit, MI: Detroit Institute of Arts in association with D. Giles Ltd., London, 2005.

Brown, B. L., ed. *The Genius of Rome, 1592–1623*. Exh. cat. London: Royal Academy of Arts; New York: Dist. in the United States and Canada by Harry N. Abrams, 2001.

Brown, J. *Francisco de Zurbaran*. New York: Harry N. Abrams, 1991.

———. *Painting in Spain, 1500–1700*. Pelican History of Art. New Haven: Yale University Press, 1998.

———. *Velázquez: The Technique of Genius*. New Haven: Yale University Press, 1998.

Dempsey, C. *Annibale Carracci and the Beginnings of Baroque Style*. 2d ed. Fiesole, Italy: Cadmo, 2000.

Enggass, R., and J. Brown. *Italy and Spain, 1600–1750: Sources and Documents*. Reprint of 1970 ed. Evanston, IL: Northwestern University Press, 1992.

Freedberg, S. *Circa 1600: A Revolution of Style in Italian Painting*. Cambridge, MA: Harvard University Press, 1983.

Garrard, M. D. *Artemisia Gentileschi: The Image of the Female Hero in Italian Baroque Art*. Princeton, NJ: Princeton University Press, 1989.

Marder, T. A. *Bernini and the Art of Architecture*. New York: Abbeville Press, 1998.

Montagu, J. *Roman Baroque Sculpture: The Industry of Art*. New Haven: Yale University Press, 1989.

Nicolson, B. *Caravaggism in Europe*. Ed. L. Vertova. 3 vols. 2d ed., rev. and enl. Turin, Italy: Allemandi, 1989.

Schroth, S., R. Baer, et al. *El Greco to Velázquez: Art During the Reign of Philip III*. Exh. cat. Boston: Museum of Fine Arts; MFA Publications, 2008.

Smith, G. *Architectural Diplomacy: Rome and Paris in the Late Baroque*. Cambridge, MA: MIT Press, 1993.

Spear, R. E. *From Caravaggio to Artemisia: Essays on Painting in Seventeenth-Century Italy and France*. London: Pindar Press, 2002.

Spike, J. T. *Caravaggio*. Includes CD-ROM of all the known paintings of Caravaggio, including attributed and lost works. New York: Abbeville Press, © 2001.

Varriano, J. *Italian Baroque and Rococo Architecture*. New York: Oxford University Press, 1986.

Wittkower, R. *Art and Architecture in Italy, 1600–1750*. 4th ed. Pelican History of Art. New Haven: Yale University Press, 2000.

———. *Bernini: The Sculptor of the Roman Baroque*. 4th ed. London: Phaidon Press, 1997.

CHAPTER 20. THE BAROQUE IN FLANDERS AND HOLLAND

Alpers, S. *The Art of Describing: Dutch Art in the Seventeenth Century*. Chicago: University of Chicago Press, 1983.

———. *The Making of Rubens*. New Haven: Yale University Press, 1995.

Chapman, H. P. *Rembrandt's Self-Portraits: A Study in Seventeenth-Century Identity*. Princeton, NJ: Princeton University Press, 1990.

Fleischer, R., ed. *Rembrandt, Rubens, and the Art of Their Time: Recent Perspectives*. University Park: Pennsylvania State University, 1997.

Franits, W. E. *Dutch Seventeenth-Century Genre Painting: Its Stylistic and Thematic Evolution*. New Haven: Yale University Press, 2004.

Grijzenhout, F., ed. *The Golden Age of Dutch Painting in Historical Perspective*. New York: Cambridge University Press, 1999.

Kiers, J. and E. Runia, eds. *The Glory of the Golden Age: Dutch Art of the 17th Century*. 2 vols. Exh. cat. Rijksmuseum, Amsterdam: Waanders: 2000.

Logan, A. S. *Peter Paul Rubens: The Drawings*. Exh. cat. New York: Metropolitan Museum of Art; New Haven: Yale University Press, 2004.

Salvesen, S., ed. *Rembrandt: The Master and His Workshop*. 2 vols. Exh. cat. New Haven: Yale University Press, 1991.

Schama, S. *The Embarrassment of Riches: An Interpretation of Dutch Culture in the Golden Age*. New York: Alfred A. Knopf, 1987.

Schwartz, G. *Rembrandt: His Life, His Paintings*. New York: Viking, 1985.

Slive, S. *Dutch Painting, 1600–1800*. Pelican History of Art. New Haven: Yale University Press, 1995.

———. *Frans Hals*. Exh. cat. Munich: Prestel-Verlag, 1989.

———. *Jacob van Ruisdael: Master of Landscape*. London: Royal Academy of Arts, 2005.

Sluijter, E. J. *Rembrandt and the Female Nude*. Amsterdam University Press, 2006.

Sutton, P. *The Age of Rubens*. Exh. cat. Boston: Museum of Fine Arts, 1993.

Vlieghe, H. *Flemish Art and Architecture, 1585–1700*. Pelican History of Art. New Haven: Yale University Press, © 1998.

Westermann, M. *Art and Home: Dutch Interiors in the Age of Rembrandt*. Exh. cat. Zwolle: Waanders, 2001.

———. *Rembrandt*. Art & Ideas. London: Phaidon Press, 2000.

———. *A Worldly Art: The Dutch Republic 1585–1718*. Perspectives. New York: Harry N. Abrams, 1996.

Wheelock, A. K., ed. *Johannes Vermeer*. Exh. cat. New Haven: Yale University Press, 1995.

———., et al. *Anthony van Dyck*. Exh. cat. New York: Harry N. Abrams, 1990.

White, C. *Peter Paul Rubens*. New Haven: Yale University Press, 1987.

CHAPTER 21. THE BAROQUE IN FRANCE AND ENGLAND

Blunt, A. *Art and Architecture in France, 1500–1700*. 5th ed. Pelican History of Art. New Haven: Yale University Press, 1999.

Brusatin, M., et al. *The Baroque in Central Europe: Places, Architecture, and Art*. Venice: Marsilio, 1992.

Donovan, F. *Rubens and England*. New Haven: Published for The Paul Mellon Centre for Studies in British Art by Yale University Press, 2004.

Downes, K. *The Architecture of Wren*. Rev. ed. Reading, England: Redhedge, 1988.

Garreau, M. *Charles Le Brun: First Painter to King Louis XIV*. New York: Harry N. Abrams, 1992.

Kitson, M. *Studies on Claude and Poussin*. London: Pindar, 2000.

Lagerlöf, M. R. *Ideal Landscape: Annibale Carracci, Nicolas Poussin, and Claude Lorrain*. New Haven: Yale University Press, 1990.

Mérot, A. *French Painting in the Seventeenth Century*. New Haven: Yale University Press, 1995.

———. *Nicolas Poussin*. New York: Abbeville Press, 1990.

Porter, R. *London: A Social History*. Cambridge, MA: Harvard University Press, 1995.

Rosenberg, P., and K. Christiansen, eds. *Poussin and Nature: Arcadian Visions*. Exh. cat. New York: Metropolitan Museum of Art; New Haven: Yale University Press, 2008.

Summerson, J. *Architecture in Britain, 1530–1830*. Rev. 9th ed. Pelican History of Art. New Haven: Yale University Press, 1993.

Tinniswood, A. *His Invention So Fertile: A Life of Christopher Wren*. New York: Oxford University Press, 2001.

Verdi, R. *Nicolas Poussin 1594–1665*. London: Zwemmer in association with the Royal Academy of Arts, 1995.

Vlnas, V., ed. *The Glory of the Baroque in Bohemia: Essays on Art, Culture and Society in the 17th and 18th Centuries*. Prague: National Gallery, 2001.

Waterhouse, E. K. *The Dictionary of Sixteenth and Seventeenth Century British Painters*. Woodbridge, Suffolk, England: Antique Collectors' Club, 1988.

———. *Painting in Britain, 1530–1790*. 5th ed. Pelican History of Art. New Haven: Yale University Press, 1993.

Whinney, M. D. *Wren*. World of Art. New York: Thames & Hudson, 1998.

CHAPTER 22. THE ROCOCO

Bailey, C. B. *The Age of Watteau, Chardin, and Fragonard: Masterpieces of French Genre Painting*. New Haven: Yale University Press in association with the National Gallery of Canada, 2003.

Brunel, G. *Boucher*. New York: Vendome, 1986.

———. *Painting in Eighteenth-Century France*. Ithaca, NY: Cornell University Press, 1981.

Cuzin, J. P. *Jean-Honoré Fragonard: Life and Work: Complete Catalogue of the Oil Paintings*. New York: Harry N. Abrams, 1988.

François Boucher, 1703–1770. Exh. cat. New York: Metropolitan Museum of Art, © 1986.

Gaunt, W. *The Great Century of British Painting: Hogarth to Turner*. 2d ed. London: Phaidon Press, 1978.

Kalnein, W. von. *Architecture in France in the Eighteenth Century*. Pelican History of Art. New Haven: Yale University Press, 1995.

Levey, M. *Giambattista Tiepolo: His Life and Art*. New Haven: Yale University Press, 1986.

———. *Painting and Sculpture in France, 1700–1789*. New ed. Pelican History of Art. New Haven: Yale University Press, 1993.

———. *Painting in Eighteenth-Century Venice*. 3d ed. Pelican History of Art. New Haven: Yale University Press, 1993.

———. *Rococo to Revolution: Major Trends in Eighteenth-Century Painting*. Reprint of 1966 ed. The World of Art. New York: Thames & Hudson, 1985.

Links, J. G. *Canaletto*. Completely rev., updated, and enl. ed. London: Phaidon Press, 1994.

Paulson, R. *Hogarth*. 3 vols. New Brunswick: Rutgers University Press, 1991–1993.

Pointon, M. *Hanging the Head: Portraiture and Social Formation in Eighteenth-Century England*. New Haven: Yale University Press, 1993.

Posner, D. *Antoine Watteau*. Ithaca, NY: Cornell University Press, 1984.

Rococo to Romanticism: Art and Architecture, 1700–1850. Garland Library of the History of Art. New York: Garland, 1976.

Rosenberg, P. *Chardin*. Exh. cat. London: Royal Academy of Art; New York: Metropolitan Museum of Art, 2000.

———. *From Drawing to Painting: Poussin, Watteau, Fragonard, David & Ingres*. Princeton, NJ: Princeton University Press, 2000.

Scott, K. *The Rococo Interior: Decoration and Social Spaces in Early Eighteenth-Century Paris*. New Haven: Yale University Press, 1995.

Sheriff, M. D. *The Exceptional Woman: Elisabeth Vigée-Lebrun and the Cultural Politics of Art*. Chicago: University of Chicago Press, 1996.

Wintermute, A. *Watteau and His World: French Drawing from 1700 to 1750*. Exh. cat. London: Merrell Holberton; New York: American Federation of Arts, 1999.

PART FOUR: THE MODERN WORLD

GENERAL REFERENCES

Arnason, H. H. *History of Modern Art: Painting, Sculpture, Architecture, Photography*. 5th ed. Upper Saddle River, NJ: Pearson Prentice Hall, 2004.

Atkins, R. *Artspoke: A Guide to Modern Ideas, Movements, and Buzzwords, 1848–1944*. New York: Abbeville Press, 1993.

Baigell, M. *A Concise History of American Painting and Sculpture*. Rev. ed. New York: Icon Editions, 1996.

Banham, R. *Theory and Design in the First Machine Age*. 2d ed. Cambridge, MA: MIT Press, 1980, © 1960.

Bearden, R., and H. Henderson. *A History of African-American Artists from 1792 to the Present*. New York: Pantheon, 1993.

Bergdoll, B. *European Architecture 1750–1890*. Oxford History of Art. New York: Oxford University Press, 2000.

Bjelajac, D. *American Art: A Cultural History*. Upper Saddle River, NJ: Pearson Prentice Hall, 2005.

Boime, A. *A Social History of Modern Art. Vol. 1, Art in the Age of Revolution, 1750–1800. Vol. 2, Art in the Age of Bonapartism, 1800–1815. Vol. 3, Art in the Age of Counterrevolution, 1815–1848*. Chicago: University of Chicago Press, 1987–2004.

Bown, M. C. *A Dictionary of Twentieth Century Russian and Soviet Painters 1900–1980s*. London: Izomar, 1998.

Campany, D., ed. *Art and Photography*. Themes and Movements. London: Phaidon Press, 2003.

Castleman, R. *Prints of the Twentieth Century: A History*. Rev. ed. London: Thames & Hudson, 1988.

Chiarmonte, P. *Women Artists in the United States: A Selective Bibliography and Resource Guide to the Fine and Decorative Arts, 1750–1986*. Boston: G. K. Hall, 1990.

Chilvers, I. *A Dictionary of Twentieth-Century Art*. New York: Oxford University Press, 1998.

Chipp, H., ed. *Theories of Modern Art: A Source Book by Artists and Critics*. Berkeley: University of California Press, 1968.

Colquhoun, A. *Modern Architecture*. New York: Oxford University Press, 2002.

Crary, J. *Techniques of the Observer: On Vision and Modernity in the Nineteenth Century*. Cambridge, MA: MIT Press, 1990.

Craven, W. *American Art: History and Culture*. New York: Harry N. Abrams, 1994.

Crook, J. *The Dilemma of Style: Architectural Ideas from the Picturesque to the Post Modern*. Chicago: University of Chicago Press, 1987.

Crow, T. *Modern Art in the Common Culture*. New Haven: Yale University Press, 1996.

Cummings, P. *Dictionary of Contemporary American Artists*. New York: St. Martin's Press, 1988.

Documents of Modern Art. 14 vols. New York: Wittenborn, 1944–1961. Anthologies of primary source material. Selected titles listed individually, below.

The Documents of Twentieth-Century Art. Boston: G. K. Hall, Anthologies of primary source material. Selected titles listed individually, below.

Doss, E. *Twentieth-Century American Art*. Oxford History of Art. New York: Oxford University Press, 2002.

Drucker, J. *The Century of Artists' Books*. New York: Granary Books, 2004.

Eisenman, S. *Nineteenth Century Art: A Critical History*. New York: Thames & Hudson, 2002.

Eitner, L. *An Outline of Nineteenth-Century European Painting: From David Through Cézanne*. 2 vols. New York: Harper & Row, 1986.

Elderfield, J., ed. *Modern Painting and Sculpture: 1880 to the Present at the Museum of Modern Art*. New York: Museum of Modern Art; Dist. by D.A.P./Distributed Art Publishers, 2004.

Evans, M. M., ed. *Contemporary Photographers*. 3d ed. New York: St. James Press, 1995.

Farrington, L. E. *Creating Their Own Image: The History of African-American Women Artists*. New York: Oxford University Press, 2005.

Frampton, K. *Modern Architecture: A Critical History*. 3d ed. New York: Thames & Hudson, 1992.

Frascina, F. and J. Harris, eds. *Art in Modern Culture: An Anthology of Critical Texts*. New York: Harper & Row, 1992.

Gaiger, J., ed. *Art of the Twentieth Century: A Reader*. New Haven: Yale University Press in association with the Open University, 2003.

———. *Frameworks for Modern Art*. New Haven: Yale University Press in association with the Open University, 2003.

Goldberg, R. *Performance Art: From Futurism to the Present*. Rev. and exp. ed. The World of Art. New York: Thames & Hudson, 2001.

Goldwater, R. *Primitivism in Modern Art*. Enl. ed. Cambridge: Harvard University Press, 1986.

Gray, J. *Action Art: A Bibliography of Artists' Performance from Futurism to Fluxus and Beyond*. Westport, CT: Greenwood Press, 1993.

Harrison, C., and P. Wood, eds. *Art in Theory, 1815–1900: An Anthology of Changing Ideas*. Malden, MA: Blackwell, 1998.

————. *Art in Theory, 1900–2000: An Anthology of Changing Ideas*. New ed. Malden, MA: Blackwell, 2003.

Heller, N. *Women Artists: An Illustrated History*. New York: Abbeville Press, 2003.

Hertz, R., ed. *Theories of Contemporary Art*. 2d ed. Englewood Cliffs, NJ: Prentice Hall, 1993.

————., and N. Klein, eds. *Twentieth-Century Art Theory: Urbanism, Politics, and Mass Culture*. Englewood Cliffs, NJ: Prentice Hall, 1990.

Hitchcock, H. R. *Architecture: Nineteenth and Twentieth Centuries*. 4th rev. ed. Pelican History of Art. New Haven: Yale University Press, 1987, © 1977.

Hughes, R. *American Visions: The Epic History of Art in America*. New York: Alfred A. Knopf, 1997.

Hunter, S., and J. Jacobus. *Modern Art: Painting, Sculpture, Architecture*. 3d rev. ed. New York: Harry N. Abrams, 2000.

Igoe, L. *250 Years of Afro-American Art: An Annotated Bibliography*. New York: Bowker, 1981.

Joachimides, C., et al. *American Art in the Twentieth Century: Painting and Sculpture, 1913–1933*. Exh. cat. Munich: Prestel, 1993.

Johnson, W. *Nineteenth-Century Photography: An Annotated Bibliography, 1839–1879*. Boston: G. K. Hall, 1990.

Kostelanetz, R. *A Dictionary of the Avant-Gardes*. New York: Routledge, 2001.

Lewis, S. *African American Art and Artists*. Berkeley: University of California Press, 1990.

Marien, M. *Photography: A Cultural History*. Upper Saddle River, NJ: Pearson Prentice Hall, 2002.

McCoubrey, J. *American Art, 1700–1960: Sources and Documents*. Englewood Cliffs, NJ: Prentice Hall, 1965.

Meikle, J. L. *Design in the USA*. Oxford History of Art. New York: Oxford University Press, 2005.

Modern Arts Criticism. 4 vols. Detroit, MI: Gale Research, 1991–1994.

Newhall, B. *The History of Photography from 1830 to the Present*. Rev. and enl. 5th ed. New York: Museum of Modern Art; Dist. by Bulfinch Press/Little, Brown, 1999.

Nochlin, L. *The Politics of Vision: Essays on Nineteenth-Century Art and Society*. New York: Harper & Row, 1989.

Osborne, H., ed. *Oxford Companion to Twentieth-Century Art*. Reprint. New York: Oxford University Press, 1990.

Patton, S. F. *African-American Art*. Oxford History of Art. New York: Oxford University Press, 1998.

Pevsner, N. *Pioneers of Modern Design: From William Morris to Walter Gropius*. 4th ed. New Haven: Yale University Press, 2005.

Piland, S. *Women Artists: An Historical, Contemporary, and Feminist Bibliography*. Metuchen, NJ: Scarecrow Press, 1994.

Powell, R. J. *Black Art and Culture in the 20th Century*. New York: Thames & Hudson, 1997.

Robinson, Hilary. *Feminism-Art-Theory: An Anthology, 1968–2000*. Oxford and Malden, MA: Blackwell, 2001.

Rose, B. *American Art Since 1900*. Rev. ed. New York: Praeger, 1975.

————. *American Painting: The Twentieth Century*. New updated ed. New York: Rizzoli, 1986.

Rosenblum, N. *A World History of Photography*. 3rd ed. New York: Abbeville Press, 1997.

Rosenblum, R., and H. W. Janson. *19th Century Art*. Rev. and updated ed. Upper Saddle River, NJ: Pearson Prentice Hall, 2005.

Schapiro, M. *Modern Art: Nineteenth and Twentieth Centuries*. New York: Braziller, 1982.

Scharf, A. *Art and Photography*. Reprint. Harmondsworth, England: Penguin, 1995.

Sennott, S., ed. *Encyclopedia of 20th Century Architecture*. 3 vols. New York: Fitzroy Dearborn, 2004.

Stiles, K., and P. Selz. *Theories and Documents of Contemporary Art*. Berkeley: University of California Press, 1996.

Tafuri, M. *Modern Architecture*. 2 vols. New York: Rizzoli, 1986.

Taylor, J. *The Fine Arts in America*. Chicago: University of Chicago Press, 1979.

————., ed. *Nineteenth-Century Theories of Art*. California Studies in the History of Art. Berkeley: University of California Press, 1987.

Tomlinson, J. *Readings in Nineteenth-Century Art*. Upper Saddle River, NJ: Prentice Hall, 1995.

Upton, D. *Architecture in the United States*. New York: Oxford University Press, 1998.

Varnedoe, K., and A. Gopnik, eds. *Modern Art and Popular Culture: Readings in High and Low*. New York: Harry N. Abrams, 1990.

Waldman, D. *Collage, Assemblage, and the Found Object*. New York: Harry N. Abrams, 1992.

Weaver, M. *The Art of Photography, 1839–1989*. Exh. cat. New Haven: Yale University Press, 1989.

Wilmerding, J. *American Views: Essays on American Art*. Princeton, NJ: Princeton University Press, 1991.

Witzling, M., ed. *Voicing Our Visions: Writings by Women Artists*. New York: Universe, 1991.

CHAPTER 23. ART IN THE AGE OF THE ENLIGHTENMENT, 1750–1789

Bryson, N. *Tradition and Desire: From David to Delacroix*. Cambridge: Cambridge University Press, 1984.

————. *Word and Image: French Painting in the Ancient Régime*. Cambridge: Cambridge University Press, 1981.

Crow, T. *Painters and Public Life in Eighteenth-Century Paris*. New Haven: Yale University Press, 1985.

Eitner, L. E. A. *Neoclassicism and Romanticism, 1750–1850: Sources and Documents*. Reprint of 1970 ed. New York: Harper & Row, 1989.

Fried, M. *Absorption and Theatricality: Painting and Beholder in the Age of Diderot*. Chicago: University of Chicago Press, 1980.

Friedlaender, W. *David to Delacroix*. Reprint of 1952 ed. New York: Schocken Books, 1968.

Goncourt, E. de, and J. de Goncourt. *French Eighteenth-Century Painters*. Reprint of 1948 ed. Ithaca, NY: Cornell University Press, 1981.

Honour, H. *Neoclassicism*. Reprint of 1968 ed. London: Penguin, 1991.

Irwin, D. G. *Neoclassicism*. Art & Ideas. London: Phaidon Press, 1997.

Licht, F. *Canova*. New York: Abbeville Press, 1983.

Miles, E. G., ed. *The Portrait in Eighteenth-Century America*. Newark: University of Delaware Press, 1993.

Ottani Cavina, A. *Geometries of Silence: Three Approaches to Neoclassical Art*. New York: Columbia University Press, 2004.

Picon, A. *French Architects and Engineers in the Age of Enlightenment*. New York: Cambridge University Press, 1992.

Rebora, C., et al. *John Singleton Copley in America*. Exh. cat. New York: The Metropolitan Museum of Art, 1995.

Rosenblum, R. *Transformations in Late Eighteenth Century Art*. Princeton, NJ: Princeton University Press, 1967.

Rosenthal, M., ed. *Prospects for the Nation: Recent Essays in British Landscape, 1750–1880*. Studies in British Art. New Haven: Yale University Press, © 1997.

Saisselin, R. G. *The Enlightenment Against the Baroque: Economics and Aesthetics in the Eighteenth Century*. Berkeley: University of California Press, 1992.

Solkin, D. *Painting for Money: The Visual Arts and the Public Sphere in Eighteenth-Century England*. New Haven: Yale University Press, 1993.

Vidler, A. *The Writing of the Walls: Architectural Theory in the Late Enlightenment*. Princeton, NJ: Princeton Architectural Press, 1987.

Watkin, D., and T. Mellinghoff. *German Architecture and the Classical Ideal*. Cambridge: MIT Press, 1987.

CHAPTER 24. ART IN THE AGE OF ROMANTICISM, 1789–1848

Boime, A. *The Academy and French Painting in the Nineteenth Century*. New ed. New Haven: Yale University Press, 1986.

Brown, D. B. *Romanticism*. Art & Ideas. New York: Phaidon Press, 2001.

Chu, P. *Nineteenth-Century European Art*. Upper Saddle River, NJ: Pearson Prentice Hall, 2002.

Eitner, L. E. A. *Géricault: His Life and Work*. Ithaca, NY: Cornell University Press, 1982.

Hartley, K. *The Romantic Spirit in German Art, 1790–1990*. Exh. cat. London: South Bank Centre, © 1994.

Herrmann, L. *Nineteenth Century British Painting*. London: Giles de la Mare, 2000.

Honour, H. *Romanticism*. New York: Harper & Row, 1979.

Johnson, E. *The Paintings of Eugène Delacroix: A Critical Catalogue, 1816–1863*. 6 vols. Oxford: Clarendon Press, 1981–1989.

————. *The Paintings of Eugène Delacroix: A Critical Catalogue*. 4th supp. and reprint of 3d supp. New York: Oxford University Press, 2002.

Joll, E. *The Oxford Companion to J. M. W. Turner*. Oxford: Oxford University Press, 2001.

Koerner, J. *Caspar David Friedrich and the Subject of Landscape*. New Haven: Yale University Press, 1990.

Licht, F. *Goya: The Origins of the Modern Temper in Art*. New York: Harper & Row, 1983.

Middleton, R. *Architecture of the Nineteenth Century*. Milan: Electa, © 2003.

Noon, P. J. *Crossing the Channel: British and French Painting in the Age of Romanticism*. Exh. cat. London: Tate, 2003.

Novak, B. *Nature and Culture: American Landscape and Painting, 1825–1875*. Rev. ed. New York: Oxford University Press, 1995.

Novotny, F. *Painting and Sculpture in Europe, 1780–1880*. 3d ed. Pelican History of Art. New Haven: Yale University Press, 1992.

Pérez Sánchez, A., and E. A. Sayre. *Goya and the Spirit of Enlightenment*. Exh. cat. Boston: Bulfinch Press, 1989.

Rosenblum, R. *Jean-Auguste-Dominique Ingres*. New York: Harry N. Abrams, 1990.

Tomlinson, J. *Goya in the Twilight of Enlightenment*. New Haven: Yale University Press, 1992.

Vaughn, W. *Romanticism and Art*. World of Art. London: Thames & Hudson, © 1994.

CHAPTER 25. THE AGE OF POSITIVISM: REALISM, IMPRESSIONISM, AND THE PRE-RAPHAELITES, 1848–1885

Adriani, G. *Renoir*. Cologne: Dumont; Dist. by Yale University Press, 1999.

Broude, N. *Impressionism: A Feminist Reading*. New York: Rizzoli, 1991.

Cachin, F., et al. *Cézanne*. Exh. cat. New York: Harry N. Abrams, 1995.

Cikovsky, N., and F. Kelly. *Winslow Homer*. Exh. cat. New Haven: Yale University Press, 1995.

Clark, T. J. *The Absolute Bourgeois: Artists and Politics in France, 1848–1851*. Berkeley: University of California Press, 1999, © 1973.

————. *The Painting of Modern Life: Paris in the Art of Manet and His Followers*. Rev. ed. Princeton, NJ: Princeton University Press, 1999.

Denvir, B. *The Chronicle of Impressionism: A Timeline History of Impressionist Art*. London: Thames & Hudson, 2000, © 1993.

————. *The Thames & Hudson Encyclopaedia of Impressionism*. New York: Thames & Hudson, 1990.

Elsen, A. *Origins of Modern Sculpture*. New York: Braziller, 1974.

Fried, M. *Courbet's Realism*. Chicago: University of Chicago Press, 1990.

————. *Manet's Modernism, or, The Face of Painting in the 1860s*. Chicago: University of Chicago Press, 1996.

Goodrich, L. *Thomas Eakins*. 2 vols. Exh. cat. Cambridge, MA: Harvard University Press, 1982.

Gray, C. *The Russian Experiment in Art, 1863–1922*. Rev. ed. The World of Art. New York: Thames & Hudson, 1986.

Hamilton, G. H. *Manet and His Critics*. Reprint of 1954 ed. New Haven, CT: Yale University Press, 1986.

Hares-Stryker, C., ed. *An Anthology of Pre-Raphaelite Writings*. New York: New York University Press, 1997.

Herbert, R. *Impressionism: Art, Leisure, and Parisian Society*. New Haven: Yale University Press, 1988.

Higonnet, A. *Berthe Morisot*. New York: Harper & Row, 1990.

House, J. *Impressionism: Paint and Politics*. New Haven: Yale University Press, 2004.

————. *Monet: Nature into Art*. New Haven: Yale University Press, 1986.

Jenkyns, R. *Dignity and Decadence: Victorian Art and the Classical Inheritance*. Cambridge, MA: Harvard University Press, 1991.

Kendall, R., and G. Pollock, eds. *Dealing with Degas: Representations of Women and the Politics of Vision*. New York: Universe, 1992.

————. *Degas: Beyond Impressionism*. Exh. cat. London: National Gallery; Chicago: Art Institute of Chicago; New Haven: Dist. by Yale University Press, 1996.

Krell, A. *Manet and the Painters of Contemporary Life*. The World of Art. New York: Thames & Hudson, 1996.

Lipton, E. *Looking into Degas*. Berkeley: University of California Press, 1986.

Mainardi, P. *Art and Politics of the Second Empire: The Universal Expositions of 1855 and 1867*. New Haven: Yale University Press, 1987.

————. *The End of the Salon: Art and the State in the Early Third Republic*. Cambridge: Cambridge University Press, 1993.

Miller, D., ed. *American Iconology: New Approaches to Nineteenth-Century Art and Literature*. New Haven: Yale University Press, 1993.

Needham, G. *Nineteenth-Century Realist Art*. New York: Harper & Row, 1988.

Nochlin, L., ed. *Impressionism and Post-Impressionism, 1874–1904: Sources and Documents*. Englewood Cliffs, NJ: Prentice Hall, 1976.

————. *Realism and Tradition in Art, 1848–1900: Sources and Documents*. Englewood Cliffs, NJ: Prentice Hall, 1966.

Novak, B. *American Painting of the Nineteenth Century: Realism and the American Experience*. 2d ed. New York: Harper & Row, 1979.

————. *Nature and Culture: American Landscape and Painting, 1825–1875*. New York: Oxford University Press, 1995.

Pollock, G. *Mary Cassatt: Painter of Modern Women*. New York: Thames & Hudson, 1998.

Prettejohn, E. *The Art of the Pre-Raphaelites*. Princeton, NJ: Princeton University Press, 2000.

Reff, T. *Manet and Modern Paris*. Exh. cat. Washington, DC: National Gallery of Art, 1982.

Rewald, J. *Studies in Impressionism*. New York: Harry N. Abrams, 1986, © 1985.

Rubin, J. H. *Impressionism*. Art & Ideas. London: Phaidon Press, 1999.

Spate, V. *Claude Monet: Life and Work*. New York: Rizzoli, 1992.

Tucker, P. H. *Claude Monet: Life and Art*. New Haven: Yale University Press, 1995.

————. *The Impressionists at Argenteuil*. Washington, DC: National Gallery of Art; Hartford, CT: Wadsworth Atheneum Museum of Art, 2000.

————. *Monet in the '90s: The Series Paintings*. Exh. cat. New Haven: Yale University Press, 1989.

Walther, I., ed. *Impressionist Art, 1860–1920*. 2 vols. Cologne: Taschen, 1996.

Weisberg, G. *Beyond Impressionism: The Naturalist Impulse*. New York: Harry N. Abrams, 1992.

Werner, M. *Pre-Raphaelite Painting and Nineteenth-Century Realism*. New York: Cambridge University Press, 2005.

CHAPTER 26. PROGRESS AND ITS DISCONTENTS: POST-IMPRESSIONISM, SYMBOLISM, AND ART NOUVEAU, 1880-1905

Brettell, R., et al. *The Art of Paul Gauguin*. Exh. cat. Boston: Little, Brown, 1988.

Broude, N. *Georges Seurat*. New York: Rizzoli, 1992.

Denvir, B. *Post-Impressionism*. The World of Art. New York: Thames & Hudson, 1992.

Dorra, H., ed. *Symbolist Art Theories: A Critical Anthology*. Berkeley: University of California Press, 1994.

Gibson, M. *The Symbolists*. New York: Harry N. Abrams, 1988.

Hamilton, G. H. *Painting and Sculpture in Europe, 1880–1940*. 6th ed. Pelican History of Art. New Haven: Yale University Press, 1993.

Herbert, R. L. *Georges Seurat, 1859–1891*. New York: Metropolitan Museum of Art; Dist. by Harry N. Abrams, 1991.

Hulsker, J. *The New Complete Van Gogh: Paintings, Drawings, Sketches: Revised and Enlarged Edition of the Catalogue Raisonné of the Works of Vincent van Gogh*. Amsterdam: J. M. Meulenhoff, 1996.

Mosby, D. *Henry Ossawa Tanner*. Exh. cat. New York: Rizzoli, 1991.

Schapiro, M. *Paul Cézanne*. New York: Harry N. Abrams, 1988.

————. *Vincent Van Gogh*. New York: Harry N. Abrams, 2000, © 1983.

Shiff, R. *Cézanne and the End of Impressionism: A Study of the Theory, Technique, and Critical Evaluation of Modern Art*. Chicago: University of Chicago Press, 1984.

Silverman, D. *Art Nouveau in Fin-de-Siècle France*. Berkeley: University of California Press, 1989.

Théberge, P. *Lost Paradise, Symbolist Europe*. Exh. cat. Montreal: Montreal Museum of Fine Arts, 1995.

Troy, N. J. *Modernism and the Decorative Arts in France: Art Nouveau to Le Corbusier*. New Haven: Yale University Press, 1991.

Varnedoe, K. *Vienna 1900: Art, Architecture, and Design*. Exh. cat. New York: Museum of Modern Art, 1986.

CHAPTER 27. TOWARD ABSTRACTION: THE MODERNIST REVOLUTION, 1904-1914

Bach, F., T. Bach, and A. Temkin. *Constantin Brancusi*. Exh. cat. Cambridge: MIT Press, 1995.

Behr, S. *Expressionism*. Movements in Modern Art. Cambridge: Cambridge University Press, 1999.

Bowlt, J. E., ed. *Russian Art of the Avant-Garde: Theory and Criticism, 1902–1934*. New York: Thames & Hudson, 1988.

Brown, M. *The Story of the Armory Show*. 2d ed. New York: Abbeville Press, 1988.

Duchamp, M. *Marcel Duchamp, Notes*. The Documents of Twentieth-Century Art. Boston: G. K. Hall, 1983.

Edwards, S. *Art of the Avant-Gardes*. New Haven: Yale University Press in association with the Open University, 2004.

Elderfield, J. *Henri Matisse: A Retrospective*. Exh. cat. New York: Museum of Modern Art; Dist. by Harry N. Abrams, 1992.

Golding, J. *Cubism: A History and an Analysis, 1907–1914*. 3d ed. Cambridge, MA: Harvard University Press, 1988.

Goldwater, R. *Primitivism in Modern Art*. Enl. ed. Cambridge, MA: Belknap Press, 1986.

Gordon, D. *Expressionism: Art and Idea*. New Haven: Yale University Press, 1987.

Green, C. *Cubism and Its Enemies*. New Haven: Yale University Press, 1987.

Herbert, J. *Fauve Painting: The Making of Cultural Politics*. New Haven: Yale University Press, 1992.

Hoffman, K., ed. *Collage: Critical Views*. Ann Arbor, MI: UMI Research Press, 1989.

Kallir, J. *Egon Schiele: The Complete Works*. Exp. ed. New York: Harry N. Abrams, 1998.

Krauss, R. *The Originality of the Avant-Garde and Other Modernist Myths*. Cambridge: MIT Press, 1986.

Kuspit, D. *The Cult of the Avant-Garde Artist*. New York: Cambridge University Press, 1993.

Rosenblum, R. *Cubism and Twentieth-Century Art*. New York: Harry N. Abrams, 2001.

Rubin, W. S. *Picasso and Braque: Pioneering Cubism*. Exh. cat. New York: Museum of Modern Art, 1989.

Taylor, B. *Collage: The Making of Modern Art*. London: Thames & Hudson, 2004.

Washton, R.-C., ed. *German Expressionism: Documents from the End of the Wilhelmine Empire to the Rise of National Socialism*. The Documents of Twentieth-Century Art. Boston: G. K. Hall, 1993.

Weiss, J. *The Popular Culture of Modern Art: Picasso, Duchamp and Avant Gardism*. New Haven: Yale University Press, 1994.

CHAPTER 28. ART BETWEEN THE WARS, 1914-1940

Ades, D. *Photomontage*. Rev. and enl. ed. London: Thames & Hudson, 1986.

Arbaïzar, P. *Henri Cartier-Bresson: The Man, the Image and the World: A Retrospective*. New York: Thames & Hudson, 2003.

Bayer, H., et al., eds. *Bauhaus, 1919–1928*. Reprint of 1938 ed. Boston: New York Graphic Society, 1986.

Blaser, W. *Mies van der Rohe*. 6th exp. and rev. ed. Boston: Birkhauser Verlag, 1997.

Campbell, M., et al. *Harlem Renaissance: Art of Black America*. New York: Harry N. Abrams, 1987.

Chadwick, W., ed. *Mirror Images: Women, Surrealism, and Self-Representation*. Cambridge, MA: MIT Press, 1998.

Corn, W. *The Great American Thing: Modern Art and National Identity, 1915–1935*. Berkeley: University of California Press, 2001.

Curtis, W. *Modern Architecture Since 1900*. 3rd ed. New York: Phaidon Press, 1996.

Durozoi, G. *History of the Surrealist Movement*. Chicago: University of Chicago Press, 2002.

Fer, B., et al. *Realism, Rationalism, Surrealism: Art Between the Wars*. Modern Art—Practices and Debates. New Haven: Yale University Press, 1993.

Fiedler, J., ed. *Photography at the Bauhaus*. Cambridge, MA: MIT Press, 1990.

Foster, S. C., ed. *Crisis and the Arts: The History of Dada*. 10 vols. New York: G. K. Hall, 1996–2005.

Gale, M. *Dada & Surrealism*. Art & Ideas. London: Phaidon Press, 1997.

Gössel, P., and G. Leuthäuser. *Architecture in the Twentieth Century*. Cologne: Taschen, 1991.

Greenough, S., and J. Hamilton. *Alfred Stieglitz: Photographs and Writings*. New York: Little, Brown, 1999.

Haskell, B. *The American Century: Art & Culture, 1900–1950*. New York: W. W. Norton, 1999.

Hight, E. M. *Picturing Modernism: Moholy-Nagy and Photography in Weimar Germany*. Cambridge, MA: MIT Press, 1995.

Hitchcock, H. R., and P. Johnson. *The International Style*. With a new forward. New York: W. W. Norton, 1996.

Hochman, E. S. *Bauhaus: Crucible of Modernism*. New York: Fromm International, © 1997.

Hopkins, D. *Dada and Surrealism: A Very Short Introduction*. New York: Oxford University Press, 2004.

Kandinsky, W. *Kandinsky: Complete Writings on Art*. Orig. pub. in The Documents of Twentieth-Century Art. New York: Da Capo Press, 1994.

Krauss, R. *L'Amour Fou: Photography and Surrealism*. New York: Abbeville Press, 1985.

Kultermann, U. *Architecture in the Twentieth Century*. New York: Van Nostrand Reinhold, 1993.

Lane, B. *Architecture and Politics in Germany, 1918–1945*. New ed. Cambridge, MA: Harvard University Press, 1985.

Le Corbusier. *Towards a New Architecture*. Oxford: Architectural Press, 1997, © 1989.

Lodder, C. *Russian Constructivism*. New Haven: Yale University Press, 1983.

McEuen, M. A. *Seeing America: Women Photographers Between the Wars*. Lexington, KY: University Press of Kentucky, 2000.

Miró, J. *Joan Miró: Selected Writings and Interviews*. The Documents of Twentieth-Century Art. Boston: G. K. Hall, 1986.

Mondrian, P. *The New Art, the New Life: The Complete Writings*. Eds. and trans. H. Holtzmann and M. James. Orig. pub. in The Documents of Twentieth-Century Art. New York: Da Capo, 1993.

Motherwell, R., ed. *The Dada Painters and Poets: An Anthology*. 2d ed. Cambridge, MA: Harvard University Press, 1989.

Nadeau, M. *History of Surrealism*. Cambridge, MA: Harvard University Press, 1989.

Phillips, C., ed. *Photography in the Modern Era: European Documents and Critical Writings, 1913–1940*. New York: Metropolitan Museum of Art; Aperture, 1989.

Roskill, M. *Klee, Kandinsky, and the Thought of Their Time: A Critical Perspective*. Urbana: University of Illinois Press, 1992.

Silver, K. E. *Esprit de Corps: The Art of the Parisian Avant-Garde and the First World War, 1914–1925*. Princeton, NJ: Princeton University Press, 1989.

Spiteri, R., ed. *Surrealism, Politics and Culture*. Aldershot, Hants., England and Burlington, VT: Ashgate, 2003.

Wood, P., ed. *Varieties of Modernism*. New Haven: Yale University Press in association with the Open University, 2004.

Wright, F. L. *Frank Lloyd Wright, Collected Writings.* 5 vols. New York: Rizzoli, 1992–1995.

CHAPTER 29. POST-WORLD WAR II TO POSTMODERN, 1945-1980

Archer, M. *Art Since 1960.* World of Art. New York: Thames & Hudson, 2002.

Ashton, D. *American Art Since 1945.* New York: Oxford University Press, 1982.

Atkins, R. *Artspeak: A Guide to Contemporary Ideas, Movements, and Buzzwords, 1945 to the Present.* New York: Abbeville Press, 1997.

Baker, K. *Minimalism: Art of Circumstance.* New York: Abbeville Press, 1989.

Battcock, G., comp. *Idea Art: A Critical Anthology.* New ed. New York: Dutton, 1973.

———., ed. *Minimal Art: A Critical Anthology.* Berkeley: University of California Press, 1995.

———., and R. Nickas, eds. *The Art of Performance: A Critical Anthology.* New York: Dutton, 1984.

Beardsley, J. *Earthworks and Beyond: Contemporary Art in the Landscape.* 3d ed. New York: Abbeville Press, 1998.

———., and J. Livingston. *Hispanic Art in the United States: Thirty Contemporary Painters and Sculptors.* Exh. cat. New York: Abbeville Press, 1987.

Burgin, V., ed. *Thinking Photography.* Communications and Culture. Houndsmills, England: Macmillan Education, 1990.

Carlson, M. A. *Performance: A Critical Introduction.* 2d ed. New York: Routledge, 2004.

Causey, A. *Sculpture Since 1945.* Oxford History of Art. New York: Oxford University Press, 1998.

Crane, D. *The Transformation of the Avant-Garde: The New York Art World, 1940–1985.* Chicago: University of Chicago Press, 1987.

Crow, T. *The Rise of the Sixties: American and European Art in the Era of Dissent.* London: Laurence King, 2005, © 1996.

Frascina, F. *Pollock and After: The Critical Debate.* 2d ed. New York: Routledge, 2001.

Gilbaut, S. *How New York Stole the Idea of Modern Art.* Chicago: University of Chicago Press, 1983.

———., ed. *Reconstructing Modernism: Art in New York, Paris, and Montreal, 1945–1964.* Cambridge: MIT Press, 1990.

Greenberg, C. *Clement Greenberg: The Collected Essays and Criticism.* 4 vols. Chicago: University of Chicago Press, 1986–1993.

Griswold del Castillo, R., ed. *Chicano Art: Resistance and Affirmation, 1965–1985.* Exh. cat. Los Angeles: Wight Art Gallery, University of California, 1991.

Hopkins, D. *After Modern Art: 1945–2000.* New York: Oxford University Press, 2000.

Joselit, D. *American Art Since 1945.* The World of Art. London: Thames & Hudson, 2003.

Landau, E. G., ed. *Reading Abstract Expressionism: Context and Critique.* New Haven: Yale University Press, 2005.

Leggio, J., and S. Weiley, eds. *American Art of the 1960s.* Studies in Modern Art, 1. New York: Museum of Modern Art, 1991.

Leja, M. *Reframing Abstract Expressionism: Subjectivity and Painting in the 1940s.* New Haven: Yale University Press, 1993.

Linder, M. *Nothing Less Than Literal: Architecture After Minimalism.* Cambridge, MA: MIT Press, 2004.

Lippard, L. R., ed. *From the Center: Feminist Essays on Women's Art.* New York: Dutton, 1976.

———. *Overlay: Contemporary Art and the Art of Prehistory.* New York: Pantheon, 1983.

Livingstone, M. *Pop Art: A Continuing History.* New York: Thames & Hudson, 2000.

Lucie-Smith, E. *Movements in Art Since 1945.* The World of Art. New York: Thames & Hudson, 2001.

McCarthy, D. *Pop Art.* Movements in Modern Art. New York: Cambridge University Press, 2000.

McEvilley, T. *Sculpture in the Age of Doubt.* New York: School of Visual Arts; Allworth Press, 1999.

Meisel, L. K. *Photorealism at the Millennium.* New York: Harry N. Abrams, 2002.

Ockman, J., ed. *Architecture Culture, 1943–1968: A Documentary Anthology.* New York: Rizzoli, 1993.

Orvell, M. *American Photography.* The World of Art. New York: Oxford University Press, 2003.

Pincus-Witten, R. *Postminimalism into Maximalism: American Art, 1966–1986.* Ann Arbor, MI: UMI Research Press, 1987.

Polcari, S. *Abstract Expressionism and the Modern Experience.* New York: Cambridge University Press, 1991.

Rosen, R., and C. Brawer, eds. *Making Their Mark: Women Artists Move into the Mainstream, 1970–85.* Exh. cat. New York: Abbeville Press, 1989.

Ross, C. *Abstract Expressionism: Creators and Critics: An Anthology.* New York: Harry N. Abrams, 1990.

Sandler, I. *Art of the Postmodern Era: From the Late 1960s to the Early 1990s.* New York: Icon Editions, 1996.

———. *The New York School: The Painters and Sculptors of the Fifties.* New York: Harper & Row, 1978.

———. *The Triumph of American Painting: A History of Abstract Expressionism.* New York: Praeger, 1970.

Sayre, H. *The Object of Performance: The American Avant-Garde Since 1970.* Chicago: University of Chicago Press, 1990.

Seitz, W. *Abstract Expressionist Painting in America.* Cambridge, MA: Harvard University Press, 1983.

Self-Taught Artists of the 20th Century: An American Anthology. Exh. cat. San Franciso: Chronicle Books, 1998.

Sontag, S. *On Photography.* New York: Picador; Farrar, Straus & Giroux, 2001, © 1977.

Weintraub, L. *Art on the Edge and Over.* Litchfield, CT: Art Insights; Dist. by D.A.P., 1997.

Wood, P., et al. *Modernism in Dispute: Art Since the Forties.* New Haven: Yale University Press, 1993.

CHAPTER 30. THE POSTMODERN ERA: ART SINCE 1980

Barthes, R. *The Pleasure of the Text.* Oxford: Blackwell, 1990.

Belting, H. *Art History After Modernism.* Chicago: University of Chicago Press, 2003.

Broude, N., and M. Garrad., eds. *Reclaiming Female Agency: Feminist Art History After Postmodernism.* Berkeley: University of California Press, 2005.

Brunette, P., and D. Wills, eds. *Deconstruction and the Visual Arts: Art, Media, Architecture.* New York: Cambridge University Press, 1994.

Capozzi, R., ed. *Reading Eco: An Anthology.* Bloomington: Indiana University Press, © 1997.

Derrida, J. *Writing and Difference.* London: Routledge Classics, 2001.

Eco, U. *A Theory of Semiotics.* Bloomington: Indiana University Press, 1976.

Foster, H., ed. *The Anti-Aesthetic: Essays on Postmodern Culture.* New York: New Press; Dist. by W. W. Norton, 1998.

Ghirardo, D. *Architecture After Modernism.* New York: Thames & Hudson, 1996.

Harris, J. P. *The New Art History: A Critical Introduction.* New York: Routledge, 2001.

Jencks, C. *New Paradigm in Architecture: The Language of Post-Modernism.* New Haven: Yale University Press, 2002.

———., ed. *The Post-Modern Reader.* London: Academy Editions; New York: St. Martin's Press, 1992.

———. *What Is Post-Modernism?* 4th rev. ed. London: Academy Editions, 1996.

Lucie-Smith, E. *Art Today.* London: Phaidon Press, 1995.

Mitchell, W. J. T. *The Reconfigured Eye: Visual Truth in the Post-Photographic Era.* Cambridge, MA: MIT Press, 1992.

Norris, C., and A. Benjamin. *What Is Deconstruction?* New York: St. Martin's Press, 1988.

Papadakes, A., et al., eds. *Deconstruction: The Omnibus Volume.* New York: Rizzoli, 1989.

Paul, C. *Digital Art.* New York: Thames & Hudson, © 2003.

Pearman, H. *Contemporary World Architecture.* London: Phaidon Press, © 1998.

Risatti, H., ed. *Postmodern Perspectives.* Englewood Cliffs, NJ: Prentice Hall, 1990.

Senie, H. *Contemporary Public Sculpture: Tradition, Transformation, and Controversy.* New York: Oxford University Press, 1992.

Steele, J. *Architecture Today.* New York: Phaidon Press, 2001.

Thody, P. *Introducing Barthes.* New York: Totem Books; Lanham, MD: National Book Network, 1997.

Tomkins, C. *Post to Neo: The Art World of the 1980s.* New York: Holt, 1988.

Wallis, B., ed. *Art After Modernism: Rethinking Representation.* Documentary Sources in Contemporary Art, 1. Boston: Godine, 1984.

Credits

Victoria and Albert Museum, London; **18.26** National Portrait Gallery, London, Reproduced by Courtesy of the Trustees; **18.27** Giraudon / Art Resource, NY; **18.28** © 2005. Photo Scala, Florence/BPK, Bildagentur fuer Kunst, Kultur und Geschichte, Berlin; **18.29** © Bednorz-images; **18.30** Digital Image 2008 © The Metropolitan Museum of Art/Art Rsource New York/Scala, Florence; **18.32** akg-images / Erich Lessing; **18.33** akg-images / Erich Lessing; **18.34** Canali Photobank, Milan Italy.

CHAPTER 19

19.0 Canali Photobank, Milan ItalY; **19.2** Canali Photobank, Milan Italy; **19.3** Canali Photobank, Milan Italy; **19.4** © 2007. Image copyright The Metropolitan Museum of Art/Art Resource/Scala, Florence; **19.5** Photograph © 1984 Detroit Institute of Arts; **19.6** © Her Majesty Queen Elizabeth II; **19.7** Canali Photobank, Milan Italy; **19.8** Canali Photobank; **19.9** Canali Photobank, Milan Ital; **19.10** Canali Photobank, Milan Italy; **19.11** © Vincenzo Pirozzi, Rome fotopirozzi@inwind.it; **19.12** © 1990. Photo Scala, Florence/Fondo Edifici di Culto – Min. dell'Interno; **19.13** © Bednorz-images; **19.14** Aerocentro Varesino; **19.15** © 1990. Photo Scala, Florence; **19.16** Musei Capitolino / Index; **19.17** © Photoservice Electa/Vescovo; **19.19** Alinari Archives / Florence; **19.20** © Bednorz-images; **19.21** © Bednorz-images; **19.23** akg-images / Joseph Martin; **19.26** © 2006. Photo Scala, Florence; **19.27** Seat Archive/Alinari Archives; **19.28** © Bednorz-images; **19.29** © 1990. Photo Scala, Florence; **19.30** © 1990. Photo Scala, Florence – courtesy of the Ministero Beni e Att. Culturali; **19.31** akg-images / Pirozzi; **Box p688** © 2004 President and Fellows of Harvard College; **19.32** © 1990. Photo Scala, Florence; **19.34** V & A Images, Victoria & Albert Museum, London; **19.37** © 2007. Image copyright The Metropolitan Museum of Art/Art Resource/Scala, Florence.

CHAPTER 20

20.0 © Peter Willi / SuperStock; **20.1** © IRPA-KIK, Brussels; **20.2** © The Trustees of the British Museum; **20.3** Image © The Board of Trustees, National Gallery of Art, Washington; **20.4** Bridgeman-Giraudon / Art Resource, NY; **20.5** akg-images / Erich Lessing; **20.6** Giraudon / Bridgeman Art Library; **20.8** © Réunion des Musées Nationaux; **20.9** © 1990, Photo Scala, Florence; **20.12** Photography © The Art Institute of Chicago; **20.15** Photograph © The National Gallery, London; **20.19** Photograph by Lorene Emerson/Images © The Board of Trustees, National Gallery of Art, Washington; **20.20** © 1990. Photo Scala, Florence; **20.21** © 2005. Photo Scala, Florence/BPK, Bildagentur fuer Kunst, Kultur und Geschichte, Berlin; **20.22** akg-images / Erich Lessing; **20.24** Photograph © The Metropolitan Museum of Art; **20.25** © 2005. Photo Ann Ronan/HIP/Scala, Florence; **20.26** Copyright The Frick Collection, New York; **20.27** Photograph © 1993 The Metropolitan Museum of Art; **20.29** Photograph © 1996 Detroit Institute of Arts; **20.34** Copyright The Frick Collection, New York; **20.35** Image © The Board of Trustees, National Gallery of Art, Washington.

CHAPTER 21

21.0 The Minneapolis Institute of Arts. The William Hood Dunwoody Fund; **21.1** © The Trustees of the British Museum; **21.2** © Gerard Blott/Réunion des Musées Nationaux; **21.3** Photograph © Carnegie Museum of Art, Pittsburgh; **21.4** The Minneapolis Institute of Arts. The William Hood Dunwoody Fund; **21.5** © 2007. Image copyright The Metropolitan Museum of Art/Art Resource/Scala, Florence; **21.6** © Orsi Battaglini; **21.7** Photograph © The Art Institute of Chicago; **21.8** © 2007. Yale University Art Gallery/Art Resource, NY/Scala, Florence; **21.9** Image © The Metropolitan Museum of Art; **21.10** © Herve Lewandowski/Réunion des Musées Nationaux; **Box p747** © The Trustees of the British Museum; **21.11** akg-images / Erich lessing; **21.12** © Yann Arthus-Bertrand, Altitude; **21.13** Centre Des Monuments Nationaux, Paris; **21.14** © Réunion des Musées Nationaux/Droits reserves; **21.15** Giraudon, Art Resource, NY; **21.16** © Werner Otto, SuperStock; **21.18** Reproduced by permission of the Trustees, The Wallace Collection, London; **21.19** Giraudon, Art Resource; **21.20** akg-images / A.F.Kersting; **21.21** © News International; **21.22** akg-images / A.F.Kersting; **21.23** Dorling Kindersley Media; **21.24** akg-images / A.F.Kersting; **21.25** © Yann Arthus-Bertrand, Altitude.

CHAPTER 22

22.0 akg-images / Erich Lessing; **22.1** © Gerard Blot/Réunion des Musées Nationaux, **22.2** © 2007. Image copyright The Metropolitan Museum of Art/Art Resource/Scala, Florence; **22.3** © 2000. Photo Pierpont Morgan Library/Art Resource/Scala, Florence; **22.4** akg-images / Erich Lessing; **22.5** © Blauel/Gnamm/ARTOTHEK; **22.6** © Wallace Collection, London, UK / The Bridgeman Art Library; Box p769 John Hammond, The National Trust Photo Library; **22.7** Image © The Board of Trustees, National Gallery of Art, Washington; **22.8** © Herve Lewandowski/Réunion des Musées Nationaux; **22.9** © Réunion des Musées Nationaux /Herve Lewandowski; **22.10** The J. Paul Getty Museum, Los Angeles; **22.11** © 2007. Image copyright The Metropolitan Museum of Art/Art Resource/Scala, Florence; **22.12** © 2007. Image copyright The Metropolitan Museum of Art/Art Resource/Scala, Florence; **22.14** Image © The Metropolitan Museum of Art; **22.15** © 2009 Her Majesty Queen Elizabeth II; **22.16** © Bednorz-images; **22.18** akg-images / Erich Lessing; **22.19** akg-images / Bildarchiv Monheim; **22.22** © Bednorz-images; **22.23** © Bednorz-images.

CHAPTER 23

23.0 © STOCKFOLIO® / Alamy; **23.1** © Photoservice Electa/Sergio Anelli; **23.3** Image © The Metropolitan Museum of Art; **23.4** By Kind Permission of the Earl of Leicester and the Trustees of the Holkham Estate; Box p792 Photo courtesy of The Potteries Museum & Art Gallery, Stoke-on-Trent (top); Plate 127, The General Research Division, The New York Public Library, Astor, Lenox and Tilden Foundations (bottom); **23.5** Photograph by Katherine Wetzel; **23.6** Photo © National Gallery of Canada, Ottawa Transfer from the Canadian War Memorials, 1921; **23.7** Photograph © The Art Institute of Chicago; **23.8** © Bednorz-images; **23.9** © Graham Harrison; **23.10** © 2003. Photo Scala, Florence/HIP; **23.11** Photo by Nick Meers, The National Trust Photographic Library; **23.12** English Heritage, National Monuments Record; **23.13** akg-images / A.F.Kersting; **23.14** © 2007. Yale University Art Gallery/Art Resource, NY/Scala, Florence; **23.16** Royal Academy of Arts; **23.17** Photograph © 1996 Detroit Institute of Arts; **23.18** Image © The Board of Trustees, National Gallery of Art, Washington; **23.21** © Bednorz-images; **23.22** © STOCKFOLIO® / Alamy; **23.23** Bibliotheque Nationale de France; **23.24** Bibliotheque Nationale de France; **23.25** akg-images / Erich Lessing; **23.26** akg-images / Erich Lessing; **23.27** © Réunion des Musées Nationaux; **23.29** © Réunion des Musées Nationaux / Gerard Blot; **23.30** © C. Jean/Réunion des Musées Nationaux; **23.31** akg-images / Erich Lessing.

CHAPTER 24

24.0 © Réunion des Musées Nationaux / Rene-Gabriel Ojeda; **24.1** © 2007. Image copyright The Metropolitan Museum of Art/Art Resource/Scala, Florence; **24.4** © Tate, London 2008; **24.5** National Gallery, London, UK / The Bridgeman Art Library; **24.6** Tate, London / Art Resource, NY; **24.7** Photograph © 2010, Museum of Fine Arts, Boston; **24.8** © 2005. Photo Scala, Florence/BPK, Bildagentur fuer Kunst, Kultur und Geschichte, Berlin; **24.9** © 2007. Image copyright The Metropolitan Museum of Art/Art Resource/Scala, Florence; **24.10** © The Cleveland Museum of Art, purchase, Mr. and Mrs. William H. Marlatt Fund (1965.233); **24.11** akg-images / Erich Lessing; **24.12** akg-images / Erich Lessing; **24.13** © Herve Lewandowski/Réunion des Musées Nationaux; **24.14** © The National Gallery, London; **24.15** © Réunion des Musées Nationaux; **24.16** © Herve Lewandowski/Réunion des Musées Nationaux; **24.17** akg-images / Erich Lessing; **24.19** © LeeMage/Réunion des Musées Nationaux; **24.20** © Réunion des Musées Nationaux; **24.21** © Réunion des Musées Nationaux; **24.22** © Réunion des Musées Nationaux / Thierry Le Mage; **24.24** © Réunion des Musées Nationaux / Rene-Gabriel Ojeda; **24.26** © 1985 The Detroit Institute of Arts; **24.27** © Bernard Boutrit / Woodfin Camp & Associates; **24.29** © Stewart McKnight, Alamy Images; **24.31** The Ancient Art & Architecture Collection Ltd; **24.32** © Bednorz-images; **24.33** © Peter Aaron / Esto; Photograph by Jen Swanson-Seningen, 2009, Property of the Basilica of the Assumption Historic Trust, Inc; **24.35** Giraudon / The Bridgeman Art Library.

CHAPTER 25

25.0 © Herve Lewandowski/Réunion des Musées Nationaux; **25.1** © Herve Lewandowski/Réunion des Musées Nationaux; **25.2** © Staatliche Kunstsammlungen Dresden / The Bridgeman Art Library; **25.3** Photograph © 2010, Museum of Fine Arts, Boston; **25.5** © 2008. Image copyright The Metropolitan Museum of Art/Art Resource/Scala, Florence; **25.6** © Gerard Blot/Réunion des Musées Nationaux; **25.8** akg-images / Erich Lessing; **25.9** © Robert Harding; **25.10** © Réunion des Musées Nationaux; **25.11** © Herve Lewandowski/Réunion des Musées Nationaux; **25.12** © Herve Lewandowski/Réunion des Musées Nationaux; **25.14** © The Art Institute of Chicago; **25.15** akg-images / Erich Lessing; **25.16** © President and Fellows of the Harvard College; **25.20** Photo © The National Gallery, London; **25.21** Photography © The Art Institute of Chicago; **25.23** Tate, London / Art Resource, NY; **25.24** Tate, London / Art Resource, NY; **25.25** V & A Images, Victoria and Albert Museum, London; **25.26** © Tate, London 2008; **25.27** Tate, London / Art Resource, NY; **25.28** The Detroit Institute of Arts / Bridgeman Art Library; **25.29** © 2007. Image copyright The Metropolitan Museum of Art/Art Resource/Scala, Florence; **Box p889** © 2007. Image copyright The Metropolitan Museum of Art/Art Resource/Scala, Florence; **25.30** Art Resource/The Metropolitan Museum of Art; **25.32** © Réunion des Musées Nationaux; **25.34** V & A Images, Victoria and Albert Museum, London; **25.35** Library of Congress, Prints and Photographs Division, Washington, D.C; **25.38** Science & Society Picture Library; **25.39** The Royal Collection © 2010 Her Majesty Queen Elizabeth II; **25.40** Fay Torres-Yap, New York; **25.41** Artedia; **25.42** Getty Images.

CHAPTER 26

26.0 Photograph by C. H. Bastin and J. Evrard, Brussels. © SOFAM Brussles / artist © DACS; **26.4** Photography © The Art Institute of Chicago; **26.5** Photography © The Art Institute of Chicago; **26.6** Photography © The Art Institute of Chicago; **26.10** © 2007. Yale University Art Gallery/Art Resource, NY/Scala, Florence; **26.11** © 2009. Digital image, The Museum of Modern Art, New York/Scala, Florence; **26.13** Photograph © 2010, Museum of Fine Arts, Boston; **26.14** © ADAGP, Paris and DACS, London 2009; **26.15** © J. G. Berizzi/Réunion des Musées Nationaux; **26.16** © 2009. Digital image, The Museum of Modern Art, New York/Scala, Florence; **26.17** © 2009. Digital image, The Museum of Modern Art, New York/Scala, Florence; **26.18** © DACS; **26.19** The Art Archive / © Munch Museum/Munch – Ellingsen Group, BONO, Oslo/DACS, London; **26.20** akg-images; **26.21** © Austrian National Library/Picture Archive, Vienna, 94.905-E; **26.22** Image © The Board of Trustees, National Gallery of Art, Washington; **26.23** © 2004. Photo Smithsonian American Art Museum/Art Resource/Scala, Florence; **26.24** © Réunion des Musées Nationaux; **26.25** Musee Rodin, Paris / Bridgeman Art Library; **26.26** Image © The Board of Trustees, National Gallery of Art, Washington; **26.27** Photograph by Lee Stalsworth; **26.29** Photograph by C. H. Bastin and J. Evrard, Brussels. © SOFAM Brussles / artist © DACS; **26.30** © Bednorz-images; **26.31** SuperStock, Inc; **26.32** From Henry-Russell Hitchcock, *Architecture Nineteenth and Twentieth Centuries, Penguin Books, Yale University Press, 1968, fig. 35, p. 304*; **26.33** akg-images / A.F.Kersting; **26.35** Library of Congress, Prints and Photographs Division, Washington, D.C **26.36** © Art on File, Corbis; **26.37** Marvin Trachtenberg, Chicago Architecture Foundation; **26.39** Photography Heidrich Blessing, Chicago History Museum, © ARS, NY and DACS, London 2009; **26.41** © 2007. Image copyright The Metropolitan Museum of Art/Art Resource/Scala, Florence, © ARS, NY and DACS, London 2009; **26.43** © 2007. Image copyright The Metropolitan Museum of Art/Art Resource/Scala, Florence; **26.44** © Joanna T. Steichen, George Eastman House, courtesy Steichen-Carousel; **26.45** © 2009. Digital image, The Museum of Modern Art, New York/Scala, Florence, © Georgia O'Keeffe Museum; **26.47** Photograph by Jacques Henri Lartigue, © Ministère de la Culture – France / AAJHL; **26.50** Library of Congress, Prints & Photographs Division, Washington DC.

CHAPTER 27

27.0 © ADAGP, Paris and DACS, London 2009; **27.1** © Succession H Matisse/DACS 2009; **27.2** Image © The Board of Trustees, National Gallery of Art, Washington, © ADAGP, Paris and DACS, London 2009; **27.3** Photograph reproduced with the permission of the Barnes Foundation, © Succession H Matisse/DACS 2009; **27.4** Digital image, The Museum of Modern Art, New York/Scala, Florence, © Succession H Matisse/DACS 2009; **27.5** © 2009. Digital image, The Museum of Modern Art, New York/Scala, Florence, © Succession Picasso/DACS 2009; **27.6** © ADAGP, Paris and DACS, London 2009; **27.7** © 2008, McNay Art Museum/Art Resource, NY/Scala, Florence, © Succession Picasso/DACS 2009; **27.8** © Réunion des Musées Nationaux / © Succession Picasso/DACS 2009; **27.9** © Paula Modersohn-Becker; **27.10** © Ingeborg and Dr. Wolfgang Henze-Ketterer, Wichtrach/Bern; **27.11** © Nolde-Stiftung, Seebull; **27.12** Artothek, © DACS; **27.13** © Ingeborg and Dr. Wolfgang Henze-Ketterer, Wichtrach/Bern; **27.14** © ADAGP, Paris and DACS, London 2009; **27.16** © DACS 2009; **27.17** Artothek, © DACS 2009; **27.20** © 2009. Digital Image, The Museum of Modern Art, New York/Scala, Florence, © estate of Boccioni; **27.21** © 2009. Digital image, The Museum of Modern Art, New York/Scala, Florence, © estate of Boccioni; **27.23** © Bednorz-images; **27.24** © 2009. Digital image, The Museum of Modern Art, New York/Scala, Florence; **27.25** © 2009. Digital Image, The Museum of Modern Art, New York/Scala, Florence, © ADAGP, Paris and DACS, London 2009; **27.26** Bridgeman Art Library, © DACS; **27.27** © Succession Marcel

Duchamp/ADAGP, Paris and DACS, London 2009; **27.28** Photography © The Art Institute of Chicago; **27.29** © 2009. Digital image, The Museum of Modern Art, New York/Scala, Florence, © Succession Marcel Duchamp/ADAGP, Paris and DACS, London 2009; **27.30** © ADAGP, Paris and DACS, London 2009; **27.31** © 2009. Digital Image, The Museum of Modern Art, New York/Scala, Florence, © ADAGP, Paris and DACS, London 2009; **27.33** Image copyright The Metropolitan Museum of Art/Art Resource/Scala, Florence, © Marsden Hartley; **27.34** Gerald Zugmann Fotographie KEG, © DACS; **27.35** Bildarchiv Monheim GmbH, © DACS; **27.36** Vanni, Art Resource, NY, © DACS; **27.39** © Bednorz-images.

CHAPTER 28

28.0 © 2004. Photo The Newark Museum/Art Resource/Scala, Florence; **28.1** © DACS; **28.2** Photograph by Alfred Stieglitz, © Philadelphia Museum of Art / Art Resource, NY / © Succession Marcel Duchamp/ADAGP, Paris and DACS, London 2009; **28.3** © DACS / CNAC/MNAM/Dist. Réunion des Musées Nationaux; **28.4** Scala / Bildarchiv Preussischer Kulturbesitz, © DACS; **28.5** Photo courtesy Galerie St. Etienne, New York, © DACS; **28.6** © DACS; **28.7** Estate of Hans Arp, © ADAGP, Paris and DACS, London 2009; **28.8** © Man Ray Trust/ADAGP, Paris and DACS, London 2009; **28.9** Tate, London / Art Resource, NY, © Succession Picasso/DACS 2009; **28.10** Photography © Beatrice Hatala/Réunion des Musées Nationaux / © Succession Picasso/DACS 2009; **28.11** © 2009. Digital image, The Museum of Modern Art, New York/Scala, Florence, © ADAGP, Paris and DACS, London 2009; **28.12** © ADAGP, Paris and DACS, London 2009; **28.13** © Succession Miro/ADAGP, Paris and DACS, London 2009; **28.14** © 2009. Digital image, The Museum of Modern Art, New York/Scala, Florence, © ADAGP, Paris and DACS, London 2009; **28.15** Photograph courtesy of BFI Stills, © Salvador Dali, Gala-Salvador Dali Foundation, DACS, London 2009; **28.16** © 2009. Digital image, The Museum of Modern Art, New York/Scala, Florence, © Salvador Dali, Gala-Salvador Dali Foundation, DACS, London 2009; **28.17** © Henri Cartier-Bresson, Magnum Photos; **28.18** © 2009. Digital image, The Museum of Modern Art, New York/Scala, Florence, © Man Ray Trust/ADAGP, Paris and DACS, London 2009; **28.19** © 2009. Digital image, The Museum of Modern Art, New York/Scala, Florence, © DACS; 28.20 © 2009. Digital Image, The Museum of Modern Art, New York/Scala, Florence, © Calder Foundation, New York / DACS London 2009; **28.21** Art Resource, NY, Reproduced by Permission of the Henry Moore Foundation. www.henry-moore.org; **28.22** © Bowness, Hepworth Estate; **28.25** © 1990. Photo Scala, Florence, © Rodchenko & Stepanova Archive, DACS 2009; **28.26** © Rodchenko & Stepanova Archive, DACS 2009; **28.28** © DACS; **28.29** © Bildarchiv Monheim GmbH / Alamy, © DACS; **28.30** Bauhaus Archiv Berlin, © DACS; **28.31** Photo: Junius Beebe © President and Fellows of Harvard College, © Hattula Moholy-Nagy/DACS 2009; **28.32** Vanni, Art Resource, NY, © DACS; **28.33** Chicago Historical Museum, © DACS; **28.34** Chicago Historical Museum, © DACS; **28.35** © 2008. White Images/Scala, Florence, © FLC/ADAGP, Paris and DACS, London 2009; **Box p1013** Paul Maeyaert; **28.36** Photography © Adrian Forty/Edifice, Corbis, © FLC/ADAGP, Paris and DACS, London 2009; **28.37** © 2009. Digital image, The Museum of Modern Art, New York/Scala, Florence, © ADAGP, Paris and DACS, London 2009; **28.38** © 2006. Photo The Newark Museum/Art Resource/Scala, Florence, © ARS, NY and DACS, London 2009; **28.39** © Paul Strand estate/Aperture; **28.40** Frame enlargements from 2008 2K digital restoration of Manhatta by Lowry Digital. Courtesy Lowry Digital © 2008 The Museum of Modern Art / Anthology Film Archives; **28.41** Margaret Bourke-White/Time Life Pictures, Getty Images; **28.42** Malcom Varon, N.Y.C; **28.43** Photograph © 2010, Museum of Fine Arts, Boston, © DACS 2009; **28.44** © Nathan Benn, Woodfin Camp & Associates, Inc; **28.45** © Jeff Goldberg / Esto; **28.46** © 2007. Image copyright The Metropolitan Museum of Art/Art Resource/Scala, Florence, © Georgia O'Keeffe Museum; **28.48** Photography © The Art Institute of Chicago, VAGA; **28.49** © 2009. Digital image, The Museum of Modern Art, New York/Scala, Florence, © DACS; **28.50** © Banco de Mexico Trust. Pala / 2005. Photo Art Resource/Scala, Florence, © Year of reproduction, Banco de Mexico Diego Rivera & Frida Kahlo Museums Trust, Mexico D.F. / DACS; **28.51** Photo Art Resource/Scala, Florence, © Year of reproduction, Banco de Mexico Diego Rivera & Frida Kahlo Museums Trust, Mexico D.F. / DACS; **28.52** © Manual Alvarez Bravo, San Diego Museum of Photographic Arts. Photo © Colette Urbajtel; **28.53** Photography by Geoffrey Clements; **28.54** © 2009. Digital Image, The Museum of Modern Art, New York/Scala, Florence; **28.56** © 2009. Digital Image, The Museum of Modern Art, New York/Scala, Florence, © DACS; **28.57** © The Heartfield Community of Heirs/VG Bild-Kunst, Bonn and DACS, London; **28.58** Photo Art Resource/Scala, Florence/John Bigelow Taylor, © Succession Picasso/DACS 2009.

CHAPTER 29

29.0 © 2007. Image copyright The Metropolitan Museum of Art/Art Resource/Scala, Florence. © The Pollock-Krasner Foundation ARS, NY and DACS, London 2009; **29.1** © ADAGP, Paris and DACS, London 2009; **29.2** © 2007. Image copyright The Metropolitan Museum of Art/Art Resource/Scala, Florence / © The Pollock-Krasner Foundation ARS, NY and DACS, London 2009; **29.3** © 2009. Digital image, The Museum of Modern Art, New York/Scala, Florence, © The Willem de Kooning Foundation, New York/ ARS, NY and DACS, London 2009; **29.4** © 1998 Kate Rothko Prizel & Christopher Rothko ARS, NY and DACS, London; **29.5** Tate Gallery. © DACS; **29.6** Courtesy Pace Wildenstein, New York, Photograph by Ellen Page Wilson / © ARS, NY and DACS, London 2009; **29.7** Photography © Peter Willi, SuperStock / © ADAGP, Paris and DACS, London 2009; **29.8** Photograph The Art Institute of Chicago, © The Estate of Francis Bacon. All rights reserved. DACS 2009; **29.9** © The Estate of Francis Bacon. All rights reserved. DACS 2009; **29.10** Photograph by Geoffrey Clements, © Jasper Johns / VAGA, New York / DACS, London; **29.11** Photography Ken Heyman / Woodfin Camp; **29.12** Photography Babette Mangolte. Courtesy Dia Art Foundation; **29.13** Photo © National Gallery of Canada, Ottawa, © The George and Helen Segal Foundation/DACS, London/ VAGA, New York 2009; **29.14** © 2009. Digital Image, The Museum of Modern Art, New York/Scala, Florence / DACS; **29.15** © 2009. Digital image, The Museum of Modern Art, New York/Scala, Florence / © The Andy Warhol Foundation for the Visual Arts / Artists Rights Society (ARS), New York / DACS, London 2009; **29.16** © Richard Hamilton . All Rights Reserved, DACS 2009; **29.18** Image © The Board of Trustees,National Gallery of Art, Washington / © ARS, NY and DACS, London 2009; **29.19** Photography by Philipp Scholz Rittermann / © Ellsworth Kelly 1963, San Diego Museum of Contemporary Art; **29.20** © 2009. Digital image, The Museum of Modern Art, New York/Scala, Florence, © ARS, NY and DACS, London 2009; **29.21** Photograph by David Heald © The Solomon R Guggenheim Foundation, New York / © Judd Foundation. Licensed by VAGA, New York/DACS, London 2009; **29.22** Photograph by David Heald © The Solomon R. Guggenheim Foundation, NY / © ARS, NY and DACS, London 2009; **29.23** © Estate of Eva Hesse; **29.24** Courtesy Leo Castelli Gallery, New York, DACS; **29.26** Photograph by Wolfgang Volz / © 1976 Christo and Jeanne-Claude; **29.27** © 2009. Digital image, The Museum of Modern Art, New York/Scala, Florence, © ARS, NY and DACS, London 2009; **29.28** © Ute Klophaus, D-Wuppertal / © DACS, **29.29** © estate of Nam June Paik; **29.30** © Robert Frank from the Americans; **29.31** © Romare Bearden Foundation/DACS, London/VAGA, New York 2009; **29.32** © Melvin Edwards; **29.33** Photo courtesy Michael Rosenfeld Gallery LLC; **29.34** Photograph © Donald Woodman / © ARS, NY and DACS, London 2009; **29.35** Ezra Stoller © Esto / © DACS; **29.36** Photography © Bednorz-images / © FLC/ ADAGP, Paris and DACS, London 2009; **29.37** Photography © Bednorz-images / © FLC/ ADAGP, Paris and DACS, London 2009; **29.38** © Kurt Wyss, Switzerland.

CHAPTER 30

30.0 Richard Bryant / Arcaid; **30.1** © Matt Wargo for VSBA; **30.2** © Peter Aaron / Esto; **30.4** © Réunion des Musées Nationaux; **30.5** Gerald Zugmann; **30.8** © Roland Halbe, Artur; **30.9** SuperStock; **Box p1085** © FMGB Guggenheim, Bilbao, Museum; **30.10** © Anselm Kiefer / Photo: Carnegie Museum of Art, Pittsburgh; **30.12** Photography Douglas M. Parker Studio, Los Angeles / © ADAGP, Paris and DACS, London 2009; **30.13** © Elizabeth Murray; **30.14** © Martin Puryear; **30.15** © Frank Fournier; **30.16** © Barbara Kruger; **30.17** Metro Pictures, © Cindy Sherman; **30.18** Photograph by David Heald © The Solomon R. Guggenheim Foundation, New York / © ARS, NY and DACS, London 2009; **30.19** © Fred Wilson, courtesy PaceWildenstein, New York; **30.20** © Jeff Koons; **30.21** Courtesy Jack Tilton Gallery, New York, © David Hammons; **30.22** Photograph by Ellen Labenski, The Solomon R Guggenheim Foundation, New York / © Kara Walker; **30.23** © Gonzalez Torres Foundation; **30.24** © Kiki Smith; **30.25** Courtesy Jay Jopling/White Cube, © Damien Hirst. All rights reserved, DACS 2009; **30.26** © DACS 2009; **30.27** Image courtesy of Bill Viola Studio, © Bill Viola; **30.28** Courtesy: Monika Sprueth/Philomene Magers, Cologne / © Andreas Gursky, © DACS, London 2009; **Box p1104** Courtesy Art Basel Miami Beach; **30.29** Photography John Berens; **30.30** Courtesy Creative Time, © Cai Studio.

TEXT CREDITS

Page 461 Inscriptions on the Frescoes in the Palazzo Pubblico, Siena from *Arts of Power: Three Halls of State in Italy, 1300-1600*, edited by Randolph Starn and Loren Partridge (Berkeley: University California Press, 1992), copyright © 1992 The Regents of the University of California. Reprinted by permission of the University of California Press. **Page 494** Fray Jose de Siguenza. From *Bosch in Perspective*, edited by James Snyder (NY: Simon & Schuster, 1973), © 1973 Prentice Hall Inc. Reprinted with permission of Simon & Schuster, Inc. All rights reserved. **Page 562** Leonardo da Vinci. From his undated manuscripts from *The Literary Works of Leonardo da Vinci*, edited by Jean Paul Richter (London: Phaidon Press, 1975), © 1975 Phaidon Press Limited, reprinted by permission of the publisher. **Page 568** Michelangelo. From Commentary on his 'Pieta' by Ascanio Condivi from *Life, Letters and Poetry*, edited and translated by George Bull (Oxford: Oxford University Press, 1987). Reprinted by permision of Oxford University Press. **Page 572** From *The Poetry of Michelangelo*, translated by James Saslow (New Haven, CT: Yale University Press, 1991), copyright © 1991 by Yale University Press. Reprinted by permission of the publisher. **Page 603** Michelangelo. Sonnet, "The Smith" from *Life, Letters and Poetry*, edited and translated by George Bull (Oxford: Oxford University Press, 1987). Reprinted by permission of Oxford University Press. **Page 620** From a Session of the Inquisition Tribunal in Venice of Paolo Veronese from *A Documentary History of Art, volume 2*, edited by Elizabeth Gilmore Holt (Princeton, NJ: Princeton University Press, 1982), copyright © 1947, 1958, 1982 Princeton University Press. Reprinted by permission of Princeton University Press. **Page 656** Karel van Mander. From *Dutch and Flemish Painters*, translated by Constant van de Wall (Manchester, NH: Ayer Co, 1978). Reprinted by permission of the publisher. **Page 766** Jean de Jullienne. "A Summary of the Life of Antoine Watteau" from *A Documentary History of Art, Volume 2*, edited by Elizabeth Gilmore Holt (Princeton, NJ: Princeton University Press, 1982), copyright © 1947, 1958, 1982 by Princeton University Press. Reprinted by permission of Princeton University Press. **Page 1050** Roy Lichtenstein. Interview with Joan Marter. From *Off Limits: Rutgers University and the Avant-Garde, 1957-1963*, edited by Joan Marter (NJ: Rutgers University Press, 1999), copyright © 1999 by Rutgers, the State University and The Newark Museum. Reprinted by permission of Rutgers University Press.

Notes

Notes